BARRON'S

HOW TO PREPARE FOR

SAT II

SPANISH

8TH EDITION

BARRON'S

HOW TO PREPARE FOR

SAT II

SPANISH

8TH EDITION

Christopher Kendris
B.S., M.S., Columbia University
in the City of New York
M.A., Ph.D., Northwestern University
in Evanston, Illinois
Diplômé, Faculté des Lettres, Université de Paris
et Institut de Phonétique, Paris (en Sorbonne)

Former Assistant Professor
Department of French and Spanish
State University of New York
Albany, New York

BARRON'S

For my wife Yolanda, my two sons Alex and Ted, my
daughter-in-law Tina, and my four grandchildren Bryan,
Daniel, Matthew, and Andrew
With love

About the Author

Christopher Kendris earned his B.S. and M.S. degrees at Columbia University in the City of New York and his M.A. and Ph.D. degrees at Northwestern University in Evanston, Illinois. He also earned two diplomas with *Mention très Honorable* at the Université de Paris (en Sorbonne), Faculté des Lettres, École Supérieure de Préparation et de Perfectionnement des Professeurs de Français à l'Étranger, and at the Institut de Phonétique, Paris.

Dr. Kendris has taught French and Spanish. He has also worked as interpreter and translator for the U.S. State Department at the American Embassy in Paris and has worked at the Library of Congress, Washington, D.C., using his foreign language skills.

Dr. Kendris is the author of the following books, workbooks, study cards, and audiocassettes for the study of French and Spanish: *501 French Verbs, 501 Spanish Verbs, French Now Level I, Spanish Now Level II, Write It in Spanish, Write It in French, Master the Basics: French, Master the Basics: Spanish, Pronounce It Perfectly in French, How to Prepare for SAT II: French, How to Prepare for SAT II: Spanish*, new editions completely revised and enlarged with ten practice tests and listening comprehension practice on CD, *Spanish Grammar, French Grammar, French Vocabulary, Card Guide to Spanish Grammar, Spanish Fundamentals, French Fundamentals, Spanish on the Road*, and others, all published by Barron's Educational Series, Inc. He is listed in *Contemporary Authors*.

Directions to the test questions are reprinted by permission of
Educational Testing Service. However, such permission does not
constitute review or endorsement by Educational Testing Service
or the College Board of this publication as a whole or any
other test questions or testing information it contains.

All inquiries should be addressed to:
Barron's Educational Series, Inc.
250 Wireless Boulevard
Hauppauge, New York 11788
http://www.barronseduc.com

Library of Congress Catalog Card No. 98-39421

International Standard Book No. 0-7641-7142-9

Library of Congress Cataloging-in-Publication Data
Kendris, Christopher
    How to prepare for SAT II: Spanish / by Christopher Kendris. —
8th ed.
        p.   cm.
    English and Spanish
    Includes index.
    ISBN 0-7641-7142-9
    1. Spanish language—Examinations, questions, etc   I. Title.
PC4119.K46   1998
468'.0076—dc21
                                                98-39421
                                                  CIP
                                                  AC

PRINTED IN THE UNITED STATES OF AMERICA
9 8 7 6 5 4 3 2

TABLE OF CONTENTS

PREFACE TO THE EIGHTH EDITION

This new 1998 edition has been revised and updated with new features so you can get the most benefit to help yourself do your best on the next SAT II Spanish test that you take.

If you plan to take the SAT II Spanish test with Listening Comprehension, Part VI of this book provides considerable practice with fifty questions based on ten pictures, ten short dialogues, and six long dialogues and monologues. This new feature conforms to the expectations on the actual test that you take. Everything in the listening comprehension part of the test is contained in the compact disc (CD), which is in an envelope on the inside of the back cover of this book. Also provided are answer keys, analysis charts, and answer sheets.

This new edition is divided into nine parts.

Part I contains a diagnostic test modeled on the actual Spanish SAT test. Used with the analysis charts, answer keys and explained answers, it will help you assess your strengths and weaknesses.

Part II contains nine more practice tests. That makes ten full-length practice tests in all. There is an answer key and explained answers for each test plus analysis charts for your use.

Part III contains additional reading comprehension passages and visual material with questions based on them to give you extra practice. Compare your answers on your answer sheet with the answer keys and analysis chart to see how many new words you are learning and how much progress you are making.

Part IV is a mini review book that contains the essentials of Spanish grammar, extensive vocabularies including synonyms, antonyms, idioms, and idiomatic expressions, sentence structure, use of verbs and tenses, and other basic elements that are always found on the actual SAT II test. If you study thoroughly all the features in Part IV, you will be able to achieve a high score on the actual test. The general review is arranged in a decimal system, making it easy to locate a particular topic and subtopic with explanations and examples. In addition, the explained answers of all the tests contain many references to specific sections in the review, allowing you to refresh quickly your knowledge of a specific grammatical element or to learn it for the first time.

Part V is a new feature consisting of definitions of basic grammatical terms with examples in English and Spanish. The purpose of that section is to prepare you to become aware of the different parts of a sentence and the grammatical terms used when you analyze the structure of a sentence in Spanish to figure out the correct answer to a question.

Part VI contains the Listening Comprehension test and Part VII contains the complete compact disc (CD) script of the listening test. Part VIII consists of a Spanish-English Vocabulary and Part IX contains a detailed index to help you make the best possible use of this book.

Special thanks go out to my friend and colleague, Dr. Hilda Garcerán de Vall, a professor of the Spanish language. Her distinguished late husband, Dr. Julio Garcerán, was also a teacher of Spanish. They wrote the book *Guía del idioma español*, published by Las Americas Publishing Company. I sincerely appreciate their helpful suggestions while reading the manuscript to make sure that the Spanish contained in this book is *correcto como debe ser*.

Christopher Kendris
B.S., M.S., M.A., Ph.D.

HOW TO USE THIS BOOK

You should begin preparing for SAT II Spanish well in advance of the test. This book has been designed to make studying quick, easy, and effective, and the following step-by-step approach will help assure you of your best performance on the test.

Step 1   As the first step in using this book, study the General Review (Part IV of the book). Establish a schedule, aiming perhaps to review ten pages a day or whatever pace is comfortable. Spend more time on sections that contain unfamiliar material. In addition, study the Spanish-English Vocabulary in the back of the book to make sure you know the Spanish words listed there.

Step 2   After your preliminary review, take the diagnostic test in Part I of the book. It's similar to the actual SAT II: Spanish test and will give you a good idea of what to expect. Use the answer sheet at the end of the test and correct your answers by referring to the Answer Key. Then consult the Analysis Charts to help spot your strengths and weaknesses in the three main areas covered by the test—vocabulary in context, grammar, and reading comprehension. Study the Explained Answers for help with questions that gave you difficulty.

Step 3   Refer to the Analysis Charts of the Diagnostic Test as well as to suggestions in the Explained Answers, study the General Review again, concentrating on those areas with which you had difficulty. You'll want to review the Spanish-English Vocabulary too.

Step 4   After completing the review outlined in Step 3, take Practice Test 1 in Part II of this book. Use the Analysis Charts to gauge your performance, consult the Explained Answers for help on specific questions, do some more reviewing, and then take Practice Test 2. Repeat this procedure until you have completed Practice Test 9. You'll very likely see your score improve steadily as you take the tests. By the time you complete Practice Test 9 you'll be well prepared for the real thing—you'll be familiar with the format of the test and you'll have a more solid grasp of the Spanish language. The ten full-length practice tests in this book consist of the diagnostic test in Part I and the nine practice tests in Part II.

Step 5   After you have completed the ten practice tests and have analyzed your scores based on the Analysis Charts, you may feel the need for additional practice. In Part III, there are extra reading comprehension passages (some with pictures), consisting of one hundred questions with an Answer Sheet, Analysis Chart, and Answers. It would be a good idea to do those also.

Step 6   If you plan to take the Listening Comprehension Test, Part VI contains considerable practice consisting of fifty questions based on pictures, short dialogues, long dialogues, and monologues. In this part, you are provided with an Answer Sheet, Analysis Chart, Answers, and a compact disc (CD), which is in an envelope on the inside of the back cover of this book. The complete script of the CD is in Part VII.

TIPS AND STRATEGIES TO PREP YOU FOR THE SAT II SPANISH TEST

The Purpose in Taking the SAT II Spanish Test

The purpose in taking this standardized test is to find out how extensive your knowledge is of the Spanish language. What have your grades been in high school in your Spanish classes? Around 75? 85? 95? Your score on the SAT II Spanish Test will not be significantly lower or higher because that test is fair and it contains Spanish words that are of various levels of difficulty. The test is not all easy, not all difficult. It will be easy for you if you have an extensive knowledge of Spanish vocabulary. But, *amigo mío/amiga mía,* it will be difficult if your vocabulary needs to be expanded. If that's the case, you have a lot of studying to do in this book.

If you think that the extent of your knowledge of the Spanish language is less than you would like it to be, if you are honest with yourself and say that there is a lot of vocabulary you still have not learned, if you are telling yourself that you would like some day—before the real test—to be able to understand and use correctly the basic pronouns, adjectives, verbs, and other essential elements of the Spanish language, then you will reach your goal if you prepare yourself for the test beginning today, right now, *ahora mismo,* by using this book seriously and wisely, by studying everything in it from the beginning to the end.

Every once in a while, ask yourself if you are prepared and ready for the real test. Do you think you have acquired a sufficient command of the Spanish language to earn a high score? Will you take the test this year or next year when you will have learned more of the language? Normally, a student does better on a foreign language SAT II test after several years of study because knowledge of a language is cumulative. It is very easy to forget vocabulary, idioms, phrases, and grammar if you do not use the language. When that happens, you need to do a lot of reviewing and you need to learn a lot of new words—not just to communicate—but to do your best on the SAT II Spanish Test.

The day will come when you will take the official test prepared by the Educational Testing Service (ETS) for the College Board. In the meantime, you must start today to take all the ten practice tests that I have prepared for you in this book to help you expand your knowledge of the Spanish language. After you have finished them all, do them again! Use the Explained Answers section to understand your mistakes, consult the General Review in Part IV for in-depth explanations that contain plenty of examples, and study the vocabulary lists in this book. Too much to do? Enjoy it!

The score you earn on the official test will help the college of your choice to determine the level of the Spanish course that is best for you when you begin your college program.

What to Expect on the Test

On the test, you can expect a total of 85 multiple-choice questions to answer in 60 minutes. When you take the official test on a specified date in the future, you may find that there are more than the traditional 85 questions, maybe something like 85 to 90 on the entire test. Some questions are easy, some are somewhat difficult, and some are definitely difficult. From my experience as a teacher of

Spanish, I can say that the test includes extensive Spanish vocabulary and elements of Spanish grammar that are on all three levels: beginning, intermediate, and advanced—all pretty much equally distributed.

In the past, there have been three types of questions. Now, a new type of question is being added. Therefore, on some tests to be given in the future, there will be four types of questions. Let me say this: No matter how many different types of questions you find on the official test you take, they all test your knowledge of vocabulary, which includes idiomatic phrases and idiomatic expressions, and all parts of speech (for example, nouns, pronouns, adjectives, prepositions, conjunctions), as well as elements of Spanish grammar.

If you find three types of questions on the official test you will take, they will be arranged in Parts A, B, and C. If you find four types, they will be arranged in Parts A, B, C, and D on the test. Remember that all are multiple-choice questions. You will not have to write anything in Spanish and you will not have to write any translations from English to Spanish or from Spanish to English—at least, not as of now—according to the latest types of questions they include on their test.

Does it matter to you in what order the different types of questions are arranged? I shouldn't think so. Maybe, in the future, the type of question in Part B will be moved to Part C, or vice versa.

Traditionally, Part A has tested your knowledge of Spanish vocabulary in a variety of short, simple sentences.

Part B has tested primarily grammar in a variety of short sentences.

Part C has tested vocabulary and grammar combined in a single paragraph where you are expected to fill in the blanks with the correct verb form, or correct adverb, or correct form of an appropriate adjective, or the correct preposition, or the correct idiomatic expression, or other elements of the Spanish language—all in multiple-choice questions; in other words, you have to choose the correct missing word or words. In Part C, you may also find a reading selection that contains a picture or an advertisement from a Spanish newspaper or magazine, or a railroad ticket or an airline ticket with Spanish words printed on it. If that is what you find in the test you take, you will be expected to base your answer in the multiple-choice question on what you read in the selection.

Part D has traditionally tested reading comprehension in the form of paragraphs, some short, some long.

I am not a prophet and I am not a magician (sometimes I wish I were!) to predict exactly all the Spanish words, all the Spanish verb tenses, and all the elements of Spanish grammar that will appear on the next official SAT II Spanish test. And I don't have a crystal ball to predict exactly the order of the different types of questions you may expect to find on the actual official SAT II Spanish Test that you will take. Nobody knows. Only the members of the official committee who make up the test questions know what they will include on the test. Things change from test to test and from year to year.

I have done my homework. I have thoroughly examined the sample Spanish questions found in the most current official booklet entitled, *SAT Program: Taking the SAT II Subject Tests,* prepared and produced by Educational Testing Service (ETS), which is available from The College Board SAT Program. If you want to examine that booklet for yourself (and I urge you to do so), all you have to do is ask your Spanish teacher or a member of the Guidance Department in your school.

Remember that the sample issue they have on file in your school may not be the same issue that I consulted; it may be an older issue or even a newer issue, maybe one that has been issued since I wrote this book. Let's hope that there aren't any changes in the types of questions, the number of questions, and the order of the different types of questions on the official test that you will take in the future. I have done my research in trying to find out what you may expect on the test and I have shared the information with you here. Also, please remember that Barron's Educational Series, the publisher of this book, always does its best to keep up with major changes in standardized tests given on a state or national level. When it does so, a new edition of a book is issued as quickly as possible, as in the case of this book you are using, which is now in its eighth edition. A new edition of a test prep book that contains the latest new information available is not produced instantly or overnight as if it were a daily newspaper.

I have also done my best to provide you with lots and lots of practice selections in the ten full-length sample tests that I came up with in this new edition. Also, in Part III of this book I have given you a large section of Extra Reading Comprehension Passages for practice, all of which are of the exact same type that, hopefully, you will find on the actual test that you will take at some time in the near future.

The Four Types of Questions

The four types of questions are presented in four parts on the real official test that you will take: Parts A, B, C, and D. There have been variations in the past in the number of questions you will find in each part on the actual test. In the ten full-length practice tests I offer you in this book, I may have more or fewer questions than you will find on the actual official test when you take it. Nobody knows in advance exactly how many questions there will be of each of the four types because they vary. But you can expect a total of 85 to 90 questions in the entire 60-minute test—at least, as of now.

Let's Analyze Each Type of Question

Part A tests mainly your knowledge of vocabulary, which includes all parts of speech (for example: nouns, pronouns, adjectives, adverbs, conjunctions), as well as idiomatic expressions. It is not possible to know beforehand how many questions there will be in this part. It varies from test to test. At times there have been 26 to 28 questions, all of them given in the form of simple sentences or statements. In the ten full-length practice tests that I made up for you in this book, I have included 31 questions in this part of the test and they are also in the form of simple isolated sentences. Let's look at an example of this type:

Directions: This part contains incomplete statements. Each has four choices. Choose the correct completion and blacken the corresponding space on the answer sheet.

Aquel hombre no puede ver. Evidentemente es...
   A. ciego.
   B. ciclo.
   C. cesto.
   D. acero.

(A) The correct answer is in A because **ciego** means *blind.* B means *cycle.* C means *basket.* D means *steel.* In order to figure out that the correct completion is **ciego**, you first had to understand the meanings of the other words in the statement. I hope you understood immediately that **no puede ver** means *cannot see.* Those Spanish words are on an elementary level, in any Level One course in any school in the entire country. Did you recognize them at once? If you did, then all you had to do was to choose the Spanish word among the multiple-choice answers that means *blind.*

Now, the word **ciego** is not normally on a beginning Spanish level. But the remaining Spanish words in choices B, C, and D are elementary. You could have arrived at the correct answer by the process of elimination in this question, if you knew the meaning of the other Spanish words!

Without understanding the Spanish words in A, B, C, and D, it would have been risky for you to guess the answer because **for every wrong answer you lose a certain fraction of credit.** However, you do not lose any credit if you do not answer a question. **What matters is how many questions you answer correctly. If you are not sure of an answer, skip it and go back to it later if you have time; if you don't have time, it doesn't matter. Answer those questions whose answers you recognize immediately as being correct and you are certain you are answering correctly.** You must keep that in mind. Not many students ever complete all 85 to 90 questions. The point is **to show how much Spanish you know, not how much Spanish you don't know by guessing wrong.** If you don't go about the test this way, you will not have time to reach the last question and there may be easy questions at or toward the end of the test.

Part B tests primarily your knowledge of Spanish grammar; some people avoid the word *grammar* and they say *structure*. A variety of grammatical constructions is tested in the form of sentences. All elements of Spanish grammar are discussed in the General Review section in Part IV of this book.

Directions: The following sentence contains a blank space. Of the four choices given select the one that fits grammatically and makes sense.

Mi hermano...mañana.
  A. llegó
  B. llegué
  C. llegaré
  D. llega

(D) The correct answer is in D because **llega** means arrives or is arriving. The verb form **llega** is the present indicative tense, 3rd person singular of **llegar** (to arrive) because the subject you are given in the sentence is **hermano**, which is also 3rd person singular. The verb form in A is the preterit (past) tense, 3rd person singular but that is a wrong choice because **mañana** (tomorrow) is stated in the statement; if yesterday (**ayer**) had been used in the statement, that would have indicated past time and a past tense would have been correct. The verb form in B is the preterit tense, 1st person singular but that choice is wrong for two reasons; first of all, because the statement is not about anything that happened in the past and the verb form **llegué** is 1st person singular of the preterit. The verb form in C is the future tense, 1st person singular and that would be wrong in this sentence because the subject is in the 3rd person singular (**hermano**), not in the 1st person singular (**yo**).

In this type of question, when you think about choosing an answer that is grammatically correct and makes sense in a statement, you must examine carefully the Spanish words that appear *before and after* **the blank space that you are expected to complete—as is done here above in the explanation of how to figure out the correct answer.**

Also, review §8.14 and §8.14(e) in the General Review section in Part IV of this book where you are referred to an explanation of the correct answer.

Part C tests your knowledge of Spanish grammar (structure) and, at the same time, it tests Spanish vocabulary, all presented in one paragraph, not isolated sentences as in Parts A and B. It also tests your ability to understand what the paragraph is about by selecting the correct missing words.

Directions: Read the entire paragraph that follows to determine its general meaning. It contains blank spaces that are numbered. Of the four choices given for each numbered blank, choose the one that is grammatically correct and makes sense.

Otavalo es un pueblo al norte de Quito. El sábado es cuando todos van al mercado. En este __1__ tiene lugar probablemente el mercado más colorido de toda Sudamérica. Los indios salen de sus casas muy temprano porque las actividades del día comienzan a las cinco y media de la mañana. A __2__ hora los indios de la montaña, brillantemente vestidos con ponchos de color azul y violeta, llegan al pueblo. Muy pronto un gran número de indios __3__ las calles de Otavalo, llevando muchas cosas hechas a mano. Hacia las siete __4__ la mañana hay ruido y mucha alegría en el lugar y el mercado se ve muy animado. Todo el mundo quiere vender o comprar algo. Se ofrece una variedad de __5__ tales como ponchos, faldas, sombreros, y sandalias.

1. A. año
   B. día
   C. siglo
   D. mes

2. A. este
   B. esa
   C. esto
   D. aquello

3. A. llena
B. ilumina
C. limpia
D. rompe

4. A. por
B. para
C. de
D. al

5. A. ropa
B. bebidas
C. comida
D. cosméticos

(B) The correct answer in number 1 is B. The answer must be **día** because **el sábado** (Saturday) is mentioned in the preceding sentence. The meanings of the other choices are: **año**/year; **siglo**/century; **mes**/month. If you did not understand all the Spanish words up to this point in the reading selection, you have a lot of work to do to increase your Spanish vocabulary.

(B) The correct answer in number 2 is B. The word after the blank space is **hora** (hour), which is feminine. The only feminine form among the choices is **esa**/that (**a esa hora**/at that hour). Review demonstrative adjectives in §5.54 in the General Review section in Part IV of this book and demonstrative pronouns in §6.56 where **aquello** is given.

(A) The correct answer in number 3 is A. The meanings of the choices are: **llena**/fills; **ilumina**/illuminates; **limpia**/cleans; **rompe**/breaks. If you did not understand a reasonable number of Spanish words as far as this point in the reading selection, you have to increase your Spanish vocabulary. Farther on in this section, I give you some tips on how to learn new words.

(C) The correct answer in number 4 is C. Review the use of the preposition **de** regarding time in §14.22 where **de la mañana, de la noche, de la tarde** are listed when a specific time is mentioned. Also, review the use of the preposition **por** in §16.22 in the General Review section in Part IV of this book.

(A) The correct answer in number 5 is A. You need **ropa** (clothing) because the examples given after the blank space are items of clothing. The meanings of the other choices are: **bebidas**/beverages, drinks; **comida**/meal, dinner; **cosméticos**/cosmetics. In the last sentence of the reading selection, after the blank space for number 5, did you understand the Spanish words for the items of clothing? They are of an elementary level, including **falda**/skirt.

Part D tests your ability to understand what you read in Spanish, commonly known as reading comprehension. It involves both your knowledge of Spanish vocabulary and grammar as well as your ability to spot ideas, themes, and other elements in a reading passage.

Directions: The following passage is for reading comprehension. After the selection there are incomplete statements or questions. Of the four choices, choose the correct one based on the passage.

No recordamos ya nosotros ni por qué ni cuándo Mr. Huntington vino por primera vez a España y se enamoró de ella. El caso es que nuestro californiano vino a España y quedó prendado. En diversos y prolongados viajes, recorrió la Península, no en plan de turista de lujo, siguiendo los itinerarios de las agencias de viajes, sino a su espontáneo capricho, a lomos de caballo, mula o vulgar asno; a pie muchas veces, más que en tren o en automóvil. Bien pronto aprendió el español del pueblo, en todas sus variedades dialécticas, y hablaba con unos y con otros en mesones, posadas, tabernas y ferias. Moreno, de ojos y cabellos oscuros, solamente su robustez y elevada estatura le diferenciaban de la masa de rústicos con quienes le complacía platicar. El joven Huntington, enamorado de la España auténtica, no de la de guitarra, pudo conocerla como muy pocos españoles la conocen.

6. Mr. Huntington vino a España
   A. para casarse con una española.
   B. para representar una agencia turística.
   C. a arreglar un negocio.
   D. por motivo ya olvidado.

7. ¿Qué caracterizó su manera de hablar español?
   A. Usó un lenguaje popular muy variado.
   B. Siempre conservó un ligero acento californiano.
   C. Hablaba como un turista.
   D. Hablaba como una persona de la clase social más elevada.

8. Por preferencia personal viajaba
   A. en tren.
   B. en camiones de turistas.
   C. por automóvil.
   D. a caballo o a pie.

9. Se podía distinguirlo de los naturales del país porque
   A. no hablaba corrientemente el idioma.
   B. era más alto.
   C. tenía el pelo moreno.
   D. tenía los ojos oscuros.

10. Como resultado de su mucho viajar, Huntingon llegó a
    A. conocer muy bien la vida de la clase intelectual española.
    B. formar amistades con los individuos más ricos.
    C. tener relaciones con muchos turistas.
    D. comprender a España mejor que muchos españoles.

(D) The correct answer in number 6 is D (**por motivo ya olvidado**/for a reason, motive for-gotten already/**ya**). The clue to the answer is in the first sentence of the selection where it says: We no longer/**ya** remember why or when Mr. Huntington came to Spain for the first time and fell in love with the country (**se enamoró de ella**). If you did not understand **vino** in the opening statement in question 6, you would find it difficult to figure out what is being asked and what the answer is. The irregular verb form **vino** is the 3rd person singular, preterit (past) tense of the verb **venir.** You had to complete the opening statement that says: Mr. Huntington came to Spain....Of course, **vino** is also a noun meaning *wine* and if that's what you thought it meant, you were off to a false start. If you did not recognize it as a verb form of **venir**, you must review and study basic Spanish irregular verb forms.

Here is a tip to remember for the reading comprehension passages. Generally speaking, the an-swer to the first of a series of questions is usually in the beginning of the reading selection; the answer to the question after that one is usually a little farther on, and the answer to the last ques-tion is usually found toward the end or at the very end of the selection.

This may not always be so. Sometimes the answer to the last question of a reading selection might be found at the beginning of the selection or even in the middle. Put my tip to the test but remember that your best bet is to increase your knowledge of Spanish vocabulary. If you know what the Spanish words mean, you will have no problem. In a reading selection, look for Spanish words that are cognates and synonyms and associate them with key words in the ques-tion and in the multiple-choice answers that are also cognates and synonyms of the same words.

(A) The correct answer in number 7 is A. What characterized his manner of speaking Spanish? Choice A states that he used a popular and varied way of speaking the language. The statements in choices B, C, and D are not mentioned in the reading selection at all. You could have found the answer quickly by associating the key words in choice A (**usó**/he used; **un lenguaje**/a lan-guage, which is a synonym of **el idioma**/language; **popular, variado**) with these words near the middle of the selection: **aprendió, español del pueblo, en todas sus variedades dialécticas.**

(D) The correct answer in number 8 is D. His personal preference of traveling was on horseback or on foot. It says so around the middle of the reading selection where you find the following key words that you can associate with how he traveled through Spain: **En diversos...viajes...a lomos de caballo, mula o vulgar asno, a pie muchas veces**. He did not travel through Spain as a tourist provided by a tourist agency *but rather* (**sino**) on horseback (**a lomos de caballo**), on an **asno** (donkey, ass), and many times on foot (**a pie muchas veces**). He traveled like that more than by train or car.

(B) The correct answer in number 9 is B. It was possible to make a distinction (in appearance) between him and the native persons of the country because he was taller (**era más alto**). Associate those Spanish words in B with the following near the end of the selection: **elevada estatura** (elevated stature, very tall). Also associate the verb **distinguir** (to distinguish, make distinct) in the question with the verb **diferenciaban** (to differentiate), which is also found near the end of the selection. You must increase your knowledge of Spanish vocabulary and you must associate words with their synonyms (similar meanings) and their antonyms (opposite meanings).

(D) The correct answer in number 10 is D. As a result of his doing a lot of traveling (in Spain), Mr. Huntington arrived at (**llegó a**) or was able to understand Spain better than many Spanish persons, which is stated in answer D. Associate that statement with the following words in the last sentence of the reading selection: **pudo conocerla como muy pocos españoles la conocen**/he was able to know her (Spain) as very few Spanish persons know her (Spain).

There is another type of question that tests reading comprehension. I offer you many samples in the last few pages of Part III in this book, the section called *Extra Reading Comprehension Passages*. They are usually announcements, advertisements, pictures with Spanish words in them. Try this one:

> **Solicitamos los servicios de una
> Señorita Mecanógrafa, mayor de 21
> años, de carácter dinámico, buena
> presentación, sin problemas de
> horario, para ocupar puesto de
> recepción.
> Interesadas presentarse en De La Llave
> Nte. 1271, de 14:30 a 17:30 horas.
> Atención C.P. Octavio Mendoza.**

11. ¿Para quién es este anuncio?
   A. una camarera
   B. una secretaria
   C. una actriz
   D. una enfermera

(B) The correct answer in number 11 is B. For whom is this announcement (of an available position)? For a secretary. The key words in the announcement are: **Señorita Mecanógrafa** (Miss Typist)...**para ocupar puesto de recepción**/to fill the position of receptionist. The other choices are **una camarera**/waitress; **una actriz**/actress; **una enfermera**/nurse.

How to Increase Your Spanish Vocabulary

The best way to increase your vocabulary is to do a lot of reading and to use a dictionary to look up the meaning of words you do not know or forgot. During your three or four years of Spanish studies in school, did you read any Spanish magazines and newspapers? Did you read any short stories or novels in Spanish? If you did a lot of reading in Spanish every day, then you must have a pretty good vocabulary. If all you did was just use your textbook and do your homework in twenty minutes, that is only the minimum. If that's the case, then you have to learn many, many new words.

Now, to catch up and **learn at least 400 *new* Spanish words** before you take the next SAT II Spanish Test, I suggest you do the following:

1. Get four packs of 3 × 5 cards with no lines printed on them. There are usually 100 blank cards in a pack. Make your own flash cards. Writing the words yourself will help you remember them better. The flash cards sold in bookstores are too easy and too few. On one side of your own cards write the new Spanish word three times as you say it aloud and on the other side write the English meaning. Write not only new Spanish words but also new idiomatic expressions. If you are ambitious, on the Spanish side write a short sentence using the new word or new idiomatic expression. In doing so, the words and meanings will stick in your memory. And on the other side do the same in English.

2. Where will you find the new words and expressions to write on your flash cards? You will find them right here in this book that contains thousands of Spanish words. As you do each of all the ten practice tests, use your cards for new words. Do not use a typewriter. You must write them in your own handwriting in pen, not in pencil because they will remain legible longer if written in ink.

3. Also, you can find words and expressions that are new to you in the General Review section in Part IV of this book. For example, take a few minutes right now and turn to section §19. in that part of the review section. Just look at all the new words and their synonyms! And turn to section §20. Just look at all those new words and their antonyms! In the first paragraph of §20., I give you more tips on how to increase your Spanish vocabulary. Also, turn to section §21. about cognates and §22. about tricky words. You must also write on your cards about thirty pages of Spanish vocabulary in the back pages of this book. You say you know a lot of them already? Great. But I'll bet you don't know them *all.* You must know them *all* because they are basic and commonly used in the SAT II Spanish Tests. While studying these lists of basic vocabulary, use a blank 3 × 5 card as a ruler to guide yourself up and down the list. Also, cover one side of the line and try to recall the synonym or antonym. Then, cover the other side and try to recall the other word. Too much work, you say? Too much writing on cards? Too much to review? Too many words and idiomatic expressions to remember? You say you're overwhelmed with so much to study in this big thick book? It even contains Listening Comprehension Practice and a CD in an envelope on the inside of the back cover. It's there for your use in case you have decided to take the Listening Comprehension Part of the SAT II Spanish Test. Too much work to do?

No, it's not too much work to do. I thought you wanted to improve your knowledge of Spanish vocabulary, idioms, idiomatic expressions, and grammar so you could get a respectable score on the next SAT II Spanish Test you take. Carry the flash cards you create with you everywhere you go and test yourself by reading the Spanish words and giving the English. It might be difficult for you to give the Spanish for the English. What is most important is to recognize the meaning of the Spanish words.

How to Use Your 60 Minutes Wisely

Here are a few tips on how to use your 60 minutes wisely during the test.

1. Remember to have a wrist watch with you. There may not be a clock on the wall in the room where you take the test. If there is, it may be on the back wall behind you. Don't waste time turning around every few minutes to see what time it is.
2. Of the 60 minutes allowed for the test, you have less than one minute to spend on each of the 85 questions. Sometimes there are 90 questions.
3. Do not waste any time by dwelling on a question for more than one minute if you do not recognize the correct answer immediately among the multiple-choice answers.
4. Skip the troublesome questions and go on to the next.
5. Answer those questions whose answers you recognize immediately as being correct and you are certain you are answering correctly.

6. It is risky to guess an answer because for every wrong answer you lose a certain amount of credit.

7. Remember that you do not lose any credit if you do not answer a question. You are penalized only for wrong answers.

8. Show how much Spanish you do know. Don't show how much Spanish you don't know or don't remember by guessing wrong.

9. Skip the difficult questions and go back to them later if you have time. If you don't have time, it doesn't matter because you do not lose any credit for questions you did not answer.

10. If you waste precious minutes trying to decide on an answer you are not sure of, you will not have time to reach the last question. Sometimes there are easy questions at or toward the end of the test.

Not to Worry! Help Is on the Way!

In the ten full-length practice tests that I wrote for you in this book, I took the opportunity to help you by giving you a lot of practice in drilling certain grammatical points that you must master. The important thing for you to do is to practice, practice, practice the basic elements in Spanish grammar and vocabulary that you still have not mastered so you can do your best on the real test.

In some of the practice tests in this book there are three or four, sometimes five or six questions in the form of statements one right after the next that test a particular element in Spanish grammar that you must know. For example, question numbers 42 to 47 in Test 2 all test the use of direct and indirect object pronouns. I did that on purpose to help you drill that element of Spanish grammar, especially for students who still cannot tell a direct object pronoun from an indirect object pronoun and how and when they are used. In my Answers Explained sections, I try to help you by referring you to certain sections (indicated by the symbol § plus a number) of the General Review in Part IV of this book. All you have to do is turn to those sections, read them, study them, and examine the examples so you can finally master the use of direct and indirect object pronouns.

Also, in Test 3 there are several questions one right after the next, as in a drill, that test your knowledge of the use of the Spanish subjunctive. After you have done them, and after you have read and studied the answers explained, I think you will be able to understand better the use of the subjunctive to help you select the correct answer—even if on the official test there are only two or three questions that require an answer in the subjunctive.

In conclusion, let me say this: The tests in this book are, after all, practice tests and this is your chance to do a lot of practice so you can improve your knowledge of Spanish grammar to score high on the real test. Surely you must not expect to find on the "real official test" that you take three or four or more questions, all in a row, one right after the next, that test the same element of Spanish grammar! I did that on these practice tests for your benefit, but only as a drill, to drive home certain basic elements of Spanish grammar.

All elements of the Spanish language cannot be tested in one official test that contains only 85 to 90 questions. That is why I think you need a lot of practice on certain basic elements of Spanish grammar more than once, because once is just not enough to help you master any Spanish grammar at all.

Repetition, drilling, and practice are all extremely important. After practicing many questions on the use of particular points in grammar—let's say, for example, Spanish prepositions, in the ten practice tests in this book, maybe you will come across only one question on the real test where you will have to choose the correct preposition. And you will get it right.

Remember, your goal is not just to get an 800 on this test and then forget about Spanish for the rest of your life. Hopefully, you will go on to study more Spanish in college, or travel in a Spanish-speaking country.

Think of the test, then, as an evaluation of your *current* level of knowledge.

ABBREVIATIONS USED IN THIS BOOK

adj. adjective

adv. adverb, adverbial

ant. anterior

art. article

aux. auxiliary

cond. conditional

conj. conjunction

def. definite

dem. *or* **demons.** demonstrative

dir. direct

disj. disjunctive

e.g. for example

f. *or* **fem.** feminine

ff and the following

fut. future

i.e. that is to say

imper. imperative

imperf. imperfect

indef. indefinite

indic. indicative

indir. indirect

inf. infinitive

interj. interjection

interrog. interrogative

introd. introduction

m. *or* **masc.** masculine

n. noun

obj. object

p. page

par. paragraph

part. participle

perf. perfect

pers. person

pl. plural

plup. pluperfect

poss. possessive

prep. preposition

pres. present

pret. preterit

pron. pronoun

refl. reflexive

rel. relative

s. *or* **sing.** singular

subj. subjunctive

v. verb

DIAGNOSTIC
TEST

PART
I

The following Diagnostic Test serves several purposes. It will give you experience with the format and level of difficulty of SAT II: Spanish. It will also help you identify problem areas so you will become aware of your weaknesses and strengths. The Analysis Charts at the end of this Diagnostic Test will give you an idea of your score when you make your first attempt at taking this kind of test.

The best way to improve your knowledge of the Spanish language is to review thoroughly Part IV. You must build your vocabulary, idioms, and idiomatic expressions, and master the many elements of the structure of the language. Learn from your mistakes in this Diagnostic Test and in the nine practice tests in Part II.

This test consists of 85 questions. You have 60 minutes to complete it. An Answer Key, Analysis Charts, Explained Answers, and Answer Sheet follow the test.

PART A

Directions: This part contains incomplete statements. Each has four choices. Choose the correct completion and blacken the corresponding space on the answer sheet.

1. Ana acaba de comprar...
 A. otra falta.
 B. una nueva falsa.
 C. una falla.
 D. una falda nueva.

2. Aquel hombre no puede ver. Evidentemente es ...
 A. ciego.
 B. ciclo.
 C. cesto.
 D. acero.

3. Está lloviendo. Hace ... tiempo.
 A. buen
 B. bueno
 C. mal
 D. malo

4. José, te veré ...
 A. hay.
 B. ayer.
 C. algún día.
 D. anteayer.

5. Estos cuatro hombres son ...
 A. cortés.
 B. corteses.
 C. cortesías.
 D. cuadros.

6. Ricardo, Felipe, y Conchita están ...
 A. cansados.
 B. descansos.
 C. daños.
 D. desfiles.

GO ON TO THE NEXT PAGE

7. Nada puedo ver porque hay ...
   A. neblina.
   B. lodo.
   C. nieve.
   D. luna.

8. Voy a acostarme temprano porque tomo el tren a las tres de la ...
   A. madrugada.
   B. noche.
   C. semana.
   D. medianoche.

9. No tengo ganas de comer porque no me gusta ...
   A. el jamón.
   B. el jabón.
   C. la jaula.
   D. el jinete.

10. Tengo que limpiar la cocina y necesito ...
    A. una escoba.
    B. un ensayo.
    C. una escasez.
    D. un erudito.

11. La madre está cepillando ... de la niña.
    A. el caballo
    B. la arena
    C. el cabello
    D. la caída

12. Mi abuelito murió anoche y ya lo echo de ...
    A. mucho.
    B. más.
    C. menos.
    D. broma.

13. Aquí tiene Ud. el dinero que le ...
    A. quiero.
    B. debo.
    C. alquilo.
    D. aflijo.

14. No se olviden ustedes que mañana la tienda estará ...
    A. rota.
    B. cerradera.
    C. cerosa.
    D. cerrada.

15. Esta avenida es ...
    A. absorta.
    B. acera.
    C. aduana.
    D. ancha.

16. La Embajada Americana está en ... de esta calle.
    A. el arbusto
    B. la esquina
    C. el rincón
    D. la aguja

17. En esta ciudad hay varios medios de ... como el ómnibus y el tren subterráneo.
   A. trigo
   B. transmisión
   C. transgresor
   D. transporte

18. En la ciudad de San Francisco puedo divertirme porque hay muchos ...
   A. teatros y cines.
   B. testigos.
   C. trofeos.
   D. techos.

19. Los Reyes Magos traen ... a los niños el seis de enero.
   A. regalos
   B. refrescos
   C. refugios
   D. reglamentos

20. La cerveza se ...
   A. come.
   B. estudia.
   C. canta.
   D. bebe.

21. El alumno ... sus libros en la sala de clase.
   A. dejó
   B. partió
   C. salió
   D. se quitó

22. María tiene ... amigas como Elena.
   A. más
   B. menos
   C. tan
   D. tantas

23. Roberto es ... alto como José.
   A. tan
   B. tanto
   C. tonto
   D. más

24. Tengo un examen ...
   A. mañana por la mañana.
   B. de la mañana.
   C. al por menor.
   D. por consiguiente.

25. Pepita ... la sala de clase.
   A. dejó
   B. salió de
   C. partió
   D. se puso

26. La señora Fuentes no puede abrir la puerta porque perdió ...
   A. las llenas.
   B. el lloro.
   C. los llorones.
   D. las llaves.

GO ON TO THE NEXT PAGE

27. Los señores García, muy furiosos, llamaron a la policía porque los vecinos ...
- A. estaban durmiendo.
- B. eran extranjeros.
- C. eran amables.
- D. hacían mucho ruido.

28. Cuando Conchita supo que María había muerto, comenzó a ...
- A. llorar.
- B. llover.
- C. comer.
- D. reír a carcajadas.

29. A Pablo no le gusta trabajar. Evidentemente es ...
- A. listo.
- B. flojo.
- C. afortunado.
- D. extraño.

30. Los pájaros usan ... para volar.
- A. las plumas
- B. las uñas
- C. las alas
- D. los ojos

31. Acabo de tomar una aspirina porque ... la cabeza.
- A. me duele
- B. me cae
- C. me quito
- D. me despido de

PART B

<u>Directions:</u> *The following sentences contain blank spaces. Of the four choices given for each blank select the one that fits grammatically and makes sense.*

32. Quiero que María lo ... ahora mismo.
- A. hace
- B. haces
- C. hago
- D. haga

33. Mi hermana ... cuando yo entré en la casa.
- A. canta
- B. cantaba
- C. cantó
- D. está cantando

34. Iría a México si ... dinero.
- A. tuviera
- B. tengo
- C. tenga
- D. tiene

35. Este profesor me habla como si ... un niño.
- A. soy
- B. estoy
- C. es
- D. fuera

36. Elena ... a la iglesia esta mañana.
    A. fue
    B. fui
    C. fuera
    D. era

37. A mi tío no ... gustan los vinos.
    A. le
    B. lo
    C. les
    D. los

38. El jefe busca a un hombre que ... hablar español.
    A. sabe
    B. puede
    C. conoce
    D. sepa

39. La señora Pérez es ...
    A. contenta.
    B. hermosa.
    C. una profesora.
    D. en España.

40. Antes de ... tomé un helado.
    A. salgo
    B. salía
    C. saliendo
    D. salir

41. Mi apartamento es más grande que ...
    A. la suya
    B. la mía
    C. las suyas
    D. el de Roberto.

42. Este paquete es para ...
    A. tú.
    B. te.
    C. nosotros.
    D. yo.

43. Ricardo quiere ir al cine ...
    A. conmigo.
    B. con ti.
    C. con suyo.
    D. con tú.

44. Mi padre trabajó muchísimo y ahora tiene ...
    A. cansado.
    B. descansado.
    C. alegre.
    D. sed.

45. Alberto, me gusta mucho tu gorra. ¿Quién ... ?
    A. te lo dio
    B. se la dio
    C. te la dio
    D. dártelo

GO ON TO THE NEXT PAGE

46. ¿ . . . día es hoy?
   A. Cuál
   B. Qué
   C. Cuáles
   D. Cómo

47. ¿ . . . de estos lápices es mejor?
   A. Cuál
   B. Cuáles
   C. Qué
   D. Quién

48. ¿ . . . son buenos?
   A. Cuál
   B. Cuáles
   C. Qué
   D. Cuánto

49. Se sabe que María va a casarse . . . Juan.
   A. con
   B. de
   C. a
   D. al

50. Nuestra profesora de español es amable . . . nosotros.
   A. con
   B. de
   C. a
   D. por

51. ¿Le gusta a usted mi reloj . . . oro?
   A. de
   B. con
   C. a
   D. en

52. Dígame, por favor, ¿ . . . sirven los anteojos?
   A. por qué
   B. para qué
   C. qué
   D. porque

53. ¿Qué haces, Tomás? — . . . terminar mis lecciones.
   A. Acababa de
   B. Acabo a
   C. Acabo de
   D. Acababa a

54. Esta mañana, yo . . . tomar el desayuno cuando el teléfono sonó.
   A. acababa de
   B. acabo a
   C. acabo de
   D. acababa a

55. Yo sé jugar al tenis y mi hermana sabe . . . piano.
   A. jugar el
   B. jugar al
   C. tocar el
   D. tocar al

56. ¿A quién ... toca? — A María.
   A. le
   B. lo
   C. les
   D. la

57. Los ladrones ... robaron todo el dinero a él.
   A. le
   B. lo
   C. les
   D. la

58. Cuando vi el accidente, ... pálido.
   A. se puso
   B. me puse
   C. llegué a ser
   D. llegó a ser

59. José ... la silla de la cocina al comedor.
   A. tomó
   B. llevé
   C. tomé
   D. llevó

60. La profesora tomó el libro y ... leer a la clase.
   A. comenzó
   B. comenzó a
   C. comencé a
   D. comencé

61. El alumno estudió ... de la lección.
   A. medio
   B. el medio
   C. mitad
   D. la mitad

62. La alumna ... un lápiz al profesor.
   A. preguntó
   B. pregunté
   C. pidió
   D. pedí

63. ¿Qué piensa Ud. ... este libro?
   A. de
   B. en
   C. a
   D. por

64. Miguel, no hablas mucho; ¿ ... qué piensas?
   A. de
   B. en
   C. a
   D. sobre

65. Después de cenar, el señor ... una propina sobre la mesa para el camarero y partió.
   A. coloca
   B. colocó
   C. coloco
   D. colocaba

GO ON TO THE NEXT PAGE

PART C

Directions: Read the entire paragraph that follows to determine its general meaning. It contains blank spaces that are numbered. Of the four choices given for each numbered blank, choose the one that is grammatically correct and makes sense.

Cada vez que llego a México siento muchísima alegría. Es que tengo la esperanza de ver __66__ escritor por quien siento la admiración más grande. Recién llegada, llamé a su casa. Mercedes, su inteligente mujer, me __67__ que Gabriel estaba a punto __68__ volver de Europa y que, en estas fechas, paseaba por Madrid. Nunca nos encontramos. ¡Qué mala suerte! Cada vez que él llega a aquella __69__ yo estoy en México. En aquella época hacía yo un programa de televisión llamado "Nuevas gentes" y __70__ que quedarme en Barcelona con todo mi equipo para trabajar allí durante un mes.

66. A. el
B. al
C. la
D. lo

67. A. contestó
B. contesté
C. contestaré
D. contestaban

68. A. a
B. al
C. por
D. de

69. A. ciudad
B. país
C. casa
D. cuidado

70. A. tuvo
B. tengo
C. tuve
D. tuvimos

PART D

Directions: *The following passages are for reading comprehension. After each selection there are incomplete statements or questions. Of the four choices, choose the correct one based on the passage.*

Estudiaba Andrés en Madrid cuando, en respuesta a cariñosos mensajes de don Pedro, le puso su primera carta. En seguida, vino una carta de don Pedro, fechada 6 de abril, la cual decía:

Mi querido Andrés:

Desde mi llegada a París pregunté por usted a algunas personas que lo conocen, pero no me fue posible obtener los datos precisos de su residencia en Europa. Por lo tanto, su carta del 27 de marzo la he recibido con gran satisfacción.

Estoy comisionado, como usted sabrá, en el Instituto Internacional de Cooperación Intelectual. Creo que estaré por acá cuando menos por este año, y me dará mucho gusto que se presente la oportunidad de encontrarnos. Hay muchas cosas de que hablar. El último año que pasé en México lo dediqué a la fundación de la Universidad de Nuevo León, y esto me sirvió para descubrir otros horizontes a mis actividades.

Veo que usted trajo a Elena, en lo cual hizo muy bien. Alguna vez que estuve en Laredo traté de encontrarla, pero sin buen resultado. Sírvase saludarla con todo aprecio. También me felicito en saber que usted y Gabriela Mistral siguen escribiéndose. Ella le servirá mucho para todo lo que se refiere a México.

Quedo en espera de sus cartas y ya sabe que estoy por acá a sus órdenes y que desearía que nos viéramos pronto.

Un abrazo de su viejo amigo que mucho lo estima,

Pedro de Alba

71. ¿Por qué estaba Andrés en Madrid?
   A. Seguía cursos allí.
   B. Enseñaba en la universidad.
   C. Buscaba a un amigo.
   D. Quería conocer a Gabriela Mistral.

72. Don Pedro había tenido dificultad en
   A. hallar un lugar en donde vivir.
   B. conseguir informes precisos sobre Andrés.
   C. cumplir su comisión en el Instituto.
   D. encontrar la última carta de su amiga.

73. ¿Cómo pasó don Pedro su último año en México?
   A. Terminó sus estudios.
   B. Viajó con un amigo.
   C. Dirigió unas investigaciones sociológicas.
   D. Estableció un instituto de enseñanza.

74. Al escribir esta carta don Pedro, se encontraba Elena
   A. con Andrés en Madrid.
   B. en la Universidad de Nuevo León.
   C. trabajando de criada en casa de don Pedro.
   D. viajando con una amiga en México.

75. Don Pedro se alegraba de que
   A. fuera a reunirse con Andrés y Elena el mes próximo.
   B. pronto fuera a marcharse de París.
   C. Andrés estuviera en comunicación con Gabriela.
   D. Andrés se quedara en México.

GO ON TO THE NEXT PAGE ▷

Magda Rebull estaba delicada. Durante los últimos días de su estancia en la ciudad, cayó enferma. Joaquín Rius se interesaba todos los días por su estado de salud, y le enviaba sin falta un ramo de flores.

Durante la etapa de veraneo, Magda, convaleciente, empezó a contestar las cartas de Joaquín. En la casa solariega de Santa María del Vallés la vida transcurría plácidamente: Mercedes hacía compañía a su hermana y salían a pasear a la sombra de los álamos de la mina, o a la de los altísimos plátanos del jardín.

A finales de agosto y a requerimientos de Joaquín, Magda escribió convidándole a su casa.

Joaquín fue a Santa María el domingo siguiente por la mañana. Al bajar del tren, vio que se le acercaba el portero. Bernardo—el cual a causa de su mucha edad había sido enviado a veranear también con las muchachas.

—Tengo el encargo de acompañarle. Por aquí, señorito—y le condujo al coche de los Rebull, que aguardaba en la plaza.

76. Poco antes de abandonar la ciudad, ¿qué le sucedió a Magda?
A. Un coche la atropelló.
B. Se puso enferma.
C. Su enfermera la dejó.
D. La despidieron de la florería.

77. Todos los días Joaquín preguntaba
A. dónde se encontraba Magda.
B. cuándo iba a volver Magda.
C. cómo estaba Magda.
D. cómo se llamaba el florista.

78. ¿Qué hacía Mercedes para hacerle compañía a Magda?
A. Comían juntas en el jardín.
B. Hacía con ella visitas a los vecinos.
C. Le leía capítulos de sus novelas favoritas.
D. Daba vueltas con ella por los jardines.

79. ¿Por qué fue Joaquín a ver a Magda un domingo de agosto?
A. Bernardo le había escrito pidiéndole que viniera al campo.
B. El padre de Magda le había autorizado la visita.
C. Magda lo había invitado a visitarla.
D. Joaquín quería ver la casa antigua de Magda con su famoso jardín.

80. Bernardo había llegado a la estación para
A. recibir a Joaquín.
B. tomar el tren.
C. despedirse de Joaquín.
D. entregarle una carta a Joaquín.

—¿Te vas a bajar la basura de una vez?
—Ya voy, tía, ya voy.
Bajó al patio. Ya estaban allí cajones, cubos, latas. Un olor pestilente, insoportable.

El chico levantó la cabeza. La noche limpia. ¡Qué gusto mirar las estrellas, qué gusto saber el nombre de cada una! Y todo tan lejos. A miles y miles de kilómetros. La tierra también era una estrella y también estaba en el aire sin apoyo, pero estaba dando vueltas como un trompo. Brillaría de lejos, relucirían como espejos las aguas del mar, y las montañas se verían pequeñitas o no se verían siquiera. O tal vez desde otros astros, con anteojos mejores, se vería mejor, con todo detalle. Las calles, las casas, la gente incluso. ¿Y si lo estaban mirando a él? ¡Dios mío, si cualquier estrella le veía allí, en el patio, junto a la basura! ¿Qué importaba? Ya se harían cargo. "No, ¿qué va? No me ven." Miles y miles de kilómetros. No habría anteojos capaces. Verían la luz, sólo la luz de la tierra. Bastaba con eso.

La voz irritada de la tía sonó desde lo alto de la escalera.

—¿Quieres subir de una vez?

—Ya voy.

Llegó arriba cansado, de tanto como corrió.

—¿Se puede saber qué hacías ahí abajo tanto tiempo?

—Estaba estudiando un poco de astronomía.

Lo entró a la casa de un empujón.

—De mí no te burlas tú, ¿te enteras? Anda, desnúdate y a la cama. ¡Cómo se conoce que no te pesa el cuerpo de estar trabajando todo el día!

Se acostó el chico en silencio. Pero tardó en dormirse. La claridad de la luna, entrando por el ventanuco, le daba en la cara. Y pensaba que, tal vez, en alguna estrella lejana habría un niño como él, acostado en una cama, que no podía dormirse porque le entraba un rayo de luz de la tierra. Y así fue y le sacó la lengua.

81. ¿Por qué bajó el chico?
    A. Unos amigos le esperaban abajo.
    B. Su tía le había dado un encargo.
    C. Buscaba sus anteojos perdidos.
    D. El calor de la casa le sofocaba.

82. Mientras estaba abajo el muchacho pensaba en
    A. las bellezas celestiales.
    B. un viaje que iba a hacer.
    C. el mal genio de la tía.
    D. la dificultad de subir la escalera.

83. Sus pensamientos fueron interrumpidos por
    A. una lluvia repentina.
    B. una nube que oscureció la luna.
    C. las voces de los vecinos.
    D. el grito de su tía.

84. ¿Por qué se enojó la tía?
    A. El niño tardaba en regresar.
    B. El chico no quería volver a sus estudios.
    C. Alguien se había llevado el cubo.
    D. Alguien le había roto los anteojos al chico.

85. ¿A quién le sacó la lengua el chico?
    A. a una muchacha
    B. a la tía
    C. a un niño imaginario
    D. a los vecinos que le gritaban

END OF DIAGNOSTIC TEST

ANSWER KEY: DIAGNOSTIC TEST

PART A		PART B		PART C	PART D
1. D	17. D	32. D	49. A	66. B	71. A
2. A	18. A	33. B	50. A	67. A	72. B
3. C	19. A	34. A	51. A	68. D	73. D
4. C	20. D	35. D	52. B	69. A	74. A
5. B	21. A	36. A	53. C	70. C	75. C
6. A	22. D	37. A	54. A		76. B
7. A	23. A	38. D	55. C		77. C
8. A	24. A	39. B	56. A		78. D
9. A	25. B	40. D	57. A		79. C
10. A	26. D	41. D	58. B		80. A
11. C	27. D	42. C	59. D		81. B
12. C	28. A	43. A	60. B		82. A
13. B	29. B	44. D	61. D		83. D
14. D	30. C	45. C	62. C		84. A
15. D	31. A	46. B	63. A		85. C
16. B		47. A	64. B		
		48. B	65. B		

ANALYSIS CHARTS

After you have finished the Diagnostic Test, complete the Analysis Charts below to determine your strengths and weaknesses in the three skills tested by SAT II: Spanish. The three skill areas are vocabulary, grammar, and reading comprehension. Before you take the first Practice Test in this book, review those areas in which you had difficulties. This book's General Review (Part IV) and Spanish-English Vocabulary have been carefully designed to make reviewing as efficient and easy as possible. For pointers on specific questions in the Diagnostic Test, consult the Explained Answers that follow.

PART A (31 questions)

Part A of the Diagnostic Test mainly involves vocabulary. It tests your knowledge of all parts of speech as well as idiomatic expressions.

Enter the number of correct answers in Part A in the box ☐

In evaluating your score, use the following table.

> 29 to 31 correct: *Excellent*
> 26 to 28 correct: *Very Good*
> 23 to 25 correct: *Average*
> 20 to 22 correct: *Below Average*
> less than 20 correct: *Unsatisfactory*

You should study the Spanish-English vocabulary at the back of the book as well as relevant parts of the General Review even if your score was Excellent or Very Good. This will solidify your knowledge of Spanish and may fill in some gaps the test didn't reveal. The need to review is especially important if you start with a score of Average or less. If you review conscientiously, you should see your score improve steadily as you complete each Practice Test in this book.

PART B (34 questions)

Part B of the Diagnostic Test principally concerns your knowledge of Spanish grammar. A variety of grammatical constructions is tested. All are discussed in the General Review of this book.

Enter the number of correct answers in Part B in the box ☐
In evaluating your score, use the following table.

32 to 34 correct: *Excellent*
29 to 31 correct: *Very Good*
26 to 28 correct: *Average*
23 to 25 correct: *Below Average*
less than 23 correct: *Unsatisfactory*

You should study relevant parts of the General Review in this book even if your score was Excellent or Very Good. This will solidify your understanding of Spanish grammar and may fill in gaps the test didn't reveal. The need to review is especially important if you start with a score of Average or less. The Explained Answers will point you to specific parts of the General Review that you should study. If you study hard, you should see your score improve steadily as you complete each Practice Test in this book.

PART C (5 questions)

Part C of the Diagnostic Test deals with vocabulary and structure in a paragraph.

Enter the number of correct answers in Part C in the box ☐
In evaluating your score, use the following table.

5 correct: *Excellent*
4 correct: *Very Good*
3 correct: *Average*
2 correct: *Below Average*
1 or 0 correct: *Unsatisfactory*

If you scored fewer than 3 correct on this part of the test, you need to study thoroughly the General Review in Part IV of this book.

PART D (15 questions)

Part D of the Diagnostic Test deals with reading comprehension. It involves both your knowledge of Spanish vocabulary and grammar and your ability to spot ideas, themes, and other elements in a reading passage.
Enter the number of correct answers in Part D in the box ☐
In evaluating your score, use the following table.

14 or 15 correct: *Excellent*
12 or 13 correct: *Very Good*
10 or 11 correct: *Average*
8 or 9 correct: *Below Average*
less than 8 correct: *Unsatisfactory*

Reading comprehension involves your overall knowledge of Spanish. If you had difficulty on this part of the test, you need to review Spanish vocabulary and grammar and practice reading material in Spanish. If you study conscientiously, looking closely at the General Review and the Spanish-English vocabulary in this book as well as reading a variety of passages in Spanish, your score should improve steadily as you take each practice test in this book.

EXPLAINED ANSWERS: DIAGNOSTIC TEST

Please note: These explanations cover key items in the questions and answers. For more help, look up the relevant section (indicated by a § number) in this book's General Review. Consult the Spanish-English vocabulary at the back of this book or a dictionary for help with questions of vocabulary.

PART A

1. (D) **comprar** / to buy; **falta** / error; **falda** / skirt. Note that the adjective **nueva** (new) must come after **falda**. Review §5.15.

2. (A) **ciego** / blind. Review §5.17.

3. (C) **lloviendo** / raining; **hace mal tiempo** / the weather is bad. **Mal** is one of the masculine singular adjectives that drops the final **o** in front of a masculine singular noun. Review §5.19 and §5.20.

4. (C) **algún día** / someday; **te veré** / I will see you. Review §5.20.

5. (B) **cortés** / courteous; **corteses** / courteous (plural). Review §5.31.

6. (A) **cansados** / tired; note that **estar** is used rather than **ser** in referring to a person's condition. Note also the use of the masculine plural to describe two or more nouns of different genders. Review §5.36.

7. (A) **neblina** / fog

8. (A) **acostarse temprano** / to go to bed early; **madrugada** / dawn.

9. (A) **tener ganas de** / to feel like; **el jamón** / ham; **el jabón** / soap.

10. (A) **cocina** / kitchen; **una escoba** / a broom; **limpiar** / to clean.

11. (C) **cepillar** / to brush; **el caballo** / the horse; **el cabello** / the hair.

12. (C) **abuelito** / grandfather; **morir** / to die. Note the idiom **echar de menos** in §14.22; **lo echo de menos** / I miss him.

13. (B) **deber** / to owe; note the use of the indirect object pronoun **le** (to you) referring to **Ud.** Review §6.14–§6.20.

14. (D) **cerrar** / to close

15. (D) **ancha** / wide

16. (B) **la esquina** / the (outside) corner; **el rincón** / the (inside) corner.

17. (D) **transporte** / transportation

18. (A) **teatros y cines** / theaters and movies; note that the reflexive pronoun is attached to the infinitive **(divertirme)**; review §6.21–§6.53.

19. (A) **regalos** / gifts

20. (D) **cerveza** / beer; **beber** / to drink

21. (A) **dejar** / to leave something behind; study the differences between **dejar** and **salir** in §7.129–§7.132.

22. (D) Review §5.37–§5.53.

23. (A) **tan . . . como** / as . . . as; review comparatives in §5.38ff.

24. (A) **Mañana por la mañana** / tomorrow morning; study §14.18, §14.37, and §15.22.

25. (B) **salir de** / to leave; review §7.129–§7.132.

26. (D) **las llaves** / the keys

27. (D) **hacían mucho ruido** / were making a lot of noise

28. (A) **llorar** / to cry; note that **comenzar** requires the preposition **a** when followed by an infinitive. Review §7.16–§7.30.

29. (B) **flojo** / lazy

30. (C) **las alas** / the wings

31. (A) **Doler** / to ache; note **duelo**, *etc.* in §8.65.

PART B

32. (D) You need the present subjunctive form of the verb here because the main verb that precedes the **que** clause is **quiero,** which is one of those special verbs that requires the subjunctive of the verb in the **que** clause. Review §8.41 (e) (1) and §7.87–§7.100.

33. (B) The **imperfecto de indicativo** is used to express an action that was going on in the past when another action occurred, which is in the **pretérito.** Review §8.20 (b).

34. (A) You need the **imperfecto de subjuntivo** (Tense No. 7) of **tener** in the **si** (if) clause because the verb in the main clause is given in the **potencial simple** (conditional, Tense No. 5) which is **iría.** Review thoroughly §7.111 (2), §8.36–§8.40, in particular, §8.36 (a) and §8.50.

35. (D) You need the **imperfecto de subjuntivo** (Tense No. 7) of **ser** in the **como si** (as if) clause. Review §7.34, §7.111, and §8.50.

36. (A) You need the **pretérito** of **ir,** which is **fue.** Review §8.25 (2) and §8.30 where **ir** is listed alphabetically among verbs irregular in the preterit, including stem-changing verbs and orthographical changing verbs.

37. (A) Review the uses of the verb **gustar** in §7.143, §17.3, and §6.20. Also review the indirect object pronouns in §6.14–§6.20.

38. (D) An indefinite antecedent (**un hombre**) precedes the relative pronoun **que;** therefore, the verb in the following clause must be in the subjunctive. Review §7.54–§7.62 and §8.41 (1) 1.

39. (B) Choice A is not correct because **es** in the statement should be **está;** review §7.171. Choice C is not correct because the indefinite article is not used with an unmodified noun of nationality, profession, rank or religion; review §4.19 (d). Choice D is not correct because **es** in the statement should be **está.** Review §7.166–§7.174.

40. (D) The infinitive form of the verb follows the preposition **de.** Review §7.184.

41. (D) In this sentence you are dealing with a masculine singular noun, **el apartamento** or **el apartamiento.** Review the possessive pronouns in §6.61–§6.69.

42. (C) Review the prepositional pronouns (also known as disjunctive pronouns) in §6.30–§6.33.

43. (A) Review the prepositional pronouns (also known as disjunctive pronouns) in §6.30–§6.33.

44. (D) Review §14.42, where **tener sed** is listed.

45. (C) Review direct object pronouns in §6.7–§6.13; indirect object pronouns in §6.14–§6.20; and position of double object pronouns in §6.43–§6.53.

46. (B) Review §5.68ff.

47. (A) You need the singular here (**cuál,** not **cuáles**) because the verb **es** is singular. Review §5.68ff.

48. (B) You need the plural here (**cuáles,** not **cuál**) because the verb **son** is plural. Review §5.68ff.

49. (A) Review §7.221 and §7.23 (**casarse con**).

50. (A) Review §14.19 (**ser amable con**).

51. (A) Review §3.24.

52. (B) Review §12.5.

53. (C) Review §7.113–§7.117.

54. (A) Review §7.113–§7.117.

55. (C) Review §7.150–§7.152.

56. (A) Review §7.152, §6.14, and §6.20.

57. (A) Review §6.19.

58. (B) Review §7.153ff.

59. (D) Review §7.156ff.

60. (B) Review §7.20 and §8.30; the verb **comenzar** is listed there alphabetically.

61. (D) Review §14.12ff.

62. (C) Review §7.159ff and §8.30; the verb **pedir** is listed there alphabetically.

63. (A) Review §7.162ff and §8.19; the verb **pensar** is listed there alphabetically.

64. (B) Review §7.162ff and §8.19; the verb **pensar** is listed there alphabetically.

65. (B) You need the preterit tense because **partió** is in the preterit and the sense is that the gentleman left a tip for the waiter and then he left. Note in the statement the use of the infinitive form of the verb **cenar** because the preposition **de** is right in front of it; review §7.184. Review the **pretérito** (Tense No. 3) in §8.25–§8.30 where **colocar** is listed alphabetically among verbs irregular in the preterit, including stem-changing verbs and orthographical changing verbs.

PART C

66. (B) You need the personal **a** in front of **escritor** (writer) because it is a person and is the direct object of the verb **ver** (to see the writer). Personal **a** + definite article **el** changes to **al.** Review §11.8–§11.10 in the General Review, Part II.

67. (A) You need the preterit, 3rd person singular of **contestar** (to reply) because the subject is **Mercedes** (the woman's name). In B, the verb form is the 1st person singular preterit. The verb tenses in C and D would not fit correctly because the action is past. Review the preterit tense in §8.25–§8.30, specifically §8.28.

68. (D) You need the preposition **de** because an infinitive (**volver**/to return) is right after it. Review §14.26 where **estar a punto de + inf.** is listed.

69. (A) The only word that makes sense here is **ciudad** (city) in A. It refers to **Madrid**, which was mentioned in the paragraph.

70. (C) You need the preterit, 1st person singular of **tener**. Note that **tener que + inf.** means to have to + inf. The 1st person singular is needed because of **me** in **quedarme** (to remain) right after it. Review §7.128 where **tener que + inf.** is discussed. Also, review irregular verbs in the **preterit** in §8.30 where **tener** is listed alphabetically. In B, **tengo** is 1st person singular present tense of **tener**, but in this paragraph the narrator is talking about the past.

PART D

71. (A) See the first sentence of the passage.

72. (B) See the first sentence of paragraph three in the passage.

73. (D) See the last sentence of paragraph four in the passage.

74. (A) See the first sentence of paragraph five in the passage.

75. (C) See the fourth sentence in paragraph five of the passage.

76. (B) See the first two sentences in paragraph one of the passage.

77. (C) See the last sentence in paragraph one of the passage.

78. (D) See the last sentence in paragraph two of the passage.

79. (C) See paragraph three of the passage.

80. (A) See the second sentence in paragraph four of the passage.

81. (B) See the first two sentences of the passage.

82. (A) See sentences one to three of paragraph two of the passage.

83. (D) See paragraph five of the passage.

84. (A) See paragraph six of the passage.

85. (C) See the last two sentences of the passage.

Answer Sheet: Diagnostic Test

PART A

1 Ⓐ Ⓑ Ⓒ Ⓓ
2 Ⓐ Ⓑ Ⓒ Ⓓ
3 Ⓐ Ⓑ Ⓒ Ⓓ
4 Ⓐ Ⓑ Ⓒ Ⓓ
5 Ⓐ Ⓑ Ⓒ Ⓓ
6 Ⓐ Ⓑ Ⓒ Ⓓ
7 Ⓐ Ⓑ Ⓒ Ⓓ
8 Ⓐ Ⓑ Ⓒ Ⓓ
9 Ⓐ Ⓑ Ⓒ Ⓓ
10 Ⓐ Ⓑ Ⓒ Ⓓ
11 Ⓐ Ⓑ Ⓒ Ⓓ
12 Ⓐ Ⓑ Ⓒ Ⓓ
13 Ⓐ Ⓑ Ⓒ Ⓓ
14 Ⓐ Ⓑ Ⓒ Ⓓ
15 Ⓐ Ⓑ Ⓒ Ⓓ
16 Ⓐ Ⓑ Ⓒ Ⓓ
17 Ⓐ Ⓑ Ⓒ Ⓓ
18 Ⓐ Ⓑ Ⓒ Ⓓ
19 Ⓐ Ⓑ Ⓒ Ⓓ
20 Ⓐ Ⓑ Ⓒ Ⓓ
21 Ⓐ Ⓑ Ⓒ Ⓓ
22 Ⓐ Ⓑ Ⓒ Ⓓ
23 Ⓐ Ⓑ Ⓒ Ⓓ
24 Ⓐ Ⓑ Ⓒ Ⓓ
25 Ⓐ Ⓑ Ⓒ Ⓓ
26 Ⓐ Ⓑ Ⓒ Ⓓ
27 Ⓐ Ⓑ Ⓒ Ⓓ
28 Ⓐ Ⓑ Ⓒ Ⓓ
29 Ⓐ Ⓑ Ⓒ Ⓓ
30 Ⓐ Ⓑ Ⓒ Ⓓ
31 Ⓐ Ⓑ Ⓒ Ⓓ

PART B

32 Ⓐ Ⓑ Ⓒ Ⓓ
33 Ⓐ Ⓑ Ⓒ Ⓓ
34 Ⓐ Ⓑ Ⓒ Ⓓ
35 Ⓐ Ⓑ Ⓒ Ⓓ
36 Ⓐ Ⓑ Ⓒ Ⓓ
37 Ⓐ Ⓑ Ⓒ Ⓓ
38 Ⓐ Ⓑ Ⓒ Ⓓ
39 Ⓐ Ⓑ Ⓒ Ⓓ
40 Ⓐ Ⓑ Ⓒ Ⓓ
41 Ⓐ Ⓑ Ⓒ Ⓓ
42 Ⓐ Ⓑ Ⓒ Ⓓ
43 Ⓐ Ⓑ Ⓒ Ⓓ
44 Ⓐ Ⓑ Ⓒ Ⓓ
45 Ⓐ Ⓑ Ⓒ Ⓓ
46 Ⓐ Ⓑ Ⓒ Ⓓ
47 Ⓐ Ⓑ Ⓒ Ⓓ
48 Ⓐ Ⓑ Ⓒ Ⓓ
49 Ⓐ Ⓑ Ⓒ Ⓓ
50 Ⓐ Ⓑ Ⓒ Ⓓ
51 Ⓐ Ⓑ Ⓒ Ⓓ
52 Ⓐ Ⓑ Ⓒ Ⓓ
53 Ⓐ Ⓑ Ⓒ Ⓓ
54 Ⓐ Ⓑ Ⓒ Ⓓ
55 Ⓐ Ⓑ Ⓒ Ⓓ
56 Ⓐ Ⓑ Ⓒ Ⓓ
57 Ⓐ Ⓑ Ⓒ Ⓓ
58 Ⓐ Ⓑ Ⓒ Ⓓ
59 Ⓐ Ⓑ Ⓒ Ⓓ
60 Ⓐ Ⓑ Ⓒ Ⓓ
61 Ⓐ Ⓑ Ⓒ Ⓓ
62 Ⓐ Ⓑ Ⓒ Ⓓ
63 Ⓐ Ⓑ Ⓒ Ⓓ
64 Ⓐ Ⓑ Ⓒ Ⓓ
65 Ⓐ Ⓑ Ⓒ Ⓓ

PART C

66 Ⓐ Ⓑ Ⓒ Ⓓ
67 Ⓐ Ⓑ Ⓒ Ⓓ
68 Ⓐ Ⓑ Ⓒ Ⓓ
69 Ⓐ Ⓑ Ⓒ Ⓓ
70 Ⓐ Ⓑ Ⓒ Ⓓ

PART D

71 Ⓐ Ⓑ Ⓒ Ⓓ
72 Ⓐ Ⓑ Ⓒ Ⓓ
73 Ⓐ Ⓑ Ⓒ Ⓓ
74 Ⓐ Ⓑ Ⓒ Ⓓ
75 Ⓐ Ⓑ Ⓒ Ⓓ
76 Ⓐ Ⓑ Ⓒ Ⓓ
77 Ⓐ Ⓑ Ⓒ Ⓓ
78 Ⓐ Ⓑ Ⓒ Ⓓ
79 Ⓐ Ⓑ Ⓒ Ⓓ
80 Ⓐ Ⓑ Ⓒ Ⓓ
81 Ⓐ Ⓑ Ⓒ Ⓓ
82 Ⓐ Ⓑ Ⓒ Ⓓ
83 Ⓐ Ⓑ Ⓒ Ⓓ
84 Ⓐ Ⓑ Ⓒ Ⓓ
85 Ⓐ Ⓑ Ⓒ Ⓓ

NINE MORE
PRACTICE TESTS

PART

TEST 1

This test consists of 85 questions. You have 60 minutes to complete it. Answer Keys, Analysis Charts, Explained Answers, and Answer Sheets follow Test 9.

PART A

Directions: _This part contains incomplete statements. Each has four choices. Choose the correct completion and blacken the corresponding space on the answer sheet._

1. ¡Mira! ¡Mira! . . . está comiendo una banana.
   A. El mono
   B. La moneda
   C. El moho
   D. El mito

2. María no tiene apetito. No tiene . . . de comer.
   A. alhaja
   B. ganas
   C. ganado
   D. gangas

3. Al salir de la escuela, Jaime y Marta pasan por delante de . . . que anuncia una película nueva.
   A. un restaurante
   B. un peluquero
   C. una peluquería
   D. un cine

4. Un estudiante entra en una librería para . . .
   A. pedir prestado un libro.
   B. comer algo.
   C. escribir una carta.
   D. comprar un libro.

5. La señora González no desea comer porque . . .
   A. tiene mucha hambre.
   B. tiene que comer.
   C. no tiene apetito.
   D. no tiene anteojos.

6. No queremos ver aquella película porque no nos gusta entrar en . . .
   A. aquella piscina.
   B. aquel cine.
   C. aquel peligro.
   D. aquella pelea.

7. Juanita y Pepe hablan de los exámenes de junio y esperan tener . . .
   A. éxito.
   B. hambre.
   C. el tiempo.
   D. lugar.

GO ON TO THE NEXT PAGE

8. María, ¿no quieres ponerte ... ?
   A. la mesa
   B. los guantes
   C. el techo
   D. el suelo

9. No comer el pan, prohibir el azúcar, no beber durante las comidas es indudablemente la mejor receta para perder ...
   A. dinero.
   B. peso.
   C. dólares.
   D. piso.

10. Anoche durante una tempestad catorce personas, cuya identidad se desconoce, murieron ahogados ...
   A. en una cueva.
   B. en el techo de un edificio.
   C. en la arena.
   D. en el lago.

11. El chofer no puede manejar el coche, sin buena visibilidad, a causa de la intensa lluvia y del fuerte ...
   A. vecino.
   B. viento.
   C. vino.
   D. vientre.

12. En la escuela, Domingo estudia el inglés, el español, las matemáticas, la historia y la biología. Estudia cinco ...
   A. subjetivos.
   B. temas.
   C. materiales.
   D. asignaturas.

13. Este actor sabe bien ... de Don Quijote.
   A. hacer caso
   B. hacer falta
   C. hacer el papel
   D. hacer un viaje

14. Ud. está en un restaurante con un amigo. El camarero ... en venir y su amigo se pone muy impaciente.
   A. llega
   B. se acuesta
   C. trabaja
   D. tarda

15. Juan está en la estación de autobuses en Madrid y ... informes para ir a Toledo.
   A. pide
   B. pierde
   C. pregunta
   D. puede

16. Elena y su madre quieren . . . . Pronto van a salir de casa. Su madre dice: ¿Qué me dijiste esta mañana? Necesitamos azúcar y ¿qué otra cosa?
    A. ir a la iglesia
    B. asistir al baile
    C. ir de compras
    D. darse prisa

17. El señor Pérez habla por teléfono con el dueño de un restaurante llamado Casa Paco para . . . una reservación.
    A. preguntarle
    B. pedirle
    C. hacerla
    D. tomarle

18. La corbata se pone en . . .
    A. el cuello.
    B. el sello.
    C. el corderito.
    D. la corona.

19. Cuando una persona está muy triste . . .
    A. llueve.
    B. llora.
    C. se ríe.
    D. se sienta.

20. Para subir a un edificio alto se toma . . .
    A. el avión.
    B. la escalera.
    C. un paraguas.
    D. el ascensor.

21. Aquel hombre es mudo; no puede . . .
    A. ver.
    B. oír.
    C. hablar.
    D. pensar.

22. El padre de María le dice:—¿Estás . . . , María? Tenemos que partir y ya van a dar les diez.
    A. lista
    B. liga
    C. ligera
    D. linterna

23. Un turista norteamericano entra en una farmacia y habla con el farmacéutico. El turista le dice que tiene un fuerte . . .
    A. resto.
    B. nariz.
    C. faro.
    D. resfriado.

24. Tu tío te ha regalado dinero para tu cumpleaños. Ahora tú hablas con tu madre de cómo vas a gastar el dinero. Tu madre te dice que tu vas a necesitar . . . nueva para cuando comiencen las clases en septiembre.
    A. propina
    B. risa
    C. escala
    D. ropa

GO ON TO THE NEXT PAGE

25. Esta mañana conocí a la señorita López. Le di la mano y le dije— ...
  A. ¡No me digas!
  B. ¡Tanto gusto!
  C. ¡Déme una propina!
  D. ¡Muchas gracias, señorita!

26. La detención del criminal había sido larga y exclamó— ... a la puerta de la prisión cuando estaba para salir, mostrando mucha alegría.
  A. ¡Tengo suelto!
  B. ¡Por fin, libre!
  C. ¡Buenos días!
  D. ¡Por fin, preso!

27. Una mañana, los señores Robles decidieron ir a comprar ... . Habían podido economizar mucho dinero y estaban cansados de andar o viajar en el autobús por la ciudad y el campo.
  A. un codo
  B. un coche
  C. una cola
  D. zapatos

28. Si quiere uno ... por unas dos horas y media los graves problemas actuales, que vaya al Teatro del Bosque, donde trabaja el loco Valdés, combinación de actor cómico y de acróbata.
  A. recordar
  B. acordarse
  C. ver una película
  D. olvidar

29. La lámpara no funcionaba porque ...
  A. no tenía bombilla.
  B. había electricidad.
  C. encendieron la luz.
  D. hacía calor.

30. Una persona que arregla zapatos es ...
  A. una zapatería.
  B. un zapatero.
  C. una zapatilla.
  D. un zapateado.

31. Para lavarnos las manos usamos ...
  A. jabón.
  B. jamón.
  C. sopa.
  D. peine.

PART B

Directions: The following sentences contain blank spaces. Of the four choices given for each blank select the one that fits grammatically and makes sense.

32. Mi hermano ... mañana.
  A. llegó
  B. llegué
  C. llegaré
  D. llega

33. Hace tres horas que ... la televisión.
   A. miró
   B. miro
   C. he mirado
   D. miraré

34. Por poco me ...
   A. matan.
   B. hubiéramos matado.
   C. han matado.
   D. hubiera matado.

35. La profesora ... da los libros a los alumnos.
   A. le
   B. les
   C. los
   D. las

36. María y Pablo ... al profesor.
   A. hablaron
   B. hablamos
   C. hablasteis
   D. hemos hablado

37. Enrique salió sin ...
   A. hablar.
   B. habla.
   C. hablando.
   D. hablado.

38. Me apresuré ... tomar el tren.
   A. a
   B. de
   C. por
   D. para

39. El hombre comenzó ... llorar.
   A. a
   B. de
   C. por
   D. para

40. Mi cuarto da ... jardín.
   A. a
   B. al
   C. por el
   D. para el

41. Soy aficionado ... los deportes.
   A. a
   B. con
   C. de
   D. por

42. Mi hermano es más alto que ...
   A. la suya.
   B. el suyo.
   C. las mías.
   D. su.

GO ON TO THE NEXT PAGE

43. ¿Conoce Ud. . . . amigos?
    A. mi
    B. mis
    C. a mis
    D. de mis

44. Saldré a las tres y media a menos que . . .
    A. está lloviendo.
    B. esté lloviendo.
    C. llover.
    D. esté llorando.

45. No abriré la puerta, quienquiera que . . .
    A. es.
    B. está.
    C. sean.
    D. sea.

46. Adondequiera que Ud. . . . , dígamelo.
    A. va
    B. vaya
    C. está
    D. sea

47. ¿Conoce Ud. a alguien que . . . paciencia?
    A. tenga
    B. tiene
    C. sabe
    D. dondequiera

48. El señor Armstrong habla español muy bien . . . ser norteamericano.
    A. para
    B. por
    C. de
    D. al por

49. Si a Roma . . . , haz como vieres.
    A. fueres
    B. eres
    C. va
    D. irás

50. Más vale pájaro en mano que . . . volando.
    A. cien
    B. ciento
    C. cientos
    D. un cien

51. Juan tiene un regalo y quiere . . . a Teresa.
    A. darselo
    B. lo dar
    C. darle
    D. dárselo

52. ¿Quién? ¿La señora Martín? — Sí, sí, . . . conocí la semana pasada en el baile.
    A. lo
    B. la
    C. le
    D. se lo

53. Ayer yo . . . una carta de mi amigo Roberto.
   A. tuvo
   B. tuve
   C. recibió
   D. recibo

54. Trabajé hasta que . . . mi amigo a verme.
   A. vino
   B. viniera
   C. vine
   D. venir

55. Trabajaré hasta que . . . mi amigo a verme.
   A. vengo
   B. venga
   C. vino
   D. vine

56. Mi amigo salió del cuarto . . .
   A. sin decirme nada.
   B. nada sin decirme.
   C. sin me decir nada.
   D. me sin decir nada.

57. Queríamos todos que el prisionero . . . la verdad.
   A. dice
   B. dijera *or* dijese
   C. diga
   D. diera

58. . . . dinero tengo, tanto más necesito.
   A. Cuanto
   B. Cuanto más
   C. Tanto
   D. Lo más

59. Llegaremos a Madrid . . . las tres de la tarde.
   A. eso
   B. a eso
   C. a eso de
   D. acerca de

60. Si Ud. . . . bien anoche, habría podido pasearse hoy.
   A. ha dormido
   B. hubiera (*or* hubiese) dormido
   C. durmió
   D. duerme

61. . . . completar la tarea cuando el teléfono sonó.
   A. Acabo
   B. Acabo de
   C. Acababa
   D. Acababa de

62. Un fuego destruyó la casa . . .
   A. hace una semana.
   B. hacía una semana.
   C. hay una semana.
   D. una semana que hay.

GO ON TO THE NEXT PAGE

63. Anoche, cuando dormíamos, la voz de una mujer turbada ... en la calle.
   A. se oye
   B. se oyó
   C. oye
   D. oyó

64. Busco un apartamento que ... dos cuartos de baño.
   A. tiene
   B. tenía
   C. tenga
   D. tuviera

65. Pablo no quiere alquilar el automóvil ... comprarlo.
   A. pero
   B. sino
   C. también
   D. e

PART C

Directions: Read the entire paragraph that follows to determine its general meaning. It contains blank spaces that are numbered. Of the four choices given for each numbered blank, choose the one that is grammatically correct and makes sense.

Cada país tiene distinta manera de disfrutar del arte de cocinar. En Madrid se __66__ a todas horas. Por eso, hay tabernas y bares con una gran variedad de platos sobre el mostrador. Jamón, queso, pescados, callos a la madrileña, mariscos. ¡Qué ricas son las tapas! A los madrileños y a los turistas, en general, __67__ gusta ir a estos lugares y pedir distintas cosas. Las tapas son pequeñas porciones de comida que se acompañan con vino, con cerveza __68__ otra bebida. Estas tapas se toman especialmente como aperitivo. Los bares están llenos alrededor de las dos de la tarde antes del almuerzo y a __69__ de las nueve de la noche antes de la cena. Se dice que hay personas que van de bar en bar para probar las diferentes especialidades. Si una persona __70__ esto diariamente entonces existe el peligro de que aumente mucho de peso.

66. A. descansa
   B. come
   C. viaja
   D. pesca

67. A. les
   B. le
   C. los
   D. se

68. A. u
   B. o
   C. de
   D. al

69. A. esto
   B. ese
   C. eso
   D. esta

70. A. ve
   B. dice
   C. vende
   D. hace

PART D

<u>Directions:</u> *The following passages are for reading comprehension. After each selection there are incomplete statements or questions. Of the four choices, choose the correct one based on the passage.*

Es curioso el hecho de que mientras en Buenos Aires se habla español, no es una ciudad española. El número de inmigrantes de las dos últimas generaciones ha sido enorme, y entre las naciones que más han contribuido a aumentar la población se encuentra Italia en primer lugar. La semejanza de las lenguas española e italiana es tal, que los inmigrantes que vienen de aquel país, se adaptan fácilmente a la lengua predominante, y por esa razón el español continúa siendo el idioma oficial. Los británicos son también numerosos, así como los franceses y alemanes. Muchos turistas establecen una comparación entre Buenos Aires y París. En ambas ciudades es frecuente ver mesas y sillas en la acera, como prolongación de un café interior; los parques, las plazas y las estatuas abundan, prestándole tanto a la una como a la otra, singular belleza.

71. ¿Cómo se describiría la ciudad de Buenos Aires?
A. Es muy moderna.
B. Es muy cosmopolita.
C. No se distingue de otras ciudades.
D. Tiene origen romano.

72. ¿Qué ha contribuido al crecimiento de Buenos Aires?
A. la llegada de muchos extranjeros
B. la belleza de la ciudad
C. las diversiones que se encuentran allí
D. las familias famosas que viven en la ciudad

73. ¿Qué aspecto de interés caracteriza a las lenguas española e italiana?
A. Son lenguas parecidas.
B. Ambas lenguas son fáciles.
C. Las dos lenguas son románticas.
D. Ambas lenguas son oficiales.

74. ¿Dónde se hallan muchos cafés de la ciudad?
A. en las plazas
B. cerca de los parques
C. al aire libre
D. en el centro

75. Buenos Aires se parece mucho a París en
A. la grandeza.
B. la antigüedad.
C. lo extraño.
D. lo hermoso.

Un vecino pobre iba todos los sábados al monte a cortar leña, que traía después en su burrito y vendía en el pueblo cuando estaba seca. Uno de tantos sábados se perdió en el monte, y lo cogió la noche sin poder dar con la salida. Cansado de andar por aquí y por allá, resolvió subir a un árbol con la esperanza de dormir allí sin peligro. Ató el burrito, y subió hasta la copa. De repente vio a lo lejos una luz. Bajó y se encaminó a ella. Al acercarse vio una casa iluminada, donde se oían música, canto y risas. Sin hacer ruido, entró en la casa y se escondió detrás de una puerta.

76. El pobre se dirigía al monte para
A. recoger madera.
B. visitar a un vecino.
C. cortar el camino.
D. llegar a la aldea.

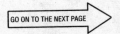
GO ON TO THE NEXT PAGE

77. ¿Qué le pasó al leñador un sábado?
    A. Vendió su asno.
    B. Se le perdió el burrito.
    C. Padeció de sed.
    D. Se desorientó.

78. ¿Por qué subió al árbol el pobre?
    A. Quería encontrar a su burro.
    B. Quería protegerse.
    C. Tenía que cortar un ramo.
    D. Esperaba esconderse.

79. ¿Qué notó el pobre a lo lejos?
    A. unos cuantos cantantes
    B. las muchas estrellas del firmamento
    C. una vivienda donde había luz
    D. un carnaval donde se oía mucha risa

80. Al entrar en la casa, ¿qué hizo el hombre?
    A. Empezó a cantar.
    B. Dio gritos.
    C. Se ocultó.
    D. Rió a carcajadas.

Pepita Montes estaba completamente engañada respecto a su novio, Curro Vázquez. Le veía joven, guapo, sonriente y humilde, sin darse cuenta de que no tenía corazón. Curro era el criado de don Francisco Calderón, el famoso negociante de caballos de Andújar. Lo había sacado del arroyo, y últimamente lo había hecho su muchacho de confianza. Le pagaba bien, y le gustaba de que vistiese con elegancia y aun con lujo. Curro se aprovechaba de ello, y enamoraba a las muchachas. Al conocer a Pepita, quedó preso de sus encantos. ¿Qué hacer para casarse con ella? Meditó mucho y al fin resolvió dejar de ser criado, negociar por su cuenta, y enriquecerse de cualquier modo.

81. ¿Cómo le parecía Curro a Pepita?
    A. bien parecido y modesto
    B. insensible y pérfido
    C. fiel y honrado
    D. cobarde y desagradable

82. ¿Cuál era el oficio de Curro?
    A. jinete
    B. sirviente
    C. propietario de negocio
    D. amo de casa

83. ¿Qué había hecho don Francisco en favor de Curro?
    A. Le había confiado su caballo.
    B. Le había presentado a Pepita.
    C. Le había dejado su riqueza.
    D. Le había posibilitado una vida mejor.

84. ¿Qué cualidad de Curro encantaba a las chicas?
    A. su risa
    B. su constancia
    C. su apariencia lujosa
    D. su firme resolución

85. ¿Por qué decidió Curro cambiar de empleo?
A. Don Francisco le había arrojado a la calle.
B. Quería hacerse rico.
C. Buscaba una esposa bien criada.
D. Le habían contado los encantos de otros empleos.

END OF TEST 1

TEST 2

This test consists of 85 questions. You have 60 minutes to complete it. Answer Keys, Analysis Charts, Explained Answers, and Answer Sheets follow Test 9.

PART A

Directions: This part contains incomplete statements. Each has four choices. Choose the correct completion and blacken the corresponding space on the answer sheet.

1. Las ... vuelan de flor en flor.
   A. rosas
   B. llaves
   C. ovejas
   D. mariposas

2. Ayer compré un reloj para saber ...
   A. el tiempo.
   B. la temperatura.
   C. la hora.
   D. la vez.

3. Ese hombre no puede ver. Es ...
   A. ciego.
   B. sordo.
   C. zurdo.
   D. mudo.

4. Este chico no habla porque es ...
   A. sordo.
   B. mudo.
   C. ciego.
   D. zurdo.

5. Aquel alumno no oye nada porque es ...
   A. mudo.
   B. ciego.
   C. zurdo.
   D. sordo.

6. Este chico escribe con la mano izquierda, por eso la gente dice que es ...
   A. manco.
   B. izquierda.
   C. zurdo.
   D. raro.

7. Usamos caña y anzuelo para ...
   A. tomar el café.
   B. pescar.
   C. comer.
   D. ir de compras.

8. Al entrar en la iglesia, la señora se cayó. Yo corrí, la ayudé a levantarse y le pregunté: ...
   A. ¿Desea Ud. rezar?
   B. ¿Es Ud. vieja?
   C. ¿Se alegra Ud.?
   D. ¿Se ha hecho Ud. daño?

9. Como yo no sabía la hora de la salida del tren, le pregunté a un empleado: ...
   A. ¿Qué hora es?
   B. ¿Cuántos trenes pasaron hoy?
   C. ¿Me hace el favor del horario?
   D. ¿Qué tiempo hace?

10. No puedo tomar la sopa porque me falta ...
   A. dinero.
   B. agua.
   C. una cuchara.
   D. un tenedor.

11. Después de ponerse los zapatos nuevos, Roberto le preguntó a su padre: ...
   A. ¿Qué te parece?
   B. ¿Me gustan mucho?
   C. ¿Cómo te van?
   D. ¿Está lloviendo?

12. Roberto, cuando salgas ... la luz, por favor.
   A. vende
   B. apaga
   C. compra
   D. come

13. Cuando llegué a casa mojado como una sopa, mi padre me dijo: ...
   A. ¿Quieres más sopa?
   B. ¿Quieres jabón?
   C. ¿Te gusta el jamón?
   D. Cámbiate de ropa.

14. Al ver que la chica se ponía pálida antes de la operación, el doctor le dijo: ...
   A. No se enfade.
   B. No te preocupes.
   C. La operación es grave.
   D. La operación salió bien.

15. Luis estaba muy nervioso por tanto que tenía que estudiar. Por eso, yo le dije: ...
   A. ¡Manos a la obra!
   B. ¡Coma!
   C. ¡Siéntate!
   D. ¡Bébelo!

16. En la calle hubo un accidente. Un hombre gritaba:...
   A. ¡Atropellaron al gato!
   B. ¡El automóvil me mató!
   C. ¡La comida es muy buena!
   D. ¡La calle es muy ancha!

17. El pobre hombre fue acusado por la policía de algo que no había cometido. Por eso, protestó: ...
   A. Soy culpable.
   B. Estoy de acuerdo.
   C. Soy inocente.
   D. Me gusta la sopa.

GO ON TO THE NEXT PAGE

18. El vino se vende en . . .
A. cristales.
B. botellas.
C. latas.
D. cartones.

19. Como es el santo de mi tía, le enviaré un ramillete de . . .
A. flores.
B. dulces.
C. pasteles.
D. zapatos.

20. Este chico es huérfano porque no tiene . . .
A. novio.
B. amigos.
C. gotas.
D. padres.

21. Para saber las noticias, compro . . .
A. un papel.
B. un periódico.
C. una rueda.
D. un borrador.

22. Después de decirle lo que quería, el camarero me trajo la comida en una . . .
A. banda.
B. bandera.
C. bandeja.
D. banderilla.

23. Todos los días antes de cenar, mi hermana . . . la mesa.
A. compra
B. vende
C. devuelve
D. pone

24. Queriendo salir del restaurante, llamamos al mozo y le pedimos . . .
A. una propina.
B. algún dinero.
C. el cuento.
D. la cuenta.

25. ¡Qué lástima! Está lloviendo. Tendré que ponerme . . . porque quiero salir.
A. el traje de baño
B. la mesa
C. el impermeable
D. pálido

26. Las naranjas tienen . . .
A. piedras.
B. juego.
C. zumo.
D. refresco.

27. Antes de echar una carta al correo, se necesita ponerle . . .
A. recuerdos.
B. un sello.
C. un fútbol.
D. en la mano.

28. Cuando mi padre fuma en la sala de nuestra casa, mi madre le dice: ...
A. ¡El humo sale por la puerta!
B. ¡Se quema la casa!
C. ¡Echa las cenizas en el cenicero!
D. ¿Es bueno fumar mucho?

29. Como el abrigo le quedaba largo, mi padre fue al sastre y le dijo: ...
A. Córtemelo, por favor.
B. Véndamelo, por favor.
C. Cómpremelo, por favor.
D. Démelo, por favor.

30. Pablo va a salir a la calle pero como hace mucho frío su madre le dice: ...
A. Ponte un vestido.
B. Ponte el abrigo.
C. Dime.
D. Yo no sé.

31. Elena habla con María después de las clases y le dice:
—María, hoy hay muchas gangas en los almacenes. Vamos ...
A. a cantar.
B. a comer.
C. de compras.
D. a las clases.

PART B

Directions: *The following sentences contain blank spaces. Of the four choices given for each blank select the one that fits grammatically and makes sense.*

32. Ricardo no alquiló el automóvil ... lo compró.
A. pero
B. sino que
C. también
D. a menos que

33. Tenemos ... trabajo hoy.
A. poco
B. pequeño
C. mudo
D. muy

34. Este niño no ... contar.
A. conoce
B. sabe
C. sabe a
D. sabe de

35. Camarero, ... una botella de vino, por favor.
A. tráigame
B. me trae
C. un traje hecho
D. pise

36. ¿Quién te dio este dinero?—Mi padre ...
A. te lo dio.
B. me lo da.
C. se lo dio.
D. me lo dio.

GO ON TO THE NEXT PAGE

37. Se lo explico a María para que lo . . .
   A. comprende.
   B. comprenda.
   C. comprendería.
   D. comprenderá.

38. Se lo explicaba a María para que lo . . .
   A. comprendiera.
   B. comprendería.
   C. comprenda.
   D. comprenderá.

39. Cuando llegué a casa, mi hermano . . .
   A. ha salido.
   B. saldrá.
   C. había salido.
   D. habrá salido.

40. Después que . . . , salió.
   A. haber hablado
   B. habrá hablado
   C. está hablando
   D. hubo hablado

41. Roberto llegará mañana y yo . . . mi trabajo.
   A. habré terminado
   B. habrá terminado
   C. habría terminado
   D. hube terminado

42. Los ladrones . . . robaron todo el dinero a él.
   A. le
   B. lo
   C. la
   D. los

43. La madre . . . quitó al niño el sombrero.
   A. le
   B. lo
   C. la
   D. los

44. . . . compré mi automóvil a ellos.
   A. Le
   B. Lo
   C. La
   D. Les

45. A Ricardo . . . gusta el helado.
   A. le
   B. lo
   C. la
   D. les

46. A Juan . . . bastan cien dólares.
   A. le
   B. lo
   C. los
   D. les

47. A los muchachos ... faltan cinco dólares.
   A. le
   B. lo
   C. los
   D. les

48. Ayer por la noche, María y yo nos ... en el cine.
   A. vimos
   B. vemos
   C. vieron
   D. vio

49. María, ¿quieres ir al cine ...
   A. con mi?
   B. con mí?
   C. con yo?
   D. conmigo?

50. Todos mis amigos van al cine menos ...
   A. mi.
   B. mí.
   C. conmigo.
   D. yo.

51. Mi hermano y ... de mi amigo son perezosos.
   A. la
   B. lo
   C. el
   D. le

52. Mis hermanos y ... de Pedro trabajan mucho.
   A. las
   B. los
   C. la
   D. lo

53. Mi hermano es más alto que ...
   A. la suya.
   B. el suyo.
   C. las mías.
   D. la nuestra.

54. Acabo de hallar un lápiz. ¿ ... es?
   A. Cuyo
   B. Cuya
   C. De cuándo
   D. De quién

55. La composición ... Ud. lee es mía.
   A. quien
   B. que
   C. el cual
   D. la cual

56. ¿Conoces a la chica con ... tomé el almuerzo?
   A. qué
   B. que
   C. quien
   D. cual

GO ON TO THE NEXT PAGE ➡

57. ¿Conoces a los chicos con ... María tomó el almuerzo?
  A. quien
  B. quienes
  C. que
  D. las cuales

58. Comprendo ... Ud. dice.
  A. el que
  B. lo que
  C. que
  D. quien

59. El señor García, ... hijos son inteligentes, es profesor.
  A. de quien
  B. de quienes
  C. cuyo
  D. cuyos

60. La muchacha, ... padre es profesor, es inteligente.
  A. cuyo
  B. cuya
  C. de quien
  D. de la cual

61. La niña, ... la madre lavó las manos, es bonita.
  A. a la cual
  B. a quien
  C. de quien
  D. cuya

62. Yo ... leyendo cuando mi hermano entró en el cuarto.
  A. estaba
  B. estoy
  C. soy
  D. era

63. Veo ... mi amigo.
  A. a
  B. al
  C. el
  D. nothing needed.

64. Antes de ... , la profesora cerró las ventanas de la sala de clase.
  A. salir
  B. saliendo
  C. sale
  D. salió

65. No hay ... en casa. Vamos a partir.
  A. alguno
  B. nunca
  C. alguien
  D. nadie

PART C

Directions: *Read the entire paragraph that follows to determine its general meaning. It contains blank spaces that are numbered. Of the four choices given for each numbered blank, choose the one that is grammatically correct and makes sense.*

Miguel Ríos tenía quince años. Era un chico normal y corriente, y __66__ poco dinero al mes trabajando en una tienda de tejidos. Todo iba bien hasta el día en que al dueño se le ocurrió abrir una pequeña sección de discos. Y ahí empezó todo. El joven dependiente vio, oyó y se convenció: Elvis Presley, Roy Orbison, discos hechos en América, rock y roll, ritmo, movimiento. A partir de aquel día, Miguel quiso ser cantante. Pasaron más __67__ diez años y Miguel Ríos, que se había llamado "Mike" durante un tiempo para acomodarse mejor a su estilo __68__, estaba ahora sentado junto al célebre presentador Johnny Carson, en el show Tonight. No por nada, sino porque había llegado al número cuatro de las listas de discos más vendidos en los Estados Unidos con la versión en inglés de su Himno a la alegría. Miguel __69__ en todo el mundo unos siete millones de discos del Himno. __70__ cantante español lo había hecho hasta entonces, y ninguno lo ha hecho después con una sola canción.

66. A. encontraba
    B. ganaba
    C. gastaba
    D. robaba

67. A. que
    B. de
    C. por
    D. para

68. A. formal
    B. tradicional
    C. musical
    D. literario

69. A. pidió
    B. perdió
    C. vendió
    D. rompió

70. A. Ninguno
    B. Nada
    C. Nadie
    D. Ningún

PART D

Directions: *The following passages are for reading comprehension. After each selection there are incomplete statements or questions. Of the four choices, choose the correct one based on the passage.*

—Juan—dijo mi padre.

—¿Qué?—respondí, adivinando de qué iba a hablarme.

—Tienes catorce años—siguió mi padre—. A tu edad ya me ganaba yo el pan que me daba mi madre. Por lo tanto, viendo que tú no te preocupas de nada, he hablado con Magín para que te admita en su taberna. Así, por lo menos, no romperás zapatos marchándote a robar manzanas con los amigotes. De modo que mañana, tempranito, te quitas la pereza, y a trabajar.

Se calló, y por un momento no se oyó sino el ruido del aceite al freírse en la sartén.

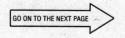

Aquella noche no pude apenas dormir. Agarré cruelmente la manta y grité: "No lo haré, no." Un pensamiento llenó como un golpetazo mi cerebro: "Me iré de casa. ¡Me iré!" Mi hermano, dormido, se estrechó a mí y me llenó de angustia. Nene, nene. Se despertó y se extrañó de verme llorar.

A la mañana siguiente Magín me consideró desde lo alto de su magnífica panza.

—Tu padre me ha dicho que si no te portas bien te doy una paliza de vez en cuando. Yo no tengo mal genio, pero me gusta que los chicos sean obedientes.

71. ¿Quién narra esta selección?
A. el padre de Juan
B. un muchacho de unos catorce años
C. el tabernero Magín
D. el hermano de Juan

72. Según el padre, Juan es un muchacho
A. serio y trabajador.
B. perezoso y travieso.
C. estudioso.
D. enfermizo.

73. ¿Qué decisión tomó su padre?
A. mandarle a vivir con los tíos
B. colocarle en una zapatería
C. conseguirle un empleo
D. hacerle admitir en un colegio interno

74. Aquella noche Juan pensaba
A. pedirle dinero a su madre.
B. marcharse a robar manzanas con sus amigos.
C. escaparse de la casa.
D. ayudar a su hermanito.

75. Magín le dijo a Juan que lo que le importaba más era
A. pagar poco dinero a los niños.
B. comer bien.
C. estar de buena salud.
D. ser obedecido.

Señor Director:

He leído en su revista, número 334, la respuesta a Luis Moreno. Como estudiante que soy, me ha llamado la atención y me ha extrañado su postura, al afirmar que "los estudiantes sólo tienen derecho a estudiar." Creo firmemente que tenemos otros derechos más importantes que el de estudiar (que al fin y al cabo es una situación pasajera) y es, por ejemplo, el formarnos intelectual y cívicamente para poder ocupar, en su día, esos puestos en la sociedad española.

En mi opinión, es muy fácil hacer afirmaciones de esa clase cuando se tiene una capacidad para suprimir, con una simple "nota de la redacción" cualquier carta que exprese un punto de vista disconforme. Se ha condenado a todos los estudiantes por actos que muchos de ellos no han realizado, y yo me pregunto si, al tiempo de condenarnos, no podían ponernos al lado unas soluciones positivas. Si el futuro de España está en nuestras manos ¿no sería interesante que alguien se preocupara de enseñarnos un poco más de esas cosas que no se aprenden en la Universidad?

Juan Pablo Zamorano

76. ¿Quién es el autor de esta carta?
A. un joven abogado
B. el Director de una revista
C. un estudiante universitario
D. Luis Moreno, un lector de la revista

77. Juan Pablo Zamorano escribe esta carta porque quiere
    A. pedir unos informes sobre la revista.
    B. darle las gracias al Director.
    C. saber las señas de su amigo, el estudiante Luis Moreno.
    D. expresar sus ideas sobre lo que ha leído en la revista.

78. ¿Qué se entiende por "situación pasajera"?
    A. la condición de estudiante
    B. el gran número de analfabetos en el campo
    C. la falta de una clase de historia
    D. la miseria de la sociedad española

79. ¿De qué abusos periodísticos se queja el autor de esta carta?
    A. Algunas revistas sólo publican cartas mandadas por subscriptores.
    B. Ciertas revistas tienden a atacar opiniones contrarias.
    C. Los precios de las revistas han subido mucho últimamente.
    D. Sólo los graduados de la Escuela de Periodismo pueden aspirar a la redacción.

80. Según Juan, las publicaciones periódicas deben dedicarse a
    A. dar enseñanza sobre materias omitidas en programas universitarios.
    B. evitar la publicación de noticias sobre delitos y crímenes.
    C. publicar solamente cosas de interés político.
    D. fomentar más interés en institutos educativos.

Valentina venía muy a menudo. Yo no podía ir a su casa con la misma frecuencia porque si su madre me quería, su padre en cambio me tenía una gran antipatía. Sabía que yo había dicho algo contra él en mi casa y que todos habían reído. Yo no podía perdonarle a don Arturo que fuera el padre de Valentina. El había publicado un libro titulado: *El amor, ensayo para un análisis psicológico.* Era su tesis de doctorado y había enviado a mi padre dos ejemplares, uno dedicado: "A don José García este libro de anticuadas ideas con un abrazo del Autor." Mi padre decía que era un libro muy bueno, pero cuando mi madre le preguntaba si lo había leído, él contestaba con vaguedades e insistía en que el libro era muy bueno. Yo estaba un día en el segundo corral donde la tía Ignacia se entretenía a veces con los conejos y las cabras y yo trataba en vano de penetrar algunos conceptos de don Arturo abriendo las páginas aquí y allá. En un descuido las cabras lo despedazaron y se lo comieron.

81. El narrador no podía visitar a Valentina muy a menudo porque
    A. ella lo detestaba.
    B. su casa distaba mucho de la de él.
    C. ella estaba enferma.
    D. el padre de la chica no le quería.

82. José García era
    A. el padre de Valentina.
    B. el padre del narrador.
    C. un profesor de Valentina.
    D. el hermano del narrador.

83. Era probable que el padre del muchacho
    A. no hubiera leído el libro.
    B. no hubiera aprendido a leer.
    C. le pidiera al autor otro ejemplar.
    D. ya tuviera un ejemplar en su biblioteca.

84. ¿Qué hacía el muchacho un día en el segundo corral?
    A. Jugaba con los animales.
    B. Tomaba la siesta.
    C. Buscaba una cabra perdida.
    D. Leía unas partes del libro.

 GO ON TO THE NEXT PAGE

85. ¿Qué le pasó al libro?
   A. La tía Ignacia se lo regaló a su hermana.
   B. Los animales lo destrozaron.
   C. El muchacho lo perdió.
   D. Don Arturo vino a buscarlo.

END OF TEST 2

TEST 3

This test consists of 85 questions. You have 60 minutes to complete it. Answer Keys, Analysis Charts, Explained Answers, and Answer Sheets follow Test 9.

PART A

Directions: This part contains incomplete statements. Each has four choices. Choose the correct completion and blacken the corresponding space on the answer sheet.

1. Llevo ... cuando llueve.
   A. impermeable
   B. la ventana
   C. a la una
   D. mis llaves

2. Me gustaría mucho ... unas semanas en la Ciudad de México.
   A. comprar
   B. llenar
   C. callarme
   D. pasar

3. Hace tres años que estudio el español y durante este ... he leído mucho sobre la capital mexicana.
   A. hora
   B. momento
   C. vez
   D. tiempo

4. Voy a entrar en este restaurante porque tengo ... de comer.
   A. dinero
   B. hambre
   C. mucho
   D. ganas

5. Ayer visité la Estatua de la Libertad en Nueva York. Al llegar, entré y subí ...
   A. la montaña.
   B. la escalera.
   C. el tren.
   D. el vapor.

6. Cuento ... tener éxito en este examen.
   A. con
   B. a
   C. de
   D. para

7. Me contento ... quedarme en casa hoy.
   A. con
   B. a
   C. de
   D. para

GO ON TO THE NEXT PAGE

8. José se casó ... Ana.
   A. con
   B. a
   C. de
   D. para

9. Mis padres acaban ... llegar.
   A. con
   B. a
   C. de
   D. para

10. Jaime dejó ... escribir la composición.
    A. con
    B. a
    C. de
    D. por

11. Vamos a aprovecharnos ... esta oportunidad.
    A. de
    B. a
    C. con
    D. en

12. La señora Pardo consintió ... asistir a la conferencia.
    A. a
    B. en
    C. con
    D. de

13. Un turista norteamericano ... la calle Salamanca en la ciudad de Madrid.
    A. sepa
    B. sabe
    C. acuerda
    D. busca

14. Un señor se acerca a un policía para...algunas direcciones y el policía lo orienta.
    A. pedirle
    B. darle
    C. preguntarle
    D. hablarle

15. La señora López entra en una tienda de ... para comprar legumbres.
    A. comparaciones
    B. comportamientos
    C. comestibles
    D. confinamientos

16. Mi madre suele hacer sus compras en ...
    A. esta cocina.
    B. este almacén.
    C. esta propina.
    D. este aceite.

17. Pienso preparar ... de jamón y huevos.
    A. una tortilla
    B. una tertulia
    C. un terreno
    D. un testigo

18. Usted está sentado en el tren que va a Madrid cuando una persona se acerca y le pide permiso para ... al lado de usted.
    A. sentirse
    B. sentarse
    C. quitarse
    D. levantarse

19. El primer concierto de la Orquestra Sinfónica Nacional no resultó ... excelente como se esperaba.
    A. tan
    B. como
    C. tanto
    D. que

20. Pablo y Enrique hablan de las vacaciones de verano. Los dos jóvenes están delante de la biblioteca y Pablo dice que él y su familia van a ... un viaje a Puerto Rico.
    A. tomar
    B. haber
    C. hacer
    D. viajar

21. Usted entra en un restaurante mexicano. El mesero le ... y Ud. va a sentarse cerca de una ventana.
    A. grita
    B. abrasa
    C. ahorra
    D. saluda

22. Una noche, el señor Pérez habla con su hijo Juan quien ... para salir.
    A. está
    B. es
    C. fue
    D. era

23. Carlos ... de saber que su amigo Manuel está en el hospital.
    A. aburre
    B. acaba
    C. abarca
    D. aclara

24. Es ... de bajar y tomar el desayuno y la mamá de Pepe lo llama varias veces porque él tiene que ir a la escuela.
    A. vez
    B. tiempo
    C. hora
    D. hasta

25. Un joven norteamericano, Robert Smith, se encuentra en un aeroplano que va de Nueva York a Barcelona y a su ... hay un joven español muy amable.
    A. lobo
    B. lodo
    C. lomo
    D. lado

26. Cuando yo ... el accidente, me puse pálido.
    A. di
    B. vi
    C. cupe
    D. caí

GO ON TO THE NEXT PAGE

27. Me gusta . . . a la pelota.
    A. tocar
    B. jugar
    C. jurar
    D. juntar

28. Carmen . . . muy bien el piano.
    A. toca
    B. juega
    C. jura
    D. junta

29. Pedro . . . a María al baile anoche.
    A. tomó
    B. llevó
    C. regaló
    D. sollozó

30. Mi padre se puso triste al oír la noticia . . .
    A. desgraciada.
    B. agradable.
    C. siquiera.
    D. sombra.

31. En una . . . se venden libros.
    A. librería
    B. biblioteca
    C. libra
    D. lectura

PART B

Directions: The following sentences contain blank spaces. Of the four choices given for each blank select the one that fits grammatically and makes sense.

32. Ahora tengo que . . . de usted.
    A. despedirme
    B. despedirse
    C. me despido
    D. despedir

33. Oí . . . de la boda de Anita.
    A. hablado
    B. hablando
    C. hablar
    D. hablo

34. ¿Qué piensa Ud. . . . nuestro profesor de español?
    A. de
    B. en
    C. a
    D. nothing needed

35. El avión tardó en . . .
    A. llegando.
    B. llegado.
    C. llega.
    D. llegar.

36. El muchacho se empeñó . . . salir.
   A. en
   B. de
   C. a
   D. con

37. ¿ . . . qué piensa Ud.?
   A. De
   B. En
   C. A
   D. Con

38. Le agradecí . . . su paciencia.
   A. por
   B. para
   C. de
   D. no preposition needed

39. ¿Qué buscas? — Busco . . . mis libros.
   A. para
   B. por
   C. de
   D. no preposition needed

40. Se lo explico a ustedes a fin de que . . . comprenderlo.
   A. pueden
   B. poder
   C. puedan
   D. podrán

41. Le daré el dinero a Roberto cuando . . .
   A. pedírmelo.
   B. me lo pida.
   C. me lo pide.
   D. me lo pedirá.

42. Le di el dinero a Roberto cuando . . .
   A. me lo pidió.
   B. me lo pedirá.
   C. me lo pide.
   D. pedírmelo.

43. Trabajaré hasta que Ud. . . .
   A. venga.
   B. viene.
   C. vendrá.
   D. venir.

44. Trabajé hasta que Ud. . . .
   A. viene.
   B. venga.
   C. vino.
   D. vendrá.

45. Por más interesante que . . . , no quiero ver esa película.
   A. es
   B. será
   C. son
   D. sea

GO ON TO THE NEXT PAGE

46. Por bien que ... Roberto, no quiero jugar con él.
   A. juega
   B. juegue
   C. jugando
   D. jugar

47. No abriré la puerta, quienquiera que ...
   A. sea.
   B. es.
   C. será.
   D. fue.

48. Dondequiera que Ud. ... , escríbame.
   A. está
   B. esté
   C. es
   D. sea

49. Adondequiera que Ud. ... , dígamelo.
   A. va
   B. está
   C. irá
   D. vaya

50. Busco un libro que ... interesante.
   A. es
   B. está
   C. esté
   D. sea

51. Tengo un libro que ... bueno.
   A. es
   B. sea
   C. está
   D. esté

52. ¿Conoce Ud. a alguien que ... paciencia?
   A. tiene
   B. tenga
   C. tendrá
   D. ten

53. No encontré a nadie que ... la respuesta.
   A. sabe
   B. sepa
   C. supiera
   D. sabrá

54. No encuentro a nadie que ... la respuesta.
   A. sabe
   B. sepa
   C. supiera
   D. sabido

55. Ayer encontré a alguien que ... la respuesta.
   A. sabe
   B. sepa
   C. supiera
   D. sabido

56. Es el mejor libro que ... leído.
   A. he
   B. haya
   C. tengo
   D. había

57. ¡Que lo ... Juan!
   A. hace
   B. hizo
   C. hará
   D. haga

58. Los niños no están aquí. ¡Ojalá que ...
   A. vienen!
   B. vendrán!
   C. vengan!
   D. han venido!

59. ¿ ... es este lápiz?
   A. Cuyo
   B. De quién
   C. Cuya
   D. El cual

60. Mamá, ¿ ... sirven los anteojos?
   A. Porque
   B. Por qué
   C. Para qué
   D. Para

61. Ayer, ... de entrar en la casa cuando el teléfono sonó.
   A. Acabo
   B. Acabamos
   C. Acaban
   D. Acabábamos

62. El soldado ... a su patria.
   A. murió
   B. haya defendido
   C. defendió
   D. hubiera defendido

63. ¿ ... a María y a su hermano?
   A. Sabe Ud.
   B. Saben Uds.
   C. Conoce Ud.
   D. Supieran Uds.

64. ¿ ... Ud. nadar bien?
   A. Sabe
   B. Saben
   C. Conoce
   D. Conocen

65. No puedo salir esta noche porque tengo ... estudiar mis lecciones.
   A. a
   B. de
   C. que
   D. nothing needed

GO ON TO THE NEXT PAGE

PART C

Directions: Read the entire paragraph that follows to determine its general meaning. It contains blank spaces that are numbered. Of the four choices given for each numbered blank, choose the one that is grammatically correct and makes sense.

Otavalo es un pueblo al norte de Quito. El sábado es cuando todos van al mercado. En este __66__ tiene lugar probablemente el mercado más colorido de toda Sudamérica. Los indios salen de sus casas muy temprano porque las actividades del día comienzan a las cinco y media de la mañana. A __67__ hora los indios de la montaña, brillantemente vestidos con ponchos de color azul y violeta, llegan al pueblo. Muy pronto un gran número de indios __68__ las calles de Otavalo, llevando muchas cosas hechas a mano. Hacia las siete __69__ la mañana hay ruido y mucha alegría en el lugar y el mercado se ve muy animado. Todo el mundo quiere vender o comprar algo. Se ofrece una variedad de __70__ tales como ponchos, faldas, sombreros, y sandalias.

66. A. año
B. día
C. siglo
D. mes

67. A. este
B. esa
C. esto
D. aquello

68. A. llena
B. ilumina
C. limpia
D. rompe

69. A. por
B. para
C. de
D. al

70. A. ropa
B. bebidas
C. comida
D. cosméticos

PART D

Directions: The following passages are for reading comprehension. After each selection there are incomplete statements or questions. Of the four choices, choose the correct one based on the passage.

Por dificultades en el último momento para adquirir billetes, llegué a Barcelona a medianoche, en un tren distinto del que yo había pensado tomar, y no me esperaba nadie.

Era la primera vez que yo viajaba sola, pero no estaba asustada; por el contrario, me parecía una aventura agradable y excitante aquella profunda libertad en la noche. Con una sonrisa de admiración, miraba la gran estación y los grupos que estaban aguardando el expreso.

El olor especial, el gran rumor de la gente, y las luces tenían para mí un gran encanto, ya que yo envolvía todas mis impresiones en la maravilla de haber llegado, por fin, a una ciudad grande, adorada en mis sueños por desconocida.

Empecé a seguir el rumbo de la masa humana que, cargada de maletas, se dirigía a la salida. Mi equipaje era un maletón muy pesado—porque estaba casi lleno de libros—y lo llevaba yo misma con toda la fuerza de mi juventud y de mi expectación.

Debía parecer una figura extraña con mi aspecto risueño y mi viejo abrigo que, a impulsos de la brisa, me golpeaba las piernas. Recuerdo que, en pocos minutos, me quedé sola en la gran avenida, mirando a la gente que corría a coger los escasos taxis o luchaba por subir al tranvía.

71. La joven llegó a Barcelona más tarde de lo que quería porque
A. tuvo que esperar a sus amistades.
B. no le fue posible conseguir un billete más temprano.
C. no había oído el anuncio de la partida del tren.
D. el tren se había detenido en todas las estaciones del camino.

72. El viaje emocionó a la joven porque
A. estaba la noche oscura y miedosa.
B. por primera vez ella hacía un viaje sin compañía.
C. estaba ansiosa de ver a sus amigos.
D. ella se equivocó de estación al bajar del tren.

73. Al llegar a la gran ciudad, ¿cómo quedó la joven?
   A. muy encantada con todo
   B. completamente desilusionada
   C. asustada de la muchedumbre y del ruido
   D. confundida y perpleja

74. ¿Qué problema se le presentó a la joven al llegar a su destinación?
   A. Tropezó contra un pobre viejo.
   B. De repente sintió un frío tremendo.
   C. Tuvo que llevar una maleta muy cargada.
   D. Se le acercó una persona conocida.

75. Una vez en la calle, ¿qué hizo la joven?
   A. Observó a los que pasaban.
   B. Le pidió ayuda a un mozo de servicio.
   C. Subió a un tranvía.
   D. Cogió un taxi que estaba cerca.

De vez en cuando siento que me gustaría olvidar que jamás salí de la ciudad de México para ir a Santa Clara, mi pueblo natal. No había vuelto desde que mi madre, recién viuda, me llevó a la capital de la República para la iniciación de mis estudios. Ni siquiera las vacaciones me habían hecho regresar a mi pueblo. Mi madre, al morir, me había dejado una pequeña herencia que me permitía vivir sin trabajar. Me hice tan hombre de ciudad que la perspectiva de una excursión a mi pueblo me llenaba de repugnancia. Y con todo, hube de emprender esa excursión cuando me llegó el telegrama anunciándome la gravedad de mi tía Enedina.

Mi tía, única hermana de mi padre, quería verme antes de morir y su llamada me causó tal impresión que me resigné a la idea de ir a soportar incomodidades y molestias. Cuando el tren me alejó de México, yo estaba muy distante de sospechar las dificultades que me aguardaban y de anticipar el sufrimiento que iba a hacer aparecer en mi cabeza los primeros cabellos blancos.

76. El que escribe había ido a la capital a
   A. ver a unos parientes.
   B. vivir con una tía.
   C. estudiar allí.
   D. buscar un empleo.

77. El escritor se oponía al pensamiento de
   A. tener que trabajar.
   B. volver a su pueblo.
   C. viajar por tren.
   D. vivir en la ciudad de México.

78. ¿Cómo supo el escritor que se moría la tía?
   A. Su padre le escribió.
   B. Se informó al llegar al pueblo natal.
   C. Un vecino trajo el mensaje.
   D. Recibió un mensaje con la noticia.

79. Viviendo en la ciudad, el escritor se acostumbró a
   A. visitar a su tía.
   B. gozar de una vida cómoda.
   C. sufrir inconveniencias.
   D. aguantar los cambios del tiempo.

GO ON TO THE NEXT PAGE

80. Nunca se había imaginado el escritor
    A. la gran distancia que tendría que viajar.
    B. la enorme herencia que iba a recibir.
    C. la alegría que le esperaba.
    D. la angustia y el dolor que iba a sufrir.

Cuando yo vine a México por primera vez, don Pepe López-Portillo se creyó obligado, por paisanaje, afecto personal y amistad literaria, a ofrecerme un almuerzo y sentar a la mesa conmigo a un numeroso grupo de escritores de Guadalajara y de la capital. Era Victoriano Salado quien debía llevarme al lugar de la cita, pero se enfermó a última hora y se excusó por teléfono de cumplir el encargo. Como Victoriano olvidó decirme el sitio de la reunión, supuse que el almuerzo sería en la casa de don Pepe, situada en la calle de Balderas, y allá fui a dar a la hora oportuna. Con gran sorpresa supe, por boca de un criado, que el señor iba a comer fuera y con amigos y que no había dejado dicho cuál iba a ser el sitio del banquete. Me encontré así desorientado y sin saber a dónde dirigirme, pues desconocía los restaurantes de la capital. Anduve por tres o cuatro restaurantes más conocidos sin resultado alguno y afligido por el desaire involuntario que me era forzoso cometer, cuando me encontré con Amado Nervo en tan difícil momento. Le referí mi apuro y solicité su amistosa ayuda de gran conocedor de la ciudad para dar con el sitio que buscaba. Pero Amado, con calma para mí desesperante, con su palabra persuasiva y elocuente, me demostró que eran ya pasadas las tres y que dar con el Señor López-Portillo y los compañeros en uno de los mil cafés de la ciudad era como dar con aguja en granero, y me convenció de que el camino más prudente en aquella ocasión trágica era dirigirnos a comer juntos a un restaurante italiano de nombre "Roma," que tenía abiertas de par en par sus puertas, listos y apetitosos los "Spaghetti," y a la temperatura debida las botellas de Chianti, en la vieja calle de Vergara. Y allá fuimos, él muy contento, y yo sumamente disgustado.

81. Este pasaje trata de un grupo de
    A. abogados que están en viaje de negocios.
    B. campesinos haciendo su primera visita a la ciudad.
    C. autores que iban a reunirse en México.
    D. arqueólogos estudiando el terreno.

82. ¿Cómo fue recibido este señor?
    A. Se le trató con frialdad y sospecha.
    B. Se le hicieron unos regalos.
    C. Fue invitado a comer en buena compañía.
    D. Fue engañado miserablemente.

83. El narrador no se encontró con el señor Salado porque éste
    A. se había olvidado completamente de la cita.
    B. se había puesto repentinamente enfermo.
    C. tenía miedo a los otros señores.
    D. estaba fuera de la ciudad con unos amigos.

84. En realidad, ¿dónde iba a tener lugar la cita?
    A. en un café de la calle de Balderas
    B. en un restaurante de la capital
    C. en la casa de Victoriano Salado
    D. en el apartamento de Amado Nervo

85. ¿Qué sucedió al encontrarse el autor con Amado Nervo?
    A. Siguieron buscando a los amigos.
    B. Comieron "spaghetti" en casa de Nervo.
    C. Fueron los dos a un restaurante conocido.
    D. Nervo se puso a recitar algunos de sus versos.

END OF TEST 3

TEST 4

This test consists of 85 questions. You have 60 minutes to complete it. Answer Keys, Analysis Charts, Explained Answers, and Answer Sheets follow Test 9.

PART A

Directions: *This part contains incomplete statements. Each has four choices. Choose the correct completion and blacken the corresponding space on the answer sheet.*

1. Me gustaría venir a tu casa esta noche ... no puedo.
   A. pero
   B. sino
   C. también
   D. ya

2. Pedro no es pequeño ... alto.
   A. pero
   B. sino
   C. también
   D. ya

3. Mi automóvil no es amarillo ... blanco.
   A. pero
   B. sino
   C. también
   D. ya

4. Pablo no alquiló el automóvil ... lo compró.
   A. pero que
   B. sino que
   C. pero
   D. sino

5. María no conoce al niño ... le habla.
   A. pero
   B. sino
   C. pero que
   D. sino que

6. Tengo ... trabajo que Ud.
   A. mas
   B. más
   C. pero
   D. mucho

7. El señor Gómez tiene ... cincuenta años.
   A. más que
   B. mas
   C. mas de
   D. más de

8. No tengo ... dos dólares.
   A. más que
   B. más de
   C. mas de
   D. mas que

GO ON TO THE NEXT PAGE

57

9. La señora Blanco goza de una vida ...
   A. dicho.
   B. dichoso.
   C. dicha.
   D. dichosa.

10. Para mañana tenemos ... trabajo en esta clase.
    A. poco
    B. poco de
    C. pequeño
    D. pequeño de

11. Mi casa es más ... que la de Ud.
    A. poco
    B. poca
    C. pequeño
    D. pequeña

12. Después de algunos minutos, Juan ... abrir la puerta.
    A. pudo
    B. pude
    C. podía
    D. puso

13. Pablo ... pálido cuando vio el accidente.
    A. puso
    B. se puso
    C. pudo
    D. se pudo

14. ¿ ... de estos lápices es mejor?
    A. Quién
    B. Cuál
    C. Qué
    D. Cuáles

15. ¿ ... de estos lápices son los mejores?
    A. Cuál
    B. Qué
    C. Cuáles
    D. Quiénes

16. Mi padre trabaja de día ... día.
    A. con
    B. de
    C. en
    D. por

17. Mi madre abrió la puerta de par ... par.
    A. con
    B. de
    C. en
    D. por

18. De hoy ... adelante, vamos a hablar en español.
    A. con
    B. de
    C. en
    D. por

19. Mi hermanita trabaja en el jardín . . . cuando en cuando.
    A. con
    B. de
    C. en
    D. por

20. Estudio mis lecciones día . . . día.
    A. con
    B. de
    C. en
    D. por

21. La semana pasada estuve ausente en la clase de español. Póngame . . . día, por favor.
    A. a
    B. al
    C. en
    D. de

22. La mujer abrió la puerta y . . . a los invitados.
    A. despidió
    B. gritó
    C. ató
    D. saludó

23. Cuando una persona está muy triste . . .
    A. se ríe.
    B. llora.
    C. llueve.
    D. lo celebra.

24. Luisa tiene mucha vergüenza y cuando habla con un muchacho guapo siempre . . .
    A. se sonroja.
    B. habla en voz alta.
    C. pide una cita.
    D. pide el número de teléfono.

25. Generalmente, las mujeres se ponen . . . en las orejas.
    A. collares
    B. ojales
    C. ojeras
    D. pendientes

26. Roberto y Ricardo han estudiado para un examen de francés. . . . es su primer examen en esta clase, los dos están muy nerviosos.
    A. Como
    B. Cuando
    C. A menos que
    D. Mientras

27. Un matrimonio está en el campo . . . un paseo en coche cuando de repente se para el coche.
    A. haciendo
    B. habiendo
    C. siendo
    D. dando

28. La señora González, profesora de español, ha . . . retirarse porque ya tiene setenta y cinco años.
    A. dicho
    B. sido
    C. decidido
    D. devuelto

GO ON TO THE NEXT PAGE

29. Pedro acaba de llegar a Buenos Aires donde lo está ... en el aeropuerto su amigo, Raúl.
    A. esperando
    B. huyendo
    C. vistiendo
    D. mintiendo

30. La señora Pérez es ...
    A. una profesora.
    B. mexicana simpática.
    C. de España.
    D. contenta.

31. Jorge llevó a ... sus responsabilidades.
    A. caber
    B. cabo
    C. cabeza
    D. cabra

PART B

Directions: The following sentences contain blank spaces. Of the four choices given for each blank select the one that fits grammatically and makes sense.

32. El alumno ... sus libros en la sala de clase.
    A. dejó
    B. partió
    C. salió
    D. cayó

33. No me gusta ... mucho dinero cuando voy de compras.
    A. gastar
    B. pasar
    C. gastando
    D. pasando

34. A Roberto y a María ... gusta el helado.
    A. le
    B. lo
    C. los
    D. les

35. ... chico le gusta bailar.
    A. El
    B. Al
    C. A
    D. nothing needed

36. A mi amigo le ... los chocolates.
    A. gusta
    B. gustaron
    C. gustar
    D. gastar

37. Mis amigos han ... traer sus discos.
    A. de
    B. a
    C. con
    D. nothing needed

38. Hay ... estudiar para aprender.
  A. de
  B. que
  C. para
  D. nothing needed

39. ¿Cuánto tiempo ... que Ud. estudia español?
  A. hacía
  B. hube
  C. hubo
  D. hace

40. ¿Cuánto tiempo hace que Ud. ... el autobús?
  A. espera
  B. esperaba
  C. esperé
  D. esperó

41. Hace tres años que ... español.
  A. estudiaba
  B. estudiaré
  C. estudio
  D. estudió

42. ¿Desde cuándo ... Ud. español?
  A. estudia
  B. estudié
  C. estudió
  D. estudiará

43. Estudio español desde ... tres años.
  A. cuando
  B. hace
  C. hay
  D. nothing needed

44. ¿Cuánto tiempo ... que Ud. hablaba cuando entré en la sala de clase?
  A. hace
  B. hacía
  C. hubo
  D. hice

45. Hacía una hora que yo ... cuando Ud. entró en la sala.
  A. hablaba
  B. hablo
  C. hablaré
  D. hablaría

46. Yo hablaba desde ... una hora cuando Ud. entró.
  A. hace
  B. hacía
  C. hubo
  D. nothing needed

47. ¿A qué ... vamos al baile?
  A. tiempo
  B. vez
  C. hora
  D. veces

GO ON TO THE NEXT PAGE

48. ¿Juega Ud. . . . ?
   A. el piano
   B. al tenis
   C. la guitarra
   D. el violín

49. Carmen . . . muy bien el piano.
   A. juega
   B. toca
   C. conoce
   D. llena

50. ¿A quién . . . toca?
   A. lo
   B. la
   C. los
   D. le

51. Mi hermano quiere llegar . . . ser doctor.
   A. de
   B. por
   C. para
   D. a

52. Cuando vi el accidente, . . . pálido.
   A. me puse
   B. me hice
   C. seré
   D. me pondré

53. José . . . la silla de la cocina al comedor.
   A. tomé
   B. llevó
   C. vendió
   D. compró

54. La profesora . . . el libro y comenzó a leer a la clase.
   A. llevó
   B. tomó
   C. tomé
   D. vendió

55. Necesito . . . docena de huevos.
   A. medio
   B. media
   C. mitad
   D. mediodía

56. El alumno estudió . . . de la lección de español.
   A. la mitad
   B. el medio
   C. el mediodía
   D. la mediana

57. La alumna . . . un lápiz al profesor.
   A. preguntó
   B. pidió
   C. pedí
   D. pregunté

58. Los alumnos ... a la profesora cómo estaba.
   A. preguntaron
   B. pidieron
   C. pediremos
   D. preguntamos

59. ¿Qué piensa Ud. ... este libro?
   A. de
   B. en
   C. a
   D. no preposition needed

60. María, no hablas mucho; ¿ ... qué piensas?
   A. de
   B. en
   C. a
   D. no preposition needed

61. Pienso ... las vacaciones de verano.
   A. de
   B. en
   C. a
   D. no preposition needed

62. Mi hermano ... leyendo cuando entré en la cocina.
   A. está
   B. estaba
   C. es
   D. era

63. Si tengo bastante dinero, ... a verle.
   A. vendré
   B. vendría
   C. viniera
   D. habría venido

64. Si yo ... bastante tiempo, vendría a verle.
   A. tengo
   B. tuviera
   C. tuvieses
   D. hubiera tenido

65. Si yo ... bastante tiempo, habría venido a verle.
   A. tengo
   B. tenía
   C. hubiera tenido
   D. tuviera

PART C

Directions: Read the entire paragraph that follows to determine its general meaning. It contains blank spaces that are numbered. Of the four choices given for each numbered blank, choose the one that is grammatically correct and makes sense.

Joan Serrat, Victor Manuel y Miguel Ríos, tres cantantes españoles, cubren todo el espectro de la música "pop" desde el rock fuerte a las baladas íntimas. No le deben __66__ nadie una nota musical ni un solo fragmento de inspiración, porque ellos son los __67__ de sus propias canciones. Su __68__ refleja las ilusiones, las preocupaciones y las esperanzas de la sociedad española. Uno suele hablar de amor, otro de la política y el tercero canta su convicción que es la vida y no el dinero, el hombre y no la máquina, los que han de protagonizar el futuro. Los tres tienen __69__ ideas musicales, personales y políticas, pero todos __70__ de acuerdo que se puede tocar, conmover, inspirar la sensibilidad de la gente por medio de la música.

GO ON TO THE NEXT PAGE

66. A. por
B. de
C. a
D. no preposition needed

67. A. hombres
B. autores
C. lectores
D. actores

68. A. locura
B. música
C. manera
D. fantasía

69. A. diferentes
B. antiguas
C. conocidas
D. sorprendentes

70. A. piden
B. hacen
C. son
D. están

PART D

Directions: The following passages are for reading comprehension. After each selection there are incomplete statements or questions. Of the four choices, choose the correct one based on the passage.

—Vengo a pedirle un favor ... un favor de que depende mi vida acaso ... ¡Soy un apasionado, un amigo de usted! ...

—Por supuesto ... —siendo el favor de tanto interés para usted ...

—Yo soy un joven ... que quiere ser cómico ...

—Cierto. ¿Y qué sabe usted? ¿Qué ha estudiado usted?

—¿Cómo? ¿Se necesita saber algo?

—No; para ser actor, ciertamente, no necesita saber usted cosa mayor ...

—¿Sabe usted castellano?

—Lo que usted ve ... para hablar, las gentes me entienden ...

—¿Aprendió usted la historia?

—No, señor, no sé lo que es.

—Por consiguiente, no sabrá usted lo que son trajes, ni épocas, ni caracteres históricos ...

—Nada, nada, no, señor. Le diré a usted ... en cuanto a trajes, ya sé que en siendo muy antiguo, siempre a la romana.

—Esto es: aunque sea griego el asunto.

—Sí, señor: si no es tan antiguo, a la antigua francesa o a la antigua española.

—¿Y cómo presentará usted un carácter histórico?

—Mire usted; el rol lo dirá, luego como el muerto no se ha de tomar el trabajo de resucitar sólo para desmentirle a uno ...

—Y de educación, de modales y usos de sociedad, ¿a qué altura se halla usted?

—Mal; porque si va a decir verdad, yo soy un pobrecillo: yo era escribiente en una mala administración; me echaron por holgazán, y me quiero meter a cómico; porque se me figura a mí que es oficio en que no hay nada que hacer ...

—Y tiene usted razón.

71. El joven dice que es un amigo del señor porque
A. conoce íntima y personalmente al señor.
B. viene a pedirle dinero prestado.
C. cree que el señor podrá ayudarle en sus ambiciones.
D. quiere dedicarse a escribir artículos.

72. De las respuestas del joven puede deducirse que
A. sabe muy bien la historia de España.
B. por lo regular puede hacerse comprender.
C. sabe el español a fondo.
D. habla un español elegante.

73. Si el asunto de la comedia fuera griego, el joven se vestiría a la
A. española.
B. romana.
C. griega.
D. francesa.

74. Al joven se le figura que la manera más fácil de representar un personaje de la historia es atendiendo
   A. al papel.
   B. al argumento.
   C. a la moda.
   D. a la época.

75. El joven escoge la carrera de actor porque es
   A. muy trabajador
   B. mal administrador.
   C. escribiente bueno.
   D. perezoso.

Vi el ejército rojo entrar en Sofía, la devastada capital de Bulgaria, el 16 de septiembre, a las cuatro y diez de la tarde. Permanecí en Bulgaria ocho meses más, pues deseaba observar de cerca lo que ocurre en una nación cuando los rusos se hacen cargo de ella.

Como representante de la prensa, había llegado yo a Bulgaria el 7 de septiembre, procedente de Turquía. En el consulado búlgaro de Istanbul, parecía interesarles que, cuando llegasen los rusos a Bulgaria, hubiese ya allí periodistas norteamericanos. En la frontera me esperaban en un automóvil dos agentes de la policía secreta, los cuales tenían ametralladoras ligeras. Juntos tomamos en ese coche el camino que conduce a Sofía.

76. ¿Cómo estaba Sofía?
   A. en ruinas
   B. cubierta de edificios nuevos
   C. nadando en sangre
   D. en pleno verano

77. ¿Por qué pasó algún tiempo en Bulgaria el que narra la aventura?
   A. Quería ver cómo los rusos ocupan un país.
   B. Observaba el sistema de educación militar entre los búlgaros.
   C. Estudiaba las costumbres de Bulgaria.
   D. Permanecía allí por su salud.

78. ¿Qué les interesaba a los búlgaros?
   A. que el autor se quedase en el consulado
   B. que las gentes no se quedasen en Turquía
   C. que los norteamericanos supiesen muy poco de los movimientos rusos
   D. que los norteamericanos llegasen antes que las tropas rusas

79. ¿Qué hacía el narrador para ganarse la vida?
   A. Era soldado.
   B. Era agente soviético.
   C. Era periodista.
   D. Era comerciante.

80. ¿Qué llevaban los agentes búlgaros?
   A. unos periódicos
   B. unos documentos secretos
   C. armas de fuego
   D. abrigos ligeros

Estimado maestro y amigo:

Espero que ésta le encuentre contento y feliz. Tal vez le sorprenda saber que a los pocos días de salir Ud. de Segovia determiné viajar también hacia el norte, a Santiago de Compostela, en vez de ir a Burgos como tenía planeado. Permítame que le explique por qué he cambiado de planes. En primer lugar porque aquí, en Santiago, no hace tanto calor como en Burgos, y en segundo lugar porque desde que leímos en su clase aquella novela *La casa de la Troya* he sentido deseos de ver esta ciudad. Además, mi profesor de historia de España en Madrid contó las glorias de Santiago, diciendo que durante la Edad

Media había sido una de las ciudades más importantes, un lugar de peregrinación adonde acudían peregrinos de todo el mundo. Según una leyenda se descubrió aquí, a principios del siglo IX, el sepulcro del apóstol Santiago. De todas maneras, en dicho lugar se edificó una ermita que más tarde se convirtió en catedral.

Temo que se esté riendo de mí al leer estas cosas. Pero no me importa que se ría. Me alegro de haber venido. El Pórtico de la Gloria de la catedral, ejemplo magnífico del arte románico, es lo que más me ha impresionado hasta ahora. Ayer, imitando a millares de peregrinos que han pasado por aquí, puse los cinco dedos de la mano derecha en la columna central de este pórtico. También fui a ver la imagen del Apóstol detrás del altar mayor, pero no la abracé ni la besé como hacían otros.

Quedo como siempre a sus órdenes,
Carlos Maldonado

81. El amigo y alumno había decidido ir hacia el norte porque
    A. quería conocer a Segovia.
    B. Burgos estaba en sus planes.
    C. deseaba asistir a una clase de historia.
    D. hacía mejor tiempo allá.

82. Por lo que se dice en esta carta es muy probable que en *La casa de la Troya* haya descripciones de
    A. Madrid.
    B. Santiago.
    C. Segovia.
    D. Burgos.

83. La fama de Santiago se debe a
    A. su casa de Dios.
    B. un profesor de historia.
    C. su ambiente peligroso.
    D. sus ruinas romanas.

84. La costumbre de los peregrinos que dejó de seguir el escritor de esta carta fue
    A. poner la mano derecha en la columna central.
    B. contemplar la estatua del Santo.
    C. visitar el Pórtico de la Gloria.
    D. abrazar y besar la imagen.

85. Lo que le llamó más la atención fue
    A. la alegría de los peregrinos.
    B. los millares de visitas.
    C. lo artístico de la catedral.
    D. la imagen del Apóstol.

END OF TEST 4

TEST 5

This test consists of 85 questions. You have 60 minutes to complete it. Answer Keys, Analysis Charts, Explained Answers, and Answer Sheets follow Test 9.

PART A

Directions: This part contains incomplete statements. Each has four choices. Choose the correct completion and blacken the corresponding space on the answer sheet.

1. El muchacho más alto ... la clase es Roberto.
   A. en
   B. de
   C. por
   D. según

2. Este ... me robó todo el dinero.
   A. ladrillo
   B. lado
   C. ladrón
   D. lejano

3. Carlota dice a Juan:— ... que tú me amas.
   A. Dame
   B. Dime
   C. Veme
   D. Sígueme

4. Esta mañana mi padre ... y ya no tiene barba.
   A. se afeitó
   B. se burló
   C. se acercó
   D. se bañó

5. Pablo parece un poco tímido porque no habla con ... en el baile.
   A. nada
   B. alguien
   C. algún
   D. nadie

6. El padre dice a su hijo:—Yo sé que sabes ... pero me parece que eres muy joven para tener coche.
   A. dirigir
   B. conducir
   C. acelerar
   D. acertar

7. Juanita no quería que le viesen desde la calle; por eso, dijo— ... las cortinas.
   A. Dame
   B. Dime
   C. Abra
   D. Baje

GO ON TO THE NEXT PAGE

8. La niña gritó "¡Socorro! ¡Socorro!" porque estaba ... en el lago.
   A. ahogándose
   B. alegrándose
   C. ahorrando
   D. aguantando

9. La señora López estaba ... la televisión cuando alguien llamó a la puerta.
   A. viendo
   B. viendo a
   C. mirando
   D. mirando a

10. Cuando Pablo dice a Roberto que no podrá asistir a la tertulia de su cumpleaños, Roberto contesta: —Te ... de menos.
   A. ejerceremos
   B. editaremos
   C. bailaremos
   D. echaremos

11. María dijo " ... " cuando subió al tren.
   A. ¡Hola!
   B. ¡Adiós!
   C. ¡Mira!
   D. ¡Ay!

12. La señorita Santiago se pone ... para leer el periódico.
   A. la peluca
   B. la gorra
   C. los lentes
   D. los periodistas

13. Pepe se puso a ... cuando su juguete se le rompió.
   A. sollozar
   B. cantar
   C. bailar
   D. reír

14. La Embajada de México en la ciudad de Guatemala concedió ... a seis personas que se refugiaron.
   A. protección
   B. polvo
   C. refresco
   D. reglamento

15. Las casas de moda de París venden a precios ... los vestidos que ellas hacen en gran escala; así no hay mujer que no pueda vestirse ahora de una manera muy elegante.
   A. redondos
   B. reducidos
   C. reemplazados
   D. de escaleras

16. El dentista pidió veinte dólares a don Ramón ... la extracción de un diente.
   A. por
   B. para
   C. pues
   D. a

17. Es costumbre de casi todos los españoles echar ... después del almuerzo.
   A. un cesto
   B. un cestillo
   C. una siesta
   D. de menos

18. En un café, cuando el mozo ... caer una taza de café sobre el vestido de una dama, el mozo dijo: —¡Perdóneme!
  A. dejó
  B. dejó de
  C. salió
  D. salió de

19. Son las once y media de la noche y mi padre tiene que...; por eso, va a acostarse.
  A. llenarse
  B. sentarse
  C. sentirse
  D. madrugar

20. Cuando la señora Sierra, una dama de ochenta años, se mira en..., se dice:—¡Cuántas arrugas tengo en el rostro!
  A. la espera
  B. el espanto
  C. el espejo
  D. la esperanza

21. Cuando el señor Pérez sufrió ..., se cayó súbitamente en la acera.
  A. un desayuno
  B. un aceite
  C. un chiste
  D. un desmayo

22. Un ... , que quiere cruzar la calle, dice a una persona: —¿Puede usted ayudarme?
  A. cero
  B. ciego
  C. cepillo
  D. mono

23. Carlota llegó a ser gran artista, gracias a ... de sus padres.
  A. los esfuerzos
  B. los fuegos
  C. los espejos
  D. las espadas

24. Cierto hombre recibió un premio en una fiesta. El premio consistía en poder cortarse el pelo gratis durante un año. Lo extraño del caso es que a él no le ... ni un solo pelo en la cabeza. ¡Qué lástima!
  A. quedaba
  B. quemaba
  C. quería
  D. quebraba

25. Los esquimales son todavía el grupo aborigen más disperso de las Américas. Se encuentran diseminados desde Groenlandia hasta Alaska. Muchos de ellos, ... que se los encuentre, se dedican a la caza y al comercio de pieles.
  A. dondequiera
  B. adondequiera
  C. cualquiera
  D. cuandoquiera

26. Un mayordomo es un ...
  A. presidente.
  B. secretario.
  C. cocinero.
  D. sirviente.

GO ON TO THE NEXT PAGE

27. Un ... ambulante de enciclopedias trata de hacer una venta en casa de Federico.
    A. veneno
    B. verano
    C. médico
    D. vendedor

28. Usted entra en un banco y habla con ... que le dice:—¿En qué puedo servirle?
    A. un cajero
    B. un cajón
    C. un calcetín
    D. una caja

29. La Embajada de los Estados Unidos anuncia que mañana ... en el canal 12 de televisión un curso de inglés que se presentará todos los lunes, miércoles y viernes a las 19.00 horas.
    A. se acercará
    B. se abrazará
    C. se acordará
    D. se iniciará

30. Celedonio Romero y su famoso grupo ..., integrado por sus hijos Celín, Pepe y Angel, se presentarán pasado mañana en el exclusivo Town Hall de Nueva York. Este famoso conjunto de guitarristas españoles, bajo la dirección de Celedonio Romero, ofrecerá un extraordinario concierto de obras clásicas de autores españoles, alemanes e italianos.
    A. literario
    B. de poetas
    C. comercial
    D. musical

31. Los de Mallorca son aficionados a los bailes folklóricos. Los trajes que llevan en estas ocasiones son sumamente pintorescos, y pintorescas también las largas trenzas que adornan ... de las mujeres.
    A. la esperanza
    B. la espalda
    C. la espada
    D. el espejo

PART B

Directions: The following sentences contain blank spaces. Of the four choices given for each blank select the one that fits grammatically and makes sense.

32. Deseo que usted ...
    A. canta.
    B. cante.
    C. cantara.
    D. cantase.

33. Le diré a Ana que ...
    A. baile.
    B. baila.
    C. bailara.
    D. bailase.

34. Le he dicho a Pablo que ...
    A. cante y baila.
    B. canta y baile.
    C. cantara y bailase.
    D. cante y baile.

35. Dígale a Pepita que ...
   A. cante y baila.
   B. canta y baile.
   C. cantara y bailase.
   D. cante y baile.

36. Dudo que mi madre ... el tren.
   A. toma
   B. tome
   C. ha tomado
   D. había tomado

37. Dudo que mi padre ... el autobús.
   A. ha tomado
   B. haya tomado
   C. había tomado
   D. tomará

38. Le gustaría a la profesora que los alumnos ... los ejercicios.
   A. hacen
   B. hagan
   C. hicieran *or* hiciesen
   D. harán

39. Yo sentía que su madre ... enferma.
   A. está
   B. esté
   C. es
   D. estuviera *or* estuviese

40. Yo dudé que mi madre ... el tren.
   A. hubiera tomado *or* hubiese tomado
   B. toma
   C. tome
   D. tomó

41. Si tengo bastante tiempo, ... a verle.
   A. vendré
   B. vengo
   C. viniera *or* viniese
   D. vine

42. Si yo tuviese bastante tiempo, ... a verle.
   A. vendría
   B. vengo
   C. vendré
   D. vine

43. Si yo hubiese tenido bastante tiempo, ... a verle.
   A. hube venido
   B. habría venido
   C. he venido
   D. vengo

44 ¿Dónde están los niños? — ¡Ojalá que ...
   A. vienen!
   B. vendrán!
   C. han venido!
   D. vengan!

GO ON TO THE NEXT PAGE

45. Ahora voy . . . casa.
    A. a
    B. en
    C. por
    D. al

46. Esta noche me quedo . . . casa.
    A. a
    B. en
    C. por
    D. al

47. Los muchachos no quisieron hacerlo . . . miedo.
    A. por
    B. a
    C. para
    D. al

48. ¡Vámonos! El tren . . . a punto de salir.
    A. es
    B. está
    C. esté
    D. va

49. Vamos a comer en este restaurante. Preparan las comidas
    A. en francés.
    B. en la francesa.
    C. a la francesa.
    D. al francés.

50. Ahora vamos a comer . . . aire libre.
    A. a
    B. al
    C. en
    D. por

51. Mi padre gana mil dólares . . . mes.
    A. en
    B. por
    C. al
    D. a

52. Basta que los alumnos . . . la lección.
    A. saben
    B. sé
    C. sepan
    D. conocen

53. Conviene que Mariano . . . ahora mismo.
    A. venga
    B. viene
    C. vino
    D. vine

54. Es aconsejable que los estudiantes . . . inmediatamente.
    A. salen
    B. salgan
    C. llegan
    D. saldrán

55. Es probable que María ... a las tres de la tarde.
   A. regresa
   B. regrese
   C. regresará
   D. llega

56. Es necesario que Ud. ... la composición ahora mismo.
   A. escriba
   B. escribe
   C. escriben
   D. escriban

57. Yo no creo que ... urgente.
   A. es
   B. estará
   C. está
   D. sea

58. Mi madre quiere que yo ... a la escuela ahora.
   A. vaya
   B. voy
   C. estoy
   D. iré

59. Espero que mi perrito ... pronto.
   A. vuelve
   B. vuelva
   C. volver
   D. volverá

60. Hace tres horas que ... la televisión.
   A. miro
   B. miraba
   C. miré
   D. miró

61. Mi hermano ... y mi padre hablaba cuando yo entré en la casa.
   A. leyó
   B. leía
   C. leerá
   D. lee

62. La señora Rivera ... lista para salir. Quiere ir de compras.
   A. es
   B. está
   C. estando
   D. yendo

63. Este hombre está ...
   A. muere.
   B. muerto.
   C. murió.
   D. morir.

64. Ahora voy a ... a casa porque tengo mucho trabajo.
   A. volver
   B. devolver
   C. vuelta
   D. vuelto

GO ON TO THE NEXT PAGE

65. Voy a . . . este libro a la biblioteca esta tarde.
   A. volver
   B. devolver
   C. vuelta
   D. vuelto

PART C

Directions: Read the entire paragraph that follows to determine its general meaning. It contains blank spaces that are numbered. Of the four choices given for each numbered blank, choose the one that is grammatically correct and makes sense.

A muchas personas __66__ encanta viajar. El turismo ha aumentado enormemente durante las últimas dos décadas. Según las estadísticas del Ministerio de Información y Turismo, el mejoramiento económico de muchas personas ha __67__ un turista contemporáneo que viaja al exterior con mucha frecuencia. Abundan en la tierra lugares de interés para el turista. En casi todos __68__ del mundo vemos paisajes de exótica belleza natural, montañas, playas, ciudades pintorescas y capitales modernas. Encontramos monumentos y huellas históricas de civilizaciones anteriores. Además, podemos observar costumbres singulares, fiestas, danzas, música típica y una __69__ variedad de atracciones populares. Algo de esto __70__ en todas partes. Sin embargo, los turistas prefieren ir a unos sitios y a otros no.

66. A. les
   B. le
   C. los
   D. las

67. A. aumentado
   B. aprendido
   C. trabajado
   D. producido

68. A. los países
   B. los edificios
   C. los mares
   D. los bosques

69. A. grande
   B. gran
   C. fiesta
   D. pintorescas

70. A. se juega
   B. se compra
   C. se encuentra
   D. se fabrica

PART D

Directions: The following passages are for reading comprehension. After each selection there are incomplete statements or questions. Of the four choices, choose the correct one based on the passage.

Llegó el momento decisivo. Se quedaría con él.
—¿Cuánto?
—Por ser para usted—dijo el gitano—lo dejaremos en cuarenta.
Batiste, como hombre acostumbrado a tales discusiones, sonrió:
—Bueno: por ser tú ¿quieres veinticinco?

—¡Veinticinco duros! ¿Pero se ha fijado usted en el animal? Pero voy a hacerle lo que no haría por nadie. ¿Conviene en treinta y cinco duros?

Batiste se alejó fingiendo haber desistido de la compra. Se acercó a un caballito fuerte y de pelo brillante, que no pensaba comprar adivinando su alto precio.

—Treinta y tres . . . —sintió a sus orejas un aliento ardoroso que murmuraba.

—Veintiocho.

—Ni lo de usted ni lo mío. Treinta y bien sabe Dios que nada gano. Vamos . . . Choque usted.

Batiste agarró la cuerda y tendió una mano al vendedor, que se la apretó expresivamente. Trato cerrado.

71. Batiste sabía de experiencia que el gitano
   A. rebajaría el precio.
   B. insistiría en el precio.
   C. no diría el precio.
   D. doblaría el precio.

72. Cuando el gitano pidió treinta y cinco duros, Batiste se alejó para
   A. irse a casa.
   B. ir a comprar otro animal.
   C. pagarle lo pedido.
   D. simular falta de interés en la compra.

73. Mientras los dos hombres se apretaban la mano, Batiste
   A. tomó posesión del caballo.
   B. dio la cuerda al gitano.
   C. montó a caballo.
   D. sacó su cartera.

74. "Trato cerrado" significa que
   A. no habían logrado nada.
   B. el gitano había realizado la venta.
   C. el vendedor había rechazado la oferta.
   D. el gitano había ganado mucho.

75. Al fin y al cabo decidió Batiste
   A. irse sin comprar nada.
   B. comprar un caballo más caro.
   C. comprar la bestia.
   D. evitar un choque.

No recordamos ya nosotros ni por qué ni cuándo Mr. Huntington vino por primera vez a España y se enamoró de ella. El caso es que nuestro californiano vino a España y quedó prendado. En diversos y prolongados viajes, recorrió la Península, no en plan de turista de lujo, siguiendo los itinerarios de las agencias de viajes, sino a su espontáneo capricho, a lomos de caballo, mula o vulgar asno; a pie muchas veces, más que en tren o en automóvil. Bien pronto aprendió el español del pueblo, en todas sus variedades dialécticas, y hablaba con unos y con otros en mesones, posadas, tabernas y ferias. Moreno, de ojos y cabellos oscuros, solamente su robustez y elevada estatura le diferenciaban de la masa de rústicos con quienes le complacía platicar. El joven Huntington, enamorado de la España auténtica, no de la de guitarra, pudo conocerla como muy pocos españoles la conocen.

76. Mr. Huntington vino a España
   A. para casarse con una española.
   B. para representar una agencia turística.
   C. a arreglar un negocio.
   D. por motivo ya olvidado.

GO ON TO THE NEXT PAGE

77. ¿Qué caracterizó su manera de hablar español?
   A. Usó un lenguaje popular muy variado.
   B. Siempre conservó un ligero acento californiano.
   C. Hablaba como un turista.
   D. Hablaba como una persona de la clase social más elevada.

78. Por preferencia personal viajaba
   A. en tren.
   B. en camiones de turistas.
   C. por automóvil.
   D. a caballo o a pie.

79. Se podía distinguirlo de los naturales del país porque
   A. no hablaba corrientemente el idioma.
   B. era más alto.
   C. tenía el pelo moreno.
   D. tenía los ojos oscuros.

80. Como resultado de su mucho viajar, Huntington llegó a
   A. conocer muy bien la vida de la clase intelectual española.
   B. formar amistades con los individuos más ricos.
   C. tener relaciones con muchos turistas.
   D. comprender a España mejor que muchos españoles.

Amanecía el día de la libertad para el Ecuador. Las tropas de Sucre cargaban contra las del Presidente Aymerich. Sobre los tejados de las casas y los campanarios de las iglesias los quiteños miraban estremecidos de entusiasmo y de ansiedad las fases del combate que bien pronto iba a aureolarse de heroísmo para la admiración de las generaciones venideras.

Comenzó el combate; el centro del ejército patriota estaba formado por los batallones Yaguachi y Paya. Abdón Calderón, un joven, casi un niño, mandaba la tercera compañía del Yaguachi. En los primeros momentos del ataque, recibió un balazo en el brazo derecho. Sin desmayar tomó la espada con la mano izquierda y siguió combatiendo. —¡Adelante!— grita, y se arroja contra el enemigo; pero otro balazo le rompe el muslo izquierdo. Calderón carga una vez más al frente de sus compañeros haciendo un esfuerzo prodigioso. En este momento, otra bala le atraviesa el corazón haciéndole caer a tierra exangüe y sin movimiento; la herida era mortal, Calderón falleció al día siguiente.

El general Sucre lo ascendió, ya muerto, a capitán. El Libertador, informado del bizarro comportamiento de aquel joven oficial ecuatoriano, ordenó que la tercera compañía del Yaguachi no tuviera otro capitán: que siempre se pasara revista en ella como vivo; y que, al nombrarle, la compañía respondiera: "¡Murió gloriosamente en Pichincha, pero vive en nuestros corazones!"

81. Los vecinos de la capital presenciaban la batalla
   A. llenos de inquietud.
   B. armados de espadas.
   C. con un mínimo de interés.
   D. sin esperar gran cosa.

82. Los patriotas ecuatorianos luchaban por
   A. la gloria.
   B. su independencia.
   C. la iglesia.
   D. el Presidente Aymerich.

83. ¿Cómo murió el joven oficial?
   A. de un balazo en el muslo
   B. de una herida en el pecho
   C. del primer balazo
   D. de haber caído a tierra

84. ¿Cómo premió Sucre a Calderón?
   A. Ordenó un entierro estupendo.
   B. Le confirió una medalla.
   C. Le nombró coronel del batallón Yaguachi.
   D. Le nombró capitán de la compañía.

85. Al enterarse del heroísmo de Calderón, El Libertador mandó que
   A. el batallón llevara el nombre del joven patriota.
   B. se celebrara el aniversario de su muerte.
   C. sus hazañas se publicasen.
   D. nunca se nombrara otro jefe de la tercera compañía.

END OF TEST 5

TEST 6

This test consists of 85 questions. You have 60 minutes to complete it. Answer Keys, Analysis Charts, Explained Answers, and Answer Sheets follow Test 9.

PART A

Directions: This part contains incomplete statements. Each has four choices. Choose the correct completion and blacken the corresponding space on the answer sheet.

1. El alumno necesita ... para corregir una falta en la carta que está escribiendo.
   A. una goma de borrar
   B. un golpe
   C. una gorra
   D. un sello de correo

2. Cuando yo no compro una cosa a plazos, yo la pago ...
   A. a largo plazo.
   B. a corto plazo.
   C. al contado.
   D. a plazos.

3. El señor González es mudo; es decir, no puede ...
   A. enfadarse.
   B. hablar.
   C. leer.
   D. oír.

4. Una cocinera es una mujer que ...
   A. cocina.
   B. habla mucho.
   C. conversa poco.
   D. duerme mucho.

5. Cuando yo compro una cosa a plazos, yo la pago ...
   A. inmediatamente.
   B. al instante.
   C. poco a poco.
   D. en seguida.

6. María, mira lo que hiciste; rompiste la silla y ahora tengo que ...
   A. repararla.
   B. reprocharla.
   C. reproducirla.
   D. silbarla.

7. Estoy jugando en el lodo. Esto no les gusta a mis padres y me dicen: ...
   A. Es hora de comer.
   B. Entra en la casa inmediatamente.
   C. Preocúpate.
   D. A nosotros, nos gusta comer.

8. El aduanero me pregunta: ...
   A. ¿Tiene usted hambre?
   B. ¿Tiene usted dinero?
   C. ¿Tiene usted cosas que declarar?
   D. ¿Tiene usted que trabajar mucho?

9. Cuando yo conduzco mi automóvil con mucha rapidez, generalmente un agente de policía me
   pide ...
   A. dinero.
   B. informes.
   C. mi licencia de conducir.
   D. mi coche.

10. Cuando yo llegué a la casa de mi amiga, ésta me recibió alegremente, y me dijo: ...
    A. Sal de ahí.
    B. Entra.
    C. Ganaría.
    D. Aquí está la puerta.

11. Usted entra en una biblioteca pública para ... un libro.
    A. preguntar
    B. conseguir
    C. vender
    D. adular

12. Federico está ... otra vez. ¿Dónde estará? —pregunta la profesora a los estudiantes.
    A. absorto
    B. absteniéndose
    C. aclarando
    D. ausente

13. Usted está en Venezuela. Hace dos semanas que Ud. no tiene noticias de casa. Ud. encuentra ...
    y le dice: —¿ Hay una carta para mí?
    A. al cartero
    B. la cartera
    C. el carrito
    D. al caudillo

14. ... de El Greco son admirables.
    A. Los cuadernos
    B. Las cuadras
    C. Los cuadros
    D. Las cuerdas

15. La leche es buena para ...
    A. la salud.
    B. los saludos.
    C. saludarse.
    D. la seda.

16. Me pongo ...
    A. la sospecha.
    B. la llena.
    C. los llantos.
    D. el sombrero.

17. La semana pasada yo ... al cine.
    A. fui
    B. vi
    C. di
    D. hice

GO ON TO THE NEXT PAGE

18. ... cantan en la primavera.
   A. Las palmadas
   B. Los pajaritos
   C. Las pajas
   D. Las cantidades

19. Los árboles tienen ... en el verano.
   A. cepillos
   B. hogares
   C. hojas
   D. joyas

20. La falda de María no está limpia; está ...
   A. sucia.
   B. suma.
   C. lista.
   D. loca.

21. Necesito ... porque quiero salir y está lloviendo.
   A. una luz
   B. un paraguas
   C. una llanta
   D. un llorón

22. ¿En qué ... hace frío, generalmente?
   A. establo
   B. estilo
   C. estrella
   D. estación

23. ¿Qué chica ... bonita!
   A. tanta
   B. tanto
   C. tan
   D. como

24. Juan está contento porque tuvo buen ... en el examen.
   A. éxito
   B. tubo
   C. turno
   D. suerte

25. ¿Sabe Ud. ... a la pregunta?
   A. la contestación
   B. el reposo
   C. el respeto
   D. el respecto

26. Batiste se acercó a un caballito fuerte y de ... brillante.
   A. palo
   B. paño
   C. peligro
   D. pelo

27. Cuando el gitano ... treinta y cinco duros, Batiste se alejó para simular falta de interés en la compra.
   A. pidió
   B. preguntó
   C. pudo
   D. puso

28. Mientras los dos hombres se apretaban ... , Batiste tomó posesión del caballo.
   A. la cuerda
   B. la mano
   C. el gitano
   D. la compra

29. Mr. Huntington ... a España por motivo ya olvidado.
   A. vino
   B. agua
   C. café
   D. fui

30. Como resultado de su mucho viajar, Mr. Huntington ... a comprender a España mejor que muchos españoles.
   A. llegó
   B. llevó
   C. llovió
   D. llenó

31. Por preferencia personal, el señor viajaba ... caballo o a pie.
   A. por
   B. ne
   C. de
   D. a

PART B

Directions: The following sentences contain blank spaces. Of the four choices given for each blank select the one that fits grammatically and makes sense.

32. Este año vamos a Europa en el mes de septiembre ... octubre.
   A. o
   B. u
   C. a
   D. e

33. En esta clase no hay muchachos ... hombres.
   A. o
   B. u
   C. a
   D. e

34. Voy a dar estos vasos a María y a José. Este vaso es ... María.
   A. por
   B. para
   C. de
   D. a

35. Esta taza es ... café. Démela, por favor.
   A. por
   B. para
   C. en
   D. par

36. La semana pasada me quedé en casa ... tres días.
   A. por
   B. para
   C. en
   D. par

GO ON TO THE NEXT PAGE

37. ¿Cuánto dinero me dará Ud. . . . mi trabajo?
    A. por
    B. para
    C. en
    D. par

38. Soy un muchacho argentino de dieciséis años . . . interés principal es mantener la paz en el mundo y hacer amistades en la América latina y los Estados Unidos.
    A. de quien
    B. de quién
    C. cuyo
    D. cuya

39. La ventana . . . abierta por el ladrón.
    A. fue
    B. hizo
    C. fui
    D. hice

40. El ladrón . . . la puerta.
    A. abrí
    B. abrió
    C. fue
    D. hice

41. Estas composiciones . . . escritas por Juana.
    A. fui
    B. fue
    C. fueron
    D. hicieron

42. Aquí en esta tienda . . . hablan español e inglés.
    A. su
    B. se
    C. sus
    D. nosotros

43. . . . dice que va a llover.
    A. Se
    B. Fue
    C. Fui
    D. Hizo

44. ¿ . . . libro tiene usted?
    A. Cuál
    B. Qué
    C. Cuáles
    D. Cómo

45. La señora Gómez es respetada . . . todos los alumnos.
    A. por
    B. para
    C. a
    D. con

46. El alumno salió de la sala de clase sin . . . nada.
    A. diciendo
    B. decir
    C. dijo
    D. dije

47. ¿Dónde están las niñas? Las vi . . .
   A. salir.
   B. saliendo.
   C. salen.
   D. salieron.

48. Tres por cinco . . . quince.
   A. son
   B. es
   C. harán
   D. harían

49. Mi gato se llama Sasha. Siempre viene cuando . . .
   A. chiflo.
   B. chiflaba.
   C. chiflé
   D. chiflaré.

50. Sasha . . . ayer.
   A. se perdía
   B. se perdió
   C. se pierde
   D. se perderá

51. A mi gato . . . gusta comer la comida seca.
   A. lo
   B. le
   C. se
   D. se lo

52. Sasha se . . . de la casa cuando alguien abrió la ventana anteayer.
   A. escape
   B. escapa
   C. escapando
   D. escapó

53. Si Ud. lo halla, puede . . . por teléfono al número 123–4568.
   A. me llama
   B. llamarme
   C. llamándome
   D. llámeme

54. Sobre los tejados de las casas y los campanarios de las iglesias, los quiteños miraban estremecidos de entusiasmo y de ansiedad las fases del combate que . . . pronto a aureolarse de heroísmo para la admiración de las generaciones venideras.
   A. iban
   B. iba
   C. fueron
   D. fue

55. En este momento, otra bala . . . atraviesa el corazón al soldado.
   A. le
   B. lo
   C. se lo
   D. se la

56. El Libertador ordenó que la tercera compañía no . . . otro capitán.
   A. tiene
   B. tenga
   C. tendrá
   D. tuviera

GO ON TO THE NEXT PAGE

57. Los indios han de ... gratuitamente los "trabajos de la república."
   A. realizando
   B. realizar
   C. realizaron
   D. realizado

58. Catorce alcaldes se presentaron ... del abuso.
   A. protestándose
   B. al protestar
   C. protestar
   D. a protestar

59. Los catorce alcaldes ... encarcelados, flagelados y maltratados.
   A. fueron
   B. fueren
   C. estén
   D. estuvieran

60. Los alumnos se quedaron sin esperar ...
   A. una grande cosa.
   B. grande cosa.
   C. cosa gran.
   D. gran cosa.

61. Al ... en la escuela, Dorotea fue a su clase de español.
   A. entrando
   B. entra
   C. entrar
   D. entrándose

62. Se sabe que Elena va a casarse ... Juan.
   A. a
   B. de
   C. pues
   D. con

63. La maestra seguía ... a los estudiantes.
   A. leer
   B. a leer
   C. leyendo
   D. leyera

64. Soy aficionado ... béisbol.
   A. al
   B. a
   C. de
   D. del

65. ¡Qué lo ... Ud. bien!
   A. pase
   B. pasar
   C. hace
   D. haces

PART C

Directions: Read the entire paragraph that follows to determine its general meaning. It contains blank spaces that are numbered. Of the four choices given for each numbered blank, choose the one that is grammatically correct and makes sense.

Europa es el continente de mayor volumen turístico desde __66__ muchos años. A principios de este siglo los únicos que podían viajar eran los aristócratas y otras gentes ricas que no necesitaban __67__. Para ser turista durante las primeras décadas de este siglo, se necesitaba mucho dinero y mucho tiempo porque los medios de transporte __68__ pocos y muy __69__. Por ejemplo, un viaje que actualmente puede durar cinco horas en automóvil, podía tardar dos semanas a caballo. En los últimos veinte años las características de __70__ han cambiado radicalmente. Hoy en día, los turistas se componen de millones de personas de todas las clases sociales, desde el trabajador hasta el millonario.

66. A. como
B. cuando
C. hace
D. falta

67. A. trabajar
B. estudiar
C. manejar
D. enseñar

68. A. fue
B. fuimos
C. eran
D. fui

69. A. cómodos
B. lentos
C. pintorescos
D. divertidos

70. A. los nadadores
B. los estudiantes
C. los escritores
D. los viajeros

PART D

Directions: *The following passages are for reading comprehension. After each selection there are incomplete statements or questions. Of the four choices, choose the correct one based on the passage.*

Ocho días después de la muerte de don José, la separación de Martín renovó el dolor de la familia, en la que el llanto resignado había sucedido a la desesperación. Martín tomó pasaje en la cubierta del vapor, y llegó a Valparaíso, animado del deseo del estudio. Nada de lo que vio en aquel puerto ni en Santiago, la capital, llamó su atención. Sólo pensaba en su madre y en su hermana, y le parecía oír en el aire las últimas y sencillas palabras de su padre. De altivo carácter y concentrada imaginación, Martín había vivido hasta entonces, aislado por su pobreza y separado de su familia, en casa de un viejo tío que residía en Coquimbo, donde el joven había hecho sus estudios mediante la protección de aquel pariente. Los únicos días de felicidad eran los que las vacaciones le permitían pasar al lado de su familia.

En ese aislamiento todos sus afectos se habían concentrado en ésta, y al llegar a Santiago juró regresar de abogado a Copiapó y cambiar la suerte de los que necesitaban de su auxilio.

—Dios premiará mi constancia y mi trabajo—decía, repitiéndose las palabras llenas de fe con que su padre se había despedido.

Con tales ideas arreglaba Martín su modesto equipaje en la pieza de los altos de la hermosa casa de don Dámaso Encina.

71. La familia se entristeció otra vez a causa de la
A. muerte del padre.
B. muerte del hijo.
C. ausencia de Martín.
D. vuelta del hijo.

72. Todo lo que vio en Valparaíso y Santiago le
A. impresionó muy poco.
B. causó mucha pena.
C. hizo pensar en Coquimbo.
D. llenó de entusiasmo por sus estudios.

73. ¿Por qué se quedó tanto tiempo en Coquimbo?
A. Su hermana menor vivía allí.
B. Quería aislarse por completo de su familia.
C. Había ido allí para estudiar.
D. Había ido allí para proteger a un tío anciano.

GO ON TO THE NEXT PAGE

74. ¿Por qué le gustaban a Martín las vacaciones?
 A. Llegaba a conocer mejor a Santiago.
 B. Regresaba a Copiapó para estar con los suyos.
 C. No tenía que asistir a las clases.
 D. Los estudios no iban bien.

75. ¿Qué pensaba hacer al hacerse abogado?
 A. buscar clientes en Santiago
 B. despedirse de su madre y hermana
 C. casarse con la hermosa hija de don Dámaso
 D. ayudar a su familia

—Me parece muy bien que pintes; pero antes termina tu carrera de ingeniero—dijo el padre secamente.

—A mí no me interesa nada más que pintar—replicó el hijo.

—Te engañas si crees que vas a poder vivir de la pintura. Y ¿qué va a ser de la fábrica? Piensa que eres el único hijo, y si más adelante tú no te pusieras al frente de ella, tendría que dirigirla un extraño.

—Que la dirija.

—Yo no soy un obstáculo para que en los ratos que te dejen libre los estudios hagas lo que quieras.

—A la pintura hay que dedicarle todo el día.

—Mira, vete por ahí—mandó malhumorado el padre.

Aquella noche, a las diez y media, como Alfonso no había llegado aún ni mandado aviso, su madre, asustada, llamaba a las casas de todos sus amigotes. Ninguno le supo dar noticia.

—¿Le habrá ocurrido alguna desgracia? ¿Tal vez un atropello?—se preguntó la madre aterrorizada.

—Me figuro lo que ha pasado—dijo su marido.

—¿Qué?

—Que se ha largado. Hemos tenido esta mañana una discusión violenta y le dije que se fuera.

76. El padre quería que su hijo dejara la idea de ser pintor porque
 A. no había artistas en la familia.
 B. la mamá se oponía a ello.
 C. muy pocos artistas alcanzaban un éxito inmediato.
 D. le resultaría difícil ganarse la vida.

77. El padre esperaba que algún día su hijo
 A. dirigiera la fábrica.
 B. se casara y que tuviera un hijo.
 C. hiciera un viaje al extranjero.
 D. se hiciera profesor.

78. El hijo no quería ir a la universidad porque
 A. era hijo único.
 B. quería ponerse al frente de la fábrica ahora mismo.
 C. quería pasar todo el tiempo pintando.
 D. no había quien se lo costeara.

79. El padre creía que su hijo
 A. había tenido un accidente con su coche.
 B. había tenido una disputa con su mamá.
 C. se había muerto violentamente.
 D. se había marchado de la casa.

80. La discusión violenta era entre
 A. el padre y el hijo.
 B. el hijo y la madre.
 C. la madre y el padre.
 D. el hijo y la hermana.

El turismo en España no es precisamente una "industria." El español no se viste de lujo, no se pone "guapo" porque sabe que millones de extranjeros —o españoles e hijos de la España extraterritorial— visitan permanentemente su país. ¡Pero qué servicios, qué atención! —nos dicen quienes estuvieron tres semanas o tres meses en la península. Y esa atención reina todo el año, es el resultado de la más natural forma de ser de un pueblo fiel a sí mismo, a una misión y a un destino. Muchos visitantes notaron que jamás se pierde una carta; la rapidez y precisión con que se obtiene una comunicación telefónica de un extremo a otro del país; la comodidad y puntualidad de los trenes; la atención en el hotel, de la categoría que fuere. Pero hay algo más. La buena predisposición, la espontaneidad con que se saca al turista de una dificultad, orientándolo y hasta acompañándolo si no interpreta bien dónde queda tal o cual lugar. Esa suerte de colaboración franca y fraternal levanta a cada español o española en un guía. Todo hombre empieza a percibir en España que tiene algo de español. No es país de rascacielos —toda la Europa clásica no lo es— y detesta la acumulación vertical de cemento si no lo guía algún gran argumento humano que se traduzca en creación.

81. El tratamiento del español para con el turista revela que
    A. el español le desprecia al turista.
    B. el español se considera superior al turista.
    C. el turismo es menos comercial en España.
    D. la cortesía ya no existe en España.

82. El servicio telefónico dentro del país
    A. da origen a gran número de quejas.
    B. funciona casi perfectamente.
    C. no alcanza de un extremo a otro.
    D. no se ha instalado todavía.

83. Se dice que los trenes parten y llegan
    A. a la hora debida.
    B. con varias horas de retraso.
    C. según los caprichos de los ferrocarrileros.
    D. sin horario fijo.

84. El turista que se encuentra perdido o en un apuro
    A. debe dirigirse a la Embajada Americana.
    B. debe dirigirse a un rascacielos próximo.
    C. puede contar con la ayuda de todo español.
    D. puede orientarse mediante los montes de la sierra.

85. Para el español todo rascacielos tiene que
    A. reflejar el espíritu creativo y humano.
    B. manifestar un deseo de dar las gracias a Dios.
    C. imitar el estilo clásico europeo.
    D. ser creación de arquitectos europeos.

END OF TEST 6

TEST 7

This test consists of 85 questions. You have 60 minutes to complete it. Answer Keys, Analysis Charts, Explained Answers, and Answer Sheets follow Test 9.

PART A

Directions: This part contains incomplete statements. Each has four choices. Choose the correct completion and blacken the corresponding space on the answer sheet.

1. Andrés tuvo una carta de don Pedro, ... el 22 de agosto.
   A. fachada
   B. fechada
   C. fijada
   D. finca

2. Desde mi llegada a Madrid, ... usted a algunas personas.
   A. pregunté por
   B. pedí por
   C. miré
   D. busqué

3. ¿Cuánto tiempo ... que usted estudia esta lengua?
   A. hay
   B. ha
   C. hace
   D. desde

4. Elena estaba delicada. Durante los últimos días de su estancia en la ciudad, ... enferma.
   A. cayó
   B. se apresuró
   C. se apoyó
   D. aportó

5. Durante la enfermedad de Elena, su amigo le enviaba todos los días ... de flores.
   A. un bosque
   B. un ramo
   C. un rato
   D. un rayo

6. Para hacerle compañía a María, Hilda daba ... con ella por los jardines.
   A. vuelos
   B. voces
   C. viudos
   D. vueltas

7. Alfonso había llegado a la estación para ... de Alberto.
   A. despedazar
   B. despertarse
   C. destrozar
   D. despedirse

8. La ... irritada de la tía sonó desde lo alto de la escalera.
   A. vez
   B. voz
   C. luz
   D. vida

9. El chico se acostó en silencio pero tardó en ...
   A. dormirse.
   B. doblar la esquina.
   C. disculpar.
   D. discurrir.

10. El niño le sacó ... a otro niño.
   A. la lengua
   B. el lenguaje
   C. la leña
   D. el lechero

11. El señor Morales se ajustaba ... de la corbata.
   A. la nube
   B. la nuez
   C. el odio
   D. el nudo

12. La vieja tiendecita que el señor Morales posee no puede sostener la competencia de los grandes ...
   A. almacenes.
   B. alfombras.
   C. almohadas.
   D. almuerzos.

13. Una mujer entra en la tienda, mira en torno, como buscando a alguien y, sin comprar ... , sale.
   A. algo
   B. alguien
   C. nada
   D. nudo

14. Nuestra profesora de español es muy amable ... nosotros.
   A. para con
   B. para
   C. por
   D. de

15. Los alumnos asisten ... la escuela cinco días por semana.
   A. en
   B. a
   C. de
   D. con

16. Los hombres no quisieron hacerlo ... miedo.
   A. para
   B. por el
   C. por
   D. al

17. Estaremos en Málaga ... julio.
   A. el medio de
   B. la medida de
   C. la media de
   D. a mediados de

GO ON TO THE NEXT PAGE

18. Estaremos en Barcelona . . . la semana que viene.
   A. a principios de
   B. al príncipe de
   C. a saltos de
   D. a toda brida de

19. Cuanto más estudio . . . más aprendo.
   A. tan
   B. tanto
   C. tanta
   D. cuanto

20. ¿Mi libro? Yo no sé donde está. Lo doy por . . .
   A. pierdo.
   B. perder.
   C. perdido.
   D. piedra.

21. Tomo el desayuno a las siete . . . la mañana.
   A. de
   B. por
   C. a
   D. en lo alto

22. No puedo hablarle ahora porque estoy . . . salir.
   A. a punto de
   B. en los puntos de
   C. en punto para
   D. en el punto de

23. ¡Vámonos! . . . tarde.
   A. Está
   B. Sea
   C. Se hizo
   D. Se hace

24. No comprendo . . . subjuntivo.
   A. lo del
   B. lo de
   C. el de
   D. el del

25. El señor Pardo llega . . . temprano.
   A. de la noche
   B. por la mañana
   C. de la mañana
   D. lo mismo

26. ¡Vámonos! El autobús . . . salir.
   A. es para
   B. está para
   C. es por
   D. está por

27. Me gusta . . . la televisión por la noche.
   A. ver
   B. mirar
   C. viendo
   D. viniendo

28. El chico se quedó ... porque había corrido tan rápidamente.
    A. sin aliento
    B. sin alimento
    C. sin aliviar
    D. sin algodón

29. Soy ... ; te escucho con atención.
    A. todas orejas
    B. todos ojos
    C. todas olas
    D. todo oídos

30. Tengo ... de tomar un helado.
    A. ganaderías
    B. ganaría
    C. ganados
    D. ganas

31. El accidente ... lugar anoche.
    A. tuvo
    B. hizo
    C. fue
    D. fui

PART B

Directions: *The following sentences contain blank spaces. Of the four choices given for each blank select the one that fits grammatically and makes sense.*

32. Esta muchacha no ... cantar.
    A. conoce
    B. sabe a
    C. sabe de
    D. sabe

33. ¿Quién te dio este dinero? — Mi madre ...
    A. me lo dio
    B. me lo da.
    C. se lo da.
    D. se lo dio.

34. Se lo explico a Juan para que lo ...
    A. comprenda.
    B. comprende.
    C. comprenderá.
    D. comprendería.

35. Se lo explicaba a José para que lo ...
    A. comprendería.
    B. comprenda.
    C. comprenderá.
    D. comprendiese.

36. Después que ... el profesor, salió.
    A. hubo hablado
    B. haber hablado
    C. hablando
    D. está hablando

GO ON TO THE NEXT PAGE

37. Felipe llegará pasado mañana y yo ... mis tareas.
    A. hube terminado
    B. habré terminado
    C. habría terminado
    D. habrá terminado

38. El padre ... quitó a la niña el zapato.
    A. la
    B. lo
    C. le
    D. los

39. Los ladrones ... robaron todo el dinero a él.
    A. le
    B. lo
    C. la
    D. los

40. Yo ... compré mi automóvil a ellos.
    A. le
    B. lo
    C. la
    D. les

41. Ayer por la tarde, Elena y yo nos ... en el cine.
    A. vimos
    B. vemos
    C. vieron
    D. vio

42. A las muchachas ... faltan diez dólares.
    A. les
    B. los
    C. le
    D. las

43. A Guillermo ... bastan cien dólares.
    A. le
    B. lo
    C. los
    D. les

44. Son las dos y media y ya tengo ... hambre.
    A. mucha
    B. mucho
    C. muy
    D. buen

45. No ... el conejo; por eso, no tengo ganas de comer.
    A. me gusto
    B. me gusta
    C. gustarme
    D. me gustar

46. Ayer, mis padres ... al campo para visitar a mis abuelos.
    A. irán
    B. irían
    C. se vayan
    D. se fueron

47. Voy ... el libro a la biblioteca.
- A. regresar
- B. a regresar
- C. devolver
- D. a devolver

48. Perro que ... no muerde.
- A. labra
- B. ladra
- C. lata
- D. malgasta

49. Si a Roma fueres, ... como vieres.
- A. hace
- B. haces
- C. haz
- D. hiciera

50. ¿Nos la ... Juan?
- A. dimos
- B. dio
- C. damos
- D. dar

51. ¿Quién quiere dar el dinero a Pablo? — Roberto quiere ...
- A. lo dar.
- B. darlo.
- C. dárselo.
- D. dándoselo.

52. ¡No ... Ud., por favor!
- A. me hable
- B. hábleme
- C. me habla
- D. háblame

53. ¿Quién escribe la carta a María? — Juan ...
- A. está la escribiendo.
- B. está escribiéndola.
- C. está escribiéndoselo.
- D. se la está escribiendo.

54. Me gustan ... guantes porque son elegantes.
- A. estos
- B. éstos
- C. estas
- D. éstas

55. Estas camisas y ... son hermosas.
- A. aquellas
- B. aquéllas
- C. estos
- D. ésos

56. ¿Qué es ... ? — Es una goma.
- A. este
- B. ésto
- C. esto
- D. esta

GO ON TO THE NEXT PAGE

57. Roberto y Antonio son inteligentes; éste es alto y ... es pequeño.
   A. este
   B. esto
   C. aquello
   D. aquél

58. Mi hermano y ... mi amigo son abogados.
   A. lo de
   B. él de
   C. el uno
   D. el de

59. Mis hermanas y ... Isabel son bonitas.
   A. las que
   B. las de
   C. las
   D. aquéllas

60. ¿Quién es la muchacha que está bailando con Roberto? — ... baila con Roberto es mi hermana.
   A. La de
   B. La que
   C. Quien que
   D. La muchacha

61. Mi hermano es más alto que ...
   A. su.
   B. lo suyo.
   C. suyo.
   D. el suyo.

62. Tu coche es más grande que ...
   A. el mío.
   B. la mía.
   C. mío.
   D. mía.

63. ¿De quién es esta casa? — Es ... tío.
   A. mi
   B. de mi
   C. a mi
   D. mí

64. ¿De quién es este lápiz? — Es ...
   A. mío.
   B. de mi.
   C. de mí.
   D. el mío.

65. ¿De quién son estas camisas? — Son ...
   A. las suyas.
   B. suyas.
   C. sus.
   D. suyos.

PART C

Directions: Read the entire paragraph that follows to determine its general meaning. It contains blank spaces that are numbered. Of the four choices given for each numbered blank, choose the one that is grammatically correct and makes sense.

El tenor madrileño, Plácido Domingo, ha obtenido en Viena un __66__ fantástico en la ópera. Después de cantar La Bohème, de Puccini, tuvo que salir para __67__ a la gente ochenta veces. Los aplausos duraron exactamente una hora y cuarto, lo que demuestra la popularidad __68__ ha alcanzado Plácido Domingo en los últimos años. Plácido Domingo tiene tres hijos, José, el mayor, Plácido y Alvaro. Su hijo Plácido es __69__; escribió una de las canciones de su nuevo álbum titulada "There Will Be Love." La compañía discográfica le ha preparado al tenor una cena para __70__ dos medallas de oro por haber vendido los primeros 50.000 ejemplares de sus discos "Perhaps Love" y "Canciones mexicanas."

66. A. sucesor.
B. sucio
C. sucoso
D. éxito

67. A. despertar
B. consolar
C. saludar
D. imitar

68. A. que
B. lo que
C. quien
D. cual

69. A. pintor
B. compositor
C. bailarín
D. periodista

70. A. darlo
B. darle
C. darlos
D. darles

PART D

<u>*Directions:*</u> *The following passages are for reading comprehension. After each selection there are incomplete statements or questions. Of the four choices, choose the correct one based on the passage.*

Hoy, que lloro amargamente la muerte de Mariano Benlliure, me voy a limitar a referir cómo y cuándo él ganó su primer dinero.

En nuestras charlas íntimas hubo de contármelo hace muchísimo tiempo. Habitaba la familia de Mariano en Valencia en el piso más alto de una casa, en cuya planta baja existía una tienda de comestibles, famosa por el buen chocolate que vendía. El dueño del establecimiento era un viejo carlista que había peleado en la primera guerra civil con fanático entusiasmo.

Benlliure, que tenía a la sazón nueve años, ya modelaba unas figurillas muy delicadas, y el chocolatero, que admiraba la habilidad del niño, le dijo un día:

—Mariano, si me copias estos dos retratos, te daré una peseta—y le entregó un retrato de San José otro del célebre caudillo carlista Pascual Cucala.

Mariano cumplió el encargo perfectamente, y gustó tanto su obra al veterano guerrillero, que le manifestó:

—Toma le peseta, que está bien ganada, y de propina, por lo parecido que están los retratos, te regalo una onza de chocolate.

Así obtuvo su primera ganancia quien en el curso de más de setenta años había de llenar el mundo entero de bustos, estatuas y monumentos, que han hecho célebre su nombre.

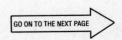

GO ON TO THE NEXT PAGE

71. ¿Dónde vivía Benlliure en aquella época?
    A. el la planta baja de la casa
    B. en el despacho del chocolatero
    C. detrás de una tienda de comestibles
    D. en la parte superior de una casa

72. ¿A quién pertenecía la tienda?
    A. a la familia de Mariano
    B. a los Valencia
    C. a un antiguo soldado
    D. a Pascual Cucala

73. ¿Cómo estimuló el chocolatero la carrera de Benlliure?
    A. Le dio al muchacho una pequeña comisión.
    B. Le ofreció empleo en su tienda de comestibles.
    C. Le presentó a un gran artista.
    D. Le compró todas las figurillas que modelaba.

74. Para demostrar lo satisfecho que estaba, el chocolatero le
    A. regaló los retratos que había copiado.
    B. pagó lo prometido y le dio unos dulces.
    C. ofreció hacer el gasto de la carrera.
    D. dio otros tres retratos para copiar.

75. Benlliure era uno de los más famosos
    A. pintores de España.
    B. escultores del mundo.
    C. soldados españoles.
    D. arquitectos valencianos.

El extrajero llegó rendido a la estación desierta. Su gran maleta, que nadie quiso llevar, le había fatigado en extremo. Se limpió el rostro con un pañuelo, y miró los rieles del ferrocarril que se perdían en el horizonte. Desanimado y pensativo consultó su reloj: la hora justa en que el tren debía partir.

Alguien, salido de quién sabe dónde, le dio una palmada muy suave. Al volverse, el extranjero se halló ante un viejecillo de vago aspecto ferrocarrilero. Llevaba en la mano una linterna roja, pero tan pequeña, que parecía de juguete. Miró sonriendo al viajero, y éste le dijo ansioso su pregunta:

—Usted perdone, ¿ha salido ya el tren?

—¿Lleva usted poco tiempo en este país?

—Necesito salir inmediatamente. Debo hallarme en Toledo mañana mismo.

—Se ve que usted ignora por completo lo que ocurre. Lo que debe hacer ahora es buscar alojamiento en un hotel.

—Pero yo no quiero alojarme, sino salir en el tren.

—Alquile usted un cuarto inmediatamente, si es que lo hay. En caso de que pueda conseguirlo, contrátelo por mes, le resultará más barato y recibirá mejor atención.

—¿Está usted loco? Yo debo llegar a Toledo mañana mismo.

—Francamente, you debería abandonarle a su suerte. Sin embargo, le daré unos informes.

—Por favor . . .

—Este país es famoso por sus ferrocarriles, como usted sabe. Falta solamente que los trenes cumplan las indicaciones contenidas en las guías y que pasen efectivamente por las estaciones. Los habitantes del país así lo esperan; mientras tanto, aceptan las irregularidades del servicio y su patriotismo les impide expresar cualquier manifestación de desagrado.

76. ¿Por qué llegó cansado el extranjero?
    A. Se había perdido en el desierto.
    B. Había viajado una gran distancia.
    C. Lo que llevaba pesaba mucho.
    D. La escalera de la estación era muy alta.

77. ¿Cuándo llegó el viajero a la estación?

    A. dos horas antes de partir el tren

    B. después de hallar un cuarto

    C. a la hora exacta

    D. momentos después de salir el tren

78. ¿Qué le recomendó el viejo al extranjero?

    A. que buscase dónde vivir mientras esperaba

    B. que alquilara un cuarto en otro pueblo

    C. que consiguiese pasaje en el próximo tren

    D. que echara ojo a su maleta

79. El viejo ofreció

    A. llevarle al extranjero a su propia casa.

    B. decirle por qué le hizo tal recomendación.

    C. llevarle él mismo a Toledo.

    D. servirle de guía.

80. El anciano acabó por decirle que

    A. los trenes no llegaban ni partían a tiempo.

    B. el servicio de ferrocarriles en Toledo era mejor.

    C. se había suspendido la distribución de guías impresas.

    D. todo español protestaba del servicio irregular.

Entre los regalos que la vida contemporánea nos ha dado está la obra de Walt Disney. Sus películas han duplicado el número de nuestros domingos, es decir, nuestros días de alegría. Todos estamos en deuda con él, porque nos ha regalado su genio a todos y no sólo a los niños. Gracias a Disney, principalmente, los chicos de todo el mundo han podido ir al cine sin que sus padres se sintieran avergonzados de comprar los billetes y entrar en el cine. He ahí quien siempre ha sabido algo muy sencillo, pero que sólo conoce una minoría de poetas: que en el viejo corazón del hombre respira todavía el niño que ese hombre fue.

Ante un film de Disney, el niño experimenta dos tipos de placer: el que proviene de la obra y el que le proporciona ver divertirse a los mayores tanto como él. Disney es, pues, universal en más de un sentido: le conocen todos, porque se dirige a todos. La violencia es una fuerza de atracción innegable, como el miedo o la risa; pero todavía por encima de ella existe una fuerza de atracción angélica que comunica algo que vale más: la alegría.

81. Lo que dice el autor de los domingos significa que

    A. se dan regalos a todos los que van al cine los domingos.

    B. con sólo comprar un billete pueden entrar dos niños.

    C. se dan dos películas de Disney los domingos.

    D. Disney nos ha proporcionado muchísmas horas alegres.

82. Los padres no se sienten avergonzados

    A. de que no ganen tanto como Disney.

    B. de que no les gusten las películas de Disney.

    C. de acompañar a sus hijos al cine.

    D. de prohibir que sus hijos vayan al cine.

83. Disney se da cuenta de que

    A. a todos no les gustan sus películas.

    B. todo hombre es un niño grande.

    C. pocos poetas van al cine.

    D. los niños prefieren películas policíacas.

GO ON TO THE NEXT PAGE

84. ¿En qué consiste la universalidad de Disney?
  A. Muchas de sus películas han sido premiadas.
  B. Conoce a todos los actores del mundo cinematográfico.
  C. Todo el mundo puede apreciar el arte de Disney.
  D. No cuesta mucho la entrada en el cine donde se dan sus filmes.

85. La atracción más fuerte de las películas de Disney es
  A. la alegría.
  B. la violencia.
  C. la vergüenza.
  D. el miedo.

END OF TEST 7

TEST 8

This test consists of 85 questions. You have 60 minutes to complete it. Answer Keys, Analysis Charts, Explained Answers, and Answer Sheets follow Test 9.

PART A

Directions: This part contains incomplete statements. Each has four choices. Choose the correct completion and blacken the corresponding space on the answer sheet.

1. Alguna vez que estuve en Laredo, . . . encontrar a Elena pero sin buen resultado.
   A. traje
   B. toqué
   C. tendí
   D. traté de

2. Me felicito en saber que usted y Gabriela . . . escribiéndose.
   A. siguen
   B. acarician
   C. abrazan
   D. abaten

3. Al . . . del tren, Joaquín vio que se le acercaba el portero.
   A. acostar
   B. acelerar
   C. bajar
   D. calentar

4. Le . . . el cochero al hombre hasta el coche que aguardaba en la plaza.
   A. dijo
   B. condujo
   C. brotó
   D. borró

5. ¡Qué gusto mirar . . . en el cielo!
   A. los cepillos
   B. las estrellas
   C. las ciegas
   D. las citas

6. ¡Qué . . . pestilente, insoportable que viene de la basura!
   A. olor
   B. orgullo
   C. oído
   D. orador

7. En la zona entre las dos ciudades, en . . . que bordea el mar, existe una zona de apartamentos para turistas.
   A. la misma carrera
   B. la misma carretera
   C. el mismo carrito
   D. la misma cartera

GO ON TO THE NEXT PAGE

8. Hoy, el sol no ... como de costumbre porque hay muchas nubes.
   A. alaba
   B. ajusta
   C. ahorra
   D. alumbra

9. Tráigame una cuchara para sacar ... que está en mi sopa.
   A. la mosca
   B. el moho
   C. el mozo
   D. la finca

10. Quisiera ir a la playa con ustedes pero no tengo ... de baño.
    A. traje
    B. trigo
    C. trofeo
    D. testigo

11. ... es mi fruta favorita.
    A. La toronja
    B. El queso
    C. La frazada
    D. El clavel

12. El profesor don Pedro fue invitado a ... conferencias en varias universidades.
    A. academias
    B. aguardar
    C. alcanzar
    D. pronunciar

13. En Madrid y París es frecuente ver mesas y sillas en ... , como prolongación de un café interior.
    A. el aceite
    B. la acera
    C. el acero
    D. la abeja

14. Pepita veía a José joven, guapo, sonriente y humilde, sin darse ... de que no tenía corazón.
    A. cuenta
    B. cuento
    C. cuello
    D. cuerda

15. Obtenemos miel de las ... obreras.
    A. abejas
    B. aduanas
    C. aguas
    D. águilas

16. La madre de Valentina me quería; su padre, ... , me tenía una gran antipatía.
    A. en cuanto
    B. en cambio
    C. en broma
    D. en cuanto a

17. Todo el mundo estaba ... cuando entré en la iglesia esta mañana.
    A. de rodillas
    B. de nuevo
    C. de madrugada
    D. de repente

18. Quisiera un café con ... y crema, por favor.
   A. aceite
   B. suelto
   C. suceso
   D. azúcar

19. No comprendo lo que usted dice; ¿qué ... decir?
   A. queja
   B. quiere
   C. quebra
   D. queso

20. Para ... vieja, la señora Molina es muy ágil.
   A. ser tan
   B. ser tanta
   C. estar tan
   D. estando tan

21. El tiempo da ... consejo.
   A. bien
   B. buen
   C. bienestar
   D. bizarro

22. Mi tía Ignacia me ... un libro para mi cumpleaños.
   A. regaló
   B. regateó
   C. pidió
   D. regresó

23. El escritor norteamericano Waldo Frank ha ... a los setenta y siete años de edad.
   A. roto
   B. muerto
   C. visto
   D. resuelto

24. En el interior de este castillo, se han instalado ... eléctrica, un teléfono y otras diversas innovaciones.
   A. la altura
   B. la lucha
   C. la luz
   D. la apuesta

25. La ... de agua este verano ha provocado una crisis.
   A. escasez
   B. escoba
   C. escala
   D. espada

26. Por haber desaparecido recientemente el puente de madera, ... del río Quetzala se hace actualmente en un barco pequeño de servicio particular.
   A. la cruz
   B. el cruce
   C. la cruzada
   D. el agua

27. La niña besó ... que su abuela le había regalado para su cumpleaños.
   A. la muñeca
   B. el polvo
   C. la pena
   D. el jurado

GO ON TO THE NEXT PAGE

28. Los bracitos de la niña enferma parecían blancos y trémulos como . . . de un pajarito.
    A. las albas
    B. los álamos
    C. las aldeas
    D. las alas

29. Al despedirse se abrazaron y la mujer le dio al médico . . . de olorosas manzanas.
    A. un colchón
    B. una colina
    C. un cesto
    D. un afán

30. Los viajeros, . . . de maletas, se dirigieron a la salida de la estación.
    A. cargados
    B. cariñosos
    C. caros
    D. casados

31. Mi padre murió hace poco; mi madre, recién . . . , me llevó a la escuela para comenzar mis estudios.
    A. viuda
    B. zurda
    C. zopenca
    D. vivienda

PART B

Directions: The following sentences contain blank spaces. Of the four choices given for each blank select the one that fits grammatically and makes sense.

32. ¿Qué hora . . . cuando sus padres regresaron a casa?
    A. fue
    B. era
    C. hizo
    D. hice

33. Mis zapatos están sucios porque . . . lodo afuera.
    A. hay
    B. hace
    C. es
    D. está

34. En este momento estoy mirando las estrellas que . . . en el cielo.
    A. brilla
    B. brillaban
    C. brillaba
    D. brillan

35. No puedo adelantar porque . . . neblina.
    A. hay
    B. hace
    C. es
    D. está

36. ¿Son amigos Pedro y Pablo? —Sí, . . . son.
    A. los
    B. lo
    C. ellos
    D. ellos los

37. ¿Quién quiere escribir una carta a Juanita? —Juan quiere . . . a Juanita.
   A. la escribir
   B. escribírsela
   C. está escribiéndosela
   D. le escribir

38. ¿Quién está escribiendo la carta? —José . . . escribiendo.
   A. lo está
   B. está lo
   C. la está
   D. se lo está

39. ¿El libro? María . . . ha dado.
   A. no lo me
   B. no me lo
   C. no lo te
   D. lo me

40. El señor Molina es el profesor . . . admiro.
   A. que
   B. quien
   C. lo cual
   D. cual

41. La cama . . . duermo es grande.
   A. la cual
   B. que
   C. en que
   D. en la cual

42. La señora Gómez, . . . es profesora, conoce a mi madre.
   A. lo cual
   B. que
   C. a quien
   D. a que

43. ¿Conoces a la chica con . . . tomé el almuerzo?
   A. que
   B. quien
   C. a quien
   D. a que

44. En este cuarto, hay una gran ventana . . . se ve el sol por la mañana.
   A. por la cual
   B. por que
   C. por quien
   D. la cual

45. Mi hijo Juan estudia sus lecciones todos los días, . . . es bueno.
   A. que
   B. lo cual
   C. cual
   D. las que

46. Comprendo perfectamente . . . usted dice.
   A. que
   B. lo que
   C. el que
   D. cual

GO ON TO THE NEXT PAGE

47. El señor García, ... son inteligentes, es profesor.
   A. cuyos hijos
   B. de quien los hijos
   C. cuyo hijos
   D. los hijos de que

48. La muchacha, ... es profesor, es inteligente.
   A. cuya padre
   B. cuyo padre
   C. de quien el padre
   D. cuya el padre

49. El muchacho, ... es profesora, es inteligente.
   A. cuyo madre
   B. cuya madre
   C. de quien la madre
   D. cuyo la madre

50. ¿ ... es este libro?
   A. De cuyo
   B. Cuyo
   C. De quién
   D. A quién

51. El niño, ... la madre lavó los pies, es hermoso.
   A. cuyo
   B. cuya
   C. a quien
   D. que

52. Cuando mi hermanito entró en mi dormitorio, yo ... leyendo.
   A. estoy
   B. soy
   C. estaba
   D. estuve

53. Antes de ... , la profesora cerró las ventanas de la sala de clase.
   A. salir
   B. saliendo
   C. salido
   D. sale

54. ¿Dio usted los libros a los alumnos? —Sí, ... di.
   A. los
   B. les
   C. les los
   D. se los

55. Cuando mi madre supo la noticia desgraciada, ... a llorar.
   A. se echó
   B. se dedicó
   C. aspiró
   D. acabó

56. El profesor ... a abrir la puerta.
   A. se olvidó
   B. trató
   C. se acordó
   D. se dirigió

57. El señor González ... a ir a la fiesta.
   A. se negó
   B. amenazó
   C. se contentó
   D. soñó

58. Enrique ... a ser profesor de matemáticas.
   A. soñó
   B. contó
   C. llegó
   D. sonó

59. Sueño ... a España.
   A. ir
   B. con ir
   C. yendo
   D. a ir

60. Siempre ... con mi promesa.
   A. cumplo
   B. ceso
   C. me canso
   D. me descanso

61. Mi padre ... de preparar la comida para toda la familia.
   A. se queda
   B. se ocupa
   C. cuenta
   D. contenta

62. Vamos ... de esta oportunidad.
   A. consentir
   B. a aprovecharnos
   C. complacernos
   D. apoyarnos

63. ¿En ... piensas? —Pienso en mi juguete perdido.
   A. quién
   B. qué
   C. quiénes
   D. lo cual

64. El avión ... en llegar.
   A. se quejó
   B. salió
   C. disfrutó
   D. tardó

65. La señora Pardo ... en salir.
   A. se empeñó
   B. acabó
   C. se dio
   D. tuvo

PART C

Directions: _Read the entire paragraph that follows to determine its general meaning. It contains blank spaces that are numbered. Of the four choices given for each numbered blank, choose the one that is grammatically correct and makes sense._

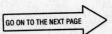GO ON TO THE NEXT PAGE

Alvaro Sauna, niño madrileño de doce añõs, quería una computadora personal, pero no tenía bastante dinero. Necesitaba un préstamo. Solicitó un crédito bancario para __66__ una computadora y ofreció, como garantía, el dinero que recibe de su familia cada semana. El Banco de Bilbao en Madrid, por primera vez en su historia, __67__ crédito a una persona no adulta. Alvaro inició el negocio por medio de una carta al director general del banco en la que decía: "Le __68__ porque tengo un problema económico. Tengo muchos deseos de comprar una computadora que cuesta 39.000 pesetas, pero sólo __69__ 7.000 pesetas. Mi padre no me puede ayudar económicamente, y por eso, recurro a sus servicios. Mi padre me da 60 pesetas semanales, y mi abuelo 100. Si ustedes me prestan lo que necesito, yo podré pagar 640 pesetas al mes." El banco le __70__ el dinero que necesitaba, y le fijó la cantidad de 500 pesetas al mes para la restitución del crédito.

66. A. vender
    B. comprar
    C. encontrar
    D. construir

67. A. ofreció
    B. corrió
    C. colgó
    D. cepilló

68. A. contesto
    B. compro
    C. escribo
    D. llamo

69. A. pierdo
    B. gasto
    C. miro
    D. tengo

70. A. compró
    B. tuvo
    C. dio
    D. tomó

PART D

Directions: The following passages are for reading comprehension. After each selection there are incomplete statements or questions. Of the four choices, choose the correct one based on the passage.

A los doce añós, peleando Juan Peña con unos chicos, le tiraron una piedra en los dientes; la sangre corrió lavándole lo sucio de la cara, y un diente se le quebró en forma de sierra. Desde ese día empieza la edad de oro de Juan Peña.

Con la punta de la lengua, Juan tocaba continuamente el diente roto; el cuerpo inmóvil, la mirada vaga sin pensar. Así, de malicioso y juguetón, se tornó en callado y tranquilo.

Los padres de Juan, cansados de escuchar quejas de los vecinos y las víctimas de las maldades del chico, y habiendo agotado toda clase de reprimendas y castigos, estaban ahora estupefactos y angustiados con la transformación de Juan.

—El niño no está, Pablo —decía la madre al marido. —Hay que llamar al médico.

Llegó el médico, grave y solemne, y procedió al diagnóstico: buen pulso, excelente apetito, ningún síntoma de enfermedad.

—Señora —terminó por decir el sabio, después de un largo examen —, su hijo está mejor que una manzana. Lo que sí es indiscutible —continuó con voz misteriosa —es que estamos en presencia de un caso fenomenal: su hijo, mi estimable señora, sufre de lo que llamamos hoy el mal de pensar. Su hijo es un filósofo precoz, un genio tal vez.

Parientes y amigos se hicieron eco de la opinión del médico, recibida con júbilo indecible por los padres de Juan. Pronto, en el pueblo se citó el caso admirable del "niño prodigio" y su fama se aumentó.

71. ¿Qué le pasó a Juan Peña a los doce años?
   A. Recibió un hermoso regalo de sus amigos.
   B. Se le rompió un diente en una pelea.
   C. Unos chicos le lavaron la cara con agua sucia.
   D. Halló un pedazo de oro en las montañas.

72. ¿Qué efecto produjo el incidente?
   A. Se puso reservado el niño.
   B. Juan se puso aun más malicioso.
   C. Siempre se miraba el diente en el espejo.
   D. Le quedó lastimada la lengua.

73. ¿Por qué quedaron sorprendidos los padres de Juan?
   A. Los vecinos se quejaron más que antes.
   B. Los severos castigos acabaron por corregirle.
   C. El niño había sufrido un cambio de genio.
   D. El niño se negó a hacer caso de las reprimendas.

74. ¿Cuál fue el diagnóstico del médico?
   A. Juan tenía varios síntomas de enfermedades graves.
   B. El niño se había comido muchas manzanas podridas.
   C. Había que estimularse su apetito.
   D. El estado de Juan era rarísimo.

75. ¿Qué ocurrió como resultado de la visita del doctor?
   A. Los parientes del prodigio lo desconocieron.
   B. Se vieron contrariados los padres del niño.
   C. Se extendió la celebridad del niño.
   D. Acudieron filósofos y genios de todas partes a verlo.

Para escribir la historia completa de la Vuelta a Colombia se necesitan noventa páginas y media. Sin embargo, para un periódico se puede hacer un relato breve de lo que es la competencia, la máxima del deporte colombiano, y lo que hacen los miembros de la llamada "familia de la Vuelta."

Cada año—durante la estación más fría del año—parten de Bogotá, generalmente, cincuenta, sesenta o más ciclistas en busca de un triunfo para los colores deportivos de sus regiones.

Muchos de ellos saben, de antemano, que sólo tendrán un éxito muy relativo en la carrera. Algunos llegan hasta adivinar las penalidades que van a pasar en las jornadas. Pero salen.

Otros, los biciclistas y "dedicados", tienen por lo menos las capacidades necesarias para luchar por los primeros lugares en la clasificación general.

Los ciclistas inician la Vuelta y con ellos cerca de seiscientas personas más. La "gran familia" está compuesta por unas setecientas en total.

Cuando ya han transcurrido cinco o seis fases, los ganadores usualmente se han identificado. En algunos casos—por ejemplo este año—el campeón de la Vuelta comenzó a tener nombre propio en Medellín.

76. La Vuelta a Colombia es una competencia deportiva de
   A. automóviles.
   B. caballos.
   C. bicicletas.
   D. motocicletas.

GO ON TO THE NEXT PAGE

77. El autor dice que se necesitarían más de noventa páginas porque
   A. Colombia fue fundada en el siglo XV.
   B. hay tanto que contar sobre la Vuelta.
   C. los premios son ofrecidos por el periódico.
   D. el periodista era ciclista él mismo.

78. La Vuelta se efectúa
   A. en un club deportivo colombiano.
   B. en el Palacio de los Deportes de Medellín.
   C. por las calles de Bogotá.
   D. por las carreteras de Colombia.

79. ¿Quiénes son los "dedicados"?
   A. los que esperan ganar la Vuelta
   B. los que tienen el apellido de Medellín
   C. los que no saben qué penalidades van a pasar
   D. los dueños de las fábricas de bicicletas

80. Se sabe quienes serán los ganadores
   A. al formarse los ciclistas.
   B. al salir de Bogotá.
   C. después de un día.
   D. después de varias etapas.

Sin hacer ruido, llegó don Paco a la casilla y desde afuera vio la puerta que estaba cerrada con cerradura que había por dentro. La luz salía desde adentro por una ventana pequeña, donde, en vez de vidrios, se había puesto una tela sucia para protección contra la lluvia y el frío. Con el obstáculo de la tela no se podían ver los objetos de dentro; pero don Paco se aproximó y observó en la tela tres o cuatro agujeros. Aplicó el ojo al más cercano, que era bastante espacioso y lo que vio por dentro le llenó de susto. Imaginó que veía a Lucifer en persona, aunque vestido de campesino andaluz, con sombrero grande, chaqueta larga y pantalones amplios. La cara del así vestido era casi negra, inmóvil, con espantosa y ancha boca y con colosales narices en forma de pico de pájaro. Don Paco se tranquilizó, no obstante, al reconocer que aquello era una máscara de las que ponen en las procesiones religiosas.

En otra silla estaba otra persona, en quien reconoció al instante don Paco a don Ramón, el comerciante más importante de su lugar que era también el hombre más rico después de cierto don Andrés y el más enorme hablador que por entonces existía en nuestro planeta.

Notó don Paco que tenía don Ramón las manos atadas con una cuerda a las espaldas, y dedujo que le habían llevado allí y que le retenían por violencia.

81. Al acercarse a la casilla, Paco descubrió que
   A. no se podía entrar por la puerta.
   B. se le había olvidado la llave.
   C. la casilla no tenía puerta.
   D. la puerta no tenía cerradura.

82. ¿Por qué no podía ver bien lo que había en la casilla?
   A. Los vidrios estaban sucios.
   B. Una tela cubría la ventana.
   C. No había luz en la casilla.
   D. La ventana estaba cubierta de madera.

83. ¿Por qué se asustó don Paco?
   A. Oyó acercarse una procesión ruidosa.
   B. Oyó gritar a una persona.
   C. Vio unos pájaros muertos en la casilla.
   D. Vio una figura grotesca dentro de la casilla.

84. ¿A quién reconoció Paco sentado en una silla?
    A. don Andrés
    B. el sacerdote
    C. un hombre de negocios
    D. la mujer de don Ramón

85. Don Paco se dio cuenta de que una persona que estaba en el cuarto era
    A. prisionero.
    B. mendigo.
    C. astrónomo.
    D. el dueño de la casilla.

END OF TEST 8

TEST 9

This test consists of 85 questions. You have 60 minutes to complete it. Answer Keys, Analysis Charts, Explained Answers, and Answer Sheets follow Test 9.

PART A

Directions: This part contains incomplete statements. Each has four choices. Choose the correct completion and blacken the corresponding space on the answer sheet.

1. A los doce años, ... Juan Peña con unos chicos, le tiraron una piedra en los dientes; la sangre corrió lavándole lo sucio de la cara, y un diente se le quebró en forma de sierra.
   A. andando
   B. hablando
   C. lavando
   D. peleando

2. Con ... de la lengua, Juan tocaba continuamente el diente roto en la boca.
   A. el punto
   B. la punta
   C. el puño
   D. el pulmón

3. Los padres de Juan estaban ... de escuchar quejas de los vecinos y las víctimas de las maldades del chico.
   A. casados
   B. cansados
   C. cantando
   D. luchando

4. Hay que ... al médico.
   A. llamar
   B. llenar
   C. levantarse
   D. lavarse

5. A los quince años, Pedro recibió un hermoso ... de sus amigos.
   A. regreso
   B. regalo
   C. reino
   D. relato

6. Me gusta mucho su reloj.—Muchas gracias. Es de ... este reloj.
   A. odio
   B. orilla
   C. oro
   D. palo

7. A José se le rompió un diente en una ... con unos chicos.
   A. pelea
   B. paja
   C. paleta
   D. panza

110

8. José siempre se miraba el diente quebrado en el … del cuarto de baño.
   A. beso
   B. balazo
   C. baño
   D. espejo

9. Los vecinos se quejaron más que … a causa de las maldades de unos chicos.
   A. menos
   B. antes
   C. afuera
   D. siquiera

10. La familia de don Pedro está … por unas quince personas.
   A. compuesta
   B. puesta
   C. rota
   D. acostumbrado

11. Esta ciudad fue … en el siglo XV.
   A. fundada
   B. furia
   C. ganado
   D. gota

12. Sin … ruido, llegó don Paco a la casilla y desde afuera vio la puerta que estaba cerrada.
   A. formar
   B. cepillar
   C. criar
   D. hacer

13. La luz salía desde dentro por una ventana pequeña donde, en vez de … , se había puesto una tela sucia para protección contra la lluvia y el frío.
   A. vides
   B. vidrios
   C. vieres
   D. viento

14. Con el obstáculo de la tela en la ventana, no se … ver los objetos de dentro.
   A. adulaban
   B. podían
   C. ponía
   D. asustaban

15. Paco se aproximó y observó en la tela tres o cuatro … ; aplicó el ojo al más cercano, que era bastante espacioso, y lo que vio por dentro le llenó de susto.
   A. agujas
   B. águilas
   C. agujeros
   D. alhajas

16. En una silla estaba una persona, en quien don Paco reconoció … a don Ramón.
   A. al por mayor
   B. al por menor
   C. al anochecer
   D. al instante

GO ON TO THE NEXT PAGE

17. Notó don Paco que tenía don Ramón las manos ... con una cuerda a las espaldas.
    A. atadas
    B. aterrizadas
    C. aterrorizadas
    D. asustadas

18. Un ... no sabe leer ni escribir.
    A. analfabeto
    B. lector
    C. escritor
    D. lento

19. Por dificultades en el último momento para ... billetes, llegué a Barcelona a medianoche en un tren distinto del que yo había pensado tomar y no me esperaba nadie.
    A. adular
    B. adquirir
    C. admitir
    D. afeitarme

20. Mi equipaje era un maletón muy ... porque estaba lleno de libros.
    A. ligero
    B. pesado
    C. limpio
    D. viejo

21. Al bajar del tren, empecé a seguir ... de los viajeros porque yo no sabía donde estaba la salida.
    A. el ruido
    B. la rueda
    C. el riel
    D. el rumbo

22. A impulsos de la brisa, mi viejo ... me golpeaba las piernas.
    A. abrazo
    B. brazo
    C. abrigo
    D. brazalete

23. María Luisa debía parecer una ... extraña con su aspecto risueño.
    A. figura
    B. abeja
    C. bala
    D. balsa

24. Recuerdo que, en pocos minutos, me quedé sola en la gran avenida, ... a la gente que corría a coger los escasos taxis.
    A. corrigiendo
    B. cosiendo
    C. chafando
    D. mirando

25. De vez en cuando siento que me gustaría olvidar que jamás salí de la Ciudad de México para ir a Santa Clara, mi ... natal.
    A. penoso
    B. pueblo
    C. puente
    D. madre

26. Yo no había ... a la ciudad desde que mi madre murió.
    A. roto
    B. hecho
    C. malhecho
    D. vuelto

27. Cuando el tren me ... de México, yo estaba muy distante de sospechar las dificultades que me aguardaban.
    A. acostó
    B. alejó
    C. abrasó
    D. abrazó

28. Viviendo en la ciudad, Claudio se acostumbró a ... de una vida cómoda.
    A. gozar
    B. ceñir
    C. cenar
    D. callarse

29. Usted prefiere comer ... pero a mí me gustaría cenar en casa.
    A. fugaz
    B. fuera
    C. fuerte
    D. fresco

30. Mi familia y yo vamos a ... porque mi padre halló trabajo en otra ciudad.
    A. mudarnos
    B. cambiarnos de ropa
    C. mojar
    D. mordernos

31. Rodolfo ... todo el dinero que había recibido de su patrón.
    A. gimió
    B. gustó
    C. gastó
    D. disgustó

PART B

Directions: The following sentences contain blank spaces. Of the four choices given for each blank select the one that fits grammatically and makes sense.

32. Hay ... estudiar para aprender.
    A. que
    B. que hace
    C. hace
    D. necesario

33. ¿Cuánto tiempo ... usted espera un taxi?
    A. hace que
    B. hace
    C. que hace
    D. está

34. ... veinte minutos que espero un taxi.
    A. Hace
    B. Hacía
    C. Es
    D. Está

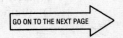

35. ¿Desde ... vives en esta casa?
    A. cuánto
    B. cuándo
    C. cuántos
    D. hace que

36. Vivo en esta casa desde ... tres años.
    A. hace
    B. cuanto
    C. cuando
    D. hay

37. ¿Cuánto tiempo ... que usted hablaba cuando yo entré?
    A. hace
    B. hacía
    C. es
    D. estaba

38. Hacía dos horas que yo ... cuando el profesor entró en la biblioteca.
    A. hablo
    B. estudiaba
    C. estudié
    D. habló

39. ¿Nadar? ¿Yo? No ... nadar. ¿Y tú?
    A. sé
    B. conozco
    C. saber
    D. conocer

40. Sentía que tu madre ... enferma.
    A. es
    B. está
    C. estuviera
    D. fuera

41. Dudé que Carlota ... sin decir nada.
    A. se fue
    B. iba
    C. iría
    D. se fuera

42. Seis menos dos ... cuatro.
    A. son
    B. están
    C. hace
    D. hagan

43. ¿Qué supones tú? —Yo ... que está bien.
    A. me parece
    B. me parecía
    C. me visto
    D. supongo

44. Cuando vivíamos en California, ... a la playa todos los días.
    A. vamos
    B. iríamos
    C. iremos
    D. íbamos

45. Salí de casa, tomé el autobús, y ... a la escuela a las ocho en punto.
   A. llego
   B. he llegado
   C. llegué
   D. llegaré

46. Graciela es ... alta como Clara.
   A. tanta
   B. tan
   C. así
   D. si

47. Rita es menos alta ... Camila.
   A. que
   B. como
   C. de
   D. tan

48. Roberto y Claudia son ... inteligentes de la clase.
   A. las más
   B. los más
   C. más
   D. menos

49. Tengo ... tíos como usted.
   A. tan
   B. tantos
   C. como
   D. que

50. Estos libros son ... interesantes como ésos.
   A. tan
   B. tantos
   C. tantas
   D. como

51. Esta frase es más fácil ... usted cree.
   A. que
   B. de lo que
   C. de la que
   D. del que

52. Paula trabaja mejor ... usted cree.
   A. que
   B. de lo que
   C. de la que
   D. del que

53. María tiene más libros ... usted tiene.
   A. de los que
   B. de lo que
   C. de las que
   D. que

54. Roberto tiene más amigas ... tiene Juan.
   A. de los que
   B. de lo que
   C. de las que
   D. que

GO ON TO THE NEXT PAGE

55. Clara trabaja . . . pero Felipe trabaja poco.
    A. mucho
    B. poco
    C. mucha
    D. poca

56. Claudio, ¿qué buscas? — . . . mis libros.
    A. Busco para
    B. Busco por
    C. Busco a
    D. Busco

57. Oscar, ¿qué pides? — . . . dinero.
    A. Pido para
    B. Pido por
    C. Pido a
    D. Pido

58. Juanita, ¿qué miras? — . . . guantes.
    A. Miro a estos
    B. Miro estas
    C. Miro a estas
    D. Miro estos

59. Le daré el dinero a Roberto cuando me lo . . .
    A. pide.
    B. pida.
    C. pidiera.
    D. pedirá.

60. Di el dinero a Carlos cuando me lo . . .
    A. pidió.
    B. pidiera.
    C. pida.
    D. pide.

61. Encontré a alguien que . . . la respuesta.
    A. sabe
    B. sepa
    C. conoce
    D. conozca

62. No encuentro a nadie que . . . la respuesta.
    A. sabe
    B. sepa
    C. conoce
    D. conozca

63. No encontré a nadie que . . . la respuesta.
    A. supiera
    B. sabe
    C. sepa
    D. conozca

64. ¿Conoce usted a alguien que . . . paciencia?
    A. tiene
    B. tuviera
    C. tenga
    D. tendrá

65. Quienquiera que ... no abriré la puerta.

    A. será

    B. es

    C. sería

    D. sea

PART C

<u>Directions:</u> *Read the entire paragraph that follows to determine its general meaning. It contains blank spaces that are numbered. Of the four choices given for each numbered blank, choose the one that is grammatically correct and makes sense.*

Mi padre era carnicero. Mi abuelo y mis tíos eran carniceros también. Mi madre era la cajera de la carnicería y trabajaba con mi padre. Los hermanos de mi madre tambíen hacían este trabajo. Al nacer yo, mi madre dijo que yo podría ser __66__ yo quisiera, menos carnicero. Durante mi niñez, me pasaba la vida __67__. Pos eso, mi madre resolvió que estudiaría en la escuela de arte. Yo viajaba hora y media de mi casa a la Escuela Secundaria de Música y Artes, que estaba situada al otro extremo de la ciudad. Mi padre siempre me presentaba a sus clientes como "mi hijo el __68__." Al mismo tiempo que you asistía a la escuela secundaria, trabajaba cada sábado en el negocio de mi padre. Cuando __69__ anuncié a mi padre que me había ganado una beca de mucho dinero para la escuela de arte en la universidad, y que yo deseaba continuar con mis __70__, él se quedó sorprendido.

66. A. lo que

    B. que

    C. quien

    D. cual

67. A. cocinando

    B. escribiendo

    C. leyendo

    D. dibujando

68. A. carnicero

    B. zapatero

    C. artista

    D. periodista

69. A. le

    B. lo

    C. les

    D. los

70. A. vacaciones

    B. exámenes

    C. estudios

    D. novelas

PART D

<u>Directions:</u> *The following passages are for reading comprehension. After each selection there are incomplete statements or questions. Of the four choices, choose the correct one based on the passage.*

Si hay un momento emocionante en la historia americana, es el instante en que la lengua castellana, puesta en labios de los misioneros, se acerca al indio. ¡Qué aire de milagro y de drama envuelve al padre Gante, delgado y mal vestido, de blanca barba bíblica, que en la plaza mayor de Tenochtitlán, bajo un sol de justicia predica un sermón a grandes voces sin que nadie le comprenda aún!

Estos momentos los vivió el padre Gante, entre otros religiosos, de manera especial. Él se inquietó ante el abismo de incomprensión que le separaba del indio. Se acercó al niño, que tiene el alma pura y la memoria fresca. Palabra a palabra, gesto a gesto, un poco en castellano, otro poco en azteca recién conocido, va el padre hablando. Va cambiando las duras palabras largas del indio, los vocablos difíciles y guturales por el claro, sonoro castellano. Señala las cosas, pinta figuras, busca el gesto elocuente y traduce. Es una escena conmovedora: el padre suda explicando y se atormenta; el indiecito, serio, callado, le escucha, y a veces una luz de comprensión brilla en sus ojos oscuros. ¡Cuántos días así!

—Mira, Juan —ya casi todos los indios se llamaban Juan—. Ese que tú llamas Tloque Nahuaque es Dios, el Señor. Y no son muchos dioses, sino uno solo. Uno. Y aquello, no "mictlan," sino infierno. Y ésta —dibuja en la arena una mujer— es la Virgen.

GO ON TO THE NEXT PAGE

71. El autor describe el primer encuentro entre
    A. religiosos e indios.
    B. padre e historiador.
    C. conquistador y misionero.
    D. misionero y universitario.

72. El sermón predicado por el misionero
    A. enojó a los indios.
    B. fue publicado en lengua indígena.
    C. fue dirigido a los españoles.
    D. no fue entendido por los indios.

73. Para poder hablar con el niño azteca, el padre Gante
    A. le enseñaba el latín.
    B. comunicaba con él mediante un jefe indio.
    C. había aprendido algo del idioma de los indios.
    D. había llevado un intérprete de España.

74. El misionero sabe que el niño le entiende
    A. por la expresión de la cara.
    B. por las palabras que pronuncia.
    C. por las señas que hace con las manos.
    D. por las figuras que dibuja.

75. Las lecciones dadas por el padre Gante tenían por objeto
    A. enseñar los misterios de la religión azteca.
    B. enseñar el arte del dibujo.
    C. enseñar la religión y la lengua de los españoles.
    D. instruir a los indios en el idioma latino.

María se lo estaba repitiendo siempre:

—No, Casimiro; esto no puede seguir así. Como tú comprenderás, hay que tomar una decisión. Después de todo, ese don Filomeno es un ladrón que te está robando el dinero pagándote lo menos posible; sí, no pongas esa cara; robando el dinero. Y si fuera por nosotros solos, mal estaría ya; pero piensa en la niña.

Casimiro Lobato no respondía nada. Demasiado sabía él que su mujer tenía toda la razón, que había que decidirse. Pero ¿cómo?, ¿cuándo? Ahí estaba el problema. Porque él no era de los que saben hablar alto, y hacerse valer, y ponerse cara a cara con el jefe. No; él tenía horror a las escenas, a las discusiones. Sobre todo a las discusiones materiales, de dinero. Lo malo era que—como decía María—, estaba la niña, esa criatura de cinco años, flaca, con unos ojos siempre asustados, bajo el pelo de color de paja. Le daba pena mirarla; y vergüenza. Vergüenza de ser un pobretón; de no haber conseguido (a pesar de que uno ha hecho también sus estudios) una posición más importante, y tener que depender todavía, a los treinta y seis años cumplidos, de los deseos extravagantes de don Filomeno. (Don Filomeno Porras, agente comercial; importación y exportación; automóvil; cincuenta y ocho años; noventa kilos; soltero; hombre de medios económicos, persona de orden.)

76. María insistía en que Casimiro tomara una decisión porque
    A. don Filomeno no le pagaba bastante.
    B. ella no tenía buena salud.
    C. ella no podía seguir trabajando.
    D. ella iba perdiendo la razón.

77. María le decía a su marido que
    A. pensara en el porvenir de su hija.
    B. confesara su crimen.
    C. denunciara a don Filomeno a la policía.
    D. pidiera ayuda a sus padres.

78. Casimiro no le respondía a su mujer porque
    A. fingía no oírla bien.
    B. era verdad lo que decía ella.
    C. no quería despertar a la niña.
    D. ella no comprendía el problema.

79. ¿De qué tenía vergüenza Casimiro?
    A. de ser dependiente en un almacén
    B. de no haber ayudado a los pobres
    C. de su poca instrucción
    D. de su condición humilde

80. Se le consideraría a don Filomeno un
    A. buen marido.
    B. buen profesor.
    C. hombre próspero.
    D. patrón benévolo.

No hace mucho, en una tertulia, un joven expresó su deseo de trabajar en determinado sitio, y preguntó qué posibilidades había de lograr su anhelo.
—Es sencillo—le contestaron—. Hazte amigo de don Crescencio.
—Bueno. Pero si interesa lo que yo puedo aportar a esa empresa, no es preciso hacerse amigo de don Crescencio.
—¡Oh, sí! Hay que ser amigo de don Crescencio. A ver si lo entiendes. Poco importa que tus proyectos valgan o no. Lo importante es que le caigas bien a don Crescencio.
En el café acababa de entrar un hombre, pálido el rostro, el cabello revuelto. Se acercó a nuestra tertulia y, cayendo en una silla, gimió desesperado:
—Creo que ya no soy amigo de don Crescencio.
Hubo un eco de lamentaciones. El recién llegado lloriqueó:
—Vosotros sabéis cómo lo he tratado, cómo le reía sus gracias, cómo asentía a sus opiniones, la de veces que acudí a sus comidas y le llevé flores a su esposa. Sabéis también que cuando él cogía odio a alguien, yo ejecutaba sus silenciosas órdenes y disponía el boicot contra el infeliz. ¡Pues hoy se ha negado a verme!
Corrieron los comentarios y consejos:
—Yo creo que si hablases con don Manuel, que manda en don Crescencio.
—Tendrías que hacerte amigo de don Manuel.

81. ¿Qué quería el joven?
    A. encontrar empleo
    B. conocer a una señorita
    C. tomar un vaso de vino
    D. ser invitado a una fiesta

82. ¿Qué le sugirieron los tertulianos?
    A. pagar la nota
    B. aportar dinero a un proyecto
    C. conseguir la amistad de cierto señor
    D. presentarse en persona en el Ministerio

83. ¿Por qué entró pálido el recién llegado?
    A. Temía que se le muriera su padre.
    B. Temía que don Crescencio se hubiera marchado.
    C. Temía haberle desagradado a don Crescencio.
    D. Temía haberle ofendido a don Manuel.

84. ¿Qué había hecho el recién llegado para complacer a don Crescencio?
    A. Le había invitado a comer.
    B. Había trabajado horas extraordinarias.
    C. Había trabajado en su jardín.
    D. Había hecho todo lo ordenado.

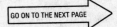
GO ON TO THE NEXT PAGE

85. Los amigos quedaron en que sería mejor
   A. preparar un proyecto para la empresa.
   B. hacerse amigo del jefe de don Crescencio.
   C. dejar su cargo y buscar otro.
   D. guardar silencio y olvidar el asunto.

END OF TEST 9

ANSWER KEYS

TEST 1

PART A

1. A
2. B
3. D
4. D
5. C
6. B
7. A
8. B
9. B
10. D
11. B
12. D
13. C
14. D
15. A
16. C
17. B
18. A
19. B
20. D
21. C
22. A
23. D
24. D
25. B
26. B
27. B
28. D
29. A
30. B
31. A

PART B

32. D
33. B
34. A
35. B
36. A
37. A
38. A
39. A
40. B
41. A
42. B
43. C
44. B
45. D
46. B
47. A
48. A
49. A
50. B
51. D
52. B
53. B
54. A
55. B
56. A
57. B
58. B
59. C
60. B
61. D
62. A
63. B
64. C
65. B

PART C

66. B
67. A
68. A
69. C
70. D

PART D

71. B
72. A
73. A
74. C
75. D
76. A
77. D
78. B
79. C
80. C
81. A
82. B
83. D
84. C
85. B

TEST 2

PART A

1. D
2. C
3. A
4. B
5. D
6. C
7. B
8. D
9. C
10. C
11. A
12. B
13. D
14. B
15. A
16. A
17. C
18. B
19. A
20. D
21. B
22. C
23. D
24. D
25. C
26. C
27. B
28. C
29. A
30. B
31. C

PART B

32. B
33. A
34. B
35. A
36. D
37. B
38. A
39. C
40. D
41. A
42. A
43. A
44. D
45. A
46. A
47. D
48. A
49. D
50. D
51. C
52. B
53. B
54. D
55. B
56. C
57. B
58. B
59. D
60. A
61. B
62. A
63. A
64. A
65. D

PART C

66. B
67. B
68. C
69. C
70. D

PART D

71. B
72. B
73. C
74. C
75. D
76. C
77. D
78. A
79. B
80. A
81. D
82. B
83. A
84. D
85. B

TEST 3

PART A

1. A
2. D
3. D
4. D
5. B
6. A
7. A
8. A
9. C
10. C
11. A
12. B
13. D
14. C
15. C
16. B
17. A
18. B
19. A
20. C
21. D
22. A
23. B
24. C
25. D
26. B
27. B
28. A
29. B
30. A
31. A

PART B

		41. B	52. B	63. C	**PART D**	80. D				
		42. A	53. C	64. A		81. C				
32. A		43. A	54. B	65. C	71. B	82. C				
33. C		44. C	55. A		72. B	83. B				
34. A		45. D	56. A	**PART C**	73. A	84. B				
35. D		46. B	57. D		74. C	85. C				
36. A		47. A	58. C	66. B	75. A					
37. B		48. B	59. B	67. B	76. C					
38. D		49. D	60. C	68. A	77. B					
39. D		50. D	61. D	69. C	78. D					
40. C		51. A	62. C	70. A	79. B					

TEST 4

PART A

	15. C	31. B	44. B	60. B	**PART D**		
	16. C		45. A	61. B			
1. A	17. C	**PART B**	46. B	62. B	71. C		
2. B	18. C		47. C	63. A	72. B		
3. B	19. B	32. A	48. B	64. B	73. B		
4. B	20. D	33. A	49. B	65. C	74. A		
5. A	21. B	34. D	50. D		75. D		
6. B	22. D	35. B	51. D	**PART C**	76. A		
7. D	23. B	36. B	52. A		77. A		
8. A	24. A	37. A	53. B	66. C	78. D		
9. D	25. D	38. B	54. B	67. B	79. C		
10. A	26. A	39. D	55. B	68. B	80. C		
11. D	27. D	40. A	56. A	69. A	81. D		
12. A	28. C	41. C	57. B	70. D	82. B		
13. B	29. A	42. A	58. A		83. A		
14. B	30. C	43. B	59. A		84. D		
					85. C		

TEST 5

PART A

	15. B	31. B	44. D	60. A	**PART D**		
	16. A		45. A	61. B			
1. B	17. C	**PART B**	46. B	62. B	71. A		
2. C	18. A		47. A	63. B	72. D		
3. B	19. D	32. B	48. B	64. A	73. A		
4. A	20. C	33. A	49. C	65. B	74. B		
5. D	21. D	34. D	50. B		75. C		
6. B	22. B	35. D	51. C	**PART C**	76. D		
7. D	23. A	36. B	52. C		77. A		
8. A	24. A	37. B	53. A	66. A	78. D		
9. C	25. A	38. C	54. B	67. D	79. B		
10. D	26. D	39. D	55. B	68. A	80. D		
11. B	27. D	40. A	56. A	69. B	81. A		
12. C	28. A	41. A	57. D	70. C	82. B		
13. A	29. D	42. A	58. A		83. B		
14. A	30. D	43. B	59. B		84. D		
					85. D		

TEST 6

PART A					PART D
	15. A	31. D	44. B	60. D	
	16. D		45. A	61. C	
1. A	17. A	PART B	46. B	62. D	71. C
2. C	18. B		47. A	63. C	72. A
3. B	19. C	32. B	48. A	64. A	73. C
4. A	20. A	33. B	49. A	65. A	74. B
5. C	21. B	34. B	50. B		75. D
6. A	22. D	35. B	51. B	PART C	76. D
7. B	23. C	36. A	52. D		77. A
8. C	24. A	37. A	53. B	66. C	78. C
9. C	25. A	38. C	54. B	67. A	79. D
10. B	26. D	39. A	55. A	68. C	80. A
11. B	27. A	40. B	56. D	69. B	81. C
12. D	28. B	41. C	57. B	70. D	82. B
13. A	29. A	42. B	58. D		83. A
14. C	30. A	43. A	59. A		84. C
					85. A

TEST 7

PART A					PART D
	15. B	31. A	44. A	60. B	
	16. C		45. B	61. D	
1. B	17. D	PART B	46. D	62. A	71. D
2. A	18. A		47. D	63. B	72. C
3. C	19. B	32. D	48. B	64. A	73. A
4. A	20. C	33. A	49. C	65. B	74. B
5. B	21. A	34. A	50. B		75. B
6. D	22. B	35. D	51. C	PART C	76. C
7. D	23. D	36. A	52. A		77. C
8. B	24. A	37. B	53. D	66. B	78. A
9. A	25. B	38. C	54. A	67. C	79. B
10. A	26. B	39. A	55. B	68. A	80. A
11. D	27. B	40. D	56. C	69. B	81. D
12. A	28. A	41. A	57. D	70. B	82. C
13. C	29. D	42. A	58. D		83. B
14. A	30. D	43. A	59. B		84. C
					85. A

TEST 8

PART A					PART D
	15. A	31. A	44. A	60. A	
	16. B		45. B	61. B	
1. D	17. A	PART B	46. B	62. B	71. B
2. A	18. D		47. A	63. B	72. A
3. C	19. B	32. B	48. B	64. D	73. C
4. B	20. A	33. A	49. B	65. A	74. D
5. B	21. B	34. D	50. C		75. C
6. A	22. A	35. A	51. C	PART C	76. C
7. B	23. B	36. B	52. C		77. B
8. D	24. C	37. B	53. A	66. B	78. D
9. A	25. A	38. C	54. D	67. A	79. A
10. A	26. B	39. B	55. A	68. C	80. D
11. A	27. A	40. A	56. D	69. D	81. A
12. D	28. D	41. C	57. A	70. C	82. B
13. B	29. C	42. B	58. C		83. D
14. A	30. A	43. B	59. B		84. C
					85. A

TEST 9

PART A	15. C	31. C	44. D	60. A	PART D
	16. D		45. C	61. A	
1. D	17. A	PART B	46. B	62. B	71. A
2. B	18. A		47. A	63. A	72. D
3. B	19. B	32. A	48. B	64. C	73. C
4. A	20. B	33. A	49. B	65. D	74. A
5. B	21. D	34. A	50. A		75. C
6. C	22. C	35. B	51. B	PART C	76. A
7. A	23. A	36. A	52. B		77. A
8. D	24. D	37. B	53. A	66. A	78. B
9. B	25. B	38. B	54. C	67. D	79. D
10. A	26. D	39. A	55. A	68. C	80. C
11. A	27. B	40. C	56. D	69. A	81. A
12. D	28. A	41. D	57. D	70. C	82. C
13. B	29. B	42. A	58. D		83. C
14. B	30. A	43. D	59. B		84. D
					85. B

ANALYSIS CHARTS

As you finish each Practice Test, complete the Analysis Charts below to determine your strengths and weaknesses in the three main skills tested by SAT II: Spanish. The three skill areas are vocabulary, grammar, and reading comprehension. Before you take the next test, review those areas in which you had difficulties. For pointers on specific questions, consult the Explained Answers that follow.

PART A (31 questions)

Part A of each Practice Test mainly involves vocabulary in context. It tests your knowledge of all parts of speech as well as idiomatic expressions.

As you complete each test, fill in the number of correct answers in the appropriate space.

TEST NUMBER	CORRECT ANSWERS
Practice Test 1	
Practice Test 2	
Practice Test 3	
Practice Test 4	
Practice Test 5	
Practice Test 6	
Practice Test 7	
Practice Test 8	
Practice Test 9	

In evaluating your score, use the following table.

29 to 31 correct: *Excellent*
26 to 28 correct: *Very Good*
23 to 25 correct: *Average*
20 to 22 correct: *Below Average*
fewer than 19 correct: *Unsatisfactory*

After the first few tests, study the Spanish-English Vocabulary beginning on page 417, as well as relevant parts of the General Review, even if your score was Excellent or Very Good. This will solidify your knowledge of Spanish and may fill in some gaps the test didn't reveal. The need to review is especially important if you start with a score of Average or less. If you study the General Review conscientiously, you should see your score improve steadily on the chart as you complete each Practice Test.

PART B (34 questions)

Part B of each Practice Test principally concerns your knowlege of Spanish grammar. A variety of grammatical constructions is tested. All are discussed in the General Review of this book.

As you finish each test, fill in the correct answers in the appropriate space.

TEST NUMBER	CORRECT ANSWERS
Practice Test 1	
Practice Test 2	
Practice Test 3	
Practice Test 4	
Practice Test 5	
Practice Test 6	
Practice Test 7	
Practice Test 8	
Practice Test 9	

In evaluating your score, use the following table.

32 to 34 correct: *Excellent*
29 to 31 correct: *Very Good*
26 to 28 correct: *Average*
23 to 25 correct: *Below Average*
fewer than 22 correct: *Unsatisfactory*

After the first few tests, study relevant parts of the General Review in this book even if your score was Excellent or Very Good. This will solidify your understanding of Spanish grammar and may fill in gaps the test didn't reveal. The need to review is especially important if you start with a score of Average or less. If you study hard, you should see your score improve steadily on the chart as you complete each Practice Test.

PART C (5 questions)

Part C of each Practice Test deals with vocabulary and structure in a paragraph. It involves your ability to determine the thought expressed in the paragraph and to select the appropriate vocabulary and elements of grammar to fill in the blank spaces.

As you complete each test, fill in the number of correct answers in the appropriate space.

TEST NUMBER	CORRECT ANSWERS
Practice Test 1	
Practice Test 2	
Practice Test 3	
Practice Test 4	
Practice Test 5	
Practice Test 6	
Practice Test 7	
Practice Test 8	
Practice Test 9	

In evaluating your score, use the following table.

5 correct: *Excellent*
4 correct: *Very Good*
3 correct: *Average*
2 correct: *Below Average*
1 or 0 correct: *Unsatisfactory*

If you scored fewer than 3 correct on this part in any of the Practice Tests, you need to study thoroughly the General Review in Part IV of this book, specifically verb forms, basic elements of Spanish grammar, and vocabulary. Also, consult the Spanish-English Vocabulary beginning on page 417, and a standard Spanish-English dictionary.

PART D (15 questions)

Part D of each Practice Test deals with reading comprehension. It involves both your knowledge of Spanish vocabulary and grammar and your ability to spot ideas, themes, and other elements in a reading passage.

As you complete each test, fill in the number of correct answers in the appropriate space.

TEST NUMBER	CORRECT ANSWERS
Practice Test 1	
Practice Test 2	
Practice Test 3	
Practice Test 4	
Practice Test 5	
Practice Test 6	
Practice Test 7	
Practice Test 8	
Practice Test 9	

In evaluating your score, use the following table.

14 or 15 correct: *Excellent*
12 or 13 correct: *Very Good*
10 or 11 correct: *Average*
8 or 9 correct: *Below Average*
fewer than 8 correct: *Unsatisfactory*

Reading comprehension involves your overall knowledge of Spanish. If you had difficulty on this part of the test, you need to review Spanish vocabulary and grammar and practice reading material in Spanish. If you study conscientiously, looking closely at the General Review and the Spanish-English Vocabulary beginning on page 417, as well as reading a variety of passages in Spanish, your score should improve steadily with each test you take.

EXPLAINED ANSWERS

TEST 1

PART A

1. (A) **el mono** / the monkey
2. (B) **tener ganas de** / to feel like; review §14.42.
3. (D) **un cine** / movie theater, movies, cinema
4. (D) **pedir prestado** / to borrow; **una librería** / bookstore; **comprar** / to buy; study §22.
5. (C) **tener apetito** / to have an appetite
6. (B) **la película** / film (movie)
7. (A) **tener éxito** / to succeed; review §14.42.
8. (B) **los guantes** / the gloves; **ponerse** / to put on
9. (B) **el peso** / the weight
10. (D) **el lago** / the lake; **ahogados** / drowned
11. (B) **el viento** / the wind
12. (D) **la asignatura** / the subject matter, course of study
13. (C) **hacer el papel** / to play the role, part (acting)
14. (D) **tardar en** / to be late in
15. (A) **pedir** / to request, ask (for); review §8.19, where **pedir** is listed alphabetically, and study §8.65.
16. (C) **ir de compras** / to go shopping; study §14.22.
17. (B) **pedir** / to ask (for), request
18. (A) **el cuello** / the collar (neck); **una corbata** / necktie
19. (B) **llorar** / to cry, weep
20. (D) **el ascensor** / the elevator; **la escalera** / the stairs; although one might take the stairs to the top of a building, the question specifies a tall building so the best answer is elevator.
21. (C) **mudo** / mute
22. (A) **lista** / ready; study §7.171.
23. (D) **el resfriado** / common cold
24. (D) **la ropa** / clothes
25. (B) **¡Tanto gusto!** / It's a pleasure (to meet you)!
26. (B) **¡Por fin, libre!** / Free at last!
27. (B) **un coche** / a car; the clue is that Mr. and Mrs. Robles were tired of walking or taking the bus.
28. (D) **olvidar** / to forget
29. (A) **la bombilla** / light bulb; **la lámpara** / lamp
30. (B) **un zapatero** / a shoe repairer, shoemaker
31. (A) **el jabón** / soap; **el jamón** / ham

PART B

32. (D)   You need the present indicative tense; review §8.14 and §8.14(e).

33. (B)   Review **hace** + length of time + **que** + verb tense in §14.7.

34. (A)   The present indicative is needed to give **por poco** its desired meaning of *nearly* in this sentence; review §8.14(g).

35. (B)   You need the indirect object pronoun in the plural; review §6.14ff and §7.13(c).

36. (A)   You need the 3rd person plural because of the compound subject; review §7.2.

37. (A)   A verb right after a preposition takes the infinitive form; review §7.17.

38. (A)   The verb **apresurarse,** a verb of motion, takes the preposition **a** + infinitive; review §7.16ff with particular attention to §7.19.

39. (A)   The verb **comenzar** takes the preposition **a** + infinitive; review §7.16ff, with particular attention to §7.20.

40. (B)   The verb **dar** takes the preposition **a** + noun; review §7.16ff, with particular attention to §7.21. Remember that with the preposition **a** + the definite article **el** changes to **al;** review §4.7, §4.8, and §14.21.

41. (A)   The expression **ser aficionado** takes the preposition **a** + noun; review §7.16ff, with particular attention to §7.21. Study also the examples at the end of §7.21.

42. (B)   You need the masculine singular form of the possessive pronoun because the comparison is made with **hermano,** which is masculine singular. Review possessive pronouns in §6.64–§6.69.

43. (C)   Review §5.57–§5.64. Review also the use of the personal **a** in §11.8–§11.14.

44. (B)   The conjunction **a menos que** requires the subjunctive form of a verb in the clause it introduces. Review §7.34 and find **a menos que** which is listed there alphabetically. Also review the examples in §7.35 and §7.36. Review also §7.37–§7.43.

45. (D)   **Quienquiera** is one of the indefinite expressions that require the subjunctive form of a verb in the clause they introduce. Review §7.50 and note the examples in §7.51–§7.53.

46. (B)   **Adondequiera** is one of the indefinite expressions that require the subjunctive form of a verb in the clause they introduce; review §7.50–§7.53.

47. (A)   An indefinite or negative antecedent requires the subjunctive form of a verb in the clause it introduces; review §7.54–§7.65; in particular, §7.58.

48. (A)   **Para** is used when you are making a comparison; review §11.19–§11.38; particularly §11.24.

49. (A)   This is a well-known proverb; review §23ff.

50. (B)   Review §5.23–§5.26 where **cien** and **ciento** are explained. Review also §23.10 where this proverb is given.

51. (D)   The indirect pronoun **le** changes to **se** in front of a direct object pronoun in the 3rd person singular and plural; review §6.52. Remember that direct and indirect object pronouns are attached to the infinitive; review §6.49.

52. (B)   You need the direct object pronoun **la;** review §6.7ff. Remember that **conocer** in the preterit means *met;* review §8.26(1).

53. (B)   The preterit is required to give **tener** the required meaning of *received;* review §8.26(7).

54. (A)   The conjunction **hasta que** requires the indicative rather than the subjunctive because **mi amigo** did come; review §7.37ff, particularly §7.43.

55. (B)   Here **hasta que** requires the subjunctive because there is some doubt that **mi amigo** will come; review §7.37ff, especially §7.42.

56. (A)   The indirect object pronoun is attached to the infinitive; review §6.14–§6.20 and §6.34–§6.53.

57. (B) You need the imperfect subjunctive because the main verb in the preceding clause is **querer** in the imperfect indicative; review §7.33–§7.111, especially §7.87–§7.100. Study also the imperfect subjunctive in §8.50–§8.54.

58. (B) You need **cuanto más** to express the ratio; review §5.66.

59. (C) This is an idiom; review §14.15–§14.46.

60. (B) Review §7.111(3) for contrary-to-fact conditions in a **si** (if) clause.

61. (D) You need the imperfect indicative (tense no. 2); review §8.20, especially (b), and §7.112ff.

62. (A) You need the idiomatic expression **hace** + length of time, which means *ago;* review §14.28.

63. (B) You need the reflexive pronoun **se** + past tense to substitute for the passive, review §7.213–§7.222, especially §7.217.

64. (C) You need the subjunctive after an indefinite antecedent–the apartment may not exist; review §7.54–§7.65, especially §7.56.

65. (B) You need **sino** to mean *on the contrary,* followed by the infinitive; review §12.6–§12.11.

PART C

66. (B) The meanings of the choices are **descansa** / rests; **come** / eats; **viaja** / travels; **pesca** / goes fishing.

67. (A) You need **les** (to them) as the plural indirect object pronoun because it refers to **a los madrileños y a los turistas**. Review indirect object pronouns in §6.14ff and direct object pronouns in §6.7ff, as well as the use of **gustar** in §7.143 (e).

68. (A) Review the use of **o** and **u** in §12.13.

69. (C) Review idiomatic expressions with **a** in §14.16 where **a eso de** is listed alphabetically.

70. (D) The meanings of the choices are: **ve** / sees; **dice** / says; **vende** / sells; **hace** / does.

PART D

71. (B) See sentences 2–4 of the passage.
72. (A) See sentence two in the passage.
73. (A) See sentence three in the passage.
74. (C) See the last sentence in the passage.
75. (D) See the last sentence in the passage.
76. (A) See sentence one in the passage.
77. (D) See sentence two in the passage.
78. (B) See sentence three in the passage.
79. (C) See sentence seven in the passage.
80. (C) See the last sentence in the passage.
81. (A) See sentence two in the passage.
82. (B) See sentence three in the passage.
83. (D) See sentences 4–5 in the passage.
84. (C) See sentences 5–6 in the passage.
85. (B) See the last sentence in the passage.

TEST 2

PART A

1. (D) **la mariposa** / butterfly
2. (C) **la hora** / hour, time

3. (A)   **ciego** / blind

4. (B)   **mudo** / mute

5. (D)   **sordo** / deaf

6. (C)   **zurdo** / left-handed

7. (B)   **pescar** / to fish

8. (D)   **¿Se ha hecho Ud. daño?** / Have you hurt yourself? **Caer** / to fall; **levantarse** / to get up.

9. (C)   **¿Me hace el favor del horario?** / May I please have a timetable?

10. (C)   **la cuchara** / spoon

11. (A)   **¿Qué te parece?** / What do you think (of them)?

12. (B)   **apagar** / to extinguish, put out

13. (D)   **cambiar(se) de ropa** / to change clothes; **mojado como una sopa** / soaking wet (literally, *wet as soup*)

14. (B)   **preocuparse** / to worry

15. (A)   **¡Manos a la obra!** / To work!

16. (A)   **atropellar (al gato)** / to run over (the cat); **matar** / to kill

17. (C)   **ser inocente** / to be innocent

18. (B)   **las botellas** / bottles; **el vino** / wine; **se vende** / is sold

19. (A)   **las flores** / flowers; **el ramillete** / bouquet

20. (D)   **los padres** / parents; **un huérfano** / orphan

21. (B)   **el periódico** / newspaper; **el papel** / paper (for writing)

22. (C)   **la bandeja** / tray; **el camarero** / waiter

23. (D)   **poner (la mesa)** / to set (the table)

24. (D)   **la cuenta** / the bill (at a restaurant); **el mozo** / waiter

25. (C)   **el impermeable** / the raincoat

26. (C)   **el zumo** / juice; **un juego** / game

27. (B)   **un sello** / a stamp

28. (C)   **echar las cenizas en el cenicero** / to put the ashes in the ashtray

29. (A)   **córtemelo** / cut (shorten) it for me; **el sastre** / the tailor; **largo** / long

30. (B)   **ponte,** verb form of **ponerse** / to put on (clothing)

31. (C)   **ir de compras** / to go shopping

PART B

32. (B)   You need **sino que** to mean *but rather;* review §12.6–§12.11, especially §12.9.

33. (A)   You need **poco** rather than **pequeño**; review §5.69–§5.71.

34. (B)   You need a form of **saber. Saber** does not take a preposition + infinitive. Review §7.29, §7.118, and §7.165(b).

35. (A)   You need the present subjunctive to express a command; review **traer** in §8.67, especially Tense No. 6. Review also §8.41(a) to (n) and §8.62.

36. (D)   The indirect object pronoun precedes the direct object pronoun; the verb **dar** is in the 3rd person preterit; review §6.7–§6.13, §6.14–§6.20, and §6.34–§6.53.

37. (B)   You need the present subjunctive; review §7.33–§7.111, especially §7.34 where **para que** is listed, and §7.35. Also review §8.41–§8.49, especially §8.41(i).

38. (A)   You need the imperfect subjunctive; review §7.33–§7.111, especially §7.34 where **para que** is listed. Review also §8.50–§8.54, especially §8.50, example #2.

39. (C)   You need the pluperfect indicative; review §8.56, and note example #1.

40. (D)   You need the past anterior *or* preterit perfect, which is translated into English the same as the pluperfect indicative. Review §8.57 and the example given at the end of that section.

41. (A) You need the future perfect; review §8.58 and the examples given there.

42. (A) You need the indirect object pronoun to indicate that something was stolen from someone; review §6.14–§6.20, especially §6.19.

43. (A) You need the indirect object pronoun to indicate that something is being taken off someone; review §6.14–§6.20, especially §6.19.

44. (D) You need the indirect object pronoun to indicate that something was purchased from someone; review §6.14–§6.20, especially §6.19.

45. (A) You need the indirect object pronoun to indicate that something is pleasing to someone; review §6.14–§6.20, especially §6.20.

46. (A) You need the indirect object pronoun to indicate that something is sufficient for someone; review §6.14–§6.20, especially §6.20.

47. (D) You need the indirect object pronoun to indicate that something is lacking to someone; review §6.14–§6.20, especially §6.20.

48. (A) You need the 1st person plural in the preterit; review §7.2, §7.3, and §8.25.

49. (D) You need the prepositional pronoun; review §6.30–§6.33, especially §6.33.

50. (D) You need the prepositional pronoun; review §6.30–§6.33, especially §6.33.

51. (C) You need the masculine singular **el** in front of **de** in place of the understood masculine singular noun **hermano;** review §6.60.

52. (B) You need the masculine plural **los** in front of **de** in place of the understood masculine plural noun **hermanos;** review §6.60.

53. (B) You need the masculine singular possessive pronoun; review §6.61–§6.66, especially §6.65.

54. (D) You need **¿De quién . . . ?** to express possession; review §6.67–§6.69.

55. (B) You need the relative pronoun **que;** review §6.70–§6.105.

56. (C) You need the relative pronoun **quien** after the preposition **con** to indicate *who;* review §6.80–§6.87.

57. (B) You need the plural relative pronoun **quienes** after the preposition **con** to indicate *whom;* review §6.80–§6.87.

58. (B) You need the neuter compound relative pronoun **lo que;** review §6.93.

59. (D) You need the masculine plural, **cuyos,** to agree in gender and number with what is possessed **(hijos),** review §6.97–§6.100.

60. (A) You need the masculine singular, **cuyo,** to agree in gender and number with what is possessed **(padre);** review §6.97–§6.100.

61. (B) **A quien** is required instead of **cuya** when referring to parts of the body; review §6.102.

62. (A) You need the imperfect indicative; review §8.20–§8.24, especially §8.20(b), and §8.63(3).

63. (A) You need the personal **a;** review §11.8–§11.14 and §7.7(a).

64. (A) You need the infinitive after a preposition **(de);** review §7.181(d), §7.7(d), and §7.17.

65. (D) You need the negative **nadie;** review §6.13, §6.105, and §9.

PART C

66. (B) The meanings of the choices are: **encontraba** / met; **ganaba** / earned; **gastaba** / spent; **robaba** / stole.

67. (B) Review §5.52.

68. (C) The meanings of the choices are; **formal** / formal; **tradicional** / traditional; **musical** / musical; **literario** / literary.

69. (C) The meanings of the choices are: **pidió** / requested, asked for **(pedir)**; **perdió** / lost; **vendió** / sold; **rompió** / broke.

70. (D) Review the use of **ninguno** and **ningún** in §5.20. Review also §6.105.

PART D

71. (B)   See paragraph three, sentence one of the passage.
72. (B)   See paragraph three, sentence three of the passage.
73. (C)   See paragraph three, sentences 3–5 of the passage.
74. (C)   See paragraph five, sentences 3–4 of the passage.
75. (D)   See the last sentence of the passage.
76. (C)   See sentence number two and the last sentence of the passage.
77. (D)   See paragraph one, sentence one, and paragraph two, sentence two in the passage.
78. (A)   See sentence three in the passage.
79. (B)   See sentence one of paragraph two.
80. (A)   See the last sentence in the passage.
81. (D)   See sentences one and two in the passage.
82. (B)   See sentence six in the passage.
83. (A)   See sentence seven in the passage.
84. (D)   See sentence eight in the passage.
85. (B)   See sentence nine in the passage.

TEST 3

PART A

1. (A)   **el impermeable** / raincoat; **llevo** / I wear; **llueve** / it rains
2. (D)   **pasar** / to spend (time); review §7.142.
3. (D)   **tiempo** / time; review §3.27ff.
4. (D)   **tener ganas de** / to feel like; review **tener ganas de** + infinitive in §14.42.
5. (B)   **la escalera** / the stairs
6. (A)   **contar con** / to count on; review §7.22.
7. (A)   **contentarse con** / to be satisfied with; review §7.22.
8. (A)   **casarse con** / to marry; review §7.23.
9. (C)   **acabar de** / to have just; review §7.24.
10. (C)   **dejar de** / to stop; review §7.24.
11. (A)   **aprovecharse de** / to take advantage of; review §7.25.
12. (B)   **consentir en** / to consent to; review §7.26.
13. (D)   **buscar** / to look for; review §7.30.
14. (C)   **pedir** / to ask for; review the difference between **pedir** and **preguntar** in §7.159ff.
15. (C)   **una tienda de comestibles** / a grocery store
16. (B)   **este almacén** / this department store, general store
17. (A)   **una tortilla** / an omelet
18. (B)   **sentarse** / to sit down
19. (A)   **tan excelente como** / as excellent as; review the difference in use between **tan** + adjective in §5.39. Review also §5.53.
20. (C)   **hacer un viaje** / to take a trip; review §14.28.
21. (D)   **saludar** / to greet

22. (A) **estar para** / to be about to; review §14.26.
23. (B) **acabar de** / to have just; review §7.112ff.
24. (C) **la hora** / time; review §3.27ff.
25. (D) **el lado** / side
26. (B) **ver** / to see; review §8.30 for the preterit of **ver**. Review also §7.155.
27. (B) **jugar** / to play; review §7.150–§7.152 to understand the uses of **jugar** and **tocar.**
28. (A) **tocar** / to play; review §7.150–§7.152 to understand the uses of **jugar** and **tocar.**
29. (B) **llevar** / to take (a person somewhere); review §7.156–§7.158.
30. (A) **desgraciada** / unfortunate; review §7.155.
31. (A) **una librería** / a bookstore

PART B

32. (A) You need the infinitive after **tener que.** Review §7.25, where **despedirse** is listed, and §7.125.
33. (C) You need the infinitive. Review §7.25 where **oír hablar de** + noun or pronoun is listed.
34. (A) Review the grammatical construction **pensar de** + noun or pronoun in §7.25.
35. (D) You need the infinitive. Review §7.26 where **tardar en** + infinitive is listed.
36. (A) Review **empeñarse en** + infinitive in §7.26.
37. (B) Review **pensar en** in §7.27.
38. (D) No preposition is needed in Spanish, even though one is used in English; review §7.30.
39. (D) No preposition is needed in Spanish, even though one is used in English; review §7.30.
40. (C) You need the present subjunctive after the conjunction **a fin de que**; review §7.33–§7.35 and §8.41–§8.44.
41. (B) You need the present subjunctive; review §7.37–§7.43.
42. (A) You do not need the subjunctive; review §7.39ff.
43. (A) You need the subjunctive; review §7.33–§7.42.
44. (C) You do not need the subjunctive. Review §7.43, §8.25–§8.29, and §8.30, where **venir** is listed as irregular in the preterit.
45. (D) You need the subjunctive; review §7.33ff and §7.47ff.
46. (B) You need the subjunctive; review §7.33ff and §7.49ff.
47. (A) You need the subjunctive; review §7.33ff, §7.50–§7.53, and §8.41ff. Find **sea** in §8.65 and study **ser** in §8.67.
48. (B) You need the subjunctive because of **adondequiera;** review §7.33ff, §7.50, §7.52, and §8.41ff. Study **estar** in §7.166ff and §8.67.
49. (D) You need the subjunctive because of an indefinite antecedent; review §7.33ff, §7.50, §7.53, and §8.41ff. Study **ir** in §8.67.
50. (D) You need the subjunctive because of an indefinite antecedent; review §7.33ff, §7.54–§7.65, and §8.41ff. Study **ser** in §7.166ff and §8.67.
51. (A) You do not use the subjunctive; review §7.57–§7.65 and §8.14ff.
52. (B) You need the subjunctive because of an indefinite antecedent; review §7.58 and §8.41ff.
53. (C) You need the subjunctive after a negative antecedent; review §7.60 and §8.50ff.
54. (B) You need the subjunctive after a negative antecedent; review §7.61 and §8.41ff, especially §8.45.
55. (A) You do not need the subjunctive; review §7.62.
56. (A) You need the present perfect indicative; review §8.55 and §8.–§8.11.
57. (D) You need the subjunctive because of a command; review §7.66, §8.41, and §8.62(a).

58. (C) You need the subjunctive because of **Ojalá que**; review §7.67–§7.70 and §8.41(n).
59. (B) **De quién** is required to express possession; review §6.101 and §6.103.
60. (C) **Para qué** is required; review §12.5.
61. (D) You need the imperfect indicative; review §7.112ff.
62. (C) You need the preterit of **defender**; review §3.26, §8.25, and §8.29.
63. (C) **Conocer** is required when speaking of people; review §7.118.
64. (A) **Saber** is required, in the 3rd person singular to agree with **Ud**; review §7.118.
65. (C) You need the grammatical construction **tener que**; review §7.125ff.

PART C

66. (B) The meanings of the choices are: **año** / year; **día** / day; **siglo** / century; **mes** / month. They are all masculine. The answer must be **día** because **el sábado** (Saturday) is mentioned in the preceding sentence.

67. (B) The word after the blank space is **hora** (hour) which is feminine. The only feminine form among the choices is **esa** / that. Review demonstrative adjectives in §5.54. Review also demonstrative pronouns in §6.56 where **aquello** is given.

68. (A) The meanings of the choices are: **llena** / fills; **ilumina** / illuminates; **limpia** / cleans; **rompe** / breaks.

69. (C) Review the use of **de** regarding time in §14.22 where **de la mañana, de la noche, de la tarde** are listed when a specific time is mentioned. And review §16.22 when **por** is used.

70. (A) The meanings of the choices are: **ropa** / clothing; **bebidas** / beverages, drinks; **comida** / meal, dinner; **cosméticos** / cosmetics. You need **ropa** because the examples given after the blank space are items of clothing.

PART D

71. (B) See paragraph one in the passage.
72. (B) See paragraph two in the passage.
73. (A) See paragraph three in the passage.
74. (C) See paragraph four in the passage.
75. (A) See paragraph five in the passage.
76. (C) See sentence two in the passage.
77. (B) See sentences 3–5 in the passage.
78. (D) See sentence six in the passage.
79. (B) See sentence four in the passage.
80. (D) See the last sentence in the passage.
81. (C) See sentence one in the passage.
82. (C) See sentence one in the passage.
83. (B) See sentence two in the passage.
84. (B) See sentence four in the passage.
85. (C) See sentence eight in the passage.

TEST 4

PART A

1. (A) **pero** / but; review the differences between **pero** and **sino** in §12.6–§12.11.
2. (B) **sino** / but; review §12.6–§12.11.

3. (B) **sino** / but; review §12.6–§12.11.

4. (B) **sino que** / but rather; review §12.9.

5. (A) **pero** / but; review §12.11.

6. (B) **más** / more; review comparatives and superlatives in §5.37–§5.53, especially §5.41. Also review the differences between **pero** and **mas** in §12.12.

7. (D) **más de** / more than; the preposition **de** (not **que**) is required in front of a number; review §5.52.

8. (A) **más que** is required when the desired meaning is *only* + a number; review §5.52.

9. (D) **dichosa** / fortunate, happy; the feminine ending is required for agreement. Review the differences in the uses of **dicho, dichoso, dicha** in §7.119–§7.124, especially §7.123. Also review **gozar de** + noun or pronoun in §7.25.

10. (A) **poco** / little; review the uses of **poco** and **pequeño** in §5.69–§5.71.

11. (D) **pequeño** / little; review the uses of **poco** and **pequeño** in §5.69–§5.71.

12. (A) **poder** (in the preterit) / to succeed; review §7.165(c).

13. (B) **ponerse** + adjective / to become; review §7.153–§7.155. Also review **ponerse** in §8.30.

14. (B) **cuál** / which (singular because the verb is **es**); review §5.68(d) and §6.103.

15. (C) **cuáles** / which (plural because the verb is **son**); review §5.68(e) and §6.103.

16. (C) **de día en día** / from day to day; review the idioms in §14.25.

17. (C) **abrir de par en par** / to open wide; review the idioms in §14.25.

18. (C) **de hoy en adelante** / from today on; review the idioms in §14.25.

19. (B) **de cuando en cuando** / from time to time; review the idioms in §14.22.

20. (D) **día por día** / day by day; review the idioms in §14.24.

21. (B) **al día** / current, up to date; review the idioms in §14.24.

22. (D) **saludar** / to greet

23. (B) **llorar** / to cry, weep

24. (A) **sonrojarse** / to blush

25. (D) **los pendientes** / earrings

26. (A) **como** / as, since; review §12.–§12.3.

27. (D) **dar un paseo en coche** / to go for a drive; review the idioms in §14.21. Review also present participles in §7.189–§7.205.

28. (C) **decidir** / to decide; review past participles in §7.204–§7.206ff.

29. (A) **esperar** / to wait (for); review present participles in §7.189–§7.205.

30. (C) **de España** / from Spain; to understand why (A) is wrong, review §4.19(d); to see why (B) is wrong, review §4.18(b); to see why (D) is wrong, review §7.171.

31. (B) **llevar a cabo** / to carry out, accomplish; review §7.21.

PART B

32. (A) You need **dejar;** review §7.129ff.

33. (A) You need the infinitive **gastar;** review §7.138ff.

34. (D) Review the use of indirect object pronouns with **gustar** in §7.143(a) through (g). Review also §6.14–§6.20.

35. (B) Review the use of indirect object pronouns with **gustar** in §7.143(g). Review also §6.14–§6.20.

36. (B) The form of **gustar** must agree with the subject (**los chocolates**); review §7.143ff.

37. (A) The correct grammatical construction is **haber de** + infinitive; review §7.148.

38. (B) The correct idiomatic construction is **hay que** + infinitive; review §14.9–§14.11.

39. (D) The correct idiomatic construction is **Cuánto tiempo hace que** + present tense; review §14.1.

40. (A) You need the present indicative tense; review §14.1.

41. (C) You need the present indicative tense; review §14.1.

42. (A) You need the present indicative tense; review §14.3.

43. (B) You need **desde hace**; review §14.4.

44. (B) You need **hacía que** + imperfect indicative tense; review §14.2(a)–(c), especially (b).

45. (A) You need the imperfect indicative tense; review §14.8(a) and (b).

46. (B) You need **desde hacía** + length of time because of the preterit **entró**; review §14.6.

47. (C) You need **hora** because *hour* is meant; review §3.27ff.

48. (B) **Jugar** is used with a sport; review §7.150ff.

49. (B) **Tocar** is used with musical instruments; review §7.150ff.

50. (D) You need the indirect object **le**; review §7.152 and §6.14ff.

51. (D) You need **llegar a ser**; review §7.154.

52. (A) You need **ponerse**; review §7.155.

53. (B) You need the preterit form of **llevar**; review §7.156ff.

54. (B) You need **tomar**; review §7.158.

55. (B) You need **media** in the feminine to agree with **docena**; review §14.12ff.

56. (A) You need **la mitad**; review §14.12ff.

57. (B) You need the 3rd person singular preterit of **pedir**; review §7.159ff. Study the irregular preterit of **pedir** in §8.30.

58. (A) You need the 3rd person plural preterit of **preguntar**; review §7.159ff.

59. (A) You need **pensar de** in this construction; review §7.163.

60. (B) **Pensar** with the preposition **en** is needed in this construction; review §7.164.

61. (B) **Pensar** with the preposition **en** is needed in this construction; review §7.164.

62. (B) You need the progressive past tense; review §7.174.

63. (A) When the verb in the **si** (if) clause is present indicative, you need the future tense in the result clause; review §7.111(1).

64. (B) You need the imperfect subjunctive; review §7.111(2).

65. (C) You need the pluperfect subjunctive when the verb in the result clause is in the conditional perfect form; review §7.111(3).

PART C

66. (C) Review the use of the **personal a** in §11.11.

67. (B) The meanings of the words in the choices are: **hombres** / men; **autores** / authors; **lectores** / readers; **actores** / actors. You need **autores** because it is stated in the first part of the sentence that they do not owe (**deben**) to anybody a musical note or a single fragment of inspiration.

68. (B) The meanings of the words in the choices are: **locura** / madness, insanity; **música** / music; **manera** / manner; **fantasía** / fantasy.

69. (A) The meanings of the words in the choices are: **diferentes** / different; **antiguas** / ancient, old; **conocidas** / known; **sorprendentes** / surprising.

70. (D) The meanings of the verbs in the choices are: **piden** / ask, request (**pedir**); **hacen** / make, do; **son** / are; **están** / are. You must know the differences in the uses of **son** (**ser**) and **están** (**estar**). Review §7.166–§7.174. Review also §14.26 where **estar de acuerdo** is listed alphabetically.

PART D

71. (C) See sentence one of the passage.

72. (B) See sentence nine of the passage. Choices (A), (C), and (D) are not supported by the passage.

73. (B) See paragraph 11, sentence two, through paragraph 14 of the passage.

74. (A) See paragraphs 15 through 16 of the passage.

75. (D) See the next-to-last sentence of the passage.

76. (A) See sentence one of the passage.

77. (A) See sentence two of the passage.

78. (D) See sentence four of the passage.

79. (C) See sentence three of the passage.

80. (C) See sentence five of the passage.

81. (D) See sentence four of the passage.

82. (B) See sentence four of the passage.

83. (A) See the last two sentences of the first paragraph.

84. (D) See the last sentence in the second paragraph.

85. (C) See sentence 11 of the passage.

TEST 5

PART A

1. (B) After a superlative in Spanish, *in* is expressed by **de**, not **en**; review §5.45 and §5.46.

2. (C) **el ladrón** / the thief

3. (B) **decir** / to tell, say; in the imperative, second singular, **dime** / tell me.

4. (A) **afeitarse** / to shave oneself; **la barba** / beard

5. (D) **nadie** / no one, not anyone

6. (B) **conducir** / to drive (a car)

7. (D) **bajar** / to lower

8. (A) **ahogarse** / to drown

9. (C) **mirar** / to watch; no preposition is required. Review §7.30.

10. (D) **echar de menos** / to miss; review §14.22.

11. (B) **adiós** / goodbye; **subir a** / to get on, into; review §7.21.

12. (C) **los lentes** / the eyeglasses

13. (A) **sollozar** / to sob

14. (A) **la protección** / the protection; **conceder** / to grant

15. (B) **reducido** / reduced

16. (A) **por** / for; review §11.19ff, especially §11.26 and §11.28.

17. (C) **la siesta** / the nap; **echar una siesta** / to take a nap

18. (A) **dejar caer** / to drop; review §7.133 and §7.134.

19. (D) **madrugar** / to get up very early in the morning; **tener que** / to have to. Review §7.128.

20. (C) **el espejo** / the mirror.

21. (D) **un desmayo** / a fainting spell

22. (B) **un ciego** / a blind man

23. (A) **el esfuerzo** / effort

24. (A) **quedar** / to remain

25. (A) **dondequiera** / wherever

26. (D)　**el sirviente** / servant
27. (D)　**el vendedor ambulante** / traveling salesman
28. (A)　**el cajero** / bank teller
29. (D)　**iniciarse** / to begin
30. (D)　**musical** is the key word.
31. (B)　**la espalda** / back (of a person's body)

PART B

32. (B)　You need the subjunctive in the dependent clause when the verb in the main clause is **desear**; review §7.33ff, §7.87ff, §7.101, and §7.102.

33. (A)　You need the subjunctive in the dependent clause when the verb in the main clause implies a wish or desire that somebody do something; review §7.33ff, §7.87ff, §7.101, and §7.103.

34. (D)　You need the subjunctive in the dependent clause when the verb in the main clause implies that somebody do something; review §7.33ff, §7.87ff, §7.101, and §7.104.

35. (D)　You need the subjunctive in the dependent clause when the verb in the main clause tells someone to do something; review §7.33ff, §7.87ff, §7.101, and §7.105.

36. (B)　You need the subjunctive in the dependent clause when the verb in the main clause expresses doubt or uncertainty; review §7.33ff, §7.78ff, §7.101, and §7.106.

37. (B)　You need the subjunctive in the dependent clause when the verb in the main clause expresses doubt or uncertainty; review §7.33ff, §7.78ff, §7.101, and §7.107.

38. (C)　You need the subjunctive in the dependent clause when the verb in the main clause expresses a desire that somebody do something; review §7.33ff, §7.87, §7.101, and §7.108.

39. (D)　You need the subjunctive in the dependent clause when the verb in the main clause expresses an emotion; review §7.33ff, §7.82ff, §7.101, and §7.109.

40. (A)　You need the subjunctive in the dependent clause when the verb in the main clause expresses doubt or uncertainty; review §7.33ff, §7.78ff, §7.101, and §7.110.

41. (A)　When the verb in the **si** clause is present indicative, you need the future tense in the result clause; review §7.111(1).

42. (A)　When the verb in the **si** clause is imperfect subjunctive, you need the conditional or imperfect subjuntive in the result clause; review §7.111(2).

43. (B)　When the verb in the **si** clause is pluperfect subjunctive, you need the conditional perfect or pluperfect subjunctive in the result clause; review §7.111(3).

44. (D)　You need the present subjunctive; review §7.67–§7.70, §8.41(n), and §8.42ff.
45. (A)　You need **a**; review §7.19.
46. (B)　You need **en**; review §14.25.
47. (A)　You need **por**; review §11.19ff and §11.35.
48. (B)　You need **estar**; review §14.16 and §14.26.
49. (C)　You need **a la francesa**; review §14.17.
50. (B)　You need **al**; review §14.18.
51. (C)　You need **al**; review §14.18.
52. (C)　You need the present subjunctive; review §7.33ff. Also review §7.71–§7.72.
53. (A)　You need the present subjunctive; review §7.71–§7.74.
54. (B)　You need the present subjunctive; review §7.71–§7.75.
55. (B)　You need the present subjunctive; review §7.71–§7.76.
56. (A)　You need the present subjunctive; review §7.71–§7.77.
57. (D)　You need the present subjunctive; review §7.33ff. Also review §7.78–§7.80.
58. (A)　You need the present subjunctive; reivew §7.33ff. Also review §7.87–§7.90.

59. (B) You need the present subjunctive; review §7.33ff. Also review §7.87–§7.98.
60. (A) You need the present indicative; review §8.14(f).
61. (B) You need the imperfect indicative; review §8.20ff, especially §8.20(a).
62. (B) You need the verb **estar**; review §7.166ff, especially §7.171.
63. (B) You need the past participle; review §7.171 and §7.205.
64. (A) You need **volver**; review §7.175–§7.177.
65. (B) You need **devolver**; review §7.175–§7.177.

PART C

66. (A) You need **les** (to them) as the plural indirect object pronoun because it refers to **a muchas personas**. Review indirect object pronouns in §6.14ff, in particular §6.18, and direct object pronouns in §6.7ff.

67. (D) The meanings of the verb choices are: **aumentado** / increased, augmented; **aprendido** / learned; **trabajado** / worked; **producido** / produced. Choice D is the only past participle that makes sense. Review the present perfect indicative tense in §8.55.

68. (A) The meanings of the word choices are: **países** / countries; **edificios** / buildings; **mares** / seas; **bosques** / forests.

69. (B) Review the use of **gran** and **grande** in §5.22. The meanings of the other word choices are: **fiesta** / holiday, feast, celebration; **pintorescas** / picturesque.

70. (C) The meanings of the verb choices are: **se juega** / is played; **se compra** / is bought; **se encuentra** / is found; **se fabrica** / is made, is manufactured. Choice C is the only one that makes sense.

PART D

71. (A) See sentence five in the passage.
72. (D) See sentences 11–12 in the passage.
73. (A) See sentence 19 in the passage.
74. (B) See sentence 19 in the passage.
75. (C) See sentences 19–20 in the passage.
76. (D) See sentence one in the passage.
77. (A) See sentence four in the passage.
78. (D) See sentence three in the passage.
79. (B) See sentence five in the passage.
80. (D) See sentence six in the passage.
81. (A) See sentence three in the passage.
82. (B) See sentence three in the passage.
83. (B) See the last sentence of paragraph two in the passage.
84. (D) See paragraph three, sentence one in the passage.
85. (D) See paragraph three, sentence two in the passage.

TEST 6

PART A

1. (A) **una goma de borrar** / an eraser
2. (C) **al contado** / cash payment
3. (B) **hablar** / to speak; **mudo** / mute
4. (A) **cocinar** / to cook; **una cocinera** / a cook

5. (C) **poco a poco** / little by little; review §14.16.
6. (A) **repararla** / to repair it.
7. (B) **entrar en la casa inmediatamente** / to come into the house immediately; **el lodo** / the mud
8. (C) **tener cosas que declarar** / to have things to declare; **el aduanero** / the customs officer
9. (C) **una licencia de conducir** / a driver's license
10. (B) **Entra.** / Come in.
11. (B) **conseguir** / to obtain
12. (D) **ausente** / absent
13. (A) **el cartero** / the postman (mailman)
14. (C) **el cuadro** / the painting. Note that if the definite article **el** is part of a proper name there is no contraction with **a** or **de** (for example, **a El Greco, de El Greco**); review §4.8.
15. (A) **la salud** / health; review §4.9(b).
16. (D) **el sombrero** / hat; review §4.9(h).
17. (A) **ir** / to go; preterit: **yo fui** / I went.
18. (B) **los pajaritos** / the little birds
19. (C) **la hoja** / leaf (on a tree branch)
20. (A) **sucia** / dirty
21. (B) **el paraguas** / the umbrella
22. (D) **la estación** / the season
23. (C) **¿Qué chica tan bonita!** / What a pretty girl! Review §13.1.
24. (A) **tener éxito** / to be successful
25. (A) **la contestación** / the answer
26. (D) **el pelo** / the hair
27. (A) **pedir** / to ask for, request
28. (B) **apretarse la mano** / to shake hands
29. (A) **venir** / to come
30. (A) **llegar a** / to come to
31. (D) **a caballo; a pie** / on horseback; on foot

PART B

32. (B) You need **u**; review §12.13.
33. (B) You need **u**; review §12.13.
34. (B) You need **para**; review §11.22.
35. (B) You need **para**; review §11.22.
36. (A) You need **por**; review §11.27.
37. (A) You need **por**; review §11.28.
38. (C) You need **cuyo**; review §6.97–§6.102.
39. (A) You need **fue**; review §7.213–§7.222, especially §7.214.
40. (B) You need **abrió**; review §7.215 and §8.25ff.
41. (C) You need **fueron**; review §7.213–§7.216.
42. (B) You need **se**; review §7.213–§7.217.
43. (A) You need **se**; review §7.220.
44. (B) You need **que**; review §5.68, especially (h).
45. (A) You need **por**; review §11.39— §11.43. More and more Spanish persons are using **por** instead of **de** in this type of construction.

46. (B)   You need **decir**; review §7.181(d) and §7.184.

47. (A)   You need **salir**; review §7.185 and §8.30, where **ver** is listed.

48. (A)   You need **son**; review §18.2.

49. (A)   You need **chiflo**; review §8.12–§8.67.

50. (B)   You need **se perdió**; review §8.25–§8.30 for the preterit.

51. (B)   You need the indirect object pronoun **le**; review §6.14–§6.20.

52. (D)   You need the preterit; review §8.25–§8.30.

53. (B)   The indirect object pronoun is attached to the infinitive; review §6.34–§6.53.

54. (B)   Review the third reading comprehension selection in Test No. 5, paragraph one. The subject of **iba** is **el combate**.

55. (A)   You need the indirect object pronoun **le**. Review §6.14–§6.20. The direct object is **el corazón**.

56. (D)   You need the imperfect subjunctive; review §8.50–§8.53. Study §7.101.

57. (B)   You need the infinitive; review §7.181(d) and §7.184.

58. (D)   Review verb forms and prepositions.

59. (A)   Review verb forms.

60. (D)   The adjective precedes the noun in this construction; review §5.15 and §5.22.

61. (C)   You need the infinitive; review §7.186.

62. (D)   You need **con**; review §7.23. Also review §7.221 for **se sabe que.**

63. (C)   You need the present participle because the helping verb is **seguía**; review §7.198.

64. (A)   You need **al**; review the idioms in §14.40.

65. (A)   You need **pase**; review the idioms in §14.39. Study §7.33ff, especially §7.66.

PART C

66. (C)   Review §14.4 for the use of **desde hace** + length of time when the main verb is in the present tense, and §14.6 for the use of **desde hacía** + length of time when the main verb is in the imperfect tense.

67. (A)   The meanings of the verb choices are: **trabajar** / work; **estudiar** / to study; **manejar** / to manage, to operate, to drive (a car); **enseñar** / to teach, to show. The only one that makes sense in the statement is **trabajar.**

68. (C)   The verb form choices are: **fui, fue, fuimos,** which are all in the preterit tense of **ir** and **ser.** Review the preterit tense forms of **ir** and **ser** in §8.67 where commonly used irregular verbs are conjugated in all the tenses. Note that **eran** (were) is the 3rd person plural, imperfect indicative of **ser** and its meaning is the only one that makes sense in the sentence.

69. (B)   The meanings of the word choices are: **cómodos** / comfortable, convenient; **lentos** / slow; **pintorescos** / picturesque; **divertidos** / amusing, entertaining.

70. (D)   The meanings of the word choices are: **nadadores** / swimmers; **estudiantes** / students; **escritores** / writers; **viajeros** / travelers.

PART D

71. (C)   See sentence one in the passage.

72. (A)   See sentence three in the passage.

73. (C)   See sentence five in the passage.

74. (B)   See sentence six in the passage.

75. (D)   See sentence seven in the passage.

76. (D)   See sentence three in the passage.

77. (A)   See sentences 4–5 in the passage.

78. (C)   See sentences 7–8 in the passage.

79. (D)   See sentences 16–17 in the passage.

80. (A)   See sentence 17 in the passage.

81. (C)   See sentence one in the passage.

82. (B)   See sentence five in the passage.

83. (A)   See sentence five in the passage.

84. (C)   See sentences 7–8 in the passage.

85. (A)   See sentence ten in the passage.

TEST 7

PART A

1. (B)   **fechada** / dated

2. (A)   **preguntar por** / to ask for; review §7.28.

3. (C)   **¿Cuánto tiempo hace que . . . ?** / How long . . . ? Review §14.1.

4. (A)   **caer enfermo(a)** / to fall ill (feminine)

5. (B)   **un ramo** / bunch (of flowers)

6. (D)   **dar una vuelta** / to go for a stroll

7. (D)   **despedirse de** / to say goodbye to

8. (B)   **la voz** / the voice

9. (A)   **dormirse** / to fall asleep; **tardar en** + infinitive / to take long to; review §7.26.

10. (A)   **sacar la lengua** / to stick out one's tongue

11. (D)   **el nudo** / the knot

12. (A)   **un almacén** / a department store

13. (C)   **nada** / nothing

14. (A)   **para con** / to, toward; review §11.15.

15. (B)   **asistir a la escuela** / to attend school; review §7.21 and §11.36.

16. (C)   **por miedo** / out of fear; review §11.35.

17. (D)   **a mediados de** / around the middle of; review §14.16.

18. (A)   **a principios de** / around the beginning of; review §14.16.

19. (B)   **cuanto más . . . tanto más** / the more . . . the more; review §14.20.

20. (C)   **dar por perdido** / to consider someone or something lost; review §14.21.

21. (A)   **de la mañana** / in the morning; review §14.22.

22. (A)   **estar a punto de** / to be about to; review §14.26.

23. (D)   **hacerse tarde** / to be getting late; review §14.28.

24. (A)   **lo del subjuntivo** / "that business of the subjunctive"; review §14.30.

25. (B)   **por la mañana** / in the morning; review §14.32.

26. (B)   **estar para** / to be about to; review §14.35.

27. (B)   **mirar** / to watch; review §14.37 for idioms with **por.**

28. (A)   **sin aliento** / out of breath; review §14.41.

29. (D)   **ser todo oídos** / to be all ears; review §14.40.

30. (D)   **tener ganas de** / to feel like; review §14.42.

31. (A)   **tener lugar** / to take place; review §14.42.

PART B

32. (D)   You need **saber** with no preposition; review §7.29, §7.118, and §7.165.

33. (A)   The indirect object pronoun **me** is required; review §6.14–§6.20 and §6.43–§6.53.

34. (A)   You need the present subjunctive after the conjunction **para que**; review §7.33–§7.35 and §8.41(i).

35. (D) You need the imperfect subjunctive after the conjunction **para que**; review §8.50(2)–§8.53.

36. (A) You need the past anterior; review §8.57.

37. (B) You need the future perfect; review §8.58.

38. (C) You need the indirect object pronoun **le**; review §6.19.

39. (A) You need the indirect object pronoun **le**; review §6.19.

40. (D) You need the indirect object pronoun **les**; review §6.19.

41. (A) You need the preterit of **ver**; review §7.2, §8.25ff, and §8.30, where **ver** is listed.

42. (A) You need the indirect object pronoun **les**; review §6.20.

43. (A) You need the indirect object pronoun **le**; review §6.20.

44. (A) You need the feminine, **mucha**; review §5.2.

45. (B) **Me gusta . . .** / I like . . . ; review §7.143.

46. (D) You need **irse** in the preterit 3rd plural; review §7.135–§7.137.

47. (D) You need **devolver** + the preposition **a**; review §7.19 and §7.177.

48. (B) You need the present tense; review §8.14ff and §23.14.

49. (C) You need the imperative; review §8.62(d) and §23.18.

50. (B) You need the preterit 3rd singular; review §8.25ff.

51. (C) You must attach both the direct and indirect pronouns to the infinitive; review §6.49 and §6.52.

52. (A) In the negative imperative, object pronouns are placed in front of the verb; review §6.42.

53. (D) Review §6.52.

54. (A) You need the masculine plural demonstrative adjective; review §5.54–§5.56.

55. (B) You need the feminine plural demonstrative pronoun; review §6.54–§6.59.

56. (C) You need the neuter demonstrative pronoun; review §6.58.

57. (D) You need **aquél**; review §6.59.

58. (D) You need **el de**; review §6.60.

59. (B) You need **las de**; review §6.60.

60. (B) You need **la que**; review §6.60.

61. (D) A possessive pronoun agrees in gender and number with the noun it replaces; review §6.64 and §6.65.

62. (A) A possessive pronoun agrees in gender and number with the noun it replaces; review §6.64 and §6.65.

63. (B) You need **de mi**; review §6.67.

64. (A) You need **mío**; review §6.69.

65. (B) You need **suyas**; review §6.69.

PART C

66. (D) The meanings of the words in the choices are: **sucesor** / successor; **sucio** / dirty; **sucoso** / juicy; succulent; **éxito** / success.

67. (C) The meanings of the verbs in the choices are: **despertar** / to awaken; **consolar** / to console; **saludar** / to greet, to take a bow; **imitar** / to imitate.

68. (A) Review relative pronouns in §6.72-§6.103. Review also §5.68

69. (B) The meanings of the words in the choices are: **pintor** / painter; **compositor** / composer; **bailarín** / dancer; **periodista** / journalist. It is evident that Plácido's son is a composer because it is stated after the blank space that he wrote songs.

70. (B) Review the position of a pronoun as object of an infinitive in §6.49. The indirect object pronoun **le** is needed because it means "to him" and the sentence states that a dinner was prepared to give (to) him two gold medals. Review the indirect object pronouns in §6.14. In A and C **lo** and **los** are direct object pronouns. Review them in §6.7.

PART D

71. (D)   See sentence three in the passage.

72. (C)   See sentence four in the passage.

73. (A)   See sentences 6–7 in the passage.

74. (B)   See sentence eight in the passage.

75. (B)   See sentence nine in the passage.

76. (C)   See sentence two in the passage.

77. (C)   See sentence four in the passage.

78. (A)   See sentence 14 in the passage.

79. (B)   See sentence 21 in the passage.

80. (A)   See sentence 24 in the passage.

81. (D)   See sentence two in the passage.

82. (C)   See sentence four in the passage.

83. (B)   See sentence five in the passage.

84. (C)   See sentence seven in the passage.

85. (A)   See sentence eight in the passage.

TEST 8

PART A

1. (D)   **tratar de** / to try to

2. (A)   **seguir** / to continue; **escribiéndose** / writing to each other

3. (C)   **bajar** / to get off a moving vehicle

4. (B)   **conducir** / to lead

5. (B)   **las estrellas** / the stars

6. (A)   **el olor** / the odor, smell

7. (B)   **la carretera** / the highway

8. (D)   **alumbrar** / to shine

9. (A)   **la mosca** / the fly

10. (A)   **el traje de baño** / the bathing suit

11. (A)   **la toronja** / the grapefruit

12. (D)   **pronunciar conferencias** / to give lectures

13. (B)   **la acera** / the sidewalk

14. (A)   **darse cuenta de** / to realize

15. (A)   **la abeja** / the bee

16. (B)   **en cambio** / on the other hand

17. (A)   **estar de rodillas** / to kneel

18. (D)   **el azúcar** / the sugar

19. (B)   **querer decir** / to mean

20. (A)   **para ser tan . . .** / for being so . . . , in spite of being so . . .

21. (B)   **buen** / good

22. (A)   **regalar** / to present, to give as a gift

23. (B)   **morir** / to die

24. (C)   **la luz** / the light

25. (A)   **la escasez** / the scarcity

26. (B)   **el cruce** / the crossing

27. (A) **la muñeca** / the doll
28. (D) **las alas** / the wings
29. (C) **el cesto** / the basket
30. (A) **cargado** / loaded
31. (A) **la viuda** / the widow

PART B

32. (B) You need the imperfect indicative form of **ser**; review §16.ff, especially §16.19.
33. (A) The correct idiom is **hay lodo**; review §17.2.
34. (D) You need **brillar** in the present indicative, 3rd person plural because of **estoy mirando**; review §17.3.
35. (A) The correct idiom is **hay neblina**; review §17.2.
36. (B) You need the neuter **lo** direct object pronoun; review §6.12.
37. (B) The direct and indirect object pronouns are attached to the infinitive; review §6.37ff and §6.52.
38. (C) The object pronoun may be placed in front of the main verb if it is a progressive form with **estar** or another auxiliary; review §6.39 and §6.40.
39. (B) The indirect object pronoun is placed in front of the direct object pronoun and the negation **no** in front of both; review §6.45.
40. (A) You need **que**; review §6.76.
41. (C) You need **en que**; review §6.79.
42. (B) You need **que**; review §6.85.
43. (B) You need **quien**; review §6.87.
44. (A) You need **por la cual**; review §6.91.
45. (B) You need **lo cual**; review §6.94.
46. (B) You need **lo que**; review §6.95.
47. (A) You need **cuyos hijos**; review §6.98.
48. (B) The relative possessive adjective agrees with what is possessed; review §6.99.
49. (B) The relative possessive adjective agrees with what is possessed; review §6.100.
50. (C) You need **de quién**; review §6.101.
51. (C) You need **a quien**; review §6.102.
52. (C) You need the imperfect indicative; review §7.1 and §8.20–§8.24.
53. (A) You need the infinitive; review §7.7(d) and §7.181(d).
54. (D) You need **se los**; review §6.52 and §7.13(d).
55. (A) You need the preterit 3rd singular of **echarse**; review §7.20. For the preterit, review §8.25–§8.30.
56. (D) Verbs of motion take the preposition **a** + infinitive; review §7.19.
57. (A) **Negarse** is the only choice that fits with the preposition **a** + infinitive; reivew §7.20, §7.21, and §7.22.
58. (C) You need the preterit 3rd singular of **llegar**; review §7.21 and §7.22.
59. (B) **Soñar** takes the preposition **con** + infinitive; review §7.22.
60. (A) **Cumplir** is the only choice that fits with the preposition **con** + noun (or pronoun); review §7.23 and §7.24.
61. (B) **Ocuparse** is the only choice that fits with the preposition **de** + infinitive; review §7.22 and §7.24.

62. (B) **Aprovecharse** is the only choice that fits with the prepostion **de** + noun; review §7.25, §7.26, and §7.27.

63. (B) You need **qué**; review §7.27.

64. (D) **Tardar** is the only choice that fits with the preposition **en** + infinitive; review §7.25 and §7.26.

65. (A) **Empeñarse** is the only choice that fits with the preposition **en** + infinitive; review §7.26 and §7.28.

PART C

66. (B) The meanings of the choices of verbs are: **vender** / to sell; **comprar** / to buy; **encontrar** / to meet; **construir** / to construct.

67. (A) All the verbs in the choices are in the preterit tense, 3rd person, singular. The only one that makes sense in the statement is **ofreció** / offered; the others are: **corrió** / ran; **colgó** / hung up; **cepilló** / brushed. Review the preterit in §8.25–§8.30.

68. (C) All the verbs in the choices are in the present indicative tense, 1st person, singular. The only one that makes sense in the statement is **escribo** / I'm writing; the others are: **contesto** / I'm answering; **compro** / I'm buying; **llamo** / I'm calling. In the preceding sentence there is mention of **una carta** / a letter. Review the present indicative tense in §8.14–§8.19.

69. (D) All the verbs in the choices are in the present indicative tense, 1st person, singular. The only one that fits sensibly in the statement is **tengo** / I have; the others are: **pierdo** / I'm losing (**perder** / to lose); **gasto** / I spend; **miro** / I look. Review the present indicative tense in §8.14–§8.19.

70. (C) All the verbs in the choices are in the preterit tense, 3rd person, singular. The only one that fits sensibly in the statement is **dio** / gave (**dar** / to give); the others are: **compró** / bought; **tuvo** / had (**tener** / to have); **tomó** / took. Review the preterit tense in §8.25–§8.30.

PART D

71. (B) See sentence one in the passage.
72. (A) See sentences 3–4 in the passage.
73. (C) See sentence five in the passage.
74. (D) See sentences 10–11 in the passage.
75. (C) See sentence 13 in the passage.
76. (C) See sentence three in the passage.
77. (B) See sentence one in the passage.
78. (D) See sentence one and the rest of the passage.
79. (A) See sentence seven in the passage.
80. (D) See sentence ten in the passage.
81. (A) See sentence one in the passage.
82. (B) See sentence two in the passage.
83. (D) See sentences 5–7 in the passage.
84. (C) See sentence eight in the passage.
85. (A) See sentence nine in the passage.

TEST 9

PART A

1. (D) **pelear** / to fight
2. (B) **la punta** / the tip (of the child's tongue)

3. (B) **cansado** / tired

4. (A) **llamar** / to call

5. (B) **el regalo** / the gift

6. (C) **el oro** / the gold

7. (A) **una pelea** / a fight

8. (D) **el espejo** / the mirror

9. (B) **antes** / before

10. (A) **componer** / to compose; **compuesta** is the feminine past participle.

11. (A) **fundar** / to found, establish

12. (D) **hacer** / to make; **el ruido** / the noise

13. (B.) **el vidrio** / the glass window pane

14. (B) **poder** / to be able

15. (C) **el agujero** / the hole

16. (D) **al instante** / instantly

17. (A) **atadas** / tied

18. (A) **un analfabeto** / an illiterate

19. (B) **adquirir** / to get, acquire, obtain

20. (B) **pesado** / heavy

21. (D) **el rumbo** / the direction

22. (C) **el abrigo** / the overcoat

23. (A) **una figura** / a figure

24. (D) **mirar** / to look (at)

25. (B) **el pueblo** / the town

26. (D) **volver** / to return; past participle, **vuelto**

27. (B) **alejarse** / to carry away, separate

28. (A) **gozar** / to enjoy

29. (B) **fuera** / outside

30. (A) **mudarse** / to move (from one place to another)

31. (C) **gastar** / to spend (money; to spend time, **pasar**)

PART B

32. (A) The correct idiom is **hay que**; review §14.11.

33. (A) You need **hace que**; review §14.1.

34. (A) You need **hace**; review §14.7.

35. (B) You need **cuándo**; review §14.3.

36. (A) You need **hace**; review §14.4.

37. (B) You need **hacía**; review §14.2(b).

38. (B) You need the imperfect indicative; review §14.8(b).

39. (A) You need **saber** in the present indicative; review §7.118.

40. (C) You need the imperfect subjunctive of **estar**; review §7.101(2) and §7.109.

41. (D) You need the imperfect subjunctive of **irse**; review §7.101(2) and §7.110.

42. (A) You need the present indicative of **ser**; review §8.14(c)(1).

43. (D) You need the present indicative of **suponer**; review §8.19, where **suponer** is listed.

44. (D) You need the imperfect indicative of **ir**; review §8.20(c)(2) and §8.24.

45. (C) You need the preterit 1st singular of **llegar**; review §8.25(5).

46. (B) You need **tan**; review §5.39.

47. (A) You need **que**; review §5.40.

48. (B) You need **los más,** masculine plural, because the subject is mixed gender, review §5.44.

49. (B) You need **tantos,** because **tíos** is masculine plural; review §5.53.

50. (A) You need **tan**; review §5.39.

51. (B) You need **de lo que**; review §5.67(a).

52. (B) You need **de lo que**; review §5.67(a).

53. (A) You need **de los que**; review §5.67(b).

54. (C) You need **de las que**; review §5.67(b).

55. (A) You need **mucho**; review §10.7.

56. (D) No preposition is required; review §7.30.

57. (D) No preposition is required; review §7.30.

58. (D) No preposition is required; review §7.30.

59. (B) Use the subjunctive after **cuando** when uncertainty is expressed; review §7.38.

60. (A) You need the preterit; review §7.39.

61. (A) You need the indicative; review §7.62.

62. (B) You need the subjunctive; review §7.61.

63. (A) You need the subjunctive; review §7.60.

64. (C) You need the subjunctive; review §7.58.

65. (D) You need the subjunctive; review §7.51.

PART C

66. (A) Review again relative pronouns in §6.72-§6.103 and, in particular, §5.68. The verb form **quisiera** (I would like) after the blank space is the imperfect subjunctive of **querer**. The boy's mother told him he could be what (**lo que**) he wanted. Study carefully §6.95. You must also study the irregular verbs conjugated fully in all the tenses in §8.67 because they are commonly used. The verb **querer** is listed among them alphabetically.

67. (D) The meanings of the words in the choices are: **cocinando** / cooking; **escribiendo** / writing; **leyendo** / reading; **dibujando** / drawing. They are all present participles. Review how to form a present participle in §7.189 and the irregulars in §7.190 where you will find **leyendo (leer)**.

68. (C) The meanings of the words in the choices are: **carnicero** / butcher; **zapatero** / shoe repairman; **artista** / artist; **periodista** / journalist. The boy's father referred to him as " my son the artist " because the boy won a scholarship (**una beca**) to study art at the university.

69. (A) You need **le** (to him) as the indirect object pronoun because it refers to **a mi padre**. The boy announced to him (to his father) that he had won a scholarship to study art. Review again indirect object pronouns in §6.14ff and direct object pronouns in §6.7ff to understand that the choices **lo** and **los** are direct object pronouns.

70. (C) The meanings of the choices are: **vacaciones** / vacation; **exámenes** / exams; **estudios** / studies; **novelas** / novels.

PART D

71. (A) See sentence one in the passage.

72. (D) See sentence four in the passage.

73. (C) See sentence six in the passage.

74. (A) See sentence nine in the passage.

75. (C) See sentence one and the last paragraph in the passage.

76. (A) See sentences 3–4 in the passage.

77. (A) See sentence five in the passage.

78. (B) See sentence seven in the passage.

79. (D) See sentences 13–14 in the passage.

80. (C) See sentence 15 in the passage.

81. (A) See sentence one in the passage.

82. (C) See sentence three in the passage.

83. (C) See sentences 10–11 in the passage.

84. (D) See sentence 15 in the passage.

85. (B) See sentences 18–19 in the passage.

75. (C) See sentence one and the last one given in the passage.
76. (A) See sentences two in the passage.
77. (A) See sentence five in the passage.
78. (D) See sentence seven in the passage.
79. (D) See sentences 13-14 in the passage.
80. (D) See sentence 15 in the passage.
81. (A) See sentence one in the passage.
82. (C) See sentence three in the passage.
83. (C) See sentence 10-11 in the passage.
84. (D) See sentence 17 in the passage.
85. (D) See sentences 18-19 in the passage.

Answer Sheet: Test 1

PART A

1 Ⓐ Ⓑ Ⓒ Ⓓ
2 Ⓐ Ⓑ Ⓒ Ⓓ
3 Ⓐ Ⓑ Ⓒ Ⓓ
4 Ⓐ Ⓑ Ⓒ Ⓓ
5 Ⓐ Ⓑ Ⓒ Ⓓ
6 Ⓐ Ⓑ Ⓒ Ⓓ
7 Ⓐ Ⓑ Ⓒ Ⓓ
8 Ⓐ Ⓑ Ⓒ Ⓓ
9 Ⓐ Ⓑ Ⓒ Ⓓ
10 Ⓐ Ⓑ Ⓒ Ⓓ
11 Ⓐ Ⓑ Ⓒ Ⓓ
12 Ⓐ Ⓑ Ⓒ Ⓓ
13 Ⓐ Ⓑ Ⓒ Ⓓ
14 Ⓐ Ⓑ Ⓒ Ⓓ
15 Ⓐ Ⓑ Ⓒ Ⓓ
16 Ⓐ Ⓑ Ⓒ Ⓓ
17 Ⓐ Ⓑ Ⓒ Ⓓ
18 Ⓐ Ⓑ Ⓒ Ⓓ
19 Ⓐ Ⓑ Ⓒ Ⓓ
20 Ⓐ Ⓑ Ⓒ Ⓓ
21 Ⓐ Ⓑ Ⓒ Ⓓ
22 Ⓐ Ⓑ Ⓒ Ⓓ
23 Ⓐ Ⓑ Ⓒ Ⓓ
24 Ⓐ Ⓑ Ⓒ Ⓓ
25 Ⓐ Ⓑ Ⓒ Ⓓ
26 Ⓐ Ⓑ Ⓒ Ⓓ
27 Ⓐ Ⓑ Ⓒ Ⓓ
28 Ⓐ Ⓑ Ⓒ Ⓓ
29 Ⓐ Ⓑ Ⓒ Ⓓ
30 Ⓐ Ⓑ Ⓒ Ⓓ
31 Ⓐ Ⓑ Ⓒ Ⓓ

PART B

32 Ⓐ Ⓑ Ⓒ Ⓓ
33 Ⓐ Ⓑ Ⓒ Ⓓ
34 Ⓐ Ⓑ Ⓒ Ⓓ
35 Ⓐ Ⓑ Ⓒ Ⓓ
36 Ⓐ Ⓑ Ⓒ Ⓓ
37 Ⓐ Ⓑ Ⓒ Ⓓ
38 Ⓐ Ⓑ Ⓒ Ⓓ
39 Ⓐ Ⓑ Ⓒ Ⓓ
40 Ⓐ Ⓑ Ⓒ Ⓓ
41 Ⓐ Ⓑ Ⓒ Ⓓ
42 Ⓐ Ⓑ Ⓒ Ⓓ
43 Ⓐ Ⓑ Ⓒ Ⓓ
44 Ⓐ Ⓑ Ⓒ Ⓓ
45 Ⓐ Ⓑ Ⓒ Ⓓ
46 Ⓐ Ⓑ Ⓒ Ⓓ
47 Ⓐ Ⓑ Ⓒ Ⓓ
48 Ⓐ Ⓑ Ⓒ Ⓓ
49 Ⓐ Ⓑ Ⓒ Ⓓ
50 Ⓐ Ⓑ Ⓒ Ⓓ
51 Ⓐ Ⓑ Ⓒ Ⓓ
52 Ⓐ Ⓑ Ⓒ Ⓓ
53 Ⓐ Ⓑ Ⓒ Ⓓ
54 Ⓐ Ⓑ Ⓒ Ⓓ
55 Ⓐ Ⓑ Ⓒ Ⓓ
56 Ⓐ Ⓑ Ⓒ Ⓓ
57 Ⓐ Ⓑ Ⓒ Ⓓ
58 Ⓐ Ⓑ Ⓒ Ⓓ
59 Ⓐ Ⓑ Ⓒ Ⓓ
60 Ⓐ Ⓑ Ⓒ Ⓓ
61 Ⓐ Ⓑ Ⓒ Ⓓ
62 Ⓐ Ⓑ Ⓒ Ⓓ
63 Ⓐ Ⓑ Ⓒ Ⓓ
64 Ⓐ Ⓑ Ⓒ Ⓓ
65 Ⓐ Ⓑ Ⓒ Ⓓ

PART C

66 Ⓐ Ⓑ Ⓒ Ⓓ
67 Ⓐ Ⓑ Ⓒ Ⓓ
68 Ⓐ Ⓑ Ⓒ Ⓓ
69 Ⓐ Ⓑ Ⓒ Ⓓ
70 Ⓐ Ⓑ Ⓒ Ⓓ

PART D

71 Ⓐ Ⓑ Ⓒ Ⓓ
72 Ⓐ Ⓑ Ⓒ Ⓓ
73 Ⓐ Ⓑ Ⓒ Ⓓ
74 Ⓐ Ⓑ Ⓒ Ⓓ
75 Ⓐ Ⓑ Ⓒ Ⓓ
76 Ⓐ Ⓑ Ⓒ Ⓓ
77 Ⓐ Ⓑ Ⓒ Ⓓ
78 Ⓐ Ⓑ Ⓒ Ⓓ
79 Ⓐ Ⓑ Ⓒ Ⓓ
80 Ⓐ Ⓑ Ⓒ Ⓓ
81 Ⓐ Ⓑ Ⓒ Ⓓ
82 Ⓐ Ⓑ Ⓒ Ⓓ
83 Ⓐ Ⓑ Ⓒ Ⓓ
84 Ⓐ Ⓑ Ⓒ Ⓓ
85 Ⓐ Ⓑ Ⓒ Ⓓ

Answer Sheet: Test 2

PART A

1 Ⓐ Ⓑ Ⓒ Ⓓ
2 Ⓐ Ⓑ Ⓒ Ⓓ
3 Ⓐ Ⓑ Ⓒ Ⓓ
4 Ⓐ Ⓑ Ⓒ Ⓓ
5 Ⓐ Ⓑ Ⓒ Ⓓ
6 Ⓐ Ⓑ Ⓒ Ⓓ
7 Ⓐ Ⓑ Ⓒ Ⓓ
8 Ⓐ Ⓑ Ⓒ Ⓓ
9 Ⓐ Ⓑ Ⓒ Ⓓ
10 Ⓐ Ⓑ Ⓒ Ⓓ
11 Ⓐ Ⓑ Ⓒ Ⓓ
12 Ⓐ Ⓑ Ⓒ Ⓓ
13 Ⓐ Ⓑ Ⓒ Ⓓ
14 Ⓐ Ⓑ Ⓒ Ⓓ
15 Ⓐ Ⓑ Ⓒ Ⓓ
16 Ⓐ Ⓑ Ⓒ Ⓓ
17 Ⓐ Ⓑ Ⓒ Ⓓ
18 Ⓐ Ⓑ Ⓒ Ⓓ
19 Ⓐ Ⓑ Ⓒ Ⓓ
20 Ⓐ Ⓑ Ⓒ Ⓓ
21 Ⓐ Ⓑ Ⓒ Ⓓ
22 Ⓐ Ⓑ Ⓒ Ⓓ
23 Ⓐ Ⓑ Ⓒ Ⓓ
24 Ⓐ Ⓑ Ⓒ Ⓓ
25 Ⓐ Ⓑ Ⓒ Ⓓ
26 Ⓐ Ⓑ Ⓒ Ⓓ
27 Ⓐ Ⓑ Ⓒ Ⓓ
28 Ⓐ Ⓑ Ⓒ Ⓓ
29 Ⓐ Ⓑ Ⓒ Ⓓ
30 Ⓐ Ⓑ Ⓒ Ⓓ
31 Ⓐ Ⓑ Ⓒ Ⓓ

PART B

32 Ⓐ Ⓑ Ⓒ Ⓓ
33 Ⓐ Ⓑ Ⓒ Ⓓ
34 Ⓐ Ⓑ Ⓒ Ⓓ
35 Ⓐ Ⓑ Ⓒ Ⓓ
36 Ⓐ Ⓑ Ⓒ Ⓓ
37 Ⓐ Ⓑ Ⓒ Ⓓ
38 Ⓐ Ⓑ Ⓒ Ⓓ
39 Ⓐ Ⓑ Ⓒ Ⓓ
40 Ⓐ Ⓑ Ⓒ Ⓓ
41 Ⓐ Ⓑ Ⓒ Ⓓ
42 Ⓐ Ⓑ Ⓒ Ⓓ
43 Ⓐ Ⓑ Ⓒ Ⓓ
44 Ⓐ Ⓑ Ⓒ Ⓓ
45 Ⓐ Ⓑ Ⓒ Ⓓ
46 Ⓐ Ⓑ Ⓒ Ⓓ
47 Ⓐ Ⓑ Ⓒ Ⓓ
48 Ⓐ Ⓑ Ⓒ Ⓓ
49 Ⓐ Ⓑ Ⓒ Ⓓ
50 Ⓐ Ⓑ Ⓒ Ⓓ
51 Ⓐ Ⓑ Ⓒ Ⓓ
52 Ⓐ Ⓑ Ⓒ Ⓓ
53 Ⓐ Ⓑ Ⓒ Ⓓ
54 Ⓐ Ⓑ Ⓒ Ⓓ
55 Ⓐ Ⓑ Ⓒ Ⓓ
56 Ⓐ Ⓑ Ⓒ Ⓓ
57 Ⓐ Ⓑ Ⓒ Ⓓ
58 Ⓐ Ⓑ Ⓒ Ⓓ
59 Ⓐ Ⓑ Ⓒ Ⓓ
60 Ⓐ Ⓑ Ⓒ Ⓓ
61 Ⓐ Ⓑ Ⓒ Ⓓ
62 Ⓐ Ⓑ Ⓒ Ⓓ
63 Ⓐ Ⓑ Ⓒ Ⓓ
64 Ⓐ Ⓑ Ⓒ Ⓓ
65 Ⓐ Ⓑ Ⓒ Ⓓ

PART C

66 Ⓐ Ⓑ Ⓒ Ⓓ
67 Ⓐ Ⓑ Ⓒ Ⓓ
68 Ⓐ Ⓑ Ⓒ Ⓓ
69 Ⓐ Ⓑ Ⓒ Ⓓ
70 Ⓐ Ⓑ Ⓒ Ⓓ

PART D

71 Ⓐ Ⓑ Ⓒ Ⓓ
72 Ⓐ Ⓑ Ⓒ Ⓓ
73 Ⓐ Ⓑ Ⓒ Ⓓ
74 Ⓐ Ⓑ Ⓒ Ⓓ
75 Ⓐ Ⓑ Ⓒ Ⓓ
76 Ⓐ Ⓑ Ⓒ Ⓓ
77 Ⓐ Ⓑ Ⓒ Ⓓ
78 Ⓐ Ⓑ Ⓒ Ⓓ
79 Ⓐ Ⓑ Ⓒ Ⓓ
80 Ⓐ Ⓑ Ⓒ Ⓓ
81 Ⓐ Ⓑ Ⓒ Ⓓ
82 Ⓐ Ⓑ Ⓒ Ⓓ
83 Ⓐ Ⓑ Ⓒ Ⓓ
84 Ⓐ Ⓑ Ⓒ Ⓓ
85 Ⓐ Ⓑ Ⓒ Ⓓ

Answer Sheet: Test 3

PART A

1 Ⓐ Ⓑ Ⓒ Ⓓ
2 Ⓐ Ⓑ Ⓒ Ⓓ
3 Ⓐ Ⓑ Ⓒ Ⓓ
4 Ⓐ Ⓑ Ⓒ Ⓓ
5 Ⓐ Ⓑ Ⓒ Ⓓ
6 Ⓐ Ⓑ Ⓒ Ⓓ
7 Ⓐ Ⓑ Ⓒ Ⓓ
8 Ⓐ Ⓑ Ⓒ Ⓓ
9 Ⓐ Ⓑ Ⓒ Ⓓ
10 Ⓐ Ⓑ Ⓒ Ⓓ
11 Ⓐ Ⓑ Ⓒ Ⓓ
12 Ⓐ Ⓑ Ⓒ Ⓓ
13 Ⓐ Ⓑ Ⓒ Ⓓ
14 Ⓐ Ⓑ Ⓒ Ⓓ
15 Ⓐ Ⓑ Ⓒ Ⓓ
16 Ⓐ Ⓑ Ⓒ Ⓓ
17 Ⓐ Ⓑ Ⓒ Ⓓ
18 Ⓐ Ⓑ Ⓒ Ⓓ
19 Ⓐ Ⓑ Ⓒ Ⓓ
20 Ⓐ Ⓑ Ⓒ Ⓓ
21 Ⓐ Ⓑ Ⓒ Ⓓ
22 Ⓐ Ⓑ Ⓒ Ⓓ
23 Ⓐ Ⓑ Ⓒ Ⓓ
24 Ⓐ Ⓑ Ⓒ Ⓓ
25 Ⓐ Ⓑ Ⓒ Ⓓ
26 Ⓐ Ⓑ Ⓒ Ⓓ
27 Ⓐ Ⓑ Ⓒ Ⓓ
28 Ⓐ Ⓑ Ⓒ Ⓓ
29 Ⓐ Ⓑ Ⓒ Ⓓ
30 Ⓐ Ⓑ Ⓒ Ⓓ
31 Ⓐ Ⓑ Ⓒ Ⓓ

PART B

32 Ⓐ Ⓑ Ⓒ Ⓓ
33 Ⓐ Ⓑ Ⓒ Ⓓ
34 Ⓐ Ⓑ Ⓒ Ⓓ
35 Ⓐ Ⓑ Ⓒ Ⓓ
36 Ⓐ Ⓑ Ⓒ Ⓓ
37 Ⓐ Ⓑ Ⓒ Ⓓ
38 Ⓐ Ⓑ Ⓒ Ⓓ
39 Ⓐ Ⓑ Ⓒ Ⓓ
40 Ⓐ Ⓑ Ⓒ Ⓓ
41 Ⓐ Ⓑ Ⓒ Ⓓ
42 Ⓐ Ⓑ Ⓒ Ⓓ
43 Ⓐ Ⓑ Ⓒ Ⓓ
44 Ⓐ Ⓑ Ⓒ Ⓓ
45 Ⓐ Ⓑ Ⓒ Ⓓ
46 Ⓐ Ⓑ Ⓒ Ⓓ
47 Ⓐ Ⓑ Ⓒ Ⓓ
48 Ⓐ Ⓑ Ⓒ Ⓓ
49 Ⓐ Ⓑ Ⓒ Ⓓ
50 Ⓐ Ⓑ Ⓒ Ⓓ
51 Ⓐ Ⓑ Ⓒ Ⓓ
52 Ⓐ Ⓑ Ⓒ Ⓓ
53 Ⓐ Ⓑ Ⓒ Ⓓ
54 Ⓐ Ⓑ Ⓒ Ⓓ
55 Ⓐ Ⓑ Ⓒ Ⓓ
56 Ⓐ Ⓑ Ⓒ Ⓓ
57 Ⓐ Ⓑ Ⓒ Ⓓ
58 Ⓐ Ⓑ Ⓒ Ⓓ
59 Ⓐ Ⓑ Ⓒ Ⓓ
60 Ⓐ Ⓑ Ⓒ Ⓓ
61 Ⓐ Ⓑ Ⓒ Ⓓ
62 Ⓐ Ⓑ Ⓒ Ⓓ
63 Ⓐ Ⓑ Ⓒ Ⓓ
64 Ⓐ Ⓑ Ⓒ Ⓓ
65 Ⓐ Ⓑ Ⓒ Ⓓ

PART C

66 Ⓐ Ⓑ Ⓒ Ⓓ
67 Ⓐ Ⓑ Ⓒ Ⓓ
68 Ⓐ Ⓑ Ⓒ Ⓓ
69 Ⓐ Ⓑ Ⓒ Ⓓ
70 Ⓐ Ⓑ Ⓒ Ⓓ

PART D

71 Ⓐ Ⓑ Ⓒ Ⓓ
72 Ⓐ Ⓑ Ⓒ Ⓓ
73 Ⓐ Ⓑ Ⓒ Ⓓ
74 Ⓐ Ⓑ Ⓒ Ⓓ
75 Ⓐ Ⓑ Ⓒ Ⓓ
76 Ⓐ Ⓑ Ⓒ Ⓓ
77 Ⓐ Ⓑ Ⓒ Ⓓ
78 Ⓐ Ⓑ Ⓒ Ⓓ
79 Ⓐ Ⓑ Ⓒ Ⓓ
80 Ⓐ Ⓑ Ⓒ Ⓓ
81 Ⓐ Ⓑ Ⓒ Ⓓ
82 Ⓐ Ⓑ Ⓒ Ⓓ
83 Ⓐ Ⓑ Ⓒ Ⓓ
84 Ⓐ Ⓑ Ⓒ Ⓓ
85 Ⓐ Ⓑ Ⓒ Ⓓ

Answer Sheet: Test 4

PART A

1 Ⓐ Ⓑ Ⓒ Ⓓ
2 Ⓐ Ⓑ Ⓒ Ⓓ
3 Ⓐ Ⓑ Ⓒ Ⓓ
4 Ⓐ Ⓑ Ⓒ Ⓓ
5 Ⓐ Ⓑ Ⓒ Ⓓ
6 Ⓐ Ⓑ Ⓒ Ⓓ
7 Ⓐ Ⓑ Ⓒ Ⓓ
8 Ⓐ Ⓑ Ⓒ Ⓓ
9 Ⓐ Ⓑ Ⓒ Ⓓ
10 Ⓐ Ⓑ Ⓒ Ⓓ
11 Ⓐ Ⓑ Ⓒ Ⓓ
12 Ⓐ Ⓑ Ⓒ Ⓓ
13 Ⓐ Ⓑ Ⓒ Ⓓ
14 Ⓐ Ⓑ Ⓒ Ⓓ
15 Ⓐ Ⓑ Ⓒ Ⓓ
16 Ⓐ Ⓑ Ⓒ Ⓓ
17 Ⓐ Ⓑ Ⓒ Ⓓ
18 Ⓐ Ⓑ Ⓒ Ⓓ
19 Ⓐ Ⓑ Ⓒ Ⓓ
20 Ⓐ Ⓑ Ⓒ Ⓓ
21 Ⓐ Ⓑ Ⓒ Ⓓ
22 Ⓐ Ⓑ Ⓒ Ⓓ
23 Ⓐ Ⓑ Ⓒ Ⓓ
24 Ⓐ Ⓑ Ⓒ Ⓓ
25 Ⓐ Ⓑ Ⓒ Ⓓ
26 Ⓐ Ⓑ Ⓒ Ⓓ
27 Ⓐ Ⓑ Ⓒ Ⓓ
28 Ⓐ Ⓑ Ⓒ Ⓓ
29 Ⓐ Ⓑ Ⓒ Ⓓ
30 Ⓐ Ⓑ Ⓒ Ⓓ
31 Ⓐ Ⓑ Ⓒ Ⓓ

PART B

32 Ⓐ Ⓑ Ⓒ Ⓓ
33 Ⓐ Ⓑ Ⓒ Ⓓ
34 Ⓐ Ⓑ Ⓒ Ⓓ
35 Ⓐ Ⓑ Ⓒ Ⓓ
36 Ⓐ Ⓑ Ⓒ Ⓓ
37 Ⓐ Ⓑ Ⓒ Ⓓ
38 Ⓐ Ⓑ Ⓒ Ⓓ
39 Ⓐ Ⓑ Ⓒ Ⓓ
40 Ⓐ Ⓑ Ⓒ Ⓓ
41 Ⓐ Ⓑ Ⓒ Ⓓ
42 Ⓐ Ⓑ Ⓒ Ⓓ
43 Ⓐ Ⓑ Ⓒ Ⓓ
44 Ⓐ Ⓑ Ⓒ Ⓓ
45 Ⓐ Ⓑ Ⓒ Ⓓ
46 Ⓐ Ⓑ Ⓒ Ⓓ
47 Ⓐ Ⓑ Ⓒ Ⓓ
48 Ⓐ Ⓑ Ⓒ Ⓓ
49 Ⓐ Ⓑ Ⓒ Ⓓ
50 Ⓐ Ⓑ Ⓒ Ⓓ
51 Ⓐ Ⓑ Ⓒ Ⓓ
52 Ⓐ Ⓑ Ⓒ Ⓓ
53 Ⓐ Ⓑ Ⓒ Ⓓ
54 Ⓐ Ⓑ Ⓒ Ⓓ
55 Ⓐ Ⓑ Ⓒ Ⓓ
56 Ⓐ Ⓑ Ⓒ Ⓓ
57 Ⓐ Ⓑ Ⓒ Ⓓ
58 Ⓐ Ⓑ Ⓒ Ⓓ
59 Ⓐ Ⓑ Ⓒ Ⓓ
60 Ⓐ Ⓑ Ⓒ Ⓓ
61 Ⓐ Ⓑ Ⓒ Ⓓ
62 Ⓐ Ⓑ Ⓒ Ⓓ
63 Ⓐ Ⓑ Ⓒ Ⓓ
64 Ⓐ Ⓑ Ⓒ Ⓓ
65 Ⓐ Ⓑ Ⓒ Ⓓ

PART C

66 Ⓐ Ⓑ Ⓒ Ⓓ
67 Ⓐ Ⓑ Ⓒ Ⓓ
68 Ⓐ Ⓑ Ⓒ Ⓓ
69 Ⓐ Ⓑ Ⓒ Ⓓ
70 Ⓐ Ⓑ Ⓒ Ⓓ

PART D

71 Ⓐ Ⓑ Ⓒ Ⓓ
72 Ⓐ Ⓑ Ⓒ Ⓓ
73 Ⓐ Ⓑ Ⓒ Ⓓ
74 Ⓐ Ⓑ Ⓒ Ⓓ
75 Ⓐ Ⓑ Ⓒ Ⓓ
76 Ⓐ Ⓑ Ⓒ Ⓓ
77 Ⓐ Ⓑ Ⓒ Ⓓ
78 Ⓐ Ⓑ Ⓒ Ⓓ
79 Ⓐ Ⓑ Ⓒ Ⓓ
80 Ⓐ Ⓑ Ⓒ Ⓓ
81 Ⓐ Ⓑ Ⓒ Ⓓ
82 Ⓐ Ⓑ Ⓒ Ⓓ
83 Ⓐ Ⓑ Ⓒ Ⓓ
84 Ⓐ Ⓑ Ⓒ Ⓓ
85 Ⓐ Ⓑ Ⓒ Ⓓ

Answer Sheet: Test 5

PART A

1 (A)(B)(C)(D)
2 (A)(B)(C)(D)
3 (A)(B)(C)(D)
4 (A)(B)(C)(D)
5 (A)(B)(C)(D)
6 (A)(B)(C)(D)
7 (A)(B)(C)(D)
8 (A)(B)(C)(D)
9 (A)(B)(C)(D)
10 (A)(B)(C)(D)
11 (A)(B)(C)(D)
12 (A)(B)(C)(D)
13 (A)(B)(C)(D)
14 (A)(B)(C)(D)
15 (A)(B)(C)(D)
16 (A)(B)(C)(D)
17 (A)(B)(C)(D)
18 (A)(B)(C)(D)
19 (A)(B)(C)(D)
20 (A)(B)(C)(D)
21 (A)(B)(C)(D)
22 (A)(B)(C)(D)
23 (A)(B)(C)(D)
24 (A)(B)(C)(D)
25 (A)(B)(C)(D)
26 (A)(B)(C)(D)
27 (A)(B)(C)(D)
28 (A)(B)(C)(D)
29 (A)(B)(C)(D)
30 (A)(B)(C)(D)
31 (A)(B)(C)(D)

PART B

32 (A)(B)(C)(D)
33 (A)(B)(C)(D)
34 (A)(B)(C)(D)
35 (A)(B)(C)(D)
36 (A)(B)(C)(D)
37 (A)(B)(C)(D)
38 (A)(B)(C)(D)
39 (A)(B)(C)(D)
40 (A)(B)(C)(D)
41 (A)(B)(C)(D)
42 (A)(B)(C)(D)
43 (A)(B)(C)(D)
44 (A)(B)(C)(D)
45 (A)(B)(C)(D)
46 (A)(B)(C)(D)
47 (A)(B)(C)(D)
48 (A)(B)(C)(D)
49 (A)(B)(C)(D)
50 (A)(B)(C)(D)
51 (A)(B)(C)(D)
52 (A)(B)(C)(D)
53 (A)(B)(C)(D)
54 (A)(B)(C)(D)
55 (A)(B)(C)(D)
56 (A)(B)(C)(D)
57 (A)(B)(C)(D)
58 (A)(B)(C)(D)
59 (A)(B)(C)(D)
60 (A)(B)(C)(D)
61 (A)(B)(C)(D)
62 (A)(B)(C)(D)
63 (A)(B)(C)(D)
64 (A)(B)(C)(D)
65 (A)(B)(C)(D)

PART C

66 (A)(B)(C)(D)
67 (A)(B)(C)(D)
68 (A)(B)(C)(D)
69 (A)(B)(C)(D)
70 (A)(B)(C)(D)

PART D

71 (A)(B)(C)(D)
72 (A)(B)(C)(D)
73 (A)(B)(C)(D)
74 (A)(B)(C)(D)
75 (A)(B)(C)(D)
76 (A)(B)(C)(D)
77 (A)(B)(C)(D)
78 (A)(B)(C)(D)
79 (A)(B)(C)(D)
80 (A)(B)(C)(D)
81 (A)(B)(C)(D)
82 (A)(B)(C)(D)
83 (A)(B)(C)(D)
84 (A)(B)(C)(D)
85 (A)(B)(C)(D)

Answer Sheet: Test 6

PART A

1 Ⓐ Ⓑ Ⓒ Ⓓ
2 Ⓐ Ⓑ Ⓒ Ⓓ
3 Ⓐ Ⓑ Ⓒ Ⓓ
4 Ⓐ Ⓑ Ⓒ Ⓓ
5 Ⓐ Ⓑ Ⓒ Ⓓ
6 Ⓐ Ⓑ Ⓒ Ⓓ
7 Ⓐ Ⓑ Ⓒ Ⓓ
8 Ⓐ Ⓑ Ⓒ Ⓓ
9 Ⓐ Ⓑ Ⓒ Ⓓ
10 Ⓐ Ⓑ Ⓒ Ⓓ
11 Ⓐ Ⓑ Ⓒ Ⓓ
12 Ⓐ Ⓑ Ⓒ Ⓓ
13 Ⓐ Ⓑ Ⓒ Ⓓ
14 Ⓐ Ⓑ Ⓒ Ⓓ
15 Ⓐ Ⓑ Ⓒ Ⓓ
16 Ⓐ Ⓑ Ⓒ Ⓓ
17 Ⓐ Ⓑ Ⓒ Ⓓ
18 Ⓐ Ⓑ Ⓒ Ⓓ
19 Ⓐ Ⓑ Ⓒ Ⓓ
20 Ⓐ Ⓑ Ⓒ Ⓓ
21 Ⓐ Ⓑ Ⓒ Ⓓ
22 Ⓐ Ⓑ Ⓒ Ⓓ
23 Ⓐ Ⓑ Ⓒ Ⓓ
24 Ⓐ Ⓑ Ⓒ Ⓓ
25 Ⓐ Ⓑ Ⓒ Ⓓ
26 Ⓐ Ⓑ Ⓒ Ⓓ
27 Ⓐ Ⓑ Ⓒ Ⓓ
28 Ⓐ Ⓑ Ⓒ Ⓓ
29 Ⓐ Ⓑ Ⓒ Ⓓ
30 Ⓐ Ⓑ Ⓒ Ⓓ
31 Ⓐ Ⓑ Ⓒ Ⓓ

PART B

32 Ⓐ Ⓑ Ⓒ Ⓓ
33 Ⓐ Ⓑ Ⓒ Ⓓ
34 Ⓐ Ⓑ Ⓒ Ⓓ
35 Ⓐ Ⓑ Ⓒ Ⓓ
36 Ⓐ Ⓑ Ⓒ Ⓓ
37 Ⓐ Ⓑ Ⓒ Ⓓ
38 Ⓐ Ⓑ Ⓒ Ⓓ
39 Ⓐ Ⓑ Ⓒ Ⓓ
40 Ⓐ Ⓑ Ⓒ Ⓓ
41 Ⓐ Ⓑ Ⓒ Ⓓ
42 Ⓐ Ⓑ Ⓒ Ⓓ
43 Ⓐ Ⓑ Ⓒ Ⓓ
44 Ⓐ Ⓑ Ⓒ Ⓓ
45 Ⓐ Ⓑ Ⓒ Ⓓ
46 Ⓐ Ⓑ Ⓒ Ⓓ
47 Ⓐ Ⓑ Ⓒ Ⓓ
48 Ⓐ Ⓑ Ⓒ Ⓓ
49 Ⓐ Ⓑ Ⓒ Ⓓ
50 Ⓐ Ⓑ Ⓒ Ⓓ
51 Ⓐ Ⓑ Ⓒ Ⓓ
52 Ⓐ Ⓑ Ⓒ Ⓓ
53 Ⓐ Ⓑ Ⓒ Ⓓ
54 Ⓐ Ⓑ Ⓒ Ⓓ
55 Ⓐ Ⓑ Ⓒ Ⓓ
56 Ⓐ Ⓑ Ⓒ Ⓓ
57 Ⓐ Ⓑ Ⓒ Ⓓ
58 Ⓐ Ⓑ Ⓒ Ⓓ
59 Ⓐ Ⓑ Ⓒ Ⓓ
60 Ⓐ Ⓑ Ⓒ Ⓓ
61 Ⓐ Ⓑ Ⓒ Ⓓ
62 Ⓐ Ⓑ Ⓒ Ⓓ
63 Ⓐ Ⓑ Ⓒ Ⓓ
64 Ⓐ Ⓑ Ⓒ Ⓓ
65 Ⓐ Ⓑ Ⓒ Ⓓ

PART C

66 Ⓐ Ⓑ Ⓒ Ⓓ
67 Ⓐ Ⓑ Ⓒ Ⓓ
68 Ⓐ Ⓑ Ⓒ Ⓓ
69 Ⓐ Ⓑ Ⓒ Ⓓ
70 Ⓐ Ⓑ Ⓒ Ⓓ

PART D

71 Ⓐ Ⓑ Ⓒ Ⓓ
72 Ⓐ Ⓑ Ⓒ Ⓓ
73 Ⓐ Ⓑ Ⓒ Ⓓ
74 Ⓐ Ⓑ Ⓒ Ⓓ
75 Ⓐ Ⓑ Ⓒ Ⓓ
76 Ⓐ Ⓑ Ⓒ Ⓓ
77 Ⓐ Ⓑ Ⓒ Ⓓ
78 Ⓐ Ⓑ Ⓒ Ⓓ
79 Ⓐ Ⓑ Ⓒ Ⓓ
80 Ⓐ Ⓑ Ⓒ Ⓓ
81 Ⓐ Ⓑ Ⓒ Ⓓ
82 Ⓐ Ⓑ Ⓒ Ⓓ
83 Ⓐ Ⓑ Ⓒ Ⓓ
84 Ⓐ Ⓑ Ⓒ Ⓓ
85 Ⓐ Ⓑ Ⓒ Ⓓ

Answer Sheet: Test 7

PART A

1 Ⓐ Ⓑ Ⓒ Ⓓ
2 Ⓐ Ⓑ Ⓒ Ⓓ
3 Ⓐ Ⓑ Ⓒ Ⓓ
4 Ⓐ Ⓑ Ⓒ Ⓓ
5 Ⓐ Ⓑ Ⓒ Ⓓ
6 Ⓐ Ⓑ Ⓒ Ⓓ
7 Ⓐ Ⓑ Ⓒ Ⓓ
8 Ⓐ Ⓑ Ⓒ Ⓓ
9 Ⓐ Ⓑ Ⓒ Ⓓ
10 Ⓐ Ⓑ Ⓒ Ⓓ
11 Ⓐ Ⓑ Ⓒ Ⓓ
12 Ⓐ Ⓑ Ⓒ Ⓓ
13 Ⓐ Ⓑ Ⓒ Ⓓ
14 Ⓐ Ⓑ Ⓒ Ⓓ
15 Ⓐ Ⓑ Ⓒ Ⓓ
16 Ⓐ Ⓑ Ⓒ Ⓓ
17 Ⓐ Ⓑ Ⓒ Ⓓ
18 Ⓐ Ⓑ Ⓒ Ⓓ
19 Ⓐ Ⓑ Ⓒ Ⓓ
20 Ⓐ Ⓑ Ⓒ Ⓓ
21 Ⓐ Ⓑ Ⓒ Ⓓ
22 Ⓐ Ⓑ Ⓒ Ⓓ
23 Ⓐ Ⓑ Ⓒ Ⓓ
24 Ⓐ Ⓑ Ⓒ Ⓓ
25 Ⓐ Ⓑ Ⓒ Ⓓ
26 Ⓐ Ⓑ Ⓒ Ⓓ
27 Ⓐ Ⓑ Ⓒ Ⓓ
28 Ⓐ Ⓑ Ⓒ Ⓓ
29 Ⓐ Ⓑ Ⓒ Ⓓ
30 Ⓐ Ⓑ Ⓒ Ⓓ
31 Ⓐ Ⓑ Ⓒ Ⓓ

PART B

32 Ⓐ Ⓑ Ⓒ Ⓓ
33 Ⓐ Ⓑ Ⓒ Ⓓ
34 Ⓐ Ⓑ Ⓒ Ⓓ
35 Ⓐ Ⓑ Ⓒ Ⓓ
36 Ⓐ Ⓑ Ⓒ Ⓓ
37 Ⓐ Ⓑ Ⓒ Ⓓ
38 Ⓐ Ⓑ Ⓒ Ⓓ
39 Ⓐ Ⓑ Ⓒ Ⓓ
40 Ⓐ Ⓑ Ⓒ Ⓓ
41 Ⓐ Ⓑ Ⓒ Ⓓ
42 Ⓐ Ⓑ Ⓒ Ⓓ
43 Ⓐ Ⓑ Ⓒ Ⓓ
44 Ⓐ Ⓑ Ⓒ Ⓓ
45 Ⓐ Ⓑ Ⓒ Ⓓ
46 Ⓐ Ⓑ Ⓒ Ⓓ
47 Ⓐ Ⓑ Ⓒ Ⓓ
48 Ⓐ Ⓑ Ⓒ Ⓓ
49 Ⓐ Ⓑ Ⓒ Ⓓ
50 Ⓐ Ⓑ Ⓒ Ⓓ
51 Ⓐ Ⓑ Ⓒ Ⓓ
52 Ⓐ Ⓑ Ⓒ Ⓓ
53 Ⓐ Ⓑ Ⓒ Ⓓ
54 Ⓐ Ⓑ Ⓒ Ⓓ
55 Ⓐ Ⓑ Ⓒ Ⓓ
56 Ⓐ Ⓑ Ⓒ Ⓓ
57 Ⓐ Ⓑ Ⓒ Ⓓ
58 Ⓐ Ⓑ Ⓒ Ⓓ
59 Ⓐ Ⓑ Ⓒ Ⓓ
60 Ⓐ Ⓑ Ⓒ Ⓓ
61 Ⓐ Ⓑ Ⓒ Ⓓ
62 Ⓐ Ⓑ Ⓒ Ⓓ
63 Ⓐ Ⓑ Ⓒ Ⓓ
64 Ⓐ Ⓑ Ⓒ Ⓓ
65 Ⓐ Ⓑ Ⓒ Ⓓ

PART C

66 Ⓐ Ⓑ Ⓒ Ⓓ
67 Ⓐ Ⓑ Ⓒ Ⓓ
68 Ⓐ Ⓑ Ⓒ Ⓓ
69 Ⓐ Ⓑ Ⓒ Ⓓ
70 Ⓐ Ⓑ Ⓒ Ⓓ

PART D

71 Ⓐ Ⓑ Ⓒ Ⓓ
72 Ⓐ Ⓑ Ⓒ Ⓓ
73 Ⓐ Ⓑ Ⓒ Ⓓ
74 Ⓐ Ⓑ Ⓒ Ⓓ
75 Ⓐ Ⓑ Ⓒ Ⓓ
76 Ⓐ Ⓑ Ⓒ Ⓓ
77 Ⓐ Ⓑ Ⓒ Ⓓ
78 Ⓐ Ⓑ Ⓒ Ⓓ
79 Ⓐ Ⓑ Ⓒ Ⓓ
80 Ⓐ Ⓑ Ⓒ Ⓓ
81 Ⓐ Ⓑ Ⓒ Ⓓ
82 Ⓐ Ⓑ Ⓒ Ⓓ
83 Ⓐ Ⓑ Ⓒ Ⓓ
84 Ⓐ Ⓑ Ⓒ Ⓓ
85 Ⓐ Ⓑ Ⓒ Ⓓ

Answer Sheet: Test 8

PART A

1 Ⓐ Ⓑ Ⓒ Ⓓ
2 Ⓐ Ⓑ Ⓒ Ⓓ
3 Ⓐ Ⓑ Ⓒ Ⓓ
4 Ⓐ Ⓑ Ⓒ Ⓓ
5 Ⓐ Ⓑ Ⓒ Ⓓ
6 Ⓐ Ⓑ Ⓒ Ⓓ
7 Ⓐ Ⓑ Ⓒ Ⓓ
8 Ⓐ Ⓑ Ⓒ Ⓓ
9 Ⓐ Ⓑ Ⓒ Ⓓ
10 Ⓐ Ⓑ Ⓒ Ⓓ
11 Ⓐ Ⓑ Ⓒ Ⓓ
12 Ⓐ Ⓑ Ⓒ Ⓓ
13 Ⓐ Ⓑ Ⓒ Ⓓ
14 Ⓐ Ⓑ Ⓒ Ⓓ
15 Ⓐ Ⓑ Ⓒ Ⓓ
16 Ⓐ Ⓑ Ⓒ Ⓓ
17 Ⓐ Ⓑ Ⓒ Ⓓ
18 Ⓐ Ⓑ Ⓒ Ⓓ
19 Ⓐ Ⓑ Ⓒ Ⓓ
20 Ⓐ Ⓑ Ⓒ Ⓓ
21 Ⓐ Ⓑ Ⓒ Ⓓ
22 Ⓐ Ⓑ Ⓒ Ⓓ
23 Ⓐ Ⓑ Ⓒ Ⓓ
24 Ⓐ Ⓑ Ⓒ Ⓓ
25 Ⓐ Ⓑ Ⓒ Ⓓ
26 Ⓐ Ⓑ Ⓒ Ⓓ
27 Ⓐ Ⓑ Ⓒ Ⓓ
28 Ⓐ Ⓑ Ⓒ Ⓓ
29 Ⓐ Ⓑ Ⓒ Ⓓ
30 Ⓐ Ⓑ Ⓒ Ⓓ
31 Ⓐ Ⓑ Ⓒ Ⓓ

PART B

32 Ⓐ Ⓑ Ⓒ Ⓓ
33 Ⓐ Ⓑ Ⓒ Ⓓ
34 Ⓐ Ⓑ Ⓒ Ⓓ
35 Ⓐ Ⓑ Ⓒ Ⓓ
36 Ⓐ Ⓑ Ⓒ Ⓓ
37 Ⓐ Ⓑ Ⓒ Ⓓ
38 Ⓐ Ⓑ Ⓒ Ⓓ
39 Ⓐ Ⓑ Ⓒ Ⓓ
40 Ⓐ Ⓑ Ⓒ Ⓓ
41 Ⓐ Ⓑ Ⓒ Ⓓ
42 Ⓐ Ⓑ Ⓒ Ⓓ
43 Ⓐ Ⓑ Ⓒ Ⓓ
44 Ⓐ Ⓑ Ⓒ Ⓓ
45 Ⓐ Ⓑ Ⓒ Ⓓ
46 Ⓐ Ⓑ Ⓒ Ⓓ
47 Ⓐ Ⓑ Ⓒ Ⓓ
48 Ⓐ Ⓑ Ⓒ Ⓓ
49 Ⓐ Ⓑ Ⓒ Ⓓ
50 Ⓐ Ⓑ Ⓒ Ⓓ
51 Ⓐ Ⓑ Ⓒ Ⓓ
52 Ⓐ Ⓑ Ⓒ Ⓓ
53 Ⓐ Ⓑ Ⓒ Ⓓ
54 Ⓐ Ⓑ Ⓒ Ⓓ
55 Ⓐ Ⓑ Ⓒ Ⓓ
56 Ⓐ Ⓑ Ⓒ Ⓓ
57 Ⓐ Ⓑ Ⓒ Ⓓ
58 Ⓐ Ⓑ Ⓒ Ⓓ
59 Ⓐ Ⓑ Ⓒ Ⓓ
60 Ⓐ Ⓑ Ⓒ Ⓓ
61 Ⓐ Ⓑ Ⓒ Ⓓ
62 Ⓐ Ⓑ Ⓒ Ⓓ
63 Ⓐ Ⓑ Ⓒ Ⓓ
64 Ⓐ Ⓑ Ⓒ Ⓓ
65 Ⓐ Ⓑ Ⓒ Ⓓ

PART C

66 Ⓐ Ⓑ Ⓒ Ⓓ
67 Ⓐ Ⓑ Ⓒ Ⓓ
68 Ⓐ Ⓑ Ⓒ Ⓓ
69 Ⓐ Ⓑ Ⓒ Ⓓ
70 Ⓐ Ⓑ Ⓒ Ⓓ

PART D

71 Ⓐ Ⓑ Ⓒ Ⓓ
72 Ⓐ Ⓑ Ⓒ Ⓓ
73 Ⓐ Ⓑ Ⓒ Ⓓ
74 Ⓐ Ⓑ Ⓒ Ⓓ
75 Ⓐ Ⓑ Ⓒ Ⓓ
76 Ⓐ Ⓑ Ⓒ Ⓓ
77 Ⓐ Ⓑ Ⓒ Ⓓ
78 Ⓐ Ⓑ Ⓒ Ⓓ
79 Ⓐ Ⓑ Ⓒ Ⓓ
80 Ⓐ Ⓑ Ⓒ Ⓓ
81 Ⓐ Ⓑ Ⓒ Ⓓ
82 Ⓐ Ⓑ Ⓒ Ⓓ
83 Ⓐ Ⓑ Ⓒ Ⓓ
84 Ⓐ Ⓑ Ⓒ Ⓓ
85 Ⓐ Ⓑ Ⓒ Ⓓ

Answer Sheet: Test 9

PART A

1 Ⓐ Ⓑ Ⓒ Ⓓ
2 Ⓐ Ⓑ Ⓒ Ⓓ
3 Ⓐ Ⓑ Ⓒ Ⓓ
4 Ⓐ Ⓑ Ⓒ Ⓓ
5 Ⓐ Ⓑ Ⓒ Ⓓ
6 Ⓐ Ⓑ Ⓒ Ⓓ
7 Ⓐ Ⓑ Ⓒ Ⓓ
8 Ⓐ Ⓑ Ⓒ Ⓓ
9 Ⓐ Ⓑ Ⓒ Ⓓ
10 Ⓐ Ⓑ Ⓒ Ⓓ
11 Ⓐ Ⓑ Ⓒ Ⓓ
12 Ⓐ Ⓑ Ⓒ Ⓓ
13 Ⓐ Ⓑ Ⓒ Ⓓ
14 Ⓐ Ⓑ Ⓒ Ⓓ
15 Ⓐ Ⓑ Ⓒ Ⓓ
16 Ⓐ Ⓑ Ⓒ Ⓓ
17 Ⓐ Ⓑ Ⓒ Ⓓ
18 Ⓐ Ⓑ Ⓒ Ⓓ
19 Ⓐ Ⓑ Ⓒ Ⓓ
20 Ⓐ Ⓑ Ⓒ Ⓓ
21 Ⓐ Ⓑ Ⓒ Ⓓ
22 Ⓐ Ⓑ Ⓒ Ⓓ
23 Ⓐ Ⓑ Ⓒ Ⓓ
24 Ⓐ Ⓑ Ⓒ Ⓓ
25 Ⓐ Ⓑ Ⓒ Ⓓ
26 Ⓐ Ⓑ Ⓒ Ⓓ
27 Ⓐ Ⓑ Ⓒ Ⓓ
28 Ⓐ Ⓑ Ⓒ Ⓓ
29 Ⓐ Ⓑ Ⓒ Ⓓ
30 Ⓐ Ⓑ Ⓒ Ⓓ
31 Ⓐ Ⓑ Ⓒ Ⓓ

PART B

32 Ⓐ Ⓑ Ⓒ Ⓓ
33 Ⓐ Ⓑ Ⓒ Ⓓ
34 Ⓐ Ⓑ Ⓒ Ⓓ
35 Ⓐ Ⓑ Ⓒ Ⓓ
36 Ⓐ Ⓑ Ⓒ Ⓓ
37 Ⓐ Ⓑ Ⓒ Ⓓ
38 Ⓐ Ⓑ Ⓒ Ⓓ
39 Ⓐ Ⓑ Ⓒ Ⓓ
40 Ⓐ Ⓑ Ⓒ Ⓓ
41 Ⓐ Ⓑ Ⓒ Ⓓ
42 Ⓐ Ⓑ Ⓒ Ⓓ
43 Ⓐ Ⓑ Ⓒ Ⓓ
44 Ⓐ Ⓑ Ⓒ Ⓓ
45 Ⓐ Ⓑ Ⓒ Ⓓ
46 Ⓐ Ⓑ Ⓒ Ⓓ
47 Ⓐ Ⓑ Ⓒ Ⓓ
48 Ⓐ Ⓑ Ⓒ Ⓓ
49 Ⓐ Ⓑ Ⓒ Ⓓ
50 Ⓐ Ⓑ Ⓒ Ⓓ
51 Ⓐ Ⓑ Ⓒ Ⓓ
52 Ⓐ Ⓑ Ⓒ Ⓓ
53 Ⓐ Ⓑ Ⓒ Ⓓ
54 Ⓐ Ⓑ Ⓒ Ⓓ
55 Ⓐ Ⓑ Ⓒ Ⓓ
56 Ⓐ Ⓑ Ⓒ Ⓓ
57 Ⓐ Ⓑ Ⓒ Ⓓ
58 Ⓐ Ⓑ Ⓒ Ⓓ
59 Ⓐ Ⓑ Ⓒ Ⓓ
60 Ⓐ Ⓑ Ⓒ Ⓓ
61 Ⓐ Ⓑ Ⓒ Ⓓ
62 Ⓐ Ⓑ Ⓒ Ⓓ
63 Ⓐ Ⓑ Ⓒ Ⓓ
64 Ⓐ Ⓑ Ⓒ Ⓓ
65 Ⓐ Ⓑ Ⓒ Ⓓ

PART C

66 Ⓐ Ⓑ Ⓒ Ⓓ
67 Ⓐ Ⓑ Ⓒ Ⓓ
68 Ⓐ Ⓑ Ⓒ Ⓓ
69 Ⓐ Ⓑ Ⓒ Ⓓ
70 Ⓐ Ⓑ Ⓒ Ⓓ

PART D

71 Ⓐ Ⓑ Ⓒ Ⓓ
72 Ⓐ Ⓑ Ⓒ Ⓓ
73 Ⓐ Ⓑ Ⓒ Ⓓ
74 Ⓐ Ⓑ Ⓒ Ⓓ
75 Ⓐ Ⓑ Ⓒ Ⓓ
76 Ⓐ Ⓑ Ⓒ Ⓓ
77 Ⓐ Ⓑ Ⓒ Ⓓ
78 Ⓐ Ⓑ Ⓒ Ⓓ
79 Ⓐ Ⓑ Ⓒ Ⓓ
80 Ⓐ Ⓑ Ⓒ Ⓓ
81 Ⓐ Ⓑ Ⓒ Ⓓ
82 Ⓐ Ⓑ Ⓒ Ⓓ
83 Ⓐ Ⓑ Ⓒ Ⓓ
84 Ⓐ Ⓑ Ⓒ Ⓓ
85 Ⓐ Ⓑ Ⓒ Ⓓ

EXTRA READING COMPREHENSION PASSAGES

PART

Directions: *The following passages are for reading comprehension. After each selection there are incomplete statements or questions. Of the four choices, choose the correct one based on the passage.*

Para la gente de la industriosa ciudad de Barcelona, el trabajo intenso es lo más vital, pero siempre hay tiempo para el arte y la fe. La prueba de esto es la extraordinaria Iglesia de la Sagrada Familia, cuya construcción ha cumplido un siglo este año y que todavía no está totalmente terminada.

Fue en el siglo pasado que se colocó la primera piedra: el 19 de marzo de 1882, es decir, en la festividad de San José. En la ceremonia, participó Don José María Bocabella, promotor de la obra. Bocabella le había encargado al arquitecto, Francisco del Villar, el proyecto de construir una iglesia de estilo gótico. Pero diferencias de opinión con Martorell, ayudante de Bocabella, hicieron que Villar renunciara el puesto. Para sustituirlo, se nombró a un arquitecto de 32 años: Antonio Gaudí.

Cuando Gaudí se encargó del proyecto, todavía no se había terminado gran parte de la construcción. Sin dudarlo un instante, Gaudí abandonó el proyecto de Villar, y diseñó algo totalmente nuevo: doce campanarios de base cuadrada y de forma larga y delgada.

Para el hombre de la calle, para el barcelonés, la Iglesia de la Sagrada Familia es algo que ha visto crecer, día a día, como parte sustancial de su pasado, de su presente y —¿por qué no?— de su futuro, en una Barcelona muy viva y progresiva.

1. ¿Cómo son los de Barcelona?
   A. Son trabajadores.
   B. Son pasivos.
   C. Son extraños.
   D. Son saludables.

2. ¿Qué sabemos de la Iglesia de la Sagrada Familia?
   A. Está al lado de una fábrica.
   B. Es una copia de otra iglesia.
   C. Es de estilo tradicional.
   D. Se está construyendo todavía.

3. ¿Cuándo empezaron a construirla?
   A. hace 32 años
   B. hace más de 100 años
   C. el año pasado
   D. este año

4. ¿Por qué dejó el empleo Francisco del Villar?
   A. Aceptó otro cargo.
   B. Quería mucho más dinero.
   C. Hubo problemas con Martorell.
   D. Tuvo que salir de Barcelona.

5. ¿Qué hizo Antonio Gaudí al aceptar el trabajo?
   A. Cambió el nombre de la iglesia.
   B. Participó en la ceremonia de inauguración.
   C. Colocó la primera piedra.
   D. Produjo un estilo distinto.

La corrida de toros sigue siendo la fiesta brava de España. Este espectáculo ha extendido su popularidad incluyendo varias repúblicas hispanoamericanas. Pero, el fútbol, con todo su dinamismo, es también una fiesta. Este deporte popular despierta gran entusiasmo en las cincuenta provincias españolas, desde Almería hasta Zamora.

No nos sorprende que *La Fiesta* sea el título del cartel oficial del Campeonato Mundial de Fútbol, del artista catalán, Joan Miró. El genial pintor nos comunica su personalísima visión del fútbol con la presentación de tres elementos básicos: el jugador, la pelota y el espectador. Joan Miró usa colores alegres e intensos para darnos la idea de la efervescencia colectiva del público.

Se ha dicho que el cartel de Miró sugiere la idea de un "ballet." Hay una estética interesante en el colorido de los uniformes y en los movimientos rudos y agresivos de los futbolistas. Esta competencia está cargada de energía. Aunque existen grandes diferencias entre este deporte y el baile clásico, sin embargo, se parecen en muchos aspectos.

Los carteles que anuncian las corridas de toros se han convertido en objetos decorativos. Nos encanta verlos, no sólo en las plazas de toros, sino en aeropuertos, restaurantes, hoteles y hasta en residencias particulares. Lo mismo ocurrirá con los carteles de este Campeonato Mundial. Mucho después de la conclusión de este magno evento deportivo del Mundial, estos carteles seguirán viéndose por todas partes. Son una elocuente afirmación de los horizontes diversos a los que pueden aspirar el espíritu humano.

Asistir a un encuentro deportivo como éste, tiene, para la persona integral, el mismo valor espiritual que admirar una obra de arte: una sinfonía de Beethoven, un cuadro de Picasso, o un cuento de Borges. En estos carteles, la emoción del deporte y los valores estéticos se dan la mano, aproximándose en un expresivo simbolismo.

6. ¿Qué se sabe del fútbol en España?
   A. Las entradas son caras.
   B. La gente no se interesa en él.
   C. Atrae a muchas personas.
   D. Es un deporte nuevo.

7. ¿Quién diseñó el cartel oficial del Mundial de Fútbol?
   A. Joan Miró
   B. un matador famoso
   C. el señor Zamora
   D. un bailador del flamenco

8. ¿Cómo es el cartel?
   A. Es de aspecto triste.
   B. Es de tres colores.
   C. Es extraño.
   D. Es muy festivo.

9. En el cartel el artista compara el fútbol a
   A. una corrida
   B. un baile
   C. una tormenta
   D. un desfile

10. ¿Qué intentan hacer con los carteles después del Campeonato Mundial?
    A. Los exhibirán en muchos sitios.
    B. Los enviarán al extranjero.
    C. Los destruirán.
    D. Los usarán en las escuelas.

El entusiasmo juvenil que comenzó con el grupo inglés Los Beatles en los años 60, está ocurriendo otra vez en los 80 con el grupo Menudo, de Puerto Rico. Este quinteto está causando un frenético delirio entre los jóvenes del mundo hispano con sólo mencionar el nombre. Pero a diferencia de los británicos, el grupo de Puerto Rico es más cariñoso y simpático.

Menudo surgió en el mundo del espectáculo en 1978, organizado por Edgardo Díaz, quien seleccionó a cinco jóvenes de talento y personalidad. El reglamento, puesto en vigor desde el principio, dice que todo miembro de Menudo debe tener menos de 15 años. Por eso, cuando alcanza esta edad, tiene que abandonar automáticamente el quinteto.

El grupo ha grabado ya 14 discos y ha ganado dos discos de oro. Venezuela ha sido uno de los mercados más lucrativos para Menudo. Los venezolanos han demostrado su preferencia por los chiquitos puertorriqueños, gastando más de $3,000,000 en discos.

En 1981, los Menudo filmaron un documental en Venezuela que se estrenó con éxito a fines del año en Nueva York. Ahora se filma en Puerto Rico "Una aventura llamada Menudo", una película dirigida por Orestes Trucco. "Una aventura llamada Menudo", con la primera actriz puertorriqueña, Gladys Rodríguez, es una mezcla de originalidad y ternura. En la película, el grupo canta muchas canciones populares como "Te imaginas", "Coquí", "Lluvia", y "A volar."

Hay clubs de admiradores en distintas regiones de las Américas, especialmente en los Estados Unidos donde hay más de cien, con bases en Los Angeles, Miami, Nueva York y Chicago. Cada vez que llegan a un aeropuerto los jóvenes de Menudo, hay tantos aficionados esperándolos que la policía necesita personal extra para mantener el órden.

11. Según el escritor de este artículo, ¿en qué consiste la diferencia entre Los Beatles y Menudo?
    A. Los Menudo son más amables.
    B. Los Beatles tienen más aficionados jóvenes.
    C. Los Menudo dieron más conciertos internacionales.
    D. Los Beatles hicieron más documentales.

12. ¿Cuándo empezó a cantar Menudo?
    A. el año pasado
    B. durante los años 70
    C. hace tres años
    D. antes de 1960

13. Cuando Edgardo Díaz organizó el grupo, él decidió que cada miembro
    A. debe hacer películas cada año
    B. tiene que ser de Venezuela
    C. tiene que participar en clubs de aficionados
    D. debe dejar el grupo al cumplir cierta edad

14. Los Menudo han ganado más dinero en
    A. Inglaterra
    B. Venezuela
    C. Puerto Rico
    D. Estados Unidos

15. Además de dar conciertos, los Menudo
    A. han cantado con Los Beatles
    B. han ayudado a los pobres
    C. han hecho unas películas
    D. han ido a Inglaterra

Alberto Salazar nació en Cuba. A la edad de dos años su familia vino a los Estados Unidos. Después de educarse en Boston, fue a vivir al estado de Oregón. Nunca ha dejado de trabajar para una de las aspiraciones más difíciles y más sacrificadas de un ser humano: establecer marcas mundiales en las carreras de maratón. Salazar representa, sin duda, un modelo de la dedicación total del atletismo mundial.

En 1980, llegó el primero en el Maratón de Nueva York. Al año siguiente repitió la hazaña, esa vez rompiendo marcas mundiales y estableciendo nuevos récords dentro de esa dura y difícil disciplina deportiva.

Salazar ha declarado que es cubano-americano, y que no podría escoger entre los dos países. Fue educado en una familia cubana dentro de un ambiente puramente norteamericano. Parece cubano, pero habla con acento estadounidense. El dice que corre porque es algo que le gusta mucho.

Alberto comprende que nadie es feliz dedicándose a actividades que no le gusten aunque gane mucho dinero. Su vida está en las carreras y todo lo que está relacionado con ellas, pero sus principales placeres provienen de su familia. Su esposa y su hijo han contribuido tanto a darle esa maravillosa sensación de bienestar absoluto que hoy siente.

Un día de rutina en la vida de Salazar empieza a las ocho y media de la mañana. Al levantarse comienza los entrenamientos con los ejercicios preliminares y después corre unos quince kilómetros. Al terminar esta serie de prácticas, Salazar está listo para tomar un gran desayuno.

En cambio, el día del evento no practica ni come mucho. Bebe algo, se baña y le pide a Dios que le ayude. Durante el evento, Salazar trata de escuchar bien las demandas de su cuerpo y su concentración. Se olvida totalmente de todo lo que está fuera de él. No piensa en ganar; sólo piensa en correr lo mejor posible.

16. ¿Qué le interesa más a Salazar?
    A. establecer nuevos récords
    B. luchar por los cubanos
    C. fundar escuelas para atletas
    D. escribir de su vida

17. Salazar es famoso porque
    A. se escapó de Cuba
    B. jugó al béisbol en Boston
    C. se ha sacrificado mucho por su país
    D. ha ganado competencias de maratón

18. ¿Por qué corre Salazar?
    A. Necesita mejorar su salud.
    B. Gana mucho dinero.
    C. Le satisface como individuo.
    D. Le gustaría recibir una beca.

19. ¿De dónde viene la felicidad mayor de Salazar?
    A. de su origen cubano
    B. de los miembros de su familia
    C. de saber que es una persona admirada de todos
    D. de haber vivido en Oregón

20. ¿Cuándo come Salazar un gran desayuno?
    A. antes de ir a la iglesia
    B. los días de entrenamiento
    C. cuando asiste a clases
    D. el día del evento

Un joven campesino de Santander, Severiano Ballesteros, famoso por todo el mundo como golfista, pasa los días cavando, plantando árboles o buscando semillas para sembrar. Ballesteros es tan popular que cuando camina por las calles de las grandes capitales del mundo, toda la gente lo reconoce. Su popularidad es comparable a la de los más famosos actores del cine. Cuando el joven santanderino sale de su pueblo, siempre se encuentra con periodistas. Es un favorito de la "jet society." Severiano ha jugado al golf varias veces con los actores Sean Connery, Christopher Lee, Telly Savalas y Bob Hope, con los astronautas Shepherd y Armstrong, y con el ex-presidente Gerald Ford. Aunque no ha estudiado en la universidad, se siente cómodo entre estas personas. A la edad de veinticinco años, ya tiene tanta fama y tanto dinero como ellos.

Seve, como lo llaman sus amigos, está considerado como una de las figuras más grandes que España ha dado al golf mundial. A pesar de que ha triunfado tanto y ha tenido éxito, todavía desea sobrepasar algunos récords en el mundo del golf. Por ejemplo quiere ganar el "Open" de Italia, Irlanda, Portugal, e Inglaterra. Estos son los cuatro récords que le faltan para ganar todos los "Open" de todos los países de Europa, cosa que no ha hecho ningún jugador. El torneo más grande y el más prestigioso es el "Open" Británico. Es el más antiguo, el de mayor tradición, el que abre las puertas a los jugadores de todo el mundo. Para Seve, el ganar estos campeonatos será más fácil que para los otros golfistas porque él es muy joven todavía.

En su pueblo nativo hay muchos vecinos que no pueden explicar cómo el joven, un modesto campesino, se haya hecho tan importante en tan poco tiempo. Según Severiano, es porque empezó de muy joven a jugar y ha tenido suerte. El añade que los miembros de su familia le han ayudado muchísimo. Es un hombre que cree en el deporte como expresión fundamental de la persona.

21. Además de ser golfista, Severiano Ballesteros es
   A. actor
   B. profesor
   C. campesino
   D. periodista

22. ¿Por qué se siente cómodo entre gente famosa?
   A. porque va al teatro a menudo
   B. porque tiene una educación universitaria
   C. porque es actor de cine
   D. porque es célebre

23. Según este artículo, ¿qué quiere Severiano?
   A. riquezas
   B. triunfos
   C. hijos
   D. amistades

24. ¿En qué país tiene lugar el torneo más importante?
   A. Inglaterra
   B. Italia
   C. Portugal
   D. España

25. Al hablar de Seve la gente del pueblo piensa en
   A. que se casará pronto
   B. cómo ha tenido tanto éxito
   C. dónde va a vivir
   D. qué hará con su tierra

UNA ENTREVISTA CON UN TORERO

Desde muy pequeño, el joven portugués, Víctor Mendes, quería ser torero. Acompañaba a su padre a las corridas de toros en Villa Francia, ciudad de Portugal donde vivían. Esta ciudad se conoce como la Sevilla portuguesa, porque tiene una tradición taurina muy importante.

Actualmente, Mendes está en Colombia practicando con maestros del toreo. La semana pasada cumplió 26 años y los celebró en una hacienda donde Mendes participó en una corrida de toros.

Entonces el reportero le preguntó:

— ¿Siente Ud. nostalgia? ¿Extraña Ud. a su familia? ¿Se siente Ud. solo?

— Algunas veces sí, Mendes dijo. — En este mundo de los toros la juventud se va rápidamente. El dedicarse completamente a esta profesión significa muchos sacrificios. La vida normal de un chico de 23 o 24 años es salir con chicas o ir de vez en cuando a una discoteca. Pero para el torero solamente existe el toro. Todavía soy muy joven y estoy haciendo planes para el futuro.

Víctor Mendes es un joven inteligente, culto y educado. Tenía mucho interés en la ley y por eso estudió varios años de abogacía, estudios que abandonó por su pasión a los toros. Habla francés, inglés, español y, claro, portugués. También le gusta mucho la poesía.

El reportero continuó la entrevista: — ¿Ha tocado el amor a su puerta?

— No, soy romántico, pero todavía no he encontrado a la mujer ideal. Sé que el amor es el sentimiento más bello que hay en el mundo; también es de gran importancia tener una familia. En este momento, sólo pienso en los toros, y algún día tendré una familia tan maravillosa como la de mis padres.

— ¿Y qué le pide a la vida?

— Para mí, el dinero no es lo más importante. La salud y el triunfo están en primer lugar.

— A propósito, ¿cuánto gana Ud. por corrida?

— Eso depende de la plaza de toros y la popularidad del torero. En general los honorarios van de uno a dos milliones de pesetas. Cuando me retire quiero una finca con caballos, pero sin toros.

26. ¿Cuándo empezó a interesarse Mendes en los toros?
    A. durante sus viajes a Francia
    B. durante su niñez
    C. a los veintiséis años
    D. cuando fue a Colombia

27. ¿Qué es lo más importante hoy día en la vida de Mendes?
    A. su interés en casarse
    B. su relación con su esposa
    C. su responsabilidad académica
    D. su dedicación al toreo

28. ¿Para qué carrera estaba preparándose Mendes?
    A. para abogado
    B. para lingüista
    C. para poeta
    D. para profesor

29. ¿Qué quiere Mendes de la vida?
    A. éxito en su profesión
    B. riquezas para su familia
    C. aprender mucho
    D. estar solo

30. ¿Qué piensa hacer Mendes cuando sea viejo?
    A. viajar por el mundo
    B. tener muchos toros
    C. comprar una hacienda
    D. enseñar a los toreros

Hay muchos que creen que los niños son la esperanza del futuro. Muchos adultos preguntan cómo pueden ayudar a los niños a llegar a su madurez con satisfacción y felicidad, aprendiendo a la vez como es la vida. Hoy día hay muchos factores que los afectan. Con el cambio diario de la familia y la influencia de la televisión, es difícil predecir su futuro.

Es cierto que el niño representa la inocencia, la simplicidad y la ternura, pero en la mayoría de los casos, los adultos no piensan así. Muchos creen que el niño es un adulto en miniatura. Por años, sociólogos, sicólogos y profesores de educación han discutido los efectos de dos grandes influencias: la herencia genética y el ambiente. Unos afirman que al nacer, el niño trae con él unas características que no cambian y que lo hacen único. Otros dicen que la sociedad, la familia y el lugar en que uno vive, moldea al individuo. En este debate frecuentemente olvidan que el niño es como una grabadora, una pequeña máquina que reproduce todo lo que ve y oye. De esta manera el niño aprende, pero, ¿qué aprende? Evidentemente absorbe lo que los adultos le enseñan. Así las personas mayores deben preguntarse si dan la guía y la dirección que los niños necesitan para enfrentar el futuro.

El pequeño debe ser responsable de sus acciones, debe amar la vida y debe tratar de conseguir lo que desea, de modo que comprenda poco a poco la realidad en que vive. Para lograr esto, el niño necesita padres que lo traten con amor, comprensión, disciplina, y sin violencia. El niño necesita padres que compartan con él sus ideas, sus deseos y sus sueños, sin olvidar que, aunque es un niño, es un miembro de la familia también. De ese modo, cuando el pequeño sea mayor, podrá enfrentar el futuro con seguridad, honestidad y amor.

31. ¿Qué le preocupa al autor de este artículo?
A. el futuro de los niños del mundo
B. la economía mundial
C. los pobres del mundo
D. la violencia en el mundo

32. Según el artículo, ¿qué piensan muchas personas de los niños?
A. Creen que los niños no estudian mucho.
B. Creen que los niños son muy violentos.
C. Creen que los niños no respetan a sus padres.
D. Creen que los niños son como las personas adultas.

33. Según el artículo, ¿cómo aprenden los niños?
A. leyendo mucho
B. imitando a sus padres
C. jugando con sus amigos
D. participando en deportes

34. Según el autor, ¿qué necesitan los niños?
A. Necesitan estar preparados para el futuro.
B. Necesitan trabajar muy fuerte.
C. Necesitan jugar con muchos juguetes.
D. Necesitan hacer nuevas amistades.

35. Para el bienestar de los niños, se recomienda
A. tratarles como adultos
B. llevarles a la escuela
C. reconocerlos como parte íntegra de la familia
D. darles muchos regalos

Diez y seis jóvenes gimnastas se preparan para el XII Campeonato Mundial que se celebra en Valladolid, España, del 10 al 13 de octubre. La vida es dura y las horas son largas para estas deportistas adolescentes que participarán en el Campeonato. La rutina está llena de ejercicios, sudor y lágrimas. Las chicas llevan más de tres meses preparándose para esta competencia.

El equipo español está compuesto por 16 chicas que tienen entre catorce y veinte años de edad, tres entrenadoras, un coreógrafo, un pianista y un psicólogo. Las gimnastas principales son Marta Cantón y Marta Bobo. Ellas son las más veteranas del equipo, y participaron en la Olimpiada de Los Angeles. Las menores del equipo se llaman Nuria Salido y Estela Martín, y las mayores son Graciela Yanes y Virginia Manzanera.

Las gimnastas no son como las demás chicas de su edad. Es difícil explicar como pueden tener tanto entusiasmo y a la vez soportar tantas dificultades: la separación de la familia y de los amigos, los duros entrenamientos, la presión de los estudios, y, además, la necesidad de sacar buenas notas.

En los días de entrenamiento las muchachas se levantan a las ocho de la mañana. Todos los días suelen comer tres platos ligeros como espárragos, pollo a la parrilla, consomé y alguna fruta. Ellas no pueden comer mucho porque pueden perder su agilidad y su bienestar.

La rutina diaria comienza a las nueve de la mañana y continúa hasta la una. Después, vuelven a las cuatro y media de la tarde y se quedan hasta las nueve y media de la noche. Cuando ha terminado la jornada, o sea, el día, cenan un poco y se acuestan temprano.

Según Emilia Boneva y Ana Roncero, dos de las entrenadoras del equipo, convivir con las gimnastas no es difícil porque son jóvenes, alegres y muy responsables. La señorita Boneva está segura de que ganarán el primer premio. Las jóvenes están sometidas a una rutina de perfeccionamiento, y por eso, repiten los ejercicios una y otra vez. Lo más importante es que cada una haga lo mejor que pueda, y que se sienta satisfecha de haber pasado tanto sacrificio.

36. ¿Cuáles son las gimnastas que tienen más experiencia?
   A. Estela Martín y Graciela Yanes
   B. Nuria Salido y Virginia Manzanera
   C. Marta Cantón y Marta Bobo
   D. Emilia Boneva y Ana Roncero

37. Estas deportistas españolas tienen
   A. horarios difíciles y rígidos
   B. vidas similares a las de otras chicas
   C. tiempo libre para divertirse
   D. apartamentos cómodos para vivir

38. ¿Cuál es un problema que tienen estas jóvenes?
   A. el costo alto del equipo moderno
   B. la ausencia de familiares y amigos
   C. la falta de interés del público
   D. la falta de maestros bien preparados

39. Según el artículo, para mantenerse ágiles, las chicas tienen que
   A. caminar unos kilómetros
   B. levantar pesas
   C. nadar cada día
   D. limitar lo que comen

40. Las entrenadoras creen que el equipo va a ganar la competencia porque las gimnastas
   A. leen libros técnicos de su deporte
   B. hablan con las otras gimnastas
   C. descansan un rato después de cada rutina
   D. practican las rutinas constantemente

Hay dos millones de puertorriqueños que residen en los Estados Unidos. Más de un millón y medio de ellos están en Nueva York. El 80% habita en la parte sur del Bronx. Es por esta razón que el grupo teatral puertorriqueño, Pregones, decidió establecerse allí, en medio de una comunidad hispana, para tener contactos con su propia cultura.

Este grupo empezó en junio de 1979 cuando tres actores puertorriqueños, Luis Menéndez, Rosalba Rolón y David Crommett, se reunieron para expresar sus raíces culturales y explicar cómo la experiencia norteamericana estaba afectando a la comunidad puertorriqueña. Pregones es una compañía que andaba de Puerto Rico a Nueva York como un teatro ambulante. Ahora el teatro se desarrolla en su propia sala, el antiguo gimnasio de la iglesia episcopal de Santa Ana en Nueva York.

Roberto Morales, ex-jugador de baloncesto en Puerto Rico y reverendo de esta iglesia, le ofreció el uso del gimnasio al grupo teatral para sus presentaciones. Poco a poco, y gracias a las donaciones de la comunidad, el gimnasio fue transformándose, y el 5 de diciembre del año pasado la transformación fue completa. Ese día Pregones estrenó *Migrantes* que es una obra bilingüe con música. Es una historieta de las dificultades que los inmigrantes puertorriqueños encontraron al llegar a los Estados Unidos durante las décadas de los 20 y de los 30.

Hay puertorriqueños en Nueva York que no hablan inglés; sin embargo, algunos de sus hijos y nietos no hablan español. Por ese motivo las obras de Pregones son bilingües. Hay escenas totalmente en español, algunas totalmente en inglés, y otras en los dos idiomas. Para que sea accesible a todos, Pregones utiliza unas técnicas teatrales destinadas a que el mensaje llegue a ambas audiencias. Por ejemplo, en algunas escenas uno de los actores canta en español, mientras otro habla en inglés.

41. ¿Por qué decidió Pregones situarse en medio de la comunidad hispana?
  A. para pagar menos impuestos
  B. para entrenar a los jugadores de baloncesto
  C. para dar clases de religión
  D. para poder comunicarse más con la gente

42. ¿Por qué se unieron los tres actores?
  A. para charlar de los contrastes culturales
  B. para hablar sobre la política
  C. para estudiar juntos
  D. para escuchar cintas de música española

43. ¿Qué hizo el señor Morales?
  A. Actuó en una obra de Pregones.
  B. Dio un lugar para producir las obras.
  C. Tradujo obras del inglés al español.
  D. Escribió obras acerca de los puertorriqueños.

44. ¿De quién recibió ayuda el grupo?
  A. del alcalde de Nueva York
  B. de una universidad del Bronx
  C. del gobernador de Puerto Rico
  D. de la comunidad puertorriqueña

45. ¿Cuál es el tema de la obra *Migrantes*?
  A. cómo ganar dinero
  B. las experiencias en una universidad
  C. los problemas que se presentan en otra cultura
  D. cómo disfrutar de amigos nuevos

The nine reading comprehension passages that you just tackled in the above section are of the traditional type that normally appears on SAT II: Spanish.

In this part there is a new type of reading comprehension passage. These passages are offered here so you can have more practice.

Directions: *There are five blank spaces in each of the following passages. Each blank space represents a missing word or expression in Spanish. For each blank space, four possible completions are provided lettered A, B, C, D. Only one of them makes sense in the context of the passage. First, read the passage in its entirety to determine its general meaning. Then read it a second time. For each blank space, choose the completion that makes the best sense and blacken the corresponding space on the Answer Sheet on page 197.*

Eran exactamente las 8:27 de la noche en la ciudad de Buenos Aires del 26 de julio de 1952, cuando el locutor de la Radio Nacional interrumpió el programa con una voz emocionante y dijo: "La Subsecretaría de Información y Prensa tiene el triste deber de anunciar que hoy, a las 8:25 de la noche dejó de existir Eva Perón, Jefa Espiritual de la Nación."

Se anunció aquella noticia por la comunidad, la ciudad, el país, hasta el _ _ _ _ _ _ entero, con una

46. A. mundo
B. territorio
C. vecindario
D. barrio

rapidez increíble. Treinta minutos después, miles de los "descamisados" que Eva había defendido en vida

se congregaban frente a la Casa Rosada; no podían creer que ella había _ _ _ _ _ _ .

47. A. huido
B. llegado
C. muerto
D. perdido

Hoy, 33 años después, Tim Rice y Andrew Lloyd Webber la han resucitado, colocándola en el corazón del teatro de Broadway. Eva Duarte de Perón luchó toda su vida, primero como actriz, después como la esposa del Presidente de la República, Juan Domingo Perón, y más tarde como Evita, la diosa de los pobres de Argentina.

Muchos dicen que era natural que una ópera basada sobre la vida de Evita tuviera tanto éxito, sobre todo una escrita por dos autores respetados. Eso en sí, es una garantía para cualquier empresario, público o compañía teatral.

Algunos opinan que la obra tiene gran mérito, mientras otros opinan lo _ _ _ _ _ _ . En lo que

48. A. mismo
B. contrario
C. corriente
D. conveniente

todos están de acuerdo, es que el personaje de Eva Perón es _ _ _ _ _ _ .

49. A. aburrido
B. fascinante
C. ordinario
D. antipático

"No me cabe ninguna duda," dice Patti Lupone, quien representaba al personaje central de la obra, "que, de punto de vista de actriz, Evita es un personaje difícil de interpretar, no sólo porque es real, es histórico y aún vive en el recuerdo de muchas personas, sino por su importancia política y social."
En Broadway no entienden cómo es posible que un personaje tan controvertido e históricamente

desconocido, ganara el interés de los amantes del _ _ _ _ _ _ norteamericano; antes de la primera

50. A. gobierno
B. país
C. cuento
D. teatro

presentación del espectáculo, habían vendido entradas por valor de dos millones de dólares.

A muchas personas les encanta viajar. El turismo ha aumentado enormemente durante las últimas dos décadas.

Según las estadísticas del Ministerio de Información y Turismo, el mejoramiento económico de muchas personas ha producido un turista contemporáneo que viaja al exterior con mucha frecuencia.

Abundan en la tierra lugares de interés para el turista. En casi todos _ _ _ _ _ _ del mundo vemos

51. A. los países
B. los edificios
C. los mares
D. los bosques

paisajes de exótica belleza natural, montañas, playas, ciudades pintorescas y capitales modernas. Encontramos monumentos y huellas históricas de civilizaciones anteriores. Además, podemos observar costumbres singulares, fiestas, danzas, música típica y una gran variedad de atracciones populares. Algo

de esto _ _ _ _ _ _ en todas partes. Sin embargo, los turistas prefieren ir a unos sitios y a otros no.

52. A. se juega
B. se compra
C. se encuentra
D. se fabrica

Europa es el continente de mayor volumen turístico desde hace muchos años. A principios de este siglo los únicos que podían viajar eran los aristócratas y otras gentes ricas que no

necesitaban _ _ _ _ _ _ .

53. A. estudiar
B. trabajar
C. manejar
D. enseñar

Para ser turista durante las primeras décadas de este siglo, se necesitaba mucho dinero y mucho

tiempo porque los medios de transporte eran pocos y muy _ _ _ _ _ _ . Por ejemplo, un viaje que

54. A. cómodos
B. lentos
C. pintorescos
D. divertidos

actualmente puede durar cinco horas en automóvil, podía tardar dos semanas a caballo.

En los últimos veinte años las características de _ _ _ _ _ _ han cambiado radicalmente. Hoy en día,

55. A. los nadadores
B. los estudiantes
C. los escritores
D. los viajeros

los turistas se componen de millones de personas de todas las clases sociales, desde el trabajador hasta el millonario.

El tenor madrileño, Plácido Domingo, ha obtenido en Viena un éxito fantástico en la ópera. Después de cantar "La Bohème", de Puccini, tuvo que salir para _ _ _ _ _ _ a la gente ochenta veces. Los

56. A. despertar
B. consolar
C. saludar
D. imitar

aplausos duraron exactamente una hora y cuarto, lo que demuestra la popularidad que ha alcanzado Plácido Domingo en los últimos años.

Plácido Domingo tiene tres hijos, José, el mayor, Plácido y Alvaro. Su hijo Plácido

es _ _ _ _ _ _ ; escribió una de las canciones de su nuevo álbum titulada "There Will Be Love."

57. A. pintor
B. compositor
C. bailarín
D. periodista

La compañía discográfica le ha preparado al tenor una cena para darle dos medallas de oro por

haber vendido los primeros 50,000 ejemplares de sus _ _ _ _ _ _ "Perhaps Love" y "Canciones

58. A. revistas
B. libros
C. pinturas
D. discos

mexicanas". También ha grabado un álbum, "Bésame mucho", con temas de la vida. No faltan en su producción musical algunas composiciones escritas por Henry Mancini y por su propio hijo.

Plácido, tenor de voz maravillosa, tiene la gran suerte de hacer lo que más le gusta, que

es _ _ _ _ _ _ , y de ser rico gracias a ello. Cuando terminó la XX temporada de la Opera de Madrid,

59. A. cantar
B. bailar
C. escribir
D. viajar

Plácido marchó a la ciudad de Ronda para filmar la ópera "Carmen". A él le gusta mucho

esta _ _ _ _ _ _ , y piensa que resultó mejor que la producción cinematográfica de "La Traviata".

60. A. canción
B. película
C. novela
D. ciudad

Cuando estaba escribiendo sus memorias siempre se reía cuando alguien le preguntaba cómo podía escribir sus memorias aún tan joven. El respondía que tenía mucho que narrar. El título de su libro es "Mis primeros cuarenta años."

Alvaro Sauna, niño madrileño de doce años, quería una computadora personal, pero no tenía bastante dinero. Necesitaba un préstamo; solicitó un crédito bancario para _ _ _ _ _ _ una computadora y

61. A. vender
B. encontrar
C. comprar
D. construir

ofreció, como garantía, el dinero que recibe de su familia cada semana. El Banco de Bilbao en Madrid, por primera vez en su historia, ofreció _ _ _ _ _ _ a una persona no adulta.

62. A. información
B. crédito
C. regalos
D. premios

Alvaro inició el negocio por medio de una carta al director general del banco en la que decía: "Le _ _ _ _ _ _ porque tengo un problema económico. Tengo muchos deseos de comprar una

63. A. contesto
B. cobro
C. escribo
D. llamo

computadora que cuesta 39.000 pesetas, pero sólo _ _ _ _ _ _ 7.000 pesetas. Mi padre no me puede

64. A. pierdo
B. gasto
C. miro
D. tengo

ayudar económicamente, y por eso, recurro a sus servicios.

Mi padre me da 60 pesetas semanales, y mi abuelo 100. Si ustedes me prestan lo que necesito, yo podré pagar 640 pesetas al mes."

El banco le dio _ _ _ _ _ _ que necesitaba, y le fijó la cantidad de 500 pesetas al mes para la

65. A. el dinero
B. el libro
C. la carta
D. la publicidad

restitución del crédito.

"Querido Felipe,

Quiero decirte, Príncipe de Asturias, que no te preocupes, que cuando seas Rey de España no tendrás complicaciones porque nosotros, que formaremos entonces el pueblo de España, no te daremos ningún problema." Esto es lo que Rocío Alonso Vallín, de diez años de edad, le ha escrito al Príncipe Felipe, hijo del Rey Juan Carlos, para felicitarle por las Navidades.

Rocío es una de las 55.000 niñas y niños asturianos que han enviado postales dibujadas y escritas por ellos mismos al Palacio de la Zarzuela donde vive el Príncipe.

Muchas de las _ _ _ _ _ son peticiones para sus escuelas y para sus pueblos. Miguel Fernández

> **66.** A. canciones
> B. revistas
> C. cuentas
> D. cartas

Rico le pide, por favor, que cuando vaya a Asturias visite el colegio de San Miguel. Le dice, "El comedor de nuestro colegio es muy pequeño. ¿Podrías ordenar que lo hicieran

más _ _ _ _ _ ?"

> **67.** A. grande
> B. bello
> C. limpio
> D. simple

El mismo problema expone Elena, que le invita a comer en su colegio, pero se lamenta que no podría hacerlo con todos a la vez, "pues no hay suficientes _ _ _ _ _ _ y por eso tenemos que comer

> **68.** A. mesas
> B. libros
> C. estudiantes
> D. discos

en dos turnos. Si tú supieras de alguien que pudiera conseguirlas nos alegraríamos mucho." Otro chico pide una clínica para su colegio, "porque el _ _ _ _ _ _ tiene su consulta en un rincón de la

> **69.** A. abogado
> B. profesor
> C. médico
> D. director

iglesia."

Susana Fernández Pérez le dice, "Príncipe, en mi casa hay un problema. Mi madre hace mucho tiempo que está mala, y mi padre está sin trabajo. No tenemos seguro y mi padre, mi madre, mi hermano y yo vivimos de las chapuzas que hace mi padre por las casas del barrio. El dinero sólo nos alcanza para comer; no nos da para más. Mi ropa me la hace mi madre. A mi madre a veces le dan unas congestiones muy grandes y le duele la cabeza. A lo mejor a ti no te interesa lo que te cuento, pero una señora me dijo que si teníamos algún problema te lo podríamos contar y tú nos ayudarías."

Las postales han sido escritas por _ _ _ _ _ _ de todos los colegios de Asturias. Estos 55.000 niños

> **70.** A. padres
> B. niños
> C. jefes
> D. artistas

que han hecho llegar al Príncipe sus sentimientos, esperan ahora la tarjeta navideña con la que el Príncipe, como ya hizo en años anteriores, les contestará.

Cada familia tiene su broma particular. En la mía, es que mi padre no entiende cómo me gano la vida.

Mi padre era carnicero. Mi abuelo y mis tíos eran carniceros también. Mi madre era la cajera de la carnicería y trabajaba con mi padre.

Los hermanos de mi madre también hacían este _ _ _ _ _ _ . Al nacer yo, mi madre dijo que yo

71. A. gasto
B. trabajo
C. viaje
D. juego

podría ser lo que yo quisiera, menos carnicero.

Durante mi niñez, me pasaba la vida _ _ _ _ _ _ . Por eso mi madre resolvió que estudiaría en la

72. A. dibujando
B. cocinando
C. escribiendo
D. leyendo

escuela de arte. Yo viajaba hora y media de mi casa a la Escuela Secundaria de Música y Artes, que estaba situada al otro extremo de la ciudad. Mi padre siempre me presentaba a sus clientes como "mi

hijo el _ _ _ _ _ _ ." Al mismo tiempo que yo asistía a la escuela secundaria, trabajaba cada sábado en

73. A. contador
B. zapatero
C. periodista
D. artista

el negocio de mi padre. Cuando le anuncié que me había ganado una beca de mucho dinero para la

escuela de arte de la universidad, y que yo deseaba continuar con mis _ _ _ _ _ _ , él se quedó

74. A. vacaciones
B. exámenes
C. estudios
D. novelas

sorprendido.

Mi padre me reafirmó que la gente se gana la vida siendo tenderos, zapateros y sobre todo, carniceros. Al fin y al cabo, la gente tiene que comer. Según él, los artistas se mueren de hambre.

Habría sido inútil explicarle que no sería yo pintor de cuadros, sino dibujante comercial. El no lo entendía. Para él un artista era un artista, y los artistas se morían de hambre.

Diez años después, mi padre vendió su carnicería y se retiró. Durante esa época yo era un director de diseño de la revista *LIFE*. Me había casado y tenía dos hijos. Yo acababa de mudarme a mi propia

casa situada en los suburbios. Cuando mi _ _ _ _ _ _ vino a visitarme en mi nueva residencia, yo le

75. A. jefe
B. padre
C. profesor
D. amigo

noté en la cara una expresión de perplejidad. El no entendía que un artista pudiera lograr ganarse la vida de esa manera. Yo sabía que él estaba muy orgulloso de su hijo, "el artista que dibujaba para la revista *LIFE*".

La última solución en la lucha contra los ladrones de las grandes tiendas es "Biónica." Es rubia, alta y atractiva. Cambia de ropa según la estación del año. Una sonrisa constante se le ve en los labios. En realidad, "Biónica" es un maniquí-biónico equipado con una cámara de televisión escondida dentro del cuerpo.

A primera vista, "Biónica" parece _ _ _ _ _ _ como cualquier otro y por eso, tiene tanto éxito. Nadie

76. A. un cuadro
B. un espejo
C. un vestido
D. un maniquí

sospecha que ella está equipada con sofisticado equipo basado en investigaciones de la NASA en los Estados Unidos. El mecanismo de "Biónica" se compone de una cámara de televisión y un micrófono que transmiten imágenes y sonidos por control remoto. Siempre hay un detective cerca

para _ _ _ _ _ _ a los ladrones.

77. A. entretener
B. ocultar
C. atrapar
D. invitar

El creador de este maniquí-biónico es Darrel Larson. El era ingeniero de la NASA y ahora es director de una compañía que fabrica alarmas para proteger a los negocios. Esta es la compañía más

importante de equipos _ _ _ _ _ _ en Gran Bretaña.

78. A. de seguridad
B. de transporte
C. médicos
D. agrícolas

El señor Larson dice que el sistema funciona con una batería recargable de doce voltios. Los lentes de la cámara son tan pequeños como la cabeza de un alfiler y se mueven en un ángulo de cincuenta grados.

La gran ventaja de este sistema, es que es posible _ _ _ _ _ _ en cualquier parte del cuerpo del

79. A. comprarlo
B. ponerlo
C. pintarlo
D. romperlo

maniquí y cubrirlo con ropa. Por eso podemos _ _ _ _ _ _ fotos a través de sus ojos, oídos y boca.

80. A. perder
B. dibujar
C. destruir
D. sacar

Por supuesto, ya se está diseñando una versión masculina de esta sensacional espía electrónica.

Su buena amiga se va a casar y Ud. quiere darle una fiesta porque la aprecia y la quiere. No hay mejor manera de compartir la felicidad de la enamorada que _ _ _ _ _ _ una fiesta de despedida de

81. A. estudiar
B. ofrecer
C. olvidar
D. perder

soltera. La fiesta de despedida de soltera es una reunión de las amigas íntimas de la novia antes de la boda. ¿Cómo se planea una fiesta tan importante?

Al principio, seleccione Ud. el día para evitar problemas con los planes de la novia y de las amigas. Esta _ _ _ _ _ _ debe ser aproximadamente un mes antes de la boda. Después de escogerla haga la

82. A. escuela
B. estrella
C. fecha
D. tempestad

lista de las _ _ _ _ _ _ que van a participar en el evento. Esto depende, por supuesto, del tipo de fiesta

83. A. invitadas
B. fotografías
C. cartas
D. monedas

que se va a organizar. Si la fiesta va a incluir a mucha gente, será más conveniente tener una cena en un restaurante.

Así, divida Ud. el trabajo entre algunas amigas para que todo resulte más fácil. Una amiga se puede encargar de la decoración; otra puede encargarse de mandar _ _ _ _ _ _ a las amistades, y también

84. A. la ropa
B. las revistas
C. la música
D. las invitaciones

recoger el dinero para los gastos. Otra amiga puede seleccionar el menú para la cena. De esta manera se elimina la confusión de última hora en el restaurante cuando tiene que pagar.

Si las amigas deciden hacer un regalo colectivo, deben ponerse de acuerdo en el tipo de regalo que se le va a dar a la _ _ _ _ _ _ . Este regalo es de gran importancia y podría ser algo como un juego de

85. A. prima
B. novia
C. abuela
D. maestra

maletas o de té de porcelana fina, o un televisor, etc.

El día del evento todos sus esfuerzos se verán recompensados al poder sentir la satisfacción de ver a su amiga llena de alegría por todo lo que Ud. ha hecho.

LA ANTOLOGIA DE LA ZARZUELA

La presencia del arte español se ha extendido por los Estados Unidos, transportada a Madison Square Garden, por la gran presentación de la "Antología de la Zarzuela". Esta obra teatral ha recorrido con gran éxito las principales ciudades estadounidenses.

Es la primera vez que España ha presentado un _ _ _ _ _ _ como éste, lleno de lujo, calidad y arte,

86. A. espectáculo
B. libro
C. periódico
D. premio

en los Estados Unidos. La Zarzuela es un tipo de obra teatral muy española que tuvo su origen en el siglo XVII. "La Antología de la Zarzuela", creada y puesta en escena por el famoso productor y director, José Tamayo, explica muy bien la vida y las costumbres de España. La Zarzuela es todo a la vez: música, comedia, drama, baile.

Los cien artistas que actúan en la compañía fueron encabezados por el primer tenor del mundo,

Plácido Domingo. El público en Madison Square Garden quedó _ _ _ _ _ _ con la grandeza artística de

87. A. enojado
B. humillado
C. impresionado
D. disgustado

esta obra.

Plácido Domingo fue excepcionalmente aclamado al terminar la función. De los miles de espectadores en el Madison Square Garden, se puede calcular que la mayoría era norteamericana y que no entendía español. Probablemente, jamás había visto una zarzuela. Sin embargo,

el _ _ _ _ _ _

88. A. ejército
B. público
C. bailarín
D. campeón

reaccionó emocionalmente a cada escena. La reacción se puede considerar como un testimonio de aprobación al espíritu alegre, de los bailes, de las canciones y de la música de la Zarzuela.

Plácido Domingo fue la figura sobresaliente, unánimamente bien recibido. Esto nos sugiere que este

tenor recibe los _ _ _ _ _ _ del público no sólo en las óperas, sino también en las obras más cercanas

89. A. pasajes
B. periódicos
C. golpes
D. aplausos

al sentimiento del pueblo español, como la Zarzuela. Don Plácido ha manifestado su deseo de presentar zarzuelas en todos los Estados Unidos. Se puede pensar que el gran éxito que tuvo en Madison Square Garden es una indicación de que "La Antología de la Zarzuela" sería bien recibida en todos los lugares donde se presentaría al público hispano. También sería bien aceptada por todas las

personas que no hablan español, pero que sí saben _ _ _ _ _ _ lo bueno en el mundo de

90. A. imitar
B. apreciar
C. describir
D. ignorar

entretenimiento.

Your skill in reading comprehension can be tested in a third type of selection. The first was the traditional type of passage that normally appears on SAT II: Spanish. The second was sentence completion of high-frequency vocabulary and idiomatic expressions, as in the above section that you just tackled for practice and experience. A third way of testing your skill in reading comprehension is the use of authentic documents, which may or may not contain illustrations, usually found in newspapers and magazines, brochures, pamphlets, announcements, or advertisements.

Here are a few to give you more practice and experience.

Directions: *Under each of the following ten selections, there is one question or incomplete statement. For each, choose the word or expression that best answers the question or completes the statement, according to the meaning of the selection, and blacken the corresponding space on the Answer Sheet on page 197.*

91.

Universidad Regiomontana

Difusión Cultural

Presenta:

La Mordaza

UNA OBRA DE
ALFONSO SASTRE

Teatro Nova

VIERNES 10-9:00 pm
SABADO 11-9:00 pm
DOMINGO 12-5:00 y
8:00 pm

91. ¿Qué profesión tiene Alfonso Sastre?
 A. Escribe obras teatrales.
 B. Es un cirujano eminente.
 C. Dibuja para los periódicos.
 D. Es director de la Universidad Regiomontana.

92.

Solicitamos los servicios de una Señorita Mecanógrafa, mayor de 21 años, de carácter dinámico, buena presentación, sin problemas de horario, para ocupar puesto de recepción.

Interesadas presentarse en De La Llave Nte. 1271, de 14:30 a 17:30 horas. Atención C.P. Octavio Mendoza.

92. ¿Para quién es este anuncio?
 A. una camarera
 B. una secretaria
 C. una actriz
 D. una enfermera

93.

<u>PERDIDO</u>

GRATIFICACIÓN: 50.000 PESOS

PERRITO DE 6 MESES, PEQUEÑO;

  CON UNA MANCHA

BLANCA EN EL PECHO, color café:

RAZA: Pastor Alemán.

DAR INFORMES: Diego Redo

Teléfono: 29 18 31

93. ¿Qué se anuncia aquí?
A. Se da un café especial.
B. Se ofrece un empleo.
C. Se ofrece un viaje a Alemania.
D. Se busca un perro desaparecido.

94.

94. ¿Qué oportunidad se presenta aquí?
A. un empleo como secretaria en una oficina
B. un empleo como vendedor de periódicos
C. un empleo como obrero en una fábrica
D. un empleo como periodista

95.

LA MEJOR OFERTA DEL VERANO

Un GRAN CRUCERO en un GRAN BUQUE

Permítanos llevarle a bordo de nuestro transatlántico, un mundo en sí mismo y un auténtico espectáculo para los ojos.

El **"IVAN FRANKO"** es un gran buque que desplaza 20.000 Tm. y que con 350 miembros de tripulación para 700 pasajeros, ofrece en sus 12 puentes un esmerado servicio del que podremos disfrutar a lo largo de un maravilloso crucero de 8 inolvidables días.

95. ¿Quiénes tienen más interés en este anuncio?
  A. los equipos de natación
  B. los historiadores del Atlántico
  C. los que van a la playa
  D. los que viajan por mar

96.

IGUALDAD DE OPORTUNIDADES EN VIVIENDAS

Conducimos Nuestros Negocios de Acuerdo con la Ley Federal de Viviendas Equitativas

(Título VIII De La Ley De Derechos Civiles de 1968 según enmendado por el Acto Nacional de Vivienda de 1974)

ES ILEGAL EL DISCRIMINAR CONTRA CUALQUIER PERSONA POR RAZÓN DE SU RAZA, COLOR, RELIGIÓN, SEXO, O SU ORIGEN NACIONAL

- En la venta o alquiler de viviendas o solares residenciales
- En anuncios para la venta o alquiler de viviendas
- En el financiamiento de viviendas
- En la provisión de servicios de agentes de bienes raíces

96. ¿Para qué sirve este anuncio?
  A. para vender casas
  B. para ofrecer préstamos
  C. para proteger los derechos humanos
  D. para alquilar viviendas

97.

Café El Pico,® con todo nuestro rico sabor latino, en su nueva super-bolsa con botón mágico: conserva el aroma y sabor natural del café tostado. Por eso es #1 en frescura.

97. En este anuncio se le ofrece al consumidor
    A. un precio reducido
    B. una receta nueva
    C. un paquete nuevo
    D. una muestra gratis

98.

TRANSPORTE TERRESTRE
TRANSPORTACION DE SU DOMICILIO AL AEROPUERTO
A CUALQUIER HORA DEL DIA O DE LA NOCHE
S E R V I C I O   A U T O R I Z A D O

LLAMENOS DE 8:00 A.M. A 21:00 HRS. AL

TEL. 571-93-44

98. Este servicio es de gran interés para personas que
    A. quieren vivir en el campo
    B. van a viajar
    C. van de compras
    D. quieren llamar a la policía

99.

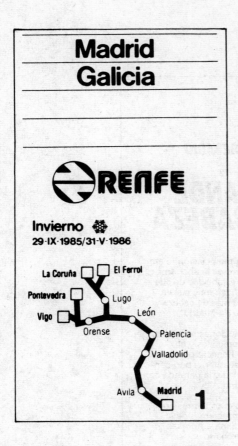

Madrid
Galicia

RENFE

Invierno ❄
29·IX·1985/31·V·1986

La Coruña — El Ferrol
Pontevedra
Lugo
Vigo
León
Orense
Palencia
Valladolid
Avila — **Madrid** **1**

TARJETA JOVEN 🚶 50%
Para jóvenes mayores de 12 años y que no hayan cumplido los 26, RENFE pone a su disposición la Tarjeta Joven.

Esta Tarjeta, cuyo precio es de 2.000 pesetas, se puede adquirir, exhibiendo el D.N.I. o pasaporte, en las estaciones y Oficinas Viajes de RENFE o en cualquiera Agencia de Viajes autorizada para su venta. Presentándola para adquirir los billetes se disfruta de las siguientes ventajas:

— 50% de reducción sobre los precios de Tarifa General (se abonan los suplementos en su totalidad).

— Un billete de litera gratuito, utilizable conjuntamente con un billete adquirido en las condiciones de la Tarjeta.

— Se puede utilizar para todo tipo de trenes y clases, en recorridos superiores a 100 Kms., en viaje sencillo o de 200 Kms. en viaje de ida y vuelta.

99. ¿Para quiénes es esta oferta especial de RENFE?
   A. las personas que tienen ciertas edades
   B. los que están retirados
   C. los recién casados
   D. los empleados de esta compañía

100.

Sr. empresario

No ANDE DE CABEZA

Si la falta de financiación le ata; si los altos intereses le ahogan; si mantener la estabilidad de su empresa se le hace muy cuesta arriba, no ande más de cabeza y venga a la Caja de Madrid.

Tenemos soluciones rentables, consejos muy prácticos y el asesoramiento financiero que usted pueda necesitar. Todo con la profesionalidad y la garantía de la Caja de Madrid.

Ponemos un gran interés en solucionar los problemas de la pequeña y mediana empresa. Venga a comprobarlo.

serviciointegral

CAJA DE MADRID

100. ¿Qué ofrece la Caja de Madrid en este anuncio?
   A. regalos para toda la familia
   B. ayuda financiera
   C. interés por su dinero en una cuenta bancaria
   D. clases especiales

ANSWER KEY

1. A	21. C	41. D	61. C	81. B
2. D	22. D	42. A	62. B	82. C
3. B	23. B	43. B	63. C	83. A
4. C	24. A	44. D	64. D	84. D
5. D	25. B	45. C	65. A	85. B
6. C	26. B	46. A	66. D	86. A
7. A	27. D	47. C	67. A	87. C
8. D	28. A	48. B	68. A	88. B
9. B	29. A	49. B	69. C	89. D
10. A	30. C	50. D	70. B	90. B
11. A	31. A	51. A	71. B	91. A
12. B	32. D	52. C	72. A	92. B
13. D	33. B	53. B	73. D	93. D
14. B	34. A	54. B	74. C	94. B
15. C	35. C	55. D	75. B	95. D
16. A	36. C	56. C	76. D	96. C
17. D	37. A	57. B	77. C	97. C
18. C	38. B	58. D	78. A	98. B
19. B	39. D	59. A	79. B	99. A
20. B	40. D	60. B	80. D	100. B

ANALYSIS CHART

In evaluating your score in the Extra Reading Comprehension passages, use the following table:

95 to 100 correct: *Excellent*
85 to 94 correct: *Very Good*
70 to 84 correct: *Average*
65 to 69 correct: *Below Average*
fewer than 64 correct: *Unsatisfactory*

Answer Sheet: Extra Reading Comprehension Passages

1 Ⓐ Ⓑ Ⓒ Ⓓ
2 Ⓐ Ⓑ Ⓒ Ⓓ
3 Ⓐ Ⓑ Ⓒ Ⓓ
4 Ⓐ Ⓑ Ⓒ Ⓓ
5 Ⓐ Ⓑ Ⓒ Ⓓ
6 Ⓐ Ⓑ Ⓒ Ⓓ
7 Ⓐ Ⓑ Ⓒ Ⓓ
8 Ⓐ Ⓑ Ⓒ Ⓓ
9 Ⓐ Ⓑ Ⓒ Ⓓ
10 Ⓐ Ⓑ Ⓒ Ⓓ
11 Ⓐ Ⓑ Ⓒ Ⓓ
12 Ⓐ Ⓑ Ⓒ Ⓓ
13 Ⓐ Ⓑ Ⓒ Ⓓ
14 Ⓐ Ⓑ Ⓒ Ⓓ
15 Ⓐ Ⓑ Ⓒ Ⓓ
16 Ⓐ Ⓑ Ⓒ Ⓓ
17 Ⓐ Ⓑ Ⓒ Ⓓ
18 Ⓐ Ⓑ Ⓒ Ⓓ
19 Ⓐ Ⓑ Ⓒ Ⓓ
20 Ⓐ Ⓑ Ⓒ Ⓓ
21 Ⓐ Ⓑ Ⓒ Ⓓ
22 Ⓐ Ⓑ Ⓒ Ⓓ
23 Ⓐ Ⓑ Ⓒ Ⓓ
24 Ⓐ Ⓑ Ⓒ Ⓓ
25 Ⓐ Ⓑ Ⓒ Ⓓ
26 Ⓐ Ⓑ Ⓒ Ⓓ
27 Ⓐ Ⓑ Ⓒ Ⓓ
28 Ⓐ Ⓑ Ⓒ Ⓓ
29 Ⓐ Ⓑ Ⓒ Ⓓ
30 Ⓐ Ⓑ Ⓒ Ⓓ
31 Ⓐ Ⓑ Ⓒ Ⓓ
32 Ⓐ Ⓑ Ⓒ Ⓓ
33 Ⓐ Ⓑ Ⓒ Ⓓ
34 Ⓐ Ⓑ Ⓒ Ⓓ

35 Ⓐ Ⓑ Ⓒ Ⓓ
36 Ⓐ Ⓑ Ⓒ Ⓓ
37 Ⓐ Ⓑ Ⓒ Ⓓ
38 Ⓐ Ⓑ Ⓒ Ⓓ
39 Ⓐ Ⓑ Ⓒ Ⓓ
40 Ⓐ Ⓑ Ⓒ Ⓓ
41 Ⓐ Ⓑ Ⓒ Ⓓ
42 Ⓐ Ⓑ Ⓒ Ⓓ
43 Ⓐ Ⓑ Ⓒ Ⓓ
44 Ⓐ Ⓑ Ⓒ Ⓓ
45 Ⓐ Ⓑ Ⓒ Ⓓ
46 Ⓐ Ⓑ Ⓒ Ⓓ
47 Ⓐ Ⓑ Ⓒ Ⓓ
48 Ⓐ Ⓑ Ⓒ Ⓓ
49 Ⓐ Ⓑ Ⓒ Ⓓ
50 Ⓐ Ⓑ Ⓒ Ⓓ
51 Ⓐ Ⓑ Ⓒ Ⓓ
52 Ⓐ Ⓑ Ⓒ Ⓓ
53 Ⓐ Ⓑ Ⓒ Ⓓ
54 Ⓐ Ⓑ Ⓒ Ⓓ
55 Ⓐ Ⓑ Ⓒ Ⓓ
56 Ⓐ Ⓑ Ⓒ Ⓓ
57 Ⓐ Ⓑ Ⓒ Ⓓ
58 Ⓐ Ⓑ Ⓒ Ⓓ
59 Ⓐ Ⓑ Ⓒ Ⓓ
60 Ⓐ Ⓑ Ⓒ Ⓓ
61 Ⓐ Ⓑ Ⓒ Ⓓ
62 Ⓐ Ⓑ Ⓒ Ⓓ
63 Ⓐ Ⓑ Ⓒ Ⓓ
64 Ⓐ Ⓑ Ⓒ Ⓓ
65 Ⓐ Ⓑ Ⓒ Ⓓ
66 Ⓐ Ⓑ Ⓒ Ⓓ
67 Ⓐ Ⓑ Ⓒ Ⓓ

68 Ⓐ Ⓑ Ⓒ Ⓓ
69 Ⓐ Ⓑ Ⓒ Ⓓ
70 Ⓐ Ⓑ Ⓒ Ⓓ
71 Ⓐ Ⓑ Ⓒ Ⓓ
72 Ⓐ Ⓑ Ⓒ Ⓓ
73 Ⓐ Ⓑ Ⓒ Ⓓ
74 Ⓐ Ⓑ Ⓒ Ⓓ
75 Ⓐ Ⓑ Ⓒ Ⓓ
76 Ⓐ Ⓑ Ⓒ Ⓓ
77 Ⓐ Ⓑ Ⓒ Ⓓ
78 Ⓐ Ⓑ Ⓒ Ⓓ
79 Ⓐ Ⓑ Ⓒ Ⓓ
80 Ⓐ Ⓑ Ⓒ Ⓓ
81 Ⓐ Ⓑ Ⓒ Ⓓ
82 Ⓐ Ⓑ Ⓒ Ⓓ
83 Ⓐ Ⓑ Ⓒ Ⓓ
84 Ⓐ Ⓑ Ⓒ Ⓓ
85 Ⓐ Ⓑ Ⓒ Ⓓ
86 Ⓐ Ⓑ Ⓒ Ⓓ
87 Ⓐ Ⓑ Ⓒ Ⓓ
88 Ⓐ Ⓑ Ⓒ Ⓓ
89 Ⓐ Ⓑ Ⓒ Ⓓ
90 Ⓐ Ⓑ Ⓒ Ⓓ
91 Ⓐ Ⓑ Ⓒ Ⓓ
92 Ⓐ Ⓑ Ⓒ Ⓓ
93 Ⓐ Ⓑ Ⓒ Ⓓ
94 Ⓐ Ⓑ Ⓒ Ⓓ
95 Ⓐ Ⓑ Ⓒ Ⓓ
96 Ⓐ Ⓑ Ⓒ Ⓓ
97 Ⓐ Ⓑ Ⓒ Ⓓ
98 Ⓐ Ⓑ Ⓒ Ⓓ
99 Ⓐ Ⓑ Ⓒ Ⓓ
100 Ⓐ Ⓑ Ⓒ Ⓓ

GENERAL REVIEW
PART
IV

In this section, a numerical decimal system has been used with the symbol § in front of it. This was done so that you may find quickly and easily the reference to a particular point in Spanish grammar when you use the General Index. For example, if you look up the entry *adjectives* in the General Index, you will find the reference given as §5., and it is in this section. If you happen to look up the entry *conjunctions, conjunctive locutions, and correlative conjunctions* in the General Index, you will find the reference given as §12., and it is in this General Review section. Sometimes additional § reference numbers are given when the entry you consulted is mentioned in other areas in this General Review section. The General Index also includes some key Spanish words if they are significant, for example **ser** and **estar**, and § references to them are also given.

§ 1. A GUIDE TO PRONOUNCING SPANISH SOUNDS

PURE VOWEL SOUNDS

	Pronounced as in the	
	Spanish word	English word
a	**la**	f*a*ther
e	**le**	l*e*t
i	**ti**	s*ee*
o	**yo**	*o*rder
u	**tu**	t*oo*

OTHER SOUNDS

h	**justo**	
	general }	*h*elp
	gigante	

The letter *h* in a Spanish word is not pronounced.

y	**yo** }	*y*es
	llave	

DIPHTHONGS (2 vowels together)

ai	**baile** }	*eye*
ay	**hay**	
au	**aula**	c*ow*
ei	**reino** }	th*ey*
ey	**ley**	
eu	**Europa**	*wa*yward
ya	**enviar** }	*ya*rd
	ya	
ye	**tiene** }	*ye*s
	yendo	
yo	**iodo** }	*yo*re
	yodo	
yu	**viuda** }	*you*
	yugo	
oi	**oigo** }	t*oy*
oy	**estoy**	
wa	**cuando**	*wa*nt
we	**bueno**	*wa*y
wi	**suizo**	*wee*k
wo	**cuota**	*wo*ke

The pronunciation given in phonetic symbols is that of most Latin American countries and of certain regions in Spain.

CONSONANT SOUNDS

	Pronounced as in the	
	Spanish word	English word
b	**bien** }	*b*oy
	va	
d	**dar**	*th*is
f	**falda**	*f*an
g	**gato** }	*g*ap
	goma	
	gusto	
k	**casa** }	*c*ap
	culpa	
	que	
	quito	
l	**la**	*l*ard
m	**me**	*m*ay
n	**no**	*n*o
ñ	**niño**	ca*ny*on
p	**papá**	*p*apa
r	**pero**	Ap*r*il
rr	**perro**	bu*rr*, g*r-r-r*
s	**sopa** }	*s*oft
	cero	
	cita	
	zumo	
t	**tu**	si*t*
ch	**mucho**	*ch*ur*ch*

TRIPHTHONGS (3 vowels together)

yai	**enviáis**	*yi*pe
yau	**miau**	m*eow*
yei	**enviéis**	*yea*
wai	**guaina** }	*wise*
	Uruguay	
wau	**guau**	*wow*
wei	**continuéis** }	*wai*t
	buey	

The accent mark (ʹ) over a vowel sound indicates that you must raise your voice on that vowel sound.

English words given here contain sounds that only approximate Spanish sounds.

§2. CAPITALIZATION, PUNCTUATION MARKS, AND DIVISION OF WORDS INTO SYLLABLES

§2.1   Generally speaking, do not capitalize days of the week, months of the year, languages, nationalities, and religions:

> **domingo, lunes, martes,** *etc.;* **enero, febrero, marzo,** *etc;* **español, francés, inglés,** *etc.;* **Roberto es español, María es española, Pierre es francés; Elena es católica.**

§2.2   Common punctuation marks in Spanish are as follows:

> **apóstrofo** / apostrophe '
> **comillas** / quotation marks " "
> **paréntesis** / parentheses ( )
> **principio de interrogación** / beginning question mark ¿
> **fin de interrogación** / final question mark ?
> **punto** / period .
> **coma** / comma ,
> **punto y coma** / semicolon ;
> **dos puntos** / colon :
> **puntos suspensivos** / suspension points . . .

§2.3   It is good to know how to divide a word into syllables (not only in Spanish but also in English) because it helps you to pronounce the word correctly and to spell it correctly. The general rules to follow when dividing Spanish words into syllables are:

§2.4   (a) A syllable must contain a vowel.

(b) A syllable may contain only one vowel and no consonant: **e / so (eso).**

(c) If you are dealing with single separate consonants, each consonant remains with the vowel that follows it: **mu / cho (mucho), ca / ba / llo (caballo), pe / ro (pero), pe / rro (perro).** Did you notice that the consonants **ch, ll,** and **rr** are considered as one consonant sound and are not separated?

(d) If you are dealing with two consonants that come together (other than **ch, ll** or **rr** as stated in (c) above), the two consonants are separated; the first remains with the preceding syllable and the second remains with the following syllable when they are split:
her / ma / no (hermano), ter / cer (tercer)
But if the second of the two consonants that come together is **l** or **r,** do not separate them:
ha / blo (hablo), a / pren / do (aprendo), li / bro (libro), a / tlas (atlas)

(e) If you are dealing with three consonants that come together, the first two remain with the preceding vowel and the third consonant remains with the vowel that follows it:
ins / ti / tu / to (instituto)
But if the third of the three consonants is **l** or **r,** do not separate that third consonant from the second; it remains with the second consonant:
com / pren / der (comprender), sas / tre (sastre), sal / dré (saldré)

(f) Two vowels that are together are generally separated if they are strong vowels. The strong vowels are: **a, e, o:**
a / e / ro / pla / no (aeroplano), o / a / sis (oasis), re /a / li / dad (realidad)
But if you are dealing with a weak vowel (**i, u**) it ordinarily remains in the same syllable with its neighboring vowel, especially if that other vowel is a strong vowel:
trein / ta (treinta), ru / bio (rubio), hue / vo (huevo)

(g) The letter **y** is considered to be a consonant when a vowel follows it. Keep it with the vowel that follows it:

a / yer (ayer), a / yu / dar (ayudar)

(h) If a vowel contains a written accent mark, it becomes strong enough (because of the stress required by the accent mark) to remain in its own syllable:

Ma / rí / a (María), re / ú / ne (reúne), dí / a (día)

(i) There are other considerations that must be made regarding syllabification of Spanish words, but those stated above are the basic essential ones that you need to know to help you pronounce and write Spanish words correctly. Of course, on the next SAT II: Spanish that you take you will not be required to pronounce any Spanish words or to write any. If you know something about the syllabification of Spanish words, it will help you become aware of words if you take a closer look at them. The Sat II: Spanish is entirely in Spanish and you are expected to choose the correct answer (multiple choice answers) based on knowledge and recognition.

§3.   NOUNS

§3.1   A noun is a word that refers to a person (**Roberto, Elena, el muchacho, la muchacha**), a thing (**el libro, la pluma**), a place (**la casa, la escuela, el parque**), a quality (**la excelencia, la honra**).

§3.2   In Spanish, a noun is either masculine or feminine. When you learn a noun in Spanish, you must learn it with the article (see §4.ff), for example: **el libro, la pluma; el muchacho, la muchacha; el hombre, la mujer**.

§3.3   A noun that refers to a male person or animal is masculine in gender, naturally: **el hombre, el toro, el tío, el padre**. A noun that refers to a female person or animal is feminine in gender, naturally: **la mujer, la chica, la tía, la vaca, la madre**. This is easy to understand. What is not so easy to understand for us English-speaking persons is that a noun referring to a thing, a place, or a quality also has a gender. You must learn the gender of a noun when you learn the word by using the article with it.

§3.4   Generally speaking, a noun that ends in **o** is masculine: **el libro**.

§3.5   Generally speaking, a noun that ends in **a** is feminine; also a noun that ends in **ción, sión, dad, tad, tud, umbre: la casa, la lección, la ilusión, la ciudad, la dificultad, la nacionalidad, la solicitud, la costumbre**.

§3.6   Generally speaking, a noun that ends in **nte** refers to a person and the gender is masculine or feminine, depending on whether it refers to a male or female person:

el estudiante / la estudiante

§3.7   Generally speaking, it is difficult to tell the gender of a noun that ends in **e**. Some are feminine, some are masculine. You must learn the gender of the noun when you learn the word with the definite or indefinite article.

MASCULINE	FEMININE
el aire / air	**la calle** / street
el arte / art	**la clase** / class
el baile / dance	**la fe** / faith
el bosque / forest	**la fuente** / fountain
el coche / car	**la gente** / people
el parque / park	**la leche** / milk

§3.8 **Irregular gender of nouns**

§3.9 Feminine nouns that end in **o**. Three common ones are:

la mano / hand; **la radio** (**la radio** is the radiotelephonic broadcast that we listen to; **el radio** is the object, the apparatus) / radio; **la foto** / photo (actually, this word is a shortened form of **la fotografía**)

§3.10 Masculine nouns that end in **a**. Four common ones are:

el día / day; **el clima** / climate; **el drama** / drama; **el mapa** / map

§3.11 Nouns that end in **ista**
These nouns are generally masculine or feminine, depending on whether they refer to male or female persons:

el dentista, la dentista / dentist; **el novelista, la novelista** / novelist

§3.12 **Plural of nouns**
To form the plural of a noun that ends in a vowel, add **s**:

el chico / **los chicos; la chica** / **las chicas; el libro** / **los libros**
la dentista / **las dentistas; el coche** / **los coches; la clase** / **las clases**

§3.13 To form the plural of a noun that ends in a consonant, add **es**:

el profesor / **los profesores; la flor** / **las flores; la ciudad** / **las ciudades**

§3.14 A noun that ends in **z** changes **z** to **c** before adding **es**:

el lápiz / **los lápices; la luz** / **las luces**

§3.15 Sometimes a masculine plural noun refers to both male and female persons:

los padres / the parents, the mother and father
los tíos / the aunt and uncle, the aunts and uncles
los niños / the children, the little boy and little girl, the little boys and little girls
los hijos / the children, the son and daughter, the sons and daughters

§3.16 Generally, a noun that ends in **ión** drops the accent mark in the plural. The accent mark is not needed in the plural because the stress naturally falls on the syllable that contained the accent mark in the singular. This happens because another syllable is added when the noun is made plural: **la lección** / **las lecciones; la ilusión** / **las ilusiones**

§3.17 Generally, a noun that ends in **és** drops the accent mark in the plural. The accent mark is not needed in the plural because the stress naturally falls on the syllable that contained the accent mark in the singular. This happens because another syllable is added when the noun is made plural: **el francés** / the Frenchman; **los franceses** / the Frenchmen

§3.18 Sometimes the accent mark is kept in the plural in order to keep the stress where it is in the singular. This generally happens when there are two vowels together and one of them is strong and the other weak: **el país** / **los países**

§3.19 Some nouns have a plural ending but are regarded as singular because they are compound nouns; that is to say, the single word is made of two words which combine into one: **el tocadiscos** / the record player; **los tocadiscos** / the record players; **el paraguas** / the umbrella; **los paraguas** / the umbrellas; **el abrelatas** / the can opener; **los abrelatas** / the can openers; **el sacapuntas** / the pencil sharpener; **los sacapuntas** / the pencil sharpeners.

§3.20 Generally speaking, a noun that ends in **s** in the singular with no stress on that final syllable remains the same in the plural: **el lunes** / **los lunes; el martes** / **los martes**

§3.21 Generally speaking, a noun that ends in **s** in the singular with the stress on that syllable (usually it is a word of one syllable) requires the addition of **es** to form the plural: **el mes** / **los meses**

§3.22   Some nouns that contain no accent mark in the singular require an accent mark in the plural in order to preserve the stress where it fell naturally in the singular: **el joven** / the young man; **los jóvenes** / the young men

§3.23   **Nouns that change meaning according to gender**
Some nouns have one meaning when masculine and another meaning when feminine. Here are two common examples:

NOUN	MASCULINE GENDER MEANING	FEMININE GENDER MEANING
capital	capital (money)	capital (city)
cura	priest	cure

§3.24   **Nouns used as adjectives**
It is common in English to use a noun as an adjective: *a history class, a silk tie, a gold watch*. When this is done in Spanish, the preposition **de** is usually placed in front of the noun that is used as an adjective and both are placed after the noun that is being described:

una clase de historia / a history class (a class of history); **una corbata de seda** / a silk tie (a tie of silk); **un reloj de oro** / a gold watch (a watch of gold)

Also note that the preposition **para** (*for*) is used in order to indicate that something is intended for something: **una taza para café** / a coffee cup (a cup for coffee). However, if the cup is filled with coffee, we say in Spanish: **una taza de café** / a cup of coffee.

§3.25   Nouns ending in **ito** or **illo**
Generally speaking, the ending **ito** or **illo** can be added to a noun to form the diminutive form of a noun. This makes the noun take on the meaning of little or small in size:

un vaso / a glass (drinking); **un vasito** / a little drinking glass; **una casa** / a house; **una casita** / a little house; **un cigarro** / a cigar; **un cigarrillo** / a cigarette

To form the diminutive in Spanish, ordinarily drop the final vowel of the noun and add **ito** or **illo**: **una casa** / **una casita**. If the final letter of the noun is a consonant, merely add **ito** or **illo**: **papel** / paper; **papelito** *or* **papelillo** / small bit of paper

At other times, these diminutive endings give a favorable quality to the noun, even a term of endearment:

una chica / a girl; **una chiquita** / a cute little girl. Here, note that before dropping the final vowel **a** to add **ita**, you must change **c** to **q** in order to preserve the hard sound of *K* in **chica; un perro** / a dog; **un perrito** / a darling little dog; **una abuela** / a grandmother; **abuelita** / "dear old granny"

In English, we do something similar to this: drop / droplet; doll / dolly *or* dollie; pig / piggy *or* piggie or piglet; bath / bathinette; book / booklet; John / Johnny; Ann / Annie.

§3.26   **Campo, país, patria, nación**
The first three nouns (**el campo, el país, la patria**) all mean *country*. However, note the following:

    (a) **campo** means *country* in the sense of countryside, where you find farmlands, as opposed to life in a city: **en el campo** / in the country; **Vamos a pasar el fin de semana en el campo** / We are going to spend the weekend in the country; **Voy al campo este verano** / I am going to the country this summer.

    (b) **país** means *country* in the meaning of a *nation*: **¿En qué país nació Ud.?** / In what country were you born?

    (c) **patria** means *country* in the sense of *native land:* **El soldado defendió a su patria** / The soldier defended his country.

    (d) **nación** means *country* in the sense of *nation*: **Las Naciones Unidas** / the United Nations; **La Sociedad de las Naciones** / The League of Nations.

§3.27   **Hora, tiempo,** and **vez**

    These three words all mean *time;* however, note the differences:

§3.28   **La hora** refers to the time (the hour) of the day: **¿A qué hora vamos al baile?** / At what time are we going to the dance? **Vamos al baile a las nueve** / We are going to the dance at nine o'clock.

    ¿Qué hora es? / What time is it? **Es la una** / It is one o'clock; **Son las dos** / It is two o'clock.

§3.29   **El tiempo** refers to a vague or indefinite duration of time; in other words, time in general: **No puedo ir contigo porque no tengo tiempo** / I cannot go with you because I don't have time.

    As you know, **tiempo** is also used to express the weather: **¿Qué tiempo hace hoy?** / What's the weather like today? **Hace buen tiempo** / The weather is fine.

§3.30   **La vez** means *time* in the sense of segmented time, different times, *e.g., the first time* / **la primera vez;** *this time* / **esta vez;** *many times* / **muchas veces;** *two times* or *twice* / **dos veces;** *again* or *another time* / **otra vez**

§4.   **ARTICLES**

§4.1   **Definite article**

§4.2   There are four forms of the definite article (the) in Spanish. They are as follows:

	SINGULAR	PLURAL
MASCULINE	el	los
FEMININE	la	las

    EXAMPLES:
    el libro (the book); **los libros** (the books)
    la pluma (the pen); **las plumas** (the pens)

§4.3   A definite article agrees in gender and number with the noun it modifies. If you do not know or do not remember what is meant by gender and number, see §5.2 and §5.5ff. (If you do not know or do not remember what the abbreviation ff means, see the list of abbreviations on page xviii.)

§4.4   If a noun is masculine singular, you must use the masculine singular form of *the*, which is **el**. If a noun is masculine plural, you must use the masculine plural form of *the*, which is **los**. If a noun is feminine singular, you must use the feminine singular form of *the*, which is **la**. If a noun is feminine plural, you must use the feminine plural form of *the*, which is **las**. See §4.2 above.

§4.5   How do you know if a noun is masculine or feminine? See §3., which is the beginning of the topic **Nouns**.

§4.6   If a feminine singular noun begins with stressed **a** or **ha**, use **el**, not **la**. This is done in order to avoid slurring the **a** in **la** with the stressed **a** or **ha** at the beginning of the noun that follows. Actually, that is what happened; the two vowel sounds **a** were not pronounced distinctly because they were slurred and **el** replaced **la**. For example, **hambre** (hunger) is a feminine noun but in the singular it is stated as **el hambre**. NOTE: **Tengo mucha hambre.** And NOTE:

el agua / the water; but **las aguas** / the waters
el hacha / the axe; but **las hachas** / the axes

However, if the def. art. is in front of an adj. that precedes the noun, this is not observed: **la alta montaña** / the high (tall) mountain; **la árida llanura** / the arid (dry) prairie.

§4.7 Contraction of the definite article **el**

§4.8 When the preposition **a** or **de** is in front of the definite article **el**, it contracts as follows:

a + el changes to **al**
de + el changes to **del**

EXAMPLES:
  Voy al parque / I am going to the park.
  Vengo del parque / I am coming from the park.

But if the def. art. **el** is part of a denomination or title of a work, there is no contraction: **Los cuadros de El Greco.**

§4.9 **The definite article is used:**

   (a) In front of each noun even if there is more than one noun stated, as in a series, which is not always done in English: **Tengo el libro, el cuaderno, y la pluma** / I have the book, notebook, and pen. See **§4.18(c)**.

   (b) With a noun when you make a general statement: **Me gusta el café** / I like coffee; **La leche es buena para la salud** / Milk is good for health.

   (c) With a noun of weight or measure: **un dólar la libra; un peso la libra** / one dollar a pound (per pound).

   (d) In front of a noun indicating a profession, rank, title followed by the name of the person: **El profesor Gómez es inteligente** / Professor Gómez is intelligent; **La señora García es muy amable** / Mrs. García is very nice; **El doctor Torres está enfermo** / Dr. Torres is sick.

   But in direct address (when talking directly to the person and you mention the rank, profession, *etc.*), do not use the definite article: **Buenas noches, señor Gómez** / Good evening, Mr. Gómez.

   (e) With the name of a language, it is optional to use the definite article: **Estudio español**. The trend in some Spanish speaking countries is not to use the definite article. However, see §4.10(b) below when **hablar** is used.

   (f) With the name of a subject matter: **Estudio la historia** / I study history. See **§4.10(c)**.

   (g) With the days of the week, when in English we use *on*: **Voy al cine el sábado** / I am going to the movies on Saturday.

   (h) With parts of the body or articles of clothing, especially if the possessor is clearly stated: **Me pongo el sombrero** / I put on my hat; **Me lavo la cara todas las mañanas** / I wash my face every morning.

   (i) With common expressions, for example: **a la escuela** / to school; **en la iglesia** / in church; **en la clase** / in class; **la semana pasada** / last week; **la semana próxima** / next week.

   (j) With the seasons of the year: **en la primavera** / in spring; **en el verano** / in summer; **en el otoño** / in autumn; **en el invierno** / in winter.

   (k) To show possession with the preposition **de** + a common noun: **el libro del alumno** / the pupil's book; **los libros de los alumnos** / the pupils' books; **los niños de las mujeres** / the women's children.

Note that when a proper noun is used, the definite article is not needed with **de** to show possession: **el libro de Juan** / John's book; **el libro de María** / Mary's book; **los libros de Juan y de María** / John's and Mary's books. See §4.10(d) below.

(l) With names of some cities, countries and continents: **la Argentina, el Brasil, el Canadá, los Estados Unidos, la Habana, la América del Norte, la América Central, la América del Sur.** See §4.10(h).

(m) With a proper noun modified by an adjective: **el pequeño José** / Little Joseph.

(n) With a noun in apposition with a pronoun: **Nosotros los norteamericanos** / We North Americans.

(o) With an infinitive used as a noun, especially when it begins a sentence: **El estudiar es bueno** / Studying is good. There are some exceptions: **Ver es creer** / Seeing is believing; and other proverbs. But you do not normally use the definite article with an infinitive if it does not begin a sentence: **Es bueno estudiar** / It is good to study. See §4.10(e) below. This is a general rule.

(p) When telling time: **Es la una** / It is one o'clock; **Son las dos** / It is two o'clock.

§4.10 **The definite article is not used:**

(a) In direct address with the rank, profession, title of the person to whom you are talking or writing: **Buenos días, señora Molina** / Good morning, Mrs. Molina.

(b) After the verb **hablar** when the name of a language is right after a form of **hablar**: **Hablo español** / I speak Spanish. See §4.9(e) above.

(c) After the prepositions **en** and **de** with the name of a language or a subject matter: **Estoy escribiendo en inglés** / I am writing in English; **La señora Johnson es profesora de inglés** / Mrs. Johnson is a teacher of English; **El señor Gómez es profesor de historia** / Mr. Gómez is a teacher of history. See §4.9(f) above.

(d) With a proper noun to show possession when using **de: los libros de Marta** / Martha's books. See §4.9(k) above.

(e) With an infinitive if the infinitive does not begin the sentence: **Es bueno trabajar** / It is good to work. **Me gusta viajar** / I like to travel. See §4.9(o). This is a general rule.

(f) With a noun in apposition with a noun: **Madrid, capital de España, es una ciudad interesante** / Madrid, capital of Spain, is an interesting city.

(g) With a numeral that denotes the order of succession of a monarch: **Carlos V (Quinto)** / Charles the Fifth.

(h) With names of some countries and continents: **España** / Spain; **Francia** / France; **México** / Mexico; **Europa** / Europe; **Asia** / Asia; **África** / Africa.

§4.11 **The neuter article lo** (See also idioms with **lo** in §14.30)

The neuter article **lo** has idiomatic uses, generally speaking.

It is used:

(a) With a masculine singular form of an adjective that is used as a noun: **lo bueno** / the good; **lo malo** / the bad; **lo simpático** / what(ever) is kind.

(b) With a past participle: **lo dicho y lo escrito** / what has been said and what has been written.

(c) With an adjective or adverb + **que**, meaning *how*: **Veo lo fácil que es** / I see how easy it is.

§4.12   Indefinite article

§4.13   In Spanish, there are four forms of the indefinite article (a, an, some, a few). They are as follows:

	SINGULAR	PLURAL
MASCULINE	**un**	**unos**
FEMININE	**una**	**unas**

EXAMPLES:

un libro (a book); **unos libros** (some books, a few books)

una naranja (an orange); **unas naranjas** (some oranges, a few oranges)

§4.14   An indefinite article agrees in gender and number with the noun it modifies. If you do not know or do not remember what is meant by gender and number, see **§5.2** and **§5.5ff**. If you do not know or do not remember what the abbreviation **ff** means, see the list of abbreviations on page xviii.

§4.15   If a noun is masculine singular, you must use the masculine singular form of *a, an* which is **un.** If a noun is masculine plural, you must use the masculine plural form of *some, a few* which is **unos.**

If a noun is feminine singular, you must use the feminine singular form of *a, an* which is **una.** If a noun is feminine plural, you must use the feminine plural form of *some, a few* which is **unas.** See **§4.13** above.

§4.16   How do you know if a noun is masculine or feminine? See **§3.**, which is the beginning of the topic **Nouns.**

§4.17   The plural of the indefinite article indicates an indefinite number: **unas treinta personas** / some thirty persons.

§4.18   The indefinite article is used:

(a) When you want to say *a* or *an*. It is also used as a numeral to mean *one:* **un libro** / a book or one book; **una pluma** / a pen or one pen. If you want to make it clear that you mean *one,* you may use **solamente** *(only)* in front of **un** or **una: Tengo solamente un libro** / I have (only) one book.

(b) With a modified noun of nationality, profession, rank, or religion: **El doctor Gómez es un médico excelente** / Dr. Gómez is an excellent doctor.

(c) In front of each noun in a series, which we do not always do in English: **Tengo un libro, un cuaderno, y una pluma** / I have a book, notebook, and pen. This use is the same for the definite article in a series of nouns. See **§4.9(a)** above.

(d) In the plural when an indefinite number is indicated: **Tengo unos dólares** / I have some (a few) dollars.

§4.19   The indefinite article is not used:

(a) With **cien** and **mil: cien libros** / a (one) hundred books; **mil dólares** / a (one) thousand dollars.

(b) With **cierto, cierta** and **tal: cierto lugar** / a certain place; **cierta persona** / a certain person; **tal hombre** / such a man; **tal caso** / such a case.

(c) With **otro, otra: otro libro** / another book; **otra pluma** / another pen.

(d) With an unmodified noun of nationality, profession, rank, or religion: **Mi hijo es dentista** / My son is a dentist; **Soy mexicano** / I am Mexican; **Es profesora** / She is a teacher. However, when the subject is qualified, the indef. art. is used. See **§4.18(b).**

(e) When you use **Qué** in an exclamation: **¡Qué hombre!** / What a man! **¡Qué lástima!** / What a pity!

(f) With some negations, particularly with the verb **tener,** or in an interrogative statement before an unmodified noun object: **¿Tiene Ud. libro?** / Do you have a book? **No tengo libro** / I don't have a book.

(g) With a noun in apposition: **Martí, gran político y más grande poeta . . .** / Martí, a great politician and greatest poet . . .

§5. ADJECTIVES

§5.1   **Definition:** An adjective is a word that describes a noun or pronoun in some way.

§5.2   **Agreement:** An adjective agrees in gender and number with the noun or pronoun it describes. **Gender** means masculine, feminine, or neuter. **Number** means singular or plural.

§5.3   **Descriptive adjectives**
    A descriptive adjective is a word that describes a noun or pronoun; **casa blanca, chicas bonitas, chicos altos; Ella es bonita.**

§5.4   **Limiting adjectives**
    A limiting adjective limits the number of the noun: **una casa, un libro, algunos muchachos, muchas veces, dos libros, pocos amigos.**

§5.5   **Gender**

§5.6   An adjective that ends in **o** in the masculine singular changes **o** to **a** to form the feminine: **rojo / roja; pequeño / pequeña**

§5.7   An adjective that expresses a person's nationality, which ends in a consonant, requires the addition of **a** to form the feminine singular: **Juan es español / María es española; Pierre Cardin es francés / Simone Signoret es francesa; El señor Armstrong es inglés / La señora Smith es inglesa.** Note that the accent mark on **francés** and **inglés** drops in the feminine because the stress falls naturally on the vowel **e.**

§5.8   An adjective that ends in **e** generally does not change to form the feminine: **un muchacho inteligente / una muchacha inteligente**

§5.9   An adjective that ends in a consonant generally does not change to form the feminine: **una pregunta difícil / un libro difícil; un chico feliz / una chica feliz** — except for an adjective of nationality, as stated above in **§5.7**, and adjectives that end in **-án, -ón, -ín, -or** (**trabajador / trabajadora,** industrious).

§5.10   **Position** (See also **§5.65**)

§5.11   Normally, a descriptive adjective is placed after the noun it describes: **una casa amarilla; un libro interesante**

§5.12   Two descriptive adjectives, **bueno** and **malo,** are sometimes placed in front of the noun. When placed in front of a masculine singular noun, the **o** drops: **un buen amigo; un mal alumno.** See **§5.18** below.

§5.13   A limiting adjective is generally placed in front of the noun: **algunos estudiantes; mucho dinero; muchos libros; cada año; tres horas; pocos alumnos; varias cosas**

§5.14   In an interrogative sentence, the predicate adjective precedes the subject when it is a noun: **¿Es bonita María? ¿Es inteligente la profesora?**

§5.15   Some adjectives have a different meaning depending on their position:

    un nuevo sombrero / a new (different, another) hat
    un sombrero nuevo / a new (brand new) hat

    un gran hombre / a great man
    un hombre grande / a large, big man

    una gran mujer / a great woman
    una mujer grande / a large, big woman

    la pobre niña / the poor girl (unfortunate, unlucky)
    la niña pobre / the poor girl (poor, not rich)

§5.16   **As nouns**

§5.17   At times, an adjective is used as a noun if it is preceded by an article or a demonstrative adjective: **el viejo** / the old man; **aquel viejo** / that old man; **la joven** / the young lady; **estos jóvenes** / these young men; **este ciego** / this blind man.

§5.18   **Shortened forms (apocopation of adjectives)**

§5.19   Certain masculine singular adjectives drop the final **o** when in front of a masculine singular noun:

§5.20
    alguno: algún día   **primero: el primer año**
    bueno: un buen amigo   **tercero: el tercer mes**
    malo: mal tiempo   **uno: un dólar**
    ninguno: ningún libro

    NOTE that when **alguno** and **ninguno** are shortened, an accent mark is required on the **u**.

§5.21   **Santo** shortens to **San** before a masculine singular saint: **San Francisco, San José;** but remains **Santo** in front of **Do-** or **To-: Santo Domingo, Santo Tomás.**

§5.22   **Grande** shortens to **gran** when in front of any singular noun, whether masc. or fem.: **un gran hombre** / a great (famous) man; **una gran mujer** / a great (famous) woman. See also **§5.15** above.

§5.23   **Ciento** shortens to **cien** when in front of any plural noun, whether masc. or fem.: **cien libros** / one (a) hundred books; **cien sillas** / one (a) hundred chairs.

§5.24   **Ciento** shortens to **cien** when in front of a number greater than itself: **cien mil** / one hundred thousand; **cien millones** / one hundred million.

§5.25   **Ciento** remains **ciento** when combined with any other number which is smaller than itself: **ciento tres dólares.**

§5.26   NOTE that in English we say *one* hundred or *a* hundred, but in Spanish no word is used in front of **ciento** or **cien** to express *one* or *a;* it is merely **ciento** or **cien.** For an explanation of when to use **ciento** or **cien**, see **§5.23 — §5.25** above.

§5.27   **Cualquiera** and **cualesquiera** lose the final **a** in front of a noun: **cualquier hombre, cualquier día,** but if after the noun, the final **a** remains: **un libro cualquiera.**

§5.28   **Plural of adjectives**

§5.29   Like nouns, to form the plural of an adjective, add **s** if the adj. ends in a vowel: **blanco / blancos; blanca / blancas.**

§5.30   If an adj. ends in a consonant, add **es** to form the plural: **español** / **españoles; difícil** / **difíciles.** NOTE that the accent on **difícil** remains in the plural in order to keep the stress there: **difíciles.**

§5.31   Some adjectives drop the accent mark in the plural because it is not needed to indicate the stress. The stress falls naturally on the same vowel in the plural: **cortés** / **corteses; alemán** / **alemanes.**

§5.32   Some adjectives add the accent mark in the plural because the stress needs to be kept on the vowel that was stressed in the singular where no accent mark was needed. In the singular, the stress falls naturally on that vowel: **joven** / **jóvenes.**

§5.33   An adjective that ends in **z** changes **z** to **c** and adds **es** to form the plural: **feliz** / **felices.** Here, there is no need to add an accent mark because the stress falls naturally on the vowel **i,** as it does in the singular.

§5.34   If an adjective describes or modifies two or more nouns that are all masculine, naturally the masculine plural is used: **Roberto y Felipe están cansados.**

§5.35   If an adjective describes or modifies two or more nouns that are all feminine, naturally the feminine plural is used: **Elena y Marta están cansadas.**

§5.36   If an adjective describes or modifies two or more nouns of different genders, the masculine plural is used: **Pablo y Juanita están cansados; María, Elena, Marta, y Roberto están cansados.**

§5.37   **Comparatives and Superlatives** (See also **§5.66** and **§5.67.**)

§5.38   **Comparatives**

§5.39   Of equality: **tan ... como** (as ... as)
  María es tan alta como Elena / Mary is as tall as Helen.

§5.40   Of a lesser degree: **menos ... que** (less ... than)
  María es menos alta que Anita / Mary is less tall than Anita.

§5.41   Of a higher degree: **más ... que** (more ... than)
  María es más alta que Isabel / Mary is taller than Elizabeth.

§5.42   **Superlatives**

§5.43   To express the superlative degree, use the comparative forms given above in **§5.38** with the appropriate definite article:

§5.44   **With a proper noun: Anita es la más alta** / Anita is the tallest.
     Roberto es el más alto / Robert is the tallest.
     Anita y Roberto son los más altos / Anita and Robert are the tallest.
     Marta y María son las más inteligentes / Martha and Mary are the most intelligent.

§5.45   **With a common noun: La muchacha más alta de la clase es Anita** / The tallest girl in the class is Anita.
     El muchacho más alto de la clase es Roberto / The tallest boy in the class is Robert.

§5.46   NOTE that after a superlative in Spanish, *in* is expressed by **de,** not **en.**

  When two or more superlative adjectives describe the same noun, **más** or **menos** is used only once in front of the first adjective: **Aquella mujer es la más pobre y vieja.**

§5.47   **Absolute superlative:** adjectives ending in **-ísimo, -ísima, -ísimos, -ísimas**

§5.48 To express an adj. in a very high degree, drop the final vowel (if there is one) and add the appropriate ending among the following, depending on the correct agreement: **-ísimo, -ísima, -ísimos, -ísimas: María está contentísima** / Mary is very (extremely) happy; **Los muchachos están contentísimos.** These forms may be used instead of **muy** + adj. (**muy contenta / muy contentos**); **una casa grandísima / una casa muy grande.**

§5.49 Never use **muy** in front of **mucho.** Say: **muchísimo. Muchísimas gracias** / many thanks; thank you very, very much.

§5.50 Irregular comparatives and superlatives

ADJECTIVE	COMPARATIVE	SUPERLATIVE
bueno (good)	**mejor** (better)	**el mejor** (best)
malo (bad)	**peor** (worse)	**el peor** (worst)
grande (large)	**más grande** (larger)	**el más grande** (largest)
	mayor (greater, older)	**el mayor** (greatest, oldest)
pequeño (small)	**más pequeño** (smaller)	**el más pequeño** (smallest)
	menor (smaller, younger)	**el menor** (smallest, youngest)

§5.51 NOTE, of course, that you must be careful to make the correct agreement in gender and number. See **§5.2** above.

NOTE also that in English, the superlative is sometimes expressed with definite article *the* and sometimes it is not. See **§5.43**.

§5.52 **Más que** (more than) or **menos que** (less than) becomes **más de, menos de** + a number:

El Señor Gómez tiene más de cincuenta años.
Mi hermano tiene más de cien dólares.
BUT: **No tengo más que dos dólares** / I have only two dollars.
In this example, the meaning is *only,* expressed by **no** in front of the verb; in this case, you must keep **que** to express *only.*

§5.53 **Tanto, tanta, tantos, tantas** + noun + **como:** as much (as many) . . . as

Tengo tanto dinero como usted / I have as much money as you.
Tengo tantos libros como usted / I have as many books as you.
Tengo tanta paciencia como usted / I have as much patience as you.
Tengo tantas plumas como usted / I have as many pens as you.

§5.54 **Demonstrative adjectives**

A demonstrative adjective is used to point out someone or something. Like other adjectives, a demonstrative adjective agrees in gender and number with the noun it modifies. The demonstrative adjectives are:

ENGLISH MEANING	MASCULINE	FEMININE
this *(here)*	**este libro**	**esta pluma**
these *(here)*	**estos libros**	**estas plumas**
that *(there)*	**ese libro**	**esa pluma**
those *(there)*	**esos libros**	**esas plumas**
that *(farther away or out of sight)*	**aquel libro**	**aquella pluma**
those *(farther away or out of sight)*	**aquellos libros**	**aquellas plumas**

§5.55 If there is more than one noun, a demonstrative adjective is ordinarily used in front of each noun: **este hombre y esta mujer** / this man and (this) woman.

§5.56 The demonstrative adjectives are used to form the demonstrative pronouns. See **§6.54ff.**

§5.57 **Possessive adjectives**

A possessive adjective is a word that shows possession, and it agrees in gender and number with the noun, not with the possesor. A short form of a possessive adjective is placed in front of the noun. If there is more than one noun stated, a possessive adjective is needed in front of each noun: **mi madre y mi padre** / my mother and (my) father.

§5.58   There are two forms for the possessive adjectives: the short form and the long form. **The short form is placed in front of the noun.** The short forms are:

ENGLISH MEANING	BEFORE A SINGULAR NOUN	BEFORE A PLURAL NOUN
1. my	**mi amigo, mi amiga**	**mis amigos, mis amigas**
2. your	**tu amigo, tu amiga**	**tus amigos, tus amigas**
3. your, his, her, its	**su amigo, su amiga**	**sus amigos, sus amigas**
1. our	**nuestro amigo** **nuestra amiga**	**nuestros amigos** **nuestras amigas**
2. your	**vuestro amigo** **vuestra amiga**	**vuestros amigos** **vuestras amigas**
3. your, their	**su amigo, su amiga**	**sus amigos, sus amigas**

§5.59   In order to clarify the meanings of **su** or **sus**, when there might be ambiguity, do the following: Replace **su** or **sus** with the definite article + the noun and add **de Ud., de él, de ella, de Uds., de ellos, de ellas:**

su libro OR **el libro de Ud., el libro de él, el libro de ella; el libro de Uds., el libro de ellos, el libro de ellas**

sus libros OR **los libros de Ud., los libros de él, los libros de ella; los libros de Uds., los libros de ellos, los libros de ellas**

§5.60   **The long form is placed after the noun.** The long forms are:

ENGLISH MEANING	AFTER A SINGULAR NOUN	AFTER A PLURAL NOUN
1. my; (of) mine	**mío, mía**	**míos, mías**
2. your; (of) yours	**tuyo, tuya**	**tuyos, tuyas**
3. your, his, her, its; (of yours, of his, of hers, of its)	**suyo, suya**	**suyos, suyas**
1. our; (of) ours	**nuestro, nuestra**	**nuestros, nuestras**
2. your; (of) yours	**vuestro, vuestra**	**vuestros, vuestras**
3. your, their; (of yours, of theirs)	**suyo, suya**	**suyos, suyas**

Examples: **amigo mío** / my friend; **un amigo mío** / a friend of mine

§5.61   The long forms are used primarily:

(a) In direct address, that is to say, when you are talking directly to someone or when writing a letter to someone:

¡Hola, amigo mío! ¿Qué tal? / Hello, my friend! How are things? **Queridos amigos míos** / My dear friends

(b) When you want to express *of mine, of yours, of his, of hers,* etc. See **§5.60.**

(c) With the verb **ser: Estos libros son míos** / These books are mine.

(d) In the expression: **¡Dios mío!** / My heavens! My God!

§5.62   In order to clarify the meanings of **suyo, suya, suyos, suyas** (since they are third person singular or plural), do the same as for **su** and **sus** in **§5.59** above: **dos amigos suyos** can be clarified as: **dos amigos de Ud., dos amigos de él, dos amigos de ella, dos amigos de Uds., dos amigos de ellos, dos amigos de ellas** / two friends of yours, of his, of hers, *etc.*

§5.63   The long forms of the possessive adjectives are used to serve as possessive pronouns. See **§6.63** and **§6.64ff.**

§5.64   A possessive adjective is ordinarily not used when referring to an article of clothing being worn or to parts of the body, particularly when a reflexive verb is used: **Me lavo las manos antes de comer** / I wash my hands before eating.

§5.65   **Two or more descriptive adjectives** (See also **§5.10** and **§12.6**).

Two or more descriptive adjectives of equal importance are placed after the noun. If there are two, they are joined by **y** (or **e**). If there are more than two, the last two are connected by **y** (or **e**):

un hombre alto y hermoso / a tall, handsome man

una mujer alta, hermosa e inteligente / a tall, beautiful and intelligent woman

§5.66   **Cuanto más (menos) . . . tanto más (menos)** / the more (the less) . . . the more (less) (See also **§5.37ff**).

A proportion or ratio is expressed by **cuanto más (menos) . . . tanto más (menos)** / the more (the less) . . . the more (less):

Cuanto más dinero tengo, tanto más necesito / The more money I have, the more I need.

Cuanto menos dinero tengo, tanto menos necesito / The less money I have, the less I need.

§5.67   **Comparison between two clauses** (See also **§5.37ff**)

(a) Use **de lo que** to express *than* when comparing two clauses with different verbs if an adjective or adverb is the comparison:

Esta frase es más fácil de lo que Ud. cree / This sentence is easier than you think.

Paula trabaja mejor de lo que Ud. cree / Paula works better than you think.

(b) Use the appropriate form of **de lo que, de los que, de la que, de las que** when comparing two clauses with the same verbs if a noun is the comparison:

Tengo más dinero de lo que Ud. tiene / I have more money than you have.

María tiene más libros de los que Ud. tiene / Mary has more books than you have.

Roberto tiene más amigas de las que tiene Juan / Robert has more girl friends than John has.

§5.68   **¿Qué . . . ?** and **¿cuál . . . ?**

(a) These two interrogative words both mean *what* or *which* but there is a difference in their use:

(b) Use **¿Qué . . . ?** as a pronoun (when there is no noun right after it) if you are inquiring about something, if you want an explanation about something, if you want something defined or described, *e.g.:* **¿Qué es esto?** / What is this?

(c) Use **¿Qué . . . ?** as an adjective, when there is a noun right after it: **¿Qué día es hoy?** /What day is it today?

(d) Use **¿Cuál . . . ?** as a pronoun, when there is no noun right after it. If by *what* you mean *which* or *which one,* it is better Spanish to use **¿Cuál . . . ?** For example: **¿Cuál de estos lápices es mejor?** / Which (Which one) of these pencils is better?

(e) The same is true in the plural: **¿Cuáles son buenos?** / Which ones are good?

(f) Do not use **cuál** if there is a noun right after it; in that case, you must use **qué,** as in **§5.68(c)** above.

(g) Do not assume, just because you can use *what* or *which* interchangeably in English, that you can do the same in Spanish. If by *what* or *which* you mean *which one,* you must use **cuál** because in that case there is no noun right after **cuál.** Note the following examples:

(h) **¿Qué libro tiene Ud.?** / What book do you have? *or* Which book do you have? You must use **qué** here because there is a noun right after it.

(i) **Cuál** and **cuáles** are pronouns and there cannot be a noun right after these words. In colloquial Spanish they are sometimes used as adjectives (when there is a noun right after them), but this does not mean that it is correct Spanish.

(j) Certain words need accent marks when they are used in interrogative sentences. For other interrogative words, see **§10.10, §12.5.**

§5.69   **Poco** and **pequeño**

These two words mean *little,* but note the difference in use.

§5.70   **Poco** means *little* in terms of quantity: **Tenemos poco trabajo hoy** / We have little work today.

§5.71   **Pequeño** means *little* in terms of size; in other words, *small:* **Mi casa es pequeña** / My house is small.

§6.   PRONOUNS

§6.1   **Definition:** A pronoun is a word that takes the place of a noun; for example, in English there are these common pronouns: I, you, he, she, it they, me, him, her, us, them — just to mention a few.

§6.2   **Pronouns are divided into certain types:** personal, prepositional, relative, interrogative, demonstrative, possessive, indefinite and negative.

§6.3   A personal pronoun is used as the subject of a verb, direct or indirect object of a verb or verb form, as a reflexive pronoun object, and as object of a preposition.

Correct use of pronouns in Spanish is not easy — nor in English, for that matter. For example, in English, you can often hear people using pronouns incorrectly: "between you and *I*" ought to be stated as "between you and *me*"; "if you have any questions, see *myself*" ought to be stated as "if you have any questions, see *me*"; "*Who* did you see?" ought to be stated as "*Whom* did you see?" And there are many more incorrect uses of pronouns in English.

§6.4   **Personal pronouns**

Subject pronouns

SINGULAR	EXAMPLES
1. **yo** / I	**Yo** hablo.
2. **tú** / you *(familiar)*	**Tú** hablas.
3. **usted** / you *(polite)*	**Usted** habla.
él / he, it	**Él** habla.
ella / she, it	**Ella** habla.
PLURAL	
1. **nosotros (nosotras)** / we	**Nosotros** hablamos.
2. **vosotros (vosotras)** / you *(fam.)*	**Vosotros** habláis.
3. **ustedes** / you *(polite)*	**Ustedes** hablan.
ellos / they	**Ellos** hablan.
ellas / they	**Ellas** hablan.

As you can see in the examples given here, a subject pronoun is ordinarily placed in front of the main verb. For other positions, see **§6.34ff.**

§6.5 In Spanish, subject pronouns are not used at all times. The ending of the verb tells you if the subject is 1st, 2nd, or 3rd person in the singular or plural. Of course, in the 3rd person sing. and pl. there is more than one possible subject with the same ending on the verb form. In that case, if there is any doubt as to what the subject is, it is mentioned for the sake of clarity. At other times, subject pronouns in Spanish are used when you want to be emphatic, to make a contrast between this person and that person, or out of simple courtesy. To prepare yourself for SAT II: Spanish, you must be certain to know the endings of the verb forms in all the tenses (see the entry **Verbs** in the General Index) in the three persons of the singular and of the plural so that you can figure out the subject if it is not clearly stated. In addition to pronouns as subjects, nouns are also used as subjects. Any noun—whether common (el hombre, la mujer, el cielo, la silla, *etc.*) or proper (María, Juan y Elena, los Estados Unidos, *etc.*)—is always 3rd person, either singular or plural.

§6.6 Generally speaking, in Latin American countries **ustedes** (3rd pers., pl.) is used in place of **vosotros** or **vosotras** (2nd pers., pl.)

§6.7 ### Direct object pronouns

SINGULAR

1. **me** / me
2. **te** / you *(fam.)*
3. **lo, la** / you
   lo / him; **lo** / him, it
   la / her, it

PLURAL

1. **nos** / us
2. **os** / you *(fam.)*
3. **los, las** / you
   los / them
   las / them

EXAMPLES

María me ha visto / Mary has seen me.
María te había visto / Mary had seen you.
María lo (la) ve / Mary sees you.
María lo (lo) ve / Mary sees him (it).
María la ve / Mary sees her (it).

María nos había visto / Mary had seen us.
María os ha visto / Mary has seen you.
María los (las) ve / Mary sees you.
María los ve / Mary sees them.
María las ve / Mary sees them.

§6.8 In Latin American countries, **lo** is generally used instead of **le** to mean *him.* You can tell from the context of what is written or said if **lo** means *him* or *it* (masc.).

§6.9 NOTE that in the 3rd pers., plural, the direct objects **los** (masc.) and **las** (fem.) refer to people and things.

§6.10 ALSO NOTE that in the 3rd pers. singular, the direct object pronoun **lo** is masc. and **la** is fem. and both mean *you.* You can tell from the context of what is written or said if **lo** means *you* (masc. sing.) or if it means *him.*

§6.11 Here is a summing up of the various meanings of the direct object pronouns, **lo, la, los, las:**

lo: him, you, it *(masc.)*
la: her, you *(fem.)*, it *(fem.)*
los: you *(masc. pl.)*, them *(people or things, masc., pl.)*
las: you *(fem. pl.)*, them *(people or things, fem., pl.)*

As you can see in the examples given in **§6.7,** a direct object pronoun ordinarily is placed in front of the main verb. For other positions, see **§6.34ff.**

§6.12 There is also the neuter **lo** direct object pronoun. It does not refer to any particular noun that is f. or m.; that is why it has no gender and is called *neuter.* It usually refers to an idea or a statement:

¿Está Ud. enfermo? / Are you sick?   **Sí, lo estoy** / Yes, I am.
¿Son amigos? / Are they friends?   **Sí, lo son** / Yes, they are.

Of course, your reply could be **Sí, estoy enfermo** and **Sí, son amigos.** But because your verb is a form of **estar** or **ser,** you do not have to repeat what was mentioned; neuter **lo** takes its place as a direct object pronoun. This neuter **lo** direct object pronoun is also used with other verbs, *e.g.,* **pedir, preguntar** and **parecer:**

María parece contenta / Mary seems happy. **Sí, lo parece** / Yes, she does (Yes, she does seem *so*).

§6.13   To make the examples in Spanish given above in §6.7 negative, place **no** in front of the direct object pronouns: **María no me ve,** *etc.* To make the examples negative in §6.4, place **no** in front of the verb.

§6.14   **Indirect Object Pronouns**

SINGULAR	EXAMPLES
1. **me** / to me	**Pablo me ha hablado** / Paul has talked to me.
2. **te** / to you *(fam.)*	**Pablo te habla** / Paul talks to you.
3. **le** / to you, to him, to her, to it	**Pablo le habla** / Paul talks to you (to him, to her, to it).

PLURAL |
---|---
1. **nos** / to us | **Pablo nos ha hablado** / Paul has talked to us.
2. **os** / to you *(fam.)* | **Pablo os habla** / Paul talks to you.
3. **les** / to you, to them | **Pablo les habla** / Paul talks to you (to them).

§6.15   To make these sentences negative, place **no** in front of the indirect object pronouns: **Pablo no me habla** / Paul does not talk to me.

§6.16   NOTE that **me, te, nos, os** are direct object pronouns and indirect object pronouns. See **§6.7ff.**

§6.17   NOTE that **le** as an indirect object pronoun has more than one meaning. If there is any doubt as to the meaning, merely add after the verb any of the following accordingly to clarify the meaning: **a Ud., a él, a ella: Pablo le habla a usted** / Paul is talking to you.

§6.18   NOTE that **les** has more than one meaning. If there is any doubt as to the meaning, merely add after the verb any of the following, accordingly: **a Uds. a ellos, a ellas: Pablo no les habla a ellos** / Paul is not talking to them.

As you can see in the examples given in §6.14, an indirect object pronoun ordinarily is placed in front of the main verb. For other positions, see **§6.34ff.**

§6.19   An indirect object pronoun is needed when you use a verb that indicates a person is being deprived of something, *e.g.,* to steal something *from* someone, to take something *off* or *from* someone, to buy something from someone, and actions of this sort. The reason why an indirect object pronoun is needed is that you are dealing with the preposition **a + noun** or **pronoun** and it must be accounted for. Examples:

Los ladrones le robaron todo el dinero a él / The robbers stole all the money from him.
La madre le quitó al niño el sombrero / The mother took off the child's hat.
Les compré mi automóvil a ellos / I bought my car from them.

§6.20   The indirect object pronouns are used with the verb **gustar** (see §7.143) and with the following verbs: **bastar, faltar** or **hacer falta, sobrar, quedarle (a uno), tocarle (a uno), placer, parecer.**

EXAMPLES:

A Ricardo le gusta el helado / Richard likes ice cream (*i.e.,* Ice cream is pleasing to him, to Richard).

A Juan le bastan cien dólares / One hundred dollars are enough for John.

A los muchachos les faltan cinco dólares / The boys need five dollars (*i.e.,* Five dollars are lacking to them, to the boys). OR: **A la mujer le hacen falta cinco dólares** / The woman needs five dollars (*i.e.,* Five dollars are lacking to her, to the woman).

To put it simply, the indirect object pronoun is needed in the examples given in §6.19 and §6.20 above because some kind of action is being done *to* someone.

§6.21 Reflexive pronouns

SINGULAR	EXAMPLES
1. **me** / myself	**Me lavo** / I wash myself.
2. **te** / yourself	**Te lavas** / You wash yourself.
3. **se** / yourself, himself, herself, itself	**Ud. se lava** / You wash yourself; **Pablo se lava** / Paul washes himself, *etc.*

PLURAL	
1. **nos** / ourselves	**Nosotros (-as) nos lavamos.**
2. **os** / yourselves	**Vosotros (-as) os laváis.**
3. **se** / yourselves, themselves	**Uds. se lavan** / You wash yourselves; **Ellos (Ellas) se lavan** / They wash themselves.

§6.22 A reflexive verb contains a reflexive pronoun, and the action of the verb falls on the subject and its reflexive pronoun either directly or indirectly. For that reason the reflexive pronoun must agree with the subject: **yo me . . . , tú te . . . , Ud. se . . . , él se . . . , ella se . . . , nosotros nos . . . , vosotros os . . . , Uds. se . . . , ellos se . . . , ellas se . . .**

A reflexive pronoun is ordinarily placed in front of the verb form, as you can see in the examples given in §6.21. For other positions, see §6.34ff.

§6.23 To make these sentences negative, place **no** in front of the reflexive pronoun: **Yo no me lavo, Tú no te lavas, Ud. no se lava,** *etc.*

§6.24 NOTE that **me, te, nos, os** are not only reflexive pronouns but they are also direct object pronouns and indirect object pronouns. See §6.16.

§6.25 A reflexive verb in Spanish is not always reflexive in English, for example:

SPANISH	ENGLISH
levantarse	to get up
sentarse	to sit down

§6.26 There are some reflexive verbs in Spanish that are also reflexive in English, for example:

SPANISH	ENGLISH
bañarse	to bathe oneself
lavarse	to wash oneself

§6.27 The following reflexive pronouns are also used as reciprocal pronouns, meaning "each other" or "to each other": **se, nos, os.** Examples:

Ayer por la noche, María y yo nos vimos en el cine / Yesterday evening, Mary and I saw each other at the movies.

Roberto y Teresa se escriben todos los días / Robert and Teresa write to each other every day.

§6.28   If the meaning of these three reflexive pronouns (**se, nos, os**) is not clear when they are used in a reciprocal meaning, any of the following may be added accordingly to express the idea of "each other" or "to each other": **uno a otro, una a otra, unos a otros,** *etc.*

§6.29   For the position of reflexive pronouns with reflexive verbs in the imperative (command) and for other comments on reflexive verbs, see Imperative, with reflexive verbs in **§8.62** and verbs, reflexive in **§5.64, §6.21 — §6.29, §6.53, §8.62 (h), (k),** and **(l).**

§6.30   **Prepositional pronouns**

§6.31   Pronouns that are used as objects of prepositions are called prepositional pronouns or disjunctive pronouns. They are as follows:

SINGULAR	PLURAL
1. **para mí** / for me, for myself	1. **para nosotros (nosotras)** / for us, for ourselves
2. **para ti** / for you, for yourself	2. **para vosotros (vosotras)** / for you, for yourselves
3. **para usted (Ud.)** / for you **para él** / for him, for it **para ella** / for her, for it	3. **para ustedes (Uds.)** / for you **para ellos** / for them **para ellas** / for them

§6.32   Also note the following:

SINGULAR	PLURAL
3. **para sí** / for yourself, for himself, for herself, for itself	3. **para sí** / for yourselves, for themselves

§6.33   NOTE the following exceptions with the prepositions **con, entre,** and **menos:**

conmigo / with me
contigo / with you *(fam.)*
consigo / with yourself, with yourselves, with himself, with herself, with themselves
entre tú y yo / between you and me
menos yo / except me

§6.34   **Position of object pronouns**

§6.35   In preparation for the next SAT II: Spanish, you surely must review pronouns and their positions beginning with §6. above. You can expect to find them in short sentences and in reading passages in the Spanish test because they are used very commonly in the Spanish language. In the reading passages, you will have to recognize their meaning according to their position with regard to a verb form. In sentences, sometimes short or long, you will probably have to choose the correct pronoun to fit in the blank space. All the questions, by the way, on the test are multiple choice type and if you do not recognize the correct answer from among the choices it will mean that you did not review this section and other sections in this General Review thoroughly enough.

     In the sections above, I reviewed for you single object pronouns and their position, beginning in **§6.7.** In this section, there is a summary review of the position of a single object pronoun and a review of double object pronouns and their position with regard to a verb or verb form. By double object pronouns is meant one direct object pronoun and one indirect object pronoun. Which one comes first and where do you put them?

§6.36   **Positon of a single object pronoun: a summary**

     Review the normal position of a single object pronoun as given above in the examples beginning in **§6.7** when dealing with a simple tense or a compound tense.

§6.37 Attach the single object pronoun to an infinitive: **Juan quiere escribirlo** / John wants to write it.

OR

§6.38 If the main verb is **poder, querer, saber, ir a,** you may place the object pronoun in front of the main verb:

Juan lo quiere escribir / John wants to write it; **¿Puedo levantarme?** or **¿Me puedo levantar?** / May I get up?

§6.39 Attach the single object pronoun to a present participle: **Juan está escribiéndolo** / John is writing it.

NOTE that when you attach an object pronoun to a present participle, you must add an accent mark on the vowel that was stressed in the present participle before the object pronoun was attached. The accent mark is needed to keep the stress where it originally was.

OR

§6.40 If the main verb is a progressive form with **estar** or another auxiliary, you may place the object pronoun in front of the main verb:

Juan lo está escribiendo / John is writing it.

§6.41 When you are dealing with a verb form in the affirmative imperative (command), you must attach the single object pronoun to the verb form and add an accent mark on the vowel that was stressed in the verb form before the single object pronoun was added. The accent mark is needed to keep the stress where it originally was:

¡Hábleme Ud., por favor! / Talk to me, please!

§6.42 When you are dealing with a verb form in the negative imperative (command), you must place the object pronoun in front of the verb form, where it normally goes:

¡No me hable Ud., por favor! / Do not talk to me, please!

§6.43 **Position of double object pronouns: a summary**

§6.44 An indirect object pronoun is always placed in front of a direct object pronoun. They are never separated from each other.

§6.45 **With a verb in a simple tense or in a compound tense in the affirmative or negative:**

The indirect object pronoun is placed in front of the direct object pronoun and both are placed in front of the verb form:

Juan me lo da / John is giving it to me.
Juan te la daba / John was giving it to you.
Juan nos los dio / John gave them to us.
Juan os las dará / John will give them to you.

María no me lo ha dado / Mary has not given it to me.
María no te la había dado / Mary had not given it to you.
María no nos los habrá dado / Mary will not have given them to us.
María no os las habría dado / Mary would not have given them to you.

§6.46 **With a verb in a simple tense or in a compound tense in the interrogative:**

The indirect object pronoun still remains in front of the direct object pronoun and both still remain in front of the verb form. The subject (whether a noun or pronoun) is placed after the verb form:

¿Nos la dio Juan? / Did John give it to us?
¿Te lo ha dado Juan? / Has John given it to you?

§6.47   **With a verb in the affirmative imperative (command):**

The object pronouns are still in the same order (indirect object + direct object) but they are attached to the verb form and an accent mark is added on the vowel that was stressed in the verb form before the two object pronouns were added. The accent mark is needed to keep the stress where it originally was:

¡Dígamelo Ud., por favor! / Tell it to me, please!

§6.48   **With a verb in the negative imperative (command):**

The position of **no** and the two object pronouns is still the same as usual, in front of the verb form:

¡No me lo diga Ud., por favor! / Don't tell it to me, please!

§6.49   **When dealing with an infinitive,** attach both object pronouns (indirect, direct) to the infinitive:

Juan quiere dármelo / John wants to give it to me.
Juan no quiere dármelo / John does not want to give it to me.

OR

If the main verb is **poder, querer, saber, ir a,** you may place the two object pronouns in front of the main verb:

Juan me lo quiere dar / John wants to give it to me.
Juan no me lo quiere dar / John does not want to give it to me.

§6.50   **When dealing with a present participle,** attach both object pronouns (indirect, direct) to the present participle:

Juan está escribiéndomelo / John is writing it to me.
Juan no está escribiéndomelo / John is not writing it to me.

OR

§6.51   If the main verb is a progressive form with **estar** or another auxiliary, you may place the two object pronouns (indirect, direct) in front of the main verb:

Juan me lo está escribiendo / John is writing it to me.
Juan no me lo está escribiendo / John is not writing it to me.
Juana me lo estaba escribiendo / Jane was writing it to me.

§6.52   When an indirect object pronoun and a direct object pronoun are both 3rd person, either singular or plural or both singular or both plural, the indirect object pronoun (**le** or **les**) changes to **se** because it cannot stand as **le** or **les** in front of a direct object pronoun beginning with the letter "l". Review the direct object pronouns, 3rd person sing. and plural in **§6.7.** Also, review the indirect object pronouns, 3rd person sing. and plural in **§6.14.**

Juan se lo da / John is giving it to you (to him, to her, to it, to you *plural,* to them).

¡Dígaselo Ud.! / Tell it to him!
¡No se lo diga Ud.! / Don't tell it to him!

Juan quiere dárselo.
Juan se lo quiere dar. } John wants to give it to her.

Juan está escribiéndoselo.
Juan se lo está escribiendo. } John is writing it to them.

Since the form **se** can have more than one meaning (to him, to her, to them, *etc.*), in addition to the fact that it looks exactly like the reflexive pronoun **se,** any doubt as to its meaning can be clarified merely by adding any of the following accordingly: **a Ud., a él, a ella, a Uds., a ellos, a ellas.**

§6.53 If you are dealing with a reflexive pronoun, it is normally placed in front of an object pronoun:

Yo me lo puse / I put it on (me, on myself).

§6.54 Demonstrative pronouns

§6.55 Demonstrative pronouns are formed from the demonstrative adjectives. To form a demonstrative pronoun write an accent mark on the stressed vowel of a demonstrative adjective. See **§5.54** and **§5.55.**

§6.56 A demonstrative pronoun is used to take the place of a noun. It agrees in gender and number with the noun it replaces. The demonstrative pronouns are:

MASCULINE	FEMININE	NEUTER	ENGLISH MEANING
éste	**ésta**	**esto**	this one *(here)*
éstos	**éstas**		these *(here)*
ése	**ésa**	**eso**	that one *(there)*
ésos	**ésas**		those *(there)*
aquél	**aquélla**	**aquello**	that one ⎫ *(farther away or*
aquéllos	**aquéllas**		those ⎭ *out of sight)*

§6.57 EXAMPLES:

Me gustan este cuadro y ése / I like this picture and that one.
Me gustan estos guantes y aquéllos / I like these gloves and those.
Esta falda y ésa son bonitas / This skirt and that one are pretty.
Estas camisas y aquéllas son hermosas / These shirts and those are beautiful.

§6.58 NOTE that the neuter forms do not have an accent mark. They are not used when you are referring to a particular noun. They are used when referring to an idea, a statement, a situation, a clause, a phrase. Never use the neuter pronouns to refer to a person.

EXAMPLES:

¿Qué es esto? / What is this?
¿Qué es eso? / What is that?
¿Qué es aquello? / What is that (way over there)?

Eso es fácil de hacer / That is easy to do.
Es fácil hacer eso / It is easy to do that.
Eso es / That's right.

Juan no estudia y esto me inquieta / John does not study and this worries me.

§6.59 NOTE also that the English term *the latter* is expressed in Spanish as **éste, ésta, éstos,** or **éstas;** and the *former* is expressed in Spanish as **aquél, aquélla, aquéllos, aquéllas**—depending on the gender and number of the noun referred to.

AND NOTE that in English the order is generally "the former . . . the latter"—in other words, "the one that was mentioned first . . . the one that was mentioned last". In Spanish, however, the stated order is the opposite: "the latter . . . the former"—in other words, "the one that was just mentioned last . . . the one that was mentioned first:

Roberto y Antonio son inteligentes; éste (meaning Antonio) **es alto y aquél es pequeño** / Robert and Anthony are intelligent; the former (meaning Roberto) is short and the latter is tall.

§6.60 The pronouns **el de, la de, los de, las de; el que, la que, los que, las que**
These pronouns are used in place of nouns.

EXAMPLES:

mi hermano y el *(hermano)* **de mi amigo** / my brother and my friend's (the one of my friend *or* that of my friend)

mi hermana y la *(hermana)* **de mi amigo** / my sister and my friend's (the one of my friend *or* that of my friend)

mis hermanos y los *(hermanos)* **del muchacho** / my brothers and the boy's (the ones of the boy *or* those of the boy)

mis hermanas y las *(hermanas)* **de la muchacha** / my sisters and the girl's (the ones of the girl *or* those of the girl)

El *(muchacho)* **que baila con María es mi hermano** / The one who (The boy who) is dancing with Mary is my brother.

La *(muchacha)* **que baila con Roberto es mi hermana** / The one who (The girl who) is dancing with Robert is my sister.

Los *(muchachos)* **que bailan son mis amigos** / The ones who (The boys who) are dancing are my friends.

Las *(muchachas)* **que bailan son mis amigas** /The ones who (The girls who) are dancing are my friends.

§6.61   Possessive pronouns

§6.62   **Definition:** A possessive pronoun is a word that takes the place of a noun to show possession, as in English: *mine, yours,* etc., instead of saying *my mother, your car,* etc.

§6.63   You form a possessive pronoun by using the appropriate definite article (**el, la, los, las**) + the long form of the possessive adj., all of which are given in **§5.60.** As you realize by now, a pronoun must agree in gender and number with the noun it takes the place of. Therefore, a possessive pronoun must agree in gender and number with the noun it replaces. It does not agree with the possessor.

§6.64   **The possessive pronouns are:**

ENGLISH MEANING	SINGULAR FORM (agreement in gender and number with the noun it replaces)	PLURAL FORM (agreement in gender and number with the noun it replaces)
1. mine	**el mío, la mía**	**los míos, las mías**
2. yours *(fam. sing.)*	**el tuyo, la tuya**	**los tuyos, las tuyas**
3. yours, his, hers, its	**el suyo, la suya**	**los suyos, las suyas**
1. ours	**el nuestro, la nuestra**	**los nuestros, las nuestras**
2. yours *(fam. pl.)*	**el vuestro, la vuestra**	**los vuestros, las vuestras**
3. yours, theirs	**el suyo, la suya**	**los suyos, las suyas**

EXAMPLES:

§6.65   **Mi hermano es más alto que el suyo** / My brother is taller than yours (his, hers, theirs)

Su hermana es más alta que la mía / Your sister is taller than mine.

Mi casa es más grande que la suya / My house is larger than yours (his, hers, theirs).

§6.66   In order to clarify the meanings of **el suyo, la suya, los suyos, las suyas** (since they can mean *yours, his, hers, its, theirs*), do the following: drop the **suyo** form, keep the appropriate definite article (**el, la, los, las**), and add, appropriately, any of the following: **de Ud., de él, de ella, de Uds., de ellos, de ellas:**

mi libro y el de Ud., mi casa y la de él, mis amigos y los de ella, mis amigas y las de Uds., mis libros y los de ellos, mis cuadernos y los de ellas / my book and yours, my house and his, my friends and hers, my friends and yours, *etc.* See also **§5.59.**

§6.67   ¿De quién es . . . ? ¿De quiénes es . . . ? ¿De quién son . . . ? ¿De quiénes son . . . ? / Whose is . . . ? Whose are . . . ?

Whose, when asking a question (usually at the beginning of a sentence), is expressed by any of the above. If you believe that the possessor is singular, use **¿De quién es . . . ?** If you think that the possessor is plural, use **¿De quiénes es . . . ?** And if the noun you have in mind (**whose . . .**) is plural, use the third person plural form of **ser:**

¿De quién es esta casa? / Whose is this house?   **Es de mi tío** / It is my uncle's.

¿De quiénes es esta casa? / Whose is this house?   **Es de mis amigos** / It is my friends'.

¿De quién son estos guantes? / Whose are these gloves?   **Son de Juan** / They are John's.

¿De quiénes son estos niños? / Whose are these children?   **Son de los Señores Pardo** / They are Mr. and Mrs. Pardo's.

§6.68   NOTE that the verb **ser** is used in these expressions showing possession.

§6.69   ALSO NOTE that if a possessive pronoun is used with the verb **ser,** the definite article is dropped:

¿De quién es este lápiz? / Whose is this pencil?   **Es mío** / It is mine.

¿De quién son estas camisas? / Whose are these shirts?   **Son suyas** / They are theirs (yours, his, hers). OR, to clarify **suyas,** say: **Son de Ud., Son de él, Son de ella,** *etc.* / They are yours, They are his, They are hers, *etc.* See also **§6.66.**

§6.70   **Relative pronouns**

§6.71   **Definition:** A pronoun is a word that takes the place of a noun (see **§6.1**). A relative pronoun is a pronoun that refers (relates) to an **antecedent.** An antecedent is something that comes before something; it can be a word, a phrase, a clause which is replaced by a pronoun or some other substitute. Example: *Is it Mary who did that?* In this sentence, *who* is the relative pronoun and *Mary* is the antecedent. Another example, a longer one: *It seems to me that you are right, which is what I had thought right along.* The relative pronoun in this example is *which* and the antecedent of it is the clause, *that you are right.*

In Spanish, a relative pronoun can refer to an antecedent which is a person or a thing, or an idea. A relative pronoun can be subject or object of a verb, or object of a preposition.

§6.72   **Common relative pronouns**

§6.73   **que** / who, that, whom, which. This is the most common relative pronoun.

§6.74   **As subject referring to a person:** / La muchacha **que** habla con Juan es mi hermana / The girl **who** is talking with John is my sister.

Here, the relative pronoun **que** is subject of the verb **habla** and it refers to **la muchacha,** which is the subject of the verb **es.**

§6.75   **As subject referring to a thing:** El libro **que** está en la mesa es mío / The book **which** (**that**) is on the table is mine.

Here, the relative pronoun **que** is subject of the verb **está** and it refers to **el libro,** which is the subject of **es.**

§6.76   **As direct object of a verb referring to a person:** El señor Molina es el profesor **que** admiro / Mr. Molina is the professor **whom** I admire.

Here, the relative pronoun **que** is object of the verb form **admiro.** It refers to **el profesor.**

§6.77   **As direct object of a verb referring to a thing:** La composición **que** Ud. lee es mía / The composition (**that, which**) you are reading is mine.

Here, the relative pronoun **que** is object of the verb form **lee.** It refers to **la composición,** which is the subject of **es.** The subject of **lee** is **Ud.**

§6.78   NOTE here, in the English translation of this example, that we do not always have to use a relative pronoun in English. In Spanish, it must be stated.

§6.79   **As object of a preposition referring only to a thing:** La cama **en que** duermo es grande / The bed **in which** I sleep is large.

Here, the relative pronoun **que** is object of the preposition **en.** It refers to **la cama.** Other prepositions used commonly with **que** are **a, con, de.**

As object of a preposition, **que** refers to a thing only—not to a person. Use **quien** or **quienes** as object of a preposition referring to persons. See **§6.87.**

§6.80   **quien** / who (after a preposition, whom)

§6.81   **As subject of a verb referring only to persons:** Yo sé **quien** lo hizo / I know **who** did it.

Here, **quien** is the subject of **hizo.** It does not refer to a specific antecedent. Here, **quien** includes its antecedent.

§6.82   When used as a subject, **quien** (or **quienes,** if plural) can also mean *he who, she who, the one who, the ones who, those who.* In place of **quien** or **quienes** in this sense, you can also use **el que, la que, los que, las que:**

§6.83   **Quien escucha** oye / Who listens hears; He who listens hears; She who listens hears; The one who listens hears.

OR: **El que escucha** oye / He who listens hears; **La que escucha** oye / She who listens hears; The one who listens hears.

§6.84   **Quienes escuchan** oyen / Who listen hear; Those who listen hear; The ones who listen hear.

OR: **Los que escuchan** oyen; **Las que escuchan** oyen / Those who listen hear; The ones who listen hear.

§6.85   **As subject of a verb,** the relative pronoun **quien** may be used instead of **que** referring only to persons (see also **§6.74**) when it is the subject of a non-restrictive dependent clause set off by commas: La señora Gómez, **quien** (or **que**) es profesora, conoce a mi madre / Mrs. Gómez, who is a teacher, knows my mother.

§6.86   **As direct object of a verb referring only to persons,** the relative pronoun **quien** or **quienes** may be used with the personal **a** (**a quien, a quienes**) instead of **que** (see also **§6.76**): La muchacha **que** (*or* **a quien**) Ud. vio al baile es mi hermana / The girl **whom** you saw at the dance is my sister.

§6.87   **As object of a preposition referring only to persons:** ¿Conoces a la chica **con quien** tomé el almuerzo? / Do you know the girl **with whom** I had lunch? ¿Conoces a los chicos **con quienes** María tomó el almuerzo? / Do you know the boys **with whom** Mary had lunch? ¿Conoce Ud. a los hombres **de quienes** hablo? / Do you know the men **of whom** (**about whom**) I am talking?

§6.88   **el cual, la cual, los cuales, las cuales** / who, that, whom, which, the one which, the ones which, the one who, the ones who.

These relative pronouns may be used in place of **que,** as given in **§6.73ff.** This can be especially needed when it is desired to clarify the gender and number of **que:** La madre de José, **la cual** es muy inteligente, es dentista / Joseph's mother, **who** is very intelligent, is a dentist.

§6.89   These substitute relative pronouns may also refer to things: El libro, **el cual** está sobre la mesa, es mío / The book, **which** (**the one which**) is on the table, is mine.

§6.90   These relative pronouns may also be used as substitutes for **el que, la que, los que, las que** (see **§6.82**) when used as the subject of a non-restrictive dependent clause set off by commas, as given in **§6.85**: La señora Gómez, **la cual** (or **la que**, or **quien**, or **que**) es profesora, conoce a mi madre / Mrs. Gómez, **who** is a teacher, knows my mother.

§6.91   These relative pronouns, as well as **el que, la que, los que, las que**, are used as objects of prepositions except with **a, con, de, en** — in which case the relative pronoun **que** is preferred with things (see **§6.79**). These relative pronouns (**el cual, la cual, los cuales, las cuales** and **el que, la que, los que, las que**) are commonly used with the following prepositions: **para, por, sin, delante de, cerca de,** and **sobre**: En este cuarto, hay una gran ventana **por la cual** se ve el sol por la mañana / In this room, there is a large window **through which** you (one, anyone) can see the sun in the morning.

§6.92   These compound relative pronouns (**el cual, el que,** *etc.*) refer to persons as well as things and can be used as subject of a verb or direct object of a verb when used in a non-restrictive dependent clause separated from its antecedent and set off with commas, as in **§6.88.** See also **§6.89 — §6.91.**

§6.93   **lo cual** / which; **lo que** / what, that which
These are neuter compound relative pronouns. They do not refer to an antecedent of any gender or number. That is why they are called *neuter.*

§6.94   **Lo cual** and **lo que** are used to refer to a statement, a clause, an idea: Mi hijo Juan estudia sus lecciones todos los días, **lo cual** es bueno / My son John studies his lessons every day, **which** is good.   Mi hija recibió buenas notas, **lo que** me gustó / My daughter received good marks, **which** pleased me.

§6.95   **Lo que** is also used to express *what* in the sense of *that which:* Comprendo **lo que** Ud. dice / I understand **what** (**that which**) you say.   **Lo que** Ud. dice es verdad / **What** (**That which**) you say is true.

§6.96   **cuanto = todo lo que** / all that
As a relative pronoun, **cuanto** may be used in place of **todo lo que; Todo lo que** Ud. dice es verdad; OR: **Cuanto** Ud. dice es verdad / All that (All that which) you say is true. See also **§6.95.**

§6.97   **cuyo, cuya, cuyos, cuyas** / whose
This word (and its forms as given) refers to persons and things. Strictly speaking, **cuyo,** *etc.* is not regarded as as relative pronoun but rather as a relative possessive adjective. It agrees in gender and number with what is possessed (whose . . .), not with the possessor. Its position is directly in front of the noun it modifies. Examples:

§6.98   El señor García, **cuyos hijos** son inteligentes, es profesor / Mr. García, **whose children** are intelligent, is a professor.

§6.99   La muchacha, **cuyo padre** es profesor, es inteligente / The girl, **whose father** is a professor, is intelligent.

§6.100   El muchacho, **cuya madre** es profesora, es inteligente / The boy, **whose mother** is a professor, is intelligent.

§6.101   The forms of **cuyo** cannot be used as an interrogative when you ask: Whose is . . . ? You must use **de quién: ¿De quién es este libro?** See also **§6.67 — §6.69.**

§6.102   When referring to parts of the body, use **a quien** instead of **cuyo**: La niña, **a quien** la madre lavó las manos, es bonita / The child, **whose** hands the mother washed, is pretty.

§6.103   **Interrogative pronouns.** See also specific interrogatives, *e.g.,* **qué, cuál,** *etc.,* in the General Index.

Here are a few common interrogatives that you should be aware of when preparing to take the Spanish SAT. NOTE the required accent mark on these words when used in a question:

¿qué . . . ? what . . . ? (See also **§5.68.**)
¿cuál . . . ? which, which one . . . ? (See also **§5.68.**)
¿cuáles . . . ? which, which ones . . . ? (See also **§5.68.**)
¿quién . . . ? ¿quiénes . . . ? who . . . ?
¿a quién . . . ? ¿a quiénes . . . ? whom . . . ? to whom . . . ?
¿de quién . . . ? of whom, from whom, by whom, whose . . . ? (**¿De quién es este lápiz?** / Whose is this pencil?)

§6.104 **Indefinite pronouns.** See also specific indefinite words, *e.g.,* **algo, alguien,** *etc.,* in the General Index.

algo / something, anything (with **sin,** use **nada; sin nada** / without anything)
alguien / anybody, anyone, someone, somebody (with **sin** use **nadie; sin nadie** / without anyone)
alguno, alguna, algunos, algunas / some, any (See also **§5.20.**)

§6.105 **Negative pronouns.** See also **§9.** and specific negative words, *e.g.,* **nada, nadie,** in the General Index.

nada / nothing (**sin nada** / without anything; after **sin, nada** is used instead of **algo; Ella no quiere nada** / She does not want anything.)
nadie / nobody, no one, not anyone, not anybody (**sin nadie** / without anybody; after **sin, nadie** is used instead of **alguien**)
ninguno, ninguna / no one, none, not any, not anybody (See also **§5.20.**)

§7. **VERBS**

§7.1 **Introduction**

A verb is where the action is! A verb is a word that expresses an action (like *go, eat, write*) or a state of being (like *think, believe, be*). Tense means time. Spanish and English verb tenses are divided into three main groups of time: past, present, and future. A verb tense shows if an action or state of being took place, is taking place, or will take place.

Spanish and English verbs are also used in moods, or modes. (There is also the Infinitive Mood, but we are not concerned with that here.) Mood has to do with the *way* a person regards an action or a state that he expresses. For example, a person may merely make a statement or ask a question—this is the Indicative Mood, which we use most of the time in Spanish and English. A person may say that he *would do* something if something else were possible or that he *would have done* something if something else had been possible—this is the Conditional. A person may use a verb *in such a way* that a wish, a fear, a regret, a joy, a request, a supposition, or something of this sort is indicated—this is the Subjunctive Mood. The Subjunctive Mood is used in Spanish much more than in English. Finally, a person may command someone to do something or demand that something be done—this is the Imperative Mood. English Conditional is not a mood.

There are six verb tenses in English: Present, Past, Future, Present Perfect, Past Perfect, and Future Perfect. The first three are simple tenses. The other three tenses are compound and are based on the simple tenses. In Spanish, however, there are fourteen tenses, seven of which are simple and seven of which are compound. The seven compound tenses are based on the seven simple tenses. In Spanish and English a verb tense is simple if it consists of one verb form, *e.g.,* **estudio.** A verb tense is compound if it consists of two parts—the auxiliary (or helping) verb plus the past participle of the verb you have in mind, *e.g.* **he estudiado.** See the list of **Verb Tenses and Moods in Spanish with English Equivalents** in **§8.**

In Spanish there is also another tense which is used to express an action in the present. It is called the *Progressive Present.* It is used only if an action is actually in progress at the present time; for example, **Estoy leyendo,** *I am reading (right now).* It is formed by using the *Present Indicative* of **estar** plus the present participle of the verb you have in mind. There is still another tense in Spanish which is used to express an action that was taking place in the past. It is called the *Progressive Past.* It is used if an action was actually in progress at a certain moment in the past; for example, **Estaba leyendo cuando mi hermano entró,** *I was reading when my brother came in.* The *Progressive Past* is formed by using the *Imperfect Indicative* of **estar** plus the present participle of the verb you have in mind.

In **§8.** and beginning with **§8.14,** the tenses and moods are given in Spanish and the equivalent name or names in English are given in parentheses. Although some of the names given in English are not considered to be tenses (for there are only six), they are given for the purpose of identification as they are related to the Spanish names. The comparison includes only the essential points you need to know about the meanings and uses of Spanish verb tenses and moods as related to English usage to help prepare you for the Spanish test. I shall use examples to illustrate their meanings and uses. This is not intended to be a treatise in detail. It is merely a summary. I hope you find it helpful so that you can understand Spanish verbs better.

But first here are some essential points you need to know about Spanish verbs.

§7.2 Agreement of subject and verb

A subject and verb form must agree in person and number. By *person* is meant 1st, 2nd, or 3rd; by *number* is meant singular or plural. To get a picture of the three persons in the singular and in the plural, see Subject pronouns, **§6.4ff.** This may seem elementary and obvious to you, but too often students become careless on a Spanish test and they neglect to watch for the correct ending of a verb form to agree with the subject in person and number. You must be aware of this. For example, if you had to select the correct subject for the verb form **hablaron** on the next Spanish test you take, and if you were offered the following choices, which would you select? **(A) Ud. (B) vosotros (C) María y Pablo (D) José y yo.** First, you have to look at the ending of the verb form that is given: **hablaron** is 3rd plural because the ending is **-aron,** which is preterit. Therefore, the correct choice for an answer is (C). You do not really have to memorize verb form endings in all the tenses (unless you want to!). All you have to do is open your eyes and observe the verb form by looking at the ending. After constant practice (haven't you been studying Spanish for about three years already?), you should be able *to recognize* the endings and know right away what the subject would have to be: 1st, 2nd or 3rd person, singular or plural.

§7.3 Agreement of subject and reflexive pronoun of a reflexive verb

A subject and reflexive pronoun must agree in person and number. Here, too, students often are careless on a Spanish test and neglect to select the proper reflexive pronoun that matches the subject. To get a picture of the correct reflexive pronoun that goes with the subject, according to the person you need (1st, 2nd or 3rd, singular or plural), see Reflexive pronouns in **§6.21–§6.29.** You must be aware of this so that you can choose the correct answer for the easy questions that test this on the next Spanish test.

§7.4 Formation of past participle

The past participle is regularly formed from the infinitive:

ar ending verbs, drop the **ar** and add **ado: hablar, hablado**
er ending verbs, drop the **er** and add **ido: beber, bebido**
ir ending verbs, drop the **ir** and add **ido: recibir, recibido**

§7.5 Common irregular past participles

For a listing of some commonly used irregular past participles, see **§7.205.** You ought to know them so that you may be able to recognize them on the next Spanish test that you take.

§7.6 Auxiliary verb: haber (to have)

The auxiliary verb **haber** (also called *helping verb*) is used in any of the seven simple tenses + the past participle of the main verb to form the seven compound tenses. For a complete picture of **haber** in the seven simple tenses, see **§8.11.**

§7.7   Transitive verbs

A transitive verb is a verb that takes a direct object. Such a verb is called *transitive* because the action passes over from the subject and directly affects someone or something in some way:

(a) **Veo a mi amigo** / I see my friend.

(b) **Abro la ventana** / I open the window.

(c) **Estudié mis lecciones esta mañana en la biblioteca** / I studied my lessons this morning in the library.

(d) **Antes de salir, la profesora cerró las ventanas de la sala de clase** / Before going out, the teacher closed the classroom windows.

NOTE that in the above examples, the direct object is a noun in every sentence. Let me diagram them for you so you can see that a transitive verb performs an action that passes over from the subject and affects someone or something:

(a)
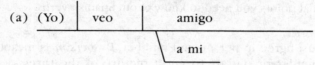

Here, **Yo** is the subject understood; it does not have to be mentioned because the verb ending is 1st person singular and we know it must be **yo**. The verb is **veo**; **amigo** is the direct object; **mi** is a possessive adjective that modifies **amigo**; **a** is the *personal a* used in front of the noun direct object because the direct object is a person.

(b)
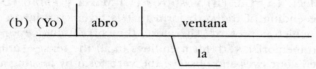

Here, **Yo** is the subject understood; **abro** is the verb; **ventana** is the direct object; **la** is the definite article fem. sing. used with the fem. sing. noun **ventana.**

(c)
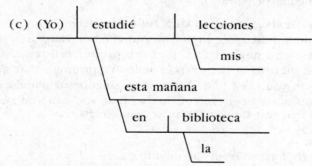

Here, **Yo** is the subject understood; **estudié** is the verb; **lecciones** is the direct object; **mis** is a possessive adjective that modifies **lecciones; esta mañana** has an adverbial value that tells you when the action of the verb took place; **en la biblioteca** is an adverbial prepositional phrase that tells you where the action of the verb took place; hence, they are placed under the words they are related to.

(d)
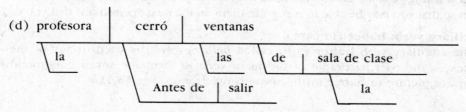

Here, **profesora** is the subject; **la** is the def. art. fem. sing. used with the fem. sing. noun **profesora; cerró** is the verb; **antes de salir** is an adverbial prepositional phrase that tells you when the action of the verb took place; **ventanas** is the direct object; **las** is the def. art. fem. plural used with the fem. plural noun **ventanas** so it is placed under it because it is related to it; **de la sala de clase** is an adjectival prepositional phrase that describes the noun **ventanas; la** is the def. art. sing. fem. used with the fem. sing. noun **sala** and it is placed under it because it is related to it.

§7.8   When the direct object of the verb is a pronoun, it is placed in front of the verb most of the time, generally speaking; at other times it is attached to an infinitive (see **§6.37**); if the main verb is **poder, querer, saber, ir a** + inf., the direct object pronoun may be placed in front of the main verb instead of attaching it to the infinitive (see **§6.38**); at other times, the direct object pronoun is attached to a present participle (see **§6.39**). For an in-depth analysis of the word order of elements in Spanish sentences, particularly pronouns, review **§6.4–§6.53**.

§7.9   Let me diagram the same sentences given above in **§7.7** using them with direct object pronouns instead of direct object nouns so that you may see their position, as in a picture:

   (a) **(Yo) le veo** / I see him.

| (Yo) | le | veo |

The subject is **yo** understood; the verb is **veo**; the direct object pronoun is **le** and it is placed directly in front of the verb. Here, you can use **lo** instead of **le** as a dir. obj. pronoun, masc. sing.

   (b) **(Yo) la abro** / I open it.

| (Yo) | la | abro |

The subject is **yo** understood; the verb is **abro**; the direct object pronoun is **la** (referring to **la ventana**) and it is placed directly in front of the verb.

   (c) **(Yo) las estudié esta mañana en la biblioteca** / I studied them this morning in the library.

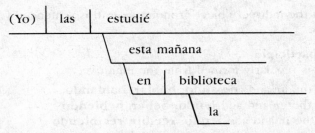

The direct object pronoun **las** (referring to **lecciones**) is placed directly in front of the verb. The other elements in the sentence are the same as in **§7.7(c)**.

   (d) **Antes de salir, la profesora las cerró** / Before going out, the professor closed them.

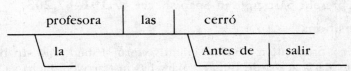

The direct object pronoun **las** (referring to **las ventanas**) is placed directly in front of the verb.

§7.10   For the position of pronouns in other types of sentences in Spanish, review **§6.4–§6.53**.

§7.11 **Intransitive verbs**

An intransitive verb is a verb that does not take a direct object. Such a verb is called *intransitive* because the action does not pass over from the subject and directly affect anyone or anything.

(a) **La profesora está hablando** / The teacher is talking.

(b) **La señora Gómez salió temprano** / Mrs. Gómez left early.

§7.12 **An intransitive verb takes an indirect object:**

(a) **La profesora está hablando a los alumnos** / The teacher is talking to the students.

Here, the indirect object noun is **alumnos** because it is preceded by **a los** (to the).

(b) **La profesora les está hablando** / The teacher is talking to them (meaning, of course, **a los alumnos** / to the students).

Here, the indirect object is the pronoun **les**, meaning *to them*.

For a review of direct object pronouns, see **§6.7–§6.13;** for a review of indirect object pronouns, see **§6.14–§6.20.**

§7.13 **Of course, a transitive verb can take an indirect object, too:**

(a) **La profesora da los libros a los alumnos** / The teacher is giving the books to the pupils.

The direct object is **los libros** and the indirect object is **a los alumnos.**

(b) **La profesora los da a los alumnos** / The teacher is giving them to the pupils.

The direct object pronoun is **los** (meaning **los libros**) and the indirect object noun is still **a los alumnos.**

(c) **La profesora les da los libros** / The teacher is giving the books to them.

The indirect object pronoun is **les** (meaning *to them, i.e.,* **a los alumnos**).

(d) **La profesora se los da** / The teacher is giving them to them.

The indirect object pronoun **les** changes to **se** because **les** is 3rd person and it is followed by **los**, a direct object pronoun, which is also 3rd person. For a review of this point in Spanish grammar, see Position of double object pronouns, beginning in **§6.43;** specifically **§6.52.**

You may clarify the indirect object pronoun **se** in this sentence by adding **a ellos** or **a los alumnos.**

§7.14 **Formation of present participle**

The present participle is regularly formed from the infinitive:

ar ending verbs, drop the **ar** and add **ando: hablar, hablando**
er ending verbs, drop the **er** and add **iendo: beber, bebiendo**
ir ending verbs, drop the **ir** and add **iendo: recibir, recibiendo**

§7.15 **Common irregular present participles**

For a listing of all commonly used irregular present participles, see **§7.190.** You ought to know them so that you may be able to recognize them on the next Spanish SAT that you take.

For uses of the present participle in Spanish, see **§7.191–§7.203**

§7.16 **Verbs with prepositions**

§7.17 A verb right after a preposition is in the infinitive form: Pablio salió **sin hablar** / Paul went out without talking; María acaba **de llegar** / Mary has just arrived; Elena va **a jugar** / Helen is going to play.

§7.18 On the Spanish Test you may be asked to fill in a blank space by selecting the appropriate preposition that is required after a particular verb. Note the following.

§7.19 **Verbs of motion take the prep. a + inf.**

    apresurarse a / to hasten to, to hurry to
    dirigirse a / to go to, to go toward
    ir a / to go to
    regresar a / to return to
    salir a / to go out to
    venir a / to come to
    volver a / to return to

      EXAMPLES:

        Me apresuré a tomar el tren / I hurried to take the train.
        El profesor se dirigió a abrir la puerta / The teacher went to open the door.
        María fue a comer / Mary went to eat.

§7.20 **The following verbs take the prep. a + inf.**

    acertar a / to happen to
    acostumbrarse a / to become used to, to become accustomed to
    aficionarse a hacer algo / to become fond of doing something
    alcanzar a / to succeed in (doing something)
    aprender a / to learn to, to learn how to
    aspirar a / to aspire to
    atreverse a / to dare to
    ayudar a (hacer algo) / to help to
    comenzar a / to begin to
    condenar a / to condemn to
    convidar a / to invite to
    decidirse a / to decide to
    dedicarse a / to devote oneself to
    detenerse a / to pause to, to stop to
    disponerse a / to get ready to
    echarse a / to begin to, to start to
    empezar a / to begin to, to start to
    enseñar a / to teach to
    exponerse a / to run the risk of
    invitar a / to invite to
    negarse a / to refuse to
    obligar a / to oblige to, to obligate to
    ponerse a / to begin to, to start to
    prepararse a / to prepare (oneself) to
    principiar a / to begin to, to start to
    resignarse a / to resign oneself to
    resolverse a / to make up one's mind to
    someter a / to submit to, to subdue to
    venir a / to end up by
    volver a / to (do something) again

      EXAMPLES:

        Me acostumbré a estudiar mis lecciones todas las noches / I became used to studying my lessons every evening.
        No me atreví a responder / I did not dare to answer.
        El hombre comenzó a llorar / The man began to cry.
        Me dispuse a salir / I got ready to go out.
        Me eché a llorar / I began to cry.
        El señor Gómez se negó a ir / Mr. Gómez refused to go.

Juana se puso a correr / Jane began to run.
El muchacho volvió a jugar / The boy played again.

§7.21   **The following verbs take the prep. a + noun** (or pronoun if that is the required dependent element)

acercarse a / to approach
acostumbrarse a / to become accustomed to, to become used to
aficionarse a / to become fond of
asemejarse a / to resemble, to look like
asistir a / to attend, to be present at
asomarse a / to appear at
cuidar a alguien / to take care of someone
dar a / to face, to overlook, to look out upon, to look out over
dedicarse a / to devote oneself to
echar una carta al correo / to mail, to post a letter
echar la culpa a alguien / to blame someone, to put the blame on someone
jugar a / to play (a game, sport, cards)
llegar a ser / to become
llevar a cabo / to carry out, to accomplish
oler a / to smell of, to smell like
parecerse a / to resemble, to look like
querer a / to love
saber a / to taste of, to taste like, to have the flavor of
ser aficionado a / to be fond of, to be a fan of
sonar a / to sound like
subir a / to get on, to get into (a bus, a train, a vehicle)
tocarle a una persona / to be a person's turn

EXAMPLES:

Nos acercamos a la ciudad / We are approaching the city.
Una muchacha bonita se asomó a la puerta / A pretty girl appeared at the door.
Mi cuarto da al jardín / My room faces the garden.
Me dedico a mis estudios / I devote myself to my studies.
Me gusta jugar al tenis / I like to play tennis.
Enrique llegó a ser profesor de matemáticas / Henry became a mathematics teacher.
Jorge llevó a cabo sus responsabilidades / George carried out his responsibilities.
Mi hermano se parece a mi padre y yo me parezco a mi madre / My brother resembles my father and I resemble my mother.
Quiero a mi patria / I love my country.
Soy aficionado a los deportes / I am fond of sports.
Subí al tren / I got on the train.
Le toca a Juan / It is John's turn.

§7.22   **The following verbs take the prep. con + inf.**

amenazar con / to threaten to
contar con / to count on, to rely on
contentarse con / to be satisfied with
soñar con / to dream of, to dream about

EXAMPLES:

Cuento con tener éxito / I am counting on being successful.
Me contento con quedarme en casa / I am satisfied with staying at home.
Sueño con ir a Chile / I dream of going to Chile.

§7.23   **The following verbs take the prep. con + noun** (or pronoun if that is the required dependent element)

acabar con / to finish, to put an end to, to make an end of, to finish off
casarse con / to marry, to get married to
conformarse con / to put up with
contar con / to count on, to rely on
contentarse con / to be satisfied with
cumplir con / to fulfill
dar con / to meet, to find, to come upon
encontrarse con / to run into, to meet by chance
entenderse con / to come to an understanding with
meterse con / to pick a quarrel with
quedarse con / to keep, to hold on to
soñar con / to dream of, to dream about
tropezar con / to come upon, to run across unexpectedly, to run into

EXAMPLES:

José se casó con Ana / Joseph married Anna.
Me conformo con tus ideas / I put up with your ideas.
Contamos con nuestros padres / We count on our parents.
Me contento con poco dinero / I am satisfied with little money.
Siempre cumplo con mi promesa / I always fulfill my promise.
Anoche di con mis amigos en el cine / Last night I met my friends at the movies.
Ayer por la tarde me encontré con un amigo mío / Yesterday afternoon I ran into a friend of mine.
Me quedo con el dinero / I am keeping the money; I am holding on to the money.
Sueño con un verano agradable / I am dreaming of a pleasant summer.

§7.27   **The following verbs take the prep. de + inf.**

acabar de / to have just
acordarse de / to remember to
alegrarse de / to be glad to
arrepentirse de / to repent
cansarse de / to become tired of
cesar de / to cease, to stop
dejar de / to stop, to fail to
encargarse de / to take charge of
haber de / *see* §7.144
ocuparse de / to be busy with, to attend to
olvidarse de / to forget to
tratar de / to try to
tratarse de / to be a question of

EXAMPLES:

Guillermo acaba de llegar / William has just arrived.
Felipe acababa de partir / Philip had just left.
Me alegro de hablarle / I am glad to talk to you.
Me canso de esperar el autobús / I'm getting tired of waiting for the bus.
Cesó de llover / It stopped raining.
Jaime dejó de escribir la redacción / James failed to write the composition.
Mi padre se ocupa de preparar la comida / My father is busy preparing the meal.
Andrés se olvidó de estudiar / Andrew forgot to study.
Siempre trato de hacer un buen trabajo / I always try to do a good job.
Se trata de abstenerse / It is a question of abstaining.

§7.25   **The following verbs take the prep. de + noun** (or pronoun if that is the required dependent element)

abusar de / to abuse, to overindulge in
acordarse de / to remember
alejarse de / to go away from
apartarse de / to keep away from
apoderarse de / to take possession of
aprovecharse de / to take advantage of
bajar de / to get out of, to descend from, to get off
burlarse de / to make fun of
cambiar de / to change (trains, buses, clothes, *etc.*)
cansarse de / to become tired of
carecer de / to lack
compadecerse de / to feel sorry for, to pity, to sympathize with
constar de / to consist of
cuidar de algo / to take care of something
depender de / to depend on
despedirse de / to say good-bye to, to take leave of
despojarse de / to take off (clothing)
disfrutar de / to enjoy
enamorarse de / to fall in love with
encogerse de hombros / to shrug one's shoulders
enterarse de / to find out about
fiarse de alguien / to trust someone
gozar de algo / to enjoy something
ocuparse de / to be busy with, to attend to
oír hablar de / to hear of, to hear about
olvidarse de / to forget
pensar de / to think of [**pensar de** is used when asking for an opinion]
perder de vista / to lose sight of
ponerse de acuerdo / to come to an agreement
preocuparse de / to worry about, to be concerned about
quejarse de / to complain about
reírse de / to laugh at
saber de memoria / to know by heart, to memorize
salir de / to go out of, to leave from
servir de / to serve as
servirse de / to make use of, to use
tratarse de / to be a question of, to deal with

EXAMPLES:

Me acuerdo de aquel hombre / I remember that man.
Vamos a aprovecharnos de esta oportunidad / Let's take advantage of this opporunity.
Después de bajar del tren, fui a comer / After getting off the train, I went to eat.
Todos los días cambio de ropa / Every day I change my clothes.
Me canso de este trabajo / I am getting tired of this work.
Esta composición carece de calidad / This composition lacks quality.
Me compadezco de ese pobre hombre / I pity that poor man.
Ahora tengo que despedirme de usted / Now I have to say good-bye.
Eduardo se enamoró de Carmen / Edward fell in love with Carmen.
Mi madre se ocupa de mi padre que está enfermo / My mother is busy with my father who is sick.
Oí hablar de la boda de Anita / I heard about Anita's wedding.

Carlos se olvidó del aniversario de sus padres / Charles forgot about his parents' anniversary.

¿Qué piensa Ud. de nuestro profesor de español? / What do you think of our Spanish teacher?

¡Mira! El mono se ríe de nosotros / Look! The monkey is laughing at us.

Siempre salgo de casa a las ocho de la mañana / I always leave (from, go out of) the house at eight in the morning.

En nuestro club, Cristóbal sirve de presidente / In our club, Christopher serves as president.

§7.26 **The following verbs generally take the prep. en + inf.**

complacerse en / to be pleased to, to delight in
consentir en / to consent to
convenir en / to agree to, to agree on
empeñarse en / to persist in, to insist on
esforzarse en / to strive for, to force oneself to, to try hard to
insistir en / to insist on
quedar en / to agree to, to agree on
tardar en / to be late (to delay) in

EXAMPLES:
La señora Pardo consintió en asistir a la conferencia / Mrs. Pardo consented to attending the meeting.
El muchacho se empeñó en salir / The boy insisted on going out.
Mis amigos insistieron en venir a verme / My friends insisted on coming to see me.
El avión tardó en llegar / The plane was late in arriving.

§7.27 **The following verbs generally take the prep. en + noun** (or pronoun if that is the required dependent element)

apoyarse en / to lean against, to lean on
confiar en / to rely on, to trust in
consistir en / to consist of
convertirse en / to become, to convert to
entrar en / to enter (into), to go into
fijarse en / to stare at, to notice, to take notice, to observe
meterse en / to get involved in, to plunge into
pensar en / to think of, to think about [**pensar en** is used when asking or when stating what or whom a person is thinking of]
ponerse en camino / to set out, to start out
reparar en / to notice, to observe
volver en sí / to regain consciousness, to be oneself again

EXAMPLES:
Me apoyé en la puerta / I leaned against the door.
Entré en el restaurante / I entered (I went in) the restaurant.
¿En qué piensa Ud.? / What are you thinking of?
Pienso en mi trabajo / I am thinking of my work.
¿En quién piensa Ud.? / Whom are you thinking of?
Pienso en mi madre / I am thinking of my mother.
¿En quiénes piensa Ud.? / Whom are you thinking of?
Pienso en mis padres / I am thinking of my parents.

§7.28 **The following verbs generally take the prep. por + inf., noun, pronoun, adj., if that is the required dependent element**

acabar por / to end up by
dar por / to consider, to regard as
darse por / to pretend (to be something), to think oneself (to be something)
estar por / to be in favor of
interesarse por / to take an interest in
pasar por / to be considered as
preguntar por / to ask for, to inquire about
tener por / to consider something, to have an opinion on something
tomar por / to take someone for

EXAMPLES:

Domingo acabó por casarse con Elena / Dominic finally ended up by marrying Helen.

¿Mi libro de español? Lo doy por perdido / My Spanish book? I consider it lost.

La señorita López se da por actriz / Miss López pretends to be an actress.

Estamos por quedarnos en casa esta noche / We are in favor of staying at home this evening.

El señor Pizarro pasa por experto / Mr. Pizarro is considered an expert.

Pregunto por el señor Pardo. ¿Está en casa? / I am asking for Mr. Pardo. Is he at home?

§7.29 **Verb + NO PREPOSITION + inf. The following verbs do not ordinarily take a preposition when followed by an infinitive**

deber + inf. / must, ought to
Debo hacer mis lecciones / I must (ought to) do my lessons.
Exception: *see* **deber de + inf.** in **§7.127.**

decidir + inf. / to decide

dejar + inf. / to allow to, to let
Mi madre me dejó salir / My mother allowed me to go out.
Dejé caer mi libro / I dropped my book (I let my book fall.)

desear + inf. / to desire to, to wish to
Deseo tomar un café / I wish to have a cup of coffee.

esperar + inf. / to expect to, to hope to
Espero ir a la América del Sur este invierno / I expect to go to South America this winter.

hacer + inf. / to do, to make, to have something made or done
Tú me haces llorar / You make me cry.
Mi madre hace construir una casita / My mother is having a small house built [by someone].
NOTE that the use of **hacer + inf.** / can be described as the "causative (causal)" use of **hacer** when there is an inf. directly after it. The construction **hacer + inf.** indicates that something is being made or being done by someone. Further examples: **hacer firmar** / to have (something) signed (by someone); **hacer confesar** / to have (someone) confess or to make (someone) confess. This causative use of **hacer** is used in a verb tense that is needed + inf. form of the verb that tells what action is being done or being made: **Mi madre hizo construir una casita** / My mother had a little house built; **Le haré confesar** / I shall make him confess; **El señor López lo hizo firmar la carta** / Mr. López made him sign the letter. **Mi madre me hace estudiar** / My mother makes me study.

necesitar + inf. / to need
Necesito pasar una hora en la biblioteca / I need to spend an hour in the library.

oír + inf. / to hear

Le oí entrar por la ventana / I heard him enter through the window.
He oído hablar de su buena fortuna / I have heard (talk) about your good fortune; **He oído decir que la señora Sierra está enferma** / I have heard (tell) that Mrs. Sierra is sick.

pensar + inf. / to intend to, to plan to
Pienso hacer un viaje a México / I plan to take a trip to Mexico.

poder + inf. / to be able to, can
Puedo venir a verle a la una / I can come to see you at one o'clock.

preferir + inf. / to prefer
Prefiero quedarme en casa esta noche / I prefer to stay at home this evening.

prometer + inf. / to promise
Prometo venir a verle a las ocho / I promise to come to see you at eight o'clock.

querer + inf. / to want to, to wish to
Quiero comer ahora / I want to eat now.
¿Qué quiere decir este muchacho? / What does this boy mean?
María quiere hacerse profesora / Mary wants to become a teacher.

saber + inf. / to know how to
¿Sabe Ud. nadar? / Do you know how to swim?
Sí, yo sé nadar / Yes, I know how to swim.

ver + inf. / to see
Veo venir el tren / I see the train coming.

§7.30 **The following verbs do not ordinarily require a preposition, whereas in English a preposition is used**

agradecer / to thank for, to be thankful (to someone) for (something)
Le agradecí su paciencia / I thanked him for his patience.

aprovechar / to take advantage of
¿No quiere Ud. aprovechar la oportunidad? / Don't you want to take advantage of the opportunity?

buscar / to look for, to search for
Busco mi libro / I am looking for my book.

escuchar / to listen to
Escucho la música / I am listening to the music.

esperar / to wait for
Espero el autobús / I am waiting for the bus.

guardar cama / to stay in bed
La semana pasada guardé cama / Last week I stayed in bed.

lograr / to succeed in
El alumno logró hacerlo / The pupil succeeded in doing it.

mirar / to look at
Miro el cielo / I am looking at the sky.

pagar / to pay for
Pagué los billetes / I paid for the tickets.

pedir / to ask for
Pido un libro / I am asking for a book.

soler + inf. / to be accustomed to, to be in the habit of
(Yo) suelo acompañar a mis amigos en el autobús / I am in the habit of accompanying my friends on the bus.

§7.31   **Principal parts of some important verbs**

Infinitive	Present Participle	Past Participle	Present Indicative (yo)	Preterit (yo)
abrir	abriendo	abierto	abro	abrí
andar	andando	andado	ando	anduve
caber	cabiendo	cabido	quepo	cupe
caer	cayendo	caído	caigo	caí
conseguir	consiguiendo	conseguido	consigo	conseguí
construir	construyendo	construido	construyo	construí
corregir	corrigiendo	corregido	corrijo	corregí
creer	creyendo	creído	creo	creí
cubrir	cubriendo	cubierto	cubro	cubrí
dar	dando	dado	doy	di
decir	diciendo	dicho	digo	dije
descubrir	descubriendo	descubierto	descubro	descubrí
deshacer	deshaciendo	deshecho	deshago	deshice
despedirse	despidiéndose	despedido	me despido	me despedí
destruir	destruyendo	destruido	destruyo	destruí
devolver	devolviendo	devuelto	devuelvo	devolví
divertirse	divirtiéndose	divertido	me divierto	me divertí
dormir	durmiendo	dormido	duermo	dormí
escribir	escribiendo	escrito	escribo	escribí
estar	estando	estado	estoy	estuve
haber	habiendo	habido	he	hube
hacer	haciendo	hecho	hago	hice
huir	huyendo	huido	huyo	huí
ir	yendo	ido	voy	fui
irse	yéndose	ido	me voy	me fui
leer	leyendo	leído	leo	leí
mentir	mintiendo	mentido	miento	mentí
morir	muriendo	muerto	muero	morí
oír	oyendo	oído	oigo	oí
oler	oliendo	olido	huelo	olí
pedir	pidiendo	pedido	pido	pedí
poder	pudiendo	podido	puedo	pude
poner	poniendo	puesto	pongo	puse
querer	queriendo	querido	quiero	quise
reír	riendo	reído	río	reí
repetir	repitiendo	repetido	repito	repetí
resolver	resolviendo	resuelto	resuelvo	resolví
romper	rompiendo	roto	rompo	rompí
saber	sabiendo	sabido	sé	supe
salir	saliendo	salido	salgo	salí
seguir	siguiendo	seguido	sigo	seguí
sentir	sintiendo	sentido	siento	sentí
ser	siendo	sido	soy	fui
servir	sirviendo	servido	sirvo	serví
tener	teniendo	tenido	tengo	tuve
traer	trayendo	traído	traigo	traje
venir	viniendo	venido	vengo	vine
ver	viendo	visto	veo	vi
vestir	vistiendo	vestido	visto	vestí
volver	volviendo	vuelto	vuelvo	volví

§7.32 **Orthographical (spelling) changes in verb forms and stem-changing (radical-changing) verb forms.** See Present Indicative, **§8.19**; Preterit, **§8.30**; Present Subjunctive, **§8.42–§8.49**; Imperfect Subjunctive, **§8.51–§8.54.**

§7.33 **Subjunctive**

The subjunctive is not a tense; it is a mood or mode. Usually, when we speak in Spanish or English, we use the indicative mood. We use the subjunctive mood in Spanish for certain reasons. The following are the principal reasons.

§7.34 **After certain conjunctions**

When the following conjunctions introduce a new clause, the verb in that new clause is in the subjunctive mood:

> **a fin de que** / so that, in order that
> **a menos que** / unless
> **a no ser que** / unless
> **antes que** *or* **antes de que** / before
> **como si** / as if
> **con tal que** *or* **con tal de que** / provided that
> **en caso que** *or* **en caso de que** / in case, in case that, supposing that
> **para que** / in order that, so that
> **sin que** / without

EXAMPLES:

§7.35 **Se lo explico a ustedes a fin de que puedan comprenderlo** / I am explaining it to you so that (in order that) you may be able to understand it.

§7.36 **Saldré a las tres y media a menos que esté lloviendo** / I will go out at three thirty unless it is raining.

§7.37 When the following conjunctions introduce a new clause, the verb in that new clause is sometimes in the indicative mood, sometimes in the subjunctive mood. Use the subjunctive mood if what is being expressed indicates some sort of anxious anticipation, doubt, indefiniteness, vagueness, or uncertainty. If these are not implied and if the action was completed in the past, use the indicative mood:

> **a pesar de que** / in spite of the fact that
> **así que** / as soon as, after
> **aunque** / although, even if, even though
> **cuando** / when
> **de manera que** / so that, so as
> **de modo que** / so that, in such a way that
> **después que** *or* **después de que** / after
> **en cuanto** / as soon as
> **hasta que** / until
> **luego que** / as soon as, after
> **mientras** / while, as long as
> **siempre que** / whenever, provided that
> **tan pronto como** / as soon as

EXAMPLES:

§7.38 **Le daré el dinero a Roberto cuando me lo pida** / I shall give the money to Robert when he asks me for it. (**Pida** is in the subjunctive mood because some doubt or uncertainty is suggested and Robert may not ask for it.)

§7.39 **BUT: Se lo di a Roberto cuando me lo pidió** / I gave it to Robert when he asked me for it. (No subjunctive of **pedir** here because he actually did ask me for it.)

§7.40   **Esperaré hasta que llegue el autobús** / I shall wait until the bus arrives. (**Llegue** is in the subjunctive mood here because some doubt or uncertainty is suggested and the bus may never arrive.)

§7.41   **BUT: Esperé hasta que llegó el autobús** / I waited until the bus arrived. (No subjunctive of **llegar** here because the bus actually did arrive.)

§7.42   **Trabajaré hasta que Ud. venga** / I shall work until you come. (**venga** is used here because some doubt or uncertainty is suggested and **Ud.** may never come.)

§7.43   **BUT: Trabajé hasta que Ud. vino** / I worked until you came. (No subjunctive of **venir** here because **Ud.** actually did come.)

§7.44   **After certain adverbs**

acaso
quizá *or* **quizás**   } perhaps, maybe
tal vez

§7.45   **Tal vez hayan perdido** / Perhaps they have lost. (Subjunctive is used here because some degree of uncertainty or pessimism is implied.)

§7.46   **Tal vez han ganado** / Perhaps they have won. (No subjunctive is used here because some degree of certainty or optimism is implied.)

§7.47   **Por + adj.** or **adv. + que** / however, no matter how

§7.48   **Por (más) interesante que sea, no quiero ver esa película** / No matter how interesting it may be, I do not want to see that film.

§7.49   **Por bien que juegue Roberto, no quiero jugar con él** / However well (No matter how well) Robert plays, I do not want to play with him.

§7.50   **After certain indefinite expressions**
cualquier, cualquiera, cualesquier, cualesquiera / whatever, whichever, any (the final **a** drops in **cualquiera** and **cualesquiera** when the word is in front of a noun)
cuandoquiera / whenever
dondequiera / wherever; **adondequiera** / to wherever
quienquiera, quienesquiera / whoever
EXAMPLES:

§7.51   **No abriré la puerta, quienquiera que sea** / I will not open the door, whoever it may be.

§7.52   **Dondequiera que Ud. esté, escríbame** / Wherever you may be, write to me.

§7.53   **Adondequiera que Ud. vaya, dígamelo** / Wherever you may go, tell me.

§7.54   **After an indefinite or negative antecedent**
See **§6.71** for a brief definition of an antecedent with examples. Remember to use the General Index for references to explanations and examples located in different parts of this book.

§7.55   The reason why the subjunctive is needed after an indefinite or negative antecedent is that the person or thing desired may possibly not exist; or, if it does exist, you may never find it.
EXAMPLES:

§7.56   **Busco un libro que sea interesante** / I am looking for a book which is interesting.

§7.57   **BUT: Tengo un libro que es interesante** / I have a book which is interesting.

§7.58   **¿Conoce Ud. a alguien que tenga paciencia?** / Do you know someone who has patience?

§7.59   **BUT: Conozco a alguien que tiene paciencia** / I know someone who has patience.

§7.60   **No encontré a nadie que supiera la respuesta** / I did not find anyone who knew the answer.

§7.61   **No encuentro a nadie que sepa la respuesta** / I do not find anyone who knows the answer.

§7.62   **BUT: Encontré a alguien que sabe la respuesta** / I found someone who knows the answer.

§7.63   **No puedo encontrar a nadie que pueda prestarme dinero** / I can't meet (find) anyone who can lend me money.

§7.64   **BUT: Conozco a alguien que puede prestarme dinero** / I know somebody who can lend me money.

§7.65   **AND: Encontré a alguien que puede prestarme dinero** / I met (found) someone who can lend me money.

§7.66   **After ¡Que . . . !**
In order to express indirectly a wish, an order, a command in the 3rd person singular or plural, you may use the exclamatory **¡Que . . . !** alone to introduce the subjunctive clause. The words generally understood to be omitted are: **Quiero que . . .** or **Deje que . . .** , which mean **I want . . .** or **Let . . .** Examples:

   ¡Que lo haga Jorge! / Let George do it! (In other words, the complete statement would be: **¡Deje que lo haga Jorge!** *or* **¡Quiero que lo haga Jorge!** / I want George to do it!)
   ¡Que entre! / Let him enter! *or* I want him to enter! (**¡Quiero que entre!**)

§7.67   **After ¡Ojalá que . . . !**

§7.68   The exclamatory expression **Ojalá** is of Arabic origin meaning "Oh, God!" (Oh, Allah!).
EXAMPLES:

§7.69   **¡Ojalá que vengan!** / If only they would come! (Would that they come! Oh, God, let them come!)

§7.70   **¡Ojalá que lleguen!** / If only they would arrive! (Would that they arrive! Oh, God, let them arrive!)

§7.71   **After certain impersonal expressions**
Generally speaking, the following impersonal expressions require the subjunctive form of the verb in the clause that follows.

§7.72   **Basta que . . .** / It is enough that . . . ; It is sufficient that . . .
Conviene que . . . / It is fitting that . . . ; It is proper that . . .
Importa que . . . / It is important that . . .
Más vale que . . . / It is better that . . .
Es aconsejable que . . . / It is advisable that . . .
Es bueno que . . . / It is good that . . .
Es importante que . . . / It is important that . . .
Es imposible que . . . / It is impossible that . . .
Es lástima que . . . / It is a pity that . . .
Es malo que . . . / It is bad that . . .
Es mejor que . . . / It is better that . . .
Es menester que . . . / It is necessary that . . .
Es necesario que . . . / It is necessary that . . .
Es posible que . . . / It is possible that . . .
Es preciso que . . . / It is necessary that . . .

Es probable que . . . / It is probable that . . .
Es raro que . . . / It is rare that . . .
Es urgente que . . . / It is urgent that . . .

EXAMPLES:

§7.73 **Basta que sepan la verdad** / It is sufficient that they know the truth.

§7.74 **Conviene que venga ahora mismo** / It is proper that she come right now.

§7.75 **Es aconsejable que salga inmediatamente** / It is advisable that she leave immediately.

§7.76 **Es probable que María regrese a las tres** / It is probable that Mary will return at three o'clock.

§7.77 **Es necesario que Ud. escriba la composición** / It is necessary that you write the composition *or* It is necessary for you to write the composition.

§7.78 **After verbs or expressions that indicate denial, doubt or lack of belief, and uncertainty**

dudar que . . . / to doubt that . . .
negar que . . . / to deny that . . .
no creer que . . . / not to believe that . . .
Es dudoso que . . . / It is doubtful that . . .
Es incierto que . . . / It is uncertain that . . .
Hay duda que . . . / There is doubt that . . .
No es cierto que . . . / It is not certain that . . .
No estar seguro que . . . / Not to be sure that . . .
No suponer que . . . / Not to suppose that . . .

EXAMPLES:

§7.79 **Dudo que mis amigos vengan a verme** / I doubt that my friends are coming (will come) to see me.

§7.80 **No creo que sea urgente** / I do not believe that it is urgent.

§7.81 **Es dudoso que Pablo lo haga** / It is doubtful that Paul will do it.

§7.82 **After verbs or expressions that indicate an emotion of joy, gladness, happiness, sorrow, regret, fear, surprise**

§7.83 **estar contento que . . .** / to be happy that . . . , to be pleased that . . .
estar feliz que . . . / to be happy that . . .
estar triste que . . . / to be sad that . . .
alegrarse (de) que . . . / to be glad that . . .
sentir que . . . / to regret that . . . , to feel sorry that . . .
sorprenderse (de) que . . . / to be surprised that . . .
temer que . . . / to fear that . . .
tener miedo (de) que . . . / to be afraid that . . .

EXAMPLES:

§7.84 **Estoy muy contento de que mis amigos vengan a verme** / I am very pleased that my friends are coming (will come) to see me.

§7.85 **Me alegro de que ellos hayan venido** / I am glad that they have come.

§7.86 **Siento mucho que su madre esté enferma** / I am very sorry that your mother is ill.

§7.87 **After certain verbs that imply a wish or desire that something be done, including a command, order, preference, advice, permission, request, plea, insistence, suggestion**

aconsejar / to advise
consentir / to consent
decir / to tell (someone to do something)
dejar / to allow, to let
desear / to want, to wish
esperar / to hope
exigir / to demand, to require
hacer / to make (someone do something or something be done)
insistir (en) / to insist (on, upon)
mandar / to order, to command
pedir / to ask, to request
permitir / to allow, to permit
preferir / to prefer
prohibir / to forbid, to prohibit
querer / to want, to wish (someone to do something or that something be done)
recomendar / to recommend
rogar / to beg, to request
sugerir / to suggest
suplicar / to beg, to plead, to make a plea
EXAMPLES:

§7.88   **Les aconsejo a ellos que hagan el trabajo** / I advise them to do the work.

§7.89   **Les digo a ellos que escriban los ejercicios** / I am telling them to write the exercises.

§7.90   **Mi madre quiere que yo vaya a la escuela ahora** / My mother wants me to go to school now.

§7.91   **BUT: Yo quiero ir a la escuela ahora** / I want to go to school now.

§7.92   **NOTE:** In this example, there is no change in subject; therefore, the infinitive **ir** is used. But in the example in §7.90, there is a new subject (**yo**) in the dependent clause and **ir** is in the subjunctive because the verb **querer** is used in the main clause.

§7.93   **El capitán me manda que yo entre** / The captain orders me to come in.

§7.94   **OR: El capitán me manda entrar** / The captain orders me to come in.
        (**NOTE** that **mandar** can take a new clause in the subjunctive or it can take an infinitive.)

§7.95   **El coronel me permite que yo salga** / The colonel permits me to leave.

§7.96   **OR: El coronel me permite salir** / The colonel permits me to leave.
        (**NOTE** that **permitir** can take a new clause in the subjunctive or it can take an infinitive. You can do the same with the verbs **dejar, hacer, mandar** and **prohibir.**)

§7.97   **Mi profesor exige que yo escriba los ejercicios** / My professor demands that I write the exercises.

§7.98   **Espero que mi perrito vuelva pronto** / I hope that my little dog returns soon.

§7.99   **Le ruego a usted que me devuelva mi libro** / I beg you to return my book to me.

§7.100   **IN SUM, NOTE THAT:**

(a) Beginning with **§7.33,** the subjunctive form of the verb in the dependent clause is used because what precedes is either a certain conjunction, a certain adverb, the expression **por + adj.** or **adv. + que,** a certain indefinite expression, an indefinite or negative antecedent, a superlative, an indirect wish or command or order introduced by **¡Que . . . !** (which is short for **"Quiero que . . . "** or **"Deje que . . . "**), **¡Ojalá que . . . !** or a certain impersonal expression, or a certain verb (**§7.78–§7.99**).

(b) When you are dealing with two different subjects, you need two clauses: the main clause (also known as independent clause) and the dependent clause which contains the new subject. See, for example, **§7.90.** When there is no change in subject, there is no need for a second clause, as in **§7.91.**

(c) Generally speaking, only the verbs **dejar, hacer, mandar, permitir, prohibir** (as in **§7.93–§7.96**) can be followed by just the infinitive or a new clause with its verb in the subjunctive.

(d) In English, it is possible not to use a second clause even when the subject changes and to use an infinitive, but this is not so in Spanish—except for what is noted in **§7.93-§7.96.** Example: I want you to leave / **Quiero que Ud. salga.**

§7.101   **Sequence of tenses when the subjunctive is required: a summary**

When the verb in the main clause is in the:	The verb in the following clause (the dependent clause) most likely will be in the:
1. Present Indicative or Future or Present Perfect Indicative or Imperative (Command)	1. Present Subjunctive or Present Perfect Subjunctive
2. Conditional or a past tense (Imperfect Indicative or Preterit or Pluperfect Indicative)	2. Imperfect Subjunctive or Pluperfect Subjunctive

EXAMPLES:

§7.102   **Deseo que Ana cante** / I want Anna to sing.

§7.103   **Le diré a Ana que baile** / I will tell Anna to dance.

§7.104   **Le he dicho a Ana que cante y baile** / I have said to Anna to sing and dance.

§7.105   **Dígale a Ana que cante y baile** / Tell Anna to sing and dance.

§7.106   **Dudo que mi madre tome el tren** / I doubt that my mother is taking (*or* will take) the train.

§7.107   **Dudo que mi madre haya tomado el tren** / I doubt that my mother has taken the train.

§7.108   **Le gustaría al profesor que los alumnos hicieran los ejercicios** / The professor would like the pupils to do the exercises.

§7.109   **Sentía que su madre estuviera enferma** / I felt sorry that your mother was ill.

§7.110   **Dudé que mi madre hubiera tomado el tren** / I doubted that my mother had taken the train.

§7.111   Si clause: a summary of contrary-to-fact conditions

When the verb in the **Si** clause is:	The verb in the main or result clause is:
1. Present Indicative	1. Future

Example: **Si tengo bastante tiempo, vendré a verle** / If I have enough time, I will come to see you.

Note that the present subjunctive form of a verb is never used in a clause beginning with the conjunction **si**.

2. Imperfect Subjunctive (**-se** form or **-ra** form)	2. Conditional or Imperfect Subjunctive (**-ra** form)

Example: **Si yo tuviese** (*or* **tuviera**) **bastante tiempo, vendría a verle** / If I had enough time, I would come to see you.

OR: **Si yo tuviese** (*or* **tuviera**) **bastante tiempo, viniera a verle** / If I had enough time, I would come to see you.

3. Pluperfect Subjunctive (**-se** form or **-ra** form)	3. Conditional Perfect or Pluperfect Subjunctive (**-ra** form)

Example: **Si yo hubiese tenido** (*or* **hubiera tenido**) **bastante tiempo, habría venido a verle** / If I had had enough time, I would have come to see you.

OR: **Si yo hubiese tenido** (*or* **hubiera tenido**) **bastante tiempo, hubiera venido a verle** / If I had had enough time, I would have come to see you.

§7.112   Acabar de + inf. (See also idioms with **de** in §14.22)

The Spanish idiomatic expression **acabar de + inf.** is expressed in English as *to have just* + past participle. This is a very common expression which you surely will find on SAT II: Spanish.

§7.113   In the present indicative:

María acaba de llegar / Mary has just arrived.
Acabo de comer / I have just eaten.
Acabamos de terminar la lección / We have just finished the lesson.

§7.114   In the imperfect indicative:

María acababa de llegar / Mary had just arrived.
Acababa de comer / I had just eaten.
Acabábamos de terminar la lección / We had just finished the lesson.

NOTE:

§7.115   When you use **acabar** in the present tense, it indicates that the action of the main verb (+ inf.) has just occurred now in the present. In English, we express this by using *have just* + the past participle of the main verb: **Acabo de llegar** / I have just arrived. (See the other examples above under **present indicative**.)

§7.116   When you use **acabar** in the imperfect indicative, it indicates that the action of the main verb (+ inf.) had occurred at some time in the past when another action occurred in the past. In English, we express this by using *had just* + the past participle of the main verb: **Acabábamos de entrar en la casa cuando el teléfono sonó** / We had just entered the house when the telephone rang. (See the other examples above under **imperfect indicative**.)

§7.117   NOTE also that when **acabar** is used in the imperfect indicative + the inf. of the main verb being expressed, the verb in the other clause is usually in the preterit.

§7.118   **Conocer** and **saber** (See also §7.165)

These two verbs mean *to know,* but they are used in a distinct sense.

(a)   Generally speaking, **conocer** means to know in the sense of *being acquainted* with a person, a place, or a thing: **¿Conoce Ud. a María?** / Do you know Mary? **¿Conoce Ud. bien los Estados Unidos?** / Do you know the United States well? **¿Conoce Ud. este libro?** / Do you know (Are you acquainted with) this book?

In the preterit tense, **conocer** means *met* in the sense of *first met, first became acquainted with someone:* **¿Conoce Ud. a Elena?** / Do you know Helen? **Sí, (yo) la conocí anoche en casa de un amigo mío** / Yes, I met her [for the first time] last night at the home of one of my friends.

(b)   Generally speaking, **saber** means to know a fact, to know something thoroughly: **¿Sabe Ud. qué hora es?** / Do you know what time it is? **¿Sabe Ud. la lección?** / Do you know the lesson?

When you use **saber + inf.,** it means *to know how:* **¿Sabe Ud. nadar?** / Do you know how to swim? **Sí, (yo) sé nadar** / Yes, I know how to swim.

In the preterit tense, **saber** means *found out:* **¿Lo sabe Ud.?** / Do you know it? **Sí, lo supe ayer** / Yes, I found it out yesterday.

§7.119   **Dicho, dichoso, dicha**

§7.120   The word **dicho** is the past part. (irregular) of **decir: ¿Ha dicho Ud. la verdad?** / Have you told the truth?

§7.121   The word **dicho** is also used with the neuter article **lo** and has a special meaning: **Lo dicho y lo escrito** / what has been said and what has been written.

§7.122   The word **dicho** is also used in the following expression: **dicho y hecho** / no sooner said that done.

§7.123   The word **dichoso** is an adj. and it means fortunate, happy, lucky: **una vida dichosa** / a happy life.

§7.124   The word **dicha** is a fem. noun and it means happiness, good fortune.

§7.125   **Deber, deber de** and **tener que**

§7.126   Generally speaking, use **deber** when you want to express a moral obligation, something you ought to do but you may or may not do it: **Debo estudiar esta noche pero estoy cansado y no me siento bien** / I ought to study tonight but I am tired and I do not feel well.

§7.127   Generally speaking, **deber de + inf.** is used to express a supposition, something that is probable: **La señora Gómez debe de estar enferma porque sale de casa raramente** / Mrs. Gómez must be sick (is probably sick) because she goes out of the house rarely.

§7.128   Generally speaking, use **tener que** when you want to say that you *have to* do something: **No puedo salir esta noche porque tengo que estudiar** / I cannot go out tonight because I have to study.

§7.129   **Dejar, salir,** and **salir de**

§7.130   These verbs mean *to leave,* but notice the difference in use:

§7.131   Use **dejar** when you leave someone or when you leave something behind you: **El alumno dejó sus libros en la sala de clase** / The pupil left his books in the classroom.

Dejar also means *to let* or *to allow* or *to let go:* **¡Déjelo!** / Let it! (Leave it!)

§7.132   Use **salir de** when you mean *to leave* in the sense of *to go out of* (a place): **El alumno salió de la sala de clase** / The pupil left the classroom; **¿Dónde está su madre? Mi madre salió** / Where is your mother? My mother went out.

§7.133   **Dejar de + inf.** and **dejar caer**

§7.134   Use **dejar de + inf.** when you mean *to stop* or *to fail to:* **Los alumnos dejaron de hablar cuando la profesora entró en la sala de clase** / The students stopped talking when the teacher came into the classroom.

¡No deje Ud. de llamarme! / Don't fail to call me!

Dejar caer means *to drop:* **Luis dejó caer sus libros** / Louis dropped his books.

§7.135   **Ir, irse**

§7.136   Use **ir** when you simply mean *to go:* **Voy al cine** / I am going to the movies.

§7.137   Use **irse** when you mean *to leave* in the sense of *to go away:* **Mis padres se fueron al campo para visitar a mis abuelos** / My parents left for (went away to) the country to visit my grandparents.

§7.138   **Gastar** and **pasar**

§7.139   These two verbs mean *to spend,* but notice the difference in use:

§7.140   Use **gastar** when you spend money: **No me gusta gastar mucho dinero** / I do not like to
§7.141   spend much money.

§7.142   Use **pasar** when you spend time: **Me gustaría pasar un año en España** / I would like to spend a year in Spain.

§7.143   **Gustar**

(a) Essentially, the verb **gustar** means *to be pleasing to . . .*

(b) In English, we say, for example, *I like ice cream.* In Spanish, we say **Me gusta el helado;** that is to say, "Ice cream is pleasing to me" [To me ice cream is pleasing].

(c) In English, the thing that you like is the direct object. In Spanish, the thing that you like is the subject. Also, in Spanish, the person who likes the thing is the indirect object: to me, to you, *etc.:* **A Roberto le gusta el helado** / Robert likes ice cream; in other words, "To Robert, ice cream is pleasing to him."

(d) In Spanish, therefore, the verb **gustar** is used in the third person, either in the singular or plural, when you talk about something that you like—something that is pleasing to you. Therefore, the verb form must agree with the subject; if the thing liked is singular, the verb is third person singular; if the thing liked is plural, the verb **gustar** is third person plural: **Me gusta el café** / I like coffee; **Me gustan el café y la leche** / I like coffee and milk ["Coffee and milk are pleasing to me."]

(e) When you mention the person or the persons who like something, you must use the preposition **a** in front of the person; you must also use the indirect object pronoun of the noun which is the person:

A los muchachos y a las muchachas les gusta jugar / Boys and girls like to play; that is to say, "To play is pleasing to them, to boys and girls."

    (f) Review the indirect object pronouns which are given in §6.14–§6.20. They are: **me, te, le; nos, os, les**.

    (g) Other examples:

        Me gusta leer / I like to read.
        Te gusta leer / You (*familiar*) like to read.
        A Felipe le gusta el helado / Philip likes ice cream.
        Al chico le gusta la leche / The boy likes milk.
        A Carlota le gusta bailar / Charlotte likes to dance.
        A las chicas les gustó el libro / The girls liked the book.
        Nos gustó el cuento / We liked the story.
        ¿Le gusta a Ud. el español? / Do you like Spanish?
        A Pedro y a Ana les gustó la película / Peter and Anna liked the film.
        A mi amigo le gustaron los chocolates / My friend liked the chocolates; that is to say, the chocolates were pleasing to my friend.

§7.144   Haber, haber de + inf. and tener

§7.145   The verb **haber** (to have) is used as an auxiliary verb (or helping verb) in order to form the seven compound tenses, which are as follows:

Compound Tenses	Example (in the 1st person sing.)
Present Perfect (or Perfect) Indicative	**he hablado** (I have spoken)
Pluperfect (or Past Perfect) Indicative	**había hablado** (I had spoken)
Preterit Perfect (or Past Anterior)	**hube hablado** (I had spoken)
Future Perfect (or Future Anterior)	**habré hablado** (I will have spoken)
Conditional Perfect	**habría hablado** (I would have spoken)
Present Perfect (or Past) Subjunctive	**haya hablado** (I may have spoken)
Pluperfect (or Past Perfect) Subjunctive	**hubiera hablado** *or* **hubiese hablado** (I might have spoken)

    For an explanation of the formation of these tenses, see the names of these tenses in the General Index.

§7.146   The verb **haber** is also used to form the Perfect (or Past) Infinitive: **haber hablado** (to have spoken). As you can see, this is formed by using the infinitive form of **haber** + the past participle of the main verb.

§7.147   The verb **haber** is also used to form the Perfect Participle: **habiendo hablado** (having spoken). As you can see, this is formed by using the present participle of **haber** + the past participle of the main verb.

§7.148   The verb **haber + de + inf.** is equivalent to the English use of "to be supposed to ... " or "to be to ... ". EXAMPLES:

    María ha de traer un pastel, yo he de traer el helado, y mis amigos han de traer sus discos / Mary is supposed to bring a pie, I am supposed to bring the ice cream, and my friends are to bring their records.

§7.149   The verb **tener** is used to mean *to have* in the sense of *to possess* or *to hold*: **Tengo un perro y un gato** / I have a dog and a cat; **Tengo un lápiz en la mano** / I have (am holding) a pencil in my hand.

    In the preterit tense, **tener** can mean *received*: **Ayer mi padre tuvo un cheque** / Yesterday my father received a check.

§7.150   Jugar and **tocar**

§7.151   Both these verbs mean *to play* but they have different uses. **Jugar a** is used to play a sport, a game:

¿Juega Ud. al tenis? / Do you play tennis?   **Me gusta jugar a la pelota** / I like to play ball.

§7.152   The verb **tocar** is used to play a musical instrument: **Carmen toca muy bien el piano** / Carmen plays the piano very well.

The verb **tocar** has other meanings, too; it is commonly used as follows: *to be one's turn,* in which case it takes an indirect object: **¿A quién le toca?** / Whose turn is it?   **Le toca a Juan** / It is John's turn; *to knock on a door:* **tocar a la puerta; Alguien toca a la puerta** / Someone is knocking on (at) the door.

Essentially, **tocar** means *to touch.*

§7.153   Llegar a ser, hacerse and **ponerse**
These three verbs mean *to become.* Note the difference in use:

§7.154   Use **llegar a ser + a noun**, *e.g., to become a doctor, to become a teacher;* in other words, the noun indicates the goal that you are striving for: **Quiero llegar a ser doctor** / I want to become a doctor. **Hacerse** is used similarly: **Juan se hizo abogado** / John became a lawyer.

§7.155   Use **ponerse + an adj.**, *e.g., to become pale, to become sick;* in other words, the adj. indicates the state or condition (physical or mental) that you have become:

Cuando vi el accidente, me puse pálido / When I saw the accident, I became pale: **Mi madre se puso triste al oír la noticia desgraciada** / My mother became sad upon hearing the unfortunate news.

§7.156   Llevar and **tomar**
These two verbs mean *to take* but note the difference in use:

§7.157   **Llevar** means *to take* in the sense of carry or transport from place to place: **José llevó la silla de la cocina al comedor** / Joseph took the chair from the kitchen to the dining room.

The verb **llevar** is also used when you *take someone somewhere:* **Pedro llevó a María al baile anoche** / Peter took Mary to the dance last night.

As you probably know, **llevar** also means *to wear:* **María, ¿por qué llevas la falda nueva?** / Mary, why are you wearing your new skirt?

§7.158   **Tomar** means *to take* in the sense of grab or catch: **La profesora tomó el libro y comenzó a leer a la clase** / The teacher took the book and began to read to the class; **Mi amigo tomó el tren esta mañana a las siete** / My friend took the train this morning at seven o'clock.

§7.159   Pedir and **preguntar**
Both these verbs mean *to ask* but note the difference:

§7.160   **Pedir** means *to ask for something* or *to request:* **El alumno pidió un lápiz al profesor** / The pupil asked the teacher for a pencil.

§7.161   **Preguntar** means *to inquire, to ask a question:* **La alumna preguntó a la profesora cómo estaba** / The pupil asked the teacher how she was. See also **§11.38**.

§7.162 **Pensar de** and **pensar en**

Both these verbs mean *to think of* but note the difference:

§7.163 **Pensar** is used with the prep. **de** when you ask someone what he/she thinks of someone or something, when you ask for someone's opinion: **¿Qué piensa Ud. de este libro?** / What do you think of this book? **Pienso que es bueno** / I think that it is good.

§7.164 **Pensar** is used with the prep. **en** when you ask someone what or whom he/she is thinking about: **Miguel, no hablas mucho; ¿en qué piensas?** / Michael, you are not talking much; of what are you thinking? (what are you thinking of?) **Pienso en las vacaciones de verano** / I'm thinking of summer vacation.

§7.165 **Poder** and **saber**

Both these verbs mean *can,* but the difference in use is as follows:

(a) **Poder** means *can* in the sense of *ability:* **No puedo ayudarle; lo siento** / I cannot (am unable to) help you; I'm sorry.

(b) **Saber** means *can* in the sense of *to know how:* **Este niño no sabe contar** / This child can't (does not know how to) count.

(c) In the preterit tense **poder** has the special meaning of *succeeded:* **Después de algunos minutos, Juan pudo abrir la puerta** / After a few minutes, John succeeded in opening the door.

(d) In the preterit tense, **saber** has the special meaning of *found out:* **Lo supe ayer** / I found it out yesterday. See also **§7.118(b)**

§7.166 **Ser** and **estar**

These two verbs mean *to be* but note the differences in use:

§7.167 Generally speaking, use **ser** when you want to express *to be.*

§7.168 Use **estar** when *to be* is used in the following ways:

§7.169 Health: **¿Cómo está Ud.?** / How are you?

Estoy bien / I am well.

Estoy enfermo (enferma) / I am sick.

§7.170 Location: persons, places, things

(a) **Estoy en la sala de clase** / I am in the classroom.

(b) **La escuela está lejos** / The school is far.

(c) **Barcelona está en España** / Barcelona is (located) in Spain.

(d) **Los libros están en la mesa** / The books are on the table.

§7.171 State or condition: persons

(a) **Estoy contento (contenta)** / I am happy.

(b) **Los alumnos están cansados (Las alumnas están cansadas)** / The students are tired.

(c) **María está triste hoy** / Mary is sad today.

(d) **Estoy listo (lista)** / I am ready.

(e) **Estoy pálido (pálida)** / I am pale.

(f) **Estoy ocupado (ocupada)** / I am busy.

(g) **Estoy seguro (segura)** / I am sure.

(h) **Este hombre está vivo** / This man is alive.

(i) **Ese hombre está muerto** / That man is dead.

(j) **Este hombre está borracho** / This man is drunk.

§7.172   State or condition: things and places

      (a) **la ventana está abierta** / The window is open.

      (b) **La taza está llena** / The cup is full.

      (c) **El té está caliente** / The tea is hot.

      (d) **La limonada está fría** / The lemonade is cold.

      (e) **La biblioteca está cerrada los domingos** / The library is closed on Sundays.

§7.173   To form the progressive present of a verb, use the present tense of **estar** + the present participle of the main verb:

    Estoy estudiando en mi cuarto y no puedo salir esta noche / I am studying in my room and I cannot go out tonight.

§7.174   To form the progressive past of a verb, use the imperfect tense of **estar** + the present participle of the main verb:

    Mi hermano estaba leyendo cuando (yo) entré en el cuarto / My brother was reading when I entered (came into) the room.

§7.175 **Volver** and **devolver**

    These two verbs mean *to return* but note the difference:

§7.176   **Volver** means *to return* in the sense of *to come back:* **Voy a volver a casa** / I am going to return home. A synonym of **volver** is **regresar: Los muchachos regresaron a las ocho de la noche** / The boys came back (returned) at eight o'clock in the evening.

§7.177   **Devolver** means *to return* in the sense of *to give back:* **Voy a devolver el libro a la biblioteca** / I am going to return the book to the library.

§7.178 **Infinitives**

§7.179   **Definition:** In English, an infinitive is identified as a verb with the preposition *to* in front of it: *to talk, to eat, to live.* In Spanish, an infinitive is identified by its ending: those that end in **-ar, -er, -ir**; for example, **hablar** (to talk, to speak), **comer** (to eat), **vivir** (to live).

§7.180   **Negation:** To make an infinitive negative, place **no** in front of it: **No entrar** / Do not enter; **No fumar** / Do not smoke or No smoking; **No estacionar** / Do not park or No Parking.

§7.181   **As a verbal noun:** A verbal noun is a verb used as a noun. In Spanish, an infinitive may be used as a noun. This means that an infinitive may be used as a subject, a direct object, a predicate noun, or object of a preposition. Examples:

      (a) **As a subject: Ser o no ser es la cuestión** / To be or not to be is the question. In this sentence, the subject is **ser** and **no ser.**

      Other examples:

      El estudiar es bueno or **Estudiar es bueno** / Studying (to study) is good. Here, when the infinitive is a subject and it begins the sentence, you may use the definite article **el** in front on the inf. or you may omit it.

      But if the sentence does not begin with the inifinitive, do not (as a general rule) use the def. art. **el** in front of it: **Es bueno estudiar** / It is good to study. See also **§4.9(o)** and **§4.10(e).**

      (b) **As a direct object: No deseo comer** / I do not want to eat. Here, the inf. **comer** is used as a noun and it functions as the direct object of the verb **deseo.**

(c) **As a predicate noun: Ver es creer** / Seeing is believing (To see is to believe). Here, the inf. **ver** is used as a noun and it functions as the subject. The inf. **creer** is used as a noun and it functions as the predicate noun because the verb is a form of **ser,** which takes a predicate noun or predicate adjective.

Do you know what these grammatical terms mean? A predicate noun is a noun which has the same referent as the subject; in other words, the predicate noun and the subject are pretty much the same thing; for example, in English: He is a father. A predicate adjective is an adjective which is attributive to the subject; in other words, the predicate adjective describes the subject in some way; for example, in English: She is pretty; She is tall. A predicate adjective is also known as an attribute complement because, as an adjective, it is attributive to the subject and it complements (describes) it in some way.

One last comment: In English, we can use an infinitive as a verbal noun, as in the above examples. In English, we can also use a gerund as a noun. A gerund in English looks like a present participle (ends in *-ing,* like *seeing, believing*) and it is used as a noun. But in Spanish, we do not use gerunds as nouns; we use only infinitives as nouns, as in the above examples. The Spanish word **gerundio** is normally translated into English as *gerund.* In a word, when we use a gerund as a noun in English its equivalent use is the infinitive in Spanish: Seeing is believing / **Ver es creer.** See also **§7.189.**

(d) **As object of a preposition: después de llegar** / after arriving. Here, the infinitive (verbal noun) **llegar** is object of the prep. **de.** In English, the word *arriving* in this example is a present participle, not a gerund. In English, present participles and gerunds both end in *-ing* but there is a distinct difference in their use. The point here is that in Spanish, only an infinitive can be used as a verbal noun, not a present participle and not a gerund in the English sense of these two terms. See also **§7.189.**

§7.182   In Spanish, an infinitive is ordinarily used after such verbs as **dejar, hacer, mandar,** and **permitir** with no preposition needed: **Luis dejó caer sus libros** / Louis dropped his books; **Mi madre me hizo leerlo** / My mother made me read it; **Mi padre me mandó comerlo** / My father ordered me to eat it; **Mi profesor me permitió hacerlo** / My teacher permitted me to do it. Note that when **dejar** is followed by the prep. **de** it means *to stop* or *to cease:* **Luis dejó de trabajar** / Louis stopped working.

§7.183   The verb **pensar** is directly followed by an infinitive with no preposition required in front of the infinitive when its meaning is *to intend:* **Pienso ir a Chile** / I intend to go to Chile.

§7.184   Ordinarily, the infinitive form of a verb is used right after a preposition: **Antes de estudiar, Rita telefoneó a su amiga Beatriz** / Before studying, Rita telephoned her friend Beatrice; **El alumno salió de la sala de clase sin decir nada** / The pupil left the classroom without saying anything. Here, note **de estudiar** and **sin decir.**

§7.185   The infinitive form of a verb is ordinarily used after certain verbs of perception, such as **ver** and **oír: Las vi salir** / I saw them go out; **Las oí cantar** / I heard them singing.

§7.186   After **al,** a verb is used in the infinitive form: **Al entrar en la escuela, Dorotea fue a su clase de español** / Upon entering the school, Dorothy went to her Spanish class. See **§7.201.**

§7.187   The Perfect Infinitive (also known as the Past Infinitive) is formed by using **haber** in its inf. form + the past participle of the main verb: **haber hablado** (to have spoken), **haber comido** (to have eaten), **haber escrito** (to have written).

§7.188 Participles

§7.189 **Present participle:** A present participle is a verb form which, in English, ends in -*ing;* for example, *singing, eating, receiving.* In Spanish, a present participle is regularly formed as follows:

> drop the **ar** of an **-ar** ending verb, like **cantar,** and add **-ando: cantando** / singing
> drop the **er** of an **-er** ending verb, like **comer,** and add **-iendo: comiendo** / eating
> drop the **ir** of an **-ir** ending verb, like **recibir,** and add **-iendo: recibiendo** / receiving

In English, a gerund also ends in -*ing* but there is a distinct difference in use between a gerund and a present participle in English. In brief, it is this: In English, when a present participle is used as a noun it is called a gerund; for example: *Reading is good.* As a present participle in English: The boy fell asleep *while reading.*

In the first example (*Reading is good*), *reading* is a gerund because it is the subject of the verb *is.* In Spanish, however, we must not use the present participle form as a noun to serve as a subject; we must use the infinitive form of the verb in Spanish: **Leer es bueno.** See also **§7.178, §7.179, §7.181, §7.181(a), (c),** and **(d).**

§7.190 **Common irregular present participles are as follows.** You ought to know them so that you may be able to recognize them if they are on the next Spanish SAT that you take.

INFINITIVE	PRESENT PARTICIPLE
caer / to fall	**cayendo** / falling
conseguir / to attain, to achieve	**consiguiendo** / attaining, achieving
construir / to construct	**construyendo** / constructing
corregir / to correct	**corrigiendo** / correcting
creer / to believe	**creyendo** / believing
decir / to say, to tell	**diciendo** / saying, telling
despedirse / to say good-bye	**despidiéndose** / saying good-bye
destruir / to destroy	**destruyendo** / destroying
divertirse / to enjoy oneself	**divirtiéndose** / enjoying oneself
dormir / to sleep	**durmiendo** / sleeping
huir / to flee	**huyendo** / fleeing
ir / to go	**yendo** / going
leer / to read	**leyendo** / reading
mentir / to lie (tell a falsehood)	**mintiendo** / lying
morir / to die	**muriendo** / dying
oír / to hear	**oyendo** / hearing
pedir / to ask (for), to request	**pidiendo** / asking (for), requesting
poder / to be able	**pudiendo** / being able
reír / to laugh	**riendo** / laughing
repetir / to repeat	**repitiendo** / repeating
seguir / to follow	**siguiendo** / following
sentir / to feel	**sintiendo** / feeling
servir / to serve	**sirviendo** / serving
traer / to bring	**trayendo** / bringing
venir / to come	**viniendo** / coming
vestir / to dress	**vistiendo** / dressing

§7.191 **Uses of the present participle**

§7.192 **To form the progressive tenses:**

§7.193 **The Progressive Present** is formed by usting **estar** in the present tense plus the present participle of the main verb you are using: *e.g.,* **Estoy hablando** (*I am talking*), *i.e., I am* (in the act of) *talking* (right now).

§7.194   **The Progressive Past** is formed by using **estar** in the imperfect indicative plus the present participle of the main verb you are using; *e.g.,* **Estaba hablando** *(I was talking),* i.e., *I was* (in the act of) *talking* (then, at some point in the past.)

§7.195   The progressive forms are generally used when you want to emphasize what you are saying; if you don't want to do that, then just use the simple present or the imperfect, *e.g.,* say **Hablo,** rather than **Estoy hablando;** or **Hablaba,** rather than **Estaba hablando.** See also **Imperfect Indicative** in the General Index.

§7.196   In brief, the Progressive Present is used to describe with intensification what is happening or going on at present. The Progressive Past is used to describe with intensification what was happening, what was going on at some point in the past.

§7.197   Instead of using **estar,** as noted above, to form these two progressive tenses, sometimes **ir** is used: **Va hablando** / *He (she) keeps right on talking;* **Iba hablando** / *He (she) kept right on talking.* NOTE that they do not have the exact same meaning as **Está hablando** and **Estaba hablando,** as explained above in **§7.193–§7.195.**

§7.198   Also, at times **andar, continuar, seguir** and **venir** are used as helping verbs in the present or imperfect indicative tenses plus the present participle to express the progressive forms: **Los muchachos andaban cantando** / *The boys were walking along singing;* **La maestra seguía leyendo a la clase** / *The teacher kept right on reading to the class.*

§7.199   To express vividly an action that occurred (preterit + present participle): **El niño entró llorando en la casa** / *The little boy came crying into the house.*

§7.200   To express the English use of *by* + present participle in Spanish, we use the gerund form, which has the same ending as a present participle explained above in **§7.189: Trabajando se gana dinero** / *By working, one earns (a person earns) money;* **Estudiando mucho, Pepe recibió buenas notas** / *By studying hard, Joe received good grades.*

NOTE here that no preposition is used in front of the present participle (the Spanish gerund) even though it is expressed in English as *by* + *present participle.*

§7.201   NOTE, too, that in Spanish we use **al + infinitive** (not + present participle) to express *on* or *upon* + *present participle* in English: **Al entrar en la casa, el niño comenzó a llorar** / Upon entering the house, the little boy began to cry. See **§7.186.**

§7.202   To form the Perfect Participle: **habiendo hablado** / having talked.

§7.203   Finally, note that the only preposition that may be used in front of the Spanish gerund (English present participle) is **en** which gives the meaning of *after* + present participle in English: **En corriendo rápidamente, el viejo cayó y murió** / After running rapidly, the old man fell and died.

§7.204   **Past participle:** A past participle is a verb form which, in English, usually ends in *-ed:* for example, *worked, talked, arrived,* as in *I have worked, I have talked, I have arrived.* There are many irregular past participles in English; for example: *gone, sung,* as in *She has gone, We have sung.* In Spanish, a past participle is regularly formed as follows:

drop the **ar** of an **-ar** ending verb, like **trabajar,** and add **-ado: trabajado** / worked
drop the **er** of an **-er** ending verb, like **comer,** and add **-ido: comido** / eaten
drop the **ir** of an **-ir** ending verb, like **recibir,** and add **-ido: recibido** / received

§7.205   **Common irregular past participles are as follows.** You ought to know them so that you may be able to recognize them when you see them on the next Spanish test that you take.

Infinitive	Past Participle
abrir / to open	**abierto** / opened
caer / to fall	**caído** / fallen
creer / to believe	**creído** / believed
cubrir / to cover	**cubierto** / covered
decir / to say, to tell	**dicho** / said, told
descubrir / to discover	**descubierto** / discovered
deshacer / to undo	**deshecho** / undone
devolver / to return (something)	**devuelto** / returned (something)
escribir / to write	**escrito** / written
hacer / to do, to make	**hecho** / done, made
imponer / to impose	**impuesto** / imposed
imprimir / to print	**impreso** / printed
ir / to go	**ido** / gone
leer / to read	**leído** / read
morir / to die	**muerto** / died
oír / to hear	**oído** / heard
poner / to put	**puesto** / put
rehacer / to redo, to remake	**rehecho** / redone, remade
reír / to laugh	**reído** / laughed
resolver / to resolve, to solve	**resuelto** / resolved, solved
romper / to break	**roto** / broken
traer / to bring	**traído** / brought
ver / to see	**visto** / seen
volver / to return	**vuelto** / returned

§7.206   **Uses of the past participle**

§7.207   **To form the compound tenses:**
As in English, the past participle is needed to form the compound tenses in Spanish, of which there are seven. For the complete conjugation showing the forms of the six persons in each of the following compound tenses and for an explanation of how they are formed, see the specific name of each tense in the General Index.

The Compound Tenses / Los Tiempos compuestos

Name of tense in Spanish / English	Example (1st pers., sing.)
Perfecto de Indicativo / Present Perfect Indicative	**he hablado**
Pluscuamperfecto de Indicativo / Pluperfect Indicative	**había hablado**
Pretérito Anterior / Preterit Perfect	**hube hablado**
Futuro Perfecto / Future Perfect	**habré hablado**
Potencial Compuesto / Conditional Perfect	**habría hablado**
Perfecto de Subjuntivo / Present Perfect Subjunctive	**haya hablado**
Pluscuamperfecto de Subjuntivo / Pluperfect Subjunctive	**hubiera hablado** *or* **hubiese hablado**

§7.208   To form the Perfect Infinitive: **haber hablado** / to have spoken

§7.209   To form the Perfect Participle: **habiendo hablado** / having spoken

§7.210   To serve as an adjective, which must agree in gender and number with the noun it modifies: **El señor Molina es muy respetado de todos los alumnos** / Mr. Molina is very respected by all the students; **La señora González es muy conocida** / Mrs. González is very well known.

§7.211   To express the result of an action with **estar** and sometimes with **quedar** or **quedarse: La puerta está abierta** / The door is open; **Las cartas están escritas** / The letters are written; **Los niños se quedaron asustados** / The children remained frightened.

§7.212   To express the passive voice with **ser: La ventana fue abierta por el ladrón** / The window was opened by the robber.

§7.213   **Passive voice**

§7.214   Passive voice means that the action of the verb falls on the subject; in other words, the subject receives the action: **La ventana fue abierta por el ladrón** / The window was opened by the robber. NOTE that **abierta** (really a form of the past part. **abrir** / **abierto**) is used as an adjective and it must agree in gender and number with the subject that it describes.

§7.215   Active voice means that the subject performs the action and the subject is always stated: **El ladrón abrió la ventana** / The robber opened the window.

§7.216   To form the true passive, use **ser** + the past participle of the verb you have in mind; the past part. then serves as an adjective and it must agree in gender and number with the subject that it describes, as in the example given in **§7.214.** In the true passive, the agent (the doer) is always expressed with the prep. **por** in front of it. The formula for the true passive construction is: subject + tense of **ser** + past participle + **por** + the agent (the doer): **Estas composiciones fueron escritas por Juan** / These compositions were written by John.

§7.217   The reflexive pronoun **se** may be used to substitute for the true passive voice construction. When you use the **se** construction, the subject is a thing (not a person) and the doer (agent) is not stated: **Aquí se habla español** / Spanish is spoken here; **Aquí se hablan español e inglés** / Spanish and English are spoken here; **Se venden libros en esta tienda** / Books are sold in this store.

§7.218   There are a few standard idiomatic expressions that are commonly used with the pronoun **se.** These expressions are not truly passive, the pronoun **se** is not truly a reflexive pronoun, and the verb form is in the 3rd pers. sing. only. In this construction, there is no subject expressed; the subject is contained in the use of **se** + the 3rd pers. sing. of the verb at all times and the common translations into English are: it is ... people ... , they ... , one ... :

§7.219   **Se cree que ...** / It is believed that ... , people believe that ... , they believe that ... , one believes that ...
Se cree que este criminal es culpable / It is believed that this criminal is guilty.

§7.220   **Se dice que ...** / It is said that ... , people say that ... , they say that ... , one says that ... , you say ...
Se dice que va a nevar esta noche / They say that it's going to snow tonight; **¿Cómo se dice en español** *ice cream?* / How do you say *ice cream* in Spanish?

§7.221   **Se sabe que ...** / It is known that ... , people know that ... , they know that ... , one knows that ...
Se sabe que María va a casarse con Juan / People know that Mary is going to marry John.

§7.222   The **se** reflexive pronoun construction (see **§7.217** above) is avoided if the subject is a person because there can be ambiguity in meaning. For example, how would you translate into English the following: **Se da un regalo.** Which of the following two meanings is intended? She (he) is being given a present, *or* She (he) is giving a present to himself (to herself). In correct Spanish you would have to say: **Le da (a María, a Juan,** *etc.***) un regalo** / He (she) is giving a present to Mary (to John, *etc.*) Avoid using the **se** construction in the passive when the subject is a person; change your sentence around and state it in the active voice to make the meaning clear. Otherwise, the pronoun **se** seems to go with the verb, as if the verb itself is reflexive, which gives an entirely different meaning. Another example: **Se miró** would mean *He (she) looked at himself (herself),* not *He (she) was looked at!* If you mean to say *He (she) looked at him (at her),* say: **Lo (La) miró** or, if in the plural, say: **La miraron** / They looked at her.

§8. THE NAMES OF TENSES AND MOODS IN SPANISH WITH ENGLISH EQUIVALENTS

Spanish

Los tiempos simples	Los tiempos compuestos
1. **Presente de indicativo**	8. **Perfecto de indicativo**
2. **Imperfecto de indicativo**	9. **Pluscuamperfecto de indicativo**
3. **Pretérito**	10. **Pretérito anterior**
4. **Futuro**	11. **Futuro perfecto**
5. **Potencial simple**	12. **Potencial compuesto**
6. **Presente de subjuntivo**	13. **Perfecto de subjuntivo**
7. **Imperfecto de subjuntivo**	14. **Pluscuamperfecto de subjuntivo**

English

The simple tenses	The compound tenses
1. Present indicative	8. Present perfect indicative
2. Imperfect indicative	9. Pluperfect *or* Past perfect indicative
3. Preterit	10. Past anterior *or* Preterit perfect
4. Future	11. Future perfect *or* Future anterior
5. Conditional	12. Conditional perfect
6. Present subjunctive	13. Present perfect *or* Past subjunctive
7. Imperfect subjunctive	14. Pluperfect *or* Past perfect subjunctive

Imperative *or* Command (**Imperativo**)

§8.1 OBSERVATIONS:

§8.2   In Spanish, there are 7 simple tenses and 7 compound tenses. A simple tense means that the verb form consists of one word. A compound tense means that the verb form consists of two words (the auxiliary verb and the past participle). The auxiliary verb is also called a helping verb and in Spanish, as you know, it is any of the 7 simple tenses of **haber** *(to have).*

§8.3   Each compound tense is based on each simple tense. The 14 tenses given above are arranged in the following logical order:

§8.4   Tense number 8 is based on Tense number 1; in other words, you form the **Perfecto de indicativo** by using the auxiliary **haber** in the **Presente de indicativo** plus the past participle of the verb you are dealing with.

§8.5   Tense number 9 is based on Tense number 2; in other words, you form the **Pluscuamperfecto de indicativo** by using the auxiliary **haber** in the **Imperfecto de indicativo** plus the past participle of the verb you are dealing with.

§8.6   Tense number 10 is based on Tense number 3; in other words, you form the **Pretérito anterior** by using the auxiliary **haber** in the **Pretérito** plus the past participle of the verb you are dealing with.

§8.7   Tense number 11 is based on Tense number 4; in other words, you form the **Futuro perfecto** by using the auxiliary **haber** in the **Futuro** plus the past participle of the verb you are dealing with.

§8.8   Tense number 12 is based on Tense number 5; in other words, you form the **Potencial compuesto** by using the auxiliary **haber** in the **Potencial simple** plus the past participle of the verb you are dealing with.

§8.9   Tense number 13 is based on Tense number 6; in other words, you form the **Perfecto de subjuntivo** by using the auxiliary **haber** in the **Presente de subjuntivo** plus the past participle of the verb you are dealing with.

§8.10   Tense number 14 is based on Tense number 7, in other words, you form the **Pluscuamperfecto de subjuntivo** by using the auxiliary **haber** in the **Imperfecto de subjuntivo** plus the past participle of the verb you are dealing with.

§8.11   What does all the above mean? This: If you ever expect to know or even recognize the meaning of any of the seven compound tenses, you certainly have to know **haber** in the seven simple tenses. If you do not, you cannot form the seven compound tenses. This is one perfect example to illustrate that learning Spanish verb forms is a cumulative experience. In order to know the seven compound tenses, you must first know the forms of **haber** in the seven simple tenses, which are as follows. Study them or memorize them!

HABER (helping verb) in the seven simple tenses

Present participle: **habiendo**   Past participle: **habido**   Infinitive: **haber**

1. **Presente indicativo**

**he, has, ha;
hemos, habéis, han**

Present indicative

I have, you have, you *or* he *or* she *or* it has;
we have, you have, you *or* they have

2. **Imperfecto indicativo**

**había, habías, había;
habíamos, habíais, habían**

Imperfect indicative

I had, you had, you *or* he *or* she *or* it had;
we had, you had, you *or* they had

3. **Pretérito**

**hube, hubiste, hubo;
hubimos, hubisteis, hubieron**

Preterit

I had, you had, you *or* he *or* she *or* it had;
we had, you had, you *or* they had

4. **Futuro**

**habré, habrás, habrá;
habremos, habréis, habrán**

Future

I shall have, you will have, you *or* he *or* she *or* it will have;
we shall have, you will have, you *or* they will have

5. **Potencial simple**

**habría, habrías, habría;
habríamos, habríais, habrían**

Conditional

I would have, you would have, you *or* he *or* she *or* it would have;
we would have, you would have, you *or* they would have

6. **Presente subjuntivo**

**haya, hayas, haya;
hayamos, hayáis, hayan**

Present subjunctive

that I may have, that you may have, that you *or* he *or* she *or* it may have;
that we may have, that you may have, that you *or* they may have

7. **Imperfecto subjuntivo**

(the **-ra** form) **hubiera, hubieras, hubiera;
hubiéramos, hubierais, hubieran**

OR

(the **-se** form) **hubiese, hubieses, hubiese;
hubiésemos, hubieseis, hubiesen**

Imperfect subjunctive

that I might have, that you might have, that you *or* he *or* she *or* it might have; that we might have, that you might have, that you *or* they might have

NOTE: The subject pronouns in Spanish have been omitted above in order to emphasize the verb forms of the auxiliary verb **haber** in the seven simple tenses, which you must know so that you can form the seven compound tenses from these. As you know, the subject pronouns are as follows:

Singular: **yo, tú, Ud.** *or* **él** *or* **ella;**

Plural: **nosotros (nosotras), vosotros (vosotras), Uds.** *or* **ellos** or **ellas**

§8.12 COMPARISON OF MEANINGS AND USES OF SPANISH VERB TENSES AND MOODS AS RELATED TO ENGLISH VERB TENSES AND MOODS

§8.13   The following verb tenses and moods are presented in the same numbered order as given in **§8.–§8.11.** Compare them with these that follow here.

§8.14   **Tense No. 1: Presente de indicativo** (Present indicative)
This tense is used most of the time in Spanish and English. It indicates:

(a) An action or a state of being at the present time.
   EXAMPLES:
   1. **Hablo** español / *I speak* Spanish, or *I am speaking* Spanish, or *I do speak* Spanish.
   2. **Creo en** Dios / *I believe* in God.

(b) Habitual action.
   EXAMPLE:
   Voy a la biblioteca todos los días / *I go* to the library every day, or *I do go* to the library every day.

(c) A general truth, something which is permanently true.
   EXAMPLES:
   1. Seis menos dos **son** cuatro / Six minus two *are* four.
   2. El ejercicio **hace** maestro al novicio / Practice *makes* perfect.

(d) Vividness when talking or writing about past events.
   EXAMPLE:
   El asesino **se pone** pálido. **Tiene** miedo. **Sale** de la casa y **corre** a lo largo del río / The murderer *turns* pale. *He is* afraid. *He goes out* of the house and *runs* along the river.

(e) A near future.
   EXAMPLES:
   1. Mi hermano **llega** mañana / My brother *arrives* tomorrow.
   2. ¿**Escuchamos** un disco ahora? / Shall we listen to a record now?

(f) An action or state of being that occurred in the past and *continues up to the present.* In Spanish this is an idiomatic use of the *Present tense* of a verb with **hace,** which is also in the *Present.*
   EXAMPLE:
   Hace tres horas que **miro** la televisión / *I have been watching* television for three hours. See also **§14.1, §14.3, §14.4, §14.7.**

(g) The meaning of *almost* or *nearly* when used with **por poco.**
   EXAMPLE:
   Por poco me **matan** / They almost *killed* me.

§8.15   **This tense is regularly formed as follows:**

§8.16   Drop the **ar** ending of an infinitive, like **hablar,** and add the following endings: **o, as, a; amos, áis, an**
   You then get: **hablo, hablas, habla;**
               hablamos, habláis, hablan

§8.17 Drop the **er** ending of an infinitive, like **beber,** and add the following endings: **o, es, e; emos, éis, en**

You then get: **bebo, bebes, bebe;**
bebemos, bebéis, beben

§8.18 Drop the **ir** ending of an infinitive, like **recibir,** and add the following endings: **o, es, e; imos, ís, en**

You then get: **recibo, recibes, recibe;**
recibimos, recibís, reciben

§8.19 **Verbs irregular in the present indicative, including stem-changing verbs and orthographical changing verbs**

NOTE that the first three forms up to the semicolon are the 1st, 2nd, and 3rd persons of the singular; the three verb forms under those are the 1st, 2nd, and 3rd persons of the plural. The subject pronouns are not given in order to emphasize the verb forms. See my note at the end of **§8.11** where **haber** is given in all its forms in the seven simple tenses. See also **§6.4**.

acertar / to hit the mark, to hit upon, to do (something) right
acierto, aciertas, acierta;
acertamos, acertáis, aciertan

This is a stem-changing verb. The **e** in the stem changes to **ie** when stressed.

acordar / to agree (upon)
acuerdo, acuerdas, acuerda;
acordamos, acordáis, acuerdan

This is a stem-changing verb. The **o** in the stem changes to **ue** when stressed.

acordarse / to remember
me acuerdo, te acuerdas, se acuerda;
nos acordamos, os acordáis, se acuerdan

This is a stem-changing verb. The **o** in the stem changes to **ue** when stressed.

acostarse / to go to bed, to lie down
me acuesto, te acuestas, se acuesta;
nos acostamos, os acostáis, se acuestan

This is a stem-changing verb. The **o** in the stem changes to **ue** when stressed.

actuar / to act, to actuate
actúo, actúas, actúa;
actuamos, actuáis, actúan

This — **uar** verb is a stem-changing verb. The **u** in the stem changes to **ú** when stressed.

adquirir / to acquire, to get, to obtain
adquiero, adquieres, adquiere;
adquirimos, adquirís, adquieren

This is a stem-changing verb. The **i** in the stem changes to **ie** when stressed.

advertir / to notify, to warn, to give notice, to give warning
advierto, adviertes, advierte;
advertimos, advertís, advierten

This is a stem-changing verb. The **e** in the stem changes to **ie** when stressed. Present participle is **advirtiendo.**

afligir / to afflict, to grieve
aflijo, afliges, aflige;
afligimos, afligís, afligen

This is an orthographical changing verb, which means that it changes in spelling. The **g** changes to **j** in front of **o** or **a** in order to keep its original sound of *h,* as in the English word *hello.*

almorzar / to lunch, to have lunch
almuerzo, almuerzas, almuerza;
almorzamos, almorzáis, almuerzan

This is a stem-changing verb. The **o** in the stem changes to **ue** when stressed.

aparecer / to appear, to show up
aparezco, apareces, aparece;
aparecemos, aparecéis, aparecen

This **—cer** verb changes only in the 1st person singular where the **c** changes to **zc.**

apretar / to squeeze, to tighten, to clench
aprieto, aprietas, aprieta;
apretamos, apretáis, aprietan

This is a stem-changing verb. The **e** in the stem changes to **ie** when stressed.

ascender / to ascend
asciendo, asciendes, asciende;
ascendemos, ascendéis, ascienden

This is a stem-changing verb. The **e** in the stem changes to **ie** when stressed.

asir / to grasp, to seize
asgo, ases, ase;
asimos, asís, asen

This verb is irregular only in the 1st person singular of this tense because the letter **g** is added.

atravesar / to cross, to go through, to run through
atravieso, atraviesas, atraviesa;
atravesamos, atravesáis, atraviesan

This is a stem-changing verb. The **e** in the stem changes to **ie** when stressed.

atribuir / to attribute
atribuyo, atribuyes, atribuye;
atribuimos, atribuís, atribuyen

This **—uir** verb requires the insertion of the letter **y** in front of the regular present tense endings **o, es, e,** and **en.** Pres. part. is **atribuyendo.**

bendecir / to bless
bendigo, bendices, bendice;
bendecimos, bendecís, bendicen

In addition to the four irregular forms noted here, the past participle is ordinarily **bendecido** but it changes to **bendito** when used as an adjective with **estar** and requires an agreement in gender and number. Also, the pres. part. is **bendiciendo.**

caber / to fit, to be contained
quepo, cabes, cabe;
cabemos, cabéis, caben

Irregular in the 1st pers. sing. only in this tense.

caer / to fall
caigo, caes, cae;
caemos, caéis, caen

Irregular in the 1st pers. sing. only in this tense. Pres. part. is **cayendo.**

calentar / to warm (up), to heat
caliento, calientas, calienta;
calentamos, calentáis, calientan

A stem-changing verb. The **e** in the stem changes to **ie** when stressed.

cerrar / to close
cierro, cierras, cierra;
cerramos, cerráis, cierran

A stem-changing verb. The **e** in the stem changes to **ie** when stressed.

cocer / to cook
cuezo, cueces, cuece;
cocemos, cocéis, cuecen

A stem-changing and orthographical changing verb. The **o** in the stem changes to **ue** when stressed. Also, this **-cer** verb changes **c** to **z** in front of **o** or **a.**

coger / to seize, to grasp, to grab, to catch
cojo, coges, coge;
cogemos, cogéis, cogen

An orthographical changing verb. This **—ger** verb changes **g** to **j** in front of **o** or **a.**

colegir / to collect
colijo, coliges, colige;
colegimos, colegís, coligen

An orthographical and stem-changing verb. This **—gir** verb changes **g** to **j** in front of **o** or **a.** Also, **e** in stem changes to **i** when stressed. Pres. part. is **coligiendo.**

colgar / to hang
cuelgo, cuelgas, cuelga;
colgamos, colgáis, cuelgan

A stem-changing verb. The **o** in the stem changes to **ue** when stressed.

comenzar / to begin, to start, to commence
comienzo, comienzas, comienza;
comenzamos, comenzáis, comienzan

A stem-changing verb. The **e** in the stem changes to **ie** when stressed.

concluir / to conclude, to end
concluyo, concluyes, concluye;
concluimos, concluís, concluyen

This **—uir** verb requires the insertion of **y** in front of the regular present tense endings **o, es, e,** and **en.** Pres. part. is **concluyendo.**

conducir / to conduct, to lead, to drive
conduzco, conduces, conduce;
conducimos, conducís, conducen

This **—cir** verb changes only in the 1st pers. sing. of this tense where the **c** changes to **zc.**

confesar / to confess
confieso, confiesas, confiesa;
confesamos, confesáis, confiesan

A stem-changing verb. The **e** in the stem changes to **ie** when stressed.

confiar (en) / to rely (on), to confide (in)
confío, confías, confía;
confiamos, confiáis, confían

This **—iar** verb changes **i** to **í** in the stem when stressed in order to split the diphthongs **io, ia.**

conocer / to know, to be acquainted with
conozco, conoces, conoce;
conocemos, conocéis, conocen

An orthographical changing verb. This
—cer verb changes c to zc only in the 1st
pers. sing. of this tense.

conseguir / to get, to obtain, to attain, to
succeed in
consigo, consigues, consigue;
conseguimos, conseguís, consiguen

A stem-changing and orthographical
changing verb. The e in the stem changes
to i when stressed and the u in the stem
drops only in the 1st pers. sing. in this
tense. Pres. part. is **consiguiendo.**

consentir / to consent
consiento, consientes, consiente;
consentimos, consentís, consienten

A stem-changing verb. The e in the stem
changes to ie when stressed. Pres. part. is
consintiendo.

constituir / to constitute
constituyo, constituyes, constituye;
constituimos, constituís, constituyen

This —uir verb requires the insertion of y
in front of the regular present tense endings
o, es, e, and en. Pres. part. is
constituyendo.

construir / to construct, to build
construyo, construyes, construye;
construimos, construís, construyen

This —uir verb requires the insertion of y
in front of the regular present tense endings
o, es, e, and en. Pres. part. is
constituyendo.

contar / to count, to relate
cuento, cuentas, cuenta;
contamos, contáis, cuentan

A stem-changing verb. The o in the stem
changes to ue when stressed.

contener / to contain, to hold
contengo, contienes, contiene;
contenemos, contenéis, contienen

A stem-changing verb and an irregular form
in the 1st pers. sing. of this tense. The e in
the stem changes to ie when stressed.

continuar / to continue
continúo, continúas, continúa;
continuamos, continuáis, continúan

This —uar verb is a stem-changing verb.
The u in the stem changes to ú when
stressed.

contribuir / to contribute
contribuyo, contribuyes, contribuye;
contribuimos, contribuís, contribuyen

This —uir verb requires the insertion of y
in front of the regular present tense endings
o, es, e, and en. Pres. part. is
contribuyendo.

convencer / to convince
convenzo, convences, convence;
convencemos, convencéis, convencen

An orthographical changing verb. This
—cer verb changes c to z in front of o or a.

convertir / to convert
convierto, conviertes, convierte;
convertimos, convertís, convierten

A stem-changing verb. The e in the stem
changes to ie when stressed. Pres. part. is
convirtiendo.

corregir / to correct
corrijo, corriges, corrige;
corregimos, corregís, corrigen

An orthographical and stem-changing verb.
The g changes to j in front of o or a in
order to keep its orginal sound of *h,* as in
the English word *hello.* Also, e in stem
changes to i when stressed. Pres. part. is
corrigiendo.

costar / to cost
cuesta;
cuestan

An impersonal verb used in the 3rd pers.
sing. and plural. A stem-changing verb. The
o in the stem changes to ue because of
stress.

crecer / to grow
crezco, creces, crece;
crecemos, crecéis, crecen

An orthographical changing verb. This
—cer verb changes c to zc only in the 1st
pers. sing. of this tense.

dar / to give
doy, das, da;
damos, **dais,** dan

An irregular form in the 1st pers. sing. and
no accent mark is needed in the 2nd pers.
plural.

decir / to say, to tell
digo, dices, dice;
decimos, decís, **dicen**

An irregular form in the 1st pers. sing. Also,
the e in the stem changes to i when
stressed. Pres. part. is **diciendo.**

defender / to defend
defiendo, defiendes, defiende;
defendemos, defendéis, defienden

A stem-changing verb. The **e** in the stem changes to **ie** when stressed.

delinquir / to be guilty, to offend, to commit an offense
delinco, delinques, delinque;
delinquimos, delinquís, delinquen

An orthographical changing verb. This —**quir** verb changes **qu** to **c** in front of **o** or **a.**

desaparecer / to disappear
desaparezco, desapareces, desaparece;
desaparecemos, desaparecéis, desaparecen

This —**cer** verb changes only in the 1st pers. sing. where **c** changes to **zc.**

descender / to descend
desciendo, desciendes, desciende;
descendemos, descendéis, descienden

A stem-changing verb. The **e** in the stem changes to **ie** when stressed.

despedir / to dismiss
despido, despides, despide;
despedimos, despedís, despiden

A stem-changing verb. The **e** in the stem changes to **i** when stressed. Pres. part. is **despidiendo.**

despedirse (**de**) / to say good-bye (to), to take leave (of)
me despido, te despides, se despide;
nos despedimos, os despedís, se despiden

A stem-chaning verb. The **e** in the stem changes to **i** when stressed. Pres. part. is **despidiéndose.**

despertarse / to awaken, to wake up (oneself)
me despierto, te despiertas, se despierta;
nos despertamos, os despertáis, se despiertan

A stem-changing verb. The **e** in the stem changes to **ie** when stressed.

destruir / to destroy
destruyo, destruyes, destruye;
destruimos, destruís, destruyen

This —**uir** verb requires the insertion of **y** in front of the regular present tense endings **o, es, e,** and **en.** Pres. part is **destruyendo.**

detener / to detain, to stop (someone or something)
detengo, detienes, detiene;
detenemos, detenéis, detienen

An irregular form of the 1st pers. sing. Also, the **e** in the stem changes to **ie** when stressed in the forms noted.

devolver / to return (something), to give back (something)
devuelvo, devuelves, devuelve;
devolvemos, devolvéis, devuelven

A stem-changing verb. The **o** in the stem changes to **ue** when stessed.

dirigir / to direct
dirijo, diriges, dirige;
dirigimos, dirigís, dirigen

An orthographical changing verb. The **g** changes to **j** in front of **o** or **a** in order to keep its original sound of *h,* as in the English word *hello.*

disminuir / to diminish
disminuyo, disminuyes, disminuye;
disminuimos, disminuís, disminuyen

This —**uir** verb requires the insertion of **y** in front of the regular present tense endings **o, es, e,** and **en.** Pres. part. is **disminuyendo.**

disponer / to dispose
dispongo, dispones, dispone;
disponemos, disponéis, disponen

Irregular only in the 1st pers. sing. of this tense.

distinguir / to distinguish
distingo, distingues, distingue;
distinguimos, distinguís, distinguen

An orthographical changing verb. This —**guir** verb changes **gu** to **g** in front of **o** or **a.**

distribuir / to distribute
distribuyo, distribuyes, distribuye;
distribuimos, distribuís, distribuyen

This —**uir** verb requires the insertion of **y** in front of the regular present tense endings **o, es, e,** and **en.** Pres. part. is **distribuyendo.**

divertirse / to have a good time, to enjoy oneself
me divierto, te diviertes, se divierte;
nos divertimos, os divertís, se divierten

A stem-changing verb. The **e** in the stem changes to **ie** when stressed. Pres. part. is **divirtiéndose.**

doler / to ache, to pain, to hurt, to cause grief, to cause regret
duelo, dueles, duele;
dolemos, doléis, duelen

A stem-changing verb. The **o** in the stem changes to **ue** when stressed.

dormir / to sleep
duermo, duermes, duerme;
dormimos, dormís, duermen

A stem-changing verb. The **o** in the stem changes to **ue** when stressed. Pres. part. is **durmiendo.**

dormirse / to fall asleep
me duermo, te duermes, se duerme;
nos dormimos, os dormís, se duermen

A stem-changing verb. The **o** in the stem changes to **ue** when stressed. Pres. part. is **durmiéndose.**

ejercer / to exert, to exercise
ejerzo, ejerces, ejerce;
ejercemos, ejercéis, ejercen

An orthographical changing verb. This —**cer** verb changes **c** to **z** in front of **o** or **a.**

elegir / to elect
elijo, eliges, elige;
elegimos, elegís, eligen

An orthographical and stem-changing verb. The **g** changes to **j** in front of **o** or **a** in order to keep its original sound of *h,* as in the English word *hello.* Also, the second **e** in the stem changes to **i** when stressed. Pres. part. is **eligiendo.**

empezar / to begin, to start
empiezo, empiezas, empieza;
empezamos, empezáis, empiezan

A stem-changing verb. The second **e** in the stem changes to **ie** when stressed.

encender / to light, to incite, to inflame, to kindle
enciendo, enciendes, enciende;
encendemos, encendéis, encienden

A stem-changing verb. The second **e** in the stem changes to **ie** when stressed.

encontrar / to meet, to encounter, to find
encuentro, encuentras, encuentra;
encontramos, encontráis, encuentran

An orthographical changing verb. The **o** in the stem changes to **ue** when stressed.

entender / to understand
entiendo, entiendes, entiende;
entendemos, entendéis, entienden

A stem-changing verb. The second **e** in the stem changes to **ie** when stressed.

enviar / to send
envío, envías, envía;
enviamos, enviáis, envían

This —**iar** verb changes **i** to **í** in the stem when stressed.

envolver / to wrap
envuelvo, envuelves, envuelve;
envolvemos, envolvéis, envuelven

A stem-changing verb. The **o** in the stem changes to **ue** when stressed.

erguir / to erect, to set up straight
irgo, irgues, irgue; OR: yergo, yergues, yergue;
erguimos, erguís, irguen OR: yerguen

An orthographical and stem-changing verb, as noted here. Pres. part is **irguiendo.**

errar / to err, to wander, to roam, to miss
yerro, yerras, yerra;
erramos, erráis, yerran

An orthographical changing verb, as noted here. Pres. part. is regular: **errando.**

escoger / to choose, to select
escojo, escoges, escoge;
escogemos, escogéis, escogen

An orthographical changing verb. This —**ger** verb changes **g** to **j** in front of **o** or **a.**

espiar / to spy
espío, espías, espía;
espiamos, espiáis, espían

This —**iar** verb changes **i** to **í** in the stem when stressed.

estar / to be
estoy, estás, está;
estamos, estáis, están

exigir / to demand, to urge, to require
exijo, exiges, exige;
exigimos, exigís, exigen

An orthographical changing verb. The **g** in the stem changes to **j** in front of **o** or **a** in order to keep its original sound of *h,* as in the English word *hello.*

exponer / to expose
expongo, expones, expone;
exponemos, exponéis, exponen

Irregular only in the 1st pers. sing. of this tense.

extinguir / to extinguish
extingo, extingues, extingue;
extinguimos, extinguís, extinguen

An orthographical changing verb. This —**guir** verb changes **gu** to **g** in front of **o** or **a.**

fiarse (de) / to trust
me fío, te fías, se fía;
nos fiamos, os fiáis, se fían

This —**iar** verb changes **i** to **í** in the stem when stressed.

fingir / to pretend, to feign
finjo, finges, finge;
fingimos, fingís, fingen

An orthographical changing verb. The **g** changes to **j** in front of **o** or **a**.

freír / to fry
frío, fríes, fríe;
freímos, freís, fríen

Pres. part. is **friendo.**

gemir / to groan, to moan
gimo, gimes, gime;
gemimos, gemís, gimen

A stem-changing verb. The **e** in the stem changes to **i** when stressed. Pres. part. is **gimiendo.**

graduarse / to be graduated, to graduate
me gradúo, te gradúas, se gradúa;
nos graduamos, os graduáis, se gradúan

This —**uar** verb changes **u** in the stem to **ú** when stressed.

guiar / to guide, to drive, to lead
guío, guías, guía;
guiamos, guiáis, guían

This —**iar** verb changes **i** in the stem to **í** when stressed.

haber / to have (as an auxiliary or helping verb)
he, has, ha;
hemos, habéis, han

hacer / to do, to make
hago, haces, hace;
hacemos, hacéis, hacen

Irregular form only in the 1st pers. sing. in this tense, as noted.

helar / to freeze
hiela OR está helando (in the present progressive form)

This impersonal verb, referring to the weather, is used in the 3rd pers. The **e** in the stem changes to **ie** because it is stressed. The present progressive form may be used also when referring to weather conditions in the present, as noted here.

herir / to harm, to hurt, to wound
hiero, hieres, hiere;
herimos, herís, hieren

A stem-changing verb because the **e** in the stem changes to **ie** when stressed. Pres. part. is **hiriendo.**

hervir / to boil
hiervo, hierves, hierve;
hervimos, hervís, hierven

A stem-changing verb because the **e** in the stem changes to **ie** when stressed. Pres. part. is **hirviendo.**

huir / to flee, to escape, to run away, to slip away
huyo, huyes, huye;
huimos, huís, huyen

This —**uir** verb requires the insertion of **y** in front of the regular present tense endings **o, es, e,** and **en.** Pres. part. is **huyendo.**

impedir / to prevent, to impede, to hinder
impido, impides, impide;
impedimos, impedís, impiden

A stem-changing verb because the **e** in the stem changes to **i** when stressed. Pres. part. is **impidiendo.**

imponer / to impose
impongo, impones, impone;
imponemos, imponéis, imponen

Irregular only in the 1st pers. sing. of this tense.

incluir / to include
incluyo, incluyes, incluye;
incluimos, incluís, incluyen

This —**uir** verb requires the insertion of **y** in front of the regular present tense endings **o, es, e,** and **en.** Pres. part. is **incluyendo.**

influir / to influence
influyo, influyes, influye;
influimos, influís, influyen

This —**uir** verb requires the insertion of **y** in front of the regular present tense endings **o, es, e,** and **en.** Pres. part. is **influyendo.**

ir / to go
voy, vas, va;
vamos, vais, van

Pres. part. is **yendo**.

irse / to go away
me voy, te vas, se va;
nos vamos, os vais, se van

Pres. part. is **yéndose.**

jugar / to play
juego, juegas, juega;
jugamos, jugáis, juegan

A stem-changing verb because **u** in the stem changes to **ue** when stressed.

llover / to rain
llueve OR está lloviendo (in the present progressive form)

This impersonal verb, referring to the weather, is used in the 3rd pers. The **o** in the stem changes to **ue** because it is stressed. The present progressive form may be used also when referring to weather conditions in the present, as noted here.

medir / to measure
mido, mides, mide;
medimos, medís, miden

A stem-changing verb because **e** in the stem changes to **i** when stressed. Pres. part. is **midiendo.**

mentir / to lie, to tell a lie
miento, mientes, miente;
mentimos, mentís, mienten

A stem-changing verb because **e** in the stem changes to **ie** when stressed. Pres. part. is **mintiendo.**

morir / to die
muero, mueres, muere;
morimos, morís, mueren

A stem-changing verb because **o** in the stem changes to **ue** when stressed. Pres. part. is **muriendo.**

mostrar / to show, to point out
muestro, muestras, muestra;
mostramos, mostráis, muestran

A stem-changing verb because **o** in the stem changes to **ue** when stressed.

mover / to move, to persuade, to induce
muevo, mueves, mueve;
movemos, movéis, mueven

A stem-changing verb because **o** in the stem changes to **ue** when stressed.

nacer / to be born
nazco, naces, nace;
nacemos, nacéis, nacen

This — cer verb changes only in the 1st pers. sing. where **c** changes to **zc.**

negar / /to deny
niego, niegas, niega;
negamos, negáis, niegan

A stem-changing verb because **e** in the stem changes to **ie** when stressed.

nevar / to snow
nieva OR está nevando (in the present progressive form)

This impersonal verb, referring to the weather, is used in the 3rd pers. The **e** in the stem changes to **ie** because it is stressed. The present progressive form may be used also when referring to weather conditions in the present, as noted here.

obedecer / to obey
obedezco, obedeces, obedece;
obedecemos, obedecéis, obedecen

An orthographical changing verb. This — cer verb changes **c** to **zc** only in the 1st pers. sing. of this tense.

obtener / to obtain, to get
obtengo, obtienes, obtiene;
obtenemos, obtenéis, obtienen

The 1st pers. sing. form is irregular. As a stem-changing verb, the **e** in the stem changes to **ie** when stressed.

ofrecer / to offer
ofrezco, ofreces, ofrece;
ofrecemos, ofrecéis, ofrecen

An orthographical changing verb. This — cer verb changes **c** to **zc** only in the 1st pers. sing. of this tense.

oír / to hear
oigo, oyes, oye;
oímos, oís, oyen

An irregular verb. Pres. part. is **oyendo.**

oler / to smell
huelo, hueles, huele;
olemos, oléis, **huelen**

An orthographical and stem-changing verb because **o** in the stem changes to **ue** when stressed and *h* is added as noted. Pres. part. is regular: **oliendo.**

pedir / to ask for, to request
pido, pides, pide;
pedimos, pedís, piden

A stem-changing verb because **e** in the stem changes to **i** when stressed. Pres. part. is **pidiendo.**

pensar / to think
pienso, piensas, piensa;
pensamos, pensáis, piensan

A stem-changing verb because **e** in the stem changes to **ie** when stressed.

perder / to lose
pierdo, pierdes, pierde;
perdemos, perdéis, pierden

A stem-changing verb because **e** in the stem changes to **ie** when stressed.

perseguir / to pursue, to follow after
persigo, persigues, persigue;
perseguimos, perseguís, persiguen

An orthographical and stem-changing verb because **u** in the stem drops only in the 1st pers. sing. since it is not needed. Also, the second **e** in the stem changes to **i** when stressed. Pres. part. is **persiguiendo.**

poder / to be able, can
puedo, puedes, puede;
podemos, podéis, pueden

A stem-changing verb because **o** in the stem changes to **ue** when stressed. Pres. part. is **pudiendo.**

poner / to put, to place
pongo, pones, pone;
ponemos, ponéis, ponen

Irregular in the 1st pers. sing. only of this tense.

preferir / to prefer
prefiero, prefieres, prefiere;
preferimos, preferís, prefieren

A stem-changing verb because the second **e** in the stem changes to **ie** when stressed. Pres. part. is **prefiriendo.**

probar / to prove, to test, to try
pruebo, pruebas, prueba;
probamos, probáis, prueban

A stem-changing verb because **o** in the stem changes to **ue** when stressed.

producir / to produce
produzco, produces, produce;
producimos, producís; producen

This —**cir** verb changes **c** to **zc** only in the 1st pers. sing. of this tense.

proseguir / to continue, to proceed
prosigo, prosigues, prosigue;
proseguimos, proseguís, prosiguen

An orthographical changing verb because **u** in the stem drops only in the 1st pers. sing. Also, a stem-changing verb because **e** in the stem changes to **i** when stressed. Pres. part. is **prosiguiendo.**

proteger / to protect
protejo, proteges, protege;
protegemos, protegéis, protegen

An orthographical changing verb because this —**ger** verb changes **g** to **j** in front of **o** or **a.**

quebrar / to break
quiebro, quiebras, quiebra;
quebramos, quebráis, quiebran

A stem-changing verb because **e** in the stem changes to **ie** when stressed.

querer / to want, to wish
quiero, quieres, quiere;
queremos, queréis, quieren

A stem-changing verb because **e** in the stem changes to **ie** when stressed.

recoger / to pick, to pick up, to gather
recojo, recoges, recoge;
recogemos, recogéis, recogen

An orthographical changing verb because this —**ger** verb changes **g** to **j** in front of **o** or **a.**

recomendar / to recommend, to advise, to commend
recomiendo, recomiendas, recomienda;
recomendamos, recomendáis, recomiendan

A stem-changing verb because **e** in the stem changes to **ie** when stressed.

recordar / to remember
recuerdo, recuerdas, recuerda;
recordamos, recordáis, recuerdan

A stem-changing verb because **o** in the stem changes to **ue** when stressed.

referir / to refer
refiero, refieres, refiere;
referimos, referís, refieren

A stem-changing verb because the second **e** in the stem changes to **ie** when stressed. Pres. part. is **refiriendo.**

reír / to laugh
**río, ríes, ríe;
reímos, reís, ríen**

The pres. part. is also irregular: **riendo.**

reñir / to scold, to quarrel, to argue
riño, riñes, riñe;
reñimos, reñís, riñen

A stem-changing verb because **e** in the stem changes to **i** when stressed. Pres. part. is also irregular: **riñendo.**

renovar / to renew, to remodel
renuevo, renuevas, renueva;
renovamos, renováis, renuevan

A stem-changing verb because **o** in the stem changes to **ue** when stressed.

repetir / to repeat
repito, repites, repite;
repetimos, repetís, repiten

A stem-changing verb because the second **e** in the stem changes to **i** when stressed. Pres. part. is also irregular: **repitiendo.**

resfriarse / to catch cold
me resfrío, te resfrías, se resfría;
nos resfriamos, os resfriáis, se resfrían

This —**iar** verb changes **i** to **í** when stressed.

resolver / to resolve, to solve (a problem)
resuelvo, resuelves, resuelve;
resolvemos, resolvéis, resuelven

A stem-changing verb because **o** in the stem changes to **ue** when stressed.

reunir / to gather, to join, to unite
reúno, reúnes, reúne;
reunimos, reunís, reúnen

The **u** in the stem changes to **ú** when stressed.

rogar / to beg, to request
ruego, ruegas, ruega;
rogamos, rogáis, ruegan

A stem-changing verb because **o** in the stem changes to **ue** when stressed.

saber / to know, to know how
sé, sabes, sabe;
sabemos, sabéis, saben

Irregular only in the 1st pers. sing. of this tense.

salir / to go out
salgo, sales, sale;
salimos, salís, salen

Irregular only in the 1st pers. sing. of this tense.

seguir / to follow, to pursue, to continue
sigo, sigues, sigue;
seguimos, seguís, siguen

An orthographical changing verb because **u** in the stem drops only in the 1st pers. sing. of this tense. Also, a stem-changing verb because **e** in the stem changes to **i** when stressed. Pres. part. is also irregular: **siguiendo.**

sentarse / to sit down
me siento, te sientas, se sienta;
nos sentamos, os sentáis, se sientan

A stem-changing verb because **e** in the stem changes to **ie** when stressed.

sentir / to feel sorry, to regret, to feel, to experience, to sense
siento, sientes, siente;
sentimos, sentís, sienten

A stem-changing verb because **e** in the stem changes to **ie** when stressed. Pres. part. is also irregular: **sintiendo.**

sentirse / to feel (well, sick)
me siento, te sientes, se siente;
nos sentimos, os sentís, se sienten

A stem-changing verb because **e** in the stem changes to **ie** when stressed. Pres. part. is also irregular: **sintiéndose.**

ser / to be
soy, eres, es;
somos, sois, son

Pres. part. is **siendo.**

servir / to serve
sirvo, sirves, sirve;
servimos, servís, sirven

A stem-changing verb because **e** in the stem changes to **i** when stressed. Pres. part. is also irregular: **sirviendo.**

soler / to be in the habit of, to be accustomed to, to have the custom of
suelo, sueles, suele;
solemos, soléis, suelen

A stem-changing verb because **o** in the stem changes to **ue** when stressed. This verb is generally used in this tense, in the imperfect indicative, and in the present subjunctive. It is followed by an inf.: **Suelo lavarme las manos antes de comer** / I am in the habit of washing my hands before eating.

sonar / to ring, to sound
sueno, suenas, suena;
sonamos, sonáis, suenan

A stem-changing verb because **o** in the stem changs to **ue** when stressed.

soñar / to dream
sueño, sueñas, sueña;
soñamos, soñáis, sueñan

A stem-changing verb because **o** in the stem changes to **ue** when stressed.

sonreír / to smile
sonrío, sonríes, sonríe;
sonreímos, sonreís, sonríen

The pres. part. is also irregular: **sonriendo.**

sugerir / to suggest, to hint
sugiero, sugieres, sugiere;
sugerimos, sugerís, sugieren

A stem-changing verb because **e** in the
stem changes to **ie** when stressed. Pres.
part. is also irregular: **sugiriendo.**

suponer / to suppose, to assume
supongo, supones, supone;
suponemos, suponéis, suponen

Irregular in the 1st pers. sing. only of this
tense.

sustituir / to substitute
sustituyo, sustituyes, sustituye;
sustituimos, sustituís, sustituyen

This —**uir** verb requires the insertion of **y**
in front of the regular present tense endings
o, es, e, and **en.** Pres. part. is also
irregular: **sustituyendo.**

tener / to have, to hold
tengo, tienes, tiene;
tenemos, tenéis, tienen

An irregular form in the 1st pers. sing. of
this tense. Also, **e** in the stem changes to **ie**
when stressed.

torcer / to twist
tuerzo, tuerces, tuerce;
torcemos, torcéis, tuercen

A stem-changing verb because **o** in the stem
changes to **ue** when stressed. Also an
orthographical changing verb because **c**
changes to **z** in front of **o** or **a.**

traducir / to translate
traduzco, traduces, traduce;
traducimos, traducís, traducen

An orthographical changing verb because
this —**cer** verb changes **c** to **zc** only in the
1st pers. sing. of this tense.

traer / to bring
traigo, traes, trae;
traemos, traéis, traen

Irregular in the 1st pers. sing. only of this
tense. Also, the pres. part. is irregular:
trayendo.

tronar / to thunder
truena OR está tronando (in the present
progressive form)

This impersonal verb, referring to the weather,
is used in the 3rd pers. The **o** in the stem
changes to **ue** because it is stressed. The
present progressive form may be used also
when referring to weather conditions in the
present, as noted here.

valer / to be worth, to be worthy
valgo, vales, vale;
valemos, valéis, valen

Irregular only in the 1st pers. sing. of this
tense.

vencer / to conquer, to overcome
venzo, vences, vence;
vencemos, vencéis, vencen

An orthographical changing verb because **c**
changes to **z** in front of **o** or **a.**

venir / to come
vengo, vienes, viene;
venimos, venís, vienen

The pres. part. is also irregular: **viniendo.**

ver / to see
veo, ves, ve;
vemos, veis, ven

vestir / to clothe, to dress
visto, vistes, viste;
vestimos, vestís, visten

A stem-changing verb because **e** in the stem
changes to **i** when stressed. Pres. part. is
also irregular: **vistiendo.**

vestirse / to dress oneself, to get dressed
me visto, te vistes, se viste;
nos vestimos, os vestís, se visten

A stem-changing verb because **e** in the stem
changes to **i** when stressed. Pres. part. is
also irregular: **vistiéndose.**

volar / to fly
vuelo, vuelas, vuela;
volamos, voláis, vuelan

A stem-changing verb because **o** in the stem
changes to **ue** when stressed.

volver / to return
vuelvo, vuelves, vuelve;
volvemos, volvéis, vuelven

A stem-changing verb because **o** in the stem
changes to **ue** when stressed.

NOTE: If I have inadvertently omitted any verb you have in mind, which is irregular in the present indicative in some way, consult my book *501 Spanish verbs fully conjugated in all the tenses in a new easy to learn format,* Fourth Edition, also published by Barron's.

§8.20   **Tense No. 2: Imperfecto de indicativo** (Imperfect indicative)

This is a past tense. Imperfect suggests incomplete. The *Imperfect tense* expresses an action or a state of being that was continuous in the past and **its completion is not indicated.** This tense is used, therefore, to express:

(a) An action that was going on in the past at the same time as another action.
EXAMPLE:
Mi hermano **leía** y mi padre **hablaba** / My brother *was reading* and my father *was talking.*

(b) An action that was going on in the past when another action occurred.
EXAMPLE:
Mi hermana **cantaba** cuando yo entré / My sister *was singing* when I came in.

(c) An action that a person did habitually in the past.
EXAMPLES:
1.   Cuando **estábamos** en Nueva York, **íbamos** al cine todos los sábados / When *we were* in New York, *we went* to the movies every Saturday; When *we were* in New York, *we used to go* to the movies every Saturday.
2.   Cuando **vivíamos** en California, **íbamos** a la playa todos los días / When *we used to live* in California, *we would go* to the beach every day.

NOTE: In this last example, *we would go* looks like the Conditional, but it is not. It is the *Imperfect tense* in this sentence because habitual action in the past is expressed.

(d) A description of a mental, emotional, or physical condition in the past.
EXAMPLES:
1.   (mental condition)   **Quería** ir al cine / *I wanted* to go to the movies.
Common verbs in this use are **creer, desear, pensar, poder, preferir, querer, saber, sentir.**
2.   (emotional condition)   **Estaba** contento de verlo / *I was* happy to see him.
3.   (physical condition)   Mi madre **era** hermosa cuando **era** pequeña / My mother *was* beautiful when she *was* young.

(e) The time of day in the past.
EXAMPLES:
1.   ¿Qué hora **era?** / What time *was* it?
2.   **Eran** las tres / *It was* three o'clock.

(f) An action or state of being that occurred in the past and *lasted for a certain length of time* prior to another past action. In English it is usually translated as a Pluperfect tense and is formed with *had been* plus the present participle of the verb you are using. It is like the special use of the **Presente de indicativo** explained in the above section in paragraph **§8.14** (f), except that the action or state of being no longer exists at present. This is an idiomatic use of the *Imperfect tense* of a verb with **hacía,** which is also in the *Imperfect.*
EXAMPLE:
Hacía tres horas que **miraba** la televisión cuando mi hermano entró / *I had been watching* television for three hours when my brother came in.
See also **§14.2, §14.5, §14.8**

(g) An indirect quotation in the past.
EXAMPLE:
Present: Dice que **quiere** venir a mi casa / He says *he wants* to come to my house.
Past: Dijo que **quería** venir a mi casa / He said *he wanted* to come to my house.

§8.21   **This tense is regularly formed as follows:**

§8.22   Drop the **—ar** ending of an infinitive, like **hablar,** and add the following endings: **aba, abas, aba; ábamos, abais, aban**

You then get: **hablaba, hablabas, hablaba;**
hablábamos, hablabais, hablaban

The usual equivalent in English is: I was talking OR I used to talk OR I talked; you were talking OR you used to talk OR you talked, *etc.*

§8.23   Drop the **—er** ending of an infinitive, like **beber,** or the **—ir** ending of an infinitive, like **recibir,** and add the following endings: **ía, ías, ía; íamos, íais, ían**

You then get: **bebía, bebías, bebía;**
bebíamos, bebíais, bebían

recibía, recibías, recibía;
recibíamos, recibíais, recibían

The usual equivalent in English is: I was drinking OR I used to drink OR I drank; you were drinking OR you used to drink OR you drank, *etc.*; I was receiving OR I used to receive OR I received; you were receiving OR you used to receive OR you received, *etc.*

§8.24   Verbs irregular in the imperfect indicative

ir / to go   **iba, ibas, iba;** (I was going, I used to go, *etc.*)
íbamos, ibais, iban

ser / to be   **era, eras, era;** (I was, I used to be, *etc.*)
éramos, erais, eran

ver / to see   **veía, veías, veía;** (I was seeing, I used to see, *etc.*)
veíamos, veíais, veían

NOTE: If I have inadvertently omitted any verb you have in mind, which is irregular in the imperfect indicative in some way, consult my book *501 Spanish verbs fully conjugated in all the tenses in a new easy to learn format,* Third Edition, also published by Barron's.

§8.25   **Tense No. 3: Pretérito** (Preterit)
This tense expresses an action that was completed at some time in the past.

EXAMPLES:
1. Mi padre **llegó** ayer / My father *arrived* yesterday; My father *did arrive* yesterday.
2. María **fue** a la iglesia esta mañana / Mary *went* to church this morning: Mary *did go* to church this morning.
3. ¿Qué **pasó?** / What *happened?* What *did happen?*
4. **Tomé** el desayuno a las siete / I *had* breakfast at seven o'clock. I *did have* breakfast at seven o'clock.
5. **Salí** de casa, **tomé** el autobús y **llegué** a la escuela a las ocho / I *left* the house, I *took* the bus and I *arrived* at school at eight o'clock.

§8.26   In Spanish, some verbs that express a mental state have a different meaning when used in the Preterit.

EXAMPLES:
1. La **conocí** la semana pasada en el baile / I *met* her last week at the dance. (**Conocer,** which means *to know* or *be acquainted with,* means *met,* that is, introduced to for the first time, in the Preterit.)

2. **Pude** hacerlo / *I succeeded* in doing it. (**Poder,** which means *to be able,* means *succeeded* in the Preterit.)

3. **No pude** hacerlo / *I failed* to do it. (**Poder,** when used in the negative in the Preterit, means *failed* or *did not succeed.*)

4. **Quise** llamarlo / *I tried* to call you. (**Querer,** which means *to wish* or *want,* means *tried* in the Preterit.)

5. **No quise** hacerlo / *I refused* to do it. (**Querer,** when used in the negative in the Preterit, means *refused.*)

6. **Supe** la verdad / *I found out* the truth. (**Saber,** which means *to know,* means *found out* in the Preterit.)

7. **Tuve** una carta de mi amigo Roberto / *I received* a letter from my friend Robert. (**Tener,** which means *to have,* means *received* in the Preterit.)

§8.27   This tense is regularly formed as follows:

§8.28   Drop the **—ar** ending of an infinitive, like **hablar,** and add the following endings: **é, aste, ó; amos, asteis, aron**

You then get: **hablé, hablaste, habló;**
            hablamos, hablasteis, hablaron

The usual equivalent in English is: I talked OR I did talk; you talked OR you did talk, *etc.* OR I spoke OR I did speak; you spoke OR you did speak, *etc.*

§8.29   Drop the **—er** ending of an infinitive, like **beber,** or the **—ir** ending of an infinitive, like **recibir,** and add the following endings: **í, iste, ió; imos, isteis, ieron**

You then get: **bebí, bebiste, bebió;**
            bebimos, bebisteis, bebieron

            recibí, recibiste, recibió;
            recibimos, recibisteis, recibieron

The usual equivalent in English is: I drank OR I did drink; you drank OR you did drink, *etc.*; I received OR I did receive, *etc.*

§8.30   **Verbs irregular in the preterit, including stem-changing verbs and orthographical changing verbs**

NOTE that the first three forms up to the semicolon are the 1st, 2nd, and 3rd persons of the singular; the three verb forms under those are the 1st, 2nd, and 3rd persons of the plural. The subject pronouns are not given in order to emphasize the verb forms. See my note at the end of §8.11 where **haber** is given in all its forms in the seven simple tenses. See also §6.4.

abrazar / to embrace, to hug
abracé, abrazaste, abrazó;
abrazamos, abrazasteis, abrazaron

An orthographical changing verb because **z** changes to **c** in front of **é** in the 1st pers. sing. of this tense.

acercarse / to approach, to draw near
me acerqué, te acercaste, se acercó;
nos acercamos, os acercasteis, se acercaron

An orthographical changing verb because **c** changes to **qu** in front of **é** in the 1st pers. sing. of this tense.

advertir / to notify, to warn, to give notice, to give warning
advertí, advertiste, advirtió;
advertimos, advertisteis, advirtieron

A stem-changing verb because **e** in the stem changes to **i** in the 3rd pers. sing. and plural of this tense.

agregar / to add, to collect, to gather
agregué, agregaste, agregó;
agregamos, agregasteis, agregaron

An orthographical changing verb because **g** changes to **gu** in front of **é** in the 1st pers. sing. of this tense.

alcanzar / to reach, to overtake
alcancé, alcanzaste, alcanzó;
alcanzamos, alcanzasteis, alcanzaron

An orthographical changing verb because **z** changes to **c** in front of **é** in the 1st pers. sing. of this tense.

almorzar / to have lunch, to eat lunch
almorcé, almorzaste, almorzó;
almorzamos, almorzasteis, almorzaron

An orthographical changing verb because **z** changes to **c** in front of **é** in the 1st pers. sing. of this tense.

alzar / to heave, to lift, to pick up, to raise (prices)
alcé, alzaste, alzó;
alzamos, alzasteis, alzaron

An orthographical changing verb because **z** changes to **c** in front of **é** in the 1st pers. sing. of this tense.

amenazar / to threaten
amenacé, amenazaste, amenazó;
amenazamos, amenazasteis, amenazaron

An orthographical changing verb because **z** changes to **c** in front of **é** in the 1st pers. sing. of this tense.

andar / to walk
anduve, anduviste, anduvo;
anduvimos, anduvisteis, anduvieron

apagar / to extinguish
apagué, apagaste, apagó;
apagamos, apagasteis, apagaron

An orthographical changing verb because **g** changes to **gu** in front of **é** in the 1st pers. sing. of this tense.

aplicar / to apply
apliqué, aplicaste, aplicó;
aplicamos, aplicasteis, aplicaron

An orthographical changing verb because **c** changes to **qu** in front of **é** in the 1st pers. sing. of this tense.

arrancar / to pull out, to uproot
arranqué, arrancaste, arrancó;
arrancamos, arrancasteis, arrancaron

An orthographical changing verb because **c** changes to **qu** in front of **é** in the 1st pers. sing. of this tense.

atacar / to attack
ataqué, atacaste, atacó;
atacamos, atacasteis, atacaron

An orthographical changing verb because **c** changes to **qu** in front of **é** in the 1st pers. sing. of this tense.

atraer / to attract, to allure, to charm
atraje, atrajiste, atrajo;
atrajimos, atrajisteis, atrajeron

avanzar / to advance
avancé, avanzaste, avanzó;
avanzamos, avanzasteis, avanzaron

An orthographical changing verb because **z** changes to **c** in front of **é** in the 1st pers. sing. of this tense.

averiguar / to find out, to inquire, to investigate
averigüé, averiguaste, averiguó;
averiguamos, averiguasteis, averiguaron

An orthographical changing verb because **u** changes to **ü** in front of **é** in the 1st pers. sing. of this tense. The two dots over the **ü** are called dieresis or diaeresis; in Spanish, they are called *diéresis*. They indicate that each of the two vowels (**üé**) has a separate and distinct pronunciation. The dieresis mark is used in **averigüé** to tell you that **güé** should be pronounced as *gway*, not *gay*. Why? In order to preserve the *gw* sound in the infinitive.

bautizar / to baptize, to christen
bauticé, bautizaste, bautizó;
bautizamos, bautizasteis, bautizaron

An orthographical changing verb because **z** changes to **c** in front of **é** in the 1st pers. sing. of this tense.

bendecir / to bless
bendije, bendijiste, bendijo;
bendijimos, bendijisteis, bendijeron

bostezar / to gape, to yawn
bostecé, bostezaste, bostezó;
bostezamos, bostezasteis, bostezaron

An orthographical changing verb because **z** changes to **c** in front of **é** in the 1st pers. sing. of this tense.

buscar / to look for, to search, to seek
busqué, buscaste, buscó;
buscamos, buscasteis, buscaron

An orthographical changing verb because **c** changes to **qu** in front of **é** in the 1st pers. sing. of this tense.

caber / to fit, to be contained
cupe, cupiste, cupo;
cupimos, cupisteis, cupieron

caer / to fall
caí, caíste, cayó;
caímos, caísteis, cayeron

An orthographical changing verb because **i** in **ió**, of the 3rd pers. sing. ending, changes to **y** and **i** in **ieron** of the 3rd pers. plural ending changes to **y.** The reason for this spelling change is the strong vowel **a** right in front of those two endings.

ALSO NOTE that **i** in **iste** changes to **í** in the 2nd pers. sing. and **i** in **isteis** changes to **í** in the 2nd pers. plural because of the strong vowel **a** in front of those two endings. The same thing happens in **caímos.**

caracterizar / to characterize
caractericé, caracterizaste, caracterizó;
caracterizamos, caracterizasteis, caracterizaron

An orthographical changing verb because **z** changes to **c** in front of **é** in the 1st pers. sing. of this tense.

cargar / to load, to burden
cargué, cargaste, cargó;
cargamos, cargasteis, cargaron

An orthographical changing verb because **g** changes to **gu** in front of **é** in the 1st pers. sing. of this tense.

castigar / to punish
castigué, castigaste, castigó;
castigamos, castigasteis, castigaron

An orthographical changing verb because **g** changes to **gu** in front of **é** in the 1st pers. sing. of this tense.

certificar / to certify, to register (a letter), to attest
certifiqué, certificaste, certificó;
certificamos, certificasteis, certificaron

An orthographical changing verb because **c** changes to **qu** in front of **é** in the 1st pers. sing. of this tense.

colgar / to hang
colgué, colgaste, colgó;
colgamos, colgasteis, colgaron

An orthographical changing verb because **g** changes to **gu** in front of **é** in the 1st pers. sing. of this tense.

colocar / to place, to put
coloqué, colocaste, colocó;
colocamos, colocasteis, colocaron

An orthographical changing verb because **c** changes to **qu** in front of **é** in the 1st pers. sing. of this tense.

comenzar / to begin, to commence, to start
comencé, comenzaste, comenzó;
comenzamos, comenzasteis, comenzaron

An orthographical changing verb because **z** changes to **c** in front of **é** in the 1st pers. sing. of this tense.

componer / to compose
**compuse, compusiste, compuso;
compusimos, compusisteis, compusieron**

comunicar / to communicate
comuniqué, comunicaste, comunicó;
comunicamos, comunicasteis, comunicaron

An orthographical changing verb because **c** changes to **que** in front of **é** in the 1st pers. sing. of this tense.

conducir / to conduct, to lead, to drive
**conduje, condujiste, condujo;
condujimos, condujisteis, condujeron**

conseguir / to get, to obtain, to attain, to succeed in
conseguí, conseguiste, consiguió;
conseguimos, conseguisteis, consiguieron

A stem-changing verb because **e** in the stem changes to **i** in the 3rd pers. sing. and pl. of this tense. Pres. part. is **consiguiendo.**

constituir / to constitute
constituí, constituiste, constituyó;
constituimos, constituisteis, constituyeron

This —**uir** verb changes **i** to **y** in the 3rd pers. sing. and pl. of this tense.

construir / to construct, to build
construí, construiste, construyó;
construimos, construisteis, construyeron

This —**uir** verb changes **i** to **y** in the 3rd pers. sing. and pl. of this tense.

contener / to contain, to hold
**contuve, contuviste, contuvo;
contuvimos, contuvisteis, contuvieron**

contradecir / to contradict
**contradije, contradijiste, contradijo;
contradijimos, contradijisteis, contradijeron**

contribuir / to contribute
contribuí, contribuiste, contribuyó;
contribuimos, contribuisteis, contribuyeron

This —**uir** verb changes **i** to **y** in the 3rd pers. sing. and pl. of this tense.

convenir / to agree
**convine, conviniste, convino;
convinimos, convinisteis, convinieron**

Pres. part. is also irregular: **conviniendo.**

convertir / to convert
convertí, convertiste, convirtió;
convertimos, convertisteis, convirtieron

A stem-changing verb because **e** in the stem changes to **i** in the 3rd pers. sing. and pl. of this tense. Pres. part. is also irregular: **convirtiendo**.

convocar / to call together, to convene
convoqué, convocaste, convocó;
convocamos, convocasteis, convocaron

An orthographical changing verb because **c** changes to **qu** in front of **é** in the 1st pers. sing. of this tense.

corregir / to correct
corregí, corregiste, corrigió;
corregimos, corregisteis, corrigieron

A stem-changing verb because **e** in the stem changes to **i** in the 3rd pers. sing. and pl. of this tense. Pres. part. is also irregular: **corrigiendo**.

creer / to believe
creí, creíste, creyó;
creímos, creísteis, creyeron

An orthographical changing verb because **i** in **ió** of the 3rd pers. sing. ending changes to **y** and **i** in **ieron** of the 3rd pers. plural ending changes to **y**. Also note that **i** in **iste** changes to **í** in the 2nd pers. sing. and **i** in **isteis** changes to **í** in the 2nd pers. pl. because of the strong vowel **e** in front of those two endings. The same thing happens in **creímos**.

cruzar / to cross
crucé, cruzaste, cruzó;
cruzamos, cruzasteis, cruzaron

An orthographical changing verb because **z** changes to **c** in front of **é** in the 1st pers. sing. of this tense.

dar / to give
dí, diste, dio;
dimos, disteis, dieron

decir / to say, to tell
dije, dijiste, dijo;
dijimos, dijisteis, dijeron

dedicar / to dedicate, to devote
dediqué, dedicaste, dedicó;
dedicamos, dedicasteis, dedicaron

An orthographical changing verb because **c** changes to **qu** in front of **é** in the 1st pers. sing. of this tense.

deslizarse / to slip away, to let slip, to let slide
me deslicé, te deslizaste, se deslizó;
nos deslizamos, os deslizasteis, se deslizaron

An orthographical changing verb because **z** changes to **c** in front of **é** in the 1st pers. sing. of this tense.

despedir / to dismiss
despedí, despediste, despidió;
despedimos, despedisteis, despidieron

A stem-changing verb because **e** in the stem changes to **i** in the 3rd pers. sing. and pl. of this tense. Pres. part. is **despidiendo**.

despedirse (de) / to say good-bye (to), to take leave (of)
me despedí, te despediste, se despidió;
nos despedimos, os despedisteis, se despidieron

A stem-changing verb because **e** in the stem changes to **i** in the 3rd pers. sing. and pl. of this tense. Pres. part. is **despidiéndose**.

desperezarse / to stretch (oneself)
me desperecé, te desperezaste, se desperezó;
nos desperezamos, os desperezasteis, se desperezaron

An orthographical changing verb because **z** changes to **c** in front of **é** in the 1st pers. sing. of this tense.

destruir / to destroy
destruí, destruiste, destruyó;
destruimos, destruisteis, destruyeron

This **—uir** verb changes **i** to **y** in the 3rd pers. sing. and pl. of this tense.

desvestirse / to undress, to get undressed
me desvestí, te desvestiste, se desvistió;
nos desvestimos, os desvestisteis, se desvistieron

A stem-changing verb because **e** in the stem changes to **i** in the 3rd pers. sing. and pl. of this tense. Pres. part. is **desvistiéndose**.

detener / to detain, to stop (someone or something)
detuve, detuviste, detuvo;
detuvimos, detuvisteis, detuvieron

detenerse / to stop (oneself or itself)
me detuve, te detuviste, se detuvo;
nos detuvimos, os detuvisteis,
se detuvieron

divertirse / to have a good time, to enjoy oneself
me divertí, te divertiste, se divirtió;
nos divertimos, os divertisteis, se divirtieron

A stem-changing verb because **e** in the stem changes to **i** in the 3rd pers. sing. and pl. of this tense. Pres. part. is **divirtiéndose**.

dormir / to sleep
dormí, dormiste, durmió;
dormimos, dormisteis, durmieron

A stem-changing verb because **o** in the stem

changes to **u** in the 3rd pers. sing. and pl. of this tense. Pres. part. is **durmiendo.**

dormirse / to fall asleep
me dormí, te dormiste, se durmió;
nos dormimos, os dormisteis, se durmieron

A stem-changing verb because **o** in the stem changes to **u** in the 3rd pers. sing. and pl. of this tense. Pres. part. is **durmiéndose.**

educar / to educate
eduqué, educaste, educó;
educamos, educasteis, educaron

An orthographical changing verb because **c** changes to **qu** in front of **é** in the 1st pers. sing. of this tense.

elegir / to elect
elegí, elegiste, eligió;
elegimos, elegisteis, eligieron

A stem-changing verb because **e** in the stem changes to **i** in the 3rd pers. sing. and pl. of this tense. Pres. part. is **eligiendo.**

embarcarse / to embark
me embarqué, te embarcaste, se embarcó;
nos embarcamos, os embarcasteis,
se embarcaron

An orthographical changing verb because **c** changes to **qu** in front of **é** in the 1st pers. sing. of this tense.

empezar / to begin, to start
empecé, empezaste, empezó;
empezamos, empezasteis, empezaron

An orthographical changing verb because **z** changes to **c** in front of **é** in the 1st pers. sing. of this tense.

encargar / to entrust, to put in charge
encargué, encargaste, encargó;
encargamos, encargasteis, encargaron

An orthographical changing verb because **g** changes to **gu** in front of **é** in the 1st pers. sing. of this tense.

entregar / to surrender, to give up, to hand over, to deliver
entregué, entregaste, entregó;
entregamos, entregasteis, entregaron

An orthographical changing verb because **g** changes to **gu** in front of **é** in the 1st pers. sing. of this tense.

equivocarse / to be mistaken
me equivoqué, te equivocaste, se equivocó;
nos equivocamos, os equivocasteis,
se equivocaron

An orthographical changing verb because **c** changes to **qu** in front of **é** in the 1st pers. sing. of this tense.

erguir / to erect, to set up straight
erguí, erguiste, irguió;
erguimos, erguisteis, irguieron

A stem-changing verb because **e** in the stem changes to **i** in the 3rd pers. sing. and pl. of this tense. Pres. part. is **irguiendo.**

estar / to be
estuve, estuviste, estuvo;
estuvimos, estuvisteis, estuvieron

explicar / to explain
expliqué, explicaste, explicó;
explicamos, explicasteis, explicaron

An orthographical changing verb because **c** changes to **qu** in front of **é** in the 1st pers. sing. of this tense.

fabricar / to manufacture, to fabricate
fabriqué, fabricaste, fabricó;
fabricamos, fabricasteis, fabricaron

An orthographical changing verb because **c** changes to **qu** in front of **é** in the 1st pers. sing. of this tense.

gemir / to groan, to moan
gemí, gemiste, gimió;
gemimos, gemisteis, gimieron

A stem-changing verb because **e** in the stem changes to **i** in the 3rd pers. sing. and pl. of this tense. Pres. part. is **gimiendo.**

gozar / to enjoy
gocé, gozaste, gozó;
gozamos, gozasteis, gozaron

An orthographical changing verb because **z** changes to **c** in front of **é** in the 1st pers. sing. of this tense.

gruñir / to grumble, to grunt, to growl, to creak (as doors, hinges, *etc.*)
gruñí, gruñiste, gruñó;
gruñimos, gruñisteis, gruñeron

This —**ñir** verb drops **i** in the ending **ió** in the 3rd pers. sing. and drops **i** in the ending **ieron** in the 3rd pers. pl. because **ñ** is in front of those two endings. The sound of **ieron** is still the same without **i** because of the sound of **ñ**. Pres. part. is **gruñendo.**

haber / to have (as an auxiliary or helping verb)
hube, hubiste, hubo;
hubimos, hubisteis, hubieron

hacer / to do, to make
hice, hiciste, hizo;
hicimos, hicisteis, hicieron

herir / to harm, to hurt, to wound
herí, heriste, hirió;
herimos, heristeis, hirieron

A stem-changing verb because **e** changes to
i in the stem in the 3rd pers. sing. and pl.
of this tense. Pres. part. is **hiriendo.**

huir / to flee, to escape, to run away,
to slip away
huí, huiste, huyó;
huimos, huisteis, huyeron

This —**uir** verb changes **i** to **y** in the 3rd
pers. sing. and pl. of this tense. Pres. part. is
huyendo.

impedir / to prevent, to impede, to hinder
impedí, impediste, impidió;
impedimos, impedisteis, impidieron

A stem-changing verb because **e** in the stem
changes to **i** in the 3rd pers. sing. and pl. of
this tense. Pres. part. is **impidiendo.**

imponer / to impose
impuse, impusiste, impuso;
impusimos, impusisteis, impusieron

incluir / to enclose, to include
incluí, incluiste, incluyó;
incluimos, incluisteis, incluyeron

This —**uir** verb changes **i** to **y** in the 3rd
pers. sing. and pl. of this tense. Pres. part. is
incluyendo.

indicar / to indicate
indiqué, indicaste, indicó;
indicamos, indicasteis, indicaron

An orthographical changing verb because **c**
changes to **qu** in front of **é** in the 1st pers.
sing. of this tense.

inducir / to induce, to influence, to persuade
induje, indujiste, indujo;
indujimos, indujisteis, indujeron

influir / to influence
influí, influiste, influyó;
influimos, influisteis, influyeron

This —**uir** verb changes **i** to **y** in the 3rd
pers. sing. and pl. of this tense. Pres. part. is
influyendo.

introducir / to introduce
introduje, introdujiste, introdujo;
introdujimos, introdujisteis,
introdujeron

ir / to go
fui, fuiste, fue;
fuimos, fuisteis, fueron

NOTE that these forms are the same for **ser**
in the preterit.

irse / to go away
me fui, te fuiste, se fue;
nos fuimos, os fuisteis, se fueron

jugar / to play (game or sport)
jugué, jugaste, jugó;
jugamos, jugasteis, jugaron

An orthographical changing verb because **g**
changes to **gu** in front of **é** in the 1st pers.
sing. of this tense.

lanzar / to throw, to hurl, to fling, to launch
lancé, lanzaste, lanzó;
lanzamos, lanzasteis, lanzaron

An orthographical changing verb because **z**
changes to **c** in front of **é** in the 1st pers.
sing. of this tense.

leer / to read
leí, leíste, leyó;
leímos, leísteis, leyeron

An orthographical changing verb because **i**
in **ió** of the 3rd pers. sing. ending changes
to **y** and **i** in **ieron** of the 3rd pers. plural
ending changes to **y**. Also note that **i** in **iste**
changes to **í** in the 2nd pers. sing. and **i** in
isteis changes to **í** in the 2nd pers. pl.
because of the strong vowel **e** in front of
those two endings. The same thing happens
in **leímos**. Remember that the regular
endings in the preterit of an —**er** and —**ir**
verb are: **í, iste, ió; imos, isteis, ieron.**

llegar / to arrive
llegué, llegaste, llegó;
llegamos, llegasteis, llegaron

An orthographical changing verb because **g**
changes to **gu** in front of **é** in the 1st pers.
sing. of this tense.

marcar / to mark
marqué, marcaste, marcó;
marcamos, marcasteis, marcaron

An orthographical changing verb because **c**
changes to **qu** in front of **é** in the 1st pers.
sing. of this tense.

mascar / to mask, to chew, to masticate
masqué, mascaste, mascó;
mascamos, mascasteis, mascaron

An orthographical changing verb because **c**
changes to **qu** in front of **é** in the 1st pers.
sing. of this tense.

medir / to measure
medí, mediste, midió;
medimos, medisteis, midieron

A stem-changing verb because **e** in the stem changes to **i** in the 3rd pers. sing. and pl. of this tense. Pres. part. is **midiendo.**

mentir / to lie, to tell a lie
mentí, mentiste, mintió;
mentimos, mentisteis, mintieron

A stem-changing verb because **e** in the stem changes to **i** in the 3rd pers. sing. and pl. of this tense. Pres. part. is **mintiendo.**

morir / to die
morí, moriste, murió;
morimos, moristeis, murieron

A stem-changing verb because **o** in the stem changes to **u** in the 3rd pers. sing. and pl. of this tense. Pres. part. is **muriendo.**

negar / to deny
negué, negaste, negó;
negamos, negasteis, negaron

An orthographical changing verb because **g** changes to **gu** in front of **é** in the 1st pers. sing. of this tense.

obligar / to obligate, to compel
obligué, obligaste, obligó;
obligamos, obligasteis, obligaron

An orthographical changing verb because **g** changes to **gu** in front of **é** in the 1st per. sing. of this tense.

obtener / to obtain, to get
**obtuve, obtuviste, obtuvo;
obtuvimos, obtuvisteis, obtuvieron**

oír / to hear (sometimes can mean *to understand*)
**oí, oíste, oyó;
oímos, oísteis, oyeron**

An orthographical changing verb because **i** in **ió** of the 3rd pers. sing. ending and **i** in **ieron** of the 3rd pers. plural ending both change to **y.**

ALSO NOTE that **iste** changes to **íste, imos** to **ímos,** and **isteis** to **ísteis** because of the strong vowel **o** in front of those endings. Remember that the regular endings in the preterit of an —**er** and —**ir** verb are: **í, iste, ió, imos, isteis, ieron.**

oponer / to oppose
**opuse, opusiste, opuso;
opusimos, opusisteis, opusieron**

pagar / to pay
pagué, pagaste, pagó;
pagamos, pagasteis, pagaron

An orthographical changing verb because **g** changes to **gu** in front of **é** in the 1st pers. sing. of this tense.

pedir / to ask for, to request
pedí, pediste, pidió;
pedimos, pedisteis, pidieron

A stem-changing verb because **e** in the stem changes to **i** in the 3rd pers. sing. and pl. of this tense. Pres. part. is **pidiendo.**

pegar / to beat, to hit, to slap
pegué, pegaste, pegó;
pegamos, pegasteis, pegaron

An orthographical changing verb because **g** changes to **gu** in front of **é** in the 1st pers. sing. of this tense.

pescar / to fish
pesqué, pescaste, pescó;
pescamos, pescasteis, pescaron

An orthographical changing verb because **c** changes to **qu** in front of **é** in the 1st pers. sing. of this tense.

poder / to be able, can
**pude, pudiste, pudo;
pudimos, pudisteis, pudieron**

See also §8.26.

poner / to put, to place
**puse, pusiste, puso;
pusimos, pusisteis, pusieron**

ponerse / to put on, to become (pale, angry, *etc.*), to set (of the sun)
**me puse, te pusiste, se puso;
nos pusimos, os pusisteis, se pusieron**

poseer / to possess, to own
poseí, poseíste, poseyó;
poseímos, poseísteis, poseyeron

An orthographical changing verb because **i** in **ió** of the 3rd pers. sing. ending and **i** in **ieron** of the 3rd pers. plural ending both change to **y.**

ALSO NOTE that **iste** changes to **íste, imos** to **ímos,** and **isteis** to **ísteis** because of the strong vowel **e** in front of those endings. Remember that the regular endings in the preterit of an —**er** and —**ir** verb are: **í, iste, ió; imos, isteis, ieron.**

predecir / to predict, to forecast, to foretell
**predije, predijiste, predijo;
predijimos, predijisteis, predijeron**

predicar / to preach
prediqué, predicaste, predicó;
predicamos, predicasteis, predicaron

An orthographical changing verb because **c** changes to **qu** in front of **é** in the 1st pers. sing. of this tense.

preferir / to prefer
preferí, preferiste, prefirió;
preferimos, preferisteis, prefirieron

A stem-changing verb because **e** in the stem changes to **i** in the 3rd pers. sing. and pl. of this tense. Pres. part. is **prefiriendo.**

producir / to produce
produje, produjiste, produjo;
produjimos, produjisteis, produjeron

proponer / to propose
propuse, propusiste, propuso;
propusimos, propusisteis, propusieron

publicar / to publish
publiqué, publicaste, publicó;
publicamos, publicasteis, publicaron

An orthographical changing verb because **c** changes to **qu** in front of **é** in the 1st pers. sing. of this tense.

querer / to want, to wish
quise, quisiste, quiso;
quisimos, quisisteis, quisieron

See also §8.26.

raer / to erase, to wipe out, to scrape,
  to rub off
raí, raíste, rayó;
raímos, raísteis, rayeron

An orthographical changing verb because **i** in **ió** of the 3rd pers. sing. ending and **i** in **ieron** of the 3rd pers. plural ending both change to **y.**

ALSO NOTE that **iste** changes to **íste, imos** to **ímos,** and **isteis** to **ísteis** because of the strong vowel **a** in front of those endings. Remember that the regular endings in the preterit of an — **er** and — **ir** verb are: **í, iste, ió; imos, isteis, ieron.** Pres. part. is **rayendo.**

realizar / to realize, to carry out, to fulfill
realicé, realizaste, realizó;
realizamos, realizasteis, realizaron

An orthographical changing verb because **z** changes to **c** in front of **é** in the 1st pers. sing. of this tense.

referir / to refer
referí, referiste, refirió;
referimos, referisteis, refirieron

A stem-changing verb because **e** in the stem changes to **i** in the 3rd pers. sing. and pl. of this tense. Pres. part. is **refiriendo.**

reír / to laugh
reí, reíste, rió;
reímos, reísteis, rieron

Pres. part. is **riendo.**

reñir / to scold, to quarrel, to argue
reñí, reñiste, riñó;
reñimos, reñisteis, riñeron

Pres. part. is **riñendo.** Compare these forms of **reñir** with those of **gruñir** given above.

repetir / to repeat
repetí, repetiste, repitió;
repetimos, repetisteis, repitieron

A stem-changing verb because **e** in the stem changes to **i** in the 3rd pers. sing. and pl. of this tense. Pres. part. is **repitiendo.**

replicar / to reply
repliqué, replicaste, replicó;
replicamos, replicasteis, replicaron

An orthographical changing verb because **c** changes to **qu** in front of **é** in the 1st pers. sing. of this tense.

rezar / to pray
recé, rezaste, rezó;
rezamos, rezasteis, rezaron

An orthographical changing verb because **z** changes to **c** in front of **é** in the 1st pers. sing. of this tense.

rogar / to beg, to request
rogué, rogaste, rogó;
rogamos, rogasteis, rogaron

An orthographical changing verb because **g** changes to **gu** in front of **é** in the 1st pers. sing. of this tense.

saber / to know, to know how
supe, supiste, supo;
supimos, supisteis, supieron

See also §8.26.

sacar / to take out
saqué, sacaste, sacó;
sacamos, sacasteis, sacaron

An orthographical changing verb because **c** changes to **qu** in front of **é** in the 1st pers. sing. of this tense.

sacrificar / to sacrifice
sacrifiqué, sacrificaste, sacrificó;
sacrificamos, sacrificasteis, sacrificaron

An orthographical changing verb because **c** changes to **qu** in front of **é** in the 1st pers. sing. of this tense.

satisfacer / to satisfy
satisfice, satisficiste, satisfizo;
satisficimos, satisficisteis, satisficieron

Compare these forms of **satisfacer** with those of **hacer** given above.

secar / to dry, to wipe dry
sequé, secaste, secó;
secamos, secasteis, secaron

An orthographical changing verb because **c** changes to **qu** in front of **é** in the 1st pers. sing. of this tense.

seguir / to follow, to pursue, to continue
seguí, seguiste, siguió;
seguimos, seguisteis, siguieron

A stem-changing verb because **e** in the stem changes to **i** in the 3rd pers. sing. and pl. of this tense. Pres. part. is **siguiendo.**

sentir / to feel sorry, to regret, to feel, to experience, to sense
sentí, sentiste, sintió;
sentimos, sentisteis, sintieron

A stem-changing verb because **e** in the stem changes to **i** in the 3rd pers. sing. and pl. of this tense. Pres. part. is **sintiendo.**

ser / to be
fui, fuiste, fue;
fuimos, fuisteis, fueron

NOTE that these forms are the same for **ir** in the preterit.

servir / to serve
serví, serviste, sirvió;
servimos, servisteis, sirvieron

A stem-changing verb because **e** in the stem changes to **i** in the 3rd pers. sing. and pl. of this tense. Pres. part. is **sirviendo.**

significar / to mean, to signify
signifiqué, significaste, significó;
significamos, significasteis, significaron

An orthographical changing verb because **c** changes to **qu** in front of **é** in the 1st pers. sing. of this tense.

sollozar / to sob
sollocé, sollozaste, sollozó;
sollozamos, sollozasteis, sollozaron

An orthographical changing verb because **z** changes to **c** in front of **é** in the 1st pers. sing. of this tense.

sonreír / to smile
sonreí, sonreíste, sonrió;
sonreímos, sonreísteis, sonrieron

Pres. part. is **sonriendo.**

sugerir / to suggest, to hint
sugerí, sugeriste, sugirió;
sugerimos, sugeristeis, sugirieron

A stem-changing verb because **e** in the stem changes to **i** in the 3rd pers. sing. and pl. of this tense. Pres. part is **sugiriendo.**

suplicar / to supplicate, to beseech, to entreat, to beg
supliqué, suplicaste, suplicó;
suplicamos, suplicasteis, suplicaron

An orthographical changing verb because **c** changes to **qu** in front of **é** in the 1st pers. sing. of this tense.

suponer / to suppose
supuse, supusiste, supuso;
supusimos, supusisteis, supusieron

tener / to have, to hold
tuve, tuviste, tuvo;
tuvimos, tuvisteis, tuvieron

See also §8.26.

tocar / to touch, to play (music or a musical instrument)
toqué, tocaste, tocó;
tocamos, tocasteis, tocaron

An orthographical changing verb because **c** changes to **qu** in front of **é** in the 1st pers. sing. of this tense.

traducir / to translate
traduje, tradujiste, tradujo;
tradujimos, tradujisteis, tradujeron

traer / to bring
traje, trajiste, trajo;
trajimos, trajisteis, trajeron

Pres. part. is **trayendo.**

tropezar / to stumble
tropecé, tropezaste, tropezó;
tropezamos, tropezasteis, tropezaron

An orthographical changing verb because **z** changes to **c** in front of **é** in the 1st pers. sing. of this tense.

utilizar / to utilize
utilicé, utilizaste, utilizó;
utilizamos, utilizasteis, utilizaron

An orthographical changing verb because **z** changes to **c** in front of **é** in the 1st pers. sing. of this tense.

venir / to come
  vine, viniste, vino;
  vinimos, vinisteis, vinieron

A stem-changing verb because **e** in the stem changes to **i** in the 3rd pers. sing. and pl. of this tense. Pres. part. is **vistiendo.**

ver / to see
  vi, viste, vio;
  vimos, visteis, vieron

vestirse / to dress, to clothe (oneself)
  me vestí, te vestiste, se vistió;
  nos vestimos, os vestisteis, se vistieron

vestir / to dress, to clothe (someone)
  vestí, vestiste, vistió;
  vestimos, vestisteis, vistieron

A stem-changing verb because **e** in the stem changes to **i** in the 3rd pers. sing. and pl. of this tense. Pres. part. is **vistiéndose.**

NOTE: If I have inadvertently omitted any verb you have in mind, which is irregular in the preterit in some way, consult my book *501 Spanish verbs fully conjugated in all the tenses in a new easy to learn format*, Fourth Edition, also published by Barron's.

§8.31   Tense No. 4: Futuro (Future)
In Spanish and English, the future tense is used to express an action or a state of being that will take place at some time in the future.

EXAMPLES:
1. Lo **haré** / *I shall do* it; *I will do* it.
2. **Iremos** al campo la semana que viene / *We shall go* to the country next week; *We will go* to the country next week.

Also, in Spanish the future tense is used to indicate:

(a) Conjecture regarding the present.
  EXAMPLES:
    1. ¿Qué hora **será**? / *I wonder* what time *it is.*
    2. ¿Quién **será**? / Who *can that be? I wonder who that is.*

(b) Probability regarding the present.
  EXAMPLES:
    1. **Serán** las cinco / *It is probably* five o'clock; *It must be* five o'clock.
    2. **Tendrá** muchos amigos / *He probably has* many friends; *He must have* many friends.
    3. María **estará** enferma / Mary *is probably* sick; Mary *must be* sick.

(c) An indirect quotation.
  EXAMPLE: María dice que **vendrá** mañana / Mary says that she *will come* tomorrow.

Finally, remember that the future is never used in Spanish after *si* when *si* means *if.*

§8.32   This tense is regularly formed as follows:
Add the following endings to the whole infinitive: **é, ás, á; emos, éis, án**

NOTE that these future endings happen to be related to the endings of **haber** in the present indicative: **he, has, ha; hemos, habéis, han.** ALSO NOTE the accent marks on the future endings, except for **emos.**

§8.33   You then get: hablaré, hablarás, hablará;
            hablaremos, hablaréis, hablarán

            beberé, beberás, beberá;
            beberemos, beberéis, beberán

            recibiré, recibirás, recibirá;
            recibiremos, recibiréis, recibirán

§8.34   The usual equivalent in English is: I shall talk OR I will talk, you will talk, *etc.*; I shall drink OR I will drink, you will drink, *etc.*; I shall receive OR I will receive, you will receive, *etc.*

§8.35 Verbs irregular in the future

caber / to fit, to be contained
cabré, cabrás, cabrá;
cabremos, cabréis, cabrán

The **e** of the inf. ending drops.

decir / to say, to tell
diré, dirás, dirá;
diremos, diréis, dirán

The **e** and **c** of the inf. drop.

haber / to have (as an auxiliary or helping verb)
habré, habrás, habrá;
habremos, habréis, habrán

The **e** of the inf. ending drops.

hacer / to do, to make
haré, harás, hará;
haremos, haréis, harán

The **c** and **e** of the inf. drop.

poder / to be able, can
podré, podrás, podrá;
podremos, podréis, podrán

The **e** of the inf. ending drops.

poner / to put, to place
pondré, pondrás, pondrá;
pondremos, pondréis, pondrán

The **e** of the inf. ending drops and **d** is added.

querer / to want, to wish
querré, querrás, querrá;
querremos, querréis, querrán

The **e** of the inf. ending drops and you are left with two **r**'s.

saber / to know, to know how
sabré, sabrás, sabrá;
sabremos, sabréis, sabrán

The **e** of the inf. ending drops.

salir / to go out
saldré, saldrás, saldrá;
saldremos, saldréis, saldrán

The **i** of the inf. ending drops and **d** is added.

tener / to have, to hold
tendré, tendrás, tendrá;
tendremos, tendréis, tendrán

The **e** of the inf. ending drops and **d** is added.

valer / to be worth, to be worthy
valdré, valdrás, valdrá;
valdremos, valdréis, valdrán

The **e** of the inf. ending drops and **d** is added.

venir / to come
vendré, vendrás, vendrá;
vendremos, vendréis, vendrán

The **i** of the inf. ending drops and **d** is added.

NOTE: If I have inadvertently omitted any verb you have in mind, which is irregular in the future in some way, consult my book *501 Spanish verbs fully conjugated in all the tenses in a new easy to learn format,* Third Edition, also published by Barron's.

§8.36 **Tense No. 5: Potencial simple** (Conditional)
The Conditional is used in Spanish and in English to express:

(a) An action that you *would do* if something else were possible.

EXAMPLE:

Iría a España si tuviera dinero / *I would go* to Spain if I had money. (For an explanation of **tuviera,** imperfect subjunctive, see **§7.111(2)** and **§8.50.**)

(b) A conditional desire. This is a conditional of courtesy.

EXAMPLE:

Me **gustaría** tomar una limonada / *I would like (I should like)* to have a lemonade ... (if you are willing to let me have it).

(c) An indirect quotation.

EXAMPLES:

María *dijo* que **vendría** mañana / Mary *said* that she *would come* tomorrow.
María *decía* que **vendría** mañana / Mary *was saying* that she *would come tomorrow.*
María *había dicho* que **vendría** mañana / Mary *had said* that she *would come* tomorrow.

(d) Conjecture regarding the past.

EXAMPLE:

¿Quién **sería**? / *I wonder who that was.*

(e) Probability regarding the past.

    EXAMPLE:

        Serían las cinco cuando salieron / *It was probably* five o'clock when they went out.

See also the use of **deber de + inf.** in §7.127.

§8.37 **This tense is regularly formed as follows:**

Add the following endings to the whole infinitive: **ía, ías, ía; íamos, íais, ían**

NOTE that these conditional endings are the same endings of the imperfect indicative for **—er** and **—ir** verbs. See **§8.23.**

§8.38 You then get: **hablaría, hablarías, hablaría;**
                hablaríamos, hablaríais, hablarían

                bebería, beberías, bebería;
                beberíamos, beberíais, beberían

                recibiría, recibirías, recibiría;
                recibiríamos, recibiríais, recibirían

§8.39 The usual translation in English is: I would talk, you would talk, *etc.*; I would drink, you would drink, *etc.*; I would receive, you would receive, *etc.*

§8.40 **Verbs irregular in the conditional**

caber / to fit, to be contained
cabría, cabrías, cabría;
cabríamos, cabríais, cabrían

The **e** of the inf. ending drops.

decir / to say, to tell
diría, dirías, diría;
diríamos, diríais, dirían

The **e** and **c** of the inf. drop.

haber / to have (as an auxiliary or helping verb)
habría, habrías, habría;
habríamos, habríais, habrían

The **e** of the inf. ending drops.

hacer / to do, to make
haría, harías, haría;
haríamos, haríais, harían

The **c** and **e** of the inf. drop.

poder / to be able, can
podría, podrías, podría;
podríamos, podríais, podrían

The **e** of the inf. ending drops.

poner / to put, to place
pondría, pondrías, pondría;
pondríamos, pondríais, pondrían

The **e** of the inf. ending drops and **d** is added.

querer / to want, to wish
querría, querrías, querría;
querríamos, querríais, querrían

The **e** of the inf. ending drops and you are left with two **r**'s.

saber / to know, to know how
sabría, sabrías, sabría;
sabríamos, sabríais, sabrían

The **e** of the inf. ending drops.

salir / to go out
saldría, saldrías, saldría;
saldríamos, saldríais, saldrían

The **i** of the inf. ending drops and **d** is added.

tener / to have, to hold
tendría, tendrías, tendría;
tendríamos, tendríais, tendrían

The **e** of the inf. ending drops and **d** is added.

valer / to be worth, to be worthy
valdría, valdrías, valdría;
valdríamos, valdríais, valdrían

The **e** of the inf. ending drops and **d** is added.

venir / to come
vendría, vendrías, vendría;
vendríamos, vendríais, vendrían

The **i** of the inf. ending drops and **d** is added.

NOTE: If I have inadvertently omitted any verb you have in mind, which is irregular in the conditional in some way, consult my book *501 Spanish verbs fully conjugated in all the tenses in a new easy to learn format*, Fourth Edition, also published by Barron's.

§8.41   Tense No. 6: Presente de subjuntivo (Present subjunctive) (See also **§7.33**)

The subjunctive mood is used in Spanish much more than in English. In Spanish the present subjunctive is used:

(a) To express a command in the **usted** or **ustedes** form, either in the affirmative or negative.

EXAMPLES:

1. **Siéntese** Ud. / *Sit down.*
2. **No se siente** Ud. / *Don't sit down.*
3. **Cierren** Uds. la puerta / *Close* the door.
4. **No cierren** Uds. la puerta / *Don't close* the door.
5. **Dígame** Ud. la verdad / *Tell me* the truth.

(b) To express a negative command in the familiar form (**tú**).

EXAMPLES:

1. **No te sientes** / *Don't sit down.*
2. **No entres** / *Don't come in.*
3. **No duermas** / *Don't sleep.*
4. **No lo hagas** / *Don't do it.*

(c) To express a negative command in the second person plural (**vosotros**).

EXAMPLES:

1. **No os sentéis** / *Don't sit down.*
2. **No entréis** / *Don't come in.*
3. **No durmáis** / *Don't sleep.*
4. **No lo hagáis** / *Don't do it.*

(d) To express a command in the first person plural, either in the affirmative or negative (**nosotros**).

EXAMPLES:

1. **Sentémonos** / *Let's sit down.*
2. **No entremos** / *Let's not go in.*

See also **Imperativo** (Imperative) in **§8.62.**

(e) After a verb that expresses some kind of wish, insistence, preference, suggestion, or request. For those verbs, see **§7.87–§7.100.**

EXAMPLES:

1. *Quiero* que María lo **haga** / I want Mary to do it.

NOTE: In this example, English uses the infinitive form, *to do*. In Spanish, however, a new clause is needed introduced by *que* because there is a new subject, María. The present subjunctive of *hacer* is used (**haga**) because the main verb is *Quiero*, which indicates a wish. If there were no change in subject, Spanish would use the infinitive form, as we do in English, for example, **Quiero hacerlo** / *I want to do it.*

2. *Insisto* en que María lo **haga** / I insist that Mary *do* it.
3. *Prefiero* que María lo **haga** / I prefer that Mary *do* it.
4. *Pido* que María lo **haga** / I ask that Mary *do* it.

NOTE: In examples 2, 3, and 4 here, English also uses the subjunctive form *do*. Not so in example no. 1, however.

(f) After a verb that expresses doubt, fear, joy, hope, sorrow, or some other emotion. Notice in the following examples, however, that the subjunctive is not used in English. For those verbs, see **§7.78–§7.86.**

EXAMPLES:

1. *Dudo* que María lo **haga** / I doubt that Mary *is doing* it; I doubt that Mary *will do* it.
2. *No creo* que María **venga** / I don't believe (I doubt) that Mary *is coming;* I don't believe (I doubt) that Mary *will come.*
3. *Temo* que María **esté** enferma / I fear that Mary *is* ill.

4. *Me alegro* de que **venga** María / I'm glad that Mary *is coming*; I'm glad that Mary *will come*.

5. *Espero* que María no **esté** enferma / I hope that Mary *is* not ill.

(g) After certain impersonal expressions that show necessity, doubt, regret, importance, urgency, or possibility. Notice, however, that the subjunctive is not used in English in all of the following examples. For those impersonal expressions, see §7.71–§7.77.

EXAMPLES:

1. *Es necesario que* María lo **haga** / It is necessary for Mary to do it; It is necessary that Mary *do* it.

2. *No es cierto que* María **venga** / It is doubtful (not certain) that Mary *is coming*; It is doubtful (not certain) that Mary *will come*.

3. *Es lástima que* María **no venga** / It's too bad (a pity) that Mary *isn't coming*.

4. *Es importante que* María **venga** / It is important for Mary to come; It is important that Mary *come*.

5. *Es preciso que* María **venga** / It is necessary for Mary to come; It is necessary that Mary *come*.

6. *Es urgente que* María **venga** / It is urgent for Mary to come; It is urgent that Mary *come*.

(h) After certain conjunctions of time, such as **antes (de) que, cuando, en cuanto, después (de) que, hasta que, mientras,** and the like. The subjunctive form of the verb is used when introduced by any of these time conjunctions if the time referred to is either indefinite or is expected to take place in the future. However, if the action was completed in the past, the indicative mood is used. See §7.34–§7.43.

EXAMPLES:

1. Le hablaré a María cuando **venga** / I shall talk to Mary when she *comes*.

2. Vámonos antes (de) que **llueva** / Let's go before *it rains*.

3. En cuanto la **vea** yo, le hablaré / As soon as *I see* her, I shall talk to her.

4. Me quedo aquí hasta que **vuelva** / I'm staying here until *he returns*.

NOTE: In the above examples, the subjunctive is not used in English.

(i) After certain conjunctions that express a condition, negation, purpose, such as, **a menos que, con tal que, para que, a fin de que, sin que, en caso (de) que,** and the like. Notice, however, that the subjunctive is not used in English in the following examples. For these conjunctions, and others, see §7.34–§7.43.

EXAMPLES:

1. Démelo con tal que **sea** bueno / Give it to me provided that *it is* good.

2. Me voy a menos que **venga** / I'm leaving unless *he comes*.

(j) After certain adverbs, such as, **acaso, quizá,** and **tal vez.** See also §7.44–§7.46.

EXAMPLE:

Acaso **venga** mañana / Perhaps *he will come* tomorrow; Perhaps *he is coming* tomorrow.

(k) After **aunque** if the action has not yet occurred.

EXAMPLE:

Aunque María **venga** esta noche, no me quedo / Although Mary *may come* tonight, I'm not staying; Although Mary *is coming* tonight, I'm not staying.

(l) In an adjectival clause if the antecedent is something or someone that is indefinite, negative, vague, or nonexistent. See also §7.54–§7.62.

EXAMPLES:

1. Busco un libro que **sea** interesante / I'm looking for a book that *is* interesting.

NOTE: In this example, *que* (which is the relative pronoun) refers to *un libro* (which is the antecedent). Since *un libro* is indefinite, the verb in the following clause must be in the subjunctive (**sea**). Notice, however, that the subjunctive is not used in English.

2. ¿Hay alguien aquí que **hable** francés? / Is there anyone here who *speaks* French?

NOTE: In this example, *que* (which is the relative pronoun) refers to *alguien* (which is the antecedent). Since *alguien* is indefinite and somewhat vague — we do not know who this anyone might be — the verb in the following clause must be in the subjunctive (**hable**). Notice, however, that the subjunctive is not used in English.

3. No hay nadie que **pueda** hacerlo / There is no one who *can* do it.

NOTE: In this example, *que* (which is the relative pronoun) refers to *nadie* (which is the antecedent). Since *nadie* is nonexistent, the verb in the following clause must be in the subjunctive (**pueda**). Notice, however, that the subjunctive is not used in English.

(m) After **por más que** or **por mucho que.** See also §7.47ff.

EXAMPLES:

1. **Por más que hable usted,** no quiero escuchar / *No matter how much you talk,* I don't want to listen.

2. **Por mucho que se alegre,** no me importa / *No matter how glad he is,* I don't care.

(n) After the expression **ojalá (que),** which expresses a great desire. This interjection means *would to God!* or *may God grant!* ... It is derived from the Arabic, **ya Allah!** / (Oh, God!) See also §7.67ff.

EXAMPLE:

¡**Ojalá que vengan** mañana! / *Would to God that they come* tomorrow! *May God grant that they come* tomorrow! *How I wish that they would come* tomorrow! *If only they would come* tomorrow!

Finally, remember that the present subjunctive is never used in Spanish after *si* when *si* means *if.* See also §7.50–§7.53, §7.63–§7.66, and §7.101–§7.111.

§8.42 The present subjunctive of regular verbs and many irregular verbs is normally formed as follows:

Go to the present indicative, 1st pers. sing., of the verb you have in mind, drop the ending **o,** and

for an **—ar** ending type, add: **e, es, e; emos, éis, en**

for an **—er** or **—ir** ending type, add: **a, as, a; amos, áis, an**

As you can see, the characteristic vowel in the present subjunctive endings for an **—ar** type verb is **e** in the six persons.

As you can see, the characteristic vowel in the present subjunctive endings for an **—er** or **—ir** type verb is **a** in the six persons.

§8.43 You then get, for example: **hable, hables, hable;**
hablemos, habléis, hablen

beba, bebas, beba;
bebamos, bebáis, beban

reciba, recibas, reciba;
recibamos, recibáis, reciban

§8.44 The usual equivalent in English is: (that I) talk OR (that I) may talk, (that you) talk OR (that you) may talk, (that he/she) talk OR (that he/she) may talk, *etc.*; (that I) drink OR (that I) may drink, (that you) drink OR (that you) may drink, (that he/she) drink OR (that he/she) may drink, *etc.*; (that I) receive OR (that I) may receive, (that you) receive OR (that you) may receive, (that he/she) receive OR (that he/she) may receive, *etc.*

§8.45 **Verbs irregular in the present subjunctive commonly used**

The following verbs are irregular because if you go to the present indicative, 1st pers. sing. of these verbs, you will find a form which you cannot work with according to the process of forming the present subjunctive normally, as explained in **§8.42** above. Also, see the irregular verbs in the present indicative where they are arranged alphabetically in **§8.19.**

dar / to give
   dé, des, dé;
   demos, deis, den

estar / to be
   esté, estés, esté;
   estemos, estéis, estén

haber / to have (as an auxiliary or helping verb)
   haya, hayas, haya;
   hayamos, hayáis, hayan

ir / to go
   vaya, vayas, vaya;
   vayamos, vayáis, vayan

saber / to know, to know how
   sepa, sepas, sepa;
   sepamos, sepáis, sepan

ser / to be
   sea, seas, sea;
   seamos, seáis, sean

§8.46   Other verbs irregular in the present subjunctive

§8.47   Stem-changing verbs in the present indicative have the same stem changes in the present subjunctive, generally speaking. If you go to the present indicative, 1st. pers. sing. of those verbs, you will find the stem change there. Drop the ending **o** and add the appropriate endings of the present subjunctive, as explained in **§8.42** above. For example, to form the present subjunctive of **pensar**, go to the 1st pers. sing. of the present indicative and there you will find **pienso**. Drop the ending **o** and add: **e, es, e; emos, éis, en**. The verbs irregular in the present indicative, including stem-changing and orthographical changing verbs, are given to you alphabetically in **§8.19**.

§8.48   Orthographical changing verbs (those that change in spelling), which end in **car, gar,** and **zar** in the infinitive form, have the same spelling changes in the present subjunctive as they do in the 1st pers. sing. of the preterit. Just drop the accent mark on **é** and you have the form of the present subjunctive, generally speaking. Those verbs are given to you in **§8.30** where they are listed alphabetically under **Verbs irregular in the preterit, including stem-changing verbs and orthographical changing verbs.**

FOR EXAMPLE:

PRETERIT, 1st pers. sing.	PRESENT SUBJUNCTIVE
abracé (abra**zar**)	abrace, abraces, abrace; abracemos, abracéis, abracen
busqué (bus**car**)	busque, busques, busque; busquemos, busquéis, busquen
pagué (pa**gar**)	pague, pagues, pague; paguemos, paguéis, paguen

§8.49   However, there are some verbs of the type that end in **car, gar,** and **zar** which are stem-changing when stressed and the process described in **§8.48** above will not work for them. For example:

Take **almorzar**. If you go to the preterit, 1st pers. sing., you will find **almorcé**. If you drop the accent mark on **é**, you are left with **almorce**, which is not the correct form in the present subjunctive. The **o** in the stem is stressed and it changes to **ue**; the forms in the present subjunctive for this verb contain the stem change, which is found in the present indicative. The forms of **almorzar** in the present subjunctive, therefore, are: **almuerce, almuerces, almuerce; almorcemos, almorcéis, almuercen**.

See the verb **almorzar** in sections §8.19 and §8.30.

Finally, remember that there is really no easy perfect system of arriving at verb forms no matter what process is used because there is usually some exception—even if only one exception. The best thing for you to do, since you are preparing to take the next SAT II test, is to be sure you know the regular forms in all the tenses and the irregular forms that are commonly used just so that you can recognize them on the test. All those that you need to know and to recognize are given to you in these sections on Spanish verbs.

If I have inadvertently omitted any verb you have in mind, which is irregular in the present subjunctive in some way, consult my book *501 Spanish verbs fully conjugated in all the tenses in a new easy to learn format*, Fourth Edition, also published by Barron's.

§8.50 **Tense No. 7: Imperfecto de subjuntivo** (Imperfect subjunctive) (See also §7.33.)

This past tense past is used for the same reasons as the **presente de subjuntivo**—that is, after certain verbs, conjunctions, impersonal expressions, etc., which were explained and illustrated above in §8.41–§8.45. The main difference between these two tenses is the time of the action.

If the verb in the main clause is in the present indicative or future or present perfect indicative or imperative, the *present subjunctive* or the *present perfect subjunctive* (see §7.101, no. 1) is used in the dependent clause—provided, of course, that there is some element which requires the use of the subjunctive.

However, if the verb in the main clause is in the imperfect indicative, preterit, conditional, or pluperfect indicative, the *imperfect subjunctive* (this tense) or *pluperfect subjunctive* is ordinarily used in the dependent clause — provided, of course, that there is some element which requires the use of the subjunctive. See also §7.101, no. 2.

EXAMPLES:

1. *Insistí* en que María lo **hiciera** / I insisted that Mary *do* it.
2. Se lo *explicaba* a María **para que lo comprendiera** / I was explaining it to Mary *so that she might understand it*.

NOTE that the *imperfect subjunctive* is used after **como si** to express a condition contrary to fact. See also §7.34.

EXAMPLE:

Me habla como si **fuera** un niño / He speaks to me as if *I were* a child.

NOTE: In this last example, the subjunctive is used in English also for the same reason.

Finally, note that **quisiera** (the imperfect subjunctive of **querer**) can be used to express in a very polite way, *I should like*: **Quisiera hablar ahora** / I should like to speak now.

§8.51 **The imperfect subjunctive is regularly formed as follows:**

For all verbs, drop the **ron** ending of the 3rd pers. pl. of the preterit and add the following endings:

ra, ras, ra;
ramos, rais, ran OR **se, ses, se;**
semos, seis, sen

§8.52 The only accent mark on the forms of the imperfect subjunctive is on the 1st pers. pl. form (**nosotros**) and it is placed on the vowel which is right in front of the ending **ramos** or **semos**.

§8.53 EXAMPLES:

PRETERIT, 3rd pers. plural	IMPERFECT SUBJUNCTIVE
bebieron (beber)	**bebiera, bebieras, bebiera;** **bebiéramos, bebierais, bebieran** OR **bebiese, bebieses, bebiese;** **bebiésemos, bebieseis, bebiesen**

PRETERIT, 3rd pers. plural	IMPERFECT SUBJUNCTIVE
creyeron (creer)	**creyera, creyeras, creyera;** **creyéramos, creyerais, creyeran** OR **creyese, creyeses, creyese;** **creyésemos, creyeseis, creyesen**
dieron (dar)	**diera, dieras, diera;** **diéramos, dierais, dieran** OR **diese, dieses, diese;** **diésemos, dieseis, diesen**
dijeron (decir)	**dijera, dijeras, dijera;** **dijéramos, dijerais, dijeran** OR **dijese, dijeses, dijese;** **dijésemos, dijeseis, dijesen**
durmieron (dormir)	**durmiera, durmieras, durmiera;** **durmiéramos, durmierais, durmieran** OR **durmiese, durmieses, durmiese;** **durmiésemos, durmieseis, durmiesen**
hubieron (haber)	**hubiera, hubieras, hubiera;** **hubiéramos, hubierais, hubieran** OR **hubiese, hubieses, hubiese;** **hubiésemos, hubieseis, hubiesen**
hablaron (hablar)	**hablara, hablaras, hablara;** **habláramos, hablarais, hablaran** OR **hablase, hablases, hablase;** **hablásemos, hablaseis, hablasen**
hicieron (hacer)	**hiciera, hicieras, hiciera;** **hiciéramos, hicierais, hicieran** OR **hiciese, hicieses, hiciese;** **hiciésemos, hicieseis, hiciesen**
fueron (ir)	**fuera, fueras, fuera;** **fuéramos, fuerais, fueran** OR **fuese, fueses, fuese;** **fuésemos, fueseis, fuesen**

leyeron (leer)	leyera, leyeras, leyera; leyéramos, leyerais, leyeran OR leyese, leyeses, leyese; leyésemos, leyeseis, leyesen
recibieron (recibir)	recibiera, recibieras, recibiera; recibiéramos, recibierais, recibieran OR recibiese, recibieses, recibiese; recibiésemos, recibieseis, recibiesen
fueron (ser)	fuera, fueras, fuera; fuéramos, fuerais, fueran OR fuese, fueses, fuese; fuésemos, fueseis, fuesen
tuvieron (tener)	tuviera, tuvieras, tuviera; tuviéramos, tuvierais, tuvieran OR tuviese, tuvieses, tuviese; tuviésemos, tuvieseis, tuviesen

§8.54 Using the first three examples given above in **§8.53** (**beber, creer, dar**), the usual English equivalents are as follows:

(that I) might drink, (that you) might drink, (that he/she) might drink, *etc.*
(that I) might believe, (that you) might believe, (that he/she) might believe, *etc.*
(that I) might give, (that you) might give, (that he/she) might give, *etc.*

§8.55 Tense No. 8: Perfecto de indicativo (Present perfect indicative)

This is the first of the seven compound tenses that follow here. This tense expresses an action that took place at no definite time in the past. It is also called Past Indefinite. It is a compound tense because it is formed with the present indicative of **haber** (the auxiliary or helping verb) plus the past participle of the verb you have in mind. Note the translation into English in the examples that follow. Then compare this tense with the Perfecto de Subjuntivo and the examples given in **§8.60.** For the seven simple tenses of **haber** (which you need to know to form these seven compound tenses), see **§8.11.** See also **§8.4.**

1. (Yo) **he hablado** / *I have spoken*.
2. (Tú) no **has venido** a verme / *You have not come* to see me.
3. Elena **ha ganado** el premio / Helen *has won* the prize.

§8.56 Tense No. 9: Pluscuamperfecto de indicativo (Pluperfect *or* Past perfect indicative)

This is the second of the compound tenses. In Spanish and English, this past tense is used to express an action which happened in the past *before* another past action. Since it is used in relation to another past action, the other past action is ordinarily expressed in the preterit. However, it is not always necessary to have the other past action expressed, as in example no. 2 below.

In English, this tense is formed with the past tense of *to have* (had) plus the past participle of the verb you have in mind. In Spanish, this tense is formed with the imperfect indicative of **haber** plus the past participle of the verb you have in mind. Note the translation into English in the examples that follow. Then compare this tense with the **pluscuamperfecto de subjuntivo** and the examples given in **§8.61.** For the seven simple tenses of **haber** (which you need to know to form these seven compound tenses), see **§8.11.** See also **§8.5.**

1. Cuando **llegué** a casa, mi hermano **había salido** / When I *arrived* home, my brother *had gone out*.

   NOTE: *First*, my brother went out; *then*, I arrived home. Both actions happened in the past. The action that occurred in the past *before* the other past action is in the pluperfect, and in this example it is *my brother had gone out* (**mi hermano había salido**).

   NOTE: ALSO that **llegué** (*I arrived*) is in the preterit because it is an action that happened in the past and it was completed.

2. Juan lo **había perdido** en la calle / John *had lost* it in the street.

   NOTE: In this example, the pluperfect indicative is used even though no other past action is expressed. It is assumed that John *had lost* something **before** some other past action.

§8.57 **Tense No. 10: Pretérito anterior** (Past anterior *or* Preterit perfect)

This is the third of the compound tenses. This past tense is compound because it is formed with the preterit of **haber** plus the past participle of the verb you are using. It is translated into English like the pluperfect indicative explained in **§8.56** above. This tense is not used much in spoken Spanish. Ordinarily, the pluperfect indicative is used in spoken Spanish (and sometimes even the simple preterit) in place of the past anterior.

This tense is ordinarily used in formal writing, such as history and literature. It is normally used after certain conjunctions of time, *e.g.*, **después que, cuando, apenas, luego que, en cuanto**.

For your purposes, since you are preparing to take the next Spanish Test, you must become familiar with this tense because you will have to recognize its meaning in reading comprehension selections on the Test. Remember that it is translated into English the same as the pluperfect indicative in **§8.56** above. It is used in literature and formal writings, rarely in informal conversation. See **§8.6** and **§8.11**.

EXAMPLE:
Después que **hubo hablado**, salió / After *he had spoken*, he left.

§8.58 **Tense No. 11: Futuro perfecto** (Future perfect *or* Future anterior)

This is the fourth of the compound tenses. This compound tense is formed with the future of **haber** plus the past participle of the verb you have in mind. In Spanish and in English, this tense is used to express an action that will happen in the future *before* another future action. In English, this tense is formed by using *shall have* or *will have* plus the past participle of the verb you have in mind.

NOTE the translation into English in the examples that follow. See **§8.7** and **§8.11**.

EXAMPLE:
María llegará mañana y **habré terminado** mi trabajo / Mary will arrive tomorrow and *I shall have finished* my work.

NOTE: *First*, I shall finish my work; *then*, Mary will arrive. The action that will occur in the future *before* the other future action is in the **Futuro perfecto**, and in this example it is (yo) **habré terminado mi trabajo**.

Also, in Spanish the future perfect is used to indicate conjecture or probability regarding recent past time.

EXAMPLES:
1. María **se habrá acostado** / Mary *has probably gone to bed*; Mary *must have gone to bed*.
2. José **habrá llegado** / Joseph *has probably arrived*; Joseph *must have arrived*.

§8.59 **Tense No. 12: Potencial compuesto** (Conditional perfect)

This is the fifth of the compound tenses. It is formed with the conditional of **haber** (see **§8.8** and **§8.11**) plus the past participle of the verb you have in mind. It is used in Spanish and English to express an action that you *would have done* if something else had been possible; that is, you would have done something *on condition* that something else had been possible.

In English it is formed by using *would have* plus the past participle of the verb you have in mind. Observe the difference between the following example and the one given for the use of the **Potencial simple** which was explained and illustrated in **§8.36(a).**

EXAMPLE:

(a) **Habría ido** a España si hubiera tenido dinero / *I would have gone* to Spain if I had had money. (For an explanation of **hubiera tenido,** see **§7.111(3)** and **§8.61.**

Also, in Spanish the Conditional perfect is used to indicate probability or conjecture in the past.

EXAMPLE:

(b) **Habrían sido** las cinco cuando salieron / *It must have been* five o'clock when they went out. [Compare this with the example given for the simple conditional in **§8.36(e)**].

(c) ¿Quién **habría sido?** / Who *could that have been* (*or* I wonder *who that could have been*)? [Compare this with the example given for the simple conditional in **§8.36(d)**].

§8.60 **Tense No. 13: Perfecto de subjuntivo** (Present perfect *or* Past subjunctive) (See also **§7.33ff)**

This is the sixth of the compound tenses. It is formed by using the present subjunctive of **haber** as the helping verb (see **§8.9** and **§8.11**) plus the past participle of the verb you have in mind.

If the verb in the main clause is in the present indicative, future, or present perfect tense, the present subjunctive (see **§8.41**) is used *or* this tense is used in the dependent clause — provided, of course, that there is some element that requires the use of the subjunctive.

The present subjunctive is used if the action is not past. However, if the action is past, this tense (present perfect subjunctive) is used, as in the examples given below.

Review the present subjunctive in **§8.41** and the imperfect subjunctive in **§8.50.**

NOTE the following examples in which this tense is used. Then compare them with the examples given in **§8.55** where the **Perfecto de indicativo** is explained and illustrated:

1. María duda que yo le **haya hablado** al profesor / Mary doubts that *I have spoken* to the professor.
2. Siento que tú no **hayas venido** a verme / I am sorry that you *have not come* to see me.
3. Me alegro de que Elena **haya ganado** el premio / I am glad that Helen *has won* the prize.

In these three examples, the auxiliary verb **haber** is used in the present subjunctive because the main verb in the clause that precedes is one that requires the subjunctive mood of the verb in the dependent clause. See the special verbs that require the subjunctive form of a verb in a dependent clause in **§7.78–§7.99.**

§8.61 **Tense No. 14: Pluscuamperfecto de subjuntivo** (Pluperfect *or* Past perfect subjunctive) (See also **§7.33ff)**

This is the seventh of the compound tenses. It is formed by using the imperfect subjunctive of **haber** as the helping verb (see **§8.10** and **§8.11**) plus the past participle of the verb you have in mind.

The translation of this tense into English is often like the pluperfect indicative (see **§8.56**).

If the verb in the main clause is in a past tense, this tense is used in the dependent clause — provided, of course, that there is some element that requires the use of the subjunctive. Review **§7.101(2).**

EXAMPLES:

1. Sentí mucho que **no hubiera venido** María / I was very sorry that Mary *had not come.*
2. Me alegraba de que **hubiera venido** María / I was glad that Mary *had come.*
3. No creía que María **hubiera llegado** / I did not believe that Mary *had arrived.*

So much for the seven simple tenses and the seven compound tenses. Now, let's look at the Imperative Mood.

§8.62   Imperativo (Imperative *or* Command)

The Imperative mood is used in Spanish and in English to express a command. We saw earlier in **§8.41** that the subjunctive mood is used to express commands in the **Ud.** and **Uds.** forms, in addition to other uses of the subjunctive mood. Review **§8.41(a)** to **(d)** and **(n)**.

Here are other points you ought to know about the Imperative.

(a) An indirect command or deep desire expressed in the third pers. sing. or pl. is in the subjunctive. Notice the use of *Let* or *May* in the English translations. **Que** introduces this kind of command. EXAMPLES:

1. ¡Que lo **haga** Jorge!
   Let George do it!
2. ¡Que Dios se lo **pague**!
   May God reward you!
3. ¡Que **vengan** pronto!
   Let them come quickly!
4. ¡Que **entre** Roberto!
   Let Rober enter!
5. ¡Que **salgan**!
   Let them leave!
6. ¡Que **entren** las muchachas!
   Let the girls come in!

(b) In some indirect commands, **que** is omitted. Here, too, the subjunctive is used.
   EXAMPLE: ¡**Viva** el presidente! / Long live the president!

(c) The verb form of the affirmative sing. familiar (**tú**) is the same as the 3rd pers. sing. of the present indicative when expressing a command. EXAMPLES:

1. ¡**Entra** pronto! / *Come in* quickly!
2. ¡**Sigue** leyendo! / *Keep on* reading! or *Continue* reading!

(d) There are some exceptions, however, to (c) above. The following verb forms are irregular in the affirmative sing. imperative (**tú** form only).

di (decir)   **sal** (salir)   **val** (valer)
haz (hacer)   **sé** (ser)   **ve** (ir)
he (haber)   **ten** (tener)   **ven** (venir)
pon (poner)

(e) In the affirmative command, 1st pers. pl., instead of using the present subjunctive hortatory command, **vamos a** (*Let's* or *Let us*) + **inf.** may be used. EXAMPLES:

1. **Vamos a** comer / Let's eat.
   or: **Comamos** (1st pers. pl., present subj., hortatory command)
2. **Vamos a** cantar / Let's sing.
   or: **Cantemos** (1st pers. pl., present subj., hortatory command)

(f) In the affirmative command, 1st pers. pl., **vamos** may be used to mean *Let's go:* **Vamos** al cine / Let's go to the movies.

(g) However, if in the negative (*Let's not go*), the present subjunctive of **ir** must be used: **No vayamos** al cine / Let's not go to the movies.

(h) Note that **Vámonos** (1st pers. pl. of **irse**, imperative) means *Let's go,* or *Let's go away,* or *Let's leave.* See (m) below.

(i) Also note that **no nos vayamos** (1st pers. pl. of **irse**, present subjunctive) means *Let's not go,* or *Let's not go away,* or *Let's not leave.*

(j) The imperative in the affirmative familiar plural (**vosotros, vosotras**) is formed by dropping the final **r** of the inf. and adding **d.** EXAMPLES:

1. ¡**Hablad**! / Speak!
2. ¡**Comed**! / Eat!
3. ¡**Id**! / Go!
4. ¡**Venid**! Come!

(k) When forming the affirmative familiar plural (**vosotros, vosotras**) imperative of a reflexive verb, the final **d** on the inf. must be dropped before the reflexive pronoun **os** is added, and both elements are joined to make one word. EXAMPLES:

1. ¡**Levantaos**! / Get up!
2. ¡**Sentaos**! / Sit down!

(l) Referring to (k) above, when the final **d** is dropped in a reflexive verb ending in
—ir, an accent mark must be written on the **i**. EXAMPLES:

    1. **¡Vestíos!** / Get dressed!   2. **¡Divertíos!** / Have a good time!

(m) When forming the 1st pers. pl. affirmative imperative of a reflexive verb, the final **s**
must drop before the reflexive pronoun **os** is added, and both elements are joined to
make one word. This requires an accent mark on the vowel of the syllable that was
stressed before **os** was added. EXAMPLE:

Vamos + nos changes to: **Vámonos!** / *Let's go!* or *Let's go away!* or *Let's leave!* See
(h) above.

(n) All negative imperatives in the familiar 2nd pers. sing. (**tú**) and plural (**vosotros,
vosotras**) are expressed in the present subjunctive. Review **§8.41(b)** and **(c)**.
    EXAMPLES:

    1. **¡No corras (tú)!** / Don't run!
    2. **¡No corráis (vosotros or vosotras)!** / Don't run!
    3. **¡No vengas (tú)!** / Don't come!
    4. **¡No vengáis (vosotros or vosotras)!** / Don't come!

(o) Object pronouns (direct, indirect, or reflexive) with an imperative verb form in the
affirmative are attached to the verb form. See also **Position of object pronouns** in
§6.34–§6.53 and the entry **accent mark** in the General Index in the back pages of
this book for section references in this General Review.
    EXAMPLES:

    1. **¡Hágalo (Ud.)!** / Do it!
    2. **¡Díganoslo (Ud.)!** / Tell it to us!
    3. **¡Dímelo (tú)!** / Tell it to me!
    4. **¡Levántate (tú)!** / Get up!
    5. **¡Siéntese (Ud.)!** / Sit down!
    6. **¡Hacedlo (vosotros, vosotras)!** / Do it!
    7. **¡Démelo (Ud.)!** / Give it to me!
    8. **¡Hábleme (Ud.), por favor!** / Talk to me, please!

(p) Object pronouns (direct, indirect, or reflexive) with an imperative verb form in the
negative are placed in front of the verb form. See also **Position of object
pronouns** in **§6.34–§6.53** and the entry **accent mark** in the General Index in the
back pages of this book for section references in this General Review. Compare the
following examples with those given in (o) above:

    1. **¡No lo haga (Ud.)!** / Don't do it!
    2. **¡No nos lo diga (Ud.)!** / Don't tell it to us!
    3. **¡No me lo digas (tú)!** / Don't tell it to me!
    4. **¡No te levantes (tú)!** / Don't get up!
    5. **¡No se siente (Ud.)!** / Don't sit down!
    6. **¡No lo hagáis (vosotros, vosotras)!** / Don't do it!
    7. **No me lo dé (Ud.)!** / Don't give it to me!

(q) Note that in some countries in Latin America the 2nd pers. pl. familiar (**vosotros,
vosotras**) forms are avoided. In place of them, the 3rd pers. pl. **Uds.** forms are
customarily used.

§8.63 The Progressive forms of tenses: a note

(1) In Spanish, there are also progressive forms of tenses. They are the Progressive
Present and the Progressive Past.

(2) The Progressive Present is formed by using **estar** in the present tense plus the
present participle of your main verb; *e.g.*, **Estoy hablando** (*I am talking*), *i.e., I am*
(in the act of) *talking* (right now).

(3) The Progressive Past is formed by using **estar** in the imperfect indicative plus the present participle of your main verb; *e.g.,* **Estaba hablando** (*I was talking*), i.e., I was (in the act of) *talking* (right then).

(4) The progressive forms are used when you want to emphasize or intensify an action; if you don't want to do that, then just use the simple present or simple imperfect; *e.g.,* say **Hablo,** *not* **Estoy hablando;** or **Hablaba,** *not* **Estaba hablando**.

(5) Sometimes **ir** is used instead of **estar** to form the progressive tenses; *e.g.,* **Va hablando** (*he/she keeps right on talking*), **Iba hablando** (*he/she kept right on talking*). Note that they do not have the exact same meaning as **Está hablando** and **Estaba hablando**. See (2) and (3) above.

(6) See also the General Index in the back pages of this book for other references about these forms under the entry **Progressive forms**.

§8.64 **The Future Subjunctive and the Future Perfect Subjunctive: a note**

The Future Subjunctive and the Future Prefect Subjunctive exist in Spanish, but they are rarely used. Nowadays, instead of using the Future Subjunctive, one uses the Present Subjunctive or the Present Indicative. Instead of using the Future Perfect Subjunctive, one uses the Future Perfect Indicative or the Present Perfect Subjunctive. However, if you are curious to know how to form the Future Subjunctive and the Future Perfect Subjunctive in Spanish, the following is offered:

(1) To form the Future Subjunctive, take the third person plural of the Preterit of any Spanish verb and change the ending **ron** to **re, res, re; remos, reis, ren**. An accent mark is needed as shown below on the first person plural form to preserve the stress.

EXAMPLES:

amar	**amare, amares, amare;** **amáremos, amareis, amaren**
comer	**comiere, comieres, comiere;** **comiéremos, comiereis, comieren**
dar	**diere, dieres, diere;** **diéremos, diereis, dieren**
haber	**hubiere, hubieres, hubiere;** **hubiéremos, hubiereis, hubieren**
hablar	**hablare, hablares, hablare;** **habláremos, hablareis, hablaren**
ir *or* **ser**	**fuere, fueres, fuere;** **fuéremos, fuereis, fueren**

(2) Let's look at the forms of **amar** above to see what the English translation is of this tense:

(que) yo amare / (that) I love …
(que) tú amares / (that) you love …
(que) Ud. (él, ella) amare / (that) you (he, she) love …
(que) nosotros (—tras) amáremos / (that) we love …
(que) vosotros (—tras) amareis / (that) you love …
(que) Uds. (ellos, ellas) amaren / (that) you (they) love …

(3) To form the Future Perfect Subjunctive, use the Future Subjunctive form of **haber** (shown above) as your auxiliary plus the past participle of the verb you have in mind.

EXAMPLES:

(que) hubiere amado, hubieres amado, hubiere amado;
(que) hubiéremos amado, hubiereis amado, hubieren amado

English translation:
(that) I have *or* I shall have loved, (that) you have *or* will have loved, *etc.*

§8.65   **Common irregular Spanish verb forms and uncommon Spanish verb forms identified by infinitive**

A

abierto **abrir**
acierto, *etc.* **acertar**
acuerdo, *etc.* **acordar**
acuesto, *etc.* **acostarse**
alce, *etc.* **alzar**
andes **andar**
anduve, *etc.* **andar**
apruebo, *etc.* **aprobar**
ase, *etc.* **asir**
asgo, *etc.* **asir**
ataque, *etc.* **atacar**
ate, *etc.* **atar**

C

cabré, *etc.* **caber**
caí, *etc.* **caer**
caía, *etc.* **caer**
caigo, *etc.* **caer**
calce, *etc.* **calzar**
caliento, *etc.* **calentar**
cayera, *etc.* **caer**
cierro, *etc.* **cerrar**
cojo, *etc.* **coger**
colija, *etc.* **colegir**
consigo, *etc.* **conseguir**
cuece, *etc.* **cocer**
cuelgo, *etc.* **colgar**
cuento, *etc.* **contar**
cuesta, *etc.* **costar**
cuezo, *etc.* **cocer**
cupe, *etc.* **caber**
cupiera, *etc.* **caber**

D

da, *etc.* **dar**
dad **dar**
das **dar**
dé **dar**
demos **dar**
den **dar**
des **dar**
di, *etc.* **dar, decir**
dice, *etc.* **decir**
diciendo **decir**
dicho **decir**
diera, *etc.* **dar**
diese, *etc.* **dar**
digo, *etc.* **decir**
dije, *etc.* **decir**
dimos, *etc.* **dar**
dio **dar**
diré, *etc.* **decir**
diría, *etc.* **decir**
diste **dar**
doy **dar**
duelo, *etc.* **doler**
duermo, *etc.* **dormir**

durmamos **dormir**
durmiendo **dormir**

E

eliges, *etc.* **elegir**
eligiendo **elegir**
eligiera, *etc.* **elegir**
elijo, *etc.* **elegir**
era, *etc.* **ser**
eres **ser**
es **ser**
estoy **estar**
estuve, *etc.* **estar**
exija, *etc.* **exigir**

F

fíe, *etc.* **fiar**
finja, *etc.* **fingir**
fío, *etc.* **fiar**
friego, *etc.* **fregar**
friendo **freír**
friera, *etc.* **freír**
frío, *etc.* **freír**
frito **freír**
fue, *etc.* **ir, ser**
fuera, *etc.* **ir, ser**
fuese, *etc.* **ir, ser**
fui, *etc.* **ir, ser**

G

gima, *etc.* **gemir**
gimiendo **gemir**
gimiera, *etc.* **gemir**
gimiese, *etc.* **gemir**
gimo, *etc.* **gemir**
goce, *etc.* **gozar**
gocé **gozar**

H

ha **haber**
había, *etc.* **haber**
habré, *etc.* **haber**
haga, *etc.* **hacer**
hago, *etc.* **hacer**
han **haber**
haría, *etc.* **hacer**
has **haber**
haya, *etc.* **haber**
haz **hacer**
he **haber**
hecho **hacer**
hemos **haber**
hice, *etc.* **hacer**
hiciera, *etc.* **hacer**

hiciese, *etc.* **hacer**
hiela **helar**
hiele **helar**
hiera, *etc.* **herir**
hiero, *etc.* **herir**
hiramos **herir**
hiriendo **herir**
hiriera, *etc.* **herir**
hiriese, *etc.* **herir**
hizo **hacer**
hube, *etc.* **haber**
hubiera, *etc.* **haber**
hubiese, *etc.* **haber**
huela, *etc.* **oler**
huelo, *etc.* **oler**
huya, *etc.* **huir**
huyendo **huir**
huyera, *etc.* **huir**
huyese, *etc.* **huir**
huyo, *etc.* **huir**

I

iba, *etc.* **ir**
id **ir**
ido **ir**
idos **irse**
irgo, *etc.* **erguir**
irguiendo **erguir**
irguiera, *etc.* **erguir**
irguiese, *etc.* **erguir**

J

juego, *etc.* **jugar**
juegue, *etc.* **jugar**

L

lea, *etc.* **leer**
leído **leer**
leo, *etc.* **leer**
leyendo **leer**
leyera, *etc.* **leer**
leyese, *etc.* **leer**

LL

llueva **llover**
llueve **llover**

M

mida, *etc.* **medir**
midiendo **medir**
midiera, *etc.* **medir**
midiese, *etc.* **medir**
mido, *etc.* **medir**
mienta, *etc.* **mentir**
miento, *etc.* **mentir**
mintiendo **mentir**

mintiera, *etc.* **mentir**
mintiese, *etc.* **mentir**
muerda, *etc.* **morder**
muerdo, *etc.* **morder**
muero, *etc.* **morir**
muerto **morir**
muestre, *etc.* **mostrar**
muestro, *etc.* **mostrar**
mueva, *etc.* **mover**
muevo, *etc.* **mover**
muramos **morir**
muriendo **morir**
muriera, *etc.* **morir**
muriese, *etc.* **morir**

N

nazca, *etc.* **nacer**
nazco **nacer**
niego, *etc.* **negar**
niegue, *etc.* **negar**
nieva **nevar**
nieve **nevar**

O

oíd **oír**
oiga, *etc.* **oír**
oigo, *etc.* **oír**
oliendo **oler**
oliera, *etc.* **oler**
oliese, *etc.* **oler**
oye, *etc.* **oír**
oyendo **oír**
oyera, *etc.* **oír**
oyese, *etc.* **oír**

P

pida, *etc.* **pedir**
pidamos **pedir**
pidiendo **pedir**
pidiera, *etc.* **pedir**
pidiese, *etc.* **pedir**
pido, *etc.* **pedir**
pienso, *etc.* **pensar**
pierda, *etc.* **perder**
pierdo, *etc.* **perder**
plegue **placer**
plugo **placer**
pluguiera **placer**
pluguieron **placer**
pluguiese **placer**
ponga, *etc.* **poner**
pongámonos **ponerse**
ponte **ponerse**
pruebe, *etc.* **probar**
pruebo, *etc.* **probar**
pude, *etc.* **poder**
pudiendo **poder**
pudiera, *etc.* **poder**
pudiese, *etc.* **poder**
puedo, *etc.* **poder**
puesto **poner**
puse, *etc.* **poner**
pusiera, *etc.* **poner**
pusiese, *etc.* **poner**

Q

quepo, *etc.* **caber**
quiebro **quebrar**
quiero, *etc.* **querer**
quise, *etc.* **querer**
quisiera, *etc.* **querer**
quisiese, *etc.* **querer**

R

raí, *etc.* **raer**
raía, *etc.* **raer**
raiga, *etc.* **raer**
raigo, *etc.* **raer**
rayendo **raer**
rayera, *etc.* **raer**
rayese, *etc.* **raer**
ría, *etc.* **reír**
riamos **reír**
riego, *etc.* **regar**
riendo **reír**
riera, *etc.* **reír**
riese, *etc.* **reír**
riña, *etc.* **reñir**
riñendo **reñir**
riñera, *etc.* **reñir**
riñese, *etc.* **reñir**
riño, *etc.* **reñir**
río, *etc.* **reír**
roto **romper**
ruego, *etc.* **rogar**
ruegue, *etc.* **rogar**

S

sal, salgo, *etc.* **salir**
saque, *etc.* **sacar**
sé **saber, ser**
sea, *etc.* **ser**
sed **ser**
sepa, *etc.* **saber**
seque, *etc.* **secar**
sido **ser**
siendo **ser**
siento, *etc.* **sentar, sentir**
sigo, *etc.* **seguir**
siguiendo **seguir**
siguiera, *etc.* **seguir**
siguiese, *etc.* **seguir**
sintiendo **sentir**
sintiera, *etc.* **sentir**
sintiese, *etc.* **sentir**
sintió **sentir**
sirviendo **servir**
sirvo, *etc.* **servir**
sois **ser**
somos **ser**
son **ser**
soy **ser**
suela, *etc.* **soler**
suelo, *etc.* **soler**
suelto, *etc.* **soltar**
sueno, *etc.* **sonar**

sueño, *etc.* **soñar**
supe, *etc.* **saber**
supiera, *etc.* **saber**
supiese, *etc.* **saber**
surja, *etc.* **surgir**

T

ten, tengo **tener**
tiemblo, *etc.* **temblar**
tiendo, *etc.* **tender**
tienes, *etc.* **tener**
tiento, *etc.* **tentar**
toque, *etc.* **tocar**
traigo, *etc.* **traer**
tuesto, *etc.* **tostar**
tuve, *etc.* **tener**

U

uno, *etc.* **unir**

V

va **ir**
vais **ir**
val, valgo, *etc.* **valer**
vámonos **irse**
vamos **ir**
van **ir**
vas **ir**
vaya, *etc.* **ir**
ve **ir, ver**
vea, *etc.* **ver**
ved **ver**
ven **venir, ver**
vendré, *etc.* **venir**
venga, vengo **venir**
veo, *etc.* **ver**
ves **ver**
vete **irse**
vi **ver**
viendo **ver**
viene, *etc.* **venir**
viera, *etc.* **ver**
viese, *etc.* **ver**
vimos, *etc.* **ver**
vine, vino, *etc.* **venir**
vio **ver**
viste **ver, vestir**
vistiendo **vestir**
vistiéndose **vestirse**
vistiese, *etc.* **vestir(se)**
visto **ver, vestir**
voy **ir**
vuelo, *etc.* **volar**
vuelto **volver**
vuelvo, *etc.* **volver**

Y

yaz **yacer**
yazco, *etc.* **yacer**
yendo **ir**
yergo, *etc.* **erguir**
yerro, *etc.* **errar**

§8.66 Commonly used irregular verbs

§8.67   Here are some commonly used irregular verbs conjugated fully in all the tenses and moods. If any verbs *not* given here are of interest to you, consult my book *501 Spanish verbs fully conjugated in all the tenses in a new easy to learn format*, Fourth Edition, which contains them all, also published by Barron's.

In the format of the verbs that follow, the subject pronouns have been omitted in order to emphasize the verb forms. The subject pronouns are, as you know:

Subject Pronouns

SINGULAR	PLURAL
yo	nosotros (nosotras)
tú	vosotros (vosotras)
Ud. (él, ella)	Uds. (ellos, ellas)

caber to be contained, to fit into
Gerundio **cabiendo**   Part. pas. **cabido**

THE SEVEN SIMPLE TENSES		THE SEVEN COMPOUND TENSES	
SINGULAR	PLURAL	SINGULAR	PLURAL
1 presente de indicativo		**8 perfecto de indicativo**	
quepo	cabemos	he cabido	hemos cabido
cabes	cabéis	has cabido	habéis cabido
cabe	caben	ha cabido	han cabido
2 imperfecto de indicativo		**9 pluscuamperfecto de indicativo**	
cabía	cabíamos	había cabido	habíamos cabido
cabías	cabíais	habías cabido	habíais cabido
cabía	cabían	había cabido	habían cabido
3 pretérito		**10 pretérito anterior**	
cupe	cupimos	hube cabido	hubimos cabido
cupiste	cupisteis	hubiste cabido	hubisteis cabido
cupo	cupieron	hubo cabido	hubieron cabido
4 futuro		**11 futuro perfecto**	
cabré	cabremos	habré cabido	habremos cabido
cabrás	cabréis	habrás cabido	habréis cabido
cabrá	cabrán	habrá cabido	habrán cabido
5 potencial simple		**12 potencial compuesto**	
cabría	cabríamos	habría cabido	habríamos cabido
cabrías	cabríais	habrías cabido	habríais cabido
cabría	cabrían	habría cabido	habrían cabido
6 presente de subjuntivo		**13 perfecto de subjuntivo**	
quepa	quepamos	haya cabido	hayamos cabido
quepas	quepáis	hayas cabido	hayáis cabido
quepa	quepan	haya cabido	hayan cabido
7 imperfecto de subjuntivo		**14 pluscuamperfecto de subjuntivo**	
cupiera	cupiéramos	hubiera cabido	hubiéramos cabido
cupieras	cupierais	hubieras cabido	hubierais cabido
cupiera	cupieran	hubiera cabido	hubieran cabido
OR		OR	
cupiese	cupiésemos	hubiese cabido	hubiésemos cabido
cupieses	cupieseis	hubieses cabido	hubieseis cabido
cupiese	cupiesen	hubiese cabido	hubiesen cabido

imperativo

—	quepamos
cabe; no quepas	cabed; no quepáis
quepa	quepan

Common idiomatic expressions using this verb

Pablo no cabe en sí.   Paul has a swelled head.
No quepo aquí.   I don't have enough room here.
No cabe duda de que . . . .   There is no doubt that . . .

caer to fall
Gerundio **cayendo**   Part. pas. **caído**

THE SEVEN SIMPLE TENSES		THE SEVEN COMPOUND TENSES	
SINGULAR	PLURAL	SINGULAR	PLURAL
1 presente de indicativo		**8 perfecto de indicativo**	
caigo	caemos	he caído	hemos caído
caes	caéis	has caído	habéis caído
cae	caen	ha caído	han caído
2 imperfecto de indicativo		**9 pluscuamperfecto de indicativo**	
caía	caíamos	había caído	habíamos caído
caías	caíais	habías caído	habíais caído
caía	caían	había caído	habían caído
3 pretérito		**10 pretérito anterior**	
caí	caímos	hube caído	hubimos caído
caíste	caísteis	hubiste caído	hubisteis caído
cayó	cayeron	hubo caído	hubieron caído
4 futuro		**11 futuro perfecto**	
caeré	caeremos	habré caído	habremos caído
caerás	caeréis	habrás caído	habréis caído
caerá	caerán	habrá caído	habrán caído
5 potencial simple		**12 potencial compuesto**	
caería	caeríamos	habría caído	habríamos caído
caerías	caeríais	habrías caído	habríais caído
caería	caerían	habría caído	habrían caído
6 presente de subjuntivo		**13 perfecto de subjuntivo**	
caiga	caigamos	haya caído	hayamos caído
caigas	caigáis	hayas caído	hayáis caído
caiga	caigan	haya caído	hayan caído
7 imperfecto de subjuntivo		**14 pluscuamperfecto de subjuntivo**	
cayera	cayéramos	hubiera caído	hubiéramos caído
cayeras	cayerais	hubieras caído	hubierais caído
cayera	cayeran	hubiera caído	hubieran caído
OR		OR	
cayese	cayésemos	hubiese caído	hubiésemos caído
cayeses	cayeseis	hubieses caído	hubieseis caído
cayese	cayesen	hubiese caído	hubiesen caído

imperativo

—	caigamos
cae; no caigas	caed; no caigáis
caiga	caigan

Words and expressions related to this verb

la caída   the fall
a la caída del sol   at sunset
a la caída de la tarde   at the end of
   the afternoon
caer enfermo (enferma)   to fall sick

dejar caer   to drop
caer de espaldas   to fall backwards
decaer   to decay, decline
recaer   to relapse, fall back
caer con   to come down with

creer to believe
Gerundio **creyendo**   Part. pas. **creído**

THE SEVEN SIMPLE TENSES		THE SEVEN COMPOUND TENSES	
SINGULAR	PLURAL	SINGULAR	PLURAL
1 presente de indicativo		**8 perfecto de indicativo**	
creo	creemos	he creído	hemos creído
crees	creéis	has creído	habéis creído
cree	creen	ha creído	han creído
2 imperfecto de indicativo		**9 pluscuamperfecto de indicativo**	
creía	creíamos	había creído	habíamos creído
creías	creíais	habías creído	habíais creído
creía	creían	había creído	habían creído
3 pretérito		**10 pretérito anterior**	
creí	creímos	hube creído	hubimos creído
creíste	creísteis	hubiste creído	hubisteis creído
creyó	creyeron	hubo creído	hubieron creído
4 futuro		**11 futuro perfecto**	
creeré	creeremos	habré creído	habremos creído
creerás	creeréis	habrás creído	habréis creído
creerá	creerán	habrá creído	habrán creído
5 potencial simple		**12 potencial compuesto**	
creería	creeríamos	habría creído	habríamos creído
creerías	creeríais	habrías creído	habríais creído
creería	creerían	habría creído	habrían creído
6 presente de subjuntivo		**13 perfecto de subjuntivo**	
crea	creamos	haya creído	hayamos creído
creas	creáis	hayas creído	hayáis creído
crea	crean	haya creído	hayan creído
7 imperfecto de subjuntivo		**14 pluscuamperfecto de subjuntivo**	
creyera	creyéramos	hubiera creído	hubiéramos creído
creyeras	creyerais	hubieras creído	hubierais creído
creyera	creyeran	hubiera creído	hubieran creído
OR		OR	
creyese	creyésemos	hubiese creído	hubiésemos creído
creyeses	creyeseis	hubieses creído	hubieseis creído
creyese	creyesen	hubiese creído	hubiesen creído

imperativo

—		creamos	
cree; no creas		creed; no creáis	
crea		crean	

Words and expressions related to this verb

Ver y creer   Seeing is believing.
¡Ya lo creo!   Of course!
crédulo, crédula   credulous
descreer   to disbelieve

la credulidad   credulity
el credo   creed
dar crédito   to believe

dar to give
Gerundio **dando**   Part. pas. **dado**

THE SEVEN SIMPLE TENSES		THE SEVEN COMPOUND TENSES	
SINGULAR	PLURAL	SINGULAR	PLURAL
1 presente de indicativo		**8 perfecto de indicativo**	
doy	damos	he dado	hemos dado
das	dais	has dado	habéis dado
da	dan	ha dado	han dado
2 imperfecto de indicativo		**9 pluscuamperfecto de indicativo**	
daba	dábamos	había dado	habíamos dado
dabas	dabais	habías dado	habíais dado
daba	daban	había dado	habían dado
3 pretérito		**10 pretérito anterior**	
*di	dimos	hube dado	hubimos dado
diste	disteis	hubiste dado	hubisteis dado
dio	dieron	hubo dado	hubieron dado
4 futuro		**11 futuro perfecto**	
daré	daremos	habré dado	habremos dado
darás	daréis	habrás dado	habréis dado
dará	darán	habrá dado	habrán dado
5 potencial simple		**12 potencial compuesto**	
daría	daríamos	habría dado	habríamos dado
darías	daríais	habrías dado	habríais dado
daría	darían	habría dado	habrían dado
6 presente de subjuntivo		**13 perfecto de subjuntivo**	
dé	demos	haya dado	hayamos dado
des	deis	hayas dado	hayáis dado
dé	den	haya dado	hayan dado
7 imperfecto de subjuntivo		**14 pluscuamperfecto de subjuntivo**	
diera	diéramos	hubiera dado	hubiéramos dado
dieras	dierais	hubieras dado	hubierais dado
diera	dieran	hubiera dado	hubieran dado
OR		OR	
diese	diésemos	hubiese dado	hubiésemos dado
dieses	dieseis	hubieses dado	hubieseis dado
diese	diesen	hubiese dado	hubiesen dado

imperativo

—	demos
da; no des	dad; no deis
dé	den

Common idiomatic expressions using this verb

A Dios rogando y con el mazo dando.   Put your faith in God and keep your powder dry.
El tiempo da buen consejo.   Time will tell.
dar la mano (las manos) a alguien   to shake hands with someone
dar de comer   to feed
darse   to give oneself up, to give in

* The accent mark on **di** is preferred in order to distinguish it from **di**, which is the 2nd person singular, imperative form of **decir**.

decir to say, to tell
Gerundio **diciendo**   Part. pas. **dicho**

THE SEVEN SIMPLE TENSES		THE SEVEN COMPOUND TENSES	
SINGULAR	PLURAL	SINGULAR	PLURAL
1 presente de indicativo		**8 perfecto de indicativo**	
digo	decimos	he dicho	hemos dicho
dices	decís	has dicho	habéis dicho
dice	dicen	ha dicho	han dicho
2 imperfecto de indicativo		**9 pluscuamperfecto de indicativo**	
decía	decíamos	había dicho	habíamos dicho
decías	decíais	habías dicho	habíais dicho
decía	decían	había dicho	habían dicho
3 pretérito		**10 pretérito anterior**	
dije	dijimos	hube dicho	hubimos dicho
dijiste	dijisteis	hubiste dicho	hubisteis dicho
dijo	dijeron	hubo dicho	hubieron dicho
4 futuro		**11 futuro perfecto**	
diré	diremos	habré dicho	habremos dicho
dirás	diréis	habrás dicho	habréis dicho
dirá	dirán	habrá dicho	habrán dicho
5 potencial simple		**12 potencial compuesto**	
diría	diríamos	habría dicho	habríamos dicho
dirías	diríais	habrías dicho	habríais dicho
diría	dirían	habría dicho	habrían dicho
6 presente de subjuntivo		**13 perfecto de subjuntivo**	
diga	digamos	haya dicho	hayamos dicho
digas	digáis	hayas dicho	hayáis dicho
diga	digan	haya dicho	hayan dicho
7 imperfecto de subjuntivo		**14 pluscuamperfecto de subjuntivo**	
dijera	dijéramos	hubiera dicho	hubiéramos dicho
dijeras	dijerais	hubieras dicho	hubierais dicho
dijera	dijeran	hubiera dicho	hubieran dicho
OR		OR	
dijese	dijésemos	hubiese dicho	hubiésemos dicho
dijeses	dijeseis	hubieses dicho	hubieseis dicho
dijese	dijesen	hubiese dicho	hubiesen dicho

	imperativo	
—	digamos
di; no digas	decid; no digáis
diga	digan

Sentences using this verb and words related to it

Dicho y hecho.   No sooner said than done.
Dime con quien andas y te diré quien eres.   Tell me who your friends are and I will tell you who you are.
querer decir   to mean
un decir   a familiar saying

estar to be

Gerundio **estando**   Part. pas. **estado**

THE SEVEN SIMPLE TENSES		THE SEVEN COMPOUND TENSES	
SINGULAR	PLURAL	SINGULAR	PLURAL
1 presente de indicativo		**8 perfecto de indicativo**	
estoy	estamos	he estado	hemos estado
estás	estáis	has estado	habéis estado
está	están	ha estado	han estado
2 imperfecto de indicativo		**9 pluscuamperfecto de indicativo**	
estaba	estábamos	había estado	habíamos estado
estabas	estabais	habías estado	habíais estado
estaba	estaban	había estado	habían estado
3 pretérito		**10 pretérito anterior**	
estuve	estuvimos	hube estado	hubimos estado
estuviste	estuvisteis	hubiste estado	hubisteis estado
estuvo	estuvieron	hubo estado	hubieron estado
4 futuro		**11 futuro perfecto**	
estaré	estaremos	habré estado	habremos estado
estarás	estaréis	habrás estado	habréis estado
estará	estarán	habrá estado	habrán estado
5 potencial simple		**12 potencial compuesto**	
estaría	estaríamos	habría estado	habríamos estado
estarías	estaríais	habrías estado	habríais estado
estaría	estarían	habría estado	habrían estado
6 presente de subjuntivo		**13 perfecto de subjuntivo**	
esté	estemos	haya estado	hayamos estado
estés	estéis	hayas estado	hayáis estado
esté	estén	haya estado	hayan estado
7 imperfecto de subjuntivo		**14 pluscuamperfecto de subjuntivo**	
estuviera	estuviéramos	hubiera estado	hubiéramos estado
estuvieras	estuvierais	hubieras estado	hubierais estado
estuviera	estuvieran	hubiera estado	hubieran estado
OR		OR	
estuviese	estuviésemos	hubiese estado	hubiésemos estado
estuvieses	estuvieseis	hubieses estado	hubieseis estado
estuviese	estuviesen	hubiese estado	hubiesen estado

imperativo

—	estemos
está; no estés	estad; no estéis
esté	estén

Common idiomatic expressions using this verb

— ¿Cómo está Ud.?

— Estoy muy bien, gracias. ¿Y usted?

— Estoy enfermo hoy.

estar para + inf. to be about + inf.

  Estoy para salir. I am about to go out.

estar por to be in favor of

haber to have (as an auxiliary verb to form compound tenses)
Gerundio **habiendo**   Part. pas. **habido**

THE SEVEN SIMPLE TENSES		THE SEVEN COMPOUND TENSES	
SINGULAR	PLURAL	SINGULAR	PLURAL
1 presente de indicativo		**8 perfecto de indicativo**	
he	hemos	he habido	hemos habido
has	habéis	has habido	habéis habido
ha	han	ha habido	han habido
2 imperfecto de indicativo		**9 pluscuamperfecto de indicativo**	
había	habíamos	había habido	habíamos habido
habías	habíais	habías habido	habíais habido
había	habían	había habido	habían habido
3 pretérito		**10 pretérito anterior**	
hube	hubimos	hube habido	hubimos habido
hubiste	hubisteis	hubiste habido	hubisteis habido
hubo	hubieron	hubo habido	hubieron habido
4 futuro		**11 futuro perfecto**	
habré	habremos	habré habido	habremos habido
habrás	habréis	habrás habido	habréis habido
habrá	habrán	habrá habido	habrán habido
5 potencial simple		**12 potencial compuesto**	
habría	habríamos	habría habido	habríamos habido
habrías	habríais	habrías habido	habríais habido
habría	habrían	habría habido	habrían habido
6 presente de subjuntivo		**13 perfecto de subjuntivo**	
haya	hayamos	haya habido	hayamos habido
hayas	hayáis	hayas habido	hayáis habido
haya	hayan	haya habido	hayan habido
7 imperfecto de subjuntivo		**14 pluscuamperfecto de subjuntivo**	
hubiera	hubiéramos	hubiera habido	hubiéramos habido
hubieras	hubierais	hubieras habido	hubierais habido
hubiera	hubieran	hubiera habido	hubieran habido
OR		OR	
hubiese	hubiésemos	hubiese habido	hubiésemos habido
hubieses	hubieseis	hubieses habido	hubieseis habido
hubiese	hubiesen	hubiese habido	hubiesen habido

imperativo

—		hayamos
	hé; no hayas	habed; no hayáis
	haya	hayan

Words and expressions related to this verb

el haber   credit (in bookkeeping)
los haberes   assets, possessions, property
habérselas con alguien   to have a showdown with someone

hacer to do, to make
Gerundio **haciendo**   Part. pas. **hecho**

THE SEVEN SIMPLE TENSES		THE SEVEN COMPOUND TENSES	
SINGULAR	PLURAL	SINGULAR	PLURAL
1 presente de indicativo		**8 perfecto de indicativo**	
hago	hacemos	he hecho	hemos hecho
haces	hacéis	has hecho	habéis hecho
hace	hacen	ha hecho	han hecho
2 imperfecto de indicativo		**9 pluscuamperfecto de indicativo**	
hacía	hacíamos	había hecho	habíamos hecho
hacías	hacíais	habías hecho	habíais hecho
hacía	hacían	había hecho	habían hecho
3 pretérito		**10 pretérito anterior**	
hice	hicimos	hube hecho	hubimos hecho
hiciste	hicisteis	hubiste hecho	hubisteis hecho
hizo	hicieron	hubo hecho	hubieron hecho
4 futuro		**11 futuro perfecto**	
haré	haremos	habré hecho	habremos hecho
harás	haréis	habrás hecho	habréis hecho
hará	harán	habrá hecho	habrán hecho
5 potencial simple		**12 potencial compuesto**	
haría	haríamos	habría hecho	habríamos hecho
harías	haríais	habrías hecho	habríais hecho
haría	harían	habría hecho	habrían hecho
6 presente de subjuntivo		**13 perfecto de subjuntivo**	
haga	hagamos	haya hecho	hayamos hecho
hagas	hagáis	hayas hecho	hayáis hecho
haga	hagan	haya hecho	hayan hecho
7 imperfecto de subjuntivo		**14 pluscuamperfecto de subjuntivo**	
hiciera	hiciéramos	hubiera hecho	hubiéramos hecho
hicieras	hicierais	hubieras hecho	hubierais hecho
hiciera	hicieran	hubiera hecho	hubieran hecho
OR		OR	
hiciese	hiciésemos	hubiese hecho	hubiésemos hecho
hicieses	hicieseis	hubieses hecho	hubieseis hecho
hiciese	hiciesen	hubiese hecho	hubiesen hecho

imperativo

—	hagamos
haz; no hagas	haced; no hagáis
haga	hagan

Common idiomatic expressions using this verb

Dicho y hecho.   No sooner said than done.
La práctica hace maestro al novicio.   Practice makes perfect.
Si a Roma fueres, haz como vieres.   When in Rome do as the Romans do. Note that it is not uncommon to use the future subjunctive in proverbs, as in *fueres* (**ir** or **ser**) and *vieres* (**ver**). See §8.64.

ir to go
Gerundio **yendo**   Part. pas. **ido**

THE SEVEN SIMPLE TENSES		THE SEVEN COMPOUND TENSES	
SINGULAR	PLURAL	SINGULAR	PLURAL
1 presente de indicativo		**8 perfecto de indicativo**	
voy	vamos	he ido	hemos ido
vas	vais	has ido	habéis ido
va	van	ha ido	han ido
2 imperfecto de indicativo		**9 pluscuamperfecto de indicativo**	
iba	íbamos	había ido	habíamos ido
ibas	ibais	habías ido	habíais ido
iba	iban	había ido	habían ido
3 pretérito		**10 pretérito anterior**	
fui	fuimos	hube ido	hubimos ido
fuiste	fuisteis	hubiste ido	hubisteis ido
fue	fueron	hubo ido	hubieron ido
4 futuro		**11 futuro perfecto**	
iré	iremos	habré ido	habremos ido
irás	iréis	habrás ido	habréis ido
irá	irán	habrá ido	habrán ido
5 potencial simple		**12 potencial compuesto**	
iría	iríamos	habría ido	habríamos ido
irías	iríais	habrías ido	habríais ido
iría	irían	habría ido	habrían ido
6 presente de subjuntivo		**13 perfecto de subjuntivo**	
vaya	vayamos	haya ido	hayamos ido
vayas	vayáis	hayas ido	hayáis ido
vaya	vayan	haya ido	hayan ido
7 imperfecto de subjuntivo		**14 pluscuamperfecto de subjuntivo**	
fuera	fuéramos	hubiera ido	hubiéramos ido
fueras	fuerais	hubieras ido	hubierais ido
fuera	fueran	hubiera ido	hubieran ido
OR		OR	
fuese	fuésemos	hubiese ido	hubiésemos ido
fueses	fueseis	hubieses ido	hubieseis ido
fuese	fuesen	hubiese ido	hubiesen ido

imperativo

—		vamos (no vayamos)
	ve; no vayas	id; no vayáis
	vaya	vayan

Common idiomatic expressions using this verb

ir de compras to go shopping
ir de brazo to walk arm in arm
¿Cómo le va? How goes it? How are you?
Cuando el gato va a sus devociones,
bailan los ratones. When the cat is away,
  the mice will play.

ir a caballo to ride horseback
un billete de ida y vuelta
  return ticket
¡Qué va! Nonsense!

leer to read
Gerundio **leyendo**   Part. pas. **leído**

THE SEVEN SIMPLE TENSES		THE SEVEN COMPOUND TENSES	
SINGULAR	PLURAL	SINGULAR	PLURAL
1 presente de indicativo		**8 perfecto de indicativo**	
leo	leemos	he leído	hemos leído
lees	leéis	has leído	habéis leído
lee	leen	ha leído	han leído
2 imperfecto de indicativo		**9 pluscuamperfecto de indicativo**	
leía	leíamos	había leído	habíamos leído
leías	leíais	habías leído	habíais leído
leía	leían	había leído	habían leído
3 pretérito		**10 pretérito anterior**	
leí	leímos	hube leído	hubimos leído
leíste	leísteis	hubiste leído	hubisteis leído
leyó	leyeron	hubo leído	hubieron leído
4 futuro		**11 futuro perfecto**	
leeré	leeremos	habré leído	habremos leído
leerás	leeréis	habrás leído	habréis leído
leerá	leerán	habrá leído	habrán leído
5 potencial simple		**12 potencial compuesto**	
leería	leeríamos	habría leído	habríamos leído
leerías	leeríais	habrías leído	habríais leído
leería	leerían	habría leído	habrían leído
6 presente de subjuntivo		**13 perfecto de subjuntivo**	
lea	leamos	haya leído	hayamos leído
leas	leáis	hayas leído	hayáis leído
lea	lean	haya leído	hayan leído
7 imperfecto de subjuntivo		**14 pluscuamperfecto de subjuntivo**	
leyera	leyéramos	hubiera leído	hubiéramos leído
leyeras	leyerais	hubieras leído	hubierais leído
leyera	leyeran	hubiera leído	hubieran leído
OR		OR	
leyese	leyésemos	hubiese leído	hubiésemos leído
leyeses	leyeseis	hubieses leído	hubieseis leído
leyese	leyesen	hubiese leído	hubiesen leído

imperativo

—	leamos
lee; no leas	leed; no leáis
lea	lean

Words and expressions related to this verb

la lectura reading
Me gusta la lectura. I like reading.
la lección lesson
lector, lectora reader
leer mal to misread

releer to read again, to reread
leer entre líneas to read between the lines
un, una leccionista private tutor
leer para sí to read to oneself

oír to hear
Gerundio **oyendo**   Part. pas. **oído**

THE SEVEN SIMPLE TENSES		THE SEVEN COMPOUND TENSES	
SINGULAR	PLURAL	SINGULAR	PLURAL
1 presente de indicativo		**8 perfecto de indicativo**	
oigo	oímos	he oído	hemos oído
oyes	oís	has oído	habéis oído
oye	oyen	ha oído	han oído
2 imperfecto de indicativo		**9 pluscuamperfecto de indicativo**	
oía	oíamos	había oído	habíamos oído
oías	oíais	habías oído	habíais oído
oía	oían	había oído	habían oído
3 pretérito		**10 pretérito anterior**	
oí	oímos	hube oído	hubimos oído
oíste	oísteis	hubiste oído	hubisteis oído
oyó	oyeron	hubo oído	hubieron oído
4 futuro		**11 futuro perfecto**	
oiré	oiremos	habré oído	habremos oído
oirás	oiréis	habrás oído	habréis oído
oirá	oirán	habrá oído	habrán oído
5 potencial simple		**12 potencial compuesto**	
oiría	oiríamos	habría oído	habríamos oído
oirías	oiríais	habrías oído	habríais oído
oiría	oirían	habría oído	habrían oído
6 presente de subjuntivo		**13 perfecto de subjuntivo**	
oiga	oigamos	haya oído	hayamos oído
oigas	oigáis	hayas oído	hayáis oído
oiga	oigan	haya oído	hayan oído
7 imperfecto de subjuntivo		**14 pluscuamperfecto de subjuntivo**	
oyera	oyéramos	hubiera oído	hubiéramos oído
oyeras	oyerais	hubieras oído	hubierais oído
oyera	oyeran	hubiera oído	hubieran oído
OR		OR	
oyese	oyésemos	hubiese oído	hubiésemos oído
oyeses	oyeseis	hubieses oído	hubieseis oído
oyese	oyesen	hubiese oído	hubiesen oído

imperativo

—	oigamos
oye; no oigas	oíd; no oigáis
oiga	oigan

Words and expressions related to this verb

la oída hearing; **de oídas** by hearsay
dar oídos to lend an ear
oír decir to hear tell, to hear say
oír hablar de to hear of, to hear talk of

por oídos, de oídos by hearing
al oído confidentially
el oído hearing (sense)
desoír to ignore, to be deaf to

poder to be able, can
Gerundio **pudiendo**   Part. pas. **podido**

THE SEVEN SIMPLE TENSES		THE SEVEN COMPOUND TENSES	
SINGULAR	PLURAL	SINGULAR	PLURAL
1 presente de indicativo		**8 perfecto de indicativo**	
puedo	podemos	he podido	hemos podido
puedes	podéis	has podido	habéis podido
puede	pueden	ha podido	han podido
2 imperfecto de indicativo		**9 pluscuamperfecto de indicativo**	
podía	podíamos	había podido	habíamos podido
podías	podíais	habías podido	habíais podido
podía	podían	había podido	habían podido
3 pretérito		**10 pretérito anterior**	
pude	pudimos	hube podido	hubimos podido
pudiste	pudisteis	hubiste podido	hubisteis podido
pudo	pudieron	hubo podido	hubieron podido
4 futuro		**11 futuro perfecto**	
podré	podremos	habré podido	habremos podido
podrás	podréis	habrás podido	habréis podido
podrá	podrán	habrá podido	habrán podido
5 potencial simple		**12 potencial compuesto**	
podría	podríamos	habría podido	habríamos podido
podrías	podríais	habrías podido	habríais podido
podría	podrían	habría podido	habrían podido
6 presente de subjuntivo		**13 perfecto de subjuntivo**	
pueda	podamos	haya podido	hayamos podido
puedas	podáis	hayas podido	hayáis podido
pueda	puedan	haya podido	hayan podido
7 imperfecto de subjuntivo		**14 pluscuamperfecto de subjuntivo**	
pudiera	pudiéramos	hubiera podido	hubiéramos podido
pudieras	pudierais	hubieras podido	hubierais podido
pudiera	pudieran	hubiera podido	hubieran podido
OR		OR	
pudiese	pudiésemos	hubiese podido	hubiésemos podido
pudieses	pudieseis	hubieses podido	hubieseis podido
pudiese	pudiesen	hubiese podido	hubiesen podido

	imperativo	
—		podamos
	puede; no puedas	poded; no podáis
	pueda	puedan

Words and expressions related to this verb

el poder power
apoderar to empower
apoderarse de to take possession, to take over
poderoso, poderosa powerful
No se puede. It can't be done.

a poder de by dint of (by the power or force of)
estar en el poder to be in power
Querer es poder Where there's a will there's a way.

poner to put, to place
Gerundio **poniendo**   Part. pas. **puesto**

THE SEVEN SIMPLE TENSES		THE SEVEN COMPOUND TENSES	
SINGULAR	PLURAL	SINGULAR	PLURAL
1 presente de indicativo		**8 perfecto de indicativo**	
pongo	ponemos	he puesto	hemos puesto
pones	ponéis	has puesto	habéis puesto
pone	ponen	ha puesto	han puesto
2 imperfecto de indicativo		**9 pluscuamperfecto de indicativo**	
ponía	poníamos	había puesto	habíamos puesto
ponías	poníais	habías puesto	habíais puesto
ponía	ponían	había puesto	habían puesto
3 pretérito		**10 pretérito anterior**	
puse	pusimos	hube puesto	hubimos puesto
pusiste	pusisteis	hubiste puesto	hubisteis puesto
puso	pusieron	hubo puesto	hubieron puesto
4 futuro		**11 futuro perfecto**	
pondré	pondremos	habré puesto	habremos puesto
pondrás	pondréis	habrás puesto	habréis puesto
pondrá	pondrán	habrá puesto	habrán puesto
5 potencial simple		**12 potencial compuesto**	
pondría	pondríamos	habría puesto	habríamos puesto
pondrías	pondríais	habrías puesto	habríais puesto
pondría	pondrían	habría puesto	habrían puesto
6 presente de subjuntivo		**13 perfecto de subjuntivo**	
ponga	pongamos	haya puesto	hayamos puesto
pongas	pongáis	hayas puesto	hayáis puesto
ponga	pongan	haya puesto	hayan puesto
7 imperfecto de subjuntivo		**14 pluscuamperfecto de subjuntivo**	
pusiera	pusiéramos	hubiera puesto	hubiéramos puesto
pusieras	pusierais	hubieras puesto	hubierais puesto
pusiera	pusieran	hubiera puesto	hubieran puesto
OR		OR	
pusiese	pusiésemos	hubiese puesto	hubiésemos puesto
pusieses	pusieseis	hubieses puesto	hubieseis puesto
pusiese	pusiesen	hubiese puesto	hubiesen puesto

imperativo

—	pongamos
pon; no pongas	poned; no pongáis
ponga	pongan

Common idiomatic expressions using this verb

poner fin a to put a stop to
poner la mesa to set the table
ponerse de acuerdo to reach an
   agreement

posponer to postpone
la puesta de sol sunset
bien puesto, bien puesta well placed
reponer to replace, to put back

querer to want, to wish
Gerundio **queriendo**   Part. pas. **querido**

THE SEVEN SIMPLE TENSES		THE SEVEN COMPOUND TENSES	
SINGULAR	PLURAL	SINGULAR	PLURAL
1 presente de indicativo		8 perfecto de indicativo	
quiero	queremos	he querido	hemos querido
quieres	queréis	has querido	habéis querido
quiere	quieren	ha querido	han querido
2 imperfecto de indicativo		9 pluscuamperfecto de indicativo	
quería	queríamos	había querido	habíamos querido
querías	queríais	habías querido	habíais querido
quería	querían	había querido	habían querido
3 pretérito		10 pretérito anterior	
quise	quisimos	hube querido	hubimos querido
quisiste	quisisteis	hubiste querido	hubisteis querido
quiso	quisieron	hubo querido	hubieron querido
4 futuro		11 futuro perfecto	
querré	querremos	habré querido	habremos querido
querrás	querréis	habrás querido	habréis querido
querrá	querrán	habrá querido	habrán querido
5 potencial simple		12 potencial compuesto	
querría	querríamos	habría querido	habríamos querido
querrías	querríais	habrías querido	habríais querido
querría	querrían	habría querido	habrían querido
6 presente de subjuntivo		13 perfecto de subjuntivo	
quiera	queramos	haya querido	hayamos querido
quieras	queráis	hayas querido	hayáis querido
quiera	quieran	haya querido	hayan querido
7 imperfecto de subjuntivo		14 pluscuamperfecto de subjuntivo	
quisiera	quisiéramos	hubiera querido	hubiéramos querido
quisieras	quisierais	hubieras querido	hubierais querido
quisiera	quisieran	hubiera querido	hubieran querido
OR		OR	
quisiese	quisiésemos	hubiese querido	hubiésemos querido
quisieses	quisieseis	hubieses querido	hubieseis querido
quisiese	quisiesen	hubiese querido	hubiesen querido

imperativo

—	queramos
quiere; no quieras	quered; no queráis
quiera	quieran

Words and expressions related to this verb

querer decir   to mean; **¿Qué quiere Ud. decir?**   What do you mean?
¿Qué quiere decir esto?   What does this mean?
querido, querida   dear; **querido amigo, querida amiga**   dear friend
querido mío, querida mía   my dear
querer bien a   to love
Querer es poder   Where there's a will there's a way.

saber to know, to know how
Gerundio **sabiendo**   Part. pas. **sabido**

THE SEVEN SIMPLE TENSES		THE SEVEN COMPOUND TENSES	
SINGULAR	PLURAL	SINGULAR	PLURAL
1 presente de indicativo		**8 perfecto de indicativo**	
sé	sabemos	he sabido	hemos sabido
sabes	sabéis	has sabido	habéis sabido
sabe	saben	ha sabido	han sabido
2 imperfecto de indicativo		**9 pluscuamperfecto de indicativo**	
sabía	sabíamos	había sabido	habíamos sabido
sabías	sabíais	habías sabido	habíais sabido
sabía	sabían	había sabido	habían sabido
3 pretérito		**10 pretérito anterior**	
supe	supimos	hube sabido	hubimos sabido
supiste	supisteis	hubiste sabido	hubisteis sabido
supo	supieron	hubo sabido	hubieron sabido
4 futuro		**11 futuro perfecto**	
sabré	sabremos	habré sabido	habremos sabido
sabrás	sabréis	habrás sabido	habréis sabido
sabrá	sabrán	habrá sabido	habrán sabido
5 potencial simple		**12 potencial compuesto**	
sabría	sabríamos	habría sabido	habríamos sabido
sabrías	sabríais	habrías sabido	habríais sabido
sabría	sabrían	habría sabido	habrían sabido
6 presente de subjuntivo		**13 perfecto de subjuntivo**	
sepa	sepamos	haya sabido	hayamos sabido
sepas	sepáis	hayas sabido	hayáis sabido
sepa	sepan	haya sabido	hayan sabido
7 imperfecto de subjuntivo		**14 pluscuamperfecto de subjuntivo**	
supiera	supiéramos	hubiera sabido	hubiéramos sabido
supieras	supierais	hubieras sabido	hubierais sabido
supiera	supieran	hubiera sabido	hubieran sabido
OR		OR	
supiese	supiésemos	hubiese sabido	hubiésemos sabido
supieses	supieseis	hubieses sabido	hubieseis sabido
supiese	supiesen	hubiese sabido	hubiesen sabido

imperativo

—	sepamos
sabe; no sepas	sabed; no sepáis
sepa	sepan

Words and expressions related to this verb

sabio, sabia   wise, learned
un sabidillo, una sabidilla   a know-it-all
   individual
la sabiduría   knowledge, learning, wisdom
¿Sabe Ud. nadar?   Do you know how to
   swim?
Sí, yo sé nadar.   Yes, I know how to swim.

Que yo sepa . . .   As far as I know . . .
¡Quién sabe!   Who knows! Perhaps!
   Maybe!

salir to go out, to leave
Gerundio **saliendo**   Part. pas. **salido**

THE SEVEN SIMPLE TENSES		THE SEVEN COMPOUND TENSES	
SINGULAR	PLURAL	SINGULAR	PLURAL
1 presente de indicativo		**8 perfecto de indicativo**	
salgo	salimos	he salido	hemos salido
sales	salís	has salido	habéis salido
sale	salen	ha salido	han salido
2 imperfecto de indicativo		**9 pluscuamperfecto de indicativo**	
salía	salíamos	había salido	habíamos salido
salías	salíais	habías salido	habíais salido
salía	salían	había salido	habían salido
3 pretérito		**10 pretérito anterior**	
salí	salimos	hube salido	hubimos salido
saliste	salisteis	hubiste salido	hubisteis salido
salió	salieron	hubo salido	hubieron salido
4 futuro		**11 futuro perfecto**	
saldré	saldremos	habré salido	habremos salido
saldrás	saldréis	habrás salido	habréis salido
saldrá	saldrán	habrá salido	habrán salido
5 potencial simple		**12 potencial compuesto**	
saldría	saldríamos	habría salido	habríamos salido
saldrías	saldríais	habrías salido	habríais salido
saldría	saldrían	habría salido	habrían salido
6 presente de subjuntivo		**13 perfecto de subjuntivo**	
salga	salgamos	haya salido	hayamos salido
salgas	salgáis	hayas salido	hayáis salido
salga	salgan	haya salido	hayan salido
7 imperfecto de subjuntivo		**14 pluscuamperfecto de subjuntivo**	
saliera	saliéramos	hubiera salido	hubiéramos salido
salieras	salierais	hubieras salido	hubierais salido
saliera	salieran	hubiera salido	hubieran salido
OR		OR	
saliese	saliésemos	hubiese salido	hubiésemos salido
salieses	salieseis	hubieses salido	hubieseis salido
saliese	saliesen	hubiese salido	hubiesen salido

imperativo

—	salgamos
sal; no salgas	salid; no salgáis
salga	salgan

Words and expressions related to this verb

la salida exit
sin salida no exit, dead-end street
salir de compras to go out shopping
salir mal to go wrong, to do badly

salir a to resemble, to look like
salir al encuentro de to go to meet
salir de to leave from, to get out of

ser to be

Gerundio **siendo**   Part. pas. **sido**

THE SEVEN SIMPLE TENSES		THE SEVEN COMPOUND TENSES	
SINGULAR	PLURAL	SINGULAR	PLURAL
1 presente de indicativo		**8 perfecto de indicativo**	
soy	somos	he sido	hemos sido
eres	sois	has sido	habéis sido
es	son	ha sido	han sido
2 imperfecto de indicativo		**9 pluscuamperfecto de indicativo**	
era	éramos	había sido	habíamos sido
eras	erais	habías sido	habíais sido
era	eran	había sido	habían sido
3 pretérito		**10 pretérito anterior**	
fui	fuimos	hube sido	hubimos sido
fuiste	fuisteis	hubiste sido	hubisteis sido
fue	fueron	hubo sido	hubieron sido
4 futuro		**11 futuro perfecto**	
seré	seremos	habré sido	habremos sido
serás	seréis	habrás sido	habréis sido
será	serán	habrá sido	habrán sido
5 potencial simple		**12 potencial compuesto**	
sería	seríamos	habría sido	habríamos sido
serías	seríais	habrías sido	habríais sido
sería	serían	habría sido	habrían sido
6 presente de subjuntivo		**13 perfecto de subjuntivo**	
sea	seamos	haya sido	hayamos sido
seas	seáis	hayas sido	hayáis sido
sea	sean	haya sido	hayan sido
7 imperfecto de subjuntivo		**14 pluscuamperfecto de subjuntivo**	
fuera	fuéramos	hubiera sido	hubiéramos sido
fueras	fuerais	hubieras sido	hubierais sido
fuera	fueran	hubiera sido	hubieran sido
OR		OR	
fuese	fuésemos	hubiese sido	hubiésemos sido
fueses	fueseis	hubieses sido	hubieseis sido
fuese	fuesen	hubiese sido	hubiesen sido

imperativo

—	seamos
sé; no seas	sed; no seáis
sea	sean

Common idiomatic expressions using this verb

Dime con quien andas y te diré quien eres.   Tell me who your friends are and I will tell you who you are.

es decir   that is, that is to say; **Si yo fuera usted . . .**   If I were you . . .

¿Qué hora es?   What time is it?   **Es la una.**   It is one o'clock.   **Son las dos.**   It is two o'clock.

tener to have, to hold
Gerundio **teniendo**   Part. pas. **tenido**

THE SEVEN SIMPLE TENSES		THE SEVEN COMPOUND TENSES	
SINGULAR	PLURAL	SINGULAR	PLURAL
1 presente de indicativo		**8 perfecto de indicativo**	
tengo	tenemos	he tenido	hemos tenido
tienes	tenéis	has tenido	habéis tenido
tiene	tienen	ha tenido	han tenido
2 imperfecto de indicativo		**9 pluscuamperfecto de indicativo**	
tenía	teníamos	había tenido	habíamos tenido
tenías	teníais	habías tenido	habíais tenido
tenía	tenían	había tenido	habían tenido
3 pretérito		**10 pretérito anterior**	
tuve	tuvimos	hube tenido	hubimos tenido
tuviste	tuvisteis	hubiste tenido	hubisteis tenido
tuvo	tuvieron	hubo tenido	hubieron tenido
4 futuro		**11 futuro perfecto**	
tendré	tendremos	habré tenido	habremos tenido
tendrás	tendréis	habrás tenido	habréis tenido
tendrá	tendrán	habrá tenido	habrán tenido
5 potencial simple		**12 potencial compuesto**	
tendría	tendríamos	habría tenido	habríamos tenido
tendrías	tendríais	habrías tenido	habríais tenido
tendría	tendrían	habría tenido	habrían tenido
6 presente de subjuntivo		**13 perfecto de subjuntivo**	
tenga	tengamos	haya tenido	hayamos tenido
tengas	tengáis	hayas tenido	hayáis tenido
tenga	tengan	haya tenido	hayan tenido
7 imperfecto de subjuntivo		**14 pluscuamperfecto de subjuntivo**	
tuviera	tuviéramos	hubiera tenido	hubiéramos tenido
tuvieras	tuvierais	hubieras tenido	hubierais tenido
tuviera	tuvieran	hubiera tenido	hubieran tenido
OR		OR	
tuviese	tuviésemos	hubiese tenido	hubiésemos tenido
tuvieses	tuvieseis	hubieses tenido	hubieseis tenido
tuviese	tuviesen	hubiese tenido	hubiesen tenido

imperativo

—	tengamos
ten; no tengas	tened; no tengáis
tenga	tengan

Common idiomatic expressions using this verb

Anda despacio que tengo prisa.   Make haste slowly.
tener prisa   to be in a hurry
tener hambre   to be hungry
tener sed   to be thirsty
tener frío   to be (feel) cold (persons)
tener calor   to be (feel) warm (persons)
retener   to retain

traer to bring
Gerundio **trayendo**   Part. pas. **traído**

THE SEVEN SIMPLE TENSES		THE SEVEN COMPOUND TENSES	
SINGULAR	PLURAL	SINGULAR	PLURAL
1 presente de indicativo		**8 perfecto de indicativo**	
traigo	traemos	he traído	hemos traído
traes	traéis	has traído	habéis traído
trae	traen	ha traído	han traído
2 imperfecto de indicativo		**9 pluscuamperfecto de indicativo**	
traía	traíamos	había traído	habíamos traído
traías	traíais	habías traído	habíais traído
traía	traían	había traído	habían traído
3 pretérito		**10 pretérito anterior**	
traje	trajimos	hube traído	hubimos traído
trajiste	trajisteis	hubiste traído	hubisteis traído
trajo	trajeron	hubo traído	hubieron traído
4 futuro		**11 futuro perfecto**	
traeré	traeremos	habré traído	habremos traído
traerás	traeréis	habrás traído	habréis traído
traerá	traerán	habrá traído	habrán traído
5 potencial simple		**12 potencial compuesto**	
traería	traeríamos	habría traído	habríamos traído
traerías	traeríais	habrías traído	habríais traído
traería	traerían	habría traído	habrían traído
6 presente de subjuntivo		**13 perfecto de subjuntivo**	
traiga	traigamos	haya traído	hayamos traído
traigas	traigáis	hayas traído	hayáis traído
traiga	traigan	haya traído	hayan traído
7 imperfecto de subjuntivo		**14 pluscuamperfecto de subjuntivo**	
trajera	trajéramos	hubiera traído	hubiéramos traído
trajeras	trajerais	hubieras traído	hubierais traído
trajera	trajeran	hubiera traído	hubieran traído
OR		OR	
trajese	trajésemos	hubiese traído	hubiésemos traído
trajeses	trajeseis	hubieses traído	hubieseis traído
trajese	trajesen	hubiese traído	hubiesen traído

imperativo

—	traigamos
trae; no traigas	traed; no traigáis
traiga	traigan

Words and expressions related to this verb

el traje   costume, dress, suit
el traje de baño   bathing suit
el traje hecho   ready-made suit

traer daño   to cause damage
traer entre ojos   to hate
contraer   to contract

valer to be worth
Gerundio **valiendo**   Part. pas. **valido**

THE SEVEN SIMPLE TENSES		THE SEVEN COMPOUND TENSES	
SINGULAR	PLURAL	SINGULAR	PLURAL
1 presente de indicativo		**8 perfecto de indicativo**	
valgo	valemos	he valido	hemos valido
vales	valéis	has valido	habéis valido
vale	valen	ha valido	han valido
2 imperfecto de indicativo		**9 pluscuamperfecto de indicativo**	
valía	valíamos	había valido	habíamos valido
valías	valíais	habías valido	habíais valido
valía	valían	había valido	habían valido
3 pretérito		**10 pretérito anterior**	
valí	valimos	hube valido	hubimos valido
valiste	valisteis	hubiste valido	hubisteis valido
valió	valieron	hubo valido	hubieron valido
4 futuro		**11 futuro perfecto**	
valdré	valdremos	habré valido	habremos valido
valdrás	valdréis	habrás valido	habréis valido
valdrá	valdrán	habrá valido	habrán valido
5 potencial simple		**12 potencial compuesto**	
valdría	valdríamos	habría valido	habríamos valido
valdrías	valdríais	habrías valido	habríais valido
valdría	valdrían	habría valido	habrían valido
6 presente de subjuntivo		**13 perfecto de subjuntivo**	
valga	valgamos	haya valido	hayamos valido
valgas	valgáis	hayas valido	hayáis valido
valga	valgan	haya valido	hayan valido
7 imperfecto de subjuntivo		**14 pluscuamperfecto de subjuntivo**	
valiera	valiéramos	hubiera valido	hubiéramos valido
valieras	valierais	hubieras valido	hubierais valido
valiera	valieran	hubiera valido	hubieran valido
OR		OR	
valiese	valiésemos	hubiese valido	hubiésemos valido
valieses	valieseis	hubieses valido	hubieseis valido
valiese	valiesen	hubiese valido	hubiesen valido

imperativo

—	valgamos
val; no valgas	valed; no valgáis
valga	valgan

Sentences using this verb and words related to it

Más vale pájaro en mano que ciento volando.   A bird in the hand is worth two in the bush.
Más vale tarde que nunca.   Better late than never.
el valor   value, price, valor
valor nominal   face value

valorar   to appraise, to increase the value
No vale la pena   It's not worth the trouble.

§9. **INDEFINITE AND NEGATIVE WORDS COMMONLY USED** (See also the specific word, *e.g.,* **no, pero, sino, sin,** *etc.* in the General Index and idioms in **§14.ff**)

> **jamás** / ever, never, not ever
> **nada** / nothing (**sin nada** / without anything); after **sin, nada** is used instead of **algo; Ella no quiere nada** / She does not want anything.
> **ni** / neither, nor
> **ni . . . ni** / neither . . . nor
> **ni siquiera** / not even
> **nunca** / never, not ever, ever
> **siempre** / always
> **también** / also, too
> **tampoco** / neither; **ni yo tampoco** / nor I either
> **unos cuantos, unas cuantas** / a few, some, several

§10. **ADVERBS**

§10.1 **Definition:** An adverb is a word that modifies a verb, an adjective or another adverb.

§10.2 **Regular formation:** An adverb is regularly formed by adding the ending **mente** to the fem. sing. form of an adj.:

> **lento, lenta** / **lentamente:** slow / slowly; **rápido, rápida** / **rápidamente:** rapid / rapidly

> If the form of the adj. is the same for the fem. sing. and masc. sing. (**fácil, feliz**), add **mente** to that form. See **§5.9.**

> **fácil** (easy) / **fácilmente** (easily)
> **feliz** (happy) / **felizmente** (happily)

> NOTE that an accent mark on an adjective remains when the adjective is changed to an adverb. And note that the Spanish ending **mente** is equivalent to the ending **-ly** in English.

§10.3 An adverb remains invariable; that is to say, it does not agree in gender and number and therefore does not change in form.

§10.4 There are many adverbs that do not end in **mente.** Some common ones are:

> | | | | | |
> |---|---|---|---|---|
> | **abajo** / below | **bien** / well | **hoy** / today | **siempre** / always | **aquí** / here |
> | **arriba** / above | **mal** / badly | **mañana** / tomorrow | **nunca** / never | **allí** / there |

§10.5 The adverbial ending **ísimo**
Never use **muy** in front of **mucho.** Say **muchísimo: Elena trabaja muchísimo** / Helen works a great deal; Helen works very, very much.

§10.6 **Regular comparison of adverbs and superlative**
An adverb is compared regularly as an adjective. (See **§5.38–§5.41.**)

> **María corre tan rápidamente como Elena** / Mary runs as rapidly as Helen.

> **María corre menos rápidamente que Anita** / Mary runs less rapidly than Anita.

> **María corre más rápidamente que Isabel** / Mary runs more rapidly than Elizabeth.

> Superlative: **lo más rápidamente** / the most rapidly

§10.7 **Irregular comparative adverbs**
> **mucho, poco** / much, little: **Roberto trabaja mucho; Felipe trabaja poco.**

> **bien, mal** / well, badly: **Juan trabaja bien; Lucas trabaja mal.**

> **más, menos** / more, less: **Carlota trabaja más que Casandra; Elena trabaja menos que Marta.**

> **mejor, peor** / better, worse: **Paula trabaja mejor que Anita; Isabel trabaja peor que Elena.**

§10.8   **Con, sin** + noun (See also idioms with **con** and with **sin** in §14.19 and §14.41.)

At times, an adverb can be formed by using the prep. **con** (with) or **sin** (without) + a noun:

> **con cuidado** / carefully   **con dificultad** / with difficulty
> **sin cuidado** / carelessly   **sin dificultad** / without difficulty

§10.9   The adverb **recientemente** (recently) becomes **recién** before a past participle: **los recién llegados** / the ones recently arrived; the recently arrived (ones)

§10.10   **Interrogative adverbs**

Some common interrogative adverbs are: **¿cómo?** / how? **¿cuándo?** / when? **¿cuánto?, ¿cuánta?, ¿cuántos?, ¿cuántas?** / how much? how many? **¿por qué?** / why? **¿para qué?** / why? **¿dónde?** / where? **¿adónde?** / where to? (to where?)

§10.11   **Adverbs replaced by adjectives**

An adverb may sometimes be replaced by an adjective whose agreement is with the subject, especially if the verb is one of motion:

> **Las muchachas van y vienen silenciosas** / The girls come and go silently.

§10.12   **Ahí, allí, allá**

These three adverbs all mean *there* but they have special uses:

(a) **ahí** means *there,* not too far away from the person who says it: **El libro que Ud. quiere está ahí sobre esa mesa** / The book that you want is *there* on *that* table.

(b) **allí** means *there,* farther away from the person who says it, or even at a remote distance: **¿Quiere Ud. ir a Chicago? — Sí, porque mi padre trabaja allí** / Do you want to go to Chicago? Yes, because my father works there.

(c) **allá** means *there,* generally used with a verb of motion: **Me gustaría mucho ir allá** / I would like very much to go there; **Bueno, ¡vaya allá!** / Good, go there!

§10.13   **Aquí** and **acá**

These two adverbs both mean *here* but they have special uses:

(a) **aquí** means *here,* a place close to the person who says it: **Aquí se habla español** / Spanish is spoken here.

(b) **acá** means *here,* a place close to the person who says it, but it is used with a verb of motion: **Señor Gómez, ¡venga acá, por favor!** / Mr. Gómez, come here, please!

§11.   **PREPOSITIONS** (*See also* verbs that take certain prepositions in §7.16–§7.30)

§11.1   **Definition:** A preposition is a word that connects words and, according to the thought expressed in the sentence, serves to indicate the relationship between the words.

§11.2   **Common prepositions in Spanish are:**

a / at, to (plus other meanings, depending on idiomatic use; see **a** in idioms, §14.16–§14.18)
ante / before, in the presence of
bajo / under
con / with (plus other meanings, depending on idiomatic use; see **con** in idioms, §14.19)
contra / against
de / of, from (plus other meanings, depending on idiomatic use; see **de** in idioms, §14.22)
desde / after, from, since
durante / during
en / in, on (plus other meanings, depending on idiomatic use; see **en** in idioms, §14.25)
entre / among, between
hacia / toward
hasta / until, up to, as far as (plus other meanings, depending on idiomatic use; see **hasta** in idioms, §14.29)

menos / except

para / for, in order to (plus other meanings, depending on idiomatic use; see **para** in idioms, §14.35; see also **para** and **por** in §11.–11.18)

por / by, for (plus other meanings, depending on idiomatic use; see **por** in idioms, §14.37; see also **por** and **para** in §11.–11.18)

salvo / except, save

según / according to

sin / without (plus other meanings, depending on idiomatic use; see **sin** in idioms, §14.41); after **sin, nada** is used instead of **algo;** after **sin, nadie** is used instead of **alguien**

sobre / on, upon, over, above

tras / after, behind

§11.3   **Common prepositional phrases in Spanish are:**

acerca de / about (see **de** in idioms, §14.22, for other uses of the prep. **de**)

además de / in addition to, besides

alrededor de / around

antes de / before; (after **antes de,** use **nada** instead of **algo: antes de nada** / before anything; use **nadie** instead of **alguien: antes de nadie** / before anyone)

cerca de / near

con rumbo a / in the direction of (see **con** in idioms, §14.19, for other uses of the prep. **con**)

debajo de / underneath

delante de / in front of

dentro de / within, inside (of)

después de / after

detrás de / in back of, behind

en contra de / against (see **en** in idioms, §14.25, for other uses of the prep. **en**)

en cuanto a / as far as (see **a** in idioms, §14.16–§14.18, for other uses of the prep. **a**)

en lugar de / in place of, instead of

en medio de / in the middle of

en vez de / instead of

encima de / on top of, upon

enfrente de / opposite

frente a / in front of

fuera de / outside of

junto a / next to

lejos de / far from

por valor de / worth (see **por** in idioms, §14.37, for other uses of the prep. **por**)

§11.4   **Distinction between a preposition and an adverb**

Many prepositional phrases, such as the ones given above in §11.3, would not be prepositional if the prep. **de** were not included in the phrase; without the prep. **de,** most of them are adverbs, for example:

además / furthermore; **además de** / in addition to

alrededor / around; **alrededor de** / around

debajo / under; **debajo de** / underneath

lejos / far, far off; **lejos de** / far from

§11.5   The use of the prep. **de** with these adverbs, and others, changes the part of speech to a preposition, as in such prepositional phrases as: **lejos de la escuela** / far from the school; **alrededor de la casa** / around the house. Generally speaking, prepositions require a noun or a pronoun right after them (sometimes an infinitive, as in **sin decir nada** / without saying anything), which become objects of prepositions. In the examples cited here, **la escuela** is object of **lejos de; la casa** is object of **alrededor de.**

§11.6   Uses of prepositions

§11.7   Generally speaking, prepositions are used in the following categories:

  prep + a noun: **con María** / with Mary; **con mi amigo** / with my friend
  prep. + a pronoun: **para ella** / for her; **para usted** / for you
  prep. + inf.: **sin hablar** / without talking
  verb + prep.: **gozar de algo** / to enjoy something

§11.8   Personal a

§11.9   In Spanish, the prep. **a** is used in front of a noun direct object of a verb if the direct object is a person or something personified:

§11.10   **Conozco a su hermana Elena** / I know your sister Helen; **¿Conoce Ud. a Roberto?** / Do you know Robert? **Llamo al médico** / I am calling the doctor.

However, if the direct object is a person not definitely specified by name or noun whom you have in mind, the personal **a** is not generally used: **Llamo un médico** / I am calling a doctor. Here, no definite doctor is specified. This exception is not always observed by everyone and it is possible for you to read or hear: **Llamo a un médico.**

§11.11   The personal **a** is used in front of an indefinite pronoun when it is a direct object of a verb and it refers to a person, for example: **nadie, ninguno (ninguna), alguien, alguno (alguna), quien: Mis padres están visitando a alguien en el hospital** / My parents are visiting someone in the hospital; **¿Ve Ud. a alguien?** / Do you see anybody? **No veo a nadie** / I don't see anybody.

§11.12   The personal **a** is used in front of a geographic name if it is used as direct object: **Este verano pensamos visitar a Colombia** / This summer we plan to visit Colombia.

But if the geographic place contains a definite article in front of it (which is part of its name), the personal **a** is not used: **¿Ha visitado Ud. la Argentina?** / Have you visited Argentina? **La familia Gómez en Guadalajara quiere visitar los Estados Unidos** / The Gómez family in Guadalajara wants to visit the United States. The trend these days is not to use the prep. **a** in front of a geographic name even if it does not contain a def. art.

§11.13   The personal **a** is used in front of a noun which is a domestic animal when personified and when it is direct object: **Quiero a mi gatito** / I love my kitten.

§11.14   The personal **a** is not generally used with the verb **tener** when it means *to have:* **Tengo dos hermanas y dos hermanos** / I have two sisters and two brothers.

But when **tener** means *to hold,* the personal **a** is generally used: **La enfermera tenía al niño en los brazos** / The nurse was holding the child in her arms.

§11.15   The prepositional expression **para con,** meaning *to* or *toward,* in the sense of *with respect to* or *as regards,* is used to denote a mental attitude or feeling about a person: **Nuestra profesora de español es muy amable para con nosotros** / Our Spanish teacher is very kind to us.

§11.16   For prepositions that are used with certain verbs, see the entry Verbs in the General Index.

§11.17   For the use of prepositions with infinitives, see the entry Infinitives in the General Index.

§11.18   For additional comments, explanations and examples regarding the use of prepositions, consult the General Index under a specific preposition, of which the most commonly used are: **a, con, de, en, para, por, sin.** See also **Verbs and prepositions, §7.16–§7.30.**

§11.19 **Para** and **por** (See also §3.24 and §12. and idioms with **para** in §14.35 and with **por** in §14.37.)

These two prepositions are generally translated into English as *for*. Observe the variations in translation and the differences between the two:

§11.20 Use **para** when you mean:

§11.21 Destination: **Mañana salgo para Madrid** / Tomorrow I am leaving for Madrid.

§11.22 Intended for: **Este vaso es para María y ese vaso es para José** / This glass is for Mary and that glass is for Joseph.
Esta taza es para café; es una taza para café / This cup is for coffee; it is a coffee cup.

§11.23 Purpose (in order to): **Estudio para llegar a ser médico** / I am studying in order to become a doctor.

§11.24 A comparison of some sort: **Para ser norteamericano, habla español muy bien** / For an American, he speaks Spanish very well.

§11.25 At some point in future time: **Esta lección es para mañana** / This lesson is for tomorrow.

§11.26 Use **por** when you mean:

§11.27 A length of time: **Me quedé en casa por tres días** / I stayed at home for three days.

§11.28 In exchange for: **¿Cuánto dinero me dará Ud. por mi trabajo?** / How much money will you give me for my work?

§11.29 To send for: **Vamos a enviar por el médico** / We are going to send for the doctor.

§11.30 By: **Este libro fue escrito por dos autores** / This book was written by two authors; **Quiero enviar esta carta por avión** / I want to send this letter by air mail.

§11.31 For the sake of, as an obligation, on someone's behalf: **Quiero hacerlo por usted** / I want to do it for you.

§11.32 Through: **Dimos un paseo por el parque** / We took a walk through the park.

§11.33 Along, by the edge of: **Anduvimos por la playa** / We walked along the beach.

§11.34 To fight for: **Luché por mi amigo** / I fought for my friend.

§11.35 Out of, because of + noun: **No quisieron hacerlo por miedo** / They refused to do it out of (for) fear.

§11.36 *Per*, when expressing frequency: **Los alumnos asisten a la escuela cinco días por semana** / Students attend school five days a (per) week.

§11.37 To go for someone or something: **Mi madre fue por Carmen** / My mother went for (went to get) Carmen; **Mi madre fue por pan** / My mother went for (went to get) bread.

§11.38 To ask about, to inquire about, using **preguntar por**: **Pregunto por el médico** / I am asking for the doctor.

§11.39 **Por** or **de**

§11.40 The preposition **por** is sometimes translated into English as *by*, although it has other meanings, such as *through, for,* etc. (See §11.26–§11.37 and §14.37).

§11.41   The preposition **de** is sometimes translated into English as *by* and it has other meanings, too, such as *of, from, in,* etc. (See §5.46, §3.24, §14.22, and other references under the entry **de** in the General Index.)

§11.42   When using a passive meaning that expresses an action performed *by* someone or something, **por** is generally used. (See also §7.212 and §7.213ff.)

§11.43   Use the prep. **de** to express *by* when using a passive meaning if some emotion or feeling is expressed instead of an action:

> **La señora Gómez es respetada de todos los alumnos** / Mrs. Gómez is respected by all the students. These days more and more Spanish persons use **por** instead of **de** in this type of sentence.

> Notice, of course, that the adjective **respetada,** which is really a past participial form (**respetar / respetado**), agrees in gender and number with the subject it modifies or describes.

§12.   CONJUNCTIONS, CONJUNCTIVE LOCUTIONS, AND CORRELATIVE CONJUNCTIONS

§12.1   **Definition:** A conjunction is a word that connects words, phrases, clauses or sentences, *e.g.,* **y, pero, o, porque** / and, but, or, because.

§12.2   Certain conjunctions that introduce a clause require the subjunctive mood of the verb in that clause. See Subjunctive in §7.33ff in this General Review section to know what those conjunctions are.

§12.3   Here are some conjunctions that you certainly ought to know before you take the SAT II: Spanish test. Some require the subjunctive and are discussed under the entry Subjunctive in §7.33ff.

(a)   **a fin de que** / so that, in order that
a menos que / unless
antes (de) que / before
apenas . . . cuando / hardly, scarcely . . . when
así que / as soon as, after
aun / even, still
aunque / although
como / as, since, how
como si / as if
con tal (de) que / provided that
cuando / when
de manera que / so that
de modo que / so that, in such a way that
después (de) que / after
e / and (See the entry **y** and **e** in the General Index)
en cuanto / as soon as
hasta que / until
luego que / as soon as, after
mas / but
mas que / even if, however much
mientras / while
mientras que / while, so long as, as long as
ni / neither, nor (**ni . . . ni** / neither . . . nor)
ni siquiera / not even
ni sólo . . . (sino) también / not only . . . but also
o / or (**o . . . o** / either . . . or)
o sea . . . o sea / either . . . or
para que / in order that, so that

> **pero** / but
> **por cuanto** / inasmuch as
> **porque** / because
> **pues que** / since
> **puesto que** / although, since, inasmuch as, as long as
> **que** / that, because
> **según que** / according as
> **si** / if, whether
> **sin embargo** / nevertheless, notwithstanding, however (in whatever way)
> **sin que** / without
> **sino** / but, but rather
> **sino que** / but that, but rather that
> **siquiera** / though, although, whether, or
> **tan pronto como** / as soon as
> **u** / or (See the entry **o** and **u** in the General Index)
> **y** / and
> **ya . . . ya** / now . . . now
> **ya que** / since, seeing that

§12.4   And here are some that maybe you are not too familiar with. You ought to get acquainted with them because they are often used in the reading comprehension passages on the Spanish test. Some of them require the subjunctive form of the verb in the clause that they introduce and they are discussed under the entry Subjunctive in §7.33.

> (b) **a condición de que** / on condition that
> **a pesar de que** / in spite of
> **así . . . como** / both . . . and *or* as well . . . as
> **aun cuando** / even if
> **caso que** / in case that
> **como que** / it seems that, apparently
> **como quiera que** / although, since
> **con la condición de que** / on condition that
> **con que** / so then, and so, then
> **conque** / and so, well then, so then, now then
> **dado caso que** / supposing that
> **dado que** / supposing that
> **de condición que** / so as to
> **de suerte que** / so that, in such a manner as
> **del mismo modo que** / in the same way that
> **desde que** / since
> **empero** / yet, however, notwithstanding
> **en caso de que** / in case, in case that
> **en razón de que** / for the reason that, because of
> **entretanto que** / meanwhile, while
> **lo mismo que . . .** / as well as, the same as
> **lo mismo . . . que . . .** / both . . . and . . . *or* as well . . . as . . .
> **más bien que** / rather than
> **mientras tanto** / meanwhile, in the meantime
> **no bien . . . cuando** / no sooner . . . than
> **no obstante** / in spite of the fact that (notwithstanding)
> **por más que** / no matter how, however much
> **por razón de que** / because of, for the reason that
> **salvo que** / unless
> **siempre que** / whenever, provided that
> **supuesto que** / since, allowing that, granting that
> **tan luego como** / therefore
> **tanto . . . como** / as much . . . as

§12.5   **¿Para qué . . . ?** and **¿Por qué . . . ?** (See also the entries **para** and **por** in the General Index)

Both of these interrogatives mean *why* but they are not used interchangeably. If by *why* you mean *for what reason,* use **¿por qué . . . ?** If by *why* you mean *for what purpose (what for?)* use **¿para qué . . . ?**

Juanita, ¿por qué lloras? / Jeanie, why [for what reason] are you crying?

Mamá, ¿para qué tenemos uñas? / Mom, why [what for, for what purpose] do we have fingernails?

¿Para qué sirven los anteojos? / What [why, what for, for what purpose] are eyeglasses used for?

§12.6   **PERO** AND **SINO**

These two words are conjunctions and they both mean *but.* Note the difference in use:

§12.7   **Me gustaría venir a tu casa esta noche pero no puedo** / I would like to come to your house tonight but I can't.

§12.8   Use **sino** to mean *but rather, but on the contrary:* **Pedro no es pequeño sino alto** / Peter is not short but tall; **Mi automóvil no es amarillo sino blanco** / My car is not yellow but white.

Note that when you use **sino** the first part of the sentence is negative. Also note that **sino** may be followed by an inf.: **Pablo no quiere alquilar el automóvil sino comprarlo** / Paul does not want to rent the car but to buy it.

§12.9   If a clause follows **sino**, use **sino que**: **Pablo no alquiló el automóvil sino que lo compró** / Paul did not rent the car but bought it.

§12.10   Remember that a clause contains a subject and verb form.

§12.11   And note finally that **sino** is used instead of **pero** when you make a clear contrast between a negative thought in the first part of the sentence and a positive thought in the second part. If no contrast is made or intended, use **pero: María no conoce al niño pero le habla** / Mary does not know the child but talks to him.

§12.12   **PERO** AND **MAS**

These two words are conjunctions and they both mean *but.* In plays and poems an author may sometimes use **mas** instead of **pero**. In conversation and informal writing, **pero** is used. Note that **mas** with no accent mark means *but* and **más** (with the accent mark) means *more.*

§12.13   **O** AND **U**

These two words, which are conjunctions, mean *or.* Use **o** normally but when a word that is right after **o** begins with **o** or **ho**, use **u** instead of **o**: **muchachos u hombres** / boys or men; **septiembre u octubre** / September or October.

§12.14   **Y** AND **E**

These two words, which are conjunctions, mean *and.* Use **y** normally but when a word that is right after **y** begins with **i** or **hi**, use **e** instead of **y**: **María es bonita e inteligente** / Mary is pretty and intelligent; **Fernando e Isabel; padre e hijo** / father and son; **madre e hija** / mother and daughter.

However, if **y** is followed by a word that begins with **hie**, keep **y**: **flores y hierba** / flowers and grass. (See also **§5.65.**)

§13.   EXCLAMATORY ¡Qué . . . ! and ¡Tal . . . !

In English, when we exclaim *What a class! What a student! What an idea!* or *Such an idea!* we use the indefinite article *a* or *an*. In Spanish, however, we do not use the indefinite article:

¿Qué clase! ¡Qué alumno! ¡Qué alumna! ¡Qué idea! or **¡Tal idea!**

§13.1   If an adjective is used to describe the noun, we generally use **más** or **tan** in front of the adjective in order to intensify the exclamation.

¡Qué chica tan bonita! / What a pretty girl!
¡Qué libro más interesante! / What an interesting book!

§13.2   When we use **¡Qué!** + an adjective, the meaning in English is *How . . . !*

¡Qué difícil es! / How difficult it is!

§14.   IDIOMS

§14.1   **¿Cuánto tiempo hace que + present tense . . . ?** (See also **§14.20**)

(a) Use this formula when you want to ask *How long + the present perfect tense* in English:

¿Cuánto tiempo hace que Ud. estudia español? / How long have you been studying Spanish?

¿Cuánto tiempo hace que Ud. espera el autobús? / How long have you been waiting for the bus?

(b) When this formula is used, you generally expect the person to tell you how long a time it has been, *e.g.,* one year, two months, a few minutes.

(c) This is used when the action began at some time in the past and continues up to the present moment. That is why you must use the present tense of the verb—the action of studying, waiting, *etc.* is still going on at the present.

§14.2   **¿Cuánto tiempo hacía que + imperfect tense . . . ?**

(a) This formula is the same as the one given in **§14.1**, except that the tense of the verb is different. If the action of the verb began in the past and ended in the past, use the imperfect tense.

(b) This formula is equivalent to the English: *How long + past perfect tense:*

¿Cuánto tiempo hacía que Ud. hablaba cuando yo entré en la sala de clase? / How long had you been talking when I entered into the classroom?

(c) Note that the action of talking in this example began in the past and ended in the past when I entered the classroom.

§14.3   ¿Desde cuándo + present tense . . . ?

This is another way of asking *How long (since when) + the present perfect tense* in English, as given above in **§14.1**.

¿Desde cuándo estudia Ud. español / How long have you been studying Spanish?

§14.4   Present tense + desde hace + length of time

This formula is the usual answer to the question in **§14.3** above. It is similar to the expression given in **§14.7**.

Estudio español desde hace tres años / I have been studying Spanish for three years.

§14.5   **¿Desde cuándo + imperfect tense . . . ?**

   (a) This formula is the same as the one give in **§14.3,** except that the tense of the verb is different.

   (b) This is another way of asking the question stated in **§14.2(b)** above.

   ¿Desde cuándo hablaba Ud. cuando yo entré en la sala de clase? / How long had you been talking when I entered into the classroom?

§14.6   **Imperfect tense + desde hacía + length of time**

   (a) This formula is the same as the one given in **§14.4,** except that the tense of the verb is different.

   (b) This is another way of answering the question stated in **§14.2(b)** above.

   (Yo) hablaba desde hacía una hora cuando Ud. entró en la sala de clase / I had been talking for one hour when you entered into the classroom.

§14.7   **Hace + length of time + que + present tense**

   (a) This formula is the usual answer to the question in **§14.1** above.

   (b) Since the question is asked in terms of *how long,* the usual answer is in terms of time: a year, two years, a few days, months, minutes, *etc.*:

   Hace tres años que estudio español / I have been studying Spanish for three years.

   Hace veinte minutos que espero el autobús / I have been waiting for the bus for twenty minutes.

   (c) The same formula is used if you want to ask *how many weeks, how many months, how many minutes,* etc.:

   ¿Cuántos años hace que Ud. estudia español? / How many years have you been studying Spanish?

   ¿Cuántas horas hace que Ud. mira la televisión / How many hours have you been watching television?

§14.8   **Hacía + length of time + que + imperfect tense**

   (a) This formula is the usual answer to the question as stated in **§14.2(b)** above.

   (b) It is the same as the one give in **§14.7,** except that the tense of the verb is different. The imperfect tense of the verb is used here because the action began in the past and ended in the past; it is not going on at the present moment, as is the case with the expression given in **§14.7** above.

   Hacía una hora que yo hablaba cuando Ud. entró en la sala de clase / I had been talking for one hour when you entered the classroom.

§14.9   **Hay and hay que + infinitive**

§14.10   The word **hay** is not a verb. You might regard it as an impersonal irregular form of **haber.** Actually, the word is composed of **ha** + the archaic **y,** meaning *there.* It is generally regarded as an adverbial expression because it points out that something or someone "is there." Its English equivalent is *There is . . .* or *There are. . . .* For example:

   Hay muchos libros en la mesa / There are many books on the table; **Hay una mosca en la sopa** / There is a fly in the soup; **Hay veinte alumnos en esta clase** / There are twenty students in this class.

§14.11   **Hay que + inf.** is an impersonal expression that denotes an obligation and it is commonly translated into English as: *One must . . .* or *It is necessary to. . . .* EXAMPLES:

Hay que estudiar para aprender / It is necessary to study in order to learn; **Hay que comer para vivir** / One must eat in order to live.

§14.12   **Medio** and **mitad**

Both these words mean *half* but note the difference in use:

§14.13   **Medio** is an adj. and it agrees with the noun it modifies: **Necesito media docena de huevos** / I need half a dozen eggs; **Llegaremos en media hora** / We will arrive in a half hour (in half an hour); **Son las dos y media y ya tengo mucha hambre** / It is two thirty and already I am very hungry.

Medio is also used as an adverb: **Los caballos corrieron rápidamente y ahora están medio muertos** / The horses ran fast and now they are half dead.

§14.14   **Mitad** is a fem. noun: **El alumno estudió la mitad de la lección** / The pupil studied half (of) the lesson.

§14.15   **Idioms, including verbal, idiomatic, common, and useful expressions (arranged alphabetically by key word)**

§14.16   with **a** (See also the entry **a** in the General Index and prepositional phrases with **a** in **§11.3**)
a beneficio de / for the benefit of
a bordo / on board
a caballo / on horseback
a cada instante / at every moment, at every turn
a casa / home (Use with a verb of motion; use **a casa** if you are going *to* the house; use **en casa** if you are *in* the house: **Salgo de la escuela y voy a casa** / I'm leaving school and I'm going home; **Me quedo en casa esta noche** / I'm staying home tonight.)
a causa de / because of, on account of
a la derecha / to (on, at) the right
a eso de / about, around (**Llegaremos a Madrid a eso de las tres de la tarde** / We will arrive in Madrid at about three o'clock in the afternoon.)
a fines de / about the end of, around the end of (**Estaremos en Madrid a fines de la semana** / We will be in Madrid around the end of the week.)
a fondo / thoroughly
a fuerza de / by dint of (**A fuerza de trabajar, tuvo éxito** / By dint of working, he was successful.)
a mano / by hand
a mediados de / around the middle of (**Estaremos en Málaga a mediados de julio** / We will be in Málaga around the middle of July.)
a menudo / often, frequently
a mi parecer / in my opinion
a pesar de / in spite of
a pie / on foot
a pierna suelta / without a care
a principios de / around the beginning of (**Estaremos en México a principios de la semana que viene** / We will be in Mexico around the beginning of next week.)
a saltos / by leaps and bounds
a solas / alone
a su parecer / in your (his, her, their) opinion
a tiempo / on time
a toda brida / at top speed
a través de / across, through

            a veces / at times, sometimes
            conforme a / in accordance with
            estar a punto de / to be about to (**Estoy a punto de salir** / I am about to leave.)
            frente a / in front of
            junto a / beside, next to
            poco a poco / little by little
            ser aficionado a / to be a fan of
            uno a uno / one by one

§14.17   with **a la**
            a la derecha / to (on, at) the right
            a la española / in the Spanish style
            a la francesa / in the French style
            a la italiana / in the Italian style
            a la izquierda / to (on, at) the left
            a la larga / in the long run
            a la madrugada / at an early hour, at daybreak
            a la semana / a week, per week
            a la vez / at the same time

§14.18   with **al** (See also §4.7 and §4.8)
            al + inf. / on, upon + pres. part. (**Al entrar en la cocina, comenzó a comer** / Upon entering into the kitchen, he began to eat.)
            al aire libre / outdoors, in the open air
            al amanecer / at daybreak, at dawn
            al anochecer / at nightfall, at dusk
            al cabo / finally, at last
            al cabo de / at the end of
            al contrario / on the contrary
            al día / current, up to date, per day
            al día siguiente / on the following day, on the next day
            al fin / at last, finally
            al lado de / next to, beside
            al menos / at least
            al mes / a month, per month
            al parecer / apparently
            al por mayor / wholesale
            al por menor / retail (sales)
            al principio / at first
            al través de / across, through
            echar al correo / to mail, to post a letter

§14.19   with **con** (See also **con** in the General Index)
            con anterioridad / beforehand
            con anterioridad a / prior to
            con arreglo a / in accordance with
            con frecuencia / frequently
            con los brazos abiertos / with open arms
            con motivo de / on the occasion of
            con mucho gusto / gladly, willingly, with much pleasure
            con permiso / excuse me, with your permission
            con rumbo a / in the direction of
            con voz sorda / in a low (muffled) voice
            ser amable con / to be kind to

§14.20 with **cuanto, cuanta, cuantos, cuantas** (See also these entries in the General Index)
cuanto antes / as soon as possible
¿Cuánto cuesta? / How much is it? How much does it cost?
cuanto más ... tanto más ... / the more ... the more ... (**Cuanto más estudio tanto más aprendo** / The more I study the more I learn.)
¿Cuántos años tiene Ud.? / How old are you?
unos cuantos libros / a few books
unas cuantas flores / a few flowers

§14.21 with **dar** and **darse**
dar a / to face (**El comedor da al jardín** / The dining room faces the garden.)
dar con algo / to find something, to come upon something (**Esta mañana di con dinero en la calle** / This morning I found money in the street.)
dar con alguien / to meet someone, to run into someone, to come across someone, to find someone (**Anoche, di con mi amiga Elena en el cine** / Last night I met my friend Helen at the movies.)
dar contra / to hit against
dar cuerda al reloj / to wind a watch
dar de beber a / to give something to drink to
dar de comer a / to feed, to give something to eat to (**Me gusta dar de comer a los pájaros en el parque** / I like to feed the birds in the park.)
dar en / to hit against, to strike against
dar en el blanco / to hit the target, to hit it right
dar gritos / to shout
dar la bienvenida / to welcome
dar la hora / to strike the hour
dar la mano a alguien / to shake hands with someone
dar las buenas noches a alguien / to say good evening (good night) to someone
dar las gracias a alguien / to thank someone
dar los buenos días a alguien / to say good morning (hello) to someone
dar por + past part. / to consider (**Lo doy por perdido** / I consider it lost.)
dar recuerdos a / to give one's regards (best wishes) to
dar un abrazo / to embrace
dar un paseo / to take a walk
dar un paseo a caballo / to go horseback riding
dar un paseo en automóvil (en coche) / to go for a drive
dar un paseo en bicicleta / to ride a bicycle
dar una vuelta / to go for a short walk, to go for a stroll
dar unas palmadas / to clap one's hands
dar voces / to shout
darse cuenta de / to realize, to be aware of, to take into account
darse la mano / to shake hands with each other
darse por + past part. / to consider oneself (**Me doy por insultado** / I consider myself insulted.)
darse prisa / to hurry

§14.22 with **de** (See also the entry **de** in the General Index and prepositional phrases with **de** in §11.3)
abrir de par en par / to open wide
acabar de + inf. / to have just + past part. (**María acaba de llegar** / Mary has just arrived; **María acababa de llegar** / Mary had just arrived.) See also §7.112ff.
acerca de / about, concerning
alrededor de / around (**alrededor de la casa** / around the house)
antes de / before
aparte de / aside from
billete de ida y vuelta / round-trip ticket

cerca de / near, close to
de abajo / down, below
de acuerdo / in agreement, in accord
de ahora en adelante / from now on
de algún modo / someway
de alguna manera / someway
de antemano / ahead of time
de aquí en adelante / from now on
de arriba / upstairs
de arriba abajo / from top to bottom
de ayer en ocho días / a week from yesterday
de balde / free, gratis
de broma / jokingly
de buena gana / willingly
de común acuerdo / by mutual accord, by mutual agreement
de cuando en cuando / from time to time
de día / by day, in the daytime
de día en día / from day to day
de esa manera / in that way
de ese modo / in that way
de esta manera / in this way
de este modo / in this way
de hoy en adelante / from today on, from now on
de hoy en ocho días / a week from today
de la mañana / in the morning (Use this when a specific time is mentioned: **Tomo el desayuno a las ocho de la mañana** / I have breakfast at eight o'clock in the morning.)
de la noche / in the evening (Use this when a specific time is mentioned: **Mi amigo llega a las nueve de la noche** / My friend is arriving at nine o'clock in the evening.)
de la tarde / in the afternoon (Use this when a specific time is mentioned: **Regreso a casa a las cuatro de la tarde** / I am returning home at four o'clock in the afternoon.)
de madrugada / at dawn, at daybreak
de mal humor / in bad humor, in a bad mood
de mala gana / unwillingly
de memoria / by heart (memorized)
de moda / in fashion
de nada / you're welcome
de ningún modo / no way, in no way, by no means; see §5.19 and §5.20
de ninguna manera / no way, in no way, by no means
de noche / by night, at night, during the night
de nuevo / again
de otra manera / in another way
de otro modo / otherwise
de pie / standing
de prisa / in a hurry
de pronto / suddenly
de repente / all of a sudden
de rodillas / kneeling, on one's knees
de todos modos / anyway, in any case, at any rate
de uno en uno / one by one
de veras / really, truly
de vez en cuando / from time to time
dentro de poco / soon, shortly, within a short time
echar de menos / to miss
en lo alto de / at the top of

en lugar de / in place of, instead of
enfrente de / opposite
estar de acuerdo / to agree
fuera de sí / beside oneself, aghast
ir de compras / to go shopping
la mayor parte de / the greater part, the majority of
no hay de qué / you're welcome, don't mention it
un poco de / a little (of): **un poco de azúcar** / a little sugar

§14.23   with decir
decirle al oído / to whisper in one's ears
dicho y hecho / no sooner said than done
Es decir / That is to say . . .
querer decir / to mean ¿Qué quiere decir este muchacho? / What does this boy mean?

§14.24   with día, días
al día / current, up to date, per day
al romper el día / at daybreak
algún día / someday; see §5.19 and §5.20
de día en día / day by day
día por día / day by day
estar al día / to be up to date
hoy día / nowadays
ocho días / a week
por día / by the day, per day
quince días / two weeks
siete días / a week
un día de éstos / one of these days

§14.25   with en (See also §5.45, §5.46 and §4.10(c))
abrir de par en par / to open wide
de ayer en ocho días / a week from yesterday
de casa en casa / from house to house
de cuando en cuando / from time to time
de día en día / from day to day
de hoy en adelante / from today on
de hoy en ocho días / a week from today
de uno en uno / one by one
de vez en cuando / from time to time
en alto / high, high up, up high, on high
en balde / in vain
en bicicleta / by bicycle
en broma / jokingly, in fun
en cambio / on the other hand
en casa / at home (Use **en casa** if you are *in* the house; use **a casa** with a verb of motion,
    if you are going *to* the house: **Me quedo en casa esta noche** / I am staying home
    tonight; **Salgo de la escuela y voy a casa** / I'm leaving school and I'm going home.)
en casa de / at the house of (**María está en casa de Elena** / Mary is at Helen's house.)
en caso de / in case of
en coche / by car
en contra de / against
en cuanto / as soon as
en cuanto a / as for, with regard to, in regard to

en efecto / as a matter of fact, in fact
en el mes próximo pasado / in the month just past, this past month
en este momento / at this moment
en lo alto de / on top of, at the top of, up
en lugar de / in place of, instead of
en marcha / under way, on the way
en medio de / in the middle of
en ninguna parte / nowhere
en punto / sharp, exactly (telling time: **Son las dos en punto** / It is two o'clock sharp.)
en seguida / immediately, at once
en suma / in short, in a word
en todas partes / everywhere
en vano / in vain
en vez de / instead of
en voz alta / in a loud voice
en voz baja / in a low voice

§14.26   with **estar** (See also **§7.166ff** and other references under **estar** in the General Index)
está bien / all right, okay
estar a punto de + inf. / to be about + inf. (**Estoy a punto de salir** / I am about to go out.)
estar a sus anchas / to be comfortable
estar conforme con / to be in agreement with
estar de acuerdo / to agree
estar de acuerdo con / to be in agreement with
estar de boga / to be in fashion, to be fashionable
estar de buenas / to be in a good mood
estar de pie / to be standing
estar de vuelta / to be back
estar en boga / to be in fashion, to be fashionable
estar para + inf. / to be about to (**Estoy para salir** / I am about to go out.)
estar por / to be in favor of
no estar para bromas / not to be in the mood for jokes

§14.27   with **haber** (See also **§7.144–§7.148** and other references under **haber** in the General Index)
ha habido . . . / there has been . . . , there have been . . .
había . . . / there was . . . , there were
habrá . . . / there will be . . .
habría / there would be . . .
hubo . . . / there was . . . , there were . . .

§14.28   with **hacer** and **hacerse** (See also **§14.7** and other references under the entries **hacer** and **weather expressions** in the General Index)
hace poco / a little while ago
hace un año / a year ago
Hace un mes que partió el señor Molina / Mr. Molina left one month ago.
hace una hora / an hour ago
hacer caso de / to pay attention to
hacer daño a algo / to harm something
hacer daño a alguien / to harm someone
hacer de / to act as (**El señor González siempre hace de jefe** / Mr. González always acts as a boss.)
hacer el baúl / to pack one's trunk
hacer el favor de + inf. / please (**Haga Ud. el favor de entrar** / Please come in.)
hacer el papel de / to play the role of
hacer falta / to be wanting, lacking, needed

hacer la maleta / to pack one's suitcase
hacer pedazos / to smash, to break, to tear into pieces
hacer un viaje / to take a trip
hacer una broma / to play a joke
hacer una pregunta / to ask a question
hacer una visita / to pay a visit
hacer unos quehaceres / to do a few tasks, chores
hacerle falta / to need (**A Juan le hace falta un lápiz** / John needs a pencil.)
hacerse / to become (**Elena se hizo dentista** / Helen became a dentist.)
hacerse daño / to hurt oneself, to harm oneself
hacerse tarde / to be getting late (**Vámonos; se hace tarde** / Let's leave; it's getting late.)

§14.29   with **hasta**
hasta ahora / until now
hasta aquí / until now, up to here
hasta después / see you later, until later
hasta entonces / see you then, see you later, up to that time, until that time
hasta la vista / see you again
hasta luego / see you later, until later
hasta mañana / see you tomorrow, until tomorrow
hasta más no poder / to the utmost
hasta no más / to the utmost

§14.30   with **lo** (See also §4.11 and §6.12)
a lo largo de / along
a lo lejos / in the distance
a lo más / at most
a lo mejor / probably
a lo menos / at least
en lo alto / on top of, at the top of, up
lo bueno / what is good, the good part; **¡Lo bueno que es!** / How good it is! **¡Lo bien que está escrito!** / How well it is written!
lo de + inf., adv., or noun / "that matter of . . . ," "that business of . . . "
lo escrito / what is written
lo malo / what is bad, the bad part
lo más pronto posible / as soon as possible
lo mejor / what is best, the best part
lo primero que debo decir / the first thing I must say
lo simpático / whatever is kind
por lo común / generally, commonly, usually
por lo contrario / on the contrary
por lo general / generally, usually
por lo menos / at least
por lo pronto / in the meantime, for the time being
por lo tanto / consequently
por lo visto / apparently
¡Ya lo creo! / I should certainly think so!

§14.31   with **luego**
desde luego / naturally, of course, immediately
hasta luego / see you later, so long
luego luego / right away
luego que / as soon as, after

§14.32   with **mañana**
ayer por la mañana / yesterday morning

de la mañana / in the morning (Use this when a specific time is mentioned: **Voy a tomar el tren a las seis de la mañana** / I am going to take the train at six o'clock in the morning.)

mañana por la mañana / tomorrow morning

mañana por la noche / tomorrow night

mañana por la tarde / tomorrow afternoon

pasado mañana / the day after tomorrow

por la mañana / in the morning (Use this when no exact time is mentioned: **El señor Pardo llega por la mañana** / Mr. Pardo is arriving in the morning.)

por la mañana temprano / early in the morning

§14.33   with **mismo**

ahora mismo / right now

al mismo tiempo / at the same time

allá mismo / right there

aquí mismo / right here

así mismo / the same, the same thing

el mismo de siempre / the same old thing

eso mismo / that very thing

hoy mismo / this very day

lo mismo / the same, the same thing

lo mismo da / it makes no difference, it amounts to the same thing

lo mismo de siempre / the same old story

lo mismo que / the same as, as well as

por lo mismo / for the same reason

§14.34   with **no**

Creo que no / I don't think so, I think not

No cabe duda / No doubt about it

No es verdad / It isn't so, It isn't true; **¿No es verdad?** / Isn't that so?

No hay de qué / You're welcome

No hay remedio / There's no way, It cannot be helped

No importa / It doesn't matter

No + verb + más que + amount of money (**No tengo más que un dólar** / I have only
    one dollar)

no obstante / notwithstanding (in spite of), nevertheless

todavía no / not yet

ya no / no longer

§14.35   with **para** (See also **para** and **por** in §11.19–§11.37 and the entry **para** in the General Index)

estar para + inf. / to be about to, to be at the point of (**El autobús está para salir** / The bus is about to leave.)

no estar para bromas / not to be in the mood for jokes

no ser para tanto / not to be so important

para con (See §11.15)

para eso / for that matter

para mí / for my part

para que / in order that, so that

para ser / in spite of being (**Para ser tan viejo, él es muy ágil** / In spite of being so old, he is very agile.)

para siempre / forever

un vaso para agua / a water glass; **una taza para café** / a coffee cup; **una taza para té** / a tea cup

§14.36   with **poco** (See also the entry **poco** in the General Index)

a poco / in a short while, presently

dentro de poco / in a short while, in a little while
en pocos días / in a few days
poco a poco / little by little
poco antes / shortly before
poco después / shortly after
por poco / nearly, almost
tener poco que hacer / to have little to do
un poco de / a little (of) (**Quisiera un poco de azúcar** / I would like a little sugar.)
y por si eso fuera poco / and as if that were not enough

§14.37   with **por** (See also **para** and **por** in §11.19–§11.37 and the entry **por** in the General Index)
acabar por + inf. / to end up by + pres. part. (**Mi padre acabó por comprarlo** / My father finally ended up by buying it.)
al por mayor / wholesale
al por menor / retail (sales)
ayer por la mañana / yesterday morning
ayer por la noche / yesterday evening
ayer por la tarde / yesterday afternoon
estar por / to be in favor of
mañana por la mañana / tomorrow morning
mañana por la noche / tomorrow night, tomorrow evening
mañana por la tarde / tomorrow afternoon
por ahí / over there
por ahora / for just now, for the present
por allá / over there
por aquí / this way, around here
por avión / by air mail
por consiguiente / consequently
por desgracia / unfortunately
por Dios / for God's sake
por ejemplo / for example
por el contrario / on the contrary; or, **por lo contrario**
por escrito / in writing
por eso / for that reason, therefore
por favor / please (**Entre, por favor** / Come in, please.)
por fin / at last, finally
por hora / by the hour, per hour
por la mañana / in the morning (Use this when no exact time is mentioned: **Me quedo en casa por la mañana** / I'm staying home in the morning.)
por la mañana temprano / early in the morning
por la noche / in the evening (Use this when no exact time is mentioned: **Me gusta mirar la televisión por la noche** / I like to watch television in the evening.)
por la noche temprano / early in the evening
por la tarde / in the afternoon (Use this when no exact time is mentioned: **Tengo tres clases por la tarde** / I have three classes in the afternoon.)
por la tarde temprano / early in the afternoon
por lo común / commonly, generally, usually
por lo contrario / on the contrary; or, **por el contrario**
por lo general / generally, usually
por lo menos / at least
por lo pronto / in the meantime, for the time being
por lo tanto / consequently, therefore
por lo visto / apparently
por mi cuenta / in my way of thinking

       por mi parte / as for me, as far as I am concerned
       por nada / you're welcome
       por poco / nearly, almost
       por regla general / as a general rule
       por semana / by the week, per week
       por si acaso / in case
       por supuesto / of course
       por teléfono / by phone
       por todas partes / everywhere
       por valor de / worth

§14.38   with **pronto**
       al pronto / at first
       de pronto / suddenly
       lo más pronto posible / as soon as possible
       por de pronto / for the time being
       por el pronto or **por lo pronto** / in the meantime, for the time being
       tan pronto como / as soon as

§14.39   with **que** (See also conjunctions with **que** in **§12.3** and **§12.4** as well as the entry **que** in the General Index)
       Creo que no / I don't think so, I think not.
       Creo que sí / I think so.
       el año que viene / next year
       la semana que viene / next week
       ¡Qué lástima! / What a pity!
       ¡Qué le vaya bien! / Good luck!
       ¡Qué lo pase Ud. bien! / Good luck! (I wish you a good outcome!)

§14.40   with **ser** (See also **§7.166ff** and other references under the entry **ser** in the General Index)
       Debe de ser . . . / It is probably . . .
       Debe ser . . . / It ought to be . . .
       Es de lamentar / It's too bad.
       Es de mi agrado / It's to my liking.
       Es hora de . . . / It is time to . . .
       Es lástima or **Es una lástima** / It's a pity; It's too bad.
       Es que . . . / The fact is . . .
       para ser / in spite of being (**Para ser tan viejo, él es muy ágil** / In spite of being so old, he is very nimble.)
       sea lo que sea / whatever it may be
       ser aficionado a / to be a fan of (**Soy aficionado al béisbol** / I'm a baseball fan.)
       ser amable con / to be kind to (**Mi profesora de español es amable conmigo** / My Spanish teacher is kind to me.)
       ser todo oídos / to be all ears (**Te escucho; soy todo oídos** / I'm listening to you; I'm all ears.)
       si no fuera por . . . / if it were not for . . .

§14.41   with **sin** (See also **sin** in the General Index)
       sin aliento / out of breath
       sin cuento / endless
       sin cuidado / carelessly
       sin duda / without a doubt, undoubtedly
       sin ejemplo / unparalleled, nothing like it
       sin embargo / nevertheless, however
       sin falta / without fail
       sin fondo / bottomless
       sin novedad / nothing new, same as usual

§14.42   with **tener** (See also **tener** in the General Index)

¿**Cuántos años tienes?** ¿**Cuántos años tiene Ud.?** / How old are you? **Tengo diez y seis años** / I am sixteen years old.

¿**Qué tienes?** ¿**Qué tiene Ud.?** / What's the matter? What's the matter with you? **No tengo nada** / There's nothing wrong; There's nothing the matter (with me).

tener algo que hacer / to have something to do

tener calor / to feel (to be) warm (persons)

tener cuidado / to be careful

tener dolor de cabeza / to have a headache

tener dolor de estómago / to have a stomach ache

tener éxito / to be successful

tener frío / to feel (to be) cold (persons)

tener ganas de + inf. / to feel like + pres. part. (**Tengo ganas de tomar un helado** / I feel like having an ice cream)

tener gusto en + inf. / to be glad + inf. (**Tengo mucho gusto en conocerle** / I am very glad to meet you.)

tener hambre / to feel (to be) hungry

tener la bondad de / please; please be good enough to ... (**Tenga la bondad de cerrar la puerta** / Please close the door.)

tener la culpa de algo /to take the blame for something, to be to blame for something (**Tengo la culpa de eso** / I am to blame for that.)

tener lugar / to take place (**El accidente tuvo lugar anoche** / The accident took place last night.)

tener miedo de / to be afraid of

tener mucha sed / to feel (to be) very thirsty (persons)

tener mucho calor / to feel (to be) very warm (persons)

tener mucho frío / to feel (to be) very cold (persons)

tener mucho que hacer / to have a lot to do

tener poco que hacer / to have little to do

tener prisa / to be in a hurry

tener que + inf. / to have + inf. (**Tengo que estudiar** / I have to study.)

tener que ver con / to have to do with (**No tengo nada que ver con él** / I have nothing to do with him.)

tener razón / to be right (**Ud. tiene razón** / You are right.); **no tener razón** / to be wrong (**Ud. no tiene razón** / You are wrong.)

tener sed / to feel (to be) thirsty (persons)

tener sueño / to feel (to be) sleepy

tener suerte / to be lucky

tener vergüenza de / to be ashamed of

§14.43   with **todo, toda, todos, todas**

a todo / at most

a todo correr / at full speed

ante todo / first of all, in the first place

así y todo / in spite of everything

con todo / all in all, still, however, nevertheless

de todos modos / anyway, in any case, at any rate

del todo / completely, entirely

en todo y por todo / in each and every way

en un todo / in all its parts

ir a todo correr / to run by leaps and bounds

jugar el todo por todo / to risk everything

por todo / throughout

sobre todo / above all, especially

toda la familia / the whole family

todas las noches / every night
todas las semanas / every week
todo aquel que / whoever
todo aquello que / whatever
todo el mundo / everybody
todo el que / everybody who
todos cuantos / all those that
todos los años / every year
todos los días / every day
todos los que / all who, all those who

§14.44   with **vez** and **veces** (See also the entries **vez** and **veces** in the General Index)
a la vez / at the same time (**Carlos come y habla a la vez** / Charles eats and talks at the same time.)
a veces / sometimes, at times
alguna vez / sometime
algunas veces / sometimes
cada vez / each time
cada vez más / more and more (each time)
de vez en cuando / from time to time
dos veces / twice, two times
en vez de / instead of
las más veces / most of the time
muchas veces / many times
otra vez / again, another time, once more
raras veces / few times, rarely
repetidas veces / repeatedly, over and over again
tal vez / perhaps
una vez / once, one time
una vez más / once more, one more time
unas veces / sometimes
varias veces / several times

§14.45   with **y** (See also **y** in the General Index)
dicho y hecho / no sooner said than done
mañana y pasado / tomorrow and the following day
sano y salvo / safe and sound
un billete de ida y vuelta / round-trip ticket
¿Y bien? / And then? And so? So what?
y eso que / even though
y por si eso fuera poco ... / and as if that were not enough ...

§14.46   with **ya**
¡Hazlo ya! Hágalo ya! / Do it now!
no ya ... sino / not only ... but also
¡Pues ya! / Of course! Certainly!
si ya ... / if only ...
ya ... ya ... / now ... now ...
ya ... ya / whether ... or; as well ... as
¡Ya lo creo! / I should certainly think so! Of course!
Ya lo veré / I'll see to it.
ya no / no longer
Ya pasó / It's all over now.
ya que / since, as long as, seeing that ...
¡Ya se ve! / Yes, indeed!
¡Ya voy! / I'm coming! I'll be there in a second!

§15. DATES, DAYS, MONTHS, SEASONS

§15.1 Dates

You ought to know the following expressions in preparation for the Spanish Test :

(a) **¿Cuál es la fecha?** / What's the date?
¿Cuál es la fecha de hoy? / What's the date today?

(b) **Es el primero de junio** / It is June first.
Es el dos de mayo / It is May second.

NOTE that when stating the date, in Spanish we use **el primero,** which is an ordinal number, for the first day of any month. To state all other dates, use the cardinal numbers:
Hoy es el dos de enero, el tres de febrero, el cuatro de marzo, *etc.*

(c) **¿A cuántos estamos hoy?** / What's the date today?
Estamos a cinco de abril / It's April 5th.

(d) When stating a date, the English word (preposition) *on* is expressed in Spanish by using the definite article **el** in front of the date: **María nació** *el* **cuatro de julio** / Mary was born *on* the fourth of July.

(e) When stating the year, in Spanish we use thousands and hundreds:
el año mil novecientos ochenta y seis / the year 1986

This is very different from English, which is usually stated as nineteen eighty or nineteen hundred eighty. In Spanish we must state **mil** (one thousand) + **novecientos** (nine hundred): **mil novecientos setenta y nueve** (1979), **mil novecientos ochenta y uno** (1981).

(f) To sum it up: **Hoy es jueves, el veintidós de agosto, de mil novecientos noventa y uno** / Today is Thursday, August 22, 1991.

§15.2 Days

(a) The days of the week, which are all masculine, are:
domingo / Sunday; **lunes** / Monday; **martes** / Tuesay; **miércoles** / Wednesday; **jueves** / Thursday; **viernes** / Friday; **sábado** / Saturday

(b) In Spanish, the days of the week are ordinarily not capitalized. In newspapers, magazines, business letters, and elsewhere, you sometimes see them capitalized.

(c) When stating the day of the week in English we may use *on,* but in Spanish we use **el** or **los** in front of the day of the week:
el lunes / on Monday; **los lunes** / on Mondays, *etc.*

(d) NOTE that the days of the week whose last letter is **s** do not change in the plural; **el martes** / **los martes; el miércoles** / **los miércoles.** But: **el sábado** / **los sábados; el domingo** / **los domingos**

(e) **¿Qué día es?** / What day is it?
¿Qué día es hoy? / What day is it today?
Hoy es lunes / Today is Monday.

§15.3 Months

(a) The months of the year, which are all masculine, are:
enero / January; **febrero** / February; **marzo** / March; **abril** / April, **mayo** / May; **junio** / June; **julio** / July; **agosto** / August; **septiembre** / September; **octubre** / October; **noviembre** / November; **diciembre** / December

(b) In Spanish, the months of the year are ordinarily not capitalized. In newspapers, magazines, business letters, and elsewhere, you sometimes see them capitalized.

(c) To say *in* + the name of the month, use **en: en enero** / in January; or; **en el mes de enero** / in the month of January.

(d) The plural of **el mes** is **los meses.**

§15.4   **Seasons**

(a) The seasons of the year (**las estaciones del año**) are:

la primavera / spring; **el verano** / summer; **el otoño** / autumn, fall; **el invierno** / winter

(b) In Spanish, the seasons of the year are not capitalized.

(c) The definite article usually precedes a season of the year:

¿En qué estación hace frío? / In what season is it cold?
Generalmente, hace frío en el invierno / Generally, it is cold in winter.

§16.   **TELLING TIME**

§16.1   **¿Qué hora es?** / What time is it?

§16.2   **Es la una** / It is one o'clock. Note that the 3rd pers. sing. of **ser** is used because the time is one (o'clock), which is singular.

§16.3   **Son las dos** / It is two o'clock. Note that the 3rd pers. pl. of **ser** is used because the time is two (o'clock), which is more than one.

§16.4   **Son las tres, son las cuatro,** *etc.* / It is three o'clock, it is four o'clock, *etc.*

§16.5   When the time is a certain number of minutes after the hour, the hour is stated first (**es la una**) + **y** + the number of minutes:

Es la una y cinco / It is five minutes after one o'clock / It is 1:05.
Son las dos y diez / It is ten minutes after two o'clock / It is 2:10.

§16.6   When the hour is a quarter after, you can express it by using either **y cuarto** or **y quince (minutos):**

Son las dos y cuarto or **Son las dos y quince (minutos)** / It is 2:15.

§16.7   When it is half past the hour, you can express it by using either **y media** or **y treinta (minutos):**

Son las dos y media or **Son las dos y treinta** / It is 2:30.

§16.8   When telling time, the verb **ser** is used in the 3rd pers. sing. if the time is one and in the 3rd pers. plural if the time is more than one.

§16.9   When the time is a certain number of minutes of (to, toward, before) the hour, state the hour that it will be + **menos** + the number of minutes. If it is 15 minutes before the hour, use **menos cuarto** (a quarter of).

Son las cinco menos veinte / It is twenty minutes to five *or* It is 4:40.

Son las cuatro menos cuarto / It is a quarter of (to) four *or* It is 3:45.

§16.10   When you are not telling what time it is and you want only to say *at* a certain time, merely say: **a la una, a las dos, a las tres** / at one o'clock, at two o'clock, at three o'clock; **a la una y cuarto** / at 1:15; **a las cuatro y media** / at 4:30, *etc.*

§16.11   **¿A qué hora va Ud. a la clase de español?** / At what time do you go to Spanish class? **Voy a la clase a las dos y veinte** / I go to class at 2:20.

§16.12   **¿A qué hora toma Ud. el almuerzo?** / At what time do you have lunch? **Tomo el almuerzo a las doce en punto** / I have lunch at exactly twelve o'clock.

¿A qué hora toma Ud. el autobús para ir a la escuela? / At what time do you take the bus to go to school? **Tomo el autobús a las ocho en punto** / I take the bus at eight o'clock sharp.

§16.13   ¿Llega Ud. a la escuela a tiempo? / Do you arrive at school on time? **Llego a la escuela a eso de las ocho y media** / I arrive at school at about 8:30.

§16.14   When you state what time it is or at what time you are going to do something, sometimes you have to make it clear whether it is in the morning (A.M.), in the afternoon (P.M.), or in the evening (P.M.):

Tomo el tren a las ocho de la noche / I am taking the train at 8:00 P.M. (at eight o'clock in the evening).

Tomo el tren a las ocho de la mañana / I am taking the train at 8:00 A.M. (at eight o'clock in the morning).

Tomo el tren a las cuatro de la tarde / I am taking the train at 4:00 P.M. (at four o'clock in the afternoon).

Tomo el tren a las tres de la madrugada / I am taking the train at 3:00 A.M. (at three o'clock in the morning). Note that in Spanish we say **de la madrugada** (before daylight hours) instead of **de la noche** if the time is between midnight and the break of dawn.

§16.15   ¿Qué hora es? / What time is it? **Es mediodía** / It is noon.

§16.16   ¿Qué hora es? / What time is it? **Es medianoche** / It is midnight.

§16.17   ¿A qué hora toma Ud. el almuerzo? / At what time do you have lunch? **Tomo el almuerzo a mediodía** (or **al mediodía**).

§16.18   ¿A qué hora se acuesta Ud. por lo general? / At what time do you generally get to bed? **Generalmente, me acuesto a medianoche** (or **a la medianoche**).

§16.19   When telling time in the past, use the imperfect indicative tense of the verb **ser**: It was two o'clock when I had lunch today / **Eran las dos cuando tomé el almuerzo hoy**; It was one o'clock when I saw them / **Era la una cuando los vi**; What time was it when your parents arrived home? / **¿Qué hora era cuando sus padres llegaron a casa?** It was two in the morning / **Eran las dos de la madrugada**.

§16.20   The future tense is used when telling time in the future or when you wonder what time it is at present or when you want to state what time it probably is:

En algunos minutos serán las tres / In a few minutes it will be three o'clock.
¿Qué hora será? / I wonder what time it is; **Serán las seis** / It is probably six o'clock.

§16.21   When wondering what time it was in the past or when stating what time it probably was in the past, use the conditional: **¿Qué hora sería?**/ I wonder what time it was; **Serían las seis cuando llegaron** / It was probably six o'clock when they arrived.

§16.22   When no specific time is stated and you merely want to say *in the morning, in the afternoon, in the evening,* use the prep. **por** instead of **de**: **Los sábados estudio mis lecciones por la mañana, juego por la tarde, y salgo por la noche** / On Saturdays I study my lessons in the morning, I play in the afternoon, and I go out in the evening.

§16.23   To express *a little after the hour,* state the hour + **y pico**: **Cuando salí eran las seis y pico** / When I went out it was a little after six o'clock.

§16.24   To say *about* or *around* a particular time, say **a eso de** + the hour: **Te veré a eso de la una** / I will see you about one o'clock; **Te veré a eso de las tres** / I will see you around three o'clock.

§16.25   Instead of using **menos** (of, to, toward, before the hour)—see **§16.9** above—you may use the verb **faltar**, which means *to be lacking*: **Faltan cinco minutos para las tres** / It's five minutes to three (in other words, five minutes are lacking before it is three o'clock). In this construction, which is idiomatic, note the use of the prep. **para**.

§16.26   Finally, note another way to tell time, which is used on radio and TV, in railroad and bus stations, at airports, and at other places where many people gather:

It is the 24 hour system around the clock.

§16.27   When using the 24 hours around the clock, the stated time is perfectly clear and there is no need to say **de la madrugada, de la mañana, de la tarde,** or **de la noche** (see **§16.14**).

§16.28   When using the 24-hour system around the clock, there is no need to use **cuarto, media, menos** or **y** (except when **y** is required in the cardinal number, *e.g.,* **diez y seis**).

§16.29   When you hear or see the stated time using this system, subtract 12 from the number that you hear or see. If the number is less than 12, it is A.M. time. Midnight is **veinticuatro horas.** This system uses the cardinal numbers (see **§18.1**). EXAMPLES:

trece horas / 1 P.M.	**quince horas treinta** / 15.30, 3:30 P.M.
catorce horas / 2 P.M.	**veinte horas cuarenta y dos** / 20.42, 8:42 P.M.
veinte horas / 8 P.M.	**nueve horas diez** / 09.10, 9:10 A.M.

§17.   WEATHER EXPRESSIONS

§17.1   with **hacer**

¿Qué tiempo hace? / What is the weather like?   **Hace frío** / It is cold.
Hace buen tiempo / The weather is good.   **Hace mal tiempo** / The weather is bad.
Hace calor / It is warm (hot).   **Hace sol** / It is sunny.
Hace fresco hoy / It is cool today.   **Hace viento** / It is windy.

¿Qué tiempo hacía cuando Ud. salió esta mañana? / What was the weather like when you went out this morning?
Hacía mucho frío ayer por la noche / It was very cold yesterday evening.
Hacía mucho viento / It was very windy.
¿Qué tiempo hará mañana / What will the weather be like tomorrow?
Se dice que hará mucho calor / They say it will be very hot.

§17.2   with **haber** or **hay**

Hay lodo / It is muddy; **Había lodo** / It was muddy.
Hay luna / The moon is shining *or* There is moonlight; **Había luna ayer por la noche** / There was moonlight yesterday evening.
¿Hay mucha nieve aquí en el invierno? / Is there much snow here in winter?
Hay neblina / It is foggy; **Había mucha neblina** / It was very foggy.
Hay polvo / It is dusty; **Había mucho polvo** / It was very dusty.

§17.3   **Other weather expressions**

Está lloviendo ahora / It is raining now.
Está nevando / It is snowing.
Esta mañana llovía cuando tomé el autobús / This morning it was raining when I took the bus.
Estaba lloviendo cuando tomé el autobús / It was raining when I took the bus.
Estaba nevando cuando me desperté / It was snowing when I woke up.
¿Nieva mucho aquí en el invierno? / Does it snow much here in winter?
Las estrellas brillan / The stars are shining.
¿Le gusta a usted la lluvia? / Do you like rain?
¿Le gusta a usted la nieve? / Do you like snow?

§18. NUMBERS

§18.1 Cardinal numbers: zero to one hundred million

0	cero	62	sesenta y dos, *etc.*
1	uno, una (see **§5.18ff**)	**70**	**setenta**
2	dos	71	setenta y uno, setenta y una
3	tres	72	setenta y dos, *etc.*
4	cuatro	**80**	**ochenta**
5	cinco	81	ochenta y uno, ochenta y una
6	seis	82	ochenta y dos, *etc.*
7	siete	**90**	**noventa**
8	ocho	91	noventa y uno, noventa y una
9	nueve	92	noventa y dos, *etc.*
10	**diez**	**100**	**ciento (cien)** (see
11	once		**§5.23–§5.26 and §4.19a)**
12	doce	101	ciento uno, ciento una
13	trece	102	ciento dos, *etc.*
14	catorce	**200**	**doscientos, doscientas**
15	quince	300	trescientos, trescientas
16	**dieciséis**	400	cuatrocientos, cuatrocientas
17	**diecisiete**	500	quinientos, quinientas
18	**dieciocho**	600	seiscientos, seiscientas
19	**diecinueve**	700	setecientos, setecientas
20	**veinte**	800	ochocientos, ochocientas
21	**veintiuno**	900	novecientos, novecientas
22	**veintidós**	**1,000**	**mil** (see **§4.19a**)
23	**veintitrés**	2,000	dos mil
24	**veinticuatro**	3,000	tres mil, *etc.*
25	**veinticinco**	100,000	cien mil
26	**veintiséis**	200,000	doscientos mil, doscientas
27	**veintisiete**		mil
28	**veintiocho**	300,000	trescientos mil, trescientas
29	**veintinueve**		mil, *etc.*
30	**treinta**	**1,000,000**	**un millón (de + noun)**
31	treinta y uno, treinta y una	2,000,000	dos millones (de + noun)
32	treinta y dos, *etc.*	3,000,000	tres millones (de + noun)
40	**cuarenta**		*etc.*
41	cuarenta y uno, cuarenta y una	100,000,000	cien millones (de + noun)
42	cuarenta y dos, *etc.*		
50	**cincuenta**		Approximate numbers
51	cincuenta y uno, cincuenta y una		**unos veinte libros** / about
52	cincuenta y dos, *etc.*		(some) twenty books
60	**sesenta**		**unas treinta personas** /
61	sesenta y uno, sesenta y una		about (some) thirty persons

§18.2 Simple arithmetical expressions

dos **y** dos son cuatro	$2 + 2 = 4$
diez **menos** cinco son cinco	$10 - 5 = 5$
tres **por** cinco son quince	$3 \times 5 = 15$
diez **dividido por** dos son cinco	$10 \div 2 = 5$

§18.3   **Ordinal numbers: first to tenth**

primero, primer, primera (see §5.20, §15.1)	first	1st
segundo, segunda	second	2nd
tercero, tercer, tercera (see §5.20)	third	3rd
cuarto, cuarta	fourth	4th
quinto, quinta	fifth	5th
sexto, sexta	sixth	6th
séptimo, séptima	seventh	7th
octavo, octava	eighth	8th
noveno, novena	ninth	9th
décimo, décima	tenth	10th

§18.4   NOTE that beyond 10th the cardinal numbers are used instead of the ordinal numbers, but when there is a noun involved, the cardinal number is placed after the noun: **el día 15, el día quince** / the fifteenth day.

§18.5   NOTE also that in titles of monarchs, *etc.,* the definite article is not used between the person's name and the number, as it is in English: **Alfonso XIII, Alfonso Trece** / Alfonso the Thirteenth.

§18.6   AND NOTE that **noveno** (9th) changes to **nono** in such titles: **Luis IX, Luis Nono** / Louis the Ninth.

§19.   SYNONYMS

Another very good way to increase your Spanish vocabulary in preparation for the Spanish test is to think of a synonym (similar meaning) for every word in Spanish that you already know. Of course, there is no synonym for all words in the Spanish language — nor in English. If you hope to achieve a high score on the Spanish test, you must try now to increase your vocabulary. Study the following synonyms. You can be sure that a good number of them will be on the SAT II: Spanish. They are standard words of high frequency.

For suggestions as to how to study vocabulary, consult the entry **Vocabulary, how to study** in the General Index. Also, that entry in the Index gives you references in this General Review where you can find other vocabulary that you ought to know in preparation for the Spanish test, for example, adjectives, adverbs, antonyms, cognates, conjunctions, conjunctive locutions and correlative conjunctions, and other types of words.

acercarse (a), aproximarse (a) / to approach, to come near
acordarse (de), recordar / to remember
alabar, elogiar / to praise, to glorify, to eulogize
alimento, comida / food, nourishment
alumno (alumna), estudiante / pupil, student
andar, caminar / to walk
anillo, sortija / ring (finger)
antiguo (antigua), viejo (vieja) / ancient, old
así que, luego que, tan pronto como / as soon as
asustar, espantar / to frighten, to terrify, to scare
atreverse (a), osar / to dare, to venture
aún, todavía / still, yet, even
ayuda, socorro, auxilio / aid, succor, help, assistance
barco, buque, vapor / boat, ship

bastante, suficiente / enough, sufficient
batalla, combate, lucha / battle, combat, struggle, fight
bonito (bonita), lindo (linda) / pretty
breve, corto (corta) / brief, short
burlarse de, mofarse de / to make fun of, to mock
camarero, mozo / waiter
campesino, rústico, labrador / farmer, peasant
cara, rostro, semblante / face
cariño, amor / affection, love
cocinar, cocer, guisar / to cook
comenzar, empezar, principiar / to begin, to start, to commence
comprender, entender / to understand, to comprehend
conquistar, vencer / to conquer, to vanquish
contento (contenta), feliz, alegre / content, happy, glad
contestar, responder / to answer, to reply
continuar, seguir / to continue
cruzar, atravesar / to cross
cuarto, habitación / room
cura, sacerdote / priest
chiste, chanza, broma / jest, joke, fun
dar un paseo, pasearse / to take a walk, to go for a walk
dar voces, gritar / to shout, to cry out
de manera que, de modo que / so that
dejar de + inf., cesar de + inf. / to cease + pres. part., to stop + pres. part.
delgado, esbelto, flaco / thin, slender, slim, svelte
desafortunado, desgraciado / unfortunate
desaparecer, desvanecerse / to disappear, to vanish
desear, querer / to desire, to want, to wish
desprecio, desdén / scorn, disdain, contempt
diablo, demonio / devil, demon
diferente, distinto (distinta) / different, distinct
diligente, trabajador (trabajadora), aplicado (aplicada) / diligent, hard working, industrious
diversión, pasatiempo / diversion, pastime
dueño (dueña), propietario (propietaria), amo (ama) / owner, master, boss
echar, lanzar, tirar, arrojar / to throw, to lance, to hurl
elevar, levantar, alzar / to elevate, to raise, to lift
empleado (empleada), dependiente / employee, clerk
enojarse, enfadarse / to become angry, to become annoyed
enviar, mandar / to send
error, falta / error, mistake, fault
escoger, elegir / to choose, to select, to elect
esperar, aguardar / to wait for
esposa, mujer / wife, spouse
estrecho (estrecha), angosto (angosta) / narrow
famoso (famosa), célebre, ilustre / famous, celebrated, renowned, illustrious
fatigado (fatigada), cansado (cansada), rendido (rendida) / tired, exhausted, worn out
fiebre, calentura / fever
grave, serio (seria) / serious, grave
habilidad, destreza / ability, skill, dexterity
hablador (habladora), locuaz / talkative, loquacious
halagar, lisonjear, adular / to flatter
hallar, encontrar / to find
hermoso (hermosa), bello (bella) / beautiful, handsome

igual, semejante / equal, alike, similar
invitar, convidar / to invite
irse, marcharse / to leave, to go away
joya, alhaja / jewel, gem
lanzar, tirar, echar / to throw, to lance, to hurl
lengua, idioma / language, idiom
lentamente, despacio / slowly
luchar, combatir, pelear, pugnar / to fight, to battle, to combat, to struggle
lugar, sitio / place, site
llevar, conducir / to take, to lead
maestro (maestra), profesor (profesora) / teacher, professor
marido, esposo / husband, spouse
mendigo (mendiga), pordiosero (pordiosera), limosnero (limosnera) / beggar
miedo, temor / fear, dread
morir, fallecer, fenecer / to die, to expire
mostrar, enseñar / to show
nobleza, hidalguez, hidalguía / nobility
nunca, jamás / never
obtener, conseguir / to obtain, to get
ocurrir, suceder, acontecer, acaecer / to occur, to happen, to come about, to come to pass
odiar, aborrecer / to hate, to abhor
onda, ola / wave
país, nación / country, nation
pájaro, ave / bird
pararse, detenerse / to stop (oneself)
parecido, semejante / like, similar
pasar un buen rato, divertirse / to have a good time
pena, dolor / pain, grief
perezoso (perezosa), flojo (floja) / lazy
periódico, diario / newspaper
permiso, licencia / permission, leave
permitir, dejar / to permit, to allow, to let
poner, colocar / to put, to place
porfiado (porfiada), terco (terca), testarudo (testaruda) / obstinate, stubborn
posponer, diferir, aplazar / to postpone, to defer, to put off, to delay
premio, galardón / prize, reward
quedarse, permanecer / to remain, to stay
rapidez, prisa, velocidad / rapidity, haste, speed, velocity
regresar, volver / to return (to a place)
rezar, orar / to pray
rogar, suplicar / to beg, to implore, to entreat
romper, quebrar / to break
sin embargo, no obstante / nevertheless, however
solamente, sólo / only
sorprender, asombrar / to surprise, to astonish
suceso, acontecimiento / happening, event
sufrir, padecer / to suffer, to endure
susto, espanto / fright, scare, dread
tal vez, acaso, quizá, quizás / maybe, perhaps
terminar, acabar, concluir / to terminate, to finish, to end
tonto (tonta), necio (necia) / foolish, stupid, idiotic
trabajo, tarea, obra / work, task
tratar de, intentar / to try to, to attempt
ya que, puesto que / since, inasmuch as

§20.   ANTONYMS

One very good way to increase your Spanish vocabulary is to think of an antonym (opposite meaning) or synonym (similar meaning) for every word in Spanish that you already know. Of course, there is no antonym or synonym for all words in the Spanish language—nor in English. If you plan to achieve a high score on the next Spanish test, you must increase your vocabulary. Study the following antonyms. There are many ways to study new vocabulary. You have to find the best way that suits you. One way is to see a picture in your mind of the word when you see the Spanish word. When you hear or read the Spanish word, you will see the picture first and that will reveal the meaning to you. You can also take a few minutes and write the new Spanish word as many times as you need to at the same time as you pronounce it aloud and try to see a picture either of the word or of a situation where that word would be used. You can also examine the Spanish word very carefully and make one or two observations; for example, is there another word within the new word that you already know? Is the new word based on another word? Is it a word that sounds special and reveals the meaning by its sound? Take the simple adjective **bello / bella** (beautiful), which I am sure you already know. Have you ever stopped to wonder what the antonym of it is? Picture in your mind **una dama bella**; next to it, picture the opposite: **una dama fea.** I am sure you now know what **feo / fea** means without my telling you in English what the meaning is. To my ear, the word **fea** sounds ugly.

But for the sake of expediency, here are some antonyms that you ought to become acquainted with. As you study them, follow my suggestions given above.

I will occasionally guide you by suggesting what to see in the word and how to remember its meaning. Remember that the best way to learn vocabulary is the way that suits you best. You might think of other ways that come more naturally to you.

aburrirse / to be bored; **divertirse** / to have a good time

aceptar / to accept; **ofrecer** / to offer

acordarse de / to remember; **olvidar, olvidarse de** / to forget (Does **acordarse de** remind you of **recordar,** which means *to remember, to remind?* When you remember something or someone, don't you *record* it in your mind? As for **olvidar** and **olvidarse de,** you might think of the English words, *oblivion, oblivious.*)

admitir / to admit; **negar** / to deny

agradecido, agradecida / thankful; **ingrato, ingrata** / thankless (You might think of *grateful* and associate it with **agradecido.** As for **ingrato,** you might think of *ungrateful* or *ungracious;* there is also the word *ingrate* in English.)

alejarse de / to go away from; **acercarse a** / to approach (In **acercarse a,** do you see the word **cerca** / near, close by? In **alejarse de,** do you see the word **lejos** / far? See a picture of a person coming close to you [**acercarse a**] and then going away from you [**alejarse de**].)

algo / something; **nada** / nothing

alguien / someone; **nadie** / no one

alguno (algún) / some; **ninguno (ningún)** / none; see §5.19 and §5.20

amigo, amiga / friend; **enemigo, enemiga** / enemy

amar / to love; **odiar** / to hate

ancho, ancha / wide; **estrecho, estrecha** / narrow

antes (de) / before; **después (de)** / after

antiguo, antigua / ancient, old; **moderno, moderna** / modern

antipático, antipática / unpleasant; **simpático, simpática** / nice (people)

aparecer / to appear; **desaparecer** / to disappear

aplicado, aplicada / industrious; **flojo, floja** / lazy

apresurarse a / to hasten, to hurry; **tardar en** / to delay (Here, you have the cognate *tardy.* For **apresurarse a,** you can picture a person who is hurrying because he or she is *pressed* for time.)

aprisa / quickly; **despacio** / slowly

aquí / here; **allí** / there

arriba / above, upstairs; **abajo** / below, downstairs

atrevido, atrevida / bold, daring; **tímido, tímida** / timid, shy

aumentar / to augment, to increase; **disminuir** / to diminish, to decrease

ausente / absent; **presente** / present

bajar / to go down; **subir** / to go up

bajo, baja / low, short; **alto, alta** / high, tall

bien / well; **mal** / badly, poorly

blanco, blanca / white; **negro, negra** / black

bueno (buen), buena / good; **malo (mal), mala** / bad; see §5.19 and §5.20

caballero / gentleman; **dama** / lady

caliente / hot; **frío** / cold

caro, cara / expensive; **barato, barata** / cheap

cerca (de) / near; **lejos (de)** / far

cerrar / to close; **abrir** / to open

cielo / sky; **tierra** / earth, ground

claro, clara / light; **oscuro, oscura** / dark

cobarde / cowardly; **valiente** / valiant, brave

cómico, cómica / comic, funny; **trágico, trágica** / tragic

comprar / to buy; **vender** / to sell

común / common; **raro, rara** / rare

con / with; **sin** / without

contra / against; **con** / with

corto, corta / short; **largo, larga** / long

costoso, costosa / costly, expensive; **barato, barata** / cheap, inexpensive

culpable / guilty, culpable; **inocente** / innocent

chico / boy; **chica** / girl

dar / to give; **recibir** / to receive

débil / weak, debilitated; **fuerte** / strong

dejar caer / to drop; **recoger** / to pick up

delante de / in front of; **detrás de** / in back of

delgado, delgada / thin; **gordo, gorda** / stout, fat

dentro / inside; **fuera** / outside

derrota / defeat; **victoria** / victory

descansar / to rest; **cansar** / to tire, **cansarse** / to get tired

descubrir / to uncover; **cubrir** / to cover (Here is another word with the prefix **des** which usually makes the word opposite in meaning.)

descuido / carelessness; **esmero** / meticulousness

desgraciado, desgraciada / unfortunate; **afortunado, afortunada** / fortunate

despertarse / to wake up; **dormirse** / to fall asleep

destruir / to destroy; **crear** / to create

desvanecerse / to disappear; **aparecer** / to appear (Here, you might think of *vanish* to remind you of the meaning of **desvanecerse**; for the meaning of **aparecer**, isn't it an obvious cognate?)

distinto, distinta / different; **semejante** / similar

dulce / sweet; **amargo** / bitter

duro, dura / hard; **suave, blando, blanda** / soft

elogiar / to praise; **censurar** / to criticize (Here, you might see a picture of a clergyman reading a eulogy in praise of someone; do I need to suggest to you what word to think of in English for the Spanish **censurar**? You must remember that on the Spanish Test that you take you will be expected to recognize the meaning of the words in Spanish; you will have to recognize the meaning of the spoken word because there is a listening comprehension test on the Spanish SAT. In addition, you are not going to be asked to translate from English to Spanish or from Spanish to English. The entire Spanish SAT is in Spanish and all you have to do is recognize the meanings of the Spanish words in the test.)

empezar / to begin, to start; **terminar, acabar** / to end

encender / to light; **apagar** / to extinguish

encima (de) / on top; **debajo (de)** / under

entrada / entrance; **salida** / exit

esta noche / tonight, this evening; **anoche** / last night, yesterday evening

este / east; **oeste** / west

estúpido, estúpida / stupid; **inteligente** / intelligent

éxito / success; **fracaso** / failure

fácil / easy; **difícil** / difficult

fatigado, fatigada / tired; **descansado, descansada** / rested (Here, in **descansado**, do you see the Spanish word **cansar** within that word? See the entry **descansar** above.)

feliz / happy; **triste** / sad

feo, fea / ugly; **hermoso, hermosa** / beautiful; **bello, bella** / beautiful

fin / end; **principio** / beginning

flaco, flaca / thin; **gordo, gorda** / fat

gastar / to spend (money); **ahorrar** / to save (money) (You might see a picture of a person *hoarding* money for **ahorrar**; you might see an opposite picture of a person *wasting* money to remind you of **gastar**.)

gigante / giant; **enano, enana** / dwarf

grande (gran) / large, big; **pequeño, pequeña** / small, little; see §5.15 and §5.22

guerra / war; **paz** / peace

hablador, habladora / talkative; **taciturno, taciturna** / silent, taciturn

hablar / to talk, to speak; **callarse** / to keep silent

hembra / female; **macho** / male

hombre / man; **mujer** / woman

ida / departure; **vuelta** / return (**ida y vuelta** / round trip)

ignorar / not to know; **saber** / to know

interesante / interesting; **aburrido, aburrida** / boring

inútil / useless; **útil** / useful

ir / to go; **venir** / to come

joven / young; **viejo, vieja** / old

jugar / to play; **trabajar** / to work

juventud / youth; **vejez** / old age

lejano / distant; **cercano** / nearby (Do these two words remind you of **alejarse de** and **acercarse a**, given above?)

lentitud / slowness; **rapidez** / speed

levantarse / to get up; **sentarse** / to sit down

libertad / liberty; **esclavitud** / slavery

limpio, limpia / clean; **sucio, sucia** / dirty

luz / light; **sombra** / shadow

llegada / arrival; **partida** / departure

llenar / to fill; **vaciar** / to empty (Think of *vacate*.)

lleno, llena / full; **vacío, vacía** / empty

llorar / to cry, to weep; **reír** / to laugh

madre / mother; **padre** / father

maldecir / to curse; **bendecir** / to bless (Think of *malediction* and *benediction*.)

mañana / tomorrow; **ayer** / yesterday

marido / husband; **esposa** / wife

más / more; **menos** / less

mejor / better; **peor** / worse

menor / younger; **mayor** / older (Think of *minor* and *major*.)

mentir / to lie; **decir la verdad** / to tell the truth

mentira / lie, falsehood; **verdad** / truth (Think of *veracity*.)

meridional / southern; **septentrional** / northern

meter / to put in; **sacar** / to take out

mismo, misma / same; **diferente** / different

morir / to die; **vivir** / to live

muchacho / boy; **muchacha** / girl

mucho, mucha / much; **poco, poca** / little
nacer / to be born; **morir** / to die
natural / natural; **innatural** / unnatural
necesario / necessary; **innecesario** / unnecessary
negar / to deny; **otorgar** / to grant
noche / night; **día** / day
obeso, obesa / obese, fat; **delgado, delgada** / thin
obscuro, obscura / dark; **claro, clara** / light
odio / hate, hatred; **amor** / love
orgulloso / proud; **humilde** / humble
oriental / eastern; **occidental** / western
peligro / danger; **seguridad** / safety
perder / to lose; **ganar** / to win; **hallar** / to find
perezoso, perezosa / lazy; **diligente** / diligent
permitir / to permit; **prohibir** / to prohibit
pesado, pesada / heavy; **ligero, ligera** / light
ponerse / to put on (clothing); **quitarse** / to take off (clothing)
porvenir / future; **pasado** / past
posible / possible; **imposible** / impossible
pregunta / question; **respuesta, contestación** / answer
preguntar / to ask; **contestar** / to answer
presente / present; **ausente** / absent
prestar / to lend; **pedir prestado** / to borrow
primero (primer), primera / first; **último, última** / last; see §5.19 and §5.20
princesa / princess; **príncipe** / prince
puesta del sol / sunset; **salida del sol** / sunrise
quedarse / to remain; **irse** / to leave, to go away
quizá(s) / maybe, perhaps; **seguro, cierto** / sure, certain
recto / straight; **tortuoso** / winding
rey / king; **reina** / queen
rico, rica / rich; **pobre** / poor
riqueza / wealth; **pobreza** / poverty
romper / to break; **componer** / to repair (Here, in *romper,* you can see a picture in your mind of something *ruptured* in the sense that it is broken. In *componer,* you can see something that is put *(poner)* together in the sense that it is repaired.)
rubio, rubia / blond; **moreno, morena** / brunette
ruido / noise; **silencio** / silence
sabio, sabia / wise; **tonto, tonta** / foolish
salir (de) / to leave (from); **entrar (en)** / to enter (in, into)
seco / dry; **mojado** / wet
separar / to separate; **juntar** / to join
sí / yes; **no** / no
siempre / always; **nunca** / never
sobrino / nephew; **sobrina** / niece
subir / to go up; **bajar** / to go down
sucio / dirty; **limpio** / clean
sur / south; **norte** / north
temprano / early; **tarde** / late
tío / uncle; **tía** / aunt
tomar / to take; **dar** / to give
tonto / foolish; **listo** / clever
tranquilo / tranquil, peaceful; **turbulento** / restless, turbulent
unir / to unite; **desunir** / to disunite
usual / usual; **extraño, raro** / unusual

verano / summer; **invierno** / winter
vida / life; **muerte** / death
virtud / virtue; **vicio** / vice
y / and, plus; **menos** / minus, less
zorro / fox; **zorra** / vixen, she-fox

§21. COGNATES

Another good way to increase your vocabulary is to become aware of cognates. A cognate is a word whose origin is the same as another word in other languages. There are many cognates in Spanish and English. Their spelling is sometimes identical or very similar in both languages. Most of the time, the meaning is the same or similar; sometimes they appear to be related because of the similar or identical spelling but they are not true cognates. Those are described as "false cognates"—for example, the Spanish word **actual** means *present-day,* not *actual;* the English word *actual* is expressed in Spanish as **real, verdadero, efectivo,** or **existente.** Also, the Spanish word **pan** means *bread,* not *pan.* The English word *pan* is **cacerola, cazuela,** or **sartén** in Spanish.

You ought to get into the habit of looking for cognates on the Spanish test and, if you must guess the meaning of a Spanish word if it appears to be a cognate, then guess. There are not that many "false cognates" which would be in your way. As a matter of fact, there are many more true cognates than false ones. Here is how you can recognize a true cognate:

Generally speaking, Spanish words that have certain endings have equivalent endings in English. For example:

Spanish ending of a word	Equivalent English ending of a word
-ario	-ary
-ción	-tion
-dad	-ty
-fía	-phy
-ia	-y
-ía	-y
-io	-y
-ista	-ist
-mente	-ly
-orio	-ory
-oso	-ous

There are others, but the above seem to be the most common. Also note that Spanish words that begin with **es** are generally equivalent to an English word that begins with *s.* Just drop the **e** in the beginning of the Spanish word and you have a close equivalent to the spelling of an English word; for example, **especial** / special; **estudiante** / student.

Here are examples to illustrate true cognates whose spellings are identical or similar:

actor / actor
admiración / admiration
atención / attention
autoridad / authority
central / central
civilización / civilization
color / color
correctamente / correctly
chocolate / chocolate
dentista / dentist
doctor / doctor
dormitorio / dormitory, bedroom
escena / scene
estúpido / stupid

famoso / famous
farmacia / pharmacy
finalmente / finally
fotografia / photography
generoso / generous
geografía / geography
historia / history
hotel / hotel
idea / idea
invitación / invitation
manual / manual
nación / nation
naturalmente / naturally
necesario / necessary
necesidad / necessity
novelista / novelist
piano / piano
posibilidad / possibility
radio / radio
realidad / reality
remedio / remedy
sección / section
sociedad / society
universidad / university
violín / violin
vocabulario / vocabulary

Finally, consult the General Index under the entry **vocabulary** to find references to other sections in this General Review for other kinds of vocabulary that you ought to know for the SAT II: Spanish test.

§22.   TRICKY WORDS

NOTE well the English meanings for the following Spanish words. They often appear in the reading comprehension passages on the SAT II: Spanish.

actual *adj.* / present, of the present time, of the present day
el anciano, la anciana / old (man or woman)
antiguo, antigua / *adj.* former, old, ancient
la apología / eulogy, defense
la arena / sand
asistir a *v.* / to attend, to be present at
atender *v.* / to attend to, to take care of
el auditorio / audience
el bachiller, la bachillera / graduate of a secondary school; *also means* babbler
el bagaje / beast of burden, military equipment
la bala / bullet, shot, bale, ball
bizarro, bizarra *adj.* / brave, gallant, generous
el campo / field, country(side), military camp
el carbón / coal, charcoal, carbon
el cargo / duty, post, responsibility, burden, load
la carta / letter (to mail)
el collar / necklace
colorado, colorada *adj.* / red, ruddy
la complexión / temperament, constitution
la conferencia / lecture
la confianza / confidence, trust
la confidencia / secret, trust

constipado, constipada *adj.* / sick with a head cold or common cold
la consulta / conference
convenir *v.* / to agree, to fit, to suit, to be suitable
la chanza / joke, fun
de *prep.* / from, of
dé *irreg. v. form (imper., 3rd pers., s. and pres. subj. 1st and 3rd pers. s.) of* **dar**
la decepción / disappointment
el delito / crime
la desgracia / misfortune
el desmayo / fainting
diario, diaria *adj.* / daily; **el diario** / diary, journal, daily newspaper
disfrutar *v.* / to enjoy
divisar *v.* / to perceive indistinctly
el dormitorio / bedroom, dormitory
el editor / publisher
embarazada *adj.* / pregnant
emocionante *adj.* / touching (causing an emotion)
esperar *v.* / to hope, to expect, to wait for
el éxito / success, outcome
la fábrica / factory
hay *idiomatic form* / there is, there are
el idioma / language
ignorar *v.* / not to know, to be unaware
intoxicar *v.* / to poison, to intoxicate
el labrador / farmer
largo, larga *adj.* / long
la lectura / reading
la librería / bookstore
la maleta / valise, suitcase
el mantel / tablecloth
mayor *adj.* / greater, older
la mesura / moderation
la pala / shovel
el palo / stick, pole
el pan / bread
pasar *v.* / to happen, to pass
el pastel / pie; **la pintura al pastel** / pastel painting
pinchar *v.* / to puncture, to prick, to pierce
realizar *v.* / to achieve (to realize, in the sense of achieving something: He realized his dreams, *i.e.,* his dreams came true)
recordar *v.* / to remember
el resfriado / common cold (illness)
restar *v.* / to deduct, to subtract
sano, sana *adj.* / healthy
soportar *v.* / to tolerate, to bear, to endure, to support
suceder *v.* / to happen, to come about, to succeed (follow)
el suceso / event, happening
la tabla / board, plank, table of contents
la tinta / ink, tint
la trampa / trap, snare, cheat, trick
tu *poss. adj., 2nd pers. s., fam.* / your
tú *persl. subj. pron., 2nd pers. s., fam.* / you
el vaso / drinking glass

§23. PROVERBS

Here are a few common proverbs in Spanish that you ought to be familiar with in case you come across them in the reading sections on the SAT II: Spanish test. They also contain some essential Spanish vocabulary which you ought to look up in the back pages of this book.

§23.1   **A Dios rogando y con el mazo dando** / Put your faith in God and keep your powder dry. OR: Praise the Lord and pass the ammunition.

§23.2   **Anda despacio que tengo prisa** / Make haste slowly.

§23.3   **Cuando el gato va a sus devociones, bailan los ratones** / When the cat is away, the mice will play.

§23.4   **Dicho y hecho** / No sooner said than done.

§23.5   **Dime con quien andas y te diré quien eres** / Tell me who your friends are and I will tell you who you are.

§23.6   **La práctica hace maestro al novicio** / Practice makes perfect.

§23.7   **El que mucho abarca poco aprieta** / Do not bite off more than you can chew.

§23.8   **El que no se aventura no cruza la mar** / Nothing ventured, nothing gained.

§23.9   **El tiempo da buen consejo** / Time will tell.

§23.10   **Más vale pájaro en mano que ciento volando** / A bird in the hand is worth two in the bush.

§23.11   **Más vale tarde que nunca** / Better late than never.

§23.12   **Mientras hay vida hay esperanza** / Where there is life there is hope.

§23.13   **Mucho ruido y pocas nueces** / Much ado about nothing.

§23.14   **Perro que ladra no muerde** / A barking dog does not bite.

§23.15   **Piedra movediza, el moho no la cobija** / A rolling stone gathers no moss.

§23.16   **Quien canta su mal espanta** / When you sing you drive away your grief.

§23.17   **Quien siembra vientos recoge tempestades** / If you sow the wind, you will reap the whirlwind.

§23.18   **Si a Roma fueres, haz como vieres** / When in Rome do as the Romans do. [Note that it is not uncommon to use the future subjunctive in proverbs, as in *fueres* (*ir* or *ser*) and *vieres* (*ver*).] See **§8.64.**

§23.19   **Tal madre, tal hija** / Like mother, like daughter.

§23.20   **Tal padre, tal hijo** / Like father, like son.

DEFINITIONS OF BASIC GRAMMATICAL TERMS WITH EXAMPLES IN ENGLISH AND SPANISH

PART

V

The purpose of this section is to prepare you to become aware of the different parts of a sentence and the grammatical terms used when you analyze the structure of a sentence in Spanish. If you study this section thoroughly, it will help you train yourself to analyze sentences on the next SAT II Spanish test that you take. You can acquire this skill through practice; in other words, when you read a sentence in Spanish, you must ask yourself, for example: What is the subject of this sentence? Is there a direct object or indirect object noun or pronoun? If so, where is it? Is it in front of the verb or after it? Is it attached to the infinitive? Do I have to make it agree in gender and number with some other part of the sentence? Are there any words in the sentence that indicate the tense of the verb as being in the present, past, or future? What is the tense of the verb? Is it singular or plural? First, second, or third person? Do I know my Spanish verb forms in all the tenses? Is there a certain type of conjunction in the sentence that requires the subjunctive mood in the verb form that follows it? There are many more questions you must learn to ask yourself while analyzing a sentence in Spanish so you can be able to recognize the correct multiple-choice answer.

At the end of each of the following grammatical terms, you are referred to the various numerical sections designated with the symbol § in the General Grammar Review, which is in Part IV of this book. There, you will find in-depth explanations with additional examples.

To prepare yourself for the SAT II Spanish test, you must also know Spanish verb forms in all the tenses. Study the ones given in the General Grammar Review section of this book in §7. through §8.67. Also, study the conjugation of verbs and explanations of verb tense usage in Barron's book, *501 Spanish Verbs*, 4th edition.

Active Voice

When we speak or write in the active voice, the subject of the verb performs the action of the verb. The action falls on the direct object.

> EXAMPLE:
>
> The robber opened the window / **El ladrón abrió la ventana.**
>
> The subject is *the robber*. The verb is *opened*. The direct object is *the window*.

Study §7.215 in the General Review section. *See also* passive voice in this section. Compare the above sentence with the example in the passive voice. Review the forms in all the tenses of the verb **abrir.**

Adjective

An adjective is a word that modifies a noun or a pronoun. In grammar, to modify a word means to describe, limit, expand, or make the meaning particular. In Spanish an adjective agrees in gender (masculine or feminine) and in number (singular or plural) with the noun or pronoun it modifies.

> EXAMPLES:
>
> a beautiful garden / **un jardín hermoso;**   she is pretty / **ella es bonita.**

The adjective *beautiful*/**hermoso** modifies the noun *garden*/**jardín.** It is masculine singular because **un jardín** is masculine singular. The adjective *pretty*/**bonita** modifies the pronoun *she*/**ella.** It is feminine singular because **ella** is feminine singular.

Study adjectives in §5. and agreement of adjectives in §5.2, §5.34–§5.36. In Spanish there are different kinds of adjectives. *See also* comparative adjective, demonstrative adjective, descriptive adjective, interrogative adjective, limiting adjective, possessive adjective, superlative adjective.

Adverb

An adverb is a word that modifies a verb, an adjective, or another adverb. An adverb says something about how, when, where, to what extent, or in what way.

EXAMPLES:

Mary runs swiftly / **María corre rápidamente.**

The adverb *swiftly/ **rápidamente*** modifies the verb *runs/ **corre.*** The adverb shows *how* she runs.

John is very handsome / **Juan es muy guapo.**

The adverb *very/ **muy*** modifies the adjective *handsome/ **guapo.*** The adverb shows *how handsome* he is.

The boy is talking very fast now / **El muchacho habla muy rápidamente ahora.**

The adverb *very/ **muy*** modifies the adverb *fast/ **rápidamente.*** The adverb shows *to what extent* he is talking *fast.* The adverb *now/ **ahora*** tells us *when.*

The post office is there / **La oficina de correos está allá.**

The adverb *there/ **allá*** modifies the verb *is/ **está.*** It tells us *where* the post office is.

Mary writes meticulously / **María escribe meticulosamente.**

The adverb *meticulously/ **meticulosamente*** modifies the verb *writes/ **escribe.*** It tells us *in what way* she writes.

Study adverbs in §10.

Affirmative Statement, Negative Statement

A statement in the affirmative is the opposite of a statement in the negative. To negate an affirmative statement is to make it negative.

Example in the affirmative: I like ice cream / **Me gusta el helado.**

Example in the negative: I do not like ice cream / **No me gusta el helado.**

Review §6.13, §6.15, §6.23 for negative statements. Review the use of the verb **gustar** in §7.143.

Agreement of Adjective with Noun

Agreement is made on the adjective with the noun it modifies in gender (masculine or feminine) and number (singular or plural).

EXAMPLES:

a white house / **una casa blanca**

The adjective **blanca** is feminine singular because the noun **una casa** is feminine singular.

many white houses / **muchas casas blancas**

The adjectives **muchas** and **blancas** are feminine plural because the noun **casas** is feminine plural.

Review adjectives in §5.

Agreement of Verb with its Subject

A verb agrees in person (1st, 2nd, or 3rd) and in number (singular or plural) with its subject.

EXAMPLES:

Paul tells the truth / **Pablo dice la verdad.**

The verb **dice** (of **decir**) is 3rd person singular because the subject *Pablo/ Paul* is 3rd person singular.

Where are the tourists going? / **¿Adónde van los turistas?**

The verb **van** (of **ir**) is 3rd person plural because the subject *los turistas*/ *the tourists* is 3rd person plural.

Review §6.4 for subject pronouns in all three persons of the singular and plural.

Review §7.2 about agreement of subject and verb. Review the forms in all the tenses of the verbs **decir** and **ir.** *See also* person (1st, 2nd, 3rd).

Antecedent

An antecedent is a word to which a relative pronoun refers. It comes *before* the pronoun.

> EXAMPLES:
>
> The girl who is laughing loudly is my sister / **La muchacha que está riendo a carcajadas es mi hermana**.
>
> The antecedent is *girl*/ *la muchacha*. The relative pronoun *who*/ *que* refers to the girl.
>
> The car that I bought is very expensive / **El carro que yo compré es muy costoso**.
>
> The antecedent is *car*/ **el carro**. The relative pronoun *that*/ *que* refers to the car.

Review the conjugation in all the tenses of the verbs **comprar** and **reír**.

Note that **está riendo** is the progressive present of **reír**. Review regular and irregular present participles in §7.189 and §7.190.

Review relative pronoun in this section.

Auxiliary Verb

An auxiliary verb is a helping verb. In English grammar it is *to have*. In Spanish grammar it is **haber**/ *to have*. An auxiliary verb is used to help form the compound tenses.

> EXAMPLE IN THE PRESENT PERFECT TENSE:
>
> I *have* eaten / **(Yo)** *he* **comido**.

Review the six forms of **haber** in the present indicative tense in §8.11. You need to know them to form the present perfect tense and other compound tenses. Also, review the formation of regular and irregular past participles in §7.204 and §7.205. You need to know them to form the seven compound tenses.

Cardinal Number

A cardinal number is a number that expresses an amount, such as *one, two, three,* and so on. Review them in §18.1. *See also* ordinal number.

Clause

A clause is a group of words that contains a subject and a predicate. A predicate may contain more than one word. A conjugated verb form is revealed in the predicate. A sentence may contain more than one clause.

> EXAMPLE:
>
> Mrs. Gómez lives in a large apartment / **La señora Gómez vive en un gran apartamento**.

The subject is *Mrs. Gómez/ **la señora Gómez***. The predicate is *lives in a large apartment/ **vive en un gran apartamento***. The verb is *lives/ **vive.***

Review the conjugation in all the tenses of the verb **vivir**. *See also* dependent clause, independent clause, predicate.

Comparative Adjective

When making a comparison between two persons or things, an adjective is used to express the degree of comparison in the following ways.

> EXAMPLES:
>
> Of the same degree of comparison:
>
> Helen is *as tall as* Mary / **Elena es *tan alta como* María.**
>
> Of a lesser degree of comparison:
>
> Jane is *less intelligent than* Eva / **Juana es *menos inteligente que* Eva.**
>
> Of a higher degree of comparison:
>
> This apple is *more delicious than* that one / **Esta manzana es *más deliciosa que* ésa.**

Study comparative and superlative adjectives in §5.37–§5.50. *See also* superlative adjective.

Comparative Adverb

An adverb is compared in the same way as an adjective is compared. *See* comparative adjective above.

> EXAMPLES:
>
> Of the same degree of comparison:
>
> Mr. Robles speaks *as well as* Mr. Vega / **El señor Robles habla *tan bien como* el señor Vega.**
>
> Of a lesser degree of comparison:
>
> Alice studies *less diligently than* her sister / **Alicia estudia *menos diligentemente que* su hermana.**
>
> Of a higher degree of comparison:
>
> Albert works *more slowly than* his brother / **Alberto trabaja *más lentamente que* su hermano.**

Study comparative adverbs in §10.6 and §10.7. *See also* superlative adverb.

Complex Sentence

A complex sentence contains one independent clause and one or more dependent clauses.

> EXAMPLES:
>
> One independent clause and one dependent clause:
>
> Joseph works but his brother doesn't / **José trabaja pero su hermano no trabaja.**

The independent clause is *Joseph works*. It makes sense when it stands alone because it expresses a complete thought. The dependent clause is *but his brother doesn't*. The dependent clause, which is introduced by the conjunction *but/ pero*, does not make complete sense when it stands alone because it *depends* on the thought expressed in the independent clause.

> One independent clause and two dependent clauses:
>
> Anna is a good student because she studies but her sister never studies / **Ana es una buena alumna porque estudia pero su hermana nunca estudia.**

The independent clause is *Anna is a good student*. It makes sense when it stands alone because it expresses a complete thought. The first dependent clause is *because she studies*. This dependent clause, which is introduced by the conjunction *because/**porque***, does not make complete sense when it stands alone because it *depends* on the thought expressed in the independent clause. The second dependent clause is *but her sister never studies*. That dependent clause, which is introduced by the conjunction *but/**pero***, does not make complete sense either when it stands alone because it *depends* on the thought expressed in the independent clause.

Review the conjugations in all the tenses of the basic verbs **estudiar, ser, trabajar.** *See also* dependent clause, independent clause.

Compound Sentence

A compound sentence contains two or more independent clauses.

EXAMPLE:

Mrs. Fuentes went to the supermarket, she bought a few things, and then she went home / **La señora Fuentes fue al supermercado, compró algunas cosas, y entonces fue a casa.**

This compound sentence contains three independent clauses. They are independent because they make sense when they stand alone.

Review the conjugations in all the tenses of the basic verbs **comprar** and **ir**. *See also* clause, independent clause.

Conjugation

The conjugation of a verb is the fixed order of all its forms showing their inflections (changes) in the three persons of the singular and the three persons of the plural in a particular tense.
In Spanish there are three major types of regular verb conjugations:

1st conjugation type: regular verbs that end in **ar**, for example, **hablar**
2nd conjugation type: regular verbs that end in **er**, for example, **beber**
3rd conjugation type: regular verbs that end in **ir**, for example, **recibir**

Review §8.14–§8.20.

Conjunction

A conjunction is a word that connects words or groups of words.

EXAMPLES:

and/**y**, or/**o**, but/**pero**, because/**porque**
Charles *and* Charlotte / **Carlos *y* Carlota**
You can stay home *or* you can come with me / **(Tú) puedes quedarte en casa *o* venir conmigo.**

Note that **y** (and) changes to **e** if the word right after **y** begins with **i** or **hi**.

EXAMPLES:

María es bonita e inteligente/Mary is pretty and intelligent.
Fernando e Isabel/Fernando and Isabel
padre e hijo/father and son; **madre e hija**/mother and daughter

However, if **y** is followed by a word that begins with **hie**, keep **y**: **flores y hierba**/flowers and grass.

Review conjunctions in §12.–§12.4 and §7.34–§7.43.

Contrary to Fact

This term refers to an "if" clause. *See* if **(si)** clause.

Declarative Sentence

A declarative sentence makes a statement.

> EXAMPLE:
>
> I have finished the work / **(Yo) he terminado el trabajo.**

Review the **perfecto de indicativo**/present perfect indicative tense in §8.55. Review regular and irregular past participles in §7.4 and §7.205.

Definite Article

The definite article in Spanish has four forms and they all mean *the*. They are: **el, la, los, las.**

> EXAMPLES:
>
> **el libro**/the book,　　**la casa**/the house,　　**los libros**/the books,　　**las casas**/the houses.

The definite articles **la, los,** and **las** are also used as direct object pronouns. *See* direct object pronoun.

Demonstrative Adjective

A demonstrative adjective is an adjective that points out. It is placed in front of a noun.

> EXAMPLES:
>
> this book/**este libro**; these books/**estos libros**; this cup/**esta taza**; these flowers/**estas flores.**

Review them in §5.54–§5.56.

Demonstrative Pronoun

A demonstrative pronoun is a pronoun that points out. It takes the place of a noun. It agrees in gender and number with the noun it replaces.

> EXAMPLES:
>
> I have two oranges; do you prefer *this one* or *that one?* / **Tengo dos naranjas; ¿prefiere usted ésta o ésa?**
>
> I prefer *those* [over there] / **Prefiero aquéllas.**

Review them in §6.56. For demonstrative pronouns that are neuter, *see* neuter.

Dependent Clause

A dependent clause is a group of words that contains a subject and a predicate. It does not express a complete thought when it stands alone. It is called *dependent* because it depends on the independent clause for a complete meaning. Subordinate clause is another term for dependent clause.

EXAMPLE:

Edward is absent today because he is sick / **Eduardo está ausente hoy porque está enfermo.**

The independent clause is *Edward is absent today.* The dependent clause is *because he is sick.*
See also clause, independent clause.

Descriptive Adjective

A descriptive adjective is an adjective that describes a person, place, or thing.

EXAMPLES:

a pretty girl/**una muchacha bonita**;   a big house/**una casa grande**;   an expensive car/**un carro costoso**.

Review §5.–§5.71. *See also* adjective.

Direct Object Noun

A direct object noun receives the action of the verb *directly.* That is why it is called a direct object, as opposed to an indirect object. A direct object noun is normally placed *after* the verb.

EXAMPLE:

I am writing a letter / **Escribo una carta** or **Estoy escribiendo una carta.**

The direct object is the noun *letter/***una carta.**

Review the conjugation of **escribir** in all the tenses. Review regular and irregular present participles in §7.14 and §7.190. *See also* direct object pronoun.

Direct Object Pronoun

A direct object pronoun receives the action of the verb *directly.* It takes the place of a direct object noun. In Spanish a pronoun that is a direct object of a verb is ordinarily placed *in front of* the verb.

EXAMPLE:

I am writing it [the letter] / **La escribo.**

However, in the *affirmative imperative*, a direct object pronoun is placed *after* the verb and is joined to it, resulting in one word.

EXAMPLE:

Write it [the letter] now! / **¡Escríbala [Ud.] ahora!**

Note that an accent mark is added on the vowel **i** [**í**] in order to keep the emphasis on that vowel as it was in **escriba** before the direct object pronoun **la** was added to the verb form.

Review the direct object pronouns in §6.7.
See also direct object noun and imperative.

Disjunctive Pronoun

A disjunctive pronoun is a pronoun that is stressed; in other words, emphasis is placed on it. It is usually object of a preposition. Another term for disjunctive pronoun is prepositional pronoun.

EXAMPLES:

for me/**para mí**; for you *(fam.)*/**para ti**; with you/**con usted**; with him/**con él**; with her/**con ella**

Note the following exceptions with **con**: **conmigo**/with me; **contigo**/with you *(fam.)*; **consigo**/with yourself (yourselves, himself, herself oneself, themselves). Review §6.30–§6.33.

Ending of a Verb

In Spanish grammar the ending of a verb form changes according to the person (1st, 2nd, or 3rd) and number (singular or plural) of the subject and the tense of the verb.

EXAMPLE:

To form the present indicative tense of a regular **-ar** type verb like **hablar**, drop **ar** of the infinitive and add the following endings: **-o, -as, -a** for the 1st, 2nd, and 3rd persons of the singular; **-amos, -áis, -an** for the 1st, 2nd, and 3rd persons of the plural.

You then get: **hablo, hablas, habla; hablamos, habláis, hablan**

Review §7.–§8.67. *See also* stem of a verb.

Feminine

In Spanish grammar the gender of a noun, pronoun, or adjective is feminine or masculine, not male or female.

EXAMPLES:

	Masculine			Feminine	
noun	pronoun	adjective	noun	pronoun	adjective
el hombre	**él**	**guapo**	**la mujer**	**ella**	**hermosa**
the man	*he*	*handsome*	*the woman*	*she*	*beautiful*

See also gender, below.

Gender

Gender means masculine or feminine.

EXAMPLES:

Masculine: the boy/**el muchacho**; the book/**el libro**

Feminine: the girl/**la muchacha**; the house/**la casa**

Gerund

In English grammar, a gerund is a word formed from a verb. It ends in *ing*. Actually, it is the present participle of a verb. However, it is not used as a verb. It is used as a noun.

EXAMPLE: Seeing is believing / **Ver es creer** [*to see is to believe*]. It is sometimes stated as **Ver y creer** [*to see and to believe*].

However, in Spanish grammar, the infinitive form of the verb is used, as in the above example, when the verb is used as a noun.

The Spanish gerund is also a word formed from a verb. It is the present participle of a verb. The Spanish gerund [**el gerundio**] regularly ends in **ando** for **ar** type verbs (of the 1st conjugation), in **iendo** for **er** type verbs (of the 2nd conjugation), and **iendo** for **ir** type verbs (of the 3rd conjugation). There are also irregular present participles that end in **yendo**.

EXAMPLES OF SPANISH GERUNDS:

hablando/talking **comiendo**/eating **viviendo**/living

Review §7.189, §7.190, and §7.200.

If (Si) Clause

Another term for an "if" clause is contrary-to-fact, as in English, if I were king..., if I were rich..., if I were you...

EXAMPLE:

Si yo tuviera bastante dinero, iría a España/If I had enough money, I would go to Spain.

Review the sequence of tenses and the use of a **si** (if) clause in §7.101–§7.111.
Review the conjugation of **tener** and **ir** in all the 14 tenses. *See also* clause.

Imperative Mood

The imperative is a mood, not a tense. It is used to express a command. In Spanish it is used in the 2nd person of the singular (**tú**), the 3rd person of the singular (**usted**), the 1st person of the plural (**nosotros, nosotras**), the 2nd person of the plural (**vosotros, vosotras**), and in the 3rd person of the plural (**ustedes**).

EXAMPLE:

Call me/**Llámame.**

Review §8.62.

Indefinite Article

In English the indefinite articles are *a, an*, as in *a book, an apple.* They are indefinite because they do not refer to any definite or particular noun.

In Spanish there are two indefinite articles in the singular: one in the masculine form (**un**) and one in the feminine form (**una**).

EXAMPLES:

Masculine singular: **un libro**/*a book*
Feminine singular: **una manzana**/*an apple*

In the plural they change to **unos** and **unas**.

EXAMPLES:

unos libros/some books; **unas manzanas**/some apples

Review §4.12–§4.19.

Indefinite Pronoun

An indefinite pronoun is a pronoun that does not refer to any definite or particular noun.

EXAMPLES:

something/**algo**; someone, somebody/**alguien**

Review §11.11.

Independent Clause

An independent clause is a group of words that contains a subject and a predicate. It expresses a complete thought when it stands alone.

EXAMPLE:

The cat is sleeping on the bed / **El gato está durmiendo sobre la cama.**

Review the conjugation of **estar** and **dormir** in all the 14 tenses. Review regular and irregular present participles in §7.14 and §7.190. *See also* clause, dependent clause, predicate.

Indicative Mood

The indicative mood is used in sentences that make a statement or ask a question. It is used most of the time when we speak or write in English or Spanish.

EXAMPLES:

I am going to the movies now/**Voy al cine ahora.**
Where are you going?/**¿Adónde vas?**

Review §7.1.

Indirect Object Noun

An indirect object noun receives the action of the verb *indirectly*.

EXAMPLE:

I am writing a letter to María *or* I am writing María a letter / **Estoy escribiendo una carta a María.**
The verb is *am writing/ estoy escribiendo*. The direct object noun is *a letter/ una carta*. The indirect object noun is *to María/a María.*
See also indirect object pronoun, below.

Indirect Object Pronoun

An indirect object pronoun takes the place of an indirect object noun. It receives the action of the verb *indirectly.*

EXAMPLE:

I am writing a letter to her *or* I am writing her a letter / **Le escribo una carta a ella.**
The indirect object pronoun is *(to) her/***le.** It is clarified by adding **a ella.**
Review the indirect object pronouns in §6.14. *See also* indirect object noun.

Infinitive

An infinitive is a verb form. In English, it is normally stated with the preposition *to*, as in *to talk, to drink, to receive*. In Spanish, the infinitive form of a verb consists of three major types: those of the 1st conjugation that end in **-ar**, the 2nd conjugation that end in **-er**, and the 3rd conjugation that end in **-ir**.

In Spanish grammar, the infinitive (**el infinitivo**) is considered a mood.

EXAMPLES:

hablar/ *to talk, to speak*; **beber**/ *to drink*; **recibir**/ *to receive*

Review infinitives in §7.178–§7.187.

Interjection

An interjection is a word that expresses emotion, a feeling of joy, of sadness, an exclamation of surprise, and other exclamations consisting of one or two words.

EXAMPLES:

Ah!/**¡Ah!**   Ouch!/**¡Ay!**   Darn it!/**¡Caramba!**   My God!/**¡Dios mío!**

Interrogative Adjective

In Spanish, an interrogative adjective is an adjective that is used in a question. As an adjective, it is placed in front of a noun.

EXAMPLES:

What book do you want? / **¿*Qué* libro desea usted?**

What time is it? / **¿*Qué* hora es?**

Review §5.68.

Interrogative Adverb

In Spanish, an interrogative adverb is an adverb that introduces a question. As an adverb, it modifies the verb.

EXAMPLES:

How are you? / **¿*Cómo* está usted?**

How much does this book cost? / **¿*Cuánto* cuesta este libro?**

When will you arrive? / **¿*Cuándo* llegará usted?**

Review §10.10.

Interrogative Pronoun

An interrogative pronoun is a pronoun that asks a question. There are interrogative pronouns that refer to persons and those that refer to things.

EXAMPLES:

Who is it? / **¿*Quién* es?**

What are you saying? / **¿*Qué* dice usted?**

Review §6.103–§6.105.

Interrogative Sentence

An interrogative sentence asks a question.

EXAMPLE:

What are you doing? / **¿Qué hace usted?**

Review §5.14 and §6.4–§6.53.

Intransitive Verb

An intransitive verb is a verb that does not take a direct object.

EXAMPLE:

The professor is talking / **El profesor habla.**
An intransitive verb takes an indirect object.

EXAMPLE:

The professor is talking to us / **El profesor nos habla.**

Review §7.11–§7.13. *See also* direct object pronoun, indirect object pronoun, transitive verb.

Irregular Verb

An irregular verb is a verb that does not follow a fixed pattern in its conjugation in the various verb tenses.

EXAMPLES OF BASIC IRREGULAR VERBS IN SPANISH:

estar/to be   **hacer**/to do, to make   **ir**/to go   **ser**/to be

For many commonly used irregular verb forms, review §8.65–§8.67. *See also* conjugation, regular verb.

Limiting Adjective

A limiting adjective is an adjective that limits a quantity.

EXAMPLE:

three lemons/**tres limones**; a few candies/**algunos dulces**

Main Clause

Main clause is another term for independent clause. *See* independent clause.

Masculine

In Spanish grammar the gender of a noun, pronoun, or adjective is masculine or feminine, not male or female.

For examples, *see* gender.

Mood of Verbs

Some grammarians use the term *the mode* instead of *the mood* of a verb. Either term means *the manner or way* a verb is expressed. In English and Spanish grammar a verb expresses an action or state of being in a particular mood.

In Spanish grammar, we have the following moods (**modos**): the infinitive (**el infinitivo**), the indicative (**el indicativo**), the imperative (**el imperativo**), the conditional (**el potencial**), and the subjunctive (**el subjuntivo**).

In English grammar, there are three moods: the indicative mood, the subjunctive mood, and the imperative mood. Most of the time, in English and Spanish, we speak and write in the indicative mood.

Review §7.1.

Negative Statement, Affirmative Statement

See affirmative statement, negative statement.

Neuter

A word that is neuter is neither masculine nor feminine. Common neuter demonstrative pronouns in Spanish are **esto**/ *this*, **eso**/ *that*, **aquello**/ *that* [farther away].

EXAMPLES:

What's this? / **¿Qué es esto?**   What's that? / **¿Qué es eso?**

For demonstrative pronouns that are not neuter, *see* demonstrative pronoun.

There is also the neuter pronoun **lo**. It usually refers to an idea or statement. It is not normally translated into English but often the translation is *so*.

EXAMPLES:

¿Estás enferma, María? / Are you sick, Mary?   **Sí, lo estoy** / Yes, I am.

No lo creo / I don't think so.

Lo parece / It seems so.

Review §6.12 and §6.56–§6.60.

Noun

A noun is a word that names a person, animal, place, thing, condition or state, or quality.

EXAMPLES:

the man/**el hombre**, the woman/**la mujer**, the horse/**el caballo**, the house/**la casa**, the pencil/**el lápiz**, happiness/**la felicidad**, excellence/**la excelencia**

In Spanish the noun **el nombre** is the word for name and noun. Another word for noun in Spanish is **el sustantivo**/*substantive*.

Review §3.–§3.30.

Number

In English and Spanish grammar, number means singular or plural.

EXAMPLES:

Masc. sing.: the boy/**el muchacho**; the pencil/**el lápiz**; the eye/**el ojo**

Masc. pl.: the boys/**los muchachos**; the pencils/**los lápices**; the eyes/**los ojos**

Fem. sing.: the girl/**la muchacha**; the house/**la casa**; the cow/**la vaca**

Fem. pl.: the girls/**las muchachas**; the houses/**las casas**; the cows/**las vacas**

Ordinal Number

An ordinal number is a number that expresses position in a series, such as *first, second, third*, and so on. In English and Spanish grammar we talk about subjects and verbs as being 1st person, 2nd person, or 3rd person singular or plural.

Review them in §18.3. *See also* cardinal number and person (1st, 2nd, 3rd).

Orthographical Changes in Verb Forms

An orthographical change in a verb form is a change in spelling.

EXAMPLE:

The verb **conocer**/*to know, to be acquainted with* changes in spelling in the 1st person singular of the present indicative. The letter **z** is inserted in front of the second **c**. When formed regularly, the ending **er** of the infinitive drops and **o** is added for the 1st person singular form of the present indicative. That would result in *conoco*, a peculiar sound to the Spanish ear for a verb form of **conocer**. The letter **z** is added to keep the sound of **s** as it is in the infinitive **conocer**. Therefore, the spelling changes and the form is **yo conozco**. In the other forms of **conocer** in the present indicative **z** is not inserted because they retain the sound of **s**. There are many verb forms in Spanish that contain orthographical changes.

Review other examples in §7.32.

Participles

See past participle, present participle.

Passive Voice

When we speak or write in the active voice and change to the passive voice, the direct object becomes the subject, the subject becomes the object of a preposition, and the verb becomes *to be* plus the past participle of the active verb. The past participle functions as an adjective.

EXAMPLE:

The window was opened by the robber / **La ventana fue abierta por el ladrón.**

The subject is ***la ventana***. The verb is ***fue***. The word ***abierta*** is a feminine adjective agreeing with ***la ventana***. Actually, it is the past participle of **abrir**/*to open* but here it serves as an adjective. The object of the preposition *by*/**por** is *the robber*/**el ladrón.**

See also active voice. Compare the above sentence with the example in the active voice.

Past Participle

A past participle is derived from a verb. It is used to form the compound tenses. Its auxiliary verb in English is *to have*. In Spanish, the auxiliary verb is **haber**/*to have*. It is part of the verb tense.

EXAMPLES:

Infinitive	Past Participle	Present Perfect Indicative
hablar/to speak, to talk	spoken, talked	I have *spoken (talked)*/**he hablado**
comer/to eat	eaten	I have *eaten*/**he comido**
recibir/to receive	received	I have *received*/**he recibido**

Review §7.204 for the regular formation of a past participle and §7.205 for common irregular past participles. You need to know them to form the seven compound tenses. The present perfect tense, which is commonly used, is one of them. Review §8.55ff.

See also auxiliary verb.

Person (1st, 2nd, 3rd)

Verb forms in a particular tense are learned systematically according to person (1st, 2nd, 3rd) and number (singular, plural).

EXAMPLE:

Here is the present indicative tense of the verb **ir**/*to go* in the three persons of the singular and the three persons of the plural with the subject pronouns in parentheses.

Singular	Plural
1st person: **(yo) voy**	1st person: **(nosotros, nosotras) vamos**
2nd person: **(tú) vas**	2nd person: **(vosotros, vosotras) vais**
3rd person: **(Ud., él, ella) va**	3rd person: **(Uds., ellos, ellas) van**

Personal Pronoun

A personal pronoun is a pronoun that refers to a person. Review the personal subject pronouns above in the entry *person*: **yo**, **tú**, and so on. Review §6.4.

For examples of other types of pronouns, *see also* demonstrative pronoun, direct object pronoun, disjunctive pronoun, indefinite pronoun, indirect object pronoun, interrogative pronoun, possessive pronoun, reflexive pronoun, relative pronoun.

Plural

Plural means more than one. *See also* person (1st, 2nd, 3rd), and singular.

Possessive Adjective

A possessive adjective is an adjective that is placed in front of a noun to show possession. Review them in §5.58.

EXAMPLES:

my book/**mi libro**,   my friends/**mis amigos**,   our school/**nuestra escuela**

Possessive Pronoun

A possessive pronoun is a pronoun that shows possession. It takes the place of a possessive adjective with the noun. Its form agrees in gender (masculine or feminine) and number (singular or plural) with what it is replacing.

EXAMPLES IN ENGLISH: mine, yours, his, hers, its, ours, theirs

EXAMPLES IN SPANISH:

Possessive adjective	Possessive pronoun
my book/**mi libro**	*mine*/**el mío**
my house/**mi casa**	*mine*/**la mía**
my shoes/**mis zapatos**	*mine*/**los míos**

Review the possessive pronouns in §6.64.

Predicate

The predicate is that part of the sentence that tells us something about the subject. The main word of the predicate is the verb.

EXAMPLE:

Today the tourists are going to the Prado Museum / **Hoy los turistas van al Museo del Prado.**

The subject is *the tourists/ los turistas.* The predicate is *are going to the Prado Museum/ van al Museo del Prado.* The verb is *are going/ van.*

Preposition

A preposition is a word that establishes a rapport between words.

EXAMPLES: with, without, to, at, between

with her/ ***con* ella**,   *without* money/ ***sin* dinero**

between you and me/ ***entre* tú y yo**,   *to* Spain/ ***a* España**

Review prepositions in §11.–§11.43.

Prepositional Pronoun

A prepositional pronoun is a pronoun that is object of a preposition. The term disjunctive pronoun is also used. For examples, *see* disjunctive pronoun.

Present Participle

A present participle is derived from a verb form. In English a present participle ends in *ing*. In Spanish a present participle is called **un gerundio**.

EXAMPLES:

cantando/singing,   **comiendo**/eating,   **yendo**/going

Review §7.189 for the regular formation of a present participle and §7.190 for common irregular present participles.

Pronoun

A pronoun is a word that takes the place of a noun, such as *he, she, it, they, them*.

EXAMPLES:

el hombre/*él*   **la mujer/***ella*   **el árbol/***él*   **la casa/***ella*

the man/*he*   the woman/*she*   the tree/*it*   the house/*it*

For examples of other kinds of pronouns, *see also* demonstrative pronoun, direct object pronoun, disjunctive pronoun, indefinite pronoun, indirect object pronoun, interrogative pronoun, possessive pronoun, reflexive pronoun, relative pronoun.

Reflexive Pronoun and Reflexive Verb

In English a reflexive pronoun is a personal pronoun that contains *self* or *selves*. In Spanish and English a reflexive pronoun is used with a verb that is called reflexive because the action of the verb falls on the reflexive pronoun.

In Spanish, as in English, there is a required set of reflexive pronouns for a reflexive verb.

EXAMPLES:

lavarse   **(Yo) me lavo.**

to wash oneself   I wash myself.

afeitarse   **Pablo se ha afeitado.**

to shave oneself   Paul has shaved himself.

Review reflexive pronouns in §6.21ff.

Regular Verb

A regular verb is a verb that is conjugated in the various tenses according to a fixed pattern. Three examples of regular Spanish verbs are **hablar, aprender, vivir.** Review §8.14–§8.18. *See also* conjugation, irregular verb.

Relative Pronoun

A relative pronoun is a pronoun that refers to its antecedent.

EXAMPLE:

The girl who is talking with John is my sister / **La muchacha que está hablando con Juan es mi hermana.**

The antecedent is *girl*/ *la muchacha*. The relative pronoun *who*/ *que* refers to the girl.

Review §6.70–§6.105. *See also* antecedent.

Sentence

A sentence is a group of words that contains a subject and a predicate. The verb is contained in the predicate. A sentence expresses a complete thought.

EXAMPLE:

The train leaves at two o'clock in the afternoon / **El tren sale a las dos de la tarde.**

The subject is *train*/ *el tren*. The predicate is *leaves at two o'clock in the afternoon*/*sale a las dos de la tarde.* The verb is *leaves*/ *sale.*

Simple Sentence

A simple sentence is a sentence that contains one subject and one predicate. The verb is the core of the predicate. The verb is the most important word in a sentence because it tells us what the subject is doing.

EXAMPLE:

Mary is eating an apple from her garden / **María está comiendo una manzana de su jardín.**

The subject is *Mary*/**María.** The predicate is *is eating an apple from her garden*/ **está comiendo una manzana de su jardín.** The verb is *is eating*/ **está comiendo.** The direct object is *an apple*/ **una manzana.** *From her garden*/ **de su jardín** is an adverbial phrase. It tells you from where the apple came.

Singular

Singular means one. *See also* plural.

Stem of a Verb

The stem of a verb is what is left after we drop the ending of its infinitive form. It is needed to add to it the required endings of a regular verb in a particular verb tense.

EXAMPLES:

Infinitive	Ending of infinitive	Stem
hablar/to talk	**ar**	**habl**
comer/to eat	**er**	**com**
escribir/to write	**ir**	**escrib**

Stem-changing Verb

In Spanish there are many verb forms that change in the stem.

EXAMPLE:

The verb **dormir**/*to sleep* changes the vowel **o** in the stem to **ue** when the stress (emphasis, accent) falls on that **o**; for example, **(yo) duermo.**

When the stress does not fall on that **o**, it does not change; for example, **(nosotros) dormimos.** Here, the stress is on the vowel **i**.

Subject

A subject is that part of a sentence that is related to its verb. The verb says something about the subject.

EXAMPLE:

Clara and Isabel are working / **Clara e Isabel están trabajando.**

The subject of this sentence is **Clara e Isabel**, which is 3rd person plural. To know when to use **e** instead of **y** for *and*, review the entry *conjunction* in this section.

Subjunctive Mood

The subjunctive mood is the mood of a verb that is used for a specific reason, *e.g.,* after certain verbs expressing a wish, doubt, emotion, fear, joy, uncertainty, an indefinite expression, an indefinite antecedent, certain conjunctions, and others. The subjunctive mood is used more frequently in Spanish than in English. Review the basics of the subjunctive in §7.33–§7.100.

Subordinate Clause

Subordinate clause is another term for dependent clause. *See* dependent clause.

Superlative Adjective

A superlative adjective is an adjective that expresses the highest degree when making a comparison of more than two persons or things.

EXAMPLES:

Adjective	Comparative	Superlative
bueno/good	**mejor**/better	**el mejor**/the best
alto/tall	**más alto**/taller	**el más alto**/the tallest

Review §5.37–§5.53. *See also* comparative adjective.

Superlative Adverb

A superlative adverb is an adverb that expresses the highest degree when making a comparison of more than two persons or things.

EXAMPLE:

Adverb	Comparative	Superlative
lentamente slowly	**más lentamente** more slowly	**lo más lentamente** the most slowly

Review §10.6. *See also* comparative adverb.

Tense of Verb

In English and Spanish grammar, tense means time. The tense of the verb indicates the time of the action or state of being. The three major segments of time are past, present, and future. In Spanish there are fourteen major verb tenses, of which seven are simple tenses and seven are compound.

Review §7.–§8.67.

Transitive Verb

A transitive verb is a verb that takes a direct object.

EXAMPLE:

I am closing the window / **Cierro la ventana.**

The subject is *I/ (Yo).* The verb is *am closing/ cierro.* The direct object is *the window/ la ventana.* *See also* direct object noun, direct object pronoun, intransitive verb.

Verb

A verb is a word that expresses action or a state of being.

EXAMPLES:

Action: **Los pájaros están volando** / The birds are flying.

The verb is *están volando*/*are flying*.

State of being: **La señora López está contenta** / Mrs. López is happy.

The verb is *está*/ *is*.

Review the conjugations in all the tenses of the basic verbs **estar, haber, hacer, ir, poder, ser.** The best verb review book is Barron's *501 Spanish Verbs*, 4th edition.

LISTENING COMPREHENSION TESTS

PART
VI

The College Board offers two types of one-hour SAT II Spanish Tests. The current type consists of 85 multiple-choice reading questions that test skills in vocabulary and idiomatic expressions in context, structure (which is grammar), and general reading comprehension. This book contains ten full-length practice tests of that type, including a full-length diagnostic test.

The other type is the SAT II Spanish Test with Listening. Approximately 40% tests listening comprehension and 60% tests reading comprehension. The reading comprehension consists of the same types of questions found in the current Spanish test described above.

If you plan to take the SAT II Spanish Test with Listening, this section will give you considerable practice.

The Listening Test contains questions based on (1) pictures (**Part A**), (2) short dialogues (**Part B**), and (3) long dialogues and monologues (**Part C**).

Directions for these three types of listening questions are given below in each of the three parts: **Part A**, **Part B**, and **Part C**.

To help you do your best in all parts of the Listening Test, here is a tip: Do not attempt to translate silently into English what you hear in Spanish. If you do, you will fall behind the speaker and you will not hear everything spoken. Just concentrate on listening attentively to the Spanish.

The script of everything on the compact disc (CD) begins on page 401. The CD is in an envelope on the inside of the back cover of this book.

Photo Credits. The ten photos in this part were reprinted with permission of the Spanish Government Tourist Office, New York, N.Y.

A. TEN PICTURES

Directions: *There are ten pictures in this part. For each picture you will hear four statements, but only one statement accurately states what is in the picture.*

With your CD, listen to the speaker who will read four sentences, each designated A, B, C, and D. Examine the picture very carefully while listening to the four sentences. They will not be printed in your test booklet. You will hear them only once. Therefore, you must listen attentively and remember the letter of each statement when you choose the correct answer.

Choose the letter of the statement that accurately states what is in the picture and blacken the corresponding space on the Answer Sheet on page 399. Check your answers with the Answer Key on page 398.

Now, examine picture number one and listen to the four statements designated A, B, C, and D.

Picture number 1

Picture number 2

Picture number 3

Picture number 4

Picture number 5

Picture number 6

Picture number 7

Picture number 8

Picture number 9

Picture number 10

B. TEN SHORT DIALOGUES

<u>Directions</u>: *There are ten short dialogues in this part. You will hear a chime at the beginning of each new dialogue. Each dialogue will be spoken twice. At the end of each dialogue, you will hear one or two questions about what was stated. Each question will be followed by three possible answers, designated A, B, and C. They will be spoken only once.*

Although the complete CD script is printed farther on in this book, the dialogues for the actual test will not *be printed in your test booklet.*

Choose the letter of the statement that is the best answer and blacken the corresponding space on the Answer Sheet that you used for the ten pictures, numbered 1 to 10. The short dialogues begin with question number 11 on your practice Answer Sheet. You will hear a chime on the compact disc to indicate the beginning of a new selection.

C. SIX LONG DIALOGUES AND MONOLOGUES

<u>Directions</u>: *There are six selections in this part consisting of longer dialogues and a few monologues. Each selection will be spoken only* once. *After each selection, you will hear several questions based on what you heard. The multiple-choice answers will not be spoken on the CD but they will be printed in your booklet. The questions will also be in your booklet. Although the entire script of the long dialogues and monologues for these practice tests is in this book, the dialogues and monologues for the actual test will* not *be printed in your test booklet.*

*Choose the letter of the statement that is the best answer (A, B, C, or D) and blacken the corresponding space on the Answer Sheet. This **Part C** begins with question number 26 on your practice Answer Sheet. You will hear a chime to indicate the beginning of a new selection.*

Selection number 1. Question numbers **26** to **29**:

26. ¿Adónde fueron las dos damas ayer?
    A. al teatro
    B. a casa
    C. al cine
    D. a los almacenes

27. ¿A qué hora llegó Margarita a casa?
    A. a eso de las cinco
    B. a las tres
    C. a la una
    D. a las dos

28. ¿Qué compraron Margarita y Elena?
    A. dulces
    B. almacenes
    C. prendas de vestir
    D. cansadas

29. ¿Por qué irá Margarita a casa de Elena esta noche?
    A. para comprar un vestido largo
    B. para ver los zapatos blancos y los guantes
    C. ¡No me digas!
    D. para ver la boda de su sobrino

Selection number 2. Question numbers **30** to **34**:

30. ¿Cuándo volvió Juan del ejército?
    A. el viernes de la semana pasada
    B. el mes pasado
    C. el año pasado
    D. el viernes de la semana que viene

31. ¿Por qué la familia de Juan le invitó a Roberto Carlos a comer en su casa?
- A. porque tenía mucha hambre
- B. porque los dos jóvenes son muy buenos amigos
- C. porque Roberto Carlos volvió del ejército
- D. porque a Roberto Carlos le gusta el chocolate

32. ¿Qué personas estaban allí también?
- A. los niños
- B. la abuela y el abuelo
- C. los primos y otros parientes de Roberto Carlos
- D. los primos y otros parientes de Juan

33. ¿Dónde comieron?
- A. en la cocina
- B. en el patio
- C. en el comedor
- D. en un restaurante famoso

34. ¿De qué hablaron durante la comida?
- A. de la vida en el ejército
- B. de la madre que sirvió paella y carne asada
- C. del bizcocho de chocolate
- D. de muchas cosas

Selection number 3. Question numbers 35 to 38:

35. ¿Qué pasó en el camino?
- A. Un señor y su esposa estaban en el camino.
- B. El coche se paró de repente.
- C. No han tenido problemas hasta ahora.
- D. ¡No me eches la culpa a mí!

36. ¿Por qué se paró el coche?
- A. No hay gasolina en el tanque.
- B. No hay estación de gasolina por aquí.
- C. Hay una estación de gasolina al otro lado del camino.
- D. El señor no sabe nada.

37. ¿Quién conduce?
- A. la señora
- B. el señor
- C. el coche
- D. el camino

38. ¿Adónde va el señor para pedir ayuda?
- A. al campo
- B. a su casa
- C. a la estación de gasolina
- D. a la casa a lo lejos que vio su esposa

Selection number 4. Question numbers 39 to 42:

39. ¿De quién habla la muchacha?
- A. de una vecina que ganó mucho dinero
- B. de su hermana Isabel
- C. del artículo en la primera página del periódico
- D. del marido de la señora Rodríguez

40. ¿Por qué piensa ella llamar a la señora Rodríguez?
    A. para pedir dinero
    B. para conseguir el periódico
    C. para felicitarla
    D. para cambiar todo

41. ¿Cuánto tiempo hace que las dos muchachas se conocen?
    A. hace dos semanas
    B. hace diez años
    C. por teléfono
    D. hace algunos minutos

42. ¿Cómo es la señora Rodríguez?
    A. Es muy bella.
    B. Es inteligente.
    C. Va a llamarla.
    D. Es muy simpática y generosa.

Selection number 5. Question numbers **43** to **46**:

43. ¿Quién vende la bicicleta?
    A. Pablo
    B. Pedro
    C. el padre de Pablo
    D. los padres de Pedro

44. ¿Por qué quiere venderla el joven?
    A. Su padre va a darle un coche.
    B. Quiere comprar un automóvil.
    C. Prefiere comprar otra bicicleta en perfecta condición.
    D. Sus padres se la regalaron para su cumpleaños.

45. ¿Por cuánto dinero la vende?
    A. cuarenta dólares
    B. cien dólares
    C. cincuenta dólares
    D. sesenta dólares

46. ¿En qué condición está la bicicleta?
    A. Es casi nueva.
    B. Es vieja.
    C. Es necesario repararla.
    D. Puede pagar la semana que viene.

Selection number 6. Question numbers **47** to **50**:

47. ¿Quiénes visitaron el país?
    A. turistas alemanes
    B. representantes del Presidente
    C. líderes políticos
    D. jóvenes hispanos

48. ¿A quiénes les dio las gracias el líder juvenil?
    A. al Presidente y a su señora
    B. a la Fundación del Niño
    C. a los guías
    D. a los peruanos, colombianos y argentinos

49. ¿En qué actividades tomaron parte los jóvenes?
   A. en estudios universitarios
   B. en actividades culturales y recreativas
   C. en estudios de cocina
   D. en actividades científicas y religiosas

50. ¿A qué hijos sirve este programa?
   A. a los de familias pobres
   B. a los de militares
   C. a los de familias aristocráticas
   D. a los de profesores

ANSWER KEY

A. PICTURES	B. SHORT DIALOGUES		C. LONG DIALOGUES AND MONOLOGUES		
1. D	11. B	19. B	26. D	35. B	43. B
2. A	12. C	20. C	27. A	36. A	44. B
3. C	13. C	21. C	28. C	37. A	45. C
4. B	14. A	22. C	29. B	38. D	46. A
5. A	15. B	23. A	30. A	39. A	47. D
6. B	16. C	24. B	31. B	40. C	48. A
7. A	17. A	25. A	32. D	41. B	49. B
8. D	18. A		33. C	42. D	50. A
9. C			34. D		
10. A					

ANALYSIS CHART

In evaluating your score in the Listening Comprehension section, use the following table:

45 to 50 correct: *Excellent*

40 to 44 correct: *Very Good*

35 to 39 correct: *Average*

26 to 34 correct: *Below Average*

fewer than 25 correct: *Unsatisfactory*

Answer Sheet: Listening Comprehension

A. PICTURES

1 Ⓐ Ⓑ Ⓒ Ⓓ
2 Ⓐ Ⓑ Ⓒ Ⓓ
3 Ⓐ Ⓑ Ⓒ Ⓓ
4 Ⓐ Ⓑ Ⓒ Ⓓ
5 Ⓐ Ⓑ Ⓒ Ⓓ
6 Ⓐ Ⓑ Ⓒ Ⓓ
7 Ⓐ Ⓑ Ⓒ Ⓓ
8 Ⓐ Ⓑ Ⓒ Ⓓ
9 Ⓐ Ⓑ Ⓒ Ⓓ
10 Ⓐ Ⓑ Ⓒ Ⓓ

B. SHORT DIALOGUES

11 Ⓐ Ⓑ Ⓒ
12 Ⓐ Ⓑ Ⓒ
13 Ⓐ Ⓑ Ⓒ
14 Ⓐ Ⓑ Ⓒ
15 Ⓐ Ⓑ Ⓒ
16 Ⓐ Ⓑ Ⓒ
17 Ⓐ Ⓑ Ⓒ
18 Ⓐ Ⓑ Ⓒ
19 Ⓐ Ⓑ Ⓒ
20 Ⓐ Ⓑ Ⓒ
21 Ⓐ Ⓑ Ⓒ
22 Ⓐ Ⓑ Ⓒ
23 Ⓐ Ⓑ Ⓒ
24 Ⓐ Ⓑ Ⓒ
25 Ⓐ Ⓑ Ⓒ

C. LONG DIALOGUES AND MONOLOGUES

26 Ⓐ Ⓑ Ⓒ Ⓓ
27 Ⓐ Ⓑ Ⓒ Ⓓ
28 Ⓐ Ⓑ Ⓒ Ⓓ
29 Ⓐ Ⓑ Ⓒ Ⓓ
30 Ⓐ Ⓑ Ⓒ Ⓓ
31 Ⓐ Ⓑ Ⓒ Ⓓ
32 Ⓐ Ⓑ Ⓒ Ⓓ
33 Ⓐ Ⓑ Ⓒ Ⓓ
34 Ⓐ Ⓑ Ⓒ Ⓓ
35 Ⓐ Ⓑ Ⓒ Ⓓ
36 Ⓐ Ⓑ Ⓒ Ⓓ
37 Ⓐ Ⓑ Ⓒ Ⓓ
38 Ⓐ Ⓑ Ⓒ Ⓓ
39 Ⓐ Ⓑ Ⓒ Ⓓ
40 Ⓐ Ⓑ Ⓒ Ⓓ
41 Ⓐ Ⓑ Ⓒ Ⓓ
42 Ⓐ Ⓑ Ⓒ Ⓓ
43 Ⓐ Ⓑ Ⓒ Ⓓ
44 Ⓐ Ⓑ Ⓒ Ⓓ
45 Ⓐ Ⓑ Ⓒ Ⓓ
46 Ⓐ Ⓑ Ⓒ Ⓓ
47 Ⓐ Ⓑ Ⓒ Ⓓ
48 Ⓐ Ⓑ Ⓒ Ⓓ
49 Ⓐ Ⓑ Ⓒ Ⓓ
50 Ⓐ Ⓑ Ⓒ Ⓓ

COMPLETE CD SCRIPT FOR SAT II SPANISH WITH LISTENING COMPREHENSION

PART

VII

TRACK 1

(MUSIC)

MALE NARRATOR: Welcome to Barron's Educational Series practice for the SAT II Spanish Test with Listening Comprehension. Copyright 1999.

(CHIMES)

MN: Before beginning this part of the Listening Test, make sure that you have read and understood the directions for Part A—Pictures, printed in your book. Now, carefully examine picture number 1 in your book while listening attentively to the four statements designated A, B, C, and D. You will hear each letter and statement only *once*. Choose the letter of the statement that best describes the picture and blacken the corresponding space on the Answer Sheet in your book.

TRACK 2

(CHIMES)

Picture number 1.

FEMALE SPEAKER:
A. ¡Qué campo hermoso en el invierno! (PAUSE)
B. Hay muchos pájaros que están volando. (PAUSE)
C. El primer ciclista está llorando. (PAUSE)
D. No hay duda que estos ciclistas están contentos. (PAUSE)

TRACK 3

(CHIMES)

MN: Picture number 2.

FS 1:
A. Aquí se venden muchas cosas interesantes. (PAUSE)
B. Uno de estos dos señores lleva un sombrero. (PAUSE)
C. El señor con el mazo en la mano está sentado. (PAUSE)
D. La puerta de esta tienda está cerrada. (PAUSE)

TRACK 4

(CHIMES)

MN: Picture number 3.

FS 1:
A. Estos albaricoques son deliciosos. (PAUSE)
B. Las estrellas brillan. (PAUSE)
C. Estas uvas son maravillosas. (PAUSE)
D. Está lloviendo ahora. (PAUSE)

TRACK 5

(CHIMES)

MN: Picture number 4.

FS 1:
A. Los caballos están bañándose en el mar. (PAUSE)
B. Es muy agradable ir a caballo. (PAUSE)
C. Hay un barco en el horizonte. (PAUSE)
D. ¡Qué flores hermosas! (PAUSE)

TRACK 6

(CHIMES)

MN:	Picture number 5.
FS 1:	A. A estos hombres les gusta el juego de bolos. (PAUSE)
	B. Estos hombres son aficionados al jai alai. (PAUSE)
	C. Es una venta pública. (PAUSE)
	D. El jugador lanza el bolo con la mano izquierda. (PAUSE)

TRACK 7 (CHIMES)

MN:	Picture number 6.
FS 1:	A. El chico da de comer rebanadas de pan a los pájaros. (PAUSE)
	B. El chico está sonriendo. (PAUSE)
	C. El gran pan está en el horno. (PAUSE)
	D. El ciclista y el chico se van juntos. (PAUSE)

TRACK 8 (CHIMES)

MN:	Picture number 7.
FS 1:	A. Estos clientes están mirando los postres. (PAUSE)
	B. Es una fiesta para niños. (PAUSE)
	C. Este grupo de personas va a pasar un mal rato. (PAUSE)
	D. A estos clientes les gusta el arroz con pollo. (PAUSE)

TRACK 9 (CHIMES)

MN:	Picture number 8.
FS 1:	A. En esta orquesta hay más de treinta instrumentistas. (PAUSE)
	B. Estamos en la taquilla del Teatro Real. (PAUSE)
	C. Aquí están las entradas. (PAUSE)
	D. Asistir a un concierto es un placer. (PAUSE)

TRACK 10 (CHIMES)

MN:	Picture number 9.
FS 1:	A. Estas montañas están cubiertas de arena blanca. (PAUSE)
	B. Aquí se puede alquilar equipo de buceo. (PAUSE)
	C. Este sitio de esquiar es popular. (PAUSE)
	D. Estas personas juegan a las damas. (PAUSE)

TRACK 11 (CHIMES)

MN:	Picture number 10.
FS 1:	A. Este hombre tiene una caña de pescar en las manos. (PAUSE)
	B. El hombre está pescando en aguas tranquilas. (PAUSE)
	C. Empieza a llover. (PAUSE)
	D. Este hombre está pescando en el mar. (PAUSE)

MN:	This is the end of Part A. Now go on to Part B.

TRACK 12	**(MUSIC)**

MALE NARRATOR: This is Part B of the Listening Test. There are ten short dialogues in this part. You will hear a chime at the beginning of each new dialogue. (CHIME) Each dialogue will be spoken *twice*. They are *not* printed in your test booklet. At the end of each dialogue, you will hear one or two questions about what was stated. Each question will be followed by three possible answers, designated A, B, and C. They are not printed in your test booklet either. They will be spoken only *once*. Choose the letter of the statement that is the best answer and blacken the corresponding space on the Answer Sheet that you used for the ten pictures in **Part A**, numbered **1** to **10**. This **Part B** begins with number **11**.

TRACK 13	**(CHIMES)**

MN: Dialogue number one.

FEMALE SPEAKER 1: ¿Estás bien preparado para tus exámenes, Carlos?

MALE SPEAKER 1: ¡Cómo no! He estudiado mucho. ¿Y tú, Juanita?

FS 1: Mañana tengo un examen más, y luego empiezan las vacaciones.
¿Qué vas a hacer durante las vacaciones?

MS 1: La verdad es que no sé.

FS 1: Mi familia y yo vamos a hacer un viaje a Puerto Rico.

MS 1: El verano pasado mi familia y yo pasamos las vacaciones en las montañas.

FS 1: Voy a mandarte una tarjeta postal desde San Juan si me das tu dirección.

MS 1: Con mucho gusto.

MN: Now, listen to this dialogue again.

(PAUSE)

MN: Now, listen to the question. It is number **11** on your Answer Sheet.

FS 1: ¿Quiénes son estas dos personas?
A. una hermana y un hermano
B. dos alumnos
C. dos viajeros

TRACK 14	**(CHIMES)**

MN: Dialogue number two.

FS 1: Buenos días, señor. ¿En qué puedo servirle?

MS 1: Me gustaría comprar un libro.

FS 1: ¿Qué clase de libro busca, señor?

MS 1:	No sé. Deseo regalarle a mi primo un libro.
FS 1:	Muchos clientes prefieren libros de arte.
MS 1:	No creo que a mi primo le guste mucho el arte.
FS 1:	Tenemos un magnífico libro sobre los toros.
MS 1:	Tampoco es aficiondao a los toros.
FS 1:	¿A su primo le gusta la música?
MS 1:	Sí, sí. Es una buena idea.
FS 1:	Bueno, aquí está un libro sobre la música española.
MS 1:	Lo tomo. Muchas gracias, señorita.
MN:	Now, listen to this dialogue again.

(PAUSE)

MN:	Now, listen to question number **12** on your Answer Sheet.
FS 1:	¿Dónde está este cliente? A. en una biblioteca B. en una discoteca C. en una librería
MN:	Now, listen to another question. It is number **13** on your Answer Sheet.
FS 1:	¿Qué clase de libro compra el cliente? A. un libro sobre los toros B. un libro sobre las bellas artes C. un libro sobre la música española

TRACK 15   **(CHIMES)**

MN:	Dialogue number three.
FS 1:	Con permiso, señor. Me parece que el asiento en su lado es mío.
MS 1:	Con placer, señorita. Pase, por favor.
FS 1:	Gracias. Usted es muy amable.
MS 1:	No hay problema. El gusto es mío.
FS 1:	¡Qué día espléndido!
MS 1:	Verdad. Hoy hace un día estupendo. Llevamos una semana sin llover.
FS 1:	¡Ojalá que no llueva durante esta excursión!

MN:	Now, listen to this dialogue again.

(PAUSE)

MN:	Now, listen to question number **14**.

FS 1:	¿Quiénes son estas dos personas? A. dos turistas B. un hombre y su esposa C. un vendedor y una cliente

MN:	Now, listen to number **15**.

FS 1:	¿Qué tiempo hace? A. Está lloviendo. B. Hace buen tiempo. C. Hace mal tiempo.

TRACK 16 (CHIMES)

MN:	Dialogue number four.

FS 1:	Perdóneme, señor. Necesito cuatro lonchas de jamón, por favor.

MS 1:	En seguida, señora. ¿Algo más?

FS 1:	También, necesito mostaza, algunas aceitunas, y uvas.

MS 1:	Muy bien. Con mucho gusto, señora.

MN:	Now, listen to this dialogue again.

(PAUSE)

MN:	Now, listen to question number **16**.

FS 1:	¿Dónde está la señora? A. en una pastelería B. en un hotel C. en una tienda de comestibles

TRACK 17 (CHIMES)

MN:	Dialogue number five.

MS 1:	¿En qué puedo ayudarle, joven?

MS 2:	Debo ir a la calle Salamanca.

MS 1:	La calle Salamanca es muy larga. ¿Qué número busca usted?

MS 2:	Busco el número cien.

MS 1:	¡Ah! El número cien es la Embajada Americana. ¿Quiere ir a la Embajada?

MS 2:	Sí, señor. Eso es.
MS 1::	Pues, está en la esquina de la Avenida de los Estados Unidos.
MS 2:	¿Y cómo puedo llegar hasta allí?
MS 1:	Como queda muy lejos, le conviene ir en autobús.
MS 2:	¿Y cuál de ellos es el que me lleva?
MS 1:	Todos los autobuses que pasan por aquí van en aquella dirección.
MN:	Now, listen to this dialogue again.

(PAUSE)

MN:	Now, listen to question number 17.
FS 1:	¿Qué desea este joven? A. informaciones para ir a un lugar determinado B. donde puede conseguir un pasaporte C. algo que perdió
MN:	Now, listen to question number 18.
FS 1:	¿Dónde se halla la Embajada Americana? A. en la esquina de la Avenida de los Estados Unidos B. todos los autobuses que pasan por aquí C. muy cerca

TRACK 18	(CHIMES)
MN:	Dialogue number six.
MS 1::	La película que dan aquí me parece muy interesante.
FS 1:	Sí, actúan mis artistas favoritos.
MS 1:	¿Te gustaría ir a verla conmigo esta noche, María?
FS 1:	Lo siento, José, pero no puedo. Tengo que ir de compras.
MS 1:	¡Qué lástima!
FS 1:	Tengo una idea. Como va a darse la película toda la semana, ¿por qué no vamos el sábado?
MS 1:	¡Magnífico! ¿A qué hora vamos?
FS 1:	Estaré lista a las siete en punto.
MN:	Now, listen to this dialogue again.

(PAUSE)

MN: Now, listen to question number **19**.

FS 1: ¿Por qué no puede María aceptar la invitación de José?
A. Tiene cita con la peluquera.
B. Tiene que ir de tiendas.
C. A ella no le gusta la película.

MN: Now, listen to question number 20.

FS 1: ¿Adónde irán María y José el sábado?
A. a las tiendas
B. a un baile
C. al cine

TRACK 19 <center>(CHIMES)</center>

MN: Dialogue number seven.

MS 1: ¡Hola, Miguel! ¿Te das cuenta de que el sábado que viene es el cumpleaños de Tomás?

MS 2: Sí, Andrés, me acuerdo bien.

MS 1: Me gustaría organizar una fiesta en mi casa, pero no es posible, porque esa noche vienen unos amigos de mi padre.

MS 2: Podemos celebrarla en mi casa.

MS 1: ¿Te darán permiso tus padres?

MS 2: ¡Cómo no! Quieren mucho a Tomás.

MS 1: ¿Qué podremos servir a los invitados?

MS 2: A todos les gustan pasteles y helado.

MS 1: Y no debemos olvidarnos de darle algunos regalitos. ¿Qué sugieres?

MS 2: Podemos comprarle unos discos.

MN: Now, listen to this dialogue again.

(PAUSE)

MN: Now, listen to question number **21**.

FS 1: ¿Qué discuten Andrés y Miguel?
A. una fiesta del padre de Andrés
B. unos discos importantes
C. planes para ofrecer una fiesta a un amigo

TRACK 20 <center>(CHIMES)</center>

MN: Dialogue number eight.

MS 1: Buenos días. ¿En qué puedo servirle, señora?

FS 1:	Tengo un fuerte resfriado.
MS 1:	Le voy a dar un medicamento pero si no mejora usted, debe ver a un médico.
FS 1:	¿Hay un médico por aquí cerca?
MS 1:	A dos cuadras de aquí está el doctor López, calle de los Jardines, número trescientos cuarenta y ocho.
FS 1:	¿Cuándo puedo verle?
MS 1:	Está siempre en su consultorio hasta las ocho, menos durante las horas de siesta.
FS 1:	¿Es necesario llamarle antes?
MS 1:	No hace falta llamar. Usted no tiene que hacer más que esperar su turno en el despacho.
FS 1:	Muchísimas gracias. Usted es muy amable.
MN:	Now, listen to this dialogue again.

(PAUSE)

MN:	Now, listen to question number 22.
FS 1:	¿Con quién habla la señora? A. con un médico B. con un librero C. con un farmacéutico

TRACK 21   (CHIMES)

MN:	Dialogue number nine.
MS 1:	Ah, Rosita, tengo que hablar contigo.
FS 1:	¿De qué se trata, Roberto?
MS 1:	Acabo de saber que el señor González, nuestro profesor de español, se retirará en junio.
FS 1:	¿Pero cómo puede ser? Parece tan joven. ¿Es verdad?
MS 1:	Sí, es verdad. Le haremos un regalo.
FS 1:	Podríamos darle un reloj.
MS 1:	¿Qué más podemos hacer para mostrarle nuestro afecto?
FS 1:	Vamos a prepararle una fiesta.
MS 1:	Yo puedo tocar la guitarra en la fiesta.
FS 1:	Y nosotros cantaremos.

MN:	Now, listen to this dialogue again.

(PAUSE)

MN:	Now, listen to question number **23**.
FS 2:	¿Cuándo supo Roberto que el señor González va a retirarse? A. recientemente B. en junio C. mañana

TRACK 22   **(CHIMES)**

MN:	Dialogue number ten.
MS 1:	¡Ricardo! ¡Qué bueno verte en México, por fin!
MS 2:	Me alegro mucho de estar aquí, Ramón.
MS 1:	¿Qué tal el viaje en avión?
MS 2:	Dormí durante todo el viaje.
MS 1:	¿Tuviste algún problema en la aduana?
MS 2:	No tuve ninguno.
MS 2:	Vamos a recoger tus maletas. ¿Cuáles son?
MS 2:	Allí están. Las dos verdes.
MS 1:	Ahora, vamos a mi casa para que conozcas a mi familia.
MS 2:	Será un placer.

MN:	Now, listen to this dialogue again.

(PAUSE)

MN:	Now, listen to question number **24**.
FS 1:	¿Cómo se llama el viajero? A. Ramón B. Ricardo C. No es evidente.
MN:	Now, listen to question number **25**.
FS 1:	¿Cuántas piezas de equipaje tiene el viajero? A. dos B. tres C. cuatro
MN:	This is the end of Part B. Now go on to Part C.

(MUSIC)

MALE NARRATOR:	This is Part C of the Listening Test. There are six selections in this part consisting of longer dialogues and a few monologues. Each selection will be spoken only *once*. They are *not* printed in your test booklet. After each selection, you will hear several questions based on what you heard. The multiple-choice answers will not be spoken but they *are* printed in your booklet. The questions are also printed in your booklet. Choose the letter of the statement that is the best answer (A, B, C, or D) and blacken the corresponding space on the Answer Sheet. This **Part C** begins with question number **26** on your practice Answer Sheet. You will hear a chime to indicate the beginning of a new selection.

TRACK 23	<div align="center">(CHIMES)</div>
MN:	This is selection number one.
MALE SPEAKER 1:	En este diálogo, Elena habla por teléfono con su amiga Margarita. Hablan de las compras que cada una de ellas ha hecho el día anterior.
FEMALE SPEAKER 1:	¿Margarita? Soy yo... Elena. ¿A qué hora llegaste a casa ayer?
FEMALE SPEAKER 2:	A eso de las cinco, Elena. ¿Por qué?
FS 1:	Te llamé por teléfono y no estabas.
FS 2:	Estaba en los almacenes.
FS 1:	¡No me digas! Y yo también. Regresé a casa a las tres y estaba muy cansada. Dime, ¿qué compraste?
FS 2:	Me compré un vestido largo para la boda de mi sobrino.
FS 1:	Yo me compré unos zapatos blancos y guantes también.
FS 2:	Me gustaría verlos.
FS 1:	Esta noche estaré en casa. ¿Quieres venir?
FS 2:	Con mucho gusto. Pues, nos veremos más tarde. Hasta luego.
MN:	The following question is number **26** on your Answer Sheet.
FS 1:	¿Adónde fueron las dos damas ayer? (PAUSE TEN SECONDS)
MN:	Now, listen to question number **27**.
FS 1:	¿A qué hora llegó Margarita a casa? (PAUSE TEN SECONDS)
MN:	Question number 28.
FS 1:	¿Qué compraron Margarita y Elena? (PAUSE TEN SECONDS)

MN:	Question number **29**.
FS 1:	¿Por qué irá Margarita a casa de Elena esta noche? (PAUSE TEN SECONDS)
TRACK 24	(CHIMES)
MN:	This is selection number two.
FS 1:	En este monólogo, el narrador habla de una comida en casa de unos amigos.
MS 1:	Me llamo Roberto Carlos. Fue el viernes de la semana pasada cuando volvió Juan del ejército. Su familia me invitó a comer porque somos muy buenos amigos. Los primos y otros parientes de Juan estaban allí también. Comimos en el comedor alrededor de una mesa grande. Yo estaba sentado al lado de Juan. Su madre nos sirvió paella y carne asada. Me gustó más la paella. Durante la comida hablamos de muchas cosas. De postre, la madre había preparado un bizcocho de chocolate. Después de la comida, cantamos y tocamos la guitarra.
MN:	Question number **30**.
FS 1:	¿Cuándo volvió Juan del ejército? (PAUSE TEN SECONDS)
MN:	Question number **31**.
FS 1:	¿Por qué la familia de Juan le invitó a Roberto Carlos a comer en su casa? (PAUSE TEN SECONDS)
MN:	Question number **32**.
FS 1:	¿Qué personas estaban allí también? (PAUSE TEN SECONDS)
MN:	Question number **33**.
FS 1:	¿Dónde comieron? (PAUSE TEN SECONDS)
MN:	Question number **34**.
FS 1:	¿De qué hablaraon durante la comida? (PAUSE TEN SECONDS)
TRACK 25	(CHIMES)
MN:	This is selection number three.
FS 1:	En este diálogo, un señor y su esposa están en el campo dando un paseo en coche cuando de repente se para el coche.
MS 1:	¡Caramba! ¿Qué pasa? ¿Por qué se ha parado el motor?
FS 2:	No entiendo. No hemos tenido problemas hasta ahora.
MS 1:	Nunca tengo problemas cuando conduzco yo.

FS 2:	¡No me eches la culpa a mí!
MS 1:	Cuando lo usaste ayer andaba bien, ¿verdad? Y te dije que tenías que ponerle gasolina.
FS 2:	Eso es. Tú tienes razón. Se me olvidó.
MS 1:	Y ahora, ¿qué hacemos? No hay estación de gasolina por aquí.
FS 2:	La más cerca está a tres millas de aquí.
MS 1:	Yo lo sé. Estamos en el campo y, naturalmente, no hay estación de gasolina por aquí.
FS 2:	¡Mira! Veo una casa por allá. Puedes ir para saber si tienen teléfono.
MS 1:	Bueno, me voy.
FS 2:	Te espero aquí.
MN:	Question number 35.
FS 1:	¿Qué pasó en el camino? (PAUSE TEN SECONDS)
MN:	Question number 36.
FS 1:	¿Por qué se paró el coche? (PAUSE TEN SECONDS)
MN:	Question number 37.
FS 1:	¿Quién conduce? (PAUSE TEN SECONDS)
MN:	Question number 38.
FS 1:	¿Adónde va el señor para pedir ayuda? (PAUSE TEN SECONDS)
TRACK 26	(CHIMES)
MN:	This is selection number four.
MS 1:	En este monólogo, la muchacha habla de una mujer.
FS 1:	Acabo de leer en el periódico un artículo sobre una vecina, la señora Rodríguez. Ella ganó el premio gordo en la lotería. Me sorprendió mucho ver el artículo en la primera página. Pienso llamarla por teléfono en algunos minutos para felicitarla. Me gustaría saber lo que va hacer con el dinero que ganó. La señora Rodríguez es la madre de mi amiga, Isabel. Hace diez años que nos conocemos. Ella siempre ha sido muy simpática y generosa. Creo que no va a cambiar nada. Todos los vecinos siempre la han querido. Ahora voy a llamarla.
MN:	Question number 39.
MS 1:	¿De quién habla la muchacha?

	(PAUSE TEN SECONDS)
MN:	Question number 40.
MS 1:	¿Por qué piensa ella llamar a la señora Rodríguez? (PAUSE TEN SECONDS)
MN:	Question number 41.
MS 1:	¿Cuánto tiempo hace que las dos muchachas se conocen? (PAUSE TEN SECONDS)
MN:	Question number 42.
MS 1:	¿Cómo es la señora Rodríguez? (PAUSE TEN SECONDS)
TRACK 27	(CHIMES)
MN:	This is selection number five.
FS 1:	En este diálogo, Pedro y Pablo hablan de una bicicleta.
MS 1:	Estoy muy interesado en tu bicicleta, Pedro. Me gusta mucho. ¿En qué condición está?
MS 2:	Mi bicicleta está en perfecta condición, Pablo.
MS 1:	¿Por qué la vendes?
MS 2:	Porque voy a comprar un coche con el dinero que gané trabajando en el supermercado de mi padre.
MS 1:	¿Cuánto pides por la bicicleta?
MS 2:	Cincuenta dólares solamente.
MS 1:	Es muy cara. ¿Puedes bajar el precio?
MS 2:	No, lo siento mucho. Es casi nueva.
MS 1:	¿Cuándo la compraste?
MS 2:	Mis padres me la regalaron para mi cumpleaños hace algunos meses.
MS 1:	Me gustaría comprarla pero no tengo todo el dinero ahora.
MS 2:	Puedes dármelo la semana que viene si quieres.
MN:	Question number 43.
FS 1:	¿Quién vende la bicicleta? (PAUSE TEN SECONDS)
MN:	Question number 44.

FS 1:	¿Por qué quiere venderla el joven?
	(PAUSE TEN SECONDS)
MN:	Question number **45**.
FS 1:	¿Por cuánto dinero la vende?
	(PAUSE TEN SECONDS)
MN:	Question number **46**.
FS 1:	¿En qué condición está la bicicleta?
	(PAUSE TEN SECONDS)

TRACK 28	(CHIMES)
MN:	This is selection number six.
FS 1:	En este monólogo, el narrador habla de un grupo de jóvenes hispanos.
MS 1:	La semana pasada doscientos cincuenta chicos peruanos, colombianos y argentinos visitaron al Presidente de México. Uno de los líderes juveniles dio un simpático discurso para darles las gracias a él y a su gentil esposa por estas vacaciones pagadas. Desde su llegada hasta hoy, los jóvenes, acompañados por cincuenta guías nacionales de su misma edad, pasaron las noches en el Hotel Nacional donde tomaron comidas típicas del país. Salieron en visitas turísticas de varias y diversas actividades, por ejemplo, paseos a lugares históricos, museos, teatros y parques, así como sitios de diversión tanto en la playa como en la montaña y en la ciudad. Este intercambio internacional para jóvenes de mala situación económica forma parte de los programas de la Fundación del Niño.
MN:	Question number **47**.
FS 1:	¿Quiénes visitaron el país?
	(PAUSE TEN SECONDS)
MN:	Question number **48**.
FS 1:	¿A quiénes les dio las gracias el líder juvenil?
	(PAUSE TEN SECONDS)
MN:	Question number **49**.
FS 1:	¿En qué actividades tomaron parte los jóvenes?
	(PAUSE TEN SECONDS)
MN:	Question number **50**.
FS 1:	¿A qué hijos sirve este programa?
	(PAUSE TEN SECONDS)
MN:	This is the end of the listening portion of the SAT II Spanish test.

SPANISH-ENGLISH VOCABULARY

PART
VIII

The SAT II: Spanish test contains no English to be translated into Spanish and for that reason there is no need to include an English-Spanish vocabulary here. On the test, the student is expected to recognize the meaning of the Spanish words used. Therefore, the following Spanish-English vocabulary is included here.

If you look up a Spanish word and it is not listed in the pages that follow, consult the vocabulary given in the General Review, which is in Part IV, beginning with §2. In particular, consult the *general index* under the entry Vocabulary where you will find § references to such topics as the following: adjectives, adverbs, antonyms, cognates, conjunctions, indefinite and negative words, nouns, prepositions and prepositional phrases, common irregular present participles, pronouns, proverbs, synonyms, tricky words, and verbs with prepositions. For the most part, I have tried not to repeat in the following vocabulary Spanish words and meanings in English already given in those § numbers.

To find certain categories and types of words, especially needed for a mastery of grammatical control and idioms, including verbal, idiomatic, common and useful expressions, you must consult the *general index*. For other Spanish words of interest to you, which are not given in this book, consult your Spanish-English dictionary.

The Spanish alphabet contains the letters **ch, ll, ñ,** and **rr** which are considered separately. A Spanish word that begins with or contains **ch** is alphabetized *after* the letter **c; ll** is alphabetized after the letter **l;** and **ñ** is alphabetized after the letter **n.** Therefore, in the following alphabetical listing of words, you will find **falla** listed after **falte, mañana** after **manzana, ochenta** after **ocupar.** This rule does not apply to the double consonant **rr.**

A

a *prep.* at, to; *see also* **a** in idioms **§14.16**

abajo *adv.* below, downstairs, down below

abandonar *v.* to abandon, leave

abandono *n.m.* abandonment

abarcar *v.* to encompass, embrace, take in

abatido *adj.* dejected, unhappy

abatir *v.* to knock down, throw down

abeja *n.f.* bee

abierto *past part.* of **abrir**

abismo *n.m.* abyss

abogado *n.m.* lawyer

abolir *v.* to abolish, repeal

aborigen *adj.* aboriginal

aborrecer *v.* to abhor, hate

abracé *v. form of* **abrazar**

abrasar *v.* to burn, fire

abrazar *v.* to embrace, clamp, hug; **abrazarse** *v.* to hug (embrace) each other

abrazo *n.m.* embrace, hug

abrigar *v.* to cherish, harbor, hold

abrigo *n.m.* coat, overcoat

abril *n.m.* April

abrir *v.* to open

absolutamente *adv.* absolutely

absoluto *adj.* absolute

absolver *v.* to absolve, acquit

absorber *v.* to absorb

absorto *adj.* absorbed

abstenerse *v.* to abstain

abuelo *n.m.* grandfather; **abuela** *n.f.* grandmother; **los abuelos**/grandparents

abundancia *n.f.* abundance

abundar *v.* to abound, be abundant

aburrir *v.* to annoy, bore, vex; **aburrirse** *v.* to become bored, grow tired, grow weary

abuso *n.m.* abuse

acá *adv.* here; **por acá**/this way, through here, around here

acabar *v.* to achieve, complete, end, finish; **acabar de**/to have just; **acabar con**/to end up by (with); **acabarse** *v.* to be used up; *see also* **§7.112ff, §14.22, por** in idioms **§14.37, §7.28**

academia *n.f.* academy; **académico** *n.m.* academician, professor, teacher

acariciar *v.* to caress

acaso *adv.* maybe, perhaps

acceso *n.m.* access

accidente *n.m.* accident

acción *n.f.* action

aceite *n.m.* oil

acelerar *v.* to accelerate

acento *n.m.* accent

aceptar *v.* to accept

acera *n.f.* sidewalk

acerca de/about, concerning

acercar *v.* to bring near, place near; **acercarse** *v.* to approach, come (draw) near

acero *n.m.* steel

acertar *v.* to hit the mark, hit upon, do (something) right, succeed (in)

aclamar *v.* to acclaim, applaud, shout

aclarar *v.* to explain, clarify, make clear, rinse

acompañar *v.* to accompany, escort, go with

acondicionado *adj.* conditioned; **aire acondicionado**/air conditioned

acondicionamiento *n.m.* conditioning; **acondicionamiento de aire**/air conditioning

aconsejable *adj.* advisable; **aconsejar** *v.* to advise, counsel

acontecer *v.* to happen

acordar *v.* to accord, agree; **acordarse** *v.* to remember

acostar *v.* to put to bed; **acostarse** *v.* to go to bed, lie down

acostumbrados *adj.* accustomed; **acostumbrar** *v.* to accustom, be accustomed, be in the habit of; **acostumbrarse** *v.* to be accustomed

acróbata *n.m.f.* acrobat; *n.f.* acrobatics

actitud *n.f.* attitude, position

actividad *n.f.* activity

activo, activa *adj.* active

acto *n.m.* act

actor, actriz *n.m.f.* actor, actress

actual *adj.* actual, present, present-day

actualidad *n.f.* actuality, present time

actualmente *adv.* at present

actuar *v.* to act

acuchillar *v.* to knife, cut, slash, cut open

acudir *v.* to attend, be present at, respond (to a call), come to the rescue

acueducto *n.m.* aqueduct

acuerdo *v. form of* **acordar;** *n.m.* agreement; **de acuerdo con**/in accord with, according to; *see also* §14.26

acumulación *n.f.* accumulation

acusar *v.* to accuse

acústica *n.f.* acoustics; **acústico** *adj.* acoustic

adaptarse *v.* to adapt oneself (itself)

adecuada *adj.* adequate

adelantar(se) *v.* to advance, keep on, progress, go ahead, go forward

adelante *adv.* forward, ahead; **de hoy en adelante**/from now on

ademán *n.m.* attitude, gesture; **ademanes** *n.m.pl.* manners

además *adv.* furthermore; **además de**/in addition to

adentro *adv.* inside, within

adicional *adj.* additional

adiós *interj.* good-bye

adivinando *pres. part. of* **adivinar** *v.* to guess, divine, foretell

administración *n.f.* administration; **administrador, administradora** *n.m.f.* administrator

admiración *n.f.* admiration; **admirador, admiradora** *n.m.f.* admirer; **admirar** *v.* to admire

admitir *v.* to admit, allow, permit

adonde *adv.* to where; **adondequiera**/to wherever; see §7.50ff

adoptar *v.* to adopt

adorar *v.* to adore, worship

adornar *v.* to adorn; **adorno** *n.m.* adornment

adquiere *v. form of* **adquirir** *v.* to acquire, get, obtain

aduana *n.f.* customs, customs office; **aduanero** *n.m.* customs officer

adular *v.* to flatter

adulto, adulta *adj.* adult

adversario *n.m.* adversary, foe, opponent

advertir *v.* to advise, give notice (warning), take notice of, warn, notify

aeroplano *n.m.* airplane, plane

aeropuerto *n.m.* airport

afable *adj.* affable, friendly

afán *n.m.* anxiety, eagerness

afecto *n.m.* affection; **afectuosamente** *adv.* affectionately

afeitarse *v.* to shave oneself; **¡aféitatela!**/shave it off!

afición *n.f.* fondness; **aficionado, aficionada** *n.m.f.* amateur, fan (fond of)

afirmación *n.f.* affirmation; **afirmar** *v.* to affirm, assert

afligir *v.* to afflict, affect, grieve

afortunado *adj.* fortunate

africano, africana *n.m.f., adj.* African

afuera *adv.* outside

agarrar *v.* to grasp, get hold of, obtain, come upon, seize, clutch

agencia *n.f.* agency; **agencia de viajes**/travel agency

agente *n.m.* agent; **agente de policía**/police officer

agitado *adj.* busy; **agitar** *v.* to agitate, wave, shake up, stir; **agitarse** *v.* to become excited

agosto *n.m.* August

agotado *adj.* exhausted, used up; **agotar** *v.* to exhaust, use up

agradable *adj.* pleasant, agreeable; **agradar** *v.* to please, be pleasing

agradecer *v.* to be thankful, grateful, to show gratitude, to thank; **agradecido** *adj.* grateful, thankful; **agradecimiento** *n.m.* thankfulness

agrado *n.m.* appreciation

agrandar *v.* to enlarge, grow larger, increase

agravar *v.* to aggravate, make worse

agregar *v.* to add, collect, gather

agrícola *adj.* agricultural; **agricultura** *n.f.* agriculture

agrupar *v.* to group

agua *n.f.* water **(el agua)**

aguantar *v.* to tolerate, endure, bear

aguardar *v.* to wait, await, wait for, expect

agudo *adj.* acute, sharp

agüero *n.m.* omen, augury

águila *n.f.* eagle (el águila)

aguja *n.f.* needle

agujero *n.m.* hole

ahí *adv.* there; *see also* §10.12

ahogado *adj.* drowned; **ahogar** *v.* to choke; **ahogarse** *v.* to drown

ahora *adv.* now; **ahora mismo**/right now, right away

ahorrar *v.* to save, economize

aire *n.m.* air; **al aire libre**/in the open air, outdoors; **el acondicionamiento de aire**/air conditioning

aislado *adj.* isolated; **aislamiento** *n.m.* isolation; **aislarse** *v.* to isolate oneself

ajedrez *n.m.* chess

ajeno *adj.* foreign, alien, other, different, belonging to another

ajustar *v.* to adjust

al *contraction of* **a** + **el;** *see also* §14.18

al + **inf.**/on, upon + *pres. part.;* **al llegar**/on (upon) arriving; **al partir**/on (upon) leaving; *see also* §7.186, §7.201, §14.18

ala *n.f.* wing, brim of a hat

alabar *v.* to praise

álamo *n.m.* poplar tree

alargar *v.* to lengthen, make longer; **¡alárguemela!**/lengthen it!

alarma *n.f.* alarm

alba *n.f.* dawn **(el alba)**

alcalde *n.m.* mayor

alcanzar *v.* to arrive, reach, attain, overtake

alcoba *n.f.* bedroom

aldea *n.f.* village

alegrarse *v.* to be glad, rejoice; **alegre** *adj.* happy; **alegremente** *adv.* happily; **alegría** *n.f.* joy, happiness

alejar *v.* to move away, to be distant, separate, draw away; **alejarse** *v.* to go away

alemán *n.m., adj.* German; **alemanes, alemanas** *adj.* German; **Alemania** *n.f.* Germany

alentar *v.* to encourage

alerto, alerta *adj.* alert

alfabetizar *v.* to teach reading and writing, to alphabetize; **alfabeto** *n.m.* alphabet

alfiler *n.m.* brooch, pin

alfombra *n.f.* carpet, rug

algo *indef. pron.* something

algodón *n.m.* cotton

alguien *indef. pron.* somebody, someone

algún, alguno, alguna *adj., pron,* some, any, something; **alguna vez**/some time

alhaja *n.f.* jewel, gem

alianza *n.f.* alliance

aliento *n.m.* breath, encouragement

alimento *n.m.* food

aliviar *v.* to lighten, relieve

alma *n.f.* soul, spirit **(el alma)**

almacén *n.m.* department store, general store

almohada *n.f.* pillow

almorzar *v.* to lunch, have lunch; **almuerzo** *n.m.* lunch; *also v. form of* **almorzar**

alojamiento *n.m.* lodging; **alojarse** *v.* to find lodging

alquilar *v.* to rent

alrededor *adv.* around

altar *n.m.* altar (church)

alteración *n.f.* alteration; **alteraciones**/alterations, changes; **alterar** *v.* to alter, change; **alterado**/changed, disturbed, upset

alternativamente *adv.* alternately

altísimo *adj.* very tall, very high

altitud *n.f.* altitude

altivo *adj.* proud, haughty

alto, alta *adj.* high, tall; *n.m.* height; **lo alto**/the top; **los altos**/top floor; **las altas, los altos**/tall women, tall men, tall people; **más alto**/higher, highest

altura *n.f.* height

alumbrado, alumbrada *adj.* lighted; **alumbrar** *v.* shine, illuminate, light, enlighten; **alumbrarse** *v.* to be (get) high, get tipsy, become lively

alumna, alumno *n.f.m.* pupil, student

alzar *v.* to heave, lift, pick up, raise

allá *adv.* over there; **por allá**/that way; *see also* §10.12

allí *adv.* there; **he allí**/here you have; *see also* §10.12

amable *adj.* pleasant, nice; **amablemente** *adv.* in a friendly way

amado *adj.* loved, beloved

amanecer *v.* to dawn; *n.m.* dawn

amante *n.m.* lover; *n.f.* mistress

amar *v.* to love

amargamente *adv.* bitterly; **amargo** *adj.* bitter; **amargura** *n.f.* bitterness

amarillo *n.m., adj.* yellow

ámbar *n.m.* amber

ambas, ambos *adj.* both

ambición *n.f.* ambition

ambiente *n.m.* surroundings, atmosphere

ambulante *adj.* ambulatory; **vendedor ambulante**/traveling salesman

amenazar *v.* to menace, threaten

ameno *adj.* pleasant, pleasing

América latina *n.f.* Latin America

americano *n.m., adj.* American

ametralladora *n.f.* machine gun

amiga, amigo *n.f.m.* friend; *see also* §5.60ff

amigote *n.m.* chum, pal; **amiguitos** *n.m.pl.* little friends

amistad *n.f.* friendship, friend, amnesty; **amistoso** *adj.* friendly

amo, ama *n.m.f.* owner, master, head of household

amor *n.m.* love; **amoroso** *adj.* affectionate, loving

amotinarse *v.* to mutiny, riot, rebel

amplia, amplio, amplios *adj.* ample, full

amueblar *v.* to furnish

analfabeto *n.m., adj.* illiterate

análisis *n.m.* analysis

anciana, anciano *n.f.m.* old woman, old man; *adj.* old

ancho *n.m.* width; **ancho, ancha** *adj.* wide

andaluz *adj.* of or pertaining to Andalucía

andar *v.* to walk, to run (machine); **se anda**/one walks, a person walks; *see also* §7.198

anduve *v. form of* **andar**

anfiteatro *n.m.* amphitheater

ángel *n.m.* angel; **angélico** *adj.* angelic

angosto *adj.* narrow

ángulo *n.m.* angle, corner

angustia *n.f.* anguish; **angustiado** *adj.* distressed, in anguish; **angustiar** *v.* to distress, anguish

anhelo *n.m.* eagerness, desire, yearning, longing

anillo *n.m.* ring (finger)

animado *adj.* animated, alive, lively

animalito *n.m.* little animal

animar *v.* to animate, enliven, cheer up

aniversario *n.m.* anniversary

anoche *adv.* last night, yesterday evening

anochecer *n.m.* nightfall

ansiedad *n.f.* anxiety; **ansioso** *adj.* anxious, eager

ante *prep.* before, in front, in the presence of

anteayer *adv.* day before yesterday

antecesor *n.m.* ancestor, predecessor

antemano *adv.* **de antemano**/ beforehand, previously

anteojo *n.m.* spyglass, telescope; **anteojos**/eye glasses, binoculars

anterior *adj.* previous

antes *adv.* formerly, first, before; **antes (de)**/before, in front of; **antes (de) que** *conj.* before; **cuanto antes**/as soon as possible; *see also* §5.64, §12.3, §14.22

anticipar *v.* to anticipate

anticuada *adj.* antiquated, old

antigüedad *n.f.* antiquity

antiguo, antigua *adj.* former, ancient, old

antipatía *n.f.* dislike, antipathy; **antipático** *adj.* unfriendly

anual *adj.* annual; **anualmente** *adv.* annually

anular *v.* to annul, make void

anunciar *v.* to announce, foretell, proclaim; **anuncio** *n.m.* announcement

anzuelo *n.m.* fishhook

añadir *v.* to add

año *n.m.* year

apagar *v.* to extinguish, put out a light (flame)

aparato *n.m.* apparatus, appliance

aparecer *v.* to appear, show up

apariencia *n.f.* appearance

apartamento (apartamiento) *n.m.* apartment

apartar *v.* to separate; **apartarse de** *v.* to withdraw from, separate from

aparte *adj.* aside, apart

apasionado *adj.* impassioned person

apellido *n.m.* family name

apenas *adv.* hardly, scarcely; **apenas si**/hardly; **apenas...cuando**/hardly, scarcely...when

apetito *n.m.* appetite

apetitoso *adj.* appetizing, tasty

apiadarse de *v.* to have pity on

aplaudir *v.* to applaud

aplazar *v.* to postpone

aplicaciones *n.f.pl.* applications

aplicado *adj.* hard-working, diligent; **aplicar** *v.* to apply

apoderarse (de) *v.* to take power, take possession

aportar *v.* to contribute

apóstol *n.m.* apostle

apoyados *adj.* leaning

apoyar(se) *v.* to aid, support, lean on; **apoyo** *n.m.* support

apreciar *v.* to appreciate; **aprecio** *n.m.* esteem

aprender *v* to learn; **lo aprendido**/ what was learned; **se aprende**/is learned

apresurarse *v.* to rush, hurry, hasten

apretar(se) *v.* to clench, squeeze, tighten

aprovechar(se) *v.* to make use of; take advantage of, avail oneself

aproximadamente *adv.* approximately; **aproximarse** *v.* to approach, draw near

apuesta *n.f.* bet, wager

apuntar *v.* to begin to show, appear

apurarse *v.* to fret, grieve, worry; **apuro** *n.m.* distress, predicament, worry, concern

aquel *adj.* that; *see also* §5.54, §6.56ff

aquí *adv.* here; **por aquí**/this way, around here; **he aquí**/here you have, *see also* §10.13

árbol *n.m.* tree

arbusto *n.m.* shrub

arder *v.* to blaze, burn

ardía *v. form of* **arder**

ardiente *adj.* ardent

ardoroso *adj.* fiery

arena *n.f.* sand, arena

argentino *adj.* of or pertaining to Argentina

argumento *n.m.* argument, premise

arma *n.f.* arm, weapon

armada *n.f.* fleet

armado *adj.* armed

armar *v.* to arm

armario *n.m.* closet

armonía *n.f.* harmony

arqueólogo *n.m.* archaeologist

arquitecto *n.m.* architect

arquitectónico *adj.* architectural

arquitectura *n.f.* architecture

arrancar *v.* to pull out, tear off

arrasar *v.* to level, raze

arrastrar *v.* to drag

arrebatar *v.* to snatch, captivate

arreglar *v.* to repair, arrange, adjust, regulate, settle, put in order, put back in working condition

arreglarse *v.* to come to an agreement, compromise, conform, settle

arreglo *n.m.* arrangement; **con**

arreglo a/according to
arrepentirse de *v.* to repent
arriba *adv.* upstairs, up, high, above
arrodillados *adj.* kneeling;
  arrodillarse *v.* to kneel
arrojar *v.* to fling, hurl, throw;
  arrojarse. *v.* to throw oneself, rush
arroyo *n.m.* stream, gutter
arroz *n.m.* rice; **arroz con pollo**/
  chicken with rice
arruga *n.f.* wrinkle (on skin)
arruinado *adj.* in ruins
arte *n.m. or f.* art; **las bellas artes**/
  fine arts
artefacto *n.m.* artifact, device
articular *v.* to articulate
artículo *n.m.* article
artista *n.m.f.* artist
artístico *adj.* artistic
asaltar *v.* to assail, assault
ascender *v.* to ascend, lift, raise, go
  up, promote
ascenso *n.m.* ascent, rise, promotion
ascensor *n.m.* elevator
asciende *v. form of* **ascender**
asegurar *v.* to assure, affirm, assert,
  insure
asentir *v.* to assent, agree
así *adv.* thus, so, like this, like that; **así**
  que/as soon as, so that; **así como**/as
  well as, just as; **así...como**/both...and;
  not only...but also
asiento *n.m.* seat
asignatura *n.f.* subject, course (of
  study)
asir *v.* to grasp, seize
asistencia *n.f.* assistance
asistir *v.* to attend
asno *n.m.* ass, donkey
asomarse a *v.* to look out of
asombrar *v.* to amaze, astonish,
  frighten; **asombrarse** *v.* to be
  amazed
asombro *n.m.* amazement
aspecto *n.m.* aspect, appearance
aspiración *n.f.* aspiration
aspirar *v.* to aspire
aspirina *n.f.* aspirin
astro *n.m.* star
astronauta *n.m.f.* astronaut
astronomía *n.f.* astronomy
astrónomo *n.m.* astronomer
asturiano, asturianas *n., adj.* of or
  pertaining to Asturias
asumir *v.* to assume, take upon
  oneself
asunto *n.m.* affair, matter, subject
asustado *adj.* frightened, afraid
asustar *v.* to frighten, scare
asustarse *v.* to be (become)
  frightened, scared
atacar *v.* to attack
atadas *adj.* tied
ataque *n.m.* attack
atar *v.* to bind, tie

atención *n.f.* attention; **prestar**
  atención/to pay attention
atender *v.* to pay attention, to attend
  to
atendiendo *pres. part. of* **atender**
atenerse *v.* to rely on, depend on
atentamente *adv.* courteously
atento *adj.* attentive, helpful
aterrizar *v.* to land (airplane)
aterrorizada *adj.* full of terror,
  frightened
atlántico *adj.* Atlantic
atleta *n.m.f.* athlete
atmósfera *n.f.* atmosphere
ató *v. form of* **atar**
atormentado *adj.* tormented
atormentarse *v.* to torment (distress)
  oneself
atracción *n.f.* attraction
atractivo *adj.* attractive
atraer *v.* to attract, allure, charm
atraído *past part of* **atraer**
atrás *adv.* back, behind, to the rear
atrasarse *v.* to lag behind, be slow,
  late
atravesar *v.* to cross, go (run) through
atreverse *v.* to dare, venture
atrevido *adj.* bold, daring
atropellar *v.* to run over, trample
atropello *n.m.* car accident
auditorio *n.m.* audience
aula *n.f.* classroom (**el aula**)
aúlla *v. form of* **aullar** *v.* to howl
aumentar *v.* to increase, augment
aun, aún *adv.* also, as well, even
aunque *conj.* although
aureola *n.f.* halo
aureolarse *refl. v.* to become glorified
ausencia *n.f.* absence
ausente *adj.* absent
auténtica *adj.* authentic
autobús *n.m.* bus
automóvil *n.m.* automobile, car
automovilístico *adj.* automobile
autor, autora *n.m.f.* author
autoridad *n.f.* authority
autorizar *v.* to authorize
auxiliar *v.* to aid, assist, help
auxilio *n.m.* help
avalancha *n.f.* avalanche
avanzados *adj.* advanced
avanzar *v.* to advance
avaro *n.m., adj.* stingy, avaricious
ave *n.f.* bird
avenida *n.f.* avenue
aventura *n.f.* adventure
aventurarse *v.* to take a chance, take
  a risk
avergonzado *adj.* ashamed
avergonzarse *v.* to be (feel) ashamed
averiguar *v.* to find out, inquire,
  investigate
avión *n.m.* airplane, plane
avisar *v.* to warn
aviso *n.m.* notice, warning, word

avivar *v.* to inflame, enliven
ayer *adv.* yesterday
ayuda *n.f.* help, assistance, aid
ayudante *n.m.f.* aid, assistant, helper
ayudar *v.* to help, aid, assist;
  ¡ayúdeme!/help me!
ayuntamiento *n.m.* municipal
  government
azteca *n., adj.* Aztec
azúcar *n.m.* sugar; **la caña de azúcar**/
  sugar cane
azul *n.m., adj.* blue
azur *n.m., adj.* azure

B

bachillerato *n.m.* baccalaureate
bahía *n.f.* bay, harbor
bailar *v.* to dance; **bailarín** *n.m.*
  dancer
bailarina *n.f.* dancer
baile *n.m.* dance
bajar *v.* to go (come) down, descend,
  lower, get off a moving vehicle
bajo *adj., adv., prep.* under, below,
  beneath, short
bala *n.f.* bullet, ball, shot
balazo *n.m.* bullet wound
balbucear *v.* to stammer, hesitate (in
  speech)
balsa *n.f.* raft, barge
banco *n.m.* bank, bench
banda *n.f.* band, scarf, ribbon, sash
bandeja *n.f.* tray
bandera *n.f.* banner, flag, standard
banderilla *n.f.* banderilla (ornamental
  dart that a banderillero uses to stick
  in the neck or shoulder of a bull)
bandido *n.m.* bandit
banquero *n.m.* banker
banquete *n.m.* banquet, dinner
bañar *v.* to bathe
bañarse *v.* to bathe oneself, take a bath,
  bathe
baño *n.m.* bath; **el cuarto de baño**/
  bathroom
barato *adj.* cheap
barba *n.f.* beard
bárbaro *n.m., adj.* barbarian, rude,
  barbarous
barbero *n.m.* barber
barco *n.m.* boat
barril *n.m.* barrel
barrio *n.m.* section, quarter
base *n.f.* basis
bastante *adj., adv.* enough, sufficient
bastar *v.* to suffice, be enough,
  sufficient; *see also* **§6.20**
basura *n.f.* trash, garbage, refuse,
  sweepings
batalla *n.f.* battle
batallar *v.* to battle, fight, struggle
batallón *n.m.* battalion
batir *v.* to beat, strike

batirse *v.* to fight
baúl *n.m.* trunk (baggage)
bautizar *v.* to baptize, christen
beber *v.* to drink; **se bebe**/one drinks; **bebida** *n.f.* drink; *see also* §14.21
béisbol *n.m.* baseball
bella, bello *adj.* beautiful; **bellas artes**/fine arts
belleza *n.f.* beauty
bendecir *v.* to bless, consecrate
bendición *n.f.* blessing
bendigo *v. form of* **bendecir**
beneficiar *v.* to benefit
benévolo *adj.* benevolent
benignidad *n.f.* mildness, kindness
besar *v.* to kiss; **beso** *n.m.* kiss
bestia *n.f.* beast, animal
biblioteca *n.f.* library
bibliotecario, bibliotecaria *n.m.f.* librarian
bicicleta *n.f.* bicycle
biciclista *n.m.f.* bicycle rider, cyclist
bien *adv.* well; *n.m.* good, benefit, welfare; *see also* §10.7
bienestar *n.m.* well-being
bienvenida *n.f., adj.* welcome
billete *n.m.* ticket; **billete de ida y vuelta** /round-trip ticket
biología *n.f.* biology
bizarro *adj.* brave, gallant
bizcocho *n.m.* cake, biscuit
blanco *n.m., adj.* white
blando *adj.* bland, soft, weak
blusa *n.f.* blouse
boca *n.f.* mouth
boda(s) *n.f. (pl.)* wedding
boicot *n.m.* boycott
boliviano *n., adj.* of or pertaining to Bolivia
bolsa *n.f.* purse, stock market
bolsillo *n.m.* pocket
bombilla *n.f.* bulb (electric light)
bondad *n.f.* goodness, kindness
bondadoso *adj.* kind
bonita, bonito *adj.* pretty
borde *n.m.* border, brim, brink, edge
bordear *v.* to border
bordo *n.m.* board; **a bordo**/on board, aboard
borrador *n.m.* eraser
borrar *v.* to erase, obliterate, cross out
bosque *n.m.* forest, woods
bostezar *v.* to yawn, gape
botella *n.f.* bottle
botica *n.f.* drugstore
botón *n.m.* button
bracero *n.m.* laborer
bracito *n.m.* little arm
bravo, brava *adj.* brave
brazalete *n.m.* bracelet
brazo *n.m.* arm
breve *adj.* brief
brevedad *n.f.* brevity
brillando *adj., pres. part. of* **brillar** shining

brillar *v.* to shine, glitter, sparkle
brindar *v.* to invite, offer
brisa *n.f.* breeze
británico *adj.* British
broma *n.f.* joke
bronce *n.m.* bronze
brotar *v.* to sprout, bud
brújula *n.f.* compass
buen, bueno, buena, buenos, buenas *adj.* good; **buenos días**/hello, good day; **el visto bueno**/approval; *see also* §5.12, §5.20
bufanda *n.f.* muffler, scarf
búlgaro *adj.* of or pertaining to Bulgaria
bullir *v.* to boil
buque *n.m.* boat, ship
burla *n.f.* jest, mockery, trick
burlarse (de) *v.* to make fun (of), poke fun (at), ridicule
burrito *n.m.* little burro, donkey; **burro** *n.m.* donkey
busca *n.f.* search
buscar *v.* to look for, seek
buscase *v. form of* **buscar**
busto *n.m.* bust (sculptured work of art)
butaca *n.f.* armchair, orchestra seat

C

caballería *n.f.* cavalry; **caballero** *n.m.* gentleman, knight
caballito *n.m.* small (little) horse
caballo *n.m.* horse
cabello *n.m.* hair
caber *v.* to be contained, fit into
cabeza *n.f.* head
cabo *n.m.* end; **llevar a cabo**/to bring about, succeed in, accomplish; **al cabo de**/at the end of; **al fin y al cabo**/in the long run
cabra *n.f.* goat
cada *adj.* each
cadena *n.f.* chain
caer(se) *v.* to fall, knock down (over), to fell; **dejar caer**/to drop
café *n.f.* coffee, café
cafetería *n.f.* cafeteria
caída *n.f.* fall
caído *past part. of* **caer**
caja *n.f.* box
cajero, cajera *n.m.f.* bank teller
cajón *n.m.* box, carton
calcetín *n.m.* sock
calentar *v.* to heat, warm (up)
calentarse *v.* to warm oneself, to become (get) excited (angry)
calidad *n.f.* quality, worth
caliente *adj.* warm, hot
californiano, californiana *n.m.f., adj.* of or pertaining to California
calma *n.f.* calmness, composure

calmar *v.* to calm
calor *n.m.* heat; *see also* **hacer** in idioms §14.28 and **tener** §14.42
calorcito *n.m.* warmth
caluroso *adj.* warm
calvo *adj.* bald
calzar *v.* to shoe, wear (shoes), put on shoes
calzas *n.f.pl.* stockings, hose
callado *adj.* quiet, silent, in silence (silently)
callarse *v.* to keep quiet (still), to be quiet (still, silent)
calle *n.f.* street; **calle abajo**/down the street
calló *v. form of* **callar(se)**
cama *n.f.* bed; **guardar cama**/to remain (stay) in bed
cámara *n.f.* chamber, room
camarero *n.m.* waiter; **camarera** *n.f.* waitress
cambiar(se) *v.* to change; **cambiarse de ropa**/to change clothing
cambio *n.m.* change, exchange; **en cambio**/on the other hand; **a cambio de**/in exchange for
caminar *v.* to walk, move along
camino *n.m.* road, way, walk; **camino de**/on the way to; **en camino**/on the road
camión *n.m.* truck
camisa *n.f.* shirt; **camisa de seda**/silk shirt
campana *n.f.* bell
campanada *n.f.* striking (peal) of a bell
campanario *n.m.* belfry, bell tower
campanilla *n.f.* small hand bell
campaña *n.f.* campaign, field
campeón *n.m.* champion
campesina *n.f.* farmer's wife; **campesino, campesina** *n.m.f.* farmer; *adj.* pertaining to the country
campo *n.m.* field, campus, country (opposite of city), countryside
canal *n.m.* canal, channel
canario *n.m.* canary; **las Islas Canarias**/Canary Islands
canción *n.f.* song
candidato, candidata *n.m.f.* candidate
cansado, cansada, cansados, cansadas *adj.* tired
cansancio *n.m.* fatigue, tiredness, weariness
cansar *v.* to tire, fatigue, weary
cansarse *v.* to become tired, become weary, get tired (weary)
cantando *pres. part. of* **cantar**; **cantando a grito pelado**/singing at the top of one's lungs
cantante *n.m.f.* singer
cantar *v.* to sing
cantatriz *n.f.* singer
cantidad *n.f.* quantity

canto *n.m.* canto, epic poem, song, singing

caña *n.f.* pole, stick, cane, reed, rod; **caña de pescar**/fishing rod

cañón *n.m.* cannon

caos *n.m.* chaos

capa *n.f.* cape, cloak

capaces *pl. of* **capaz**

capacidad *n.f.* capacity

capaz *adj.* capable, competent

capilla *n.f.* chapel

capital *n.m.* capital (money, finances); **la capital**/capital city

capitán *n.m.* captain

capítulo *n.m.* chapter

capricho *n.m.* caprice, desire, whim

captada, capturados *adj.* captured

cara *n.f.* face

carácter *n.m.* character

caracteres *n.m.pl.* character; **caracteres históricos**/historical characters

características *n.f.pl.* characteristics

característico *adj.* characteristic

caracterizar *v.* to characterize

¡caramba! *interj.* Darn it! Oh, nuts!

carbón *n.m.* coal

carcajada *n.f.* guffaw, loud laughter

cárcel *n.f.* jail

carecer (de) *v.* to be in need, lack, need

cargado, cargada *adj.* loaded, heavy

cargar *v.* to charge, load, burden

cargo *n.m.* burden, task, charge, load, position, post; **hacer(se) cargo de**/to realize, take over, take charge of

Caribe *n., adj.* Caribbean

caricaturista *n.m.f.* caricaturist, cartoonist

caridad *n.f.* charity

cariño *n.m.* affection, warmth

cariñoso *adj.* affectionate, loving

carlismo *n.m.* Carlism

carlista *n.m.f.* Carlist

carnaval *n.m.* carnival

carne *n.f.* meat; **carnicería** *n.f.* butcher shop; **carnicero** *n.m.* butcher

caro *adj.* expensive

carpintero *n.m.* carpenter

carrera *n.f.* career, race, course, run

carretera *n.f.* highway

carrito *n.m.* little wagon, cart

carta *n.f.* letter, card; **una partida de cartas**/game of cards

cartera *n.f.* wallet

cartero *n.m.* mailman, postman

casa *n.f.* house; **en casa**/at home, home; **casa de correos**/post office

casados *adj.* married; **recién casados**/newlyweds; **casamiento** *n.m.* marriage, wedding

casarse *v.* to get married, marry; **casarse con**/to marry someone; **Juan se casó con María**/John married Mary

casi *adv.* almost, nearly

casilla *n.f.* hut

casita *n.f.* little house

caso *n.m.* case, matter; **en caso que**/in case that; **hacer caso a** *or* **de**/to pay attention to; **en caso de que**/in case; **en todo caso**/in any case

castañuelas *n.f.* castanets

castellano *n.m., adj.* Castilian

castigar *v.* to punish

castigo *n.m.* punishment

castillo *n.m.* castle, fortress

casualidad *n.f.* chance, coincidence; **por casualidad**/by chance

catalán *n., adj.* of or pertaining to Catalan

catástrofe *n.f.* catastrophe

catedral *n.f.* cathedral

catedrático, catedrática *n.m.f.* professor

categoría *n.f.* category

Católica *adj.* Catholic

catorce *n.m., adj.* fourteen

caucho *n.m.* rubber

caudillo *n.m.* commander, leader

causa *n.f.* cause; **a causa de**/because of, on account of

causar *v.* to cause

caverna *n.f.* cave, cavern

cayéndose *pres. part. of* **caerse**

cayó *v. form of* **caer**

caza *n.f.* hunting, hunt

ceder *v.* to cede, give in, give up, yield

celda *n.f.* cell

celebrar *v.* to celebrate

célebre *adj.* famous, celebrated

celebridad *n.f.* celebrity, fame

cementerio *n.m.* cemetery

cemento *n.m.* cement

cenar *v.* to dine, have dinner, have supper, eat supper; **cena** *n.f.* supper

cenicero *n.m.* ash tray

cenit *n.m.* zenith

cenizas *n.f.pl.* ashes

censurar *v.* to censure

centavo *n.m.* cent, penny

centenar *n.m.* hundred; **centenares**/hundreds

centenario *n.m.* centenary

centro *n.m.* center, downtown

ceñir *v.* to surround

cepillar *v.* to brush

cepillo *n.m.* brush

cerámica *n.f.* ceramics

cerca *adv.* close, near; **cerca de**/near; **de cerca**/close by, at close hand

cercanía *n.f.* proximity; **las cercanías**/surroundings

cercano, cercana *adj.* near, nearby; **más cercano**/closest, nearest

cereal *n.m.* cereal

cerebro *n.m.* brain

ceremonia *n.f.* ceremony

cereza *n.f.* cherry

cero *n.m.* zero

ceroso, cerosa *adj.* waxy, waxen

cerradera *n.f.* clasp, lock

cerrado *adj.* closed

cerradura *n.f.* lock

cerrar(se) *v.* to close

certificar *v.* to certify, register (a letter), attest

cerveza *n.f.* beer

cesar *v.* to cease, stop

cesta *n.f.* basket

cestillo *n.m.* little basket

cesto *n.m.* basket

ciclista *n.m.f.* cyclist

ciclo *n.m.* cycle

ciego, ciega *adj.* blind; *n.,* blind person

cielo *n.m.* sky; **por el cielo**/in (through) the sky

cien, ciento *n.m., adj.* (one, a) hundred; *see also* §4.19(a), §5.23ff

ciencia *n.f.* science

científico *adj.* scientific

científicos *n.m.pl.* scientists

ciento *n.m., adj.* (one, a) hundred; **ciento por ciento**/one hundred per cent

ciertamente *adv.* certainly

cierto, cierta, *n.m.f., adj.* (a) certain; *adv.,* surely, certainly; *see also* §4.19(b)

cigarrillo *n.m.* cigarette; **cigarro** *n.m.* cigar

cinco *n.m., adj.* five

cincuenta *n.m., adj.* fifty

cine *n.m.* movies

cinematográfico *adj.* cinematographic

circo *n.m.* circus

circuito *n.m.* circuit

circular *v.* to circulate, move about

círculo *n.m.* club, circle

circunstancias *n.f.pl.* circumstances

cirugía *n.f.* surgery

cita *n.f.* date, appointment

citar *v.* to cite, quote

ciudad *n.f.* city

ciudadano *adj.* pertaining to a city

cívicamente *adv.* civically

civiles *adj.* civil

civilización *n.f.* civilization

civilizado, civilizada *adj.* civilized

claridad *n.f.* clarity

claro *adj.* clear; **¡claro!** *interj.* of course!

clase *n.f.* class, type, kind

clásica *adj.* classic, classical

clasificación *n.f.* classification

clavel *n.m.* carnation

claxon *n.m.* automobile horn

cliente *n.m.f.* customer, client

clientela *n.f.* clientele, customers

clima *n.m.* climate

cobarde *adj.* cowardly, coward

cobijar *v.* to cover, shelter, protect

cobrar *v.* to charge, collect; **se cobra**/is charged, collected

cobre *n.m.* copper

cocer *v.* to cook, bake, boil
cocina *n.f.* kitchen, cooking
cocinar *v.* to cook
cocinera, cocinero *n.f.m.* cook
coche *n.m.* car, auto; **cochero** *n.m.* driver, coachman
codo *n.m.* elbow
coger *v.* to grab, grasp, get, catch, take, seize
cola *n.f.* tail, line; **hacer cola**/to stand in line
colaboración *n.f.* collaboration
colaborar *v.* to collaborate
colchón *n.m.* mattress
colega *n.m.f.* colleague
colegio *n.m.* college, school; **colegio interno**/boarding school
colegir *v.* to collect
cólera *n.f.* anger, wrath
colgar *v.* to hang (up)
colina *n.f.* hill
colocación *n.f.* job
colocar *v.* to place, put
colocase *v. form of* **colocar**
colombiano, colombiana *n.m.f., adj.* of or pertaining to Colombia
Colón *n.m.* Columbus
colonia *n.f.* colony
colonización *n.f.* colonization
colonizador *n.m.* colonizer
color, colores *n.m.s.pl.* color
colorido *n.m.* color, coloring
colosal *adj.* colossal, enormous
columna *n.f.* column
collar *n.m.* collar, necklace
comandante *n.m.* commandant, commander, major
combate *n.m.* combat, fight, struggle
combatiente *n.m.f.* fighter, combatant
combatir *v.* to combat, fight
combinación *n.f.* combination
combinar(se) *v.* to combine
comedia *n.f.* comedy
comedor *n.m.* dining room
comentar *v.* to comment (on)
comentario *n.m.* comment, commentary
comenzar *v.* to begin, start, commence
comer *v.* to eat; **se come**/one eats; **comerse** *v.* to eat up
comercial *n.m., adj.* commercial
comerciante *n.m.f.* merchant, business person
comercio *n.m.* commerce
comerse *v.* to eat up
comestible *adj.* edible, eatable; **comestibles** *n.m.* provisions; **una tienda de comestibles**/grocery store
cometer *v.* to commit
comía *v. form of* **comer**
cómico *n.m.* comedian; *adj.* comic, comical, funny
comida *n.f.* meal
comience *v. form of* **comenzar**

comiendo *pres. part. of* **comer**
comieron *v. form of* **comer**
comisión *n.f.* commission
comisionado *adj.* commissioned
como *conj., adv.* how, as, like, since; **como si**/as if; **¿cómo?** *adv.* how? what?; **tan pronto como**/as soon as; *see also* §12.ff
comodidad *n.f.* commodity, comfort
cómodo *adj.* comfortable
compadecer *v.* to pity
compañero, compañera *n.m.f.* companion, friend
compañía *n.f.* company
comparación *n.f.* comparison
comparar *v.* to compare
compasivo *adj.* compassionate, merciful
competencia *n.f.* competition, competency
compilar *v.* to compile
complacer *v.* to please, accommodate
completamente *adv.* completely
completar *v.* to complete
completo *adj.* complete; **por completo**/completely
componer *v.* to compose
comportamiento *n.m.* comportment, behavior, conduct
composición *n.f.* composition
compositor *n.m.* composer
compra *n.f.* purchase; **ir de compras**/ to go shopping
comprador, compradora *n.m.f.* buyer, customer
comprar *v.* to buy, purchase
comprender *v.* to understand, comprehend, comprise; **comprendido**/comprising, comprised of; **se comprende**/is understood
comprensión *n.f.* comprehension, understanding
comprensivo *adj.* comprehensive
compuesto *past part. of* **componer**
común *n.m., adj.* common, usual; **por lo común**/ordinarily, commonly; *n.* community, public
comunicación *n.f.* communication
comunicar *v.* to communicate
comunidad *n.f.* community
comunión *n.f.* communion
con *prep.* with; **para con**/toward, with; *see also* **con** in idioms §14.19
conceder *v.* to concede, grant
concentrado, concentrada *adj.* concentrated
concentrar *v.* to concentrate; **se concentrarán**/will concentrate
concepto *n.m.* concept
conciencia *n.f.* conscience
concierto *n.m.* concert
concluir *v.* to conclude
concretamente *adv.* concretely
conde *n.m.* count
condecoración *n.f.* decoration, medal

condenar *v.* to condemn
condesa *n.f.* countess
condición *n.f.* condition; **condicional**/conditional
conducir *v.* to drive, conduct, lead, take (a person somewhere)
condujo *v. form of* **conducir**
conejo *n.m.* rabbit
conferencia *n.f.* conference, lecture, meeting; **conferenciante** *n.m.f.* lecturer
conferenciar *v.* to confer, hold a conference
conferir *v.* to confer
confesar *v.* to confess
confianza *n.f.* confidence, trust
confiar *v.* to confide, entrust
confinamiento *n.m.* confinement
confirmar *v.* to confirm, verify
confortable *adj.* comfortable
confundido *adj.* confused
confundir *v.* to confuse, confound
confusos *adj. pl.* confused
congreso *n.m.* congress, meeting, convention
conjunto *n.m.* ensemble, group; *adj.* joint, united
conmigo/with me; *see also* §6.33
conmovedora *adj.* moving, stirring, touching
conmover(se) *v.* to stir, affect, fill with emotion, touch, disturb, rouse
conocedor, conocedora *n.m.f.* connoisseur
conocer *v.* to know, be acquainted with, to meet (a person for the first time); *see also* §11.10
conocido *adj.* known
conocimiento *n.m.* knowledge
conozco, conozca *v. forms of* **conocer**
conque *conj. adv.* now then, so then
conquista *n.f.* conquest
conquistador *n.m.* conqueror
conquistar *v.* to conquer, vanquish
consecuencia *n.f.* consequence
conseguir *v.* to attain, get, obtain
consejo *n.m.* advice, counsel
consentir *v.* to consent
consideración *n.f.* consideration, magnitude
considerar *v.* to consider, look intently at, examine, think over; **se considera**/is considered
consignar *v.* to consign, assign
consigo/*see* §6.33
consiguiente *adj.* consequent, consequential; **por consiguiente**/ therefore, consequently
consiguiese *v. form of* **conseguir**
consintió *v. form of* **consentir**
consistir *v.* to consist
consolar *v.* to console, comfort
constancia *n.f.* constancy, certainty
constantemente *adv.* constantly
constituir *v.* to constitute, make up

constituyeron *v. form of* **constituir**
construcción *n.f.* construction
construir *v.* to construct, build
construyeron *v. form of* **construir**
consuela *v. form of* **consolar;**
   consuela ver.../it is comforting to
   see...
consuelo *n.m.* consolation; *also v.*
   form of **consolar**
consulado *n.m.* consulate
consultar *v.* to consult
consumir *v.* to consume, eat
consumo *n.m.* consumption
contacto *n.m.* contact
contado *see* **contar**
contaminar *v.* to contaminate
contar *v.* to count, relate, tell about;
   contar con/to count on, rely on; **al**
   contado/cash payment
contemplar *v.* to comtemplate
contemporáneo *adj.* contemporary
contener *v.* to contain, hold
contenido *n.m.* content, contents;
   also adj. & past part. of **contener**
contentarse *v.* to content oneself, be
   content
contento *n.m.* contentment, joy; *adj.*
   pleased, content, happy
contestación *n.f.* response, reply
contestar *v.* to answer, reply (to)
contigo/with you *(familiar)*
continente *n.m.* continent
continuamente *adj.* continually
continuar *v.* to continue
contra *prep.* against
contradecir *v.* to contradict
contrariado *adj.* upset, troubled,
   annoyed
contrario *n.m., adj.* contary, opposite;
   por el contrario/on the contrary
contraste *n.m.* contrast
contratar *v.* to agree, engage, contract
   for
contribuir *v.* to contribute
convaleciente *adj., n.* convalescing,
   convalescent
convencer *v.* to convince;
   convencerse *v.* to convince oneself
conveniente *adj.* proper, fitting
convenir *v.* to agree, be fitting,
   suitable
conversación *n.f.* conversation
conversar *v.* to converse, talk
convertir *v.* to convert; **convertirse**
   v. to convert oneself (itself), to be
   converted
convidar *v.* to invite
conviene *v. form of* **convenir**
convirtió *v. form of* **convertir**
convivir *v.* to live together
convocar *v.* to convoke, call (a
   meeting), call together, convene,
   summon
cooperación *n.f.* cooperation
coordinar *v.* to coordinate
copa *n.f.* tree top, glass, cup, goblet

copiar *v.* to copy
coqueta *adj., n.f.* coquette, flirt
corazón *n.m.* heart
corbata *n.f.* tie, necktie
corderito *n.m.* little lamb
cordialidad *n.f.* cordiality
cordillera *n.f.* mountain range
Corea *n.f.* Korea
corona *n.f.* crown, wreath
coronel *n.m.* colonel
corporación *n.f.* corporation
corral *n.m.* corral, barnyard
corrección *n.f.* correction
corregir *v.* to correct
correo *n.m.* mail; **echar al correo/**to
   mail
correr *v.* to run, flow, race
correspondencia *n.f.* correspondence
corresponder *v.* to correspond;
   correspondiente/corresponding
corresponsal *n.m.f.* correspondent (of
   a newspaper)
corría *v. form of* **correr**
corrida *n.f.* race, course, bullfight
corriendo *pres. part. of* **correr**
corriente *n.f., adj.* draft, current,
   present, common, flowing; **lo**
   corriente/present; **era poco**
   corriente/not long ago
corrientemente *adv.* fluently
corrió *v. form of* **correr**
cortar *v.* to cut; **se corta/**is cut;
   cortarse el pelo/to have one's hair
   cut; **córtemela/**cut it for me
cortés, corteses *adj.* courteous
cortesía *n.f.* courtesy
corteza *n.f.* crust, bark, rind, peel
cortina *n.f.* curtain
corto *adj.* short
cosa *n.f.* thing; **no es gran cosa/**it's
   not very much
cosecha *n.f.* crop, harvest
coser *v.* to sew
cosiendo *pres. part. of* **coser**
cosmopolita *adj.* cosmopolitan
costa *n.f.* coast
costar *v.* to cost
costarricense *adj., n.* of or pertaining
   to Costa Rica
costear *v.* to defray
costoso *adj.* costly
costumbre *n.f.* custom, habit; **de**
   costumbre/customarily, usually
costura *n.f.* sewing
creación *n.f.* creation
creado *adj.* created
créame/believe me
crear *v.* to create
crecer *v.* to increase, grow
creciendo *pres. part. of* **crecer**
creciente *adj.* increasing
crecimiento *n.m.* increase
credo *n.m.* belief, creed
creer *v.* to believe; **creerse** *v.* to think
   oneself, consider (believe) onself; **se**
   cree/it is believed

creo *v. form of* **creer**
creó *v. form of* **crear**
creyó *v. form of* **creer**
criada *n.f.* maid, servant; **los criados/**
   servants
criar *v.* to breed, raise, bring up (rear
   a child)
criatura *n.f.* creature, infant
crimen *n.m.* crime
cristal *n.m.* crystal, glass window pane
cristiana *adj., n.* Christian
cristiandad *n.f.* Christendom
cristianismo *n.m.* Christianity
cristiano, cristiana *n.m.f., adj.*
   Christian
Cristo *n.m.* Christ
crítica *n.f.* critique, criticism, review
criticar *v.* to criticize
criticara *v. form of* **criticar**
crítico *n.m., adj.* critic, critical
cruce, *n.m.* crossing
crueles *adj. pl. of* **cruel**
cruz *n.f.* cross
cruzada *n.f.* crusade
cruzar *v.* to cross
cuaderno *n.m.* notebook
cuadra *n.f.* city block
cuadradas *adj.* square
cuadro *n.m.* picture, painting
cual *pron.* which (one); **tal o cual/**
   such and such
cualidad *n.f.* quality, virtue
cualquier *indef. adj. & pron.*
   whichever, whatever, any
cuando *adv.* when; **de vez en**
   cuando/from time to time; **de**
   cuando en cuando/from time to
   time; **cuando menos/**at least;
   ¡cuán...!/how...!
cuanto *pron. & rel. adj.* all that, as
   many as, as much as; **unos cuantos/**
   some; **en cuanto a/**as for, as soon
   as; **cuánto, cuánta, cuántos,**
   cuántas *adj.* how much, how many;
   cuanto antes/as soon as possible
cuarenta *n., adj.* forty; **cuarenta y**
   siete/forty-seven
cuartel *n.m.* barracks, quarters
cuarto *n.m.* room, quarter(s); **el**
   cuarto de baño/bathroom
cuatro *n.m., adj.* four
cubano, cubana *n.m.f., adj.* of or
   pertaining to Cuba
cubierta *n.f.* cover, bedspread; deck
   (of a boat); **cubierto** *past part. of*
   cubrir; cubierto, cubierta *adj.*
   covered
cubo *n.m.* cube, bucket
cubrir *v.* to cover
cuchara *n.f.* spoon
cuchillo *n.m.* knife
cuello *n.m.* neck, collar
cuenta *n.f.* account, bill, tab; **darse**
   cuenta de/to realize
cuento *n.m.* story, tale
cuerda *n.f.* cord, rope

cuero *n.m.* leather
cuerpo *n.m.* body
cuestión *n.f.* question, problem, matter
cueva *n.f.* cave, cellar
cuidado *n.m.* care; **perder cuidado/** not to care, not to worry; **cuidar** *v.* to take care of
culpa *n.f.* blame, fault, guilt; **echar la culpa a/**to blame
culpable *adj.* guilty
cultivo *n.m.* cultivation
culto *n.m.* cult, worship; *adj.* cultured, cultivated, learned
cultura *n.f.* culture
cumbre *n.f.* peak, top, summit
cumpleañero *n.m.* birthday boy
cumpleaños *n.m.* birthday
cumplida *adj.* completed, fulfilled
cumplimiento *n.m.* fulfillment, compliance, completion
cumplir *v.* to fulfill, accomplish, keep (a promise), reach one's birthday (use with **años**)
cura *n.m.* priest; **la cura/**cure
curar *v.* to cure
curiosidad *n.f.* curiosity
curioso *adj.* curious; **los curiosos/** curious people
curso *n.m.* course, race, progress
curva *n.f.* curve, bend
cuyo, cuya, cuyos, cuyas *rel. pron.* whose

CH

chafar *v.* to crease, flatten, crumple
chaleco *n.m.* vest
chaqueta *n.f.* jacket
charla *n.f.* chatting, talking
charlar *v.* to chat, prattle
cheque *n.m.* check
Chianti *n.m.* name of an Italian wine
chicle *n.m.* chewing gum
chico, chica *n.m.f.* boy, girl; *adj.* small, little; **el chico, la chica/**little boy, little girl; **los chicos/**children
chichicastecos *n.m., adj.* of or pertaining to Chichicastenango, Guatemala
chiflar *v.* to whistle
chillar *v.* to scream, shriek
chimenea *n.f.* chimney, fireplace
chiquillo, chiquilla *n.m.f.* little boy, little girl
chiquitico *adj.* tiny, very small
chistar *v.* to mumble, mutter
chiste *n.m.* joke
chistoso *adj.* humorous, witty, funny
chocar *v.* to collide, to be shocking, surprising
chocolate *n.m.* chocolate
chocolatero *n.m.* chocolate maker
chofer, chófer *n.m.* chauffeur, driver
choque *v. form of* **chocar**; *n.m.* shock

choza *n.f.* hut
chupar *v.* to suck, sip
chupete *n.m.* teething ring, pacifier
chusco *adj.* amusing, droll, funny

D

da, daba *v. forms of* **dar**
dama *n.f.* lady
dan, dando *v. forms of* **dar**
danzarina *n.f.* dancer
daño *n.m.* harm, hurt, damage; **hacer daño/**to harm, hurt; **hacerse daño/** to harm, hurt oneself
dar *v.* to give, hit, strike; **dar a/**to look out upon, face; **dar con/**to find, come upon (across); **dar contra/**to hit against; **dar las diez/**to strike ten o'clock; **dar un paseo/**to take a walk; *see also* **dar** in idioms §14.21
dará *v. form of* **dar**
darse *v.* to give oneself (itself); **darse cuenta de/**to realize; *see also* **darse** in idioms §14.21
datar *v.* to date (calendar)
dato *n.m.* datum, fact
de *prep.* of, from, by, about; *see also* **de** in idioms §14.22
dé *v. form of* **dar**
debajo *adv.* below, under, underneath; **debajo de/**under
debatida *adj.* debated
debatir *v.* to debate, argue
deber *v.* to owe, have to, must, ought, should, supposed to; **deber de/**must, probably; **se debe/**is due, is owed; **debido a/**due to; *n.m.* duty; **los deberes/**homework
debido *past part. of* **deber**; *adj.* exact
débil *adj.* weak
debilidad *n.f.* weakness
debutar *v.* to make a debut
década *n.f.* decade
decadencia *n.f.* decadence
decidir *v.* to decide; **decidirse** *v.* to decide, make up one's mind; **decidirse a/**to decide to
decir *v.* to say, tell; **es decir/**that is, that is to say; **querer decir/**to mean; **se puede decir/**it can be said; *n.m.* a saying; **decir la buenaventura/**to tell one's fortune; *see also* **decir** in idioms §14.23
decisión *n.f.* decision
decisivo, decisiva *adj.* decisive
declaración *n.f.* declaration
declarar *v.* to declare; **declararse** *v.* to declare oneself
decorar *v.* to decorate
decoro *n.m.* decorum, respect
decretada *adj.* decreed
decretar *v.* to resolve, decree
dedicación *n.f.* dedication
dedicado *adj.* dedicated, devoted; *also past part. of* **dedicar** *v.* to dedicate, devote; **dedicarse** *v.* to dedicate,

devote oneself (itself)
dediqué *v. form of* **dedicar**
dedo *n.m.* finger, toe
deducir(se) *v.* to deduce
dedujo *v. form of* **deducir**
defecto *n.m.* defect
defender *v.* to defend
defensa *n.f.* defense
defensor *n.m.* defender
definido *adj.* definite
definitivo *adj.* definitive, definite
dejar *v.* to leave, quit, let, allow, permit; **dejar caer/**to drop; **dejar de/**to stop, fail to, neglect to
del *contraction of* **de** + **el/**from the, of the
delante *adv.* ahead, before, in front; **delante de/**in front of, before
delgado *adj.* delicate, thin, slender
delicado *adj.* delicate, frail
delinquir *v.* to be guilty, offend
delito *n.m.* crime, offense
demanda *n.f.* demand
demás *adj., adv.* besides, moreover; **los (las) demás/**the others, the rest, the remaining; **por lo demás/**as for the rest
demasiado *adj., adv.* too much, too many, too
déme/give me
demonio *n.m.* demon, devil
demostrar *v.* to show, demonstrate; **demostrativo** *adj.* demonstrative
den *v. form of* **dar**
denotar *v.* to denote
dentista *n.m.f.* dentist
dentro *adv.* inside, within; **dentro de/** inside of; **dentro de poco/**in (within) a short while
denunciar *v.* to denounce
depender *v.* to depend
dependiente *n.m.f.* employee, clerk
deporte *n.m.* sport; **una tienda de deportes/**sporting goods store
deportivo *adj.* sport, sporting
depósito *n.m.* deposit, depository, storehouse, warehouse
derecho *n.m.* right, privilege; **derecho, derecha** *adj.* straight, right (opposite of left); **a la derecha/**at (to the right)
derramar *v.* to scatter, shed, spill
derribar *v.* to knock down, overthrow, tear down, throw down
derrota *n.f.* defeat; **derrotar** *v.* to defeat
desagradable *adj.* unpleasant, disagreeable
desagradar *v.* to displease
desagrado *n.m.* displeasure
desaire *n.m.* disdain, rebuff
desanimado *adj.* discouraged, disheartened
desaparecer *v.* to disappear
desaparición *n.f.* disappearance
desarrollar(se) *v.* to develop, expand,

unfold

desastre *n.m.* disaster

desastroso *adj.* disastrous

desatar *v.* to untie

desayunar(se) *v.* to breakfast, have breakfast

desayuno *n.m.* breakfast

descansado *adj.* rested

descansar(se) *v.* to rest

descanso *n.m.* rest

descender *v.* to descend, go down

descendiente *n.m.* descendant

descolorido *adj.* discolored

desconectar *v.* to disconnect

desconocer *v.* to be unaware of, not to know, not to recognize

desconocido *adj.* unknown, unrecognizable (person or thing)

descontento *n.m.* displeasure; *adj.* unhappy, discontented

descortés *adj.* discourteous

describir *v.* to describe, sketch, delineate

descripción *n.f.* description

descubierto *past part. of* **descubrir**; **descubiertos** *adj.* discovered, uncovered, open

descubrimiento *n.m.* discovery

descubrir *v.* to discover, disclose

descuento *n.m.* discount

descuido *n.m.* carelessness, neglect

desde *prep.* from, since; **desde luego**/since then, of course, at once; **desde que**/ever since; **desde hace mucho tiempo**/for a long time; *see also* §14.3ff

desear *v.* to desire, want, wish

desembarcar *v.* to disembark, unload

desempeñar *v.* to play (a part), act (a part), discharge, perform (a duty), take out of pawn

deseo *n.m.* desire, wish; *also v. form of* **desear**

desesperación *n.f.* desperation, despair, hopelessness

desesperado *adj.* desperate

desesperante *adj.* discouraging, causing despair

desesperar *v.* to despair

desfile *n.m.* parade

desgracia *n.f.* misfortune, mishap, something terrible; **por desgracia**/unfortunately

desgraciadamente *adv.* unfortunately

desgraciado *adj.* unfortunate

deshacer *v.* to undo

desierto *n.m.* desert; *adj.* deserted

designar *v.* to designate

desilusionado *adj.* disillusioned

desistir *v.* to desist

deslizar(se) *v.* to slide, slip, glide

deslumbrar *v.* to daze, dazzle

desmayar(se) *v.* to dismay, faint

desmayo *n.m.* faint

desmentir *v.* to belie, disprove

desnuda *adj.* naked, nude

desnudar *v.* to undress; **desnudarse**/to undress oneself

desobedecer *v.* to disobey

desolados *adj.* desolate

desorden *n.m.* disorder

desordenada *adj.* disorganized, in disarray, disordered, disorderly

desorientado *adj.* confused

desorientarse *v.* to become confused, get lost

despacio *adv.* slowly

despacho *n.m.* dispatch, office

despedazar *v.* to tear to pieces

despedir *v.* to dismiss; **despedirse**/to take leave, say good-bye

despertar *v.* to awaken, wake up (someone)

despertarse *v.* to wake up, awaken oneself

despidieron, despidió *v. forms of* **despedir**

despierto *v. form of* **despertar**; *adj.* awake

despreciar *v.* to despise, disdain, scorn

después *adv.* after, then, afterwards, later

destacado *adj.* outstanding

destacar(se) *v.* to emphasize, excel, stand out

desterrar *v.* to banish, drive out, exile

destinación *n.f.* destination

destinar *v.* to destine

destino *n.m.* destiy, destination, fate

destrozar *v.* to destroy, shatter

destruir *v.* to destroy

desvanecerse *v.* to faint, disappear, vanish

desvestirse *v.* to undress, get undressed

detalle *n.m.* detail

detención *n.f.* detention

detener *v.* to stop, detain (someone or something)

detenerse *v.* to stop (oneself)

determinado *adj.* definite, specific, determined

determinar *v.* to determine, decide

detestar *v.* to detest

detrás *prep.* behind, in back; **detrás de**/behind, in back of

detuvo *v. form of* **detener**

deuda *n.f.* debt

devastar *v.* to devastate

devoción *n.f.* devotion; **devocionario** *n.m.* prayer book

devolver *v.* to return (an object), refund, give back

devuelva *v. form of* **devolver**

di *v. form of* **decir, dar**

día *n.m.* day; **a los pocos días**/in a few days; **al día siguiente**/on the following day; **buenos días**/hello, good day; **hoy día**/nowadays; **todos los días**/every day; *see also* **día, días** *in* idioms §14.24

diablo *n.m.* devil

diagnóstico *n.m.* diagnosis

dialéctico *adj.* dialectical

diálogo *n.m.* dialogue

diariamente *adv.* daily

diario *n.m.* diary, newspaper; *adj.* daily

dibujar *v.* to draw, sketch

dibujo *n.m.* drawing, sketch

diccionario *n.m.* dictionary

dice *v. form of* **decir; se dice**/it is said

diciembre *n.m.* December

diciendo *pres. part. of* **decir**

dictado *n.m.* dictation; **dictados**/dictates, maxims, dictations

dictador *n.m.* dictator

dictadura *n.f.* dictatorship

dicha *n.f.* happiness; *adj.* aforementioned, above-mentioned, said, stated, *see also* §7.124

dicho *past part. of* **decir**; *see also* §7.119ff

dichoso *adj.* happy, lucky, fortunate, blessed; *see also* §7.123

dieciséis *n.m., adj.* sixteen

diente *n.m.* tooth

diera, dieron. *v. forms of* **dar**

diferencia *n.f.* difference

diferenciar *v.* to differentiate, distinguish

diferente *adj.* different

difícil *adj.* difficult

dificultad *n.f.* difficulty

dificultar *v.* to make difficult

dificultoso *adj.* difficult

difunto *adj.* dead

diga *v. form of* **decir; ¡diga!**/say! hello! (on the telephone); **dígamelo**/tell me it, tell it to me, tell me so

dignidad *n.f.* dignity

digno *adj.* worthy

digo *v. form of* **decir**

dije, dijiste, dijo *v. forms of* **decir**

diles/tell them

diligente *adj.* diligent

dime/tell me

Dinamarca *n.f.* Denmark

dinamarqués *n.m., adj.* Danish, Dane; of or pertaining to Denmark

dinamita *n.f.* dynamite

dinero *n.m.* money

dio *v. form of* **dar**

Dios *n.m.* God; **dioses** *n.m.pl.* gods

diplomático *adj.* diplomatic

diré *v. form of* **decir**

dirección *n.f.* address, direction

directamente *adv.* directly

directo *adj.* direct

director, directora *n.m.f.* director, principal

diría *v. form of* **decir**

dirigido *adj.* directed

dirigir *v.* to direct, manage; **dirigirse** *v.* to go toward, go into a direction, direct oneself, address oneself, make one's way (toward)

dirija *v. form of* **dirigir**

disciplina *n.f.* discipline

discípulo *n.m.* disciple, student

disco *n.m.* phonograph record, recording

disconforme *adj.* unconforming

discreto *adj.* discreet

disculpa *n.f.* apology, excuse

discúlpame/excuse me, pardon me

disculpar. *v.* to excuse, exculpate

discurrir *v.* to speak, ramble, discourse

discurso *n.m.* speech, discourse, lecture

discusión *n.f.* discussion

discutir *v.* to discuss

diseminados *adj.* disseminated, scattered

diseminar *v.* to disseminate

disfrutar *v.* to enjoy

disgustado *adj.* displeased

disgustar *v.* to displease

disgusto *n.m.* displeasure

disminuir *v.* to diminish, decrease

disparada *adj.* in a hurry

disparar *v.* to fire, shoot, discharge

dispensar *v.* to excuse, dispense, distribute, exempt

disperso *adj.* dispersed, scattered

disponer *v.* to dispose, arrange; **disponer de**/to have available, have at one's disposal; **disponerse a**/to get ready to

disposición *n.f.* disposition, arrangement

dispuesto *adj.* ready, disposed

disputa *n.f.* dispute, quarrel

distancia *n.f.* distance

distante *adj.* far, distant

distar *v.* to be distant

distinguir *v.* to distinguish; **distinguirse** *v.* to distinguish oneself (itself)

distinto *adj.* distinct, different

distracción *n.f.* distraction, amusement

distribución *n.f.* distribution

distribuir *v.* to distribute

distrito *n.m.* district

diversión *n.f.* amusement, diversion

diversiones *n.f.pl.* amusements, diversions; entertainment

diverso *adj.* diverse, different, various; **diversos**/several

divertido *adj.* diverting, amusing

divertir *v.* to amuse, entertain; **divertirse** *v.* to have a good time, enjoy oneself

divididos *adj.* divided

dividir *v.* to divide

divierte *v. form of* **divertir**

divinidad *n.f.* divinity

divulgado *adj.* divulged

doblar *v.* to double, fold **doblarse** *v.* to double itself; **doblar la esquina/**

to turn the corner

doble *n.m., adj.* double

doce *n.m., adj.* twelve

docena *n.f.* dozen

doctor *n.m.* doctor; **doctorado** *n.m.* doctorate

documento *n.m.* document

dólar *n.m.* dollar

doler *v.* to ache, pain, hurt, cause grief, cause regret; **dolerle a uno la cabeza**/to have a headache; **un dolor de cabeza**/headache; **tener dolor**/to have an ache, pain

doliesen *v. form of* **doler**

dolor *n.m.* ache, pain, sorrow

doméstica *adj.* domestic

domicilio *n.m.* domicile, residence

dominar *v.* to dominate, command, have a command

domingo *n.m.* Sunday

dominio *n.m.* domination, command; **dominio del español, del inglés, del francés**/command of Spanish, English, French

don, Don *n.m.* title used before a gentleman's first name, *e.g.,* **Don José**

donde *adv.* where; **¿dónde?**/where?

dondequiera *indef. & rel. adv.* wherever, anywhere; *see also* §7.50

doña *n.f.* title used before a lady's first name, *e.g.* **Doña Ana**

dorar *v.* to gild

dormido *adj.* asleep

dormir *v.* to sleep; **dormirse** *v.* to fall asleep

dormitar *v.* to nap, doze

dormitorio *n.m.* dormitory, sleeping quarters, bedroom

dos *n.m., adj.* two; **los dos**/both

doscientos *n.m., adj.* two hundred

doy *v. form of* **dar**

drama *n.m.* drama

dramaturgo *n.m.* dramatist

duda *n.f.* doubt; **sin duda**/without a doubt, doubtless; **no cabe duda**/no room for doubt, no doubt about it

dudar *v.* to doubt

dudoso *adj.* doubtful

duele *v. form of* **doler**

dueña *n.f.* owner, proprietress

dueño *n.m.* master, owner, landlord

duerme, duermen *v. forms of* **dormir**

dulce *n.m.* candy; *adj.* sweet; **dulces**/candy; **dulcemente** *adv.* sweetly

dulzura *n.f.* sweetness, gentleness, tenderness

duplicar *v.* to duplicate

dura *adj.* hard

durante *prep.* during

durar *v.* to last, endure

dureza *n.f.* harshness

durmiendo *pres. part. of* **dormir**

duro *adj.* hard; *n.m.* **duro** (Spanish coin)

E

e *conj.* and; *see also* §5.65, §12.14

eco *n.m.* echo

economía *n.f.* economy, economics; **economía doméstica**/home economics

económico *adj.* economic, economical

economista *n.m.f.* economist

economizar *v.* to economize, save (money)

ecuatoriano *n.m., adj.* of or pertaining to Ecuador

echar *v.* to cast, fling, hurl, pitch, throw; **echar al correo**/to mail; **echar de menos**/to miss; **echar la culpa**/to blame; **echar ojo a**/to glance at, keep an eye on; **echar una carta al correo**/to mail (post) a letter; **echarse a + inf.**/to begin to, start to; *see also* §14.22; **echar la siesta**/to siesta, take a siesta

edad *n.f.* age; **la Edad Media**/the Middle Ages

edición *n.f.* edition

edificar *v.* to build erect; **se edificó**/was built

edificio *n.m.* edifice, building

editar *v.* to publish; to edit: **redactar**

educación *n.f.* education

educador, educadora *n.m.f.* educator

educados *adj.* educated

educativo *adj.* educational

efectivamente *adv.* effectively

efecto *n.m.* effect; **en efecto**/in fact, as a matter of fact

efectuado *adj.* carried out

efectuar *v.* to accomplish, carry out, put into effect, to effect

egoísta *adj.* egotistical, egoistic, selfish

ejecutar *v.* to execute, carry out, perform

ejemplar *n.m.* sample, copy; *adj.* exemplary

ejemplo *n.m.* example; **por ejemplo**/for example

ejercer *v.* to exert, exercise

ejercicio *n.m.* exercise, practice

ejército *n.m.* army

el *def. art. m.s.* the; **el que**/he (she) who; *see also* §4.ff, §6.60, §6.66, §6.82ff, §6.88ff, §6.90ff

elección *n.f.* election

electricidad *n.f.* electricity

eléctrico *adj.* electric, electrical

elefante *n.m.* elephant

elegancia *n.f.* elegance; **elegante** *adj.* elegant

elegir *v.* to elect

elemental *adj.* elementary

elemento *n.m.* element

elevar *v.* to exalt, raise, elevate

eliminar *v. to eliminate*

elocuente *adj.* eloquent

elogiar *v.* to praise, eulogize

elogio *n.m.* praise

embajada *n.f.* embassy

embajador, embajadora *n.m.f.* ambassador

embarcación *n.f.* embarkation

embarcarse *v.* to embark

embargo *n.m.* embargo, seizure; **sin embargo**/nevertheless, however

embeber *v.* to soak in, soak up, suck in

emergencia *n.f.* emergency

emoción *n.f.* emotion

emocionante *adj.* moving, touching

emocionar *v.* to move, touch, thrill

emocionarse *v.* to feel emotion

empecé *v. form of* **empezar**

empeñarse *v.* to insist, persist

emperador *n.m.* emperor; **emperatriz** *n.f.* empress

empezar *v.* to begin, start

empieza *v. form of* **empezar**

empleado, empleada *n.m.f.* employee

emplear *v.* to employ, use

empleo *n.m.* job, employment

emprender *v.* to undertake, begin

empresa *n.f.* enterprise, undertaking, purpose

empresario *n.m.* impresario

empujar *v.* to push

empujón *n.m.* push, shove

en *prep.* in, on, at; *see also* **en** in idioms §14.25; in prepositional phrases §11.3

enamorado de/in love with

enamorar *v.* to enamor, court, woo; **enamorarse de**/to fall in love with

enano *n.m.* dwarf

encabezar *v.* to head, lead

encaminarse *v.* to walk (toward)

encantado *adj.* enchanted, delighted

encantador, encantadora *adj.* charming

encantar *v.* to enchant, charm

encanto *n.m.* charm, enchantment

encarcelar *v.* to jail, imprison, incarcerate

encargar *v.* to put in charge

encargarse de *v.* to take charge of

encargo *n.m.* task, charge, trust

encender *v.* to incite, inflame, kindle, light, ignite

encendidas *adj.* lighted, lit, burning

encendieron *v. form of* **encender**

encerrar *v.* to enclose, lock up, confine

enciclopedia *n.f.* encyclopedia

encima *adv.* above, over, over and above; **por encima de**/in spite of

encima de/above, on top of

encogerse de hombros/to shrug one's shoulders

encontrar *v.* to meet, encounter, find

encontrarse *v.* to be located, to be found, to meet each other, to find oneself; **se encuentra**/is found, is located; **encontrarse con**/to meet, come across, find, come upon

encuentro *v. form of* **encontrar;**

n.m. encounter, meeting

enemigo, enemiga *n.m.f.* enemy

energía *n.f.* energy

enero *n.m.* January

enfadar *v.* to anger; **enfadarse** *v.* to become (get) angry, upset, annoyed

enfado *n.m.* annoyance

enfermarse *v.* to become sick

enfermedad *n.f.* illness, sickness

enfermera *n.f.* nurse

enfermita *n.f.* sick little girl

enfermizo *adj.* sickly

enfermo *n.m* sick man; *adj.* sick, ill; **los enfermos**/the sick persons

enfrente de/in front of, opposite

engaño *n.m.* deceit

engañar *v.* to deceive, cheat, fool

engañarse *v.* to be mistaken, deceived

enojado *adj.* angry, annoyed, irritated

enojar *v.* to annoy, irritate, make angry, vex

enojarse *v.* to become angry, annoyed

enojo *n.m.* anger, trouble, annoyance, bother

enorme *adj.* enormous, big, huge

enormemente *adv.* enormously

enriquecerse *v.* to become rich, enrich oneself

enrollar *v.* to roll

ensalada *n.f.* salad

ensayar *v.* to test, try rehearse

ensayista *n.m.f.* essayist

ensayo *n.m.* essay, test

enseñanza *n.f.* teaching

enseñar *v.* to teach, show, point out

entablar *v.* to start

entender *v.* to understand, hear; **se entiende**/is understood

entenderse *v.* to understand each other, get along with each other

enterar *v.* to inform; **enterarse de**/to find out about, become aware of

enternecidamente *adv.* with compassion

entero *adj.* entire

entiende *v. form of* **entender**

entierro *n.m.* burial

entonces *adj.* well, then, at that time

entrada *n.f.* entrance, admission ticket, arrival

entrar (en) *v.* to enter (into), go (in), come (in)

entre *prep.* between, among

entrega *n.f.* delivery, handing over, giving over

entregado *adj.* delivered

entregar *v.* to deliver, hand over, give

entregarse *v.* to devote oneself

entretenerse *v.* to amuse oneself

entrevista *n.f.* interview

entristecerse *v.* to become saddened, grow sad, grieve

entristecido *adj.* saddened

entusiasmarse *v.* to feel enthusiasm

entusiasmo *n.m.* enthusiasm

enunciar *v.* to enunciate

enviado *adj., past part. of* **enviar**

enviar *v.* to send

envolver *v.* to wrap

episodio *n.m.* episode

época *n.f.* epoch, era, age; **por esta época**/at that period of time

equipaje *n.m.* equipment, luggage, baggage

equipo *n.m.* team

equivocarse *v.* to be mistaken

era, eres *v. forms of* **ser**

erguir *v.* to erect, set up straight; **erguirse** *v.* to straighten up, sit up straight, stand erect

erigir *v.* to erect, found, establish, elevate, raise

ermita *n.f.* hermitage

errante *adj.* errant, roving, wandering

errar *v.* to err, wander, roam, miss

error *n.m.* error, mistake

erudito *n.m.* scholar

esa *demons. adj., f.s.* that; **ésa** *dem. pron.* that one; *see also* §5.54, §6.56

esbelta *adj.* lithe, svelte, slender

escala *n.f.* scale

escalera *n.f.* stairs, stairway, staircase

escaparse *v.* to escape

escasez *n.f.* scarcity

escaso *adj.* scarce

escena *n.f.* scene

esclavo *n.m.* slave

escoba *n.f.* broom

escoger *v.* to choose, select

escolar *n.m.f.* school child; **escolares**/students, school children

esconder(se) *v.* to hide

escribiente *n.m.f.* clerk

escribir *v.* to write

escrito *past part. of* **escribir; por escrito**/in writing; *see also* §4.11(b), §7.5, §7.31, §7.205

escritor, escritora *n.m.f.* writer, author

escritorio *n.m.* desk

escuadrón *n.m.* squadron

escuchadas *adj.* listened to, heard

escuchar *v.* to listen (to)

escudero *n.m.* attendant, squire

escuela *n.f.* school

escultor, escultora *n.m.f.* sculptor

escultura *n.f.* sculpture

ese *demons. adj., m.s.* that; **ése** *dem. pron.* that one; *see also* §5.54, §6.56

esencial *adj.* essential

esforzar *v.* to strengthen; **esforzarse** *v.* to force oneself, make an effort

esfuerzo *n.m.* effort

eso *neuter pron.* that; **por eso**/therefore; **a eso de las tres**/at about three o'clock; *see also* §5.55, §6.56, §6.58

espacio *n.m.* space

espacioso *adj.* spacious, large

espada *n.f.* sword

espalda *n.f.* back (of shoulders)

espantar *v.* to drive away, chase away,

frighten away, scare

espantarse *v.* to become frightened

espanto *n.m.* terror, shock, dread

espantosa *adj.* dreadful

España *n.f.* Spain

español, española *adj.* Spanish, Spaniard; *n.m.* Spanish language; **todo español**/all Spanish people; **a la española**/Spanish style

esparcir *v.* to scatter, spread

especial *adj.* special

especializado *adj.* specialized; **especialista** *n.m.f.* specialist

especialmente *adv.* especially

específico *adj.* specific

espectáculo *n.m.* spectacle, theatrical presentation, show

espectador, espectadora *n.m.f.* spectator

especular *v.* to speculate

espejo *n.m.* mirror

espera *n.f.* expectation, waiting, hope

esperanza *n.f.* hope

esperar *v.* to wait (for), hope, await, expect; **la sala de espera**/waiting room; **se espera**/it is hoped

espeso *adj.* thick, dense

espiar *v.* to spy (on)

espíritu *n.m.* spirit

espontaneidad *n.f.* spontaneity

espontáneo *adj.* spontaneous

esposa *n.f.* wife; **esposo** n.m. husband; **esposos** *n.m.pl.* husband and wife, couple, Mr. and Mrs.

esquimal *n.m.f., adj.* Eskimo

esquina *n.f.* corner (outside, as a street corner); **el rincón**/corner (inside, as in a room)

esta *dem. adj. f.s.* this; **ésta** *dem. pron.* this one; *see also* §5.54, §6.56, §6.59

está, están, *v. forms of* **estar; el niño no está**/the child is not all there (there is something wrong with this child)

estable *adj.* stable

establecer *v.* to establish; **establecerse** *v.* to settle down

establecimiento *n.m.* establishment

establo *n.m.* stable (for animals)

estación *n.f.* station, season

estacionar *v.* to park (a vehicle)

estadio *n.m.* stadium

estadísticas *n.f. pl.* statistics

estado *n.m.* state, condition; also *past part. of* **estar; los Estados Unidos**/ the United States

estadounidense *adj.* of or pertaining to the United States (American)

estallar *v.* to break out

estamos *v. form of* **estar**

estancia *n.f.* stay, sojourn

estante *n.m.* shelf, bookcase

estaño *n.m.* tin

estar *v.* to be; *see also* **estar** in idioms §14.26; also consult the general

index

estatua *n.f.* statue

este *n.m.* East; also *dem. adj. m.s.* this; **éste** *dem. pron. m.s.* this one; *see also* §5.54, §6.56ff, §6.58ff

esté *v. form of* **estar**

estéril *adj.* sterile

estilo *n.m.* style

estimable, estimado *adj.* esteemed

estimar *v.* to estimate, esteem, respect, value; **se estimó**/it was estimated

estimular *v.* to stimulate

esto *neuter pron.* this; **por esto**/for this reason; *see also* §5.54, §6.56ff, §6.58ff

estómago *n.m.* stomach

estoy *v. form of* **estar**

estrechar *v.* to press, tighten, squeeze

estrecharse *v.* to become friendlier, more understanding, more intimate

estrecho *adj.* narrow, tight; *n.m.* strait

estrella *n.f.* star

estremecer *v.* to shake, tremble; **estremecerse** *v.* to shudder

estremecido *adj.* shaken, trembling

estridente *adj.* strident

estructura *n.f.* structure

estuco *n.m.* stucco

estudiante *n.m.f.* student

estudiar *v.* to study

estudio *n.m.* study; **estudioso** *adj.* studious

estupefactos *adj.* stupefied

estupendo *adj.* stupendous

estuve, estuvieron *v. forms of* **estar**

etapa *n.f.* phase, stage

eterno *adj* eternal

Europa *n.f.* Europe

europea, europeo *adj.* European, of or pertaining to Europe

evaluación *n.f.* evaluation

evidente *adj.* evident

evitar *v.* to avoid

evolución *n.f.* evolution

exactamente *adv.* exactly

exacto *adj.* exact

examen *n.m.* exam, examination, test

examinar *v.* to examine

exangüe *adj.* lifeless, bloodless

exasperado *adj.* exasperated

excelente *adj.* excellent

excepto *adv.* except, excepting

excitante *adj.* exciting

exclamación *n.f.* exclamation

exclamar *v.* to exclaim

exclusivo *adj.* exclusive

excursión *n.f.* excursion

excusarse *v.* to excuse oneself

exhibición *n.f.* exhibit, exhibition

exhibir *v.* to exhibit

exigir *v.* to demand, insist, require, urge

exilado *adj.* exiled

existencia *n.f.* existence

existente *adj.* existent, existing, extant

existir *v.* to exist

éxito *n.m.* success; **tener éxito**/to be successful

expansión *n.f.* expansion

expectación *n.f.* expectation

expedición *n.f.* expedition

experiencia *n.f.* experience

experimentación *n.f.* experimentation

experimentar *v.* to experiment, experience

explicación *n.f.* explanation

explicar *v.* to explain

exploración *n.f.* exploration

explorador, exploradora *n.m.f.* explorer

explosión *n.f.* explosion

explotación *n.f.* exploitation

exponer *v.* to expose, expound

exportar *v.* to export

exposición *n.f.* exposition, exhibit

expresar *v.* to express

expresión *n.f.* expression

expresivamente *adv.* expressively, affectionately, warmly

expreso *n.m.* express (train)

expulsar *v.* to expel

extender *v.* to extend; **extenderse** *v.* to extend, spread

extensión *n.f.* extension, extent, expanse, area, space

extenso *adj.* extensive

exterior *adj.* external; *n.m.* exterior

extinguir *v.* to extinguish, put out (light, flame)

extracción *n.f.* extraction

extracto *n.m.* extract

extranjero, extranjera *n.m.f.* foreigner, stranger; *adj.* foreign

extrañar *v.* to be strange

extrañarse *v.* to be amazed at, to wonder at

extraño *adj.* strange, foreign; **lo extraño**/the strange thing

extraordinariamente *adv.* extraordinarily

extraordinario *adj.* extraordinary

extravagante *adj.* extravagant

extremo *adj.* extreme, *n.m.* end, tip, extremity; **en extremo**/extremely

exudar *v.* to exude

exultar *v.* to exult

F

fábrica *n.f.* factory

fabricación *n.f.* manufacture

fabricar *v.* to manufacture, make

facción *n.f.* faction, opposing group

facciones *n.f.pl.* facial features

fácil *adj.* easy

fácilmente *adv.* easily

facturar *v.* to bill, invoice

facultad *n.f.* faculty

fachada *n.f.* façade

falda *n.f.* skirt

falso, falsa *adj.* false

falta *n.f.* error, mistake, fault, lack; **sin**

falta/without fail; **hacer falta**/to be lacking
faltar *v.* to be lacking, wanting, to need, lack, miss, need; *see also* **§16.25, §6.20**
falte *v. form of* **faltar**
falla *n.f.* defect, flaw
fallecer *v.* to die
fama *n.f.* fame, reputation
familia *n.f.* family
familiares *n.m.pl.* familiar persons
famoso *adj.* famous
fanático *adj.* fanatic, fanatical
fantásticas *adj.* fantastic
farmacéutico, farmacéutica *n.m.f.* pharmacist
farmacia *n.f.* pharmacy, drug store
faro *n.m.* lighthouse, headlight; **farol** *n.m.* lantern
fase *n.f.* phase
fatiga *n.f.* fatigue
fatigar *v.* to fatigue, tire
favor *n.m.* favor; **por favor**/please
favorecer *v.* to favor
favorito, favorita *adj.* favorite
fe *n.f.* faith
fea *adj.* ugly
febrero *n.m.* February
fecha *n.f.* date; **fechado** *adj.* dated
felices *pl. of* **feliz**
felicidad *n.f.* felicity, happiness
felicitaciones *n.f.pl.* congratulations
felicitar *v.* to congratulate; **felicitarse**/ to congratulate oneself
feliz *adj.* happy
femenino, femenina *adj.* feminine
fenomenal *adj.* phenomenal
feo *adj.* ugly
feria *n.f.* fair
feroz *adj.* ferocious
ferrocarril *n.m.* railroad
ferrocarrilero, ferroviario *n.m.* railroad worker
fervoroso *adj.* fervent
festejar *v.* to feast, entertain, celebrate
fiar *v.* to confide, entrust; **fiarse de**/to trust
fiebre *n.f.* fever
fiel *adj.* faithful
fiesta *n.f.* party, festival, holiday, celebration; **un día de fiesta**/holiday
fiestectia *n.f.* small party
figura *n.f.* figure, shape; face
figurar *v.* to figure
figurarse *v.* to figure out, to imagine, picture
figurilla *n.f.* figurine
fijado *adj.* fixed, set
fijar *v.* to fix, settle, set, clinch, fasten
fijarse *v.* to fix itself (oneself), take notice, pay attention, note, notice; **fijarse en**/to notice, stare
fijo, fija *adj.* fixed, firm, set
fila *n.f.* row
filipino *n.m., adj.* of or pertaining to the Philippines

filósofo *n.m.* philosopher
fin *n.m.* end; **a fin de**/in order to; **a fin de que**/so that, in order that; **a fines de**/at the end of; **al fin**/finally, at last; **al fin y al cabo**/in the long run; **por fin**/finally, at last
final *adj.* end, final; **al final de**/at the end of
finalmente *adv.* finally
financiera *adj.* financial
finca *n.f.* farm, ranch
fingir *v.* to pretend, feign
finísima *adj.* very fine
fino, fina *adj.* delicate, fine
firmamento *n.m.* firmament, sky
firmar *v.* to sign
firme *adj.* firm
firmemente *adv.* firmly
físico, física *adj.* physical
flaco *adj.* skinny, thin, weak
flagelar *v.* to flagellate, whip
flojo *adj.* lazy, indolent
flor *n.f.* flower
florecer *v.* to flourish
florería *n.f.* flower shop
florista *n.m.f.* florist
flota *n.f.* fleet
fluir *v.* to flow
folklórico *adj.* folkloristic
follaje *n.m.* foliage
fomentar *v.* to foment, foster, promote
fonda *n.f.* inn, small restaurant
fondo *n.m.* depth, bottom; **a fondo**/ thoroughly
fondos *n.m.pl.* funds
forastero *n.m.* stranger, foreigner
forma *n.f.* form
formal *adj.* formal, polite
formar *v.* to form, constitute, shape, develop; **se forma**/is formed
formular *v.* to formulate
fortaleza *n.f.* fortress, fort
fortificadas *adj.* fortified
fortificarse *v.* to fortify oneself (itself)
fortuna *n.f.* fortune
forzado *adj.* forced
forzar *v.* to force
forzoso *adj.* inevitable, necessary
fósforo *n.m.* match
foto *n.f.* photo, picture; **sacar fotos**/to take pictures
fotografía *n.f.* photograph, photography
fracaso *n.m.* failure
franca *adj.* frank
francamente *adv.* frankly
francés, francesa *adj.* French; *n.m.* French language
Francia *n.f.* France
franqueo *n.m.* postage
frase *n.f.* sentence, phrase
frazada *n.f.* blanket
frecuencia *n.f.* frequency; **con frecuencia**/frequently; *see also* idioms with **con §14.19**
frecuente *adj.* frequent

freír(se) *v.* to fry
frente *n.m.* front, forehead; **al frente**/ in front, out front; **frente a, frente de, en frente**/opposite, across; **frente a frente**/face to face; **hacer frente a**/to confront, to face
fresa *n.f.* strawberry
fresco, fresca *adj.* fresh, cool; *n.m.* fresco painting; **hacer fresco**/to be cool weather; *see also* weather expressions **§3.29, §17.ff**
fría *adj.* cold
frialdad *n.f.* coldness, coolness
fríamente *adv.* coldly
frío *n.m.* cold; **hacer frío**/to be cold weather; **tener frío**/to feel cold (person); *see also* **tener** in idioms **§14.42** and weather expressions **§3.29, §17.ff**
frontera *n.f.* frontier
fruta *n.f.* fruit
fruto *n.m.* benefit, consequence
fue *v. form of* **ser, ir**
fuego *n.m.* fire
fuente *n.f.* fountain
fuera *v. form of* **ir, ser**; *also adv.* outside, out
fuere, fueres, fueron *v. forms of* **ser, ir**
fuerte *adj.* strong
fuertemente *adv.* vigorously
fuerza *n.f.* force, strength
fugaces *pl. of* **fugaz** *adj.* fleeting
fui, fuimos *v. forms of* **ser, ir**
fumar *v.* to smoke
función *n.f.* function, performance (theatrical)
funcionar *v.* to function, (mechanical)
funcionario *n.m.* official
fundación *n.f.* foundation
fundador *n.m.* founder
fundar *v.* to found, establish
furia *n.f.* fury
fusil *n.m.* gun, rifle
fusilar *v.* to shoot
fútbol *n.m.* football, soccer
fútil *adj.* futile
futilidad *n.f.* futility
futuro *n.m., adj.* future

G

gala *n.f., adj.* finery, gala, festal, festive
galería *n.f.* gallery
gallego *n.m., adj.* of or pertaining to Galicia
gallina *n.f.* hen
gallo *n.m.* rooster
gana *n.f.* desire, inclination, appetite; **de buena gana**/willingly, with pleasure; **de mala gana**/unwillingly; **tener ganas de + inf.**/to feel like, have a desire to
ganada *adj.* earned, **ganado** *past part. of* **ganar**

ganadería *n.f.* cattle raising, animal husbandry

ganadero *n.m.* rancher

ganado *n.m.* cattle; also *past part. of* **ganar**

ganador, ganadora *n.m.f.* winner

ganancia *n.f.* profit, gain

ganar(se) *v.* to earn, gain, win; **ganada**/earned

gangas *n.f.* bargains

garantizar *v.* to guarantee

gaseosa *n.f.* soda pop, carbonated drink

gasolina *n.f.* gasoline

gastar *v.* to spend (money)

gasto *n.m.* cost, expense, expenditure

gatito *n.m.* kitten

gato *n.m.* cat

gemir *v.* to grumble, moan, groan, howl, grieve

generación *n.f.* generation

general *n.m., adj.* general; **por lo general**/generally, usually; *see also* **por** in idioms §14.37

generalmente *adv.* generally

género *n.m.* merchadise, textile, goods, gender, kind, class, type

generosidad *n.f.* generosity

generoso *adj.* generous

genio *n.m.* genius, temperament, mood

gente *n.f.* people; **las gentes**/the people, inhabitants, persons

genuino *adj.* genuine

geografía *n.f.* geography

gerente *n.m.* manager

gesto *n.m.* gesture; **gesto a gesto**/gesture by gesture

gimen, gimió *v. forms of* **gemir**

girar *v.* to rotate, turn

gitano, gitana *n.m.f.* gypsy

gloria *n.f.* glory

gloriosamente *adv.* gloriously

glorioso *adj.* glorious

gobernador *n.m.* governor

gobernar *v.* to govern, rule

gobierno *n.m.* government

gocé *v. form of* **gozar**

golpe *n.m.* blow, hit, attack, stroke

golpear *v.* to strike, hit, beat

golpetazo *n.m.* knock, knocking, blow

goma (de borrar) *n.f.* eraser

gordito *adj.* chubby

gordo, gorda *adj.* fat, plump, stout; **el premio gordo**/first prize

gorila *n.m.* gorilla

gorra *n.f.* cap (hat)

gota *n.f.* drop (of liquid)

góticas *adj.* Gothic

gozar de *v.* to enjoy

gozo *n.m.* joy; also *v. form of* **gozar**

grabar *v.* to engrave

gracia *n.f.* grace, favor, joke; **no estar para gracias**/not to be in the mood for jokes; **hacer gracia**/to be funny; **gracias**/thanks; **muchas gracias**/many thanks, thank you very much; **gracias a**/thanks to; **dar las gracias**/to thank

grado *n.m.* degree, grade, rank

graduado, graduada *adj.* graduate, graduated

gramática *n.f.* grammar

gran, grande *adj.* large, big, great; **gran cosa**/much, very much; **no es gran cosa**/it's not very much; *see also* §5.15, §5.22

grandemente *adv.* largely, grandly

grandeza *n.f.* size, greatness

granero *n.m.* granary, barn, haystack

gratificación *n.f.* gratification, bonus

gratis *adv.* free, gratis

gratitud *n.f.* gratitude

gratuitamente *adv.* gratuitously, free of charge

grave *adj.* grave, serious

gravedad *n.f.* gravity, seriousness

griego, griega *n.m.f., adj.* Greek; **el griego**/Greek language

gris *n.m., adj.* gray

gritar *v.* to shout, scream, shriek, cry out

grito *n.m.* cry, shouting; **a grito pelado**/at the top of one's lungs; **dar gritos**/to shout; *see also* **dar** in idioms §14.21

Groenlandia *n.f.* Greenland

grotesca *adj.* grotesque

grueso *adj.* stout, thick

gruñir *v.* to grumble, grunt, growl, creak

grupito *n.m.* little group

grupo *n.m.* group

guante *n.m.* glove

guapo, guapa *adj.* handsome, pretty

guardar *v.* to keep, guard; **guardar cama**/to stay in bed

guardarse de *v.* to guard against

guardia *n.f.* guard; *n.m.* policeman

guatemalteco *n.m., adj.* of or pertaining to Guatemala

guerra *n.f.* war

guerrillero *n.m.* guerrilla fighter

guía *n.m.* guide; *n.f.* guide book

guiar *v.* to guide, lead, drive

guisante *n.m.* pea

guisar *v.* to cook

guitarra *n.f.* guitar

guitarrista *n.m.f.* guitarist

gustar *v.* to be pleasing to, like, taste

gusto *n.m.* pleasure, taste; **con mucho gusto**/with much pleasure, gladly; sure, gladly

gustoso *adj.* tasty, enjoyable

gutural *adj.* guttural

H

ha *v. form of* **haber;** for words beginning with stressed **ha** or **a** see §4.6

haber *v.* to have (as a helping verb); see **haber** in idioms §14.27

había *v. form of* **haber**

hábil *adj.* skillful

habilidad *n.f.* skill

habitación *n.f.* room, dwelling

habitante *n.m.f.* inhabitant

habitar *v.* to inhabit, live, dwell, reside

hábito *n.m.* habit, clothing, attire

hablador, habladora *n.m.f.* talker, *adj.* talkative

hablar *v.* to speak, talk

habrá *v. form of* **haber**

hace *v. form of* **hacer; hace algún tiempo**/some time ago; **no hace mucho**/not long ago; **hace un año**/one year ago; **hace muchísimo tiempo**/a long time ago; **desde hace mucho tiempo**/for a long time

hacer *v.* to do, make; **se hace**/is made; **hacer falta**/to be lacking; **hacer compras**/to do shopping, **hacerse** *v.* to become, make oneself (itself); **hacerse cargo de**/to realize, take over, take charge; *see also* **hacer** and **hacerse** in idioms §14.28

hacia *prep.* toward; **hacía** *v. form of* **hacer**

hacienda *n.f.* estate, large ranch, home

hacha *n.f.* ax (el hacha); *see* §4.6

haga *v. form of* **hacer**

halagar *v.* to flatter

hallar *v.* to find; **hallarse** *v.* to be found, located, to find oneself, to be; **se halla**/is found

hambre *n.f.* hunger (el hambre); *see* §4.6; *see also* idioms with **tener** §14.42

han *v. form of* **haber; han de**/they have to; see **haber** in idioms §14.27

haré *v. form of* **hacer**

has *v. form of* **haber**

hasta *adv.* until, up to, even; **hasta que** *conj.* until

hay *idiomatic v. form of* **haber;** there is, there are; **hay que**/it is necessary

haz *v. form of* **hacer**

hazaña *n.f.* good deed, feat, exploit

hazlo/do it

hazte/become; *v. form of* **hacerse**

he *v. form of* **haber;** also, *interj.* behold; **he allí**/here you have

hecho *n.m.* deed, fact; **de hecho**/in fact; also, *past part. of* **hacer; hechos** *adj.* made

helado *n.m.* ice cream

helar *v.* to freeze

hembra *n.f.* female

hemos *v. form of* **haber**

heraldo *n.m.* herald

heredar *v.* to inherit

herencia *n.f.* inheritance

herida *n.f.* wound; **herido** *adj.* wounded

herir *v.* to wound, harm, hurt

hermano, hermana *n.m.f.* brother,

sister; **los hermanos**/brothers, brothers and sisters
hermosísimo *adj.* very handsome
hermoso, hermosa *adj.* beautiful
hermosura *n.f.* beauty
héroe *n.m.* hero
heroico, heroica *adj.* heroic
heroína *n.f.* heroine
heroísmo *n.m.* heroism
hervir *v.* to boil
hice, hiciera, hicieron, hiciste *v. forms of* **hacer**
hidráulica *adj.* hydraulic
hielo *n.m.* ice
hierba *n.f.* grass
hierro *n.m.* iron
hija *n.f.* daughter
hijo *n.m.* son; **hijos**/children, sons, sons and daughters
hilo *n.m.* thread
hispánico *adj.* Hispanic
Hispanoamérica *n.f.* Spanish America
hispanoamericano *adj.* Spanish American
historia *n.f.* history, story
historiador *n.m.* historian
histórico *adj.* historic, historical
hizo *v. form of* **hacer**
hogar *n.m.* home, house, hearth, fireplace
hoja *n.f.* leaf, sheet of paper
¡hola! *interj.* Hi! Hello!
holandeses *adj.* Dutch
holgazán *n.m.* idler, loafer
hombre *n.m.* man
hombro *n.m.* shoulder; **encogerse de hombros**/to shrug one's shoulders
homenaje *n.m.* homage
hondo *n.m.* depth, bottom; *adj.* deep
honorario *adj.* honorary
honrado *adj.* honorable, honored, honest
honrar *v.* to honor
hora *n.f.* hour, time; *see also* §3.28
horario *n.m.* timetable, schedule
horizonte *n.m.* horizon
horóscopo *n.m.* horoscope
horroroso *adj.* horrible, horrid
hospedería *n.f.* hostel, inn
hotelero *n.m.* hotel manager
hoy *adv.* today; **hoy día**/nowadays; **de hoy en adelante**/from now on; **hoy mismo**/this very day
huaracino *n.m., adj.* of or pertaining to Huaraz
hubiera, hubo *v. forms of* **haber;** *see also* §14.27, §8.65
huelga *n.f.* labor strike
huérfano, huérfana *n.m.f.* orphan
huerta *n.f.* vegetable garden
hueso *n.m.* bone, stone, pit (of fruit)
huésped *n.m.* guest
huevo *n.m.* egg
huido *past part. of* **huir** *v.* to flee, escape, run away, slip away; **huir de** *v.* to shun, avoid

humanidad *n.f.* humanity
humano *adj.* human
humedecer *v.* to moisten, dampen, lick
húmedo *adj.* humid
humilde *adj.* humble
humo *n.m.* smoke, fume, vapor
humor *n.m.* disposition, humor
hundir(se) *v.* to sink, plunge
huyeron *v. form of* **huir**

I

iba *v. form of* **ir**
iberoamericano *n.m., adj.* Latin American
ida *n.f.* departure, going; **ida y vuelta**/round trip
idea *n.f.* idea
identidad *n.f.* identity
identificación *n.f.* identification
identificarse *v.* to identify oneself (itself)
idioma *n.m.* language, **un modismo**/an idiom, idiomatic expression
idiota *n.m.f.* idiot
iglesia *n.f.* church
ignorar *v.* to ignore, to be ignorant of, not to know
igual *adj.* equal, similar; **igual que a mí**/same with me
igualmente *adv.* equally, likewise
iluminado *adj.* illuminated, lighted
iluminar *v.* to light, illuminate
ilusión *n.f.* illusion
ilusionada *adj.* deluded, given to false hopes
ilustración *n.f.* illustration
ilustre *adj.* famous, illustrious
imagen *n.f.* image, statue
imaginación *n.f.* imagination
imaginar(se) *v.* to imagine
imaginario *adj.* imaginary
imitar *v.* to imitate
impaciencia *n.f.* impatience
impacientarse *v.* to become impatient
impaciente *adj.* impatient
impedir *v.* to hinder, impede, prevent
imperativo *n.m., adj.* imperative
imperio *n.m.* empire
impermeable *n.m.* raincoat
impide *v. form of* **impedir**
implorar *v.* to beg, entreat, implore
imponer(se) *v.* to impose; **se impone**/is imposed
importado *adj.* imported
importancia *n.f.* importance
importante *adj.* important; **lo importante**/the important thing
importar *v.* to import, to be important, to matter; **no importa**/it doesn't matter; **no me importa**/it's not important to me, I don't care; **poco importa**/it's of little importance

importunar *v.* to disturb
impresas *adj.* printed
impresionado *adj.* impressed; also *past part. of* **impresionar** *v.* to impress, make an impression
imprimir *v.* to imprint, impress, print, fix in the mind
improviso, improvisto *adj.* unforeseen; **de improviso, a la improvista**/suddenly, unexpectedly
impuesto *n.m.* tax; also *past part. of* **imponer**
impulso *n.m.* impulse
impusieron *v. form of* **imponer**
inauguración *n.f.* inauguration
inaugurar *v.* to inaugurate
incendiar *v.* to set on fire
incendio *n.m.* fire
incensario *n.m.* censer (which burns incense)
incidente *n.m.* incident
incienso *n.m.* incense (for burning in a censer)
incierto *adj.* uncertain
inclinación *n.f.* inclination
inclinar *v.* to bow, incline, tilt
incluir *v.* to enclose, include; **incluirse** *v.* to be included; **incluso**/included
incomodidad *n.f.* inconvenience, discomfort
incómodos *adj.* uncomfortable
incomprensión *n.f.* lack of understanding
increíble *adj.* incredible
indecible *adj.* inexpressible
indefinidamente *adv.* indefinitely
independencia *n.f.* independence
indiada *n.f.* multitude of Indians
indicación *n.f.* indication
indicado *adj.* indicated
indicar *v.* to indicate, point out
indicativo *n.m., adj.* indicative
indiecito *n.m.* little Indian boy
indiferencia *n.f.* indifference
indiferente *adj.* indifferent
indígena *n.m.f., adj.* indigenous, native
indio *n.m.* Indian
indiscutible *adj.* unquestionable
individuo *n.m.* individual, person
índole *n.f.* kind, nature, disposition
inducir *v.* to induce, influence, persuade
indudablemente *adv.* undoubtedly, indubitably
industria *n.f.* industry
inesperado *adj.* unexpected
inestabilidad *n.f.* instability
infancia *n.f.* infancy
infanta *n.f.* legitimate daughter of a king of Spain or wife of **un infante** (legitimate son of a king of Spain who is not heir to the throne)
infeliz *n.m.* wretch; *adj.* unhappy, unfortunate

infierno *n.m.* hell, inferno
infinitivo *n.m.* infinitive
infinito *adj.* infinite
inflexión *n.f.* inflection
influencia *n.f.* influence
influir *v.* to influence
informar *v.* to inform; **informarse** *v.* to find out, inform oneself
informe *n.m.* report; **informes** *n.m.pl.* information
infracción *n.f.* infraction
ingeniería *n.f.* engineering
ingeniero *n.m.* engineer
ingenio *n.m.* wit, talent
Inglaterra *n.f.* England
inglés, inglesa *adj.* English; **el inglés/** English language
ingrato *adj.* ungrateful
ingresos *n.m.pl.* income, revenue
inhabitable *adj.* uninhabitable
inhumano *adj.* inhuman
iniciación *n.f.* initiation, beginning
iniciar *v.* to initiate, begin, start
injusticia *n.f.* injustice
injustos *adj.* unjust
inmediatamente *adv.* immediately
inmediato *adj.* immediate
inmemorial *adj.* immemorial
inmensidad *n.f.* immensity
inmenso *adj.* immense, large
inmigración *n.f.* immigration
inmigrante *n.m.f.* immigrant
inmortal *adj.* immortal
inmóvil *adj.* motionless, still
innecesario *adj.* unnecessary
innegable *adj.* undeniable
innovación *n.f.* innovation
inocente *adj.* innocent
inolvidable *adj.* unforgettable
inquietante *adj.* disturbing
inquietarse *v.* to worry, feel disturbed
inquieto *adj.* uneasy, restless
inquietud *n.f.* restlessness, uneasiness
inscribir *v.* to inscribe, record; **inscribirse** *v.* to register, enroll
insignificante *adj.* insignificant
insinuar *v.* to insinuate
insistencia *n.f.* insistence
insistir (en) *v.* to insist (on, upon)
insoportable *adj.* unbearable
inspirar *v.* to inspire
instalación *n.f.* installation
instalar *v.* to install
instante *n.m.* instant; **al instante/** instantly, at once
instituto *n.m.* institute
instrucción *n.f.* instruction, learning
instructivo *adj.* instructional
instruir *v.* to instruct
instrumento *n.m.* instrument
integrar *v.* to integrate
inteligencia *n.f.* intelligence
inteligente *adj.* intelligent
intención *n.f.* intention
intensos *adj.* intense
intentar *v.* to attempt, try, intend

intercambio *n.m.* interchange
interés *n.m.* interest
interesados *adj.* interested; **los interesados/**those interested
interesante *adj.* interesting
interesar *v.* to interest; **interesarse** *v.* to be interested, interest oneself
interno *adj.* internal; **un colegio interno/**boarding school
interpretar *v.* to interpret; **intérprete** *n.m.f.* interpreter
interrogante *adj., adv.* in a questioning way
interrumpir *v.* to interrupt; **interrumpido/**interrupted
íntimo *adj., adv.* intimate, intimately
introducir *v.* to introduce
inundar *v.* to flood, inundate
inútil *adj.* useless
invadir *v.* to invade
inválido, inválida *n.m.f.* invalid (person)
invasión *n.f.* invasion
invasores *n.m.* invaders
inventar *v.* to invent
invento *n.m.* invention
investigación *n.f.* investigation, research
investigador, investigadora *n.m.f.* investigator, researcher
invierno *n.m.* winter
invitado, invitada *n.m.f.* guest
invitar *v.* to invite
involuntario *adj.* involuntary
inyección *n.f.* injection
ir *v.* to go; *see also* §7.136, §14.22, §6.38, §6.49, §8.14, §8.24, §8.30
ira *n.f.* anger, ire
iré, iremos *v. forms of* **ir**
irregularidad *n.f.* irregularity
irreligiosidad *n.f.* irreligiousness
irresponsable *adj.* irresponsible
irritar *v.* to irritate
irse *v.* to go away; *see also* §7.137, §8.14
isla *n.f.* island; **las Islas Canarias/** Canary Islands
isleño *n.m.* islander
Italia *n.f.* Italy
italiano, italiana *adj.* Italian; **el italiano/**Italian language
itinerario *n.m.* itinerary
izquierdo, izquierda *adj.* left (opposite of right); **a la izquierda/** at (on, to) the left; **la izquierda/**left, left side, left hand

J

jabón *n.m.* soap
jamás *adv.* ever, never
jamón *n.m.* ham
jardín *n.m.* garden
jarrón *n.m.* vase
jaula *n.f.* cage
jefe *n.m.* chief, boss; **jefe del estado/**

chief of state
jinete *n.m.* horseman
jornada *n.f.* journey, day's journey
joven *adj.* young; *n.m.f.* young person, young man, young woman
joya *n.f.* jewel
júbilo *n.m.* jubilation, joy
jubiloso *adj.* jubilant
juega, juego *v. forms of* **jugar; se juega** /one plays; **un juego/**a game
jueves *n.m.* Thursday
juez *n.m.* judge
jugador, jugadora *n.m.f.* player
jugar *v.* to play, play a game; *see also* §7.151
jugo *n.m.* juice
juguete *n.m.* toy
juguetón *adj.* playful
juicio *n.m.* judgment
julio *n.m.* July
junio *n.m.* June
juntar *v.* to join, unite, connect; **juntarse (con)** *v.* to assemble, join, get together with
junto *adj.* together, joined; **junto a/** next to, beside; **junto con/**together with
juntos, juntas *adj.* together
jurado *n.m.* jury
jurar *v.* to swear, vow, take an oath
justicia *n.f.* justice
justo *adj.* just, exact, right
juventud *n.f.* youth
juzgar *v.* to judge

K

kilogramo *n.m.* kilogram
kilómetro *n.m.* kilometer
klaxon *n.m.* automobile horn

L

la *def. art. f.s.* the; also, *pron.; see* §4.ff, §6–§6.105
labio *n.m.* lip
laboratorio *n.m.* laboratory
laborioso *adj.* laborious, hard-working
labrador *n.m.* farmer
labrar *v.* to work on, build, carve
lado *n.m.* side; **al lado de/**next to, beside; **por un lado/**on the one hand; **por otro lado/**on the other hand
ladrar *v.* to bark (dog)
ladrillo *n.m.* brick
ladrón *n.m.* thief
lago *n.m.* lake
lágrima *n.f.* tear, tear drop
lamentación *n.f.* sorrow, lamentation
lamento *n.m.* lament
lámpara *n.f.* lamp
lana *n.f.* wool
lancha *n.f.* boat, launch
lanzar *v.* to throw, cast, hurl, fling; **lanzarse a/**to rush upon

lápiz *n.m.* pencil; **lápices**/pencils
largarse *v.* to go away, go far away
largo, larga, largos, largas *adj.* long
larguísima *adj.* very long
lástima *n.f.* pity, compassion; **¡Qué lástima!**/What a pity! What a shame!
lastimar *v.* to hurt, injure
lastimarse *v.* to hurt oneself, be sorry for, complain, regret
lata *n.f.* tin can
latín *n.m.* Latin
latinoamericano *adj.* Latin American
latitud *n.f.* latitude
lavar *v.* to wash; **lavarse** *v.* to wash oneself
léase/read
lección *n.f.* lesson
lector, lectora *n.m.f.* reader (person)
lectura *n.f.* reading
leche *n.f.* milk
lechero *n.m.* milkman
leer *v.* to read
legales *adj.* legal
legendario *adj.* legendary
legión *n.f.* legion
legumbre *n.f.* vegetable
leía, leímos *v. forms of* **leer**; **leído** *past part. of* **leer**
lejano *adj.* distant
lejos *adv.* far; **a lo lejos**/in the distance; **lejos de**/far from
lengua *n.f.* language, tongue; **sacar la lengua**/to stick out one's tongue
lenguaje *n.m.* language, speech
lentamente *adv.,* slowly
lente *n.m.f.* lens; **los lentes**/eyeglasses
lento *adj.* slow
leña *n.f.* firewood, kindling
leñador, leñadora *n.m.f.* woodcutter
león *n.m.* lion
letra *n.f.* letter (alphabet)
levantado *adj.* raised
levantándose *pres. part. of* **levantarse**
levantar *v.* to lift, raise, build, erect
levantarse *v.* to get up, stand up, rise; **se levanta**/it rises
ley *n.f.* law
leyenda *n.f.* legend, story
leyendo *pres. part. of* **leer**
leyó *v. form of* **leer**
liberadas *adj.* liberated; **liberar** *v.* to free, liberate
libertad *n.f.* liberty, freedom
libertador, libertadora *n.* liberator
libra *n.f.* pound
librar *v.* to free, liberate; **librarse** *v.* to escape
libre *adj.* free; **al aire libre**/in the open air, outdoors
librería *n.f.* bookstore
libro *n.m.* book
licencia *n.f.* license
líder *n.m.* leader
liga *n.f.* league

ligero *adj.* light (not heavy)
limitación *n.f.* limitation
limitado *adj.* limited
limitar *v.* to limit, restrict
límite *n.m.* border, boundary, limit
limón *n.m.* lemon
limonada *n.f.* lemonade
limosna *n.f.* alms, charity
limpiar *v.* to clean, wipe, cleanse, clear
limpiarse *v.* to clean oneself
límpiela/clean it
limpieza *n.f.* cleanliness
limpio *adj.* clean
linda, lindo *adj.* pretty
línea *n.f.* line
lingüístico *adj.* linguistic
linterna *n.f.* lantern, flashlight
líquido *n.m.* liquid
lista *n.f.* list
listo, lista *adj.* ready, clever; **estar listo**/to be ready; **ser listo**/to be clever
literario *adj.* literary
literatura *n.f.* literature
litro *n.m.* liter
lo *pron.* him, it; *see* §6.–§6.105; **lo que**/that which; *see* §6.93
lobo *n.m.* wolf
local *n.m.* location, place, premises
localidad *n.f.* locality
loco, loca *n.m.f., adj.* crazy, mad, fool, insane
lodo *n.m.* mud; *see* **hay** in weather expressions §17.ff
lograr *v.* to attain, get, obtain, procure, achieve; **lograr + inf.**/succeed in
lomo *n.m.* back of an animal
longitud *n.f.* length, longitude
lote *n.m.* lot, share
lotería *n.f.* lottery
luces *pl.* of **luz**
lucientes *adj.* lucid, shining
lucir *v.* to shine
lucha *n.f.* battle, struggle, fight, combat
luchar *v.* to fight, combat, struggle, strive, wrestle
luego *adv.* then, soon; **hasta luego**/see you later; **desde luego**/since then; **luego como, luego que**/as soon as; *see also* **luego** in idioms §14.31
lugar *n.m.* place, small village; **tener lugar**/to take place
lujo *n.m.* luxury
lujoso *adj.* luxurious
lumbre *n.f.* fire; brightness, light (from a burning fire)
luna *n.f.* moon; *see also* **hay** in weather expressions §17.ff
lunes *n.m.* Monday
luz *n.f.* light
luzco *v. form of* **lucir**

LL

llama *n.f.* flame, llama (animal)
llamada *n.f.* call; **llamado, llamada** *adj.* called, so-called
llamar *v.* to call, name; **llamar a la puerta**/to knock on the door
llamarse *v.* to be called, named
llano *adj.* smooth, flat; *n.m.* plain
llanta *n.f.* rim, tire, wheel (auto)
llanto *n.m.* crying, weeping, sobbing
llanura *n.f.* prairie, plain
llave *n.f.* key
llegada *n.f.* arrival
llegar *v.* to arrive; **llegar a**/to reach; **llegar a ser**/to become; **el llegar a ser**/becoming
llena *n.f.* flood, overflow; *adj.* full, filled
llenado *adj.* full
llenar *v.* to fill; **llenarse** *v.* to be filled
lleno *adj.* filled, full; **llenos de**/full of, filled with
llevado *adj.* carried, taken, brought
llevar *v.* to bring, carry, carry away, take away, wear, bear, to take (a person somewhere); **llevar a cabo**/to succeed in, accomplish, carry out, bring about; **llevarse** *v.* to carry away; **llevarse bien con**/to get along well with
llorar *v.* to cry, weep, whine; also *n.m.* crying, weeping
lloriquear *v.* to whine, whimper
lloro *v. form of* **llorar**; also *n.m.* weeping, crying
llorón *n.m.* weeper, whiner
llover *v.* to rain
lloviendo *pres. part. of* **llover**
lluvia *n.f.* rain; *see also* weather expressions §3.29, §17.ff

M

machete *n.m.* knife, machete
macho *n.m., adj.* male, he-man, macho, manly
madera *n.f.* wood
madre *n.f.* mother
madrileño *adj.* of or pertaining to Madrid
madrugada *n.f.* dawn, daybreak
madrugar *v.* to get up very early in the morning
maduro *adj.* mature, ripe
maestro, maestra *n.m.f.* master, teacher
magistrado *n.m.* magistrate
magnífico *adj.* magnificent
mago *n.m.* magician, wizard
maíz *n.m.* corn
majestad *n.f.* majesty
majestuoso *adj.* majestic
mal *n.m.* evil, grief, harm, illness; *adv.* badly, poorly; **mal vestido**/poorly dresssed; *see also* §5.12, §5.20, §10.7

maldad *n.f.* wickedness

maldecir *v.* to curse

maldición *n.f.* curse

maldito *adj.* cursed

maleta *n.f.* suitcase, valise

maletón *n.m.* large, heavy suitcase

malgastar *v.* to waste, misuse

malhumorado *adj.* ill humored, in a bad mood, bad temper

malicioso *adj.* malicious

malo, mala *adj.* bad, evil, sick; *n.m.* bad one, bad, evil (person); **lo malo**/the bad thing; *see also* **§5.12, §5.20, §10.7**

maltratar *v.* to mistreat

mallorquino, mallorquina *adj.* of or pertaining to Mallorca

mamá *n.f.* mom, mother

manco *adj.* maimed, crippled

mancha *n.f.* spot, stain

mandado *adj.* scent; *past part. of* **mandar** *v.* to order, command, send

manejar *v.* to drive (a vehicle), to manage

manera *n.f.* manner; **de manera que**/so that; **de todas maneras**/in any case, anyway, by all means; **de esta manera**/in this way

manga *n.f.* sleeve

manifestación *n.f.* manifestation

manifestar *v.* to manifest, show, declare

mano *n.f.* hand; **¡manos a la obra!** to work!

mansión *n.f.* mansion

manta *n.f.* blanket

mantel *n.m.* tablecloth

mantener *v.* to maintain, keep up, support, provide for

manténgase/maintain yourself

mantequilla *n.f.* butter

manzana *n.f.* apple; **manzano** *n.m.* apple tree

mañana *n.f.* morning; *adv.* tomorrow; **mañana por la mañana**/tomorrow morning; **por la mañana**/in the morning; **pasado mañana**/the day after tomorrow; *see also* **mañana** in idioms **§14.32**

mapa *n.m.* map

maquillarse *v.* to make up one's face, put make up on, put on cosmetics

máquina *n.f.* machine; **máquina de coser**/sewing machine; **máquina de escribir**/typewriter

maquinaria *n.f.* machinery

mar *n.m. or f.* sea

maravilla *n.f.* marvel, wonder

maravilloso *adj.* marvelous

marcar *v.* to mark, note, observe, designate

marcha *n.f.* march, course, progress; **ponerse en marcha**/to start (set) out

marchar *v.* to march, walk;

marcharse *v.* to leave, go away, walk away

marido *n.m.* husband

marina *n.f.* marine, navy

marinero *n.m.* sailor

mariposa *n.f.* butterfly

marítima *adj.* maritime

mármol *n.m.* marble

marqués *n.m.* marquis

marquesa *n.f.* marchioness

Marte *n.m.* Mars

martes *n.m.* Tuesday

marzo *n.m.* March

mas *conj.* but

más *adv.* more, most; **lo más**/the more; **más bien**/moreover; **más tarde**/later; **cada vez más**/more and more; **más vale tarde que nunca**/better late than never; **lo más pronto posible**/as soon as possible; *see also* **§5.40ff, §12.12,** and see this word in the general index.

masa *n.f.* mass

mascar *v.* to chew

máscara *n.f.* mask

¡Mátala!/Kill it!

matar *v.* to kill

matemáticas *n.f.* mathematics

materia *n.f.* matter

matrimonio *n.m.* married couple, marriage

máxima *adj.* maximum

mayo *n.m.* May

mayor *adj.* major, important, greater, older, larger, main

mayordomo *n.m.* steward, major-domo, servant

mayores *n.m.pl.* grown-ups

mayoría *n.f.* majority

mazo *n.m.* mallet

me *pron.* me, to me, myself; *see also* **§6.–§6.105**

mecánica *n.f.* mechanics

mecánico *n.m.* mechanic

mecha *n.f.* wick

medalla *n.f.* medal

media *n.f.* stocking, sock; *adj.* half; **la Edad Media**/Middle Ages; *see also* **§16.7**

mediano *adj.* medium size

medianoche *n.f.* midnight

mediante *adj.* mediating; *prep.* by means of, through, with the help of

medicina *n.f.* medicine

médico *n.m.* doctor, physician; **médicos** *adj.* medical

medida *n.f.* measure

medio *n.m.* middle, method, way, means; **medios literarios**/literary circles; *adj.* half; *see also* **§14.13**

mediodía *n.m.* noon

medir *v.* to measure, compare, judge, weigh, scan (verses)

meditar *v.* to meditate, think

mejicano *n.m., adj.* of or pertaining to Mexico

mejilla *n.f.* cheek

mejor *adj., adv.* better, best; **todo lo mejor**/all the best; *see also* **§10.7**

mejorar *v.* to improve, become better

melocotón *n.m.* peach

memoria *n.f.* memory, recollection; **de memoria**/by heart, from memory

mencionar *v.* to mention

mendigo *n.m.* beggar

menester *n.m.* need; **ser menester**/to be necessary

menor *adj.* younger, youngest, smaller, minor; **al por menor**/retail sale

menos *adv.* less, least; **cuando menos**/at least; **lo menos**/the least; **por lo menos**/at least; **a menos que**/unless; **echar de menos**/to miss; *see also* **§5.40ff** and this word in the general index

mensaje *n.m.* message

mensajero *n.m.* messenger

mentir *v.* to lie, tell a lie

mentira *n.f.* lie, falsehood

menudo *adj.* little, small, minute, petty; *n.m.* small change; **a menudo**/often

mercado *n.m.* market

mercancía, mercancías *n.f.* merchandise

merecer *v.* to deserve, merit

mérito *n.m.* merit

mes *n.m.* month; **al mes**/a month; **el mes próximo**/next month; **por mes**/by the month; *see also* **§15.3(d)**

mesa. *n.f.* table

mesero *n.m.* waiter

meses *n.m.pl.* of **mes**

meseta *n.f.* plateau

mesón *n.m.* inn, tavern

mestizo *n.m., adj.* mestizo (a person of mixed blood)

meter *v.* to put, place, insert

metió *v. form of* **meter**

método *n.m.* method

metro *n.m.* meter, subway

metrópoli *n.f.* metropolis

mexicano *n.m. adj.* of or pertaining to Mexico

mezcla *n.f.* mixture

mezclar *v.* to mix

mi *poss. adj.* my; *see also* **§5.58**

micrófono *n.m.* microphone

miedo *n.m.* fear; **tener miedo**/to be afraid

miedosa *adj.* fearful, scary

miel *n.f.* honey

miembro *n.m.* member, limb

mientras *adv., conj.* while, meanwhile, as, whereas; **mientras que**/while; **mientras tanto**/meanwhile, in the meantime; *see also* **§10.ff**

miércoles *n.m.* Wednesday

mil *n.m., adj.* one thousand; **miles**/

thousands; *see also* **§4.19(a)**

milagro *n.m.* miracle

militar *n.m., adj.* military, soldier

milla *n.f.* mile

millares/thousands

millón *n.m.* million

mina *n.f.* mine

mínimo *n.m.* minimum

ministerio *n.m.* ministry

ministro *n.m.* minister

minoría *n.m.* minority

minuto *n.m.* minute

¡Mira!/Look!

mirada *n.f.* glance, look, facial expression

mirar *v.* to look (at), watch; **mirarse** *v.* to look at oneself

mire *v. form of* **mirar**

miseria *n.f.* misery, poverty

misericordia *n.f.* mercy, pity

misión *n.f.* mission

misionero *n.m.* missionary

mismo *adj.* same, very; **el mismo día**/the same day; **el día mismo**/the very day; **él mismo**/he himself; **lo mismo**/the same thing, *see also* **mismo** in idioms **§14.33**

misterio *n.m.* mystery

misterioso *adj.* mysterious

mitad *n.f.* half, middle; *see also* **§14.14**

mitin *n.m.* meeting

mito *n.m.* myth

moda *n.f.* fashion, style; **de última moda**/latest style

modal *n.m.* modal; **modales**/manners

modelar *v.* to model

modelo *n.m.* model, pattern

modesta *adj.* modest

modismo *n.m.* idiom, idiomatic expression

modo *n.m.* mode, manner, way, means; **de modo que**/so that, in order that, in such a way that; **de otro modo**/otherwise; **de ningún modo**/by no means, no way; **de este modo**/in this way; *see also* **§12.ff**

moho *n.m.* mildew, mold, must, rust

mojado *adj.* wet, drenched

mojar *v.* to wet

molestar *v.* to molest, bother, annoy, disturb

molestia *n.f.* bother, annoyance, trouble

monarca *n.m.* monarch, king

monasterio *n.m.* monastery

moneda *n.f.* coin, money

mono *n.m.* monkey

montaña *n.f.* mountain

montañoso *adj.* mountainous

montar *v.* to mount, get on

monte *v.* mountain

monumento *n.m.* monument

morder *v.* to bite, gnaw

moreno *adj.* dark hair, brunette, dark skin, brown

morir(se) *v.* to die

moro, mora *n.m.f., adj.* Moor, Moorish

mosca *n.f.* fly

mostrar *v.* to show, point out, appear

motivo *n.m.* motive, reason

moto *n.f.* short for **motocicleta**/motorcycle

movedizo, movediza *adj.* moving

mover *v.* to move, persuade, induce, shake, excite

moviendo *pres. part. of* **mover**

movimiento *n.m.* movement

movió *v. form of* **mover**

moza *n.f.* maid, girl

mozo *n.m.* young man, waiter, boy

muchacha *n.f.* girl

muchacho *n.m.* boy

muchedumbre *n.f.* crowd

muchísimo *adj.* many, very many, very much; *see also* **§5.47ff**

mucho, mucha *adj.* much, many, a great deal; *see also* **§5.49, §10.5, §10.7**

mudar *v.* to change; **mudarse** *v.* to move (from one place to another), change one's clothes, change one's place of residence

mudo *adj.* mute, silent, dumb

mueble *n.m.* piece (article) of furniture; **muebles**/furniture

muerde *v. form of* **morder**

muero *v. form of* **morir**

muerte *n.f.* death

muerto *past part. of* **morir**; died; *n.* dead man, **los muertos**/dead persons

muestra *v. form of* **mostrar**; *n.f.* show, presentation, sample

mujer *n.f.* woman

mula *n.f.* female mule; **mulo** *n.m.* male mule

muleta *n.f.* cape

multa *n.f.* penalty, fine

multiplicar *v.* to multiply

multitud *n.f.* multitude, crowd

mundial *adj.* world, world-wide

mundo *n.m.* world; **todo el mundo**/everybody, everyone

municiones *n.f.pl.* munitions

municipios *n.m.* municipalities

muñeco *n.m.,* **muñeca** *n.f.* doll

muralla *n.f.* wall, rampart

murieron *v. form of* **morir**

murmurar *v.* to murmur

muro *n.m.* thick, supporting wall

musa *n.f.* muse

museo *n.m.* museum

música *n.f.* music

músico *n.m.* musician; *adj.* musical

muslo *n.m.* thigh

musulmanas *adj.* Moslem

muy *adv.* very; *see also* **§5.49, §10.5**

N

nacer *v.* to be born

nacido *past part. of* **nacer**; born

nacimiento *n.m.* birth

nación *n.f.* nation, country; *see also* **§3.26**

nacional *adj.* national

nacionalidad *n.f.* nationality

nacionalizar *v.* to nationalize

Naciones Unidas *n.f.* United Nations

nada *indef. pron.* nothing, not anything; also *v. form of* **nadar**

nadando *v. form of* **nadar**

nadar *v.* to swim

nadie *indef. pron.* no one, nobody, not anyone

naranja *n.f.* orange (fruit)

narices *n.f.pl.* nostrils

nariz *n.f.* nose

narración *n.f.* narration, story

narrador *n.m.* narrator

narrar *v.* to narrate

natal *adj.* native

naturaleza *n.f.* nature

naturalmente *adv.* naturally

navaja *n.f.* razor, folding blade, jacknife, razor clam

naval *adj.* naval, navy

nave *n.f.* ship, vessel

navegante *n.m.* navigator

navegar *v.* to sail, navigate

Navidad *n.f.* Nativity; **el día de Navidad**/Christmas Day

neblina *n.f.* fog

necesario *adj.* necessary, required

necesidad *n.f.* necessity, need

necesitar *v.* to need, necessitate, be necessary; **se necesita**/it is necessary

negar *v.* to deny; **negarse a** *v.* to refuse to, deny

negociante *n.m.* business person, merchant

negociar *v.* to negotiate

negocio *n.m.* business, business deal, transaction; **negocios** *n.m.pl.* business, businesses; **un hombre de negocios**/businessman

negro *n.m., adj.* black

nena, nene *n.m.f.* baby, child

neoyorquino *n.m., adj.* of or pertaining to New York

nerviosidad, *n.f.* nervousness

nervioso *adj.* nervous

nevar *v.* to snow

ni *conj.* neither, nor, not (one); **ni...ni**/neither...nor; **ni siquiera** *adv.* not even

nicaragüense *adj.* of or pertaining to Nicaragua

nieto *n.m.* grandson; **nieta** *n.f.* granddaughter

nieva *v. form of* **nevar**; **nieve** *n.f.* snow

ningún, ninguno, ninguna *indef. pron., adj.* not any, not one, none; *see also* **§5.20ff**

niñez *n.f.* childhood

niñita *n.f.* little girl
niño, niña *n.m.f.* child; **niños/** children
nivel *n.m.* level
no *adv.* no, not; **no obstante/** notwithstanding; *see also* **no** in idioms §14.34
nobles *adj.* noble
noche *n.f.* night, evening; **esta noche/** tonight, this evening; *see also* **de** in idioms §14.22 and **por** in idioms §14.37
nombrar *v.* to name
nombre *n.m.* name; **nombre de pila/** given name (first name)
normalizar *v.* to normalize
normalmente *adv.* normally
norte *n.m.* North
norteamericano *n.m., adj.* American, North American
nota *n.f.* note, bill, grade, mark
notable *adj.* noteworthy, notable
notar *v.* to note, notice, mark, remark, observe
noticia *n.f.* news, notice; **noticias** *n.f.pl.* news
novedad *n.f.* novelty, new thing
novela *n.f.* novel; **novela policíaca/** detective story, novel
novelista *n.m.f.* novelist
noventa *n.m., adj.* ninety
novicio *n.m.* novice, learner, beginner
noviembre *n.m.* November
novio, novia *n.* sweetheart, fiancé(e), bride, bridegroom; **novios/** sweethearts
nube *n.f.* cloud
núcleo *n.m.* nucleus
nudo *n.m.* knot
nueces *n.f.pl.* nuts, walnuts; *pl.* of **nuez**
nuestro, nuestra *poss. adj.* our; *see also* §5.58ff, §6.64ff
Nueva York/New York
nuevamente *adv.* again
nueve *n.m., adj.* nine
nuevo, nueva *adj.* new; **de nuevo/** again
nuez *n.f.* nut, walnut
número *n.m.* number; *see also* §18.ff
numeroso *adj.* numerous
nunca *adv.* never; **nunca jamás/** nevermore
nupcias *n.f.pl.* nuptials, wedding
nutrir *v.* to nourish, nurture

O

o *conj.* or; **o...o/**either...or; *see also* §12.13
obedecer *v.* to obey
objetivo *n.m.* objective, purpose; **objeto** *n.m.* object
obligación *n.f.* obligation
obligado *adj.* obligated
obligar *v.* to obligate, compel
obra *n.f.* work; **obra maestra/**

masterpiece; **¡manos a la obra!** to work!
obrero *n.m.* worker
obscurecer *v.* to obscure, darken, cloud
obscuridad *n.f.* obscurity, darkness
obscuro *adj.* obscure, dark
observación *n.f.* observation
observar *v.* to observe; **observarse** *v.* to observe oneself (each other)
obstáculo *n.m.* obstacle
obstante *adv.* **no obstante/** nevertheless
obstruir *v.* to obstruct
obstruyeron *v. form of* **obstruir**
obtener *v.* to obtain, get
obtuvo *v. form of* **obtener**
ocasión *n.f.* occasion, opportunity
occidental *adj.* western
ocasionar *v.* to occasion, provoke
océano *n.m.* ocean
octava *adj.* eighth
octubre *n.m.* October
ocultar *v.* to hide
ocupación *n.f.* trade, occupation
ocupado *adj.* busy, occupied
ocupar *v.* to occupy; **ocuparse de/**to take care of, look after, be busy with
ocurrir *v.* to occur, happen
ochenta *n.m., adj.* eighty
ocho *n.m., adj.* eight
ochocientos *n.m., adj.* eight hundred
odiar *v.* to hate
odio *n.m.* hate, hatred
oeste *n.m.* West
ofender *v.* to offend
oferta *n.f.* offer
oficial *n.m.* official, officer
oficialmente *adv.* officially
oficina *n.f.* office
oficio *n.m.* craft, occupation, trade, job
ofrecer *v.* to offer; **ofreciéndole/** offering to him
ofrecimiento *n.m.* offer
oía *v. form of* **oír**; **oído** *past part. of* **oír**
oído *n.m.* hearing, ear; **de oídas/** hearsay
oír *v.* to hear
ojal *n.m.* buttonhole
¡ojalá! *interj.* May God grant...! I hope, I hope to God...! *see also* §7.67
ojera *n.f.* eyecup
ojo *n.m.* eye
ola *n.f.* wave
oler *v.* to smell, scent
olor *n.m.* odor, smell
oloroso *adj.* fragrant, odorous
olvidado *adj.* forgotten
olvidar(se) *v.* to forget
omitir *v.* to omit; **omitido** *past part. and adj.* omitted
ómnibus *n.m.* bus
onza *n.f.* ounce
operación *n.f.* operation

operar *v.* to operate
opinar *v.* to have an opinion, think, opine
opinión *n.f.* opinion
oponer(se) *v.* oppose, be opposed, object
oportunidad *n.f.* opportunity, occasion
oportuno *adj.* opportune
optimismo *n.m.* optimism
opuesto *adj.* opposite, opposed
oración *n.f.* prayer, oration, speech, sentence
orador *n.m.* orator, speaker
orales *adj. pl.* oral
orar *v.* to pray
orden *n.m.* order, group; *n.f.* order, command; **órdenes/**orders
ordenar *v.* to order, command, put in order, arrange; **lo ordenado/**what was ordered
ordinario *adj.* ordinary
oreja *n.f.* ear
organizador, organizadora *n.m.f.* organizer
organizar *v.* to organize, set up
órgano *n.m.* organ
orgullo *n.m.* pride
orgulloso *adj.* proud
orientar *v.* to inform, orient, brief
orientarse *v.* to become informed
origen *n.m.* origin
orilla *n.f.* bank, shore, edge (of a river)
oro *n.m.* gold
orquesta *n.f.* orchestra
osar *v.* to dare, venture
oscurecer *v.* to obscure, darken, cloud
oscuridad *n.f.* obscurity, darkness
oscuro *adj.* dark
oso *n.m.* bear
otoño *n.m.* autumn, fall
otro, otra *adj.* other, another; **otra vez/**again; **de otro modo/**otherwise; **otra cosa/**something else; *see also* §4.19(c)
oveja *n.f.* ewe, sheep
oxígeno *n.m.* oxygen
oye, oyen oyó *v. forms of* **oír**

P

pabellón *n.m.* pavilion
paciencia *n.f.* patience
paciente *n.m.f.* patient
pacto *n.m.* pact
padecer *v.* to suffer
padre *n.m.* father; **los padres/**mother and father, parents
paella *n.f.* rice with seafood, meat or chicken
pagar *v.* to pay (for); **se paga/**is paid
página *n.f.* page
país *n.m.* country, nation; *see also* §3.26
paisaje *n.m.* countryside
paisanaje *n.m.* countryfolk, peasantry

paja *n.f.* straw
pajarito *n.m.* little bird
pájaro *n.m.* bird
palabra *n.f.* word; **palabra a palabra**/ word by word
palacio *n.m.* palace
paleta *n.f.* palette
pálido *adj.* pale; **ponerse pálido**/to turn pale
paliza *n.f.* spanking
palmada *n.f.* handclap, slap
palo *n.m.* pole, stick
paloma *n.f.* dove, pigeon
pan *n.m.* bread
panadería *n.f.* bakery
panadero *n.m.* baker
panamericano *n.m., adj* of or pertaining to Pan-America
pantalón *n.m.,* **pantalones**/pants, trousers
panza *n.f.* belly, paunch
paño *n.m.* cloth
pañuelo *n.m.* handkerchief
papá *n.m.* dad, papa
Papa *n.m.* Pope
papel *n.m.* paper; role (part) in a play; **hacer el papel de**/to play the role of; **papel secante**/blotter
paquete *n.m.* package, parcel
par *n.m.* pair, couple; **de par en par**/ wide open
para *prep.* for, in order to, by; **para con**/toward, with, to; *see also* §11.15; **para que**/so that, in order that; *see also* §12., §11.19ff
parado *adj.* stopped
paraguas *n.m.* umbrella
paralítica *adj.* paralyzed, paralytic
parar *v.* to stop (someone or something)
pararse *v.* to stop oneself
pardo *n.m., adj.* brown
parecer *v.* to seem, appear; **parecerse** *v.* to resemble each other, look alike, resemble; **al parecer**/apparently; **a mi parecer**/in my opinion; *see also* §6.12, §6.20
parecido *n.m.* likeness, resemblance; **bien parecido**/good-looking; *adj.* similar, like
pared *n.f.* wall
pareja *n.f.* couple
pariente *n.m.* relative
parque *n.m.* park
párrafo *n.m.* paragraph
parte *n.f.* part; **por todas partes**/ everywhere; **de todas partes**/from everywhere
participación *n.f.* participation
participar *v.* to participate
particular *adj.* particular, private
partida *n.f.* departure
partidario *n.m.* partisan
partido *n.m.* game, political party
partir *v.* to leave, depart, divide, split
pasada *n.f.* passing, passage, pass; *adj.*

past, last; **la semana pasada**/last week
pasado *n.m.* past *adj.* past, last; **pasado mañana**/the day after tomorrow
pasaje *n.m.* passage
pasajero *adj.* fleeting, temporary, passing
pasajero, pasajera *n.m.f.* passenger
pasar *v.* to pass (spend time), pass by, go by, send, happen; **¡Que lo pases bien!**/Have a good time!
pasear(se) *v.* to stroll, promenade, take a walk, parade; **pasear en automóvil**/to go for a drive
paseo *n.m.* boulevard, avenue, walk, promenade; **dar un paseo**/to take a walk
paso *n.m.* step, way, lane, path, pace, pass
pasó *v. form of* **pasar**
pastel *n.m.* pie, pastry
pata *n.f.* paw
patata *n.f.* potato
patio *n.m.* patio, courtyard
patria *n.f.* native land; *see also* §3.26
patriota *n.m.f.* patriot
patriótico *adj.* patriotic
patriotismo *n.m.* patriotism
patrón *n.m.* boss, employer, patron saint
pausadamente *adv.* in a pause, pausingly
pavo *n.m.* turkey
paz *n.f.* peace
pecado *n.m.* sin
peces *pl. of* **pez**
pecho *n.m.* chest, breast
pedazo *n.m.* piece
pedía *v. form of* **pedir; pedido** *past part. of* **pedir; lo pedido**/what was requested
pedir *v.* to request, ask for; **pedir prestado**/to borrow
pegar *v.* to beat, hit, slap, spank, attach, glue, stick
¡Péinala!/Comb it!
peinar *v.* to comb
peinarse *v.* to comb one's hair
peine *n.m.* comb
pelado *past part. of* **pelar** *v.* to pluck; **a grito pelado**/at the top of one's lungs
pelea *n.f.* fight, quarrel; **pelear** *v.* to fight, combat
película *n.f.* film, movie
peligro *n.m.* danger, peril
peligroso *adj.* dangerous, perilous
pelo *n.m.* hair
pelota *n.f.* ball; **jugar a la pelota**/to play ball
peluca *n.f.* wig
peluquería *n.f.* beauty salon, barber shop
peluquero *n.m.* barber, hairdresser
pena *n.f.* pain, sorrow, grief, trouble;

valer la pena/to be worthwhile
penalidad *n.f.* penalty
pendiente *n.m.* earring
penetrante *adj.* penetrating
penetrar *v.* to penetrate
peninsulares *n.m.pl.* inhabitants of a peninsula
penoso *adj.* painful
pensamiento *n.m.* thought
pensar *v.* to think; **pensar en**/to think about; **se ha pensado**/it has been thought; **pensar de**/to think (have an opinion) of
pensativo *adj.* pensive, thoughtful
penumbra *n.f.* twilight
peor *adj., adv.* worse, worst; *see also* §10.7
pequeño *adj.* small, little; **pequeño, pequeña** *n.m.f.* little one, little boy, little girl; *see also* §5.71
pequeñito *adj.* tiny
pera *n.f.* pear
peral *n.m.* pear tree
percibir *v.* to perceive
perder *v.* to lose; **perder cuidado**/not to care, not to worry
perderse *v.* to be lost, become lost
pérdida *n.f.* loss; **perdido**/lost
perdón *n.m.* pardon
perdonar *v.* to pardon, excuse, forgive
peregrinación *n.f.* pilgrimage
peregrina, peregrino *n.f.m.* pilgrim
pereza *n.f.* laziness, sloth
perezoso *adj.* lazy
perfeccionar *v.* to perfect
perfeccionarse *v.* to perfect oneself
perfectamente *adv.* perfectly
perfecto, perfecta *adj.* perfect
pérfido *adj.* perifidious
periódico *n.m.* newspaper; *adj.* periodic, periodical
periodismo *n.m.* journalism
periodista *n.m.f.* journalist, newspaperman, newpaperwoman
periodístico *adj.* journalistic
período *n.m.* period
perla *n.f.* pearl
permanecer *v.* to remain, stay
permanencia *n.f.* sojourn, stay, permanence
permanentemente *adv.* permanently
permiso *n.m.* permit, permission
permitir *v.* to permit, admit, allow, grant
pero *conj.* but; *see also* §12.6, §12.7, §12.12
perplejo *adj.* perplexed
perrillo, perrito *n.m.* little dog, doggie
perro *n.m.* dog
perseguido *adj.* persecuted
perseguir *v.* to persecute, pursue
persiga, persiguió *v. forms of* **perseguir**
persona *n.f.* person
personaje *n.m.* personage, character

(in literature)

personal *n.m.* personnel, staff; *adj.* personal

personalidades *n.f.* personalities

personalmente *adv.* personally

perspectiva *n.f.* perspective

pertenecer *v.* to pertain, belong, appertain

perturbar *v.* to perturb, upset, disturb

peruano *n.m., adj.* of or pertaining to Peru

pesado *adj.* heavy

pesar *v.* to weigh, be heavy; **a pesar de**/in spite of; *n.m.* grief

pesca *n.f.* fishing

pescado *n.m.* fish

pescador *n.m.* fisherman

pescar *v.* to fish

peseta *n.f.* peseta (monetary unit of Spain)

peso *n.m.* weight, peso (monetary unit)

pestilente *adj.* pestilent

pétalo *n.m.* petal

petróleo *n.m.* petroleum

pez *n.m.* fish

pianista *n.m.f.* pianist

picaresco *adj.* picaresque

pícaro *n.m.* rascal, rogue

pico *n.m.* beak, peak

pide, pidiendo, pidiera, pido *v. forms of* **pedir**

pie *n.m.* foot; **a pie**/on foot; **de pie**/standing

piedad *n.f.* piety, mercy, pity

piedra *n.f.* stone

piel *n.f.* fur, skin, hide

piensa *v. form of* **pensar**

pierda *v. form of* **perder**

pierna *n.f.* leg

pieza *n.f.* room, piece, part

pila *n.f.* font (baptismal); **nombre de pila**/given (first) name of a person

pimienta *n.f.* black pepper; **pimiento** *n.m.* red pepper

pincel *n.m.* brush, paint brush (artist's)

pintar *v.* to paint

pintarse *v.* to make up (one's face), tint, color (one's hair, lips, *etc.*)

pinte *v. form of* **pintar**

pintor, pintora *n.m.f.* painter

pintoreso *adj.* picturesque

pintura *n.f.* painting

piña *n.f.* pineapple

pipa *n.f.* pipe (smoking)

pirámide *n.f.* pyramid

pisar *v.* to tread on, step on

piscina *n.f.* swimming pool

piso *n.m.* floor, story (of a building); **piso bajo**/ground floor

pizarra *n.f.* chalkboard

placer *v.* to gratify, humor, please, be pleasing; *n.m.* pleasure; *see also* **§6.20**

plácidamente *adv.* placidly, calmly

planchar *v.* to iron, press

planear *v.* to plan

planeta *n.m.* planet

planta *n.f.* plant; **planta baja**/ground floor

plata *n.f.* silver

plátano *n.m.* plane tree, plantain tree, banana

platicar *v.* to talk informally, chat

plato *n.m.* plate, dish

playa *n.f.* beach, seashore

plaza *n.f.* plaza, square

plazo *n.m.* term, installment

plazoleta *n.f.* small plaza

pleno *adj.* full; **en pleno**/right in the middle of; **en pleno día**/in broad daylight; **en pleno labor**/right in the middle of work

pluma *n.f.* feather, pen

pluscuamperfecto *n.m.* pluperfect

población *n.f.* population

pobre *adj.* poor; *n.m.f.* poor person, poor man, poor woman

pobrecillo, pobrecilla *n.m.f.* poor little person

pobrecito, pobrecita *n.m.f.* poor little child

pobretón *n.m.* poor wretch

pobreza *n.f.* poverty

poco, poca *adj.* small, little; *n.m.* a little bit; **a poco**/shortly, soon, in a little while; **a poco de**/soon after; **poco a poco**/little by little; **poco**/some; **pocos**/a few; **por poco**/almost; *see also* **§10.7, §5.70** and **poco** in idioms **§14.36**

poder *v.* to be able, can; *n.m.* power

poderoso *adj.* powerful

podido, podrá *v. form of* **poder**

podrida *adj.* rotten

poema *n.m.* poem

poesía *n.f.* poetry, poem

poeta *n.m., poetisa* *n.f.* poet

poética *adj.* poetic

policía *n.m.* policeman; *n.f.* police

policíaco *adj.* police, mystery

política *n.f.* politics, policy; politician, woman of politics; *n.m.* **político**/man of politics, politician; *adj.* political

polvo *n.m.* dust, powder; **hay polvo**/it is dusty; **Estoy hecho polvo**/I've been beaten to a pulp

pollo *n.m.* chicken

pon *v. form of* **poner; ponte**/put on **(ponerse)**

poner *v.* to put, place; **poner la mesa**/to set the table; **ponerse** *v.* to wear, put on, become, set (of sun), begin, become, place oneself; **ponerse en marcha**/to start (set) out; **se pone**/is worn; **al ponerse el sol**/at sunset; **ponerse pálido**/to turn (become) pale

ponga *v. form of* **poner; póngase**/put on **(ponerse)**

poquito *adj.* very little; **a poquitos**/bit by bit; **poquito a poco, poquito a poquito**/little by little

por *prep.* for, by, through, because of, on account of; **tres por cinco**/three times five; *see also* **por** in idioms **§14.37** and **por** in the index for other uses

por qué *interrog. adv.* why

porcentaje *n.m.* percentage

porque *conj.* because; *see also* **§12.ff**

portal *n.m.* porch, gateway

portar *v.* to carry, bear arms

portarse *v.* to behave, conduct oneself

portero *n.m.* porter, gatekeeper

portón *n.m.* gate, large door

portugués, portuguesa *adj.* Portuguese; **el portugués**/Portuguese language

porvenir *n.m.* future

posada *n.f.* inn, tavern, lodging

poseer *v.* to possess, own

posesión *n.f.* possession

posibilidad *n.f.* possibility

posibilitar *v.* to make possible

posible *adj.* possible; **lo más pronto posible**/as soon as possible

posición *n.f.* position

positivo *adj.* positive

poste *n.m.* post, pole

posteriores *adj.* posterior

postre *n.m.* dessert

postura *n.f.* position

práctica *n.f.* practice; *adj.* practical

practicar *v.* to practice

precio *n.m.* price

precioso *adj.* precious

precisamente *adv.* precisely

preciso *adj.* precise, exact, necessary; **es preciso**/it is necessary

predecir *v.* to predict, forecast, foretell

predicar *v.* to make public, to make known publicly, preach

prefecto *n.m.* prefect, director

preferencia *n.f.* preference

preferentemente *adv.* preferably

preferida *adj.* preferred

preferir *v.* to prefer

pregunta *n.f.* question, query; **hacer una pregunta**/to ask a question

preguntar *v.* to ask, inquire, question; *see also* this verb in the index

preguntarse *v.* to ask oneself, to wonder

premiar *v.* to reward, decorate, give an award to

premio *n.m.* prize, reward; **el premio gordo**/first prize

prenda *n.f.* pledge

prendar *v.* to pledge, charm, please

prendarse *v.* to become enamored

prender *v.* to seize, arrest

prensa *n.f.* press (newspaper)

preocuparse *v.* to be concerned, to worry; **no te preocupes**/don't worry

preparar *v.* to prepare
prepararse *v.* to be prepared, get ready, prepare oneself
preparativos *n.m.* preparations
presencia *n.f.* presence
presenciar *v.* to witness, be present
presentar *v.* to present, introduce, display, show
presentarse *v.* to introduce oneself, present oneself (itself), appear
presente *n.m.* present
presidencia *n.f.* presidency
presidente *n.m.* president
presidir *v.* to preside, preside over
preso *adj.* caught up in, taken by, imprisoned
prestado *adj.* on loan; **dar prestado/** to lend; **pedir prestado/**to borrow, ask for a loan of
prestador *n.m.* lender
prestar *v.* to lend; **prestar atención/** to pay attention
presteza *n.f.* haste, promptness
pretérito *n.m.* preterit
primario *adj.* primary
primavera *n.f.* spring, springtime
primer, primero, primera *adj.* first; *see also* §5.20, §15.1
primo, prima *n.m.f.* cousin
princesa *n.f.* princess
principal *adj.* principal, main
principalmente *adv.* principally
príncipe *n.m.* prince
principiar *v.* to begin
principio *n.m.* beginning, principle; **a principios/**in (at) the beginning
prisa *n.f.* haste; **tener prisa/**to be in a hurry; **darse prisa/**to hurry; **tan de prisa/**in such a hurry
prisión *n.f.* prison
prisionero *n.m.* prisoner
privada *adj.* private
privar *v.* to deprive
pro *prefix* pro, in favor of
probar(se) *v.* to try, test, prove, try (on)
problema *n.m.* problem
procedente *adj.* originating, coming from
proceder *v.* to proceed
procedimiento *n.m.* proceeding, procedure
procesión *n.f.* procession
proceso *n.m.* process, proceedings, trial
proclamar *v.* to proclaim, promulgate
procurar *v.* to procure, secure, attempt, try, endeavor
prodigio *n.m.* prodigy
prodigioso *adj.* prodigious
producción *n.f.* production
producir *v.* to produce, cause
producto *n.m.* product
productora *adj.* productive
produjo *v. form of* **producir**
profesión *n.f.* profession

profesional *n.m.f., adj.* professional
profesionalmente *adv.* professionally
profesor, profesora *n.m.f.* professor, teacher
profesorado *n.m.* professorate, professorship
profundo *adj.* profound, deep
programar *v.* to program
progresar *v.* to progress, make progress
progreso *n.m.* progress
prohibir *v.* to prohibit, forbid
prolongación *n.f.* prolongation, extension
prolongar *v.* to prolong
promesa *n.f.* promise
prometer *v.* to promise
prometido *past part. of* **prometer; lo prometido** what was promised
pronombre *n.m.* pronoun
pronóstico *n.m.* weather forecast
pronto *adv.* quickly, soon, right away; *adj.* fast, quick; **tan pronto como/**as soon as; **de pronto/**suddenly; *see also* **pronto** in idioms §14.38
pronunciar *v.* to pronounce, deliver a speech, make a speech, state, say
propia *adj.* own, proper
propiedad *n.f.* property
propietario, propietaria *n.m.f.* owner, proprietor
propina *n.f.* tip
propio *adj.* own, proper
proponer(se) *v.* to propose, resolve, determine, suggest
proporción *n.f.* proportion
proporcionar *v.* to provide, proportion, furnish
propósito *n.m.* proposal
proseguir *v.* to continue, prosecute
próspero *adj.* prosperous
protección *n.f.* protection
proteger *v.* to protect
protestar *v.* to protest
provecho *n.m.* profit, advantage
provenir *v.* to originate, come from
proverbio *n.m.* proverb
proviene *v. form of* **provenir**
provincia *n.f.* province
provinciana *adj.* provincial
provocar *v.* to provoke
próxima *adj.* close, near, nearby, next; **el mes próximo/**next month
proyecto *n.m.* plan, project
proyector *n.m.* projector
prudente *n.m.* prudent, wise
prueba *v. form of* **probar;** *n.f.* proof, trial, test
psicológico *adj.* psychological
publicación *n.f.* publication
públicamente *adv.* publicly
publicar *v.* to publish
público *adj.* public; *n.m.* public, audience
pudo *v. form of* **poder**
pueblecito *n.m.* small town

pueblo *n.m.* town, people
puede *v. form of* **poder; se puede decir/**it can be said; **se puede/**it can be, it is possible; *see also* §8.65
puente *n.m.* bridge
puerta *n.f.* door
puerto *n.m.* port
puertorriqueño *n.m., adj.* of or pertaining to Puerto Rico
pues *adv., conj.* well, since, then; **pues bueno/**well now, well then
puesta *n.f.* setting, *adj.* placed, wearing of a garment; **puesta del sol/**sunset
puesto *adj.* placed, put; *past part. of* **poner;** *n.m.* post, station, position, place, job; **puesto que** *conj.*/since, although, inasmuch as, as long as; *see also* §12.ff
pugnar *v.* to strive, struggle, persist, be obstinate
pulida *adj.* polished
pulir *v.* to polish
pulmón *n.m.* lung
pulsera *n.f.* bracelet, wristlet; **un reloj pulsera/**wrist watch
pulso *n.m.* pulse
punta *n.f.* tip, edge
punto *n.m.* period, point, dot; **en punto/**sharp; **estar a punto de/**to be about to; *see also* **estar** in idioms §14.26
puntualidad *n.f.* punctuality
puño *n.m.* fist
pupitre *n.m.* student's desk
pusiera, puso *v. forms of* **poner**

Q

que *conj.* than; *rel. pron.* which, who, what, whom, that; *interrog. pron.* **qué/**what; **sí que/**certainly; **que** is sometimes used for **porque;** *see also* §12.ff and **que** in the index
quebrar *v.* to break
quedar(se) *v.* to remain, stay; **quedar en/**to agree; **quedarle algo a alguien/**to have something remaining to someone; **quedarse con/**to keep; *see also* §7.211, §6.20
queja *n.f.* complaint
quejarse *v.* to complain, grumble
quemar *v.* to burn, fire
querer *v.* to wish, want, love; **querer decir/**to mean; *see also* **querer** in the index
quería *v. form of* **querer**
querido *adj.* dear, beloved
queso *n.m.* cheese
quiebro *v. form of* **quebrar;** *see also* §8.65
quien *pron.* who, he (she) who, whom, someone who; *see also* **quien** in the index
quienquiera, quienesquiera *indef. pron.* whoever, whomever, whosoever; *see also* §7.50ff

quiere, quieren, quiero *v. forms of* **querer;** *see* §8.65

quietos *adj.* quiet

química *n.f.* chemistry

químico *n.m.* chemist

quince *n.m., adj.* fifteen; **quince días/** two weeks

quinientos *n.m., adj.* five hundred

quinqué *n.m.* kerosene (hurricane) lamp

quinto *n.m., adj.* fifth; **dos quintos (quintas)/**two fifths

quise, quiso *v. forms of* **querer;** *see* §8.65

quisiera *v. form of* **querer/**I should like

quitar *v.* to leave, let go (of), remove

quitarse *v.* to take off, remove (clothing), remove oneself, withdraw

quiteños *n.m.pl., adj.* of or pertaining to Quito (Ecuador)

quizá(s) *adv.* maybe, perhaps

R

raer *v.* to scrape, rub off, erase, wipe out

ramillete *n.m.* bouquet

ramo *n.m.* sprig, small branch

rampa *n.f.* ramp

rápidamente *adv.* rapidly

rapidez *n.f.* rapidity, speed, swiftness

rápido *adj.* rapid, fast, swift

raqueta *n.f.* racket

rarísimo *adj.* very rare; *see also* §5.47ff, §10.5

raro *adj.* rare; **raras veces/**rarely, seldom; **por raro/**rarely

rascacielos *n.m.s. & pl.* skyscraper(s)

rascar *v.* to scrape, scratch

rata *n.f.* rat

rato *n.m.* moment, time, free time; **al poco rato/**in a short (little) while

ratón *n.m.* **ratones** *pl.* mouse, mice

rayo *n.m.* ray

raza *n.f.* race (people)

razón *n.f.* reason; **tener razón/**to be right; **no tener razón/**to be wrong

reacción *n.f.* reaction

real *adj.* royal, real

realidad *n.f.* reality

realizar *v.* to fulfill, realize (come true), carry out

realmente *adv.* really, actually

rebajar *v.* to bring down, reduce

rebelarse *v.* to rebel, revolt

recepción *n.f.* reception

receptor *n.m.* receiver

receta *n.f.* recipe, prescription

recibir *v.* to receive, get

recibo *n.m.* receipt; also *v. form of* **recibir**

recién, reciente, recientemente *adj., adv.* recent, recently; **recién casados/**newlyweds

recitar *v.* to recite

reclamador, reclamadora *n.m.f.* protester

reclamar *v.* to claim, demand

recluido *adj.* secluded

recluir *v.* to seclude, confine, shut in

recobrar *v.* to regain, recover

recoger *v.* to gather, reap, pick up, collect, pick

recomendación *n.f.* recommendation

recomendar *v.* to recommend, commend

recompensa *n.f.* reward, recompense

reconocer *v.* to recognize, acknowledge, be grateful for

recordado *adj.* recorded, remembered

recordar *v.* to remember, remind, recall

recorrer *v.* to run through, go through, visit here and there, travel through

recorrido *n.m.* flow, run, course, route

recreativa *adj.* recreational, recreative

recreo *n.m.* recreation

recuerdo *v. form of* **recordar;** *n.m.* memory, recollection, remembrance; **recuerdos/**regards

recurso *n.m.* recourse, means, resource

rechazar *v.* to reject, repel

redacción *n.f.* editing, writing, editorial work, newspaper writing

redactar *v.* to edit

redondo *adj.* round

reducido *adj.* reduced, small, little, confined

reducir *v.* to reduce

reemplazado *adj.* replaced

reemplazar *v.* to replace

reexaminación *n.f.* reexamination

referir *v.* to refer, relate, tell about, narrate

refiere *v. form of* **referir**

reflejar *v.* to reflect

reflexivo *adj.* reflexive

reforma *n.f.* reform

reformar *v.* to reform, straighten out, alter, reshape

refresco *n.m.* refreshment

refugiarse *v.* to take refuge

refugio *n.m.* refuge, shelter

regalar *v.* to present (give) as a gift, present, make a present of

regalo *n.m.* gift, present

regatear *v.* to dicker, haggle (over a price)

región *n.f.* region

registrar(se) *v.* to register

regla *n.f.* rule, ruler

reglamento *n.m.* regulation, rule

regocijado *adj.* gladdened, rejoiced

regocijar *v.* to gladden, rejoice

regresar *v.* to return, go back; *see also* §7.176

regreso *n.m.* return; **el viaje de regreso/**trip (drive) back

regular *adj.* regular; **por lo regular/** ordinarily, usually; *v.* to regulate

rehacer *v.* to redo

reina *n.f.* queen

reinar *v.* to reign

reino *n.m.* kingdom

reír(se) *v.* to laugh; **reír a carcajadas/** to burst out laughing

relación *n.f.* relation

relámpago *n.m.* streak of lightning

relativo *adj.* relative, related

relato *n.m.* account, statement, report

religiosidad *n.f.* religiousness, religiosity

religioso *adj.* religious; *n.m.* member of a religious order

reloj *n.m.* watch, clock; **reloj pulsera/** wrist watch

relucir *v.* to shine, sparkle, glow

remediar *v.* to correct, remedy

remedio *n.m.* remedy

remitir *v.* to forward, remit, transmit

remo *n.m.* oar, paddle

remota *adj.* remote

rendido *adj.* exhausted

rendir(se) *v.* to surrender, submit, overcome

renombrados *adj.* renowned

renovación *n.f.* renovation

renovar *v.* to renew, restore, renovate, remodel

renunciar *v.* to renounce, resign

reñir *v.* to scold, quarrel

reparación *n.f.* repair

reparar *v.* to repair

repartir *v.* to distribute, divide

repente *n.m.* sudden movement; **de repente/**suddenly

repentinamente *adv.* suddenly, abruptly

repentino *adj.* abrupt, sudden

repercusión *n.f.* repercussion

repercutir *v.* to resound, rebound, have repercussions

repetir *v.* to repeat

repite, repitiéndose *v. forms of* **repetir(se)**

replicar *v.* to reply

reposar *v.* to repose, rest

reposo *n.m.* rest

representación *n.f.* representation, performance, show

representante *n.m.f.* representative

representar *v.* to represent, perform (in theater)

reprimenda *n.f.* reprimand

reprochar *v.* to reproach

reproche *n.m.* reproach

reproducir *v.* to reproduce

república *n.f.* republic, government

repudiar *v.* to repudiate

repugnancia *n.f.* repugnance

requerimiento *n.m.* request, demand

resbalar *v.* to slip, slide

resentimiento *n.m.* resentment

resfiarse *v.* to catch cold

resfriado *n.m.* cold (sick)

residencia *n.f.* residence

residir *v.* to reside, live
resignado *adj.* resigned
resignarse *v.* to resign oneself
resistir *v.* to resist
resolución *n.f.* resolution
resolver *v.* to resolve, solve
respecto *n.m.* concern, relation;
  respecto a/with respect to
respetable *adj.* respectable
respetada *adj.* respected
respetar *v.* to respect
respeto *n.m.* respect, regard
respirar *v.* to breathe; *n.m.* breathing
responder *v.* to respond, answer,
  reply
respuesta *n.f.* reply, answer
restablecimiento *n.m.* reestablishment
restauración *n.f.* restoration
restaurante *n.m.* restaurant
restaurar *v.* to restore
resto *n.m.* rest, remainder, remaining
restricción *n.f.* restriction
resucitar *v.* to resuscitate, revive,
  resurrect
resultado *n.m.* result
resultar *v.* to result
retener *v. t.* retain, keep, confine
retirados *adj.* withdrawn
retirar *v.* to withdraw; **retirarse** *v.* to
  retire, withdraw
Retiro *n.m.* retirement, retreat; name
  of a park in Madrid
retraso *n.m.* delay, slowness
retrato *n.m.* likeness, picture, portrait
retroceder *v.* to recede, turn back
reunidos *adj.* gathered together
reunión *n.f.* meeting, reunion
reunir *v.* to bring together,
  accumulate, gather, join, unite
reunirse *v.* to get together, assemble,
  meet, gather
revelación *n.f.* revelation
revelar *v.* to reveal
revista *n.f.* magazine
revocar *v.* to revoke, repeal
revolución *n.f.* revolution
revolucionario *n.m., adj.*
  revolutionist, revolutionary
revolver *v.* to mix, turn over, mix up,
  rummage through; revolve, turn
  around, turn upside down, scramble
  (eggs)
revuelto *past part. of* **revolver; el
  cabello revuelto**/hair not combed;
  huevos revueltos/scrambled eggs
rey *n.m.* king; **Los Reyes Magos**/The
  Three Wise Men, the Magi
reyes *n.m.pl.* king and queen, royalty
rezar *v.* to pray, recite a prayer
ría *v. form of* **reír(se)**
rico, rica *adj.* rich; **los ricos, las
  ricas**/rich men, rich women, rich
  people; **más rico**/richer, richest
ridículo *adj.* ridiculous
ríe *v. form of* **reír(se)**
riel *n.m.* rail; **rieles**/rails

riendo *pres. part. of* **reír(se)**
riesgo *n.m.* risk
rigor *n.m.* rigor, strictness
rincón *n.m.* corner (inside, as in a
  room); **la esquina**/corner (outside,
  as a street corner)
río *n.m.* river
rió *v. form of* **reír**
riqueza *n.f.* wealth, riches
risa *n.f.* laughter, laugh
risueño *adj.* smiling, laughing
ritmo *n.m.* rhythm
robar *v.* to rob, steal
robustez *n.f.* robustness
roca *n.f.* rock
rodar *v.* to roll, spin
rodeada *adj.* surrounded
rodear *v.* to go round, surround
rodilla *n.f.* knee; **de rodillas**/kneeling
rogar *v.* to pray, beg, ask, request
rojo *n.m., adj.* red; *pron.* red one
rol *n.m.* catalogue, list, roll; role (part)
  in a play
Roma *n.f.* Rome
románico *adj.* Romanesque
romano *adj.* Roman
romántico *adj.* romantic
¡Rómpamela!/Break it for me!
romper *v.* to break, tear, shatter, wear
  out
ropa *n.f.* clothing, clothes
ropería *n.f.* clothing store, wardrobe
ropero *n.m.* clothes dealer, clothier,
  clothes closet, wardrobe
rosa *n.f.* rose
rostro *n.m.* face
roto *past part. of* **romper;** *see* §8.65;
  adj. torn, broken
rubio *adj.* blond
rudo *adj.* rude
rueda *n.f.* wheel
ruego *v. form of* **rogar;** *n.m.* request
ruido *n.m.* noise
ruidoso *adj.* noisy
ruina *n.f.* ruin
rumbo *n.m.* direction, course
rumor *n.m.* murmur, sound, rumor
Rusia *n.f.* Russia
ruso *n.m., adj.* Russian
rústico *n.m., adj.* rustic
ruta *n.f.* route
rutina *n.f.* routine

S

sábado *n.m.* Saturday
saber *v.* to know (how); **se sabe**/it is
  known; *see also* **saber** in the index
sabio *n.m.* wise man, sage, learned;
  adj. wise
sabor *n.m.* savor, taste, flavor
sabré, sabrá *v. forms of* **saber;** *see*
  §8.65
sacar *v.* to take out; **sacar fotos, sacar
  fotografías**/to take pictures; **sacar la
  lengua**/to stick out one's tongue
sacerdote *n.m.* priest

saco *n.m.* bag, sack, jacket
sacrificar(se) *v.* to sacrifice (oneself)
sacrificio *n.m.* sacrifice
sacudir *v.* to shake, jerk, jolt
sagrado *adj.* sacred, holy
sal *n.f.* salt; also, *verb form of* **salir**
sala *n.f.* large room, living room; **sala
  de espera**/waiting room; **sala de
  clase**/classroom; **sala de recibo**/
  reception, waiting room
salario *n.m.* salary
saldré, sale, salga, salgo *v. forms of*
  salir
salida *n.f.* departure, exit; **salida del
  sol**/sunrise
salir *v.* to go out, to come out, leave;
  salir de/to go out of, leave from;
  salir bien/to come out well, to pass;
  salir mal/to come out badly, to fail;
  salir el sol/to rise (sun)
salón *n.m.* room, hall, living room
saltar *v.* to jump, leap, hop, spring
salud *n.f.* health
saludar *v.* to greet, salute; **saludarse**
  v. to greet each other
saludos *n.m.pl.* greetings
salvaje *adj.* savage, wild
salvar *v.* to rescue, save
salvo *adj.* safe; **sano y salvo**/safe and
  sound; *prep.* save, except
sangre *n.f.* blood
sanitario *adj.* sanitary
sano *adj.* healthy, sound; **sano y
  salvo**/safe and sound
santo, santa *n.m.f., adj.* saint, holy; *see
  also* §5.21
sartén *n.f.* frying pan
sastre *n.m.* tailor
sastrería *n.f.* tailor shop
satisfacción *n.f.* satisfaction
satisfacer *v.* to satisfy
satisfactoriamente *adv.* satisfactorily
satisfecho *adj.* satisfied; **lo satisfecho**/
  how much satisfied
sazón *n.f.* maturity; **a la sázon**/at the
  time, then
sea, sean *v. forms of* **ser**
secamente *adv.* dryly
secar *v.* to dry, wipe dry
secarse *v.* to dry oneself
seco *adj.* dry
secretario, secretaria *n.m.f.* secretary
secreto *n.m.* secret; *adj.* secret
secundario *adj.* secondary
sed *n.f.* thirst; **tener sed**/to be thirsty
seda *n.f.* silk
seguida *n.f.* pursuit, continuation; **en
  seguida**/immediately, at once
seguir *v.* to follow, continue, pursue;
  seguir un curso/to take a course;
  see also **seguir** in the index
según *prep.* according to
segundo *n.m., adj.* second
seguramente *adv.* surely
seguridad *n.f.* security, certainty
seguro *adj.* certain, secure, sure

seis *n.m., adj.* six

seiscientos *n.m., adj.* six hundred

selección *n.f.* selection

selva *n.f.* forest, jungle

sello *n.m.* postage stamp, seal

semana *n.f.* week; **la semana que viene**/next week; **la semana pasada**/last week; **el fin de semana**/weekend

sembrar *v.* to sow, seed, plant

semejante *adj.* similar, like, alike

semejanza *n.f.* similarity

semestral *adj.* semi-annual

sencillamente *adv.* simply

sencillez *n.f.* simplicity

sencillo *adj.* simple; plain

seno *n.m.* bosom, breast

sentado *adj.* seated

sentar *v.* to seat; **sentarse** *v.* to sit down

sentencia *n.f.* sentence, punishment

sentido *n.m.* meaning, sense; **sentido común**/common sense

sentimiento *n.m.* feeling, sentiment

sentir *v.* to feel sorry, regret, feel

sentirse *v.* to feel (well, not well, ill, sick)

seña *n.f.* sign, mark; **las señas**/address

señal *n.f.* signal, mark, sign

señalar *v.* to signal, mark, point out, indicate, show

Señor *n.m.* Lord; **señor** *n.m.* Mr., sir, mister, gentleman

señora *n.f.* Mrs., madam, lady (wife, woman)

señores *n.m.* gentlemen, Mr. and Mrs.

señorita *n.f.* Miss, young lady

señorito *n.m.* young gentleman, master, little gentleman

sepa *v. form of* **saber**; *see* §8.65

separación *n.f.* separation

separado *adj.* separated

separar *v.* to separate

separarse *v.* to draw away, withdraw

septiembre *n.m.* September

sepulcro *n.m.* sepulcher

ser *v.* to be; *n.m.* being, human being; **a no ser que**/unless; *see also* **ser** in idioms §14.40 and **ser** in the general index

será *v. form of* **ser**

serenidad *n.f.* serenity

sereno *adj.* calm, serene; *n.m.* night watchman

seria, serio *adj.* serious

sería *v. form of* **ser**

serie *n.f.* series

serio *adj.* serious

sermón *n.m.* sermon

servicio *n.m.* service

servidor *n.m.* servant

servilleta *n.f.* napkin

servir *v.* to serve; **servirle**/to serve you; **¿En qué puedo servirle?**/May I help you? How may I be of some help to you? **servir de**/to serve as;

servir para/to be used for

servirse *v.* to help oneself (itself), to serve oneself

sesenta *n.m., adj.* sixty

sesión *n.f.* session

setecientos *n.m., adj.* seven hundred

setenta *n.m., adj.* seventy

seudónimo *n.m.* pseudonym

severo *adj.* severe

sevillano *n.m., adj.* of or pertaining to Sevilla

si *conj.* if, whether; *see also* §7.111

sí *adv.* yes, indeed; **creo que sí**/I think so; **digo que sí**/I say so; **sí que**/certainly; *pron.* **sí**/oneself, yourself, yourselves, himself, *etc.;* **para sí**/to himself, herself, *etc.;* **volver en sí**/to come to, regain consciousness

siamés *n.m., adj.* Siamese

sido *past part. of* **ser**; *see* §8.65

siembra *v. form of* **sembrar**

siempre *adv.* always; **siempre que fui**/whenever I went, at all times when I went

siendo *v. form of* **ser**

siente, siento *v. forms of* **sentar, sentir**; **siento**/I'm sorry; **se siente**/it is felt

sierra *n.f.* saw, mountain range

siesta *n.f.* afternoon rest, nap; **tomar la siesta**/to take an afternoon nap

siete *n.m., adj.* seven

siga *v. form of* **seguir**

siglo *n.m.* century

significado *n.m.* meaning

significar *v.* to signify, mean

siguen *v. form of* **seguir**

siguiente *adj.* next, following; **al día siguiente**/on the following day

siguiera, siguieron, siguió *v. forms of* **seguir**

silbar *v.* to whistle

silencio *n.m.* silence

silencioso *adj.* silent

silla *n.f.* chair

sillón *n.m.* armchair

simbólicos *adj.* symbolic

simbolizar *v.* to symbolize, signify

simpatía *n.f.* sympathy, congeniality

simpático *adj.* sympathetic, pleasant, congenial, nice

simular *v.* to simulate, feign, pretend, sham

simultánea *adj.* simultaneous

sin *prep.* without; **sin embargo**/nevertheless, however; *see also* conjunctions with **sin** §12.ff, **sin** in idioms §14.41, and **sin** in the index

sincero *adj.* sincere

sinfónica *adj.* symphonic

sinfonía *n.f.* symphony

singular *adj.* singular, unique

sinnúmero *n.m.* countless number

sino *conj.* but (rather, on the contrary); **sino que**/but rather; *see also* §12.6ff

sinónimo *n.m.* synonym

sintiendo, sintieran, sintió *v. forms of* **sentir**

síntoma *n.m.* symptom

siquiera *adv.* at least; *conj.* though, although; **ni siquiera**/not even

sírvase *v. form of* **servirse**; be good enough to

sirve, sirven *v. forms of* **servir**

sirvienta, sirviente *n.f.m.* servant

sirvió *v. form of* **servir**

sistema *n.m.* system

sitio *n.m.* place, site, spot, siege

situación *n.f.* situation

situado *adj.* situated

situar *v.* to situate, place

soberano *n.m., adj.* sovereign

sobrar *v.* to exceed, be more than sufficient, be left over

sobre *prep.* on, upon, about, over; **sobre todo**/above all, especially; *n.m.* envelope

sobresaliente *adj.* outstanding

sobretodo *n.m.* overcoat

sobreviviente *n.m.f.* survivor

sobrina *n.f.* niece

sobrino *n.m.* nephew

sociedad *n.f.* society

socio *n.m.* member, partner

sociológico *adj.* sociological

socorrer *v.* to aid, assist, help, succor

socorro *n.m.* help, succor

sofocar *v.* to suffocate, choke, smother, stifle

sol *n.m.* sun; **la puesta del sol**/sunset; **la salida del sol**/sunrise

sola *adj.* along, single

solamente *adv.* only

solar *adj.* solar

solariego *adj.* ancestral; **la casa solariega**/family home, homestead

soldado *n.m.* solider

soledad *n.f.* solitude

solemne *adj.* solemn

soler + inf. *v.* to have the custom of, be in the habit of, be accustomed to; *see* §8.14

soles *pl. of* **sol**

solicitar *v.* to solicit, request, apply for

sólidas *adj.* solid

solitario *n.m.* solitary person; *adj.* solitary

solo *adj.* alone, only, single, sole; **sólo** *adv.* only

soltar *v.* to unfasten, untie, loosen, let go, let loose

soltero *n.m.* bachelor; *adj.* unmarried

solterona *n.f.* old maid; unmarried woman

solución *n.f.* solution; **soluciones** *n.f.pl.*

sollozar *v.* to sob

sombra *n.f.* shade, shadow

sombrero *n.m.* hat

someter *v.* to subdue, subject, surrender, submit

somos, son *v. forms of* **ser;** *see* **§8.65**

sonar *v.* to sound, ring, echo, resound

sonido *n.m.* sound

sonoro *adj.* sonorous, pleasant sounding

sonreír(se) *v.* to smile

sonriendo, sonrió *v. forms of* **sonreír**

sonriente *adj.* smiling

sonrisa *n.f.* smile

sonrojarse *v.* to blush

soñar *v.* to dream; **soñar con**/to dream of

sopa *n.f.* soup

soplar *v.* to blow, blow out

soportar *v.* to endure

sordo *adj.* deaf

sorprendentes *adj.* surprising, amazing

sorprender *v.* to surprise, astonish; **sorprenderse de**/to be surprised at

sorprendidos *adj.* surprised

sorpresa *n.f.* surprise

sortija *n.f.* ring (finger)

sospecha *n.f.* suspicion

sospechar *v.* to suspect

sostener *v.* to sustain, maintain, support, uphold

soviético *adj.* Soviet

soy *v. form of* **ser;** *see* **§8.65**

su, sus *poss. adj.* your, his, her, its, their; *see* **§5.58**

suave *adj.* gentle, mild, soft

suavidad *n.f.* gentleness, softness

suavizar *v.* to smooth, soften ease, temper

subir *v.* to go up, come up, climb, rise, mount, ascend, get in (a vehicle)

súbitamente *adv.* suddenly

súbito *adj.* sudden

subjetivo *adj.* subjective

subjuntivo *n.m.* subjunctive

subrayar *v.* to underline, underscore, emphasize

subscribir *v.* to subscribe, agree to, sign

subscriptor *n.m.* subscriber

subsistencia *n.f.* subsistence

subterráneo *n.m.* subway; *adj.* subterranean

suceder *v.* to happen, occur, follow, succeed

suceso *n.m.* happening, event, occurrence; (success: **éxito**)

sucio *adj.* dirty

sud *see* **sur**

sudamericano *n.m., adj.* South American

sudar *v.* to sweat, perspire

sudoeste *n.m.* southwest

sudor *n.m.* perspiration, sweat

sueldo *n.m.* salary

suele *v. form of* **soler**

suelo *n.m.* floor, ground; *also v. form of* **soler;** *see* **§8.65**

suelto *n.m.* change, small change, coins; **sueltos** *adj.* loose

sueño *n.m.* dream, sleep; **tener sueño**/to be sleepy

suerte *n.f.* luck, fate; **buena suerte**/ good luck; **tener suerte**/to be lucky

suficiente *adj., adv.* enough, sufficient

sufre *v. form of* **sufrir**

sufrido *adj.* undergone, suffered

sufrimiento *n.m.* suffering

sufrir *v.* to suffer, endure, bear up, undergo

sugerir *v.* to suggest, hint, insinuate

sugirieron *v. form of* **sugerir**

sujetar *v.* to grasp, hold, secure, subject, hold fast, overcome, subdue

suma *n.f.* sum

sumamente *adv.* extremely

sumar *v.* to add, sum up

sumergir *v.* to submerge, plunge, immerse, sink

suntuoso *ajd.* sumptuous

supe *v. form of* **saber**

superior *n.m., adj.* upper, superior

supiesen *v. form of* **saber**

suplicar *v.* to beg, implore

supo *v. form of* **saber;** found out, learned; **se supo**/it was found out, it was learned

suponer *v.* to suppose, assume

supremacía *n.f.* supremacy

suprimir *v.* to suppress, abolish, cut out, cancel (in math), eliminate

supuesto *past part. of* **suponer;** supposed; **por supuesto**/of course, certainly

supuse *v. form of* **suponer**

sur *n.m.* South

surgir *v.* to surge, appear, spout, spurt

suspender *v.* to suspend; **suspensos** *adj.* suspended

suspirar *v.* to sigh

suspiro *n.m.* sigh

sustantivo *n.m.* noun

sustituir *v.* to substitute

sustituto *n.m.* subsitute

susto *n.m.* fright

suyo, suya, suyos, suyas, *poss. pron.* yours, his, hers, *etc.; see* **§5.60ff, §6.64ff; los suyos**/one's relatives

T

taberna *n.f.* bar, pub, tavern

tabernero *n.m.* tavern keeper

tabla *n.f.* board

tal *adj.* such, such a; **¿Qué tal?**/What's up? How goes it? **tal o cual**/such and such; **tal vez**/perhaps; **con tal que**/provided that; *see* **tal** in the index

tales *pl. of* **tal**

tamaño *n.m.* size

también *adv.* also, too

tampoco *adv.* neither, nor, not either

tan *adv.* so; **tan . . . como**/as...as; **tan**

pronto como/as soon as; *see* **tan** in the index

tanque *n.m.* tank

tanta, tanto *adj., pron.* so (as) much, so (as) many; **por lo tanto**/ therefore; **tanto...como**/as much...as; **mientras tanto**/meanwhile; *see also* **§5.53**

tantísimos *adj.* so many, so much; *see also* **§5.47ff, §10.5**

tañer *v.* to play, pluck a string instrument

tapar *v.* to cover, cover up, hide, stop up, plug up

taquígrafa, taquígrafo *n.f.m.* stenographer

tardanza *n.f.* delay, tardiness, lateness

tardar (en) + inf. to be late (in), to take long (in), to delay (in)

tarde *adv.* late; **más tarde**/later; *n.f.* afternoon; **(de) por la tarde**/in the afternoon

tarea *n.f.* duty, homework, task

tarjeta *n.f.* card

tarta *n.f.* pie

taxi, taxímetro *n.m.* taxi

té *n.m.* tea

te *pron.* you, to you, yourself; *see* pronouns **§6.ff**

teatral *adj.* theatrical

teatro *n.m.* theater

técnica *n.f.* technique; **técnico** *adj.* technical

tecnología *n.f.* technology

techo *n.m.* roof

tejado *n.m.* tiled roof

tela *n.f.* fabric, cloth

telefonear *v.* to telephone

telefónico *adj.* telephonic

telefonista *n.m.f.* telephone operator

teléfono *n.m.* telephone; **por teléfono**/on the telephone

telegrafiar *v.* to telegraph, cable

telegrafista *n.m.f.* telegraph operator

telegrama *n.m.* telegram

televisión *n.f.* television

televisor *n.m.* television set

telón *n.m.* curtain (stage)

tema *n.m.* theme, subject, topic, plot

temblar *v.* to tremble, quake, quiver, shake, shiver

temer *v.* to fear, dread

temor *n.m.* dread, fear

temperatura *n.f.* temperature

tempestad *n.f.* tempest, storm

templado *adj.* temperate

templo *n.m.* temple (house of prayer)

temporada *n.f.* period of time

tempranito *adv.* very early

temprano *adv.* early

ten *v. form of* **tener**

tender *v.* to hold out, tend, extend, offer, stretch, spread out, hang out (washing)

tenderos *n.m. pl.* storekeepers

tendido *n.m.* laying out, installation

tendrá *v. form of* **tener**

tenedor *n.m.* fork, holder, keeper; **tenedor de libros** *n.m.* bookkeeper

tener *v.* to have, hold; *see also* **tener** in idioms §14.42 and **tener** in the index

tener que + inf. to have to, must

tengo, tenía, tenido *v. forms of* **tener**; *see* §8.65

tenis *n.m.* tennis

tensión *n.f.* tension

tentar *v.* to examine by touch, feel with the fingers, attempt, tempt, try

teñir(se) *v.* to dye, stain, tint, color

tercer, tercero, tercera *adj., pron.* third; *see also* §5.20

tercio *n.m.* third; **dos tercios**/two thirds

terminar *v.* to terminate, end, finish

término *n.m.* end, boundary, term, limit, terminal

terreno *n.m.* terrain, ground, land

territorio *n.m.* territory

tertulia *n.f.* party, social gathering

tertulianos *n.m.* participants in a tertulia

tesis *n.m.* thesis

tesoro *n.m.* treasure

testigo *n.m.* witness

testimonio *n.m.* testimony

tiempo *n.m.* time, weather; **a tiempo**/on time; **desde hace mucho tiempo**/for a long time; **hace muchísimo tiempo**/a long time ago; *see also* §3.29, §17.ff

tienda *n.f.* tent, store, shop; **tienda de comestibles**/grocery store; **tienda de deportes**/sporting goods store

tiende *v. form of* **tender**

tiendecita *n.f.* small store

tienden *v. form of* **tender**

tiene *v. form of* **tener**

tierra *n.f.* earth, ground, land

tigre *n.m.* tiger

tímido *adj.* timid, shy

tinta *n.f.* ink

tiña *v. form of* **teñir**

¡Tíñela!/Tint it! Color it!

tío, tía *n.m.f.* aunt, uncle; **tíos** *n.m.* aunt and uncle, aunts and uncles

típico *adj.* typical

tipo *n.m.* type

tirano *n.m.* tyrant

tirar *v.* to throw, pull, draw, pitch (a ball), shoot (a gun), fling

titulado *adj.* entitled, titled

título *n.m.* title

tiza *n.f.* chalk

toalla *n.f.* towel

tocar *v.* to touch, play (a musical instrument); **tocar las campanas**/to ring the bells; **tocarle a uno**/to be someone's turn

tocino *n.m.* bacon

todavía *adv.* yet, still, even

todo *adj.* all; *pron.;* all; **sobre todo**/above all, especially; **todo español**/all Spanish people; **todo**/everything; **todo el mundo**/everybody; *see also* §14.43, §6.96

tomar *v.* to take, have (something to eat or drink); **se toma**/one takes, it is taken, is being taken

tomé *v. form of* **tomar**

tonelada *n.f.* ton

tono *n.m.* tone, voice

tontería *n.f.* foolishness, nonsense

tonto *adj., n.* stupid, fool, foolish

torcer *v.* to twist

torero *n.m.* bullfighter

tormenta *n.f.* torment, storm

tornarse *v.* to become, to change into

torno *n.m.* turnstile, wheel; **en torno**/around

toro *n.m.* bull; **la corrida de toros**/bullfight

toronja *n.f.* grapefruit

torre *n.f.* tower

tortilla *n.f.* omelet, tortilla

tortuoso *adj.* tortuous

tortura *n.f.* torture

tostar *v.* to toast

trabajador, trabajadora *n.m.f.* worker

trabajar *v.* to work

trabajo *n.m.* work

tradicional *adj.* traditional

traducción *n.f.* translation

traducir *v.* to translate

traduzca *v. form of* **traducir**

traer *v.* to bring

tragedia *n.f.* tragedy

trágico *adj.* tragic

traidor *adj., n.* traitor, treacherous

tráigame.../bring me...

traigo *v. form of* **traer**

traje *n.m.* suit, outfit; **traje de baño**/bathing suit; also *v. form of* **traer**

trajeron, trajo *v. forms of* **traer**

tranquilidad *n.f.* tranquility

tranquilizar *v.* to calm, calm down, quiet down, tranquilize

tranquilo *adj.* quiet, tranquil, calm

transacción *n.f.* transaction

transcurrir *v.* to elapse, pass

transformar *v.* to transform

transgresor *n.m.* offender, transgressor

transmisión *n.f.* tranmission

transporte *n.m.* transportation

tranvía *n.m.* streetcar, trolley

tras *prep.* after, behind, beyond; **tras (de)**/after, behind

trascendental *adj.* important, momentous, transcendental

trasladar *v.* to transport, transfer, convey, move

tratamiento *n.m.* treatment

tratar *v.* to try, treat (a subject), deal with; **tratar de**/to try, be concerned with; **tratarse de**/to be a question of, a matter of

trato *n.m.* trade, business transaction, business deal; **trato cerrado**/deal closed

través *n.m.* slant, diagonal; **a través**/through, across

travieso *adj.* mischievous, naughty

trayendo *pres. part. of* **traer**

treinta *n.m., adj.* thirty; **treinta y cinco**/thirty-five; **treinta y tres**/thirty-three

tremendo *adj.* tremendous

trémulo *adj.* trembling

tren *n.m.* train

trenza *n.f.* braid, tress

tres *n.m., adj.* three

tribu *n.f.* tribe

trigo *n.m.* wheat

triplicar *v.* to triple

triste *adj.* sad

tristeza *n.f.* sadness

triunfar *v.* to triumph, to win

triunfo *n.m.* triumph

trofeo *n.m.* trophy

trompo *n.m.* top (spin)

tronar *v.* to thunder

tronco *n.m.* trunk (of body, tree, *etc.*)

trono *n.m.* throne

tropa *n.f.* troop

tropezar *v.* to stumble, blunder, trip; **tropezar con**/to stumble upon, meet, come across, come upon

trotar *v.* to trot

trozo *n.m.* selection, piece

trueno *n.m.* thunder

tu, tus *poss. adj. see* §5.57ff

tubo *n.m.* tube, pipe (smoking pipe: **una pipa**)

turbar *v.* to disturb, trouble; **turbarse** *v.* to feel disturbed, upset

turco *n.m., adj.* Turk, Turkish

turismo *n.m.* tourism

turista *n.m.f.* tourist

turno *n.m.* turn

Turquía *n.f.* Turkey

tuviera, tuvo *v. forms of* **tener**

tuyo, tuya, *etc.,* **el tuyo, la tuya,** *etc. poss. pron.* yours; *see* §5.60ff, §6.64ff

U

u *conj.* or; *see* §12.13

últimamente *adv.* lately, ultimately

último *adj.* latest, final, last

un, uno *see* §5.18ff

une *v. form of* **unir**

U.N.E.S.C.O. United Nations Educational, Scientific, and Cultural Organization

único *adj.* only, single, sole, unique

unidad *n.f.* unity

unidas *adj.* united

uniforme *n.m.* uniform

unión *n.f.* union, uniting, combination

unir(se) *v.* to unite, join, bind, attach, connect

universalidad *n.f.* universality

universidad *n.f.* university

universitario *n.m., adj.* university, university student

uno, una *pron.* a person, someone, somebody; **unos, unas** *adj., pron.* some, several; **unos cuantos**/some, a few, several

untar *v.* to grease, moisten, annoint, oil

uña *n.f.* fingernail

urbano *adj.* urban

urgente *adj.* urgent

urgir *v.* to urge, to be urgent

usada *adj.* used

usar *v.* to use, employ, wear

uso *n.m.* use, usage

usualmente *adv.* usually

útil *adj.* useful

utilización *n.f.* utilization

utilizar *v.* to utilize, use

uva *n.f.* grape

V

va *v. form of* **ir**

vaca *n.f.* cow

vacaciones *n.f.pl.* vacation, vacations

vaciar *v.* to empty, vacate

vacilar *v.* to hestiate, vacillate, waver, fluctuate, stagger

vacío *adj* empty

vagabundo *n.m.* vagabond

vago *adj.* vague

vaguedad *n.f.* vagueness

vale *v. form of* **valer**

valenciano *n.m., adj.* of or pertaining to Valencia

valer *v.* to be worth, to value; **valer la pena**/to be worthwhile; **más vale**/it is better (worth more); **más vale tarde que nunca**/better late than never

valerosamente *adv.* bravely, courageously

valgan *v. form of* **valer**

valiente *adj.* brave, valiant, courageous

valor *n.m.* valor, value

valle *n.m.* valley

¡Vámonos! Let's leave! Let's go away! *v. form of* **irse**; *see also* **vámonos** in the index

vamos, van *v. forms of* **ir**

vanidad *n.f.* vanity

vano *n.m.* vain; **en vano**/in vain

vapor *n.m.* steam, steamship, steamboat, vapor, boat

variado *adj.* varied

variar *v.* to vary, change

variedad *n.f.* variety

varios *adj.* several, various

varón *n.m.* male, man, male person

vaso *n.m.* glass (drinking)

vasto *adj.* vast

vaya *v. form of* **ir**; **¡Vaya un...!** **¡Vaya una...!**/What a...! What an...!

ve *v. form of* **ir, ver**; **se ve**/it is seen, it can be seen

veces *pl. of* **vez**; **a veces**/at times; **la de veces**/how many times; **pocas veces**/seldom, few times; *see also* §3.30 and **veces** in idioms §14.44

vecindad *n.f.* vicinity, neighborhood

vecino, vecina *n.m.f.* neighbor; *adj.* neighboring

vehículo *n.m.* vehicle

veinte *n.m., adj.* twenty; **veinticinco**/ twenty-five; **veintidós**/twenty-two; **veintiocho**/twenty-eight; **veintiún**/ twenty-one

vejez *n.f.* old age

vela *n.f.* candle, vigil

velar *v.* to stay awake, guard, watch (over)

veloces *adj., pl. of* **veloz** *adj.* swift, fast, speedy

vencer *v.* to conquer, vanquish, overcome

vendedor, vendedora *n.m.f.* seller, salesman, saleslady

vender *v.* to sell; **se vende**/is sold; **se venden**/are sold

veneno *n.m.* poison

venerar *v.* to venerate, to honor; **se venera**/is venerated

venezolano *n.m., adj.* of or pertaining to Venezuela

venganza *n.f.* revenge, vengeance

vengo *v. form of* **venir**

venidera *adj.* coming, future, those to come

venir *v.* to come, **hacer venir**/to send for

venta *n.f.* sale, inn

ventaja *n.f.* advantage

ventana *n.f.* window; **ventanuco** *n.m.* small opening

ver *v.* to see; **a ver**/let's see; *see also* §7.185

veraneante *n.m.f.* summer vacationer

veranear *v.* to summer, to spend the summer

veraneo *adj.* summer, summer vacation

verano *n.m.* summer

veras *n.f. pl.* fact; **de veras**/truly, really

verbo *n.m.* verb

verdad *n.f.* truth; **¿No es verdad? ¿Verdad?**/Isn't it so?

verdaderamente *adv.* truly

verdadero *adj.* real, true

verde *n.m., adj.* green

veré *v. form of* **ver**

vergüenza *n.f.* shame

vería *v. form of* **ver**

verificarse *v.* to be verified, to prove true, to take place

verso *n.m.* verse

vestíbulo *n.m.* vestibule, waiting room, lobby

vestido *past part. of* **vestir**; dressed; also *n.m.* dress, robe, suit; **mal vestido**/poorly, badly dressed

vestir *v.* to dress, clothe; also *n.m.* dressing

vestirse *v.* to get dressed, dress oneself

vete *v. form of* **irse**; go away

veterano *n.m.* veteran

veterinario *n.m., adj.* veterinarian, veterinary

vez *n.f.* time, occasion; **una vez**/once, one time; **dos veces**/twice, two times, *etc.* **en vez de**/instead of; **de vez en cuando**/from time to time; **una vez**/the moment when; **de una vez**/all at once; **otra vez**/again, once more; **a la vez**/at the same time, at once, at one time; **tal vez**/perhaps, maybe; *see also* §3.30, §14.44

vi *v. form of* **ver**

vía *n.f.* way, road

viajar *v.* to travel

viaje *n.m.* trip, voyage, journey; **hacer un viaje**/to take a trip

viajero, viajera *n.m.f.* passenger, traveler

vibrar *v.* to vibrate

vicio *n.m.* vice

víctima *n.f.* victim (refers to male or female person)

victoria *n.f.* victory

vid *n.f.* vine, grapevine

vida *n.f.* life

vidrio *n.m.* glass window pane

viejecillo *n.m.* little old man

viejo, vieja *n.m.f., adj.* old, old man, old woman; **los viejos**/old people

viendo *pres. part. of* **ver**

viene, vienen *v. forms of* **venir**; **la semana que viene**/next week

viento *n.m.* wind, *see also* weather expressions §3.29, §17.ff

vientre *n.m.* abdomen, belly

viera, viéramos *v. forms of* **ver**

vieres *fut. subj. of* **ver**; *see* §23., §23.18, §8.64

viernes *n.m.* Friday

vieron, viesen *v. forms of* **ver**

vigilar *v.* to watch (over), guard, keep guard, look out (for)

vigoroso *adj.* vigorous

vinagre *n.m.* vinegar

vine, viniera *v. forms of* **venir**

vino *n.m.* wine; also *v. form of* **venir**; *see* §8.65

vio *v. form of* **ver**

violación *n.f.* violation

violencia *n.f.* violence

violenta *adj.* violent

violentamente *adv.* violently

violeta *n.f.* violet

virgen *n.f., adj.* virgin

virtud *n.f.* virtue

visibilidad *n.f.* visibility

visita *n.f.* visit; **hacer una visita**/to pay a visit

visitante *n.m.f.* visitor

visitar *v.* to visit

víspera *n.f.* eve

vista *n.f.* view, sight; **un punto de vista**/a point of view

viste *v. form of* **ver, vestir**

vistiendo, vistiese *v. forms of* **vestir(se)**; **vistiéndome**/dressing myself

visto *past part. of* **ver**; **dar el visto bueno**/to approve; **por lo visto**/ apparently

viuda *n.f.* widow

viudo *n.m.* widower

vivienda *n.f.* home, house

vivir *v.* to live, reside

vivísimo, vivísima *adj.* very lively, bright; *see* **§5.47ff, §10.5**

vivo *adj.* alive, living

vocablo *n.m.* term, word

vocacional *adj.* vocational

voces *n.f.pl. of* **voz**; **grandes voces**/ loud voice

volando *pres. part of* **volar** *v.* to fly; **volarse**/to fly away

voltear *v.* to overturn, revolve, turn, turn around

volumen *n.m.* volume

voluntad *n.f.* will

volver *v.* to return, go back, come back; **volverse**/to turn around; **al volverse**/upon turning around

volviese *v. form of* **volver**

votante *n.m.f.* voter

votar *v.* to vote, vow

voto *n.m.* vote, vow

voy *v. form of* **ir**

voz *n.f.* voice; **en voz alta**/in a loud voice; **dar voces**/to shout

vuela, vuelan *v. forms of* **volar**

vuelo *n.m.* flight

vuelta *n.f.* stroll, walk, tour, return, turn; **dar una vuelta**/to go for a stroll; **ida y vuelta**/round trip

vuelto *past part. of* **volver**

vulgar *adj.* common, ordinary, vulgar

Y

y *conj.* and; *see* **§5.65, §12.14**; *see also* **y** in idioms **§14.45** and in telling time **§16.5**

ya *adv.* now, already, indeed; **ya que**/ as long as, since, inasmuch as, because; **ya no**/no longer; **¡Ya lo creo!** I should say so! Of course! *see also* **§14.46**

yacer *v.* to lie down, be lying down

yendo *pres. part. of* **ir**; **yéndose** *v. form of* **irse**

yugo *n.m.* yoke

Z

zapateado *n.m.* Spanish clog dance, tap dance

zapatería *n.f.* shoe store, bootery, shoe repair shop

zapatero *n.m.* shoe repair worker, shoemaker

zapatilla *n.f.* slipper

zapato *n.m.* shoe

zona *n.f.* zone

zopenco *n.m.* blockhead; *adj.* stupid

zorra *n.f.* she-fox, vixen

zorrillo *n.m.* skunk

zorro *n.m.* fox

zumbar *v.* to buzz, hum, flutter around

zumo *n.m.* juice; **zumoso** *adj.* juicy

zurcir *v.* to mend, darn

zurdo *adj.* left-handed

GENERAL INDEX

PART
IX

Most references in this index are to sections in the General Review in Part IV, indicated by the symbol § in front of a numerical decimal system. Other references are to page numbers and these are cited as p. and the number.

The abbreviation **ff** means *and the following*. Additional abbreviations can be found on page xviii.

un, uno §5.18–§5.20
una a otra, uno a otro §6.28
upon + pres. part. §7.201
useful expressions §14.15ff
ustedes in place of **vosotros, vosotras**
§6.6

vámonos §8.62(h), (m)
veces (pl. of **vez**) §3.30, in idioms
§14.44
ver §7.185
verb tenses *see* verbs and specific name
of tense, *e.g.,* preterit, future, *etc.*
verbal expressions §14.15ff
verbal nouns *see* nouns
verbs §7.–§8.65 agreement of subject and
refl. pron. of a refl. verb §7.3;
agreement of subject and verb §7.2;
and prepositions §7.181(d), §7.16ff; aux.
verb **haber** §7.6; common irregular
Spanish verb forms & uncommon
Spanish verb forms identified by inf.
§8.65; comparison of meanings & uses
of Spanish verb tenses & moods as
related to English verb tenses & moods
§8.12ff; compound tenses §8.3ff;
diagrams of sentences §7.7–§7.9;
formation of regular verbs §8.15ff,
§8.21ff, §8.27ff; forms identified by inf.
§8.65; helping §7.6; intransitive §7.11–
§7.13; introductory remarks about
verbs §7.1; irregular §8.19, §8.24,
§8.30ff, §8.35, §8.40ff, §8.42ff, §8.45ff,
§8.65; irregular Spanish verb forms &
uncommon Spanish verb forms
identified by inf. §8.65; moods §7.1; of
motion §10.11; §10.12, §10.13, §7.19; of

perception §7.185; orthographical
changing §7.32ff, §8.19ff, §8.30ff,
§8.48ff; + no prep. §7.29, §7.30,
§7.182; principal parts of some
important Spanish verbs §7.31; reflexive
§5.64, §6.21–§6.29, §6.53, §8.62(h),
(k) & (l); regular formation §8.32,
§8.37ff, §8.42ff, §8.51ff; simple tenses
§8.1ff; spelling changes §7.32ff, §8.19ff,
§8.30ff, §8.48ff; stem-changing §8.19ff,
§8.30ff, §8.46ff.
 subjunctive §7.33–§7.100; after an
indef. or negative antecedent §7.54–
§7.62; after certain adverbs §7.44; after
certain conjunctions §7.34–§7.43; after
certain impersonal expressions §7.71–
§7.77; after certain indef. expressions
§7.50–§7.53; after **¡Ojalá que . . . !**
§7.67ff; after **¡Que . . . !** §7.66ff; after
verbs implying a wish, order,
command, desire, preference, advice,
permission, request, plea, insistence,
suggestion, *etc.* §7.87–§7.99; after verbs
or expressions indicating denial, doubt,
lack of belief, uncertainty, *etc.* §7.78–
§7.81; after verbs or expressions
indicating emotion, joy, gladness,
happiness, sorrow, regret, fear, surprise,
etc. §7.82–§7.86; contrary to fact
clauses §7.111; **por + adj.** or **adv. +
que** §7.48, §7.49; sequence of tenses
§7.101–§7.110; **si clauses** §7.111;
summing up of the subjunctive §7.100.
 tenses: compound §8.3ff; English
verb tenses & moods §8.–§8.12ff;
names of tenses & moods in Spanish
with English equivalents §8.ff;
progressive forms §8.63; simple tenses

§8.1ff; tenses & moods in Spanish with
English equivalents §8.ff; *see also*
specific name of tense, *e.g.,* present
indicative, future, preterit, conditional,
etc. transitive §7.7, §7.13; with
prepositions §7.181(d), §7.16–§7.30

vez §3.30; in idioms §14.44
vocabulary pp. 370–403; antonyms §20.;
cognates §21.; how to study §20.
voice, active *see* active voice
voice, passive *see* passive voice
volver §7.176
vosotros, vosotras replaced by **ustedes**
§6.6
vuestro, vuestra, vuestros, vuestras
§5.58, §5.60; **el vuestro, la vuestra,
los vuestros, las vuestras** §6.64ff

weather expressions, §3.29, §17.ff
what a . . . ! what an . . . ! §13.
which one . . . ? which ones . . . ? §6.103,
§5.68ff
who, whom §6.80ff
whose is . . . ? whose are . . . ? §6.67–
§6.69, §6.101
word order of elements in Spanish
sentences §5.14, §6.4–§6.53
words, tricky §22.
words into syllables §2.3ff

y and **e** §5.65, §12.14, §7.217
y in idioms §14.45; in telling time §16.5
ya in idioms §14.46
yours §6.62, §6.64

NOTES